INDIAN NATIONS

OF NORTH AMERICA

Sioux chief Arvol Looking
Horse's drumbeats echo across
the snowy Cheyenne River
Sioux Reservation in Green
Grass, South Dakota.

INDIAN
NATIONS
OF NORTH AMERICA

Anton Treuer, Karenne Wood, William W. Fitzhugh,
George P. Horse Capture, Sr., Theresa Lynn Fraizer, Miles R. Miller,
Miranda Belarde-Lewis, Jill Norwood

Foreword by Herman J. Viola

NATIONAL GEOGRAPHIC

WASHINGTON, D.C.

A Nunamiut boy in Anaktuvuk Pass, Alaska, peeks from behind a mask made of caribou hide.

CONTENTS

A Navajo woman tends her flock in the Canyon de Chelly National Monument, Arizona.

ABOUT THIS BOOK

ndian Nations of North America chronicles the remarkable story of the Native inhabitants of our continent, through history and modern day. This book presents the myriad cultures, languages, traditions, and perspectives in the words of highly accomplished authors who are leaders within their own Native communities.

Every currently federally recognized tribal entity (at the time of publication) is included in this book. Though the title identifies the scope as North America, due to space limitations this book does not include indigenous communities south of the U.S. border. In addition to the comprehensive listing of all tribes in the appendix and a detailed map showing all federally recognized U.S. tribal lands, essays feature dynamic histories of selected tribes, while shorter essays tell the stories of tribes through the lens of their individual reservations.

The degree of disruption to Indian homelands caused by westward migration cannot be overestimated. Before first contact, many tribal groups ranged across broad regions that their modern descendants would not recognize as home. Forced relocations often propelled tribes vast distances to reservations shared with other tribes, even those previously considered rivals or enemies. Though Indian communities themselves would not necessarily identify themselves by the regions outlined in the chapters of this book, for purposes of categorization, the tribes are included in the regions they currently inhabit.

The text is written by eight Native authors (and one non-Native) representing the eight major geographical regions of North America. The short entries on a selection of modern federally recognized tribal lands are derived from *Tiller's Guide to Indian Country: Economic Profiles of American Indian Reservations* and used with permission of the author, Veronica Tiller (Jicarilla Apache).

The editors recognize the difficulty of trying to identify and include all Native groups. It is our desire to be as inclusive, respectful, and sensitive as possible regarding the identities of the peoples we have included in this book. For organizational purposes, we have relied on the U.S. government list entitled "Indian Tribal Entities Within the Contiguous 48 States Recognized and Eligible to Receive Services from the United States Bureau of Indian Affairs." Many state-recognized as well as unrecognized (by federal or state) communities are not included in this list.

The relationship between Natives and non-Natives on this continent has ranged over time from friendly to fraught. Many of our darkest hours as a nation were born in the suffering of people whose ancestors thrived here long before European explorers arrived on these shores. Our goal with this book is to educate and inspire, impart histories and modern stories, tell the honored traditions and share the proud triumphs of the extraordinarily diverse people who are known collectively as Native Americans.

The stories of individual reservations come to life in short entries.

Phrases and translations provide examples of spoken languages of the region.

Sidebars explore fascinating historical or modern topics related to one or more tribes of the region.

Richly illustrated maps pinpoint every currently federally recognized U.S. tribe.

Myth or Fact elements reveal surprising facts about Native American life.

Biographies feature historic and modern Indian leaders.

Full spreads focus on a single tribe, exploring its development in rich detail.

FOREWORD

When Christopher Columbus reached the Americas in 1492, he met people unknown to Europeans. Thinking he had reached the Indies, he called them Indians. This is only one of the many mistakes, misunderstandings, and misconceptions that continue to plague America's Native peoples. A fundamental mistake that persists to this day is to speak about "the American Indians" as though they are one people. Despite their small numbers, the Indian peoples of North America were as dissimilar from each other as were the peoples of Europe. In terms of language, clothes, lifestyles, militancy, and religion, the tribes in different parts of North America differed greatly from each other. These differences are considered "cultural."

One question that still perplexes the American public is the correct name for the Native peoples Columbus found here. Are they Indians or are they Native Americans? As George Horse Capture likes to say, "Everyone born here is a native American. Columbus thought he had arrived in India, so he called the people he encountered Indians, and that is the name we have lived with for five hundred years. We have gotten used to it. But we are very grateful he did not think he was in Turkey."

Some tribes, especially those living along the Atlantic coast, suffered tremendous loss of life from their initial contact with Europeans because of introduced diseases such as smallpox, measles, and influenza. Other tribes in the interior of the continent, such as the buffalo hunters of the Great Plains, temporarily enjoyed a "golden age" through the acquisition of the metal tools, horses, and weapons Europeans also introduced into the Americas, but their good fortune quickly collapsed during the expansionist era of Manifest Destiny as pioneers and Presidents conspired to take Indian lands, while well-intentioned but misguided reformers and missionaries mounted crusades to assimilate Indians into the mainstream Christian culture.

Despite the dramatic and often detrimental impact of the newcomers, Indians of many tribes have survived their long ordeal and retain much of their traditional culture—the legacy that defines them. Indians have not only survived but also reasserted their deepest values and gained renewed pride in themselves and their traditions. Nonetheless, Indians today straddle two societies, as this rapidly growing minority increases its landholdings, builds a professional class, and experiences a cultural resurgence that has caught the attention of the American public. As we enter the 21st century, certain concerns are evident.

One is the future of reservations, which are now home to less than one-fourth of all Indians. Have reservations outlived their usefulness? How long will the federal government continue to give them special status, when they serve so few Indian people—even though reservations are usually guaranteed by treaty obligations. For Indians, however, it is not a question of economic efficiency. To them, it is immaterial how many people live on the reservation permanently. What is important is simply that a reservation exists at all, a haven from the stress of the dominant society. As one Indian friend remarked: "When I hit that dirt road, I feel like I have come home. I am surrounded by friends and relatives, by people who speak my language, by people who could care less who or what I am in the white world."

Another concern is the ability of these rich and vibrant cultures to survive in the modern world. Gordon McLester of the Wisconsin Oneida is not worried. "Indians will always be part of America because of the people themselves," he promises. "They believe in their tribal governments; they believe in their tribal ways. It's not the amount of your Indian blood, it's not if you dance, it's not if you talk an Indian language. It's that you believe in what you are. No legislation can take that away. We are still here, and we will always be here."

—HERMAN J. VIOLA,
Curator emeritus, Smithsonian Institution
National Museum of Natural History

Preceding pages: A Cree hunter uses a birchbark moose call to lure an animal into rifle range during rutting season in Lac des Isles, Saskatchewan, Canada.
Opposite: A Tulalip Indian plays his drum to kick off a salmon celebration ceremony in Marysville, Washington.

RUSSIA

*Bering
Sea*

*Beaufort
Sea*

ALASKA
(U.S.)

U.S.
CANADA

YUKON

*Gulf of
Alaska*

N.W.T.

BRITISH
COLUMBIA

ALBERTA

SASK.

■ NORTHWEST
COAST
pp. 274–301

CANADA
U.S.

PACIFIC

WASH.

MONT.

N.DAK.

OCEAN

OREG.

IDAHO

S.DAK.

WYO.

■ GREAT BASIN
AND PLATEAU
pp. 240–273

NEBR.

CALIF.

NEV.

UTAH

COLO.

■ CALIFORNIA
pp. 302–349

ARIZ.

■ SOUTHWEST
pp. 194–239

N.MEX.

U.S.
MEXICO

INDIAN NATIONS

SCALE
1 : 23,500,000

0   400   800
statute miles

0   400   800
kilometers

Map Key

Canadian Indian reserves

United States Indian reservations
and Alaskan native areas

GREENLAND
(DENMARK)

*Of Greenland's population of 57,000, 88% are Inuit or
part Inuit. Greenlanders have experienced "home rule"
since 1979, and in 2009 moved to "self rule", a higher
level of autonomy from Denmark. Prime Minister Kuupik
Kleist is half Danish, half Inuit.*

Baffin
Bay

NUNAVUT

Hudson
Bay

MANITOBA

ONTARIO

QUEBEC

Labrador
Sea

NFLD. & LAB.

ARCTIC AND SUBARCTIC
pp. 102–141

P.E.I.

N.B.

ME.

N.S.

Lake Superior

CANADA
U.S.

NORTHEAST
pp. 16–65

WIS.

L. Huron

Lake Michigan

MICH.

L. Ontario

Lake Erie

N.H.

VT.

MASS.

N.Y.

R.I.

CONN.

MINN.

IOWA

ILL.

IND.

OHIO

PA.

N.J.

MD.

DEL.

KANS.

MO.

PLAINS
pp. 142–193

W.VA.

VA.

KY.

N.C.

ATLANTIC

OCEAN

OKLA.

ARK.

TENN.

S.C.

TEXAS

ALA.

GA.

MISS.

SOUTHEAST
pp. 66–101

LA.

FLORIDA

Gulf of Mexico

B A H A M A S

C U B A

CHAPTER 1

THE NORTHEAST

THE NORTHEAST

FOR THE INDIGENOUS PEOPLE IN THE NORTHEASTERN UNITED STATES AND NEARBY parts of Canada, water was the primary means of transportation for trade, diplomacy, and war. The smallest advantages in water-related technology made all the difference in the survival and dominance of groups. The Ojibwe invented the birchbark canoe, and compared with other forms of boats, it was superior—lighter, faster, and more buoyant. It helped the Ojibwe and the groups with whom they shared it (the Ottawa, Potawatomi, and Menominee) defend and expand their territories.

WATER SUSTAINED ALL LIFE IN THE REGION, AND THE LIFE IT SUSTAINED WAS AMAZING.

Water sustained all life in the region, and the life it sustained was amazing. There were more people per square mile and more diverse languages and cultures here than in Europe. The bounty of the land supported many people, but the population density created problems as well. Warfare between tribes over territory was endemic, and it forced political adaptations. The Iroquois Confederacy was created to make peace among five Native nations that were destroying one another. The Great Law of Peace united the Iroquois into a powerful union that protected the cultural differences of the member tribes but united them in political purpose and eventually in military action. Their neighbors were constantly on the defensive, and the threat from the Iroquois alliance forced the Ojibwe, Ottawa, and Potawatomi to form the Three Fires Confederacy.

DECADES OF STRIFE AND DISEASE

WHEN EUROPEANS ENTERED THE NORTHEAST, THEY FOUND THEMSELVES PLAYERS IN AN ongoing tribal struggle over the land and its resources. French-British rivalry acted as a catalyst for existing tensions and embroiled the Great Lakes in terrible conflicts for decades. The dense population in the Northeast fueled major military actions by the Iroquois Confederacy and the Three Fires Confederacy but also enabled devastating virgin-soil pandemics that ravaged the entire region. The Huron were so depopulated by disease and warfare in the 1600s that they never recovered the territory or population that had made their dominance of the eastern Great Lakes possible for centuries.

Almost every tribe in the Northeast originated from one of three mother groups—Algonquian, Iroquoian, or Siouan. The Algonquian (or Algic) people were once a single group with one language, but as they spread, they diversified in language and culture. Twenty-seven tribes trace their origins to this mother group, including the Ojibwe, Ottawa, Potawatomi, Menominee, Micmac, Wampanoag, and Powhatan. Even as the Algonquian tribes diverged, cultural

Preceding pages: A modern Iroquois man dances and chants outside a reconstructed traditional longhouse. Opposite: Indian dressed as the legendary 19th-century Iroquois chief Pau Puk Keewis

commonalities remained, including a strong, patrilineal clan system that was one of the primary determining factors in what kind of positions people assumed in life—political leadership, protection, or medicinal expert, for example. Although rapid geographic dispersal and marriage with Europeans challenged the clan system for many Algonquian peoples, clan remains an obvious surviving attribute of their culture. Algonquian tribes typically built wigwams and other domed structures. They fished more than they hunted, and farmed more than they fished.

The Iroquoian tribes formed the second largest group of Indians in the Northeast. Like the Algonquian tribes, they sprang from one mother group and diversified over time. They also maintained a sophisticated clan system. However, for Iroquoian tribes, clan was passed down matrilineally (through the

THE NORTHEAST

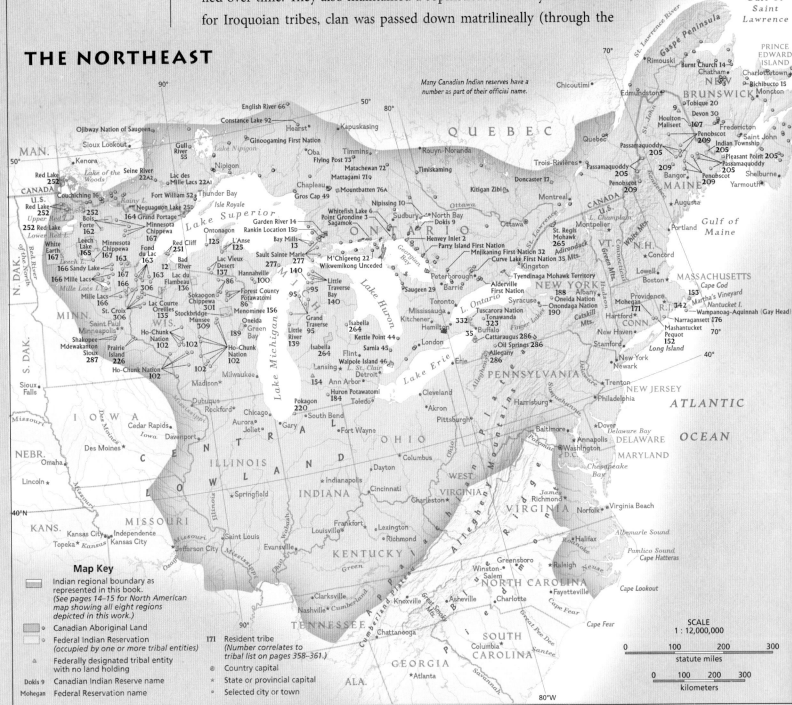

Many Canadian Indian reserves have a number as part of their official name.

Map Key

Indian regional boundary as represented in this book.
(See pages 14–15 for North American map showing all eight regions depicted in this work.)

Canadian Aboriginal Land

Federal Indian Reservation
(occupied by one or more tribal entities)

Federally designated tribal entity with no land holding

Dokis 9 Canadian Indian Reserve name

Mohegan Federal Reservation name

171 Resident tribe
(Number correlates to tribal list on pages 358–361.)

Country capital

State or provincial capital

Selected city or town

SCALE
1 : 12,000,000

0   100   200   300
statute miles

0   100   200   300
kilometers

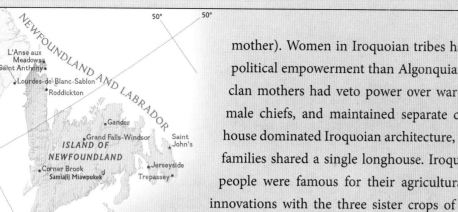

mother). Women in Iroquoian tribes had a higher degree of political empowerment than Algonquian women, as Iroquois clan mothers had veto power over war decisions, appointed male chiefs, and maintained separate councils. The longhouse dominated Iroquoian architecture, and many families shared a single longhouse. Iroquoian people were famous for their agricultural innovations with the three sister crops of corn, beans, and squash. More than other tribes in the Northeast, they relied on farming, with much less augmentation from gathering, fishing, and hunting.

The Siouan family of tribes had representative groups in the Northeast as well, such as the Ho-Chunk (formerly the Winnebago). However, Siouan tribes in the Northeast were markedly different from Siouan groups on the Great Plains. They maintained vibrant patrilineal clan systems, relied on agriculture, and never adopted the horse as a primary tool in hunting. Siouan groups in the Northeast used domed lodges for ceremonial purposes and for primary residences, but used tepee structures for travel and seasonal living.

Tribes in the Northeast had a range of experiences with American and Canadian colonization. Some, such as the Powhatan Confederacy, emerged with only shattered remnants of their political structures, land, and languages. Others, such as the Mohawk, retained vibrant languages and cultural forms. Even within tribes, there has been great diversity of experience. The Ojibwe, for example, have 125 communities in Canada and reservations in five American states. Some of those communities have no fluent speakers left; others have a 100 percent fluency rate.

> IROQUOIAN PEOPLE WERE FAMOUS FOR THEIR AGRICULTURAL INNOVATIONS WITH THE THREE SISTER CROPS OF CORN, BEANS, AND SQUASH.

DEFENDING TRIBAL SOVEREIGNTY

SOVEREIGNTY IS LEGALLY CONFIGURED VERY DIFFERENTLY IN CANADA AND THE UNITED States. The Canadian government has a legal mechanism for acknowledging tribal government but very little entrenched support for sovereignty in the courts. In the United States, Indians are mentioned in the Constitution in only two places, but from those mentions, a huge body of legal precedent has been built, giving state governments no authority on Indian land without an act of the federal Congress. That's why tribes have been so successful at developing gaming operations in the United States, but less so in Canada.

Throughout the region, tribes are realizing that their sovereign authority is vested in their languages and cultures. Language immersion programs are springing up throughout the Northeast, with the greatest strength among the Mohawk, Ottawa, and Ojibwe. The military battles that engulfed the tribes of the Northeast when Europeans first encountered them have been replaced by a new war—waged with pens, computers, and recording equipment—a war to maintain identity through revitalizing their tribal cultures and languages.

ALLEGANY RESERVATION

Tribe: Seneca Nation of New York
Current Location: New York **Total Area:** 30,189 acres
Tribal Enrollment (Tribal sources, 2004): 1,272

Seneca tribes traditionally resided on 6.5 million acres ranging from Seneca Lake to the Niagara River and from Lake Ontario to the Allegheny River in present-day New York State. The Haudenosaunee tribes' contiguous lands originally stretched across present-day New York. The Seneca were the Western Doorkeepers, controlling trade and traffic at the western edge of the Iroquois territory, while the Mohawks, who lived near the Hudson River, were the Eastern Doorkeepers. The Seneca resided in longhouses and depended heavily on a crop and diet of corn, beans, and squash, referred to as the "three sisters."

Through a series of treaties with the United States, beginning in 1784, the Seneca's traditional land base was continually diminished. In accordance with the Pickering Treaty of 1794, the State of New York continues to pay the Nation annually in cloth and cash. Throughout the 20th century, the Seneca

Ottawa, Algonquian language family

"Nwiikajitona wii-ankenmaageyaang anishnaabemowin. Mii keyaa wii-bmaadziiwingak. Mii keyaa wii-anishnaabewiyaang niigaan."

("We endeavor to transfer this native language [to future generations]. This is how it shall live. This is the key to our native identity in the future.")

have struggled to retain their independence and the rights over their land. Their adamant rejection of the Indian Reorganization Act of 1934 is indicative of this stance. In more recent years, the Seneca Nation has been occupied with renegotiating the 3,000 99-year leases on their lands in and around Salamanca, New York. The leasing of Seneca lands began in the early 1800s, first by railroad companies.

The Seneca Indians reside on three reservations in the U.S.: Allegany, Cattaraugus, and Oil Spring. The Allegany Reservation is located along the Allegheny River from the Pennsylvania border upriver to Vandalia, New York, within Cattaraugus County. It originally included 30,469 acres of land until some 10,000 acres were inundated by the Kinzua Reservoir when the Army Corps of Engineers built the Kinzua Dam in 1964. The Cattaraugus Reservation is located along the Cattaraugus Creek, from Gowanda, New York, downstream to the shore of Lake Erie in Cattaraugus, Chautauqua, and Erie Counties. The Oil Spring Reservation is situated in Cuba, New York, with access to Cuba Lake. Oil Spring is the home of the first documented oil spring in North America. Franciscan missionary Joseph de la Roche d'Allion

HOLE IN THE DAY

Assassinated Ojibwe chief

Hole in the Day (Bagone-giizhig) was one of the most powerful Ojibwe leaders of the 19th century. Most Indian chiefs held sway over a particular village, but Hole in the Day was chief over several villages in central Minnesota, including the hamlet of Crow Wing, which was half populated with whites. He negotiated almost every Ojibwe treaty with the U.S. government in Minnesota, permanently altered the nature of tribal leadership in his ascendancy to chieftainship, expanded Ojibwe territory, and used both diplomacy and force with a skill that baffled Americans and other Ojibwe leaders alike. He used the Colt .45 revolver he received as a gift from President Franklin Pierce to kill Dakota assailants and traders who exploited his people. Hole in the Day was assassinated in 1868 on his way to Washington to renegotiate Ojibwe removal to the White Earth Reservation. In testimony given as part of a land fraud case in White Earth years after the chief's death, trader Augustus Aspinwall remarked about the killing of the chief: "It was much easier for the agents to get along with these Indians after Hole-in-the-Day's death, as he was the smartest Indian chief the Chippewa [Ojibwe] Indians ever had." ■

first recorded the spring in 1627, and 300 years later the New York State Oil Producers Association dedicated a monument at the site commemorating its role in the history of the American oil industry.

AROOSTOOK BAND OF MICMAC INDIANS

Tribe: Aroostook Band of Micmac Indians of Maine
Current Location: Maine   **Total Area:** 314.38 acres
Tribal Enrollment: 999

The Aroostook Band of Micmac Indians and 28 other bands in Canada comprise the Micmac Nation. The Micmac are members of the Wabanaki Confederacy, an alliance forged among the Maliseet, Passamaquoddy, Penobscot, and Abenaki tribes in the 18th century. Tribal history and place-names suggest that the Micmac and Maliseet

Englishman William Penn's treaty with the Indians who lived in what is now Pennsylvania has been made famous by artists. The details are unknown, but the agreement was probably reached in 1682 or 1683.

peoples jointly inhabited this area for at least several thousand years. Traditionally, the Micmac people lived along the 400-mile St. John River, on the Canadian border in northern Maine. Archaeological evidence suggests that Native gatherers inhabited this region as early as 12,000 years ago.

Micmacs served as the first middlemen in French trade with the interior Native population. Competition intensified existing rivalries between the Micmac and the neighboring Abenaki, though any conflicts between the groups rarely resulted in fatalities. This changed with the introduction of guns by the French. While the colonial governments eventually attempted to limit the gun trade, the already-established pattern of trading furs for guns resulted in a deadly cycle for the area's Native people.

A migratory people, the Micmac traditionally subsisted on hunting and fishing. Throughout the 20th century, the Micmac supported themselves through seasonal labor, selling crafts—particularly splint basketry—logging, river driving, blueberry raking, and potato picking, often crossing into Canada to seek employment.

In 1970, the tribe formed the Association of Aroostook Indians to combat poverty and discrimination. They gained state recognition of their tribal status in 1973, becoming eligible for Maine's Department of Indian Affairs services, Indian scholarships, and free hunting and fishing licenses. Due to inadequate resources, documentation of Micmac history in Maine was not available when the state's other tribes participated in the 1980 settlement of the Maine

Indian land claims, and the Aroostook Band was unable to benefit. In 1982, the band incorporated the Aroostook Micmac Council, headquartered in Presque Isle.

Without reservation status, tribal members learned to retain their heritage while residing in Euro-American communities and continue to speak their native language, which is part of the Algonquian language family.

BAY MILLS INDIAN COMMUNITY

Tribe: Bay Mills Indian Community (Ojibwe)
Current Location: Michigan   **Total Area:** 3,185 acres
Tribal Enrollment: 1,646

The Bay Mills Indian Community is an Ojibwe (Chippewa) reservation. The name Chippewa, widely used in treaties and other official documents, is actually a corruption of "Ojibwe" and has many alternative spellings. The Ojibwe and their allies once commanded a vast territory in the Great Lakes region, extending as far west as the Turtle Mountains of North Dakota.

Tribal legends tell that the Ojibwe were led by the crane, *ajiijaak,* circling overhead and calling in his great voice to the people, up the St. Marys River to Lake Superior and its great schools of fish. The primary religious society of the Ojibwe is the Midewiwin (Grand Medicine Society).

In alliance with the French, the Ojibwe pushed the Dakota farther west. Then, in Pontiac's Rebellion of 1763, they drove the British from all their western outposts except Forts Pitt and Detroit. Later, Ojibwe warriors fought with Tecumseh in a major pan-Indian military campaign in the upper Midwest. After the defeat of Tecumseh in 1813, the Ojibwe entered into more than 30 treaties with the U.S. government.

The first land set aside exclusively for the Bay Mills Indian Community was purchased by the Methodist Mission Society. The sovereign status of the tribe was affirmed in treaties in

INDIAN ORIGINS IN THE AMERICAS

Many books assert that Indians came to the Western Hemisphere around 10,000 years ago by crossing an ice bridge that linked Asia to the Americas. Recent archaeological discoveries are challenging this prevailing thinking and pushing back the date of human arrival in the Americas to anywhere from 12,000 to 20,000 years ago, before the last ice bridge that connected the continents.

Archaeologists are still arguing about the dates and the validity of many sites, but increasingly the scientific community is saying that the Bering Strait theory of human migration is wrong. Ancient civilizations (such as those of Egypt, Phoenicia, Greece, and China) are typically 4,000 to 5,000 years old. There weren't even humans in the British Isles 12,000 years ago—the area was covered with ice. But Indians had established themselves in the Americas by then. Native Americans are not immigrants. They are indigenous.

As scientists struggle to explain the dates and methods of human arrival in the Americas, Indians continue to hold onto traditional stories that explain their genesis. Indigenous creation stories do not always challenge prevailing scientific thought, but they do contain tremendous symbolic meaning and present a different way of envisioning and explaining the world. All the tribes in the Northeast have creation stories that place their arrival in the world in North America. For the Iroquois and most Algonquian tribes, origin stories revolve around the creation of the Earth on the back of a giant turtle and give rise to the now pan-Indian term "Turtle Island" for North America. ∎

A close-up of a belt made around 1785 from woven wampum, the tiny beads used as currency by some Native Americans

1855 and 1860. Prior to the arrival of Europeans and the ascent of the fur trade, the Bay Mills Ojibwe subsisted primarily by hunting and fishing, along with some agricultural pursuits. The Ojibwe turned to the fur trade as a means of acquiring items to barter and solidify military alliances.

Today, the tribe accommodates an unusual mix of old and new. The Bay Mills Community continues to assert its traditional and treaty rights, including fishing rights in Lake Superior, Lake Huron, and Lake Michigan. Approximately 300 families still live in a traditional Ojibwe fishing village that is part of the Bay Mills reservation, while cultivation of wild rice on 460 acres of wetland preserve in the eastern Upper Peninsula is an increasingly innovative agricultural endeavor that yields significant revenues.

A child reads to her mother and siblings in a grassy field in the Nett Lake area of the Bois Forte Band of Chippewa reservation in northern Minnesota.

BOIS FORTE BAND OF CHIPPEWA

Tribe: Minnesota Chippewa Tribe
Current Location: Minnesota
Total Area: **43,789** acres   Tribal Enrollment: **2,988**

Six Ojibwe bands make up the Minnesota Chippewa Tribe, each with its own reservation: Bois Forte Band (Nett Lake), Fond du Lac, Grand Portage, Leech Lake, Mille Lacs (see pages 42 and 46–47), and White Earth.

The tribal language uses the terms *Ojibwe* and *Anishinaabe* for self-reference. Bois Forte is a French term that translates as "Dense [or Strong] Woods."

The Bois Forte Ojibwe were originally composed of several independent self-governing villages. The Ojibwe first encountered French explorers in the

THE NORTHEAST

WAMPANOAG

The Wampanoag (People of the First Light) were different from most other Algonquian tribes in the Northeast. While many tribes moved for seasonal rounds of harvest and hunt, the Wampanoag were sedentary farmers of corn, beans, and squash who augmented their diet with fish and game. Gender roles were also different for the Wampanoag, who sometimes had female chiefs and provided women a large voice in political functions. Men hunted, fished, and fought, but women produced 75 percent of the food at the time of European contact, and land rights were passed down through the mother. The Wampanoag population was estimated to be around 12,000 in the late 16th century—enough people to occupy and defend a large territory in southeastern Massachusetts and Rhode Island.

Friends at First

Under Chief Massasoit, the Wampanoag forged a peaceful relationship with English settlers. Tisquantum (Squanto), a Patuxet Indian, lived with the Wampanoag in the early 1600s when that relationship developed. His story has been embellished over the years, but the popular version does contain some notable truths. Massasoit, Squanto, and other Wampanoags taught the Puritans how to farm. Although farming was widespread in Europe, the climate, topography, and soil conditions were completely different in New England, and the European cereal grasses such as wheat, barley, and oats routinely failed. The Wampanoag showed the English how to rotate crops to maintain soil fertility and how to survive in the harsh New England climate. The survival of the first English settlers would have been impossible without the instruction and support of the Wampanoag.

Settlers at Plymouth, Massachusetts, received their first land from the Wampanoag in a grant arranged by treaty that gave the English 12,000 acres. Although Indians did not understand the terms of the treaty at the time, the peaceful relationship lasted for years. Tribe members actively traded with and lived near the English settlements. Many converted to Christianity.

A statue of Massasoit, a Wampanoag chief who lived in New England in the 1600s, stands near Utah's capitol.

The Wampanoag traditionally held feasts at the conclusion of each fall harvest, but it was not the same as the first Thanksgiving story so often taught to American schoolchildren. Although the romanticized version of the first Thanksgiving is often attributed to the Wampanoag-Puritan experience, archival records do not support that. The first clear evidence of a tribal-white harvest celebration appears after the Pequot War in 1637, rather than as part of the Wampanoag efforts to teach Puritans how to farm and survive their first winter in 1621.

Illness and War

Because of their frequent sustained contact with white settlers, the Wampanoag were more exposed to virgin-soil epidemics than were other tribes. European diseases wiped out as much as 90 percent of the Wampanoag population, which had no resistance to them. The pandemics rapidly and dramatically reduced the population, which in turn completely disrupted basic life functions, such as the fall harvest. That brought poverty, hunger, rapid leadership transitions, political upheaval, and grief. In addition, because the Wampanoag were at first hurt more than their Indian neighbors, they were far more vulnerable to enemy attacks than ever before. They suffered defeats at the hands of the Narragansett and were forced to cede territory.

The peaceful relationship between the Wampanoag and Puritan settlers irrevocably deteriorated after the death of Chief Massasoit. His son Wamsutta (Alexander) died immediately after his first parley with the English as chief, and his people suspected that he had been poisoned. The English-Wampanoag relationship disintegrated even further in

A young Wampanoag inside a reed hut at Plimoth Plantation in Plymouth, Massachusetts, where Indians at a re-created home site talk with tourists about their history and life

1675, when three Wampanoag men were hanged by the English for a murder they did not commit. Wamsutta's younger brother, Metacom (Philip), rallied the remaining Wampanoag population (now numbering fewer than 1,000) to resist the English colonization. Other tribes joined the cause, and an unlikely confederation of tribes that once battled each other suddenly offered the English the most formidable resistance they had encountered. The conflict, often called King Philip's War, was brutal. The Indians burned 52 of the 90 English settlements in the area. Five percent of the white population was killed, at a cost of 40 percent of the Indian population. The Wampanoag were reduced to only 400. Metacom's wife and children were sold as slaves in the West Indies, and after the English killed Metacom himself, the chief's head was displayed on a pike in the village of Plymouth for more than 20 years.

Reviving a Culture

Today there are five distinct organized groups of Wampanoag. Although all have applied for recognition by the U.S. government, only two presently have federal status—the Wampanoag Tribe of Gay Head (Martha's Vineyard) and the Mashpee Wampanoag Tribe. There are more than 2,000 tribal members. The Wampanoag language was completely stamped out, but tribal members are trying to revitalize it from missionary documents, Bibles, and other sources, augmented by knowledge of related Algonquian languages. Christianity still dominates Wampanoag religious experience, although elements of ancient tribal culture, food, and custom persist. ■

1600s near Sault Ste. Marie. Later, they prospered in the fur trade and expanded their population and territory. By the late 18th century, the Ojibwe had expanded their domain westward through Wisconsin and northeastern Minnesota and Ontario. Conflict with the Dakota continued sporadically until the mid-1860s. When Euro-American settlers arrived, the Ojibwe held undisputed control of more than two-thirds of Minnesota.

The Bois Forte reservation was established piecemeal through treaties in 1854 and 1866 with major modifications by executive orders in later years. The 1889 Nelson Act established a reservation at Red Lake and implemented allotment on all other Ojibwe reservations in Minnesota, including Bois Forte. In spite of relentless land and timber fraud by government and commercial interests, the Bois

An engraving from circa 1634 shows a wigwam in a Ho-Chunk (Winnebago) village. Animal skins are stretched over a hemispherical wooden frame, unlike the conical design of the tepees of the Plains Indians.

Forte Ojibwe survived and adapted, retaining many aspects of traditional culture, including harvesting wild rice, fishing, and hunting.

The original constitution and bylaws of the Minnesota Chippewa Tribe were ratified in 1936, in accordance with the Indian Reorganization Act. The six member reservations of the Minnesota Chippewa Tribe sought a single consolidated tribal government without relinquishing governance at the local level. Each member reservation elects its own tribal government. Public Law 280 initially sought to assert state criminal jurisdiction over all of the Minnesota Chippewa Tribe and many other tribes as well. The Bois Forte Ojibwe successfully got their reservation exempted in 1975 and proudly maintain their own police force and court system as a vibrant and strengthening dimension of their tribal sovereignty.

CAYUGA NATION RESERVATION

Tribe: Cayuga Nation of New York   Current Location: New York   Total Area: 0 acres   Tribal Enrollment: 475

Members of the Gayogoho:no, or Cayuga Nation, originated in the Cayuga Lake area of present-day New York. The Cayuga are original members of the Haudenosaunee, or Iroquois, Confederacy. *Haudenosaunee* means "People of the Longhouse." The Cayuga, or People of the Great Swamp, were the fourth of the original five nations to join the confederacy. The Mohawk, Oneida, Onondaga, and Seneca tribes were the other four original nations, and the Tuscarora joined later.

The Iroquois Confederacy is one of the world's oldest known democracies. Recent findings have encouraged some scholars to believe that the confederacy is at least 300 years older than previously thought. These theories have been supported by archaeological, scientific, and oral history evidence. The Cayuga are the Younger Brothers under the Kaianerekowa, the Great Law of Peace. The confederacy put an end to tribal warfare between the member tribes and greatly strengthened the economic, political, and military might of the Iroquois.

The Cayuga Nation Reservation was illegally seized by the State of New York in the late 1700s. The Cayuga Nation and the Seneca-Cayuga Nation of Oklahoma are engaged in a decades-long legal claim against the State of New York. Today, the tribe is still largely focused on acquiring land in Seneca and Cayuga Counties. Though the Cayuga Nation does not have a land base, many tribe members reside on or near the Seneca Nation Reservation in western New York.

The tribe is governed by the traditional Council of Chiefs and Clan Mothers. The Cayuga chiefs also sit on the Haudenosaunee Grand Council. The Cayuga Nation is made up of five clans. These clans signify family lineage, and a Cayuga citizen's clan is

This Ojibwe shoulder bag was made about 1885 from wool, silk, and muslin cloth and decorated with glass beads.

determined by the clan of his or her mother. Each is a member of one of the five clans—Bear, Heron, Snipe, Turtle, or Wolf. Each clan has a Clan Mother, whose role it is to take care of her clan members. Each clan has council representatives who form the decision-making body of the Nation. Tribally owned enterprises such as convenience stores and a thriving gaming industry contribute to the tribal economy and foster the presence of the tribe in the community.

GAY HEAD RESERVATION

Tribe: Wampanoag Tribe of Gay Head (Aquinnah) of Massachusetts   Current Location: Massachusetts   Total Area: 485 acres   Tribal Enrollment: 1,065

The Aquinnah Wampanoag people have lived in Aquinnah (Gay Head) on the island of Noepe (Martha's Vineyard) for at least hundreds of years. Tribal lands once also encompassed what is now mainland U.S. to the north and west of the island. Of eastern Algonquian linguistic stock, the Wampanoag were referred to as the Pokanokets in early documents. A horticultural people, during the early 17th century the Wampanoag occupied approximately 30 villages in southern Massachusetts and eastern Rhode Island. Best known for their relationship with the Plymouth Pilgrims, the Wampanoag leader Massasoit welcomed the English and remained at peace with them until his death in 1661. By that time the Wampanoag had suffered devastating losses due to diseases and the usurpation of ancestral land.

In retaliation for these losses, Massasoit's son, Metacom, led a coalition of New England tribes against the colonists in 1675. It was later called King Philip's War, in reference to the English name for Metacom. The Native people were initially successful, but Metacom had trouble keeping his coalition of tribes together. Despite heavy losses, the English succeeded, and Metacom was killed in 1676.

By 1800, only three Wampanoag communities remained, at Aquinnah, Christiantown, and Chappaquiddick. The Aquinnah community was the only one able to maintain control over its lands and to demand recognition as a sovereign nation. The Wampanoag Tribal Council of Gay Head was established in 1972 to fight for the recognition of tribal status, the preservation of Wampanoag culture and history, and the restoration of tribal lands. In 1987, the Wampanoag Tribe received federal recognition.

Because of sensitivity to the area's wetlands and historical and archaeological sites, not all the Wampanoag land can be developed, but a careful land development plan has been established. Joint efforts by the tribe, the Center for Economic Development, the University of Massachusetts, and Harvard University have allowed tribal members to practice traditional fishing and hunting, as well.

GRAND TRAVERSE BAND OF OTTAWA AND CHIPPEWA INDIANS RESERVATION

Tribe: Grand Traverse Band of Ottawa and Chippewa Indians   Current Location: Michigan
Total Area: 2,369 acres   Tribal Enrollment: 3,985

Historically, Michigan's Native population included three tribes, united in the Three Fires Confederacy: the Ojibwe (Chippewa), Ottawa, and Potawatomi. In the Council of Three Fires, the Ojibwe are "keepers of the faith"; the Ottawa are "keepers of trade"; and the Potawatomi are "keepers of the fire." These peoples lived by hunting and fishing in the game-rich forests surrounding the Great Lakes. Following the conflict known as the French and Indian War, contact with settlers led to declines in hunting and fishing, while farming, manufacturing, and wage work increased.

Despite outside pressures, the band's settlement areas on the Leelanau Peninsula remained constant and populated, preserving traditional lifestyles. Today, a small but revered group of tribal elders in

Ojibwe (Chippewa), Algonquian language family

"Anishinaabe ogii-wiindamaagoon manidoon ji-aabaji'aad asemaan wii-waabanda'aad manaajitood gakina gegoo mamood omaa akiing—getigaadegin, editegin, bineshiinyag, awesiinyag, bebaamikwazhiwejig igaye. Manidoo ogitigaan o'ow minis ebiitamang."

("The Indian people were told by the creator to use tobacco to show how they respect everything they take from the Earth—plants, berries, birds, animals, and water creatures. This planet we inhabit is the Great Spirit's garden.")

the community still speak the traditional Ottawa language, which they call Anishnaabemowin.

In an 1855 treaty, the eastern two-thirds of Leelanau County was ceded to the Indians of the area. Over time this land was lost, piecemeal, to fraudulent land schemes and legalized government appropriation. Federal recognition of the band was not granted until 1980, despite clear references to the Ottawa people of the area in several 19th-century treaties and a strong Indian presence throughout the Leelanau Peninsula. Since its official recognition, the band is steadily improving the quality of life for members, who live on tribal land in six counties.

HO-CHUNK NATION

Tribe: Ho-Chunk Nation of Wisconsin
Current Location: Wisconsin   Total Area: 6,018 acres
Tribal Enrollment: 6,611

The Ho-Chunk Nation, formerly the Winnebago Tribe, has resided in the Wisconsin region for hundreds of years. The people were originally a horticultural society, but eventually they began to rely upon hunting, fishing, and harvesting wild rice to augment their farming.

The Ho-Chunk tribe encountered French explorers in 1634 in the area of present-day Green Bay. During the early contact with the Euro-Americans, the Ho-Chunk suffered greatly from European diseases and intertribal warfare, reducing the population from approximately 4,500 to less than 700.

The remaining tribe settled on territory by Lake Winnebago near the Mississippi River and continued to move westward toward larger trading centers. During the 17th and 18th centuries, the Ho-Chunk traded furs with both the French and the British. During the Revolutionary War, the Ho-Chunk fought against the United States.

In the 1830s, the tribe moved into the region north of the Wisconsin River. It began ceding its territory to the federal government, and many Ho-Chunk tribal members were forcibly removed to Iowa, Minnesota, South Dakota, or Nebraska. Those who refused to go sought refuge in the forests, where they squatted in their traditional homeland and endured years of hardship. What tribal land remained in Wisconsin was allotted after 1881 and quickly passed into non-Indian hands.

During this period, many members returned to Wisconsin and refused to move again. The Ho-Chunks gradually repurchased some of their traditional land in Wisconsin. Approximately 48 percent of the tribe's members live on or near tribal lands in Wisconsin, where a number of traditional Ho-Chunk burial sites are still visible. The tribe also purchased over 600 acres of farmland in Muscoda, Wisconsin, which includes effigy mounds.

The tribe first received federal recognition in 1963 as the Wisconsin Winnebago Tribe. Then, in 1994, the Bureau of Indian Affairs (BIA) formally recognized and approved the new tribal constitution,

and the name officially changed to the Ho-Chunk Nation. Due to the Nation's nonreservation status, it is permitted to purchase lands throughout its ancestral territory and request that the BIA grant it trust status. The tribe has used revenues earned from gaming to repurchase some 2,000 acres of traditional land.

HOULTON MALISEET RESERVATION

Tribe: Houlton Band of Maliseet Indians of Maine
Current Location: Maine   Total Area: 850 acres
Tribal Enrollment: 861

The Houlton Band of Maliseet Indians has resided in present-day New England and southeastern Canada for countless years.

Ojibwe feather headgear is part of a traditional outfit worn to a modern powwow.

IROQUOIS (HAUDENOSAUNEE)

The Haudenosaunee (People of the Longhouse), often referred to as the Iroquois, are made up of six tribes. Around 1450, they organized a sophisticated ceremonial and cultural institution, usually called the Iroquois League, in which the five original member tribes held essential positions and were represented by 50 chiefs in joint council. The Mohawk were guardians of the eastern door and were represented by nine chiefs. The Seneca guarded the western door and were represented by eight chiefs. The Onondaga kept the central fire and sent 14 chiefs to the council. The Cayuga, with ten chiefs, and the Oneida, with nine, were located centrally on either side of the Onondaga. A sixth tribe, the Tuscarora (originally from North Carolina), joined in the 18th century.

Cultural Power: The Iroquois League

The Iroquois League was created primarily to make peace among the member tribes and strengthen each politically, ceremonially, and economically. Deganawida (the Great Peacemaker) and Hiawatha developed the Great Law of Peace that governed the Iroquois and strengthened all member tribes. They symbolically buried their implements of war under the Great Tree of Peace. The expression "bury the hatchet" is derived from this critical event in Iroquois history.

The Iroquois have always maintained a vibrant clan system, with anywhere from three to eight for each tribe. Clans are a matrilineal designation, passed on through the mother. Throughout Iroquois history, women have maintained a degree of political and ceremonial power that is different from most other tribes in the Northeast. Clan mothers select the 50 chiefs of the league. They can veto war decisions, initiate legislation, keep a separate formal council, and are empowered to remove chiefs from office by symbolically "knocking off the horns," a sometimes dramatic event that can be accompanied by a beating of the chief.

The military and economic power of the Iroquois existed not only because of their well-designed leadership structure but also thanks to a high population density, which was made possible by one of the world's most efficient agriculture systems. The "three sister" crops—corn,

French settlers and Algonquin Indians, allies against the Iroquois, attack an Iroquois stronghold that is protected by a stockade, July 1609.

beans, and squash—were grown in integrated fields, with bean vines growing up the cornstalks and the squash partially shaded underneath. It was a natural relationship that maintained soil fertility, moisture, the perfect combination of sun and shade, and a food yield per acre that was ten times what European farmers could achieve.

Political and Military Power: The Iroquois Confederacy

Overlapping the ceremonial and cultural functions of the Iroquois League was another entity, often called the Iroquois Confederacy. The confederacy was a formidable political and military body. It is now largely defunct, but for centuries it enabled the Iroquois to dominate a massive swath of territory.

By the year 1000, the Iroquois had exclusive control over the Finger Lakes in what is now upstate New York, and by 1200, they had pushed other tribes out of most of the Ohio Valley. The Iroquois were at the height of their military and political power by 1600, and used their military muscle and political cohesiveness to play the Dutch, French, and British against one another. In 1677, the Iroquois Confederacy allied with the British, and relations with the French went from strained to hostile.

Brutal conflict with the French from 1685 to 1689 resulted in many Iroquois

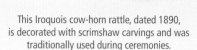

This Iroquois cow-horn rattle, dated 1890, is decorated with scrimshaw carvings and was traditionally used during ceremonies.

casualties. In a nasty feat of trickery, the French summoned the Grand Council chiefs to a meeting and captured all 50 of them, selling them as galley slaves in Marseilles and prompting major retributive warfare. The Three Fires Confederacy (Ojibwe, Ottawa, and Potawatomi) allied with the French. By 1701, the Iroquois were reeling from the conflict and signed treaties that established a lasting peace with the Three Fires Confederacy but diminished Iroquois power. The Iroquois Confederacy again sided with the British during the French and Indian War, but in spite of their assistance in evicting the French from the Great Lakes, the Iroquois were further mistreated by the British in the Treaty of Fort Stanwix (1768), as their lands came under increased colonial pressure.

Fracture and Rebuilding

The American Revolution was devastating for the Iroquois Confederacy, as some member tribes sided with the British and others with the colonists. After the war, some of those who had allied with the British moved to Canada, and the Iroquois never recovered their cohesion.

In the second half of the 18th century, the Iroquois underwent a religious revitalization through a prophet named Handsome Lake. He preached temperance, monogamy, and aversion to gambling. Some of his ideas may have been

Among northeastern tribes, lacrosse served as training for battle. Today there are intertribal competitions where Iroquois boys as young as Matthew Bennet play.

influenced by Christianity, especially because gambling and polygamy were deeply entrenched among the Iroquois. However, his ideas had wide appeal.

Today, the Iroquois Confederacy no longer functions, but the Iroquois League and longhouse culture still thrive. There are communities in Oklahoma, Wisconsin, New York, and Canada. The Iroquois population is now more than 80,000 in the United States and more than 45,000 in Canada. All the tribes are making serious initiatives with their languages. The Mohawk have made the earliest and most successful interventions, developing immersion schools and producing publications and technological innovations. ∎

There are seven bands in the Maliseet Nation, six of them based in Canada. The indigenous language of the Maliseet is an Algonquian dialect. Maliseet people call themselves Wolastoqiyik, which refers to a river that runs through the Maliseet homeland. Traditional means of sustenance included hunting, gathering, and salmon harvesting. The tribe belongs to the Wabanaki Confederacy, forged among the Penobscot, Passamaquoddy, Micmac, and Abenaki tribes in the 18th century.

The indigenous peoples of the northeastern United States began encountering Europeans in the early 17th century. The arrival of settlers brought scourges of European diseases, including smallpox, that devastated many Native American tribal populations, including that of the Maliseet.

In 1970, the Houlton Band and members of other non-reservation tribes organized the Association of Aroostook Indians to promote the recognition of their Native status. In 1973, the group was awarded access to services provided by Maine's Department of Indian Affairs. The group eventually dissolved, and the Maliseet reorganized as the Houlton Band of

MYTH OR FACT?

Indians invented the birchbark canoe.

FACT

The birchbark canoe, invented by the Ojibwe and used by the Ojibwe, Ottawa, Potawatomi, and Menominee tribes in the Northeast, was a technological development so profound (twice as buoyant and four times lighter than alternative styles of craft) that it gave those tribes a tremendous advantage in warfare with other tribes and in the fur trade. French and British traders abandoned other styles of boat in the Great Lakes region in favor of the birchbark through the fur-trade era.

Maliseet Indians. In 1980, the band was recognized in the Maine Indian Land Claim Settlement Act as the sole successor of the Maliseet Nation within the United States. Although a federally recognized tribe, the Houlton Band remains under the jurisdiction of the State of Maine. The band is required to make payments to the state in lieu of paying taxes.

More than 300 acres of tribal lands are tillable, and the tribe leases their fertile lands to farmers, who raise potatoes, peas, barley, and fiddleheads.

The Maliseet Tribe was a party to the Jay Treaty of 1794. This treaty granted tribal members the right to travel freely between the United States and Canada.

The tribe's primary environmental concerns include protecting the Meduxnekeag River watershed. The tribe hopes that restoring a clean water source will encourage the revitalization of the fish and bald eagle populations. The tribe is also a member of the Meduxnekeag Watershed Coalition.

As in many New England indigenous communities, the art of basketry continues to be practiced among the Maliseet. Tribal artists are renowned for their intricate techniques.

Clyde Bellecourt has spent his life fighting for the rights of all Indian people.

CLYDE BELLECOURT

Civil rights activist

Clyde Bellecourt (Niigaanwewidang) is cofounder of the American Indian Movement (AIM). He grew up on the White Earth Reservation (Ojibwe) in northwestern Minnesota and in Minneapolis. As an adult, he fought the poverty and racism he had encountered in childhood. AIM, created in 1968, catapulted to fame with its protests of federal Indian policy, including the Trail of Broken Treaties march from California to Washington, D.C., in 1972; the burning of the courthouse in Custer, South Dakota, in 1973; and the subsequent takeover of the Wounded Knee Trading Post on the Pine Ridge Reservation in South Dakota. These events raised awareness of Indian discontent, but did little to change policy. Bellecourt's greatest achievements with AIM are less well known. They include creating the AIM Legal Rights Center in 1968, which provided free legal counsel to more than 30,000 Indians in Minnesota. Bellecourt also helped found and still helps run AIM Patrol, which sought to police the police, assist Indians with legal grievances, and advocate for crime victims. The group evolved over time. In 1986, when a serial killer was targeting Indian women in Minneapolis, the AIM Patrol provided free protective escorts. Bellecourt now focuses on combating the use of Indians as sports mascots. ∎

This colorized 1903 postcard depicts a Native American man, identified as the Ojibwe brave Arrowmaker, in midrun with a throwing ax, or tomahawk, raised above his head. The card was printed by the Detroit Photographic Company.

rather and govenor

INDIAN TOWNSHIP
RESERVATION

Tribe: Passamaquoddy Tribe of Maine   Current Location:
Maine   Total Area: 24,570 acres   Tribal Enrollment (BIA
labor report, 2001): 1,314

In a 1921 photograph,
future U.S. President
Franklin Delano Roose-
velt meets with Iroquois
chief Francis Joseph
Neptune on Campo-
bello Island in Canada.

The Passamaquoddy tribe has inhabited the
Northeast for several thousand years. Its members speak an Algonquian language and are
closely related to the Penobscot, Maliseet, Micmac,

and Abenaki and part of the Wabenaki. The tribe
is the largest federally recognized Native American
nation in New England.

During the colonial period, traditional Passamaquoddy land and resources became a point of dispute as both the French and the English attempted to
gain control of the area. This competition escalated
into the French and Indian War. The indigenous
groups in Maine generally sided with the French, and
also sided with the American colonists during the

Revolutionary War. Passamaquoddy chief Francis Joseph Neptune led a party of tribal members in the efforts to turn back British forces in eastern Maine. The tribe further assisted the Americans in the naval attack at Machias in 1777. George Washington acknowledged the tribe's efforts and proclaimed a pledge of friendship between the Americans and the Passamaquoddy people.

By the 1960s, many tribal members were forced to leave the region in search of work and considered legal recourse for the loss of tribal lands, resulting in the Maine Indian Land Claim Settlement Act of 1980. The act enabled the tribe to buy back lands at fair market value and to invest in business ventures. Since then, the Passamaquoddy Tribe of Maine has purchased almost 134,000 acres, which include 6,000 acres of blueberry barrens. Improved conditions and enhanced services have drawn tribal members back to the reservations.

The tribe occupies two reservations in northeastern Maine. The Indian Township and Pleasant Point Reservations are situated about 50 miles apart near the eastern seaboard. The Indian Township Reservation is the largest Native American reservation in the state of Maine and consists of two neighborhoods: Peter Dana Point is located at Big Lake, and the Indian Township strip overlooks Lewy Lake. Pleasant Point Reservation consists of its original 100 acres plus 112 acres of annexed land authorized by the state of Maine. Sipayik, the main Passamaquoddy village since 1770, is situated on a promontory in Passamaquoddy Bay.

LITTLE RIVER BAND RESERVATION

Tribe: Little River Band of Ottawa Indians
Current Location: Michigan   **Total Area:** 2,763 acres
Tribal Enrollment: 3,369

The Ottawa are a member of the Algonquian language family and an important partner in the Three Fires Confederacy of the Great Lakes along with the Ojibwe and Potawatomi. Paddling birchbark canoes

This traditional Iroquois hickory bark rattle was used during ceremonial songs and dances.

over great distances, the Ottawa were intermediaries with other Algonquian tribes in the Great Lakes, and they brought the furs they collected to the French at various Huron villages. The term *ottawa* means "trader," reflecting their role as tribal traders even before contact with Europeans. By 1685, Ottawa middlemen were supplying two-thirds of the furs at Montreal. Ottawa power declined after the British takeover of French trade networks in the Great Lakes in 1760, but they remained influential. Ottawa chief Pontiac organized a pan-Indian alliance against the British in 1763 that captured nine of the eleven British forts in the Great Lakes region.

The next 100 years, however, witnessed a relentless whittling away of the Ottawa lands. Notable among the devastating "treaties" was the 1821 Treaty of Chicago—which the leader Kewaycooshkum signed, completely against the wishes of his people and their brother tribes—resulting in the cession of all Ottawa lands south of the Grand River. In 1836, the Ottawa and Ojibwe of Michigan ceded most of their remaining land in upper and lower Michigan, although they managed to retain land reservations as well as the right to continue hunting, fishing, and gathering on the lands they had ceded. The Grand River Ottawa, including the people now comprising the Little River Band, retained a large reservation along the Manistee River, referred to as the Manistee Reserve. In concert with the other tribes in Michigan and with the state, the Ottawa maintain traditions as the custodians of the Manistee River Basin and nearby Lake Michigan.

Throughout the 20th century, Grand River Ottawa leaders continued to pursue claims for both land and money. Prominent leaders during this period were Sampson Robinson, Jacob Walker Cobmoosa, and Enos Pego. Many agreements were forged and tragically broken, culminating in the de facto termination of the tribe. Finally, in 1994, the U.S. Congress enacted the Little River Act, which recognized the tribe and reaffirmed the band's rights and privileges.

MENOMINEE

The Menominee call themselves Mamaceqtaw, meaning "the people," or Kiash Matchitiwuk, meaning "the ancient ones." Their popular name, Menominee, is derived from the Ojibwe word *Omanoominii,* meaning "People of the Wild Rice." The Menominee had homes around Mackinac, Michigan, in the heart of Ojibwe country, when Europeans first encountered them, but are more closely related to the Fox and Kickapoo in terms of language. Like most Algonquian tribes, the Menominee have a patrilineal clan system, but with only five primary totems—bear, eagle, wolf, crane, and moose. The Menominee successfully avoided genocidal conflicts with both Europeans and other Indians, maintaining a significant territory in northeastern Wisconsin throughout the French and British regimes.

The Reservation Period

The U.S. government put massive pressure on Menominee land and life. Through a series of seven treaties signed between 1821 and 1848, the United States claimed title to all Menominee lands in Wisconsin, and by 1848 the people were designated for removal to central Minnesota. The Menominee were reluctant to move, not only because they loved their homeland but also because the removal location would have placed them in the center of a conflict between the much larger Ojibwe and Dakota tribes. On May 12, 1854, the Menominee ceded their reservation in Minnesota for a much smaller portion of their original territory on the Wolf River in northeastern Wisconsin. They had never actually moved to Minnesota, in spite of the removal effort, and simply remained in their old villages. The new reservation was roughly conterminous with present-day Menominee County, Wisconsin.

In 1856, the U.S. government took the southwest corner of the reservation and carved out a separate reservation for the

The Menominee American Legion parades in a Memorial Day celebration. Many Indians have served in the U.S. armed forces over the decades.

Stockbridge and Munsee Indians. In spite of the hardships caused by land loss and frequent government intrusions, the Menominee proved themselves to be culturally resilient and economically innovative. They developed one of the world's very first sustainable harvest forestry programs—designating a level of timber cutting that could be maintained every year without damaging the resource. They preserved significant tracts of land for traditional use, developing some of the largest and most productive sugar maple stands in the world. The Menominee forestry program provided jobs and a consistent source of revenue for the tribe. By the 1950s, they had banked more than $10 million from the operation for tribal use without any government support.

Termination

In 1954, the U.S. government developed a devastating national Indian policy called termination. Through that policy, the government listed tribal governments to be officially disbanded, with tribal land to be converted from a protected trust to taxable status. The Menominee tribe was terminated in 1961. Tribal members then formed a corporation to own and care for their land and look after tribal members as stockholders. This innovative development helped mitigate the damage of termination, but it could not entirely stave off the pressure on Menominee land. To pay taxes on the land, the Menominee sold significant pieces of their reservation to speculators. The tribe's sustainable forestry program was closed, and all employees were laid off. The federal

A Menominee youth rides a spirited horse. The tribe's government was terminated in 1961, but later restored.

government ended up spending more money in entitlements to increasingly impoverished tribal members than it had previously allocated to support the tribal government.

Ada Deer and other Menominee activists waged a sophisticated and persistent legal and political battle to reinstate the Menominee. They organized Menominee DRUMS (Determination of Rights and Unity for Menominee Stockholders) in the 1970s and staged protests and lobbying efforts. Sylvia Wilbur, Margaret Treuer, and other young Natives from many tribes joined the effort, soliciting letters of support from the American Civil Liberties Union and the League of

Women Voters. In 1973, with only one dissenting vote, Congress reinstated the Menominee. A new tribal government was in place by 1979.

Political, Economic, and Cultural Revitalization

The Menominee had lost a significant portion of their land; many people had moved during the termination era to find jobs. They recovered, however, and re-formed their forestry initiative with remarkable success. The government misplaced the $10 million the tribe had banked in trust, but through legal channels, the tribe was able to recover most of it. The tribe has maintained its position as a world leader in the sustainable harvesting of natural resources, even creating the Sustainable Development Institute at Menominee Nation College for training tribal members and others.

In addition to persistent pressure on their land and government, the Menominee endured relentless demands to convert to Christianity and assimilate culturally. The once widely practiced Menominee medicine dance is now defunct, although some tribal members participate in Ojibwe lodge ceremonies. The ceremonial drum culture on the Menominee reservation, however, is still very strong. It has grown in popularity, while also evolving in function—many traditional funerals are vested in drum culture now instead of medicine dance. The adaptation has filled a void and enabled the Menominee to maintain critical aspects of their culture and religion. Nearly 10,000 people identify themselves as Menominee today. ■

THE NORTHEAST

MASHANTUCKET PEQUOT RESERVATION

Tribe: Mashantucket Pequot Tribe of Connecticut
Current Location: Connecticut
Total Area: 1,403 acres   Tribal Enrollment: 796

The Mashantucket Pequot encountered English settlers in the early 17th century. In 1636, a militia from the Massachusetts Bay Colony traveled to Connecticut and burned two Pequot villages as retribution for a murder that a tribal member was involved in. The Pequot retaliated, seized Fort Saybrook, and cut off all river traffic at the mouth of the Connecticut River. On May 26, 1637, English soldiers and Mohegan, Narragansett, and Eastern Niantic warriors massacred some 300 to 400 Pequot women, children, and elderly men. Attacks against the Pequot continued. They were hunted, enslaved, executed, and virtually exterminated. Surviving tribal members signed the Hartford/Tripartite Treaty and were divided between two other tribes. The Mashantucket Pequot were forced to live within the Mohegan Nation, while the Pawcatuck Pequot were sent to the Narragansett Nation. The Pequot Tribe was declared dissolved, and the colony even forbade mention of its name. They were eventually permitted to return to their homelands, settling in New London and Groton, Connecticut, in 1650. The tribe's land was manipulated first by the settlers, and then by the state of Connecticut. By the 1970s, only two sisters who refused to leave their ancestral homelands remained on the reservation, which had been reduced to approximately 175 acres.

In 1976, the tribe received the assistance of the Native American Rights Fund and the Indian Rights Association in suing neighboring landowners to recover tribal lands. Within seven years, they reached a settlement and joined forces with tribal members to pressure the state to offer the tribe compensation. The tribe was granted recognition as well as the right to repurchase lost lands in 1983, after the state petitioned the federal government on the tribe's behalf.

The Mashantucket Pequot have rebuilt their economy and welcomed home hundreds of tribal members. The tribe is now one of the largest private

JOHN SMITH OF LEECH LAKE

One of the oldest elders

Although no one can be certain of his exact age, Leech Lake Ojibwe elder John Smith was one of the longest-lived people in history. When he was first photographed in the mid-1800s, he claimed to have been born in 1785. At that time, his image showed every mark of very old age—deep wrinkles, leathery skin, and evidence of arthritis in his hands and frame. He was photographed many more times over the next several decades until his death in 1922, making his life span as long as 137 years.

The Ojibwe word for elder, *gichi-aya'aa*, literally means "great being," underlining the respect afforded to elders in tribal culture. When queried about the secret of his longevity, Smith replied that he had never broken the Great Spirit's law, although he didn't elaborate on what the law was.

Smith had a well-known temper. As a young man, he accompanied a war party against the Dakota—one of four Ojibwe–Dakota battles he fought in during his lifetime. The party traveled to a location that a local medicine man said would bring them success. When Smith returned empty-handed, he killed the medicine man for providing false information. Once he was duped by a trader, who sold him watered-down whiskey, but got revenge by killing an aged horse and selling it to the trader as moose meat. ∎

employers in Connecticut, contributing to the region through donations, financing, and funding assistance to organizations, businesses, and townships.

In 1920, Mohegan tribal chief Lemuel Occum Fielding (center right), with his son Everett M. Fielding (left) and daughter Myrtle Germaine, met in Washington with Commissioner of Indian Affairs Cato Bells (right), to whom they presented their tribal claim to land in Connecticut.

MATCH-E-BE-NASH-SHE-WISH BAND OF POTAWATOMI INDIANS OF MICHIGAN

Tribe: Match-e-be-nash-she-wish Band of Potawatomi Indians of Michigan   Current Location: Michigan
Total Area: 326 acres   Tribal Enrollment: 305

In the 18th century, the Match-e-be-nash-she-wish (Potawatomi), commonly known as the Gun Lake Tribe, had villages along on the Grand, Thornapple, and Kalamazoo Rivers in southeast Michigan.

In 1795, the first chief known to have had extensive relations with non-Indians, Match-e-be-nash-she-wish, signed the Treaty of Greenville on behalf of the Ojibwe (Chippewa), Ottawa, and Potawatomi nations. For many years, Chief Match-e-be-nash-she-wish was a leading spokesman for all three central Algonquian nations.

Traditional religious customs have long been absent among the band, as Episcopalian and Methodist missionaries worked tirelessly at converting tribal members for many years prior to and after the band's official inception in 1836. Indigenous lay preachers served as the tribe's leaders, and missions served as central locations for tribal members who might otherwise have scattered or been absorbed by other tribes or the non-Indian community. By remaining separate from the surrounding communities, the tribe preserved its history and culture. Many families still make the tribe's traditional black ash baskets. The tribe provides cultural workshops on basketry and traditional art forms of Michigan tribes, such as cradle fire from flint, maple sugar, basswood, and hemp dogbane cordage, and Snowsnakes or *Zhoshke'nayabo,* and has developed a language program with the Pokagon and Nottawaseppi Huron bands.

Under the 1833 Treaty of Chicago, a dummy tribe sold five million acres of land in Michigan for $100,000, reportedly agreeing to move west of the Mississippi River. The fraud was so blatant that the federal government did not try to enforce removal for several years. The tribe's northern location attached it to the Grand River Ottawa for administrative purposes, which led to confusion as to the tribe's identity for the next 150 years. In the 1990s, the tribe organized a tribal government and petitioned for federal acknowledgment. The BIA recognized the tribe on October 14, 1998, finding that the residents of the Bradley community had been consistently identified since the mid-1800s as descendants of Match-e-be-nash-she-wish's band of Potawatomi.

MENOMINEE RESERVATION

Tribe: Menominee Indian Tribe of Wisconsin
Current Location: Wisconsin
Total Area: 235,062 acres   Tribal Enrollment: 8,311

Menominee is a term derived from the Ojibwe word *Omanoominii,* meaning "Wild Rice People," and indeed wild rice was a staple for the tribe, augmented by corn, squash, beans, hunting, and fishing. The Kyas-Machatiwduk, or Menominee, are the longest continuous residents of present-day Wisconsin, having resided in the area for hundreds of years. The Menominee allied themselves with the French during the French and Indian War but changed allegiances when the British won. In 1794, the British signed the Jay Treaty, clarifying the United States-Canada border, and

This jar, decorated with a design of hand and arm bones, was probably made between 1350 and 1500. It was found in Hickman County, Kentucky.

Mikmaq/ Micmac, Algonquian language family

"Msit mimajulnu'k weskwijinu'ltijik alsumsultijik aqq newte' tett wkpimte'tmut aqq koqwajo'taqnn wejkul'aqmititl."

("All human beings are born free and equal in dignity and rights. They are endowed with reason and conscience and should act towards one another in a spirit of brotherhood.") Translation of Article 1 of the Universal Declaration of Human Rights

Euro-Americans soon began arriving in the Wisconsin region. A fort was established at Green Bay in 1816, and a treaty was forged between the United States and the Menominee in 1817. By 1827, the tribe had sold about 250,000 acres of tribal lands to eastern tribes from New York and another 250,000 acres to the federal government. The Treaty of Cedars in 1836 mandated the sale of another 4.5 million acres to the government. In 1852, the tribe was moved to the Lake Poygan area, the site of its current reservation. The tribe continued to sell parcels of land over the next several decades.

After the U.S. government placed the Menominee on their reservation in 1852, it attempted to convert the tribe to full-fledged agrarians. The Menominee, however, were more interested in using logging as the basis for their economy. They began their own commercial logging operation in 1871, and by the turn of the century, the tribe was widely recognized as one of the most prosperous and progressive in the country.

Aspects of traditional culture remain vital on the reservation, and the tribe is trying to preserve and restore Menominee clan structure, the tribal creation story, and use of the Menominee language. The tribe is also a member of the Great Lakes Inter-Tribal Council, which supports member tribes in their efforts to expand self-determination and works collectively to improve the unity of tribal governments, communities, and individuals.

MILLE LACS BAND OF OJIBWE

Tribe: Minnesota Chippewa Tribe
Current Location: Minnesota
Total Area: 4,107.80 acres   Tribal Enrollment: 3,800

The Mille Lacs Band of Ojibwe is one of six constituent bands of the Minnesota Chippewa Tribe, each with its own reservation. The other five bands are Bois Forte (see above), Fond du Lac, Grand Portage, Leech Lake, and White Earth.

CASINOS

tate governments in the United States cannot intrude in tribal sovereignty, so tribes can legally develop casinos even in states that have not legalized gambling. Court rulings as well as federal legislation have affirmed tribal rights regarding casinos.

The creation of tribal gaming operations in the Northeast has had some profound effects. Unemployment dropped from 50 to 20 percent in many communities, and tribes were able to reinvest in education and social-service programs. Nevertheless, effects have varied from tribe to tribe. With only a couple hundred tribe members, the Pequot's large casino in Connecticut spawned incredible changes. On the other hand, the White Earth Ojibwe had more than 20,000 tribal members and one casino, so, aside from job creation, the effect of gaming on the daily lives of tribal members was not pronounced.

Even after casinos were established, Indians in the Northeast remained disproportionately poor. In Minnesota, for example, 30 percent of Indians from all tribes were below the poverty line as of 2000, compared with 5 percent of the overall state population. Among the Iroquois, the early 19th-century traditional prophet Handsome Lake preached the importance of abstinence from gambling, and many tribal members are upset over the cultural cost of the economic benefit. Gambling addiction is a problem, as well. There is also a misconception among non-Indians that all Indians are rich from casino profits, which has hurt grant and government funding.

Another contentious issue surrounding casinos is per capita payments—whether part of the gaming profit should be distributed to every member of a tribe. Most tribes will probably never be able to offer such payments because they have so many members relative to their income. However, some small tribes with large casinos, such as the Pequot, do. The payments have eliminated poverty for the Pequot and a few other tribes, but also have created disincentives to education and career development. In addition, they have discouraged people from augmenting their income by gardening or harvesting wild rice, berries, and fish, thus eroding healthy living and traditional tribal culture. Moreover, tribes that can't really afford to make payments have been exploring ways to cut spending on social services and education in order to offer the cash instead. ■

Gamblers play on some of the more than 6,000 slot machines at the Mohegan Sun casino in Uncasville, Connecticut, one of the nation's largest.

POWHATAN

The Powhatan were a confederacy of 30 closely related Algonquian tribes in Virginia in the 16th and 17th centuries. The term "Powhatan" has been used to refer to the largest tribe in the confederacy, the people of all tribes from the confederacy, the confederacy's principal village, and its primary chief. Confederacy nations include the Powhatan, Arrohateck, Appamattuck, Pamunkey, Mattaponi, Chiskiack, Kecoughtan, Youghtanund, Rappahannock, Moraughtacund, Weyanoak, Paspahegh, Quiyoughcohannock, and Nansemond. They numbered more than 15,000 when the British settled Jamestown in 1607, and from then on, the two cultures' histories were entangled. British soldiers fired guns at the first Indians they saw, and within weeks there were deaths on both sides.

Pocahontas

The first part of the widely embellished Pocahontas story began immediately after the establishment of Jamestown, when Capt. John Smith was captured by Opechancanough, the half brother of Wahunsunacawh, principal chief of the Powhatan Confederacy. Smith was helped to escape by Pocahontas, Wahunsunacawh's daughter. Smith wrote about his experience in 1608, 1612, and again in 1624, but only the last account claimed Smith was going to be executed when Pocahontas helped him, making it appear the story was exaggerated with each telling.

Wahunsunacawh actually seemed eager to pursue a diplomatic peace with the British. In 1608, the English invited him to a peace conference, hoping to crown him as a British vassal. Wahunsunacawh refused to kneel, though, and soldiers physically leaned on the chief's tall frame to put the crown on his head. The English saw the crowning as evidence of Powhatan subordination to English rule, but Wahunsunacawh saw it as evidence of respect and a peaceful overture.

The English expanded their colonies beyond Jamestown without permission. In 1609, Capt. John Ratcliffe came to

This portrait of Pocahontas shows her wearing a turkey-feather robe.

the Powhatan capital, demanding land and corn. A fight broke out, and all the English present were killed. The English then launched an all-out war against the Powhatan from 1610 to 1614. The second part of the Pocahontas saga evolved when the English captured her in 1614 and ransomed her to her father. The chief agreed to peace for the return of his daughter, but the English continued

to manipulate him. The teenage Pocahontas was baptized and married to English planter John Rolfe although she was already married to a Powhatan Indian. She was emotionally conflicted and never free to chart her own path. She accompanied Rolfe to England, where her beauty made her a great curiosity, but she died before she could return home. Her son, Thomas Rolfe, survived and returned to Virginia. Many families in Virginia trace their heritage to Thomas Rolfe and take pride that the blood of Pocahontas flows through their veins.

War, Slavery, and Survival

In 1618, Wahunsunacawh died, and his brother Opitchapam assumed the position of principal chief, but he died of disease soon thereafter. Wahunsunacawh's younger half brother, Opechancanough, assumed the position of chief. Warfare erupted again between the Powhatan and the English in 1622. There was a period of relative peace in the 1630s, but by the 1640s the Powhatan were once more forced to defend their homes from British raids. The English campaign from 1644 to 1646 proved especially devastating because it was accompanied by several outbreaks of disease.

In 1646, Opechancanough was captured. While being held, the elderly chief—estimated by the English to be between 90 and 100 years old—was shot in the back by a guard and died. The chief's sons, Necotowance and Totopotomoi, tried to hold the confederacy together, but the death of Opechancanough was ultimately the death of the Powhatan Confederacy. After significant numbers died from disease or left the region, the remaining Powhatan were outnumbered and overwhelmed. Many were forced into slavery—some in Virginia, others in the West Indies. The Virginia colony abolished Indian slavery in 1691, but many Powhatan slaves were converted to indentured servitude for decades more. Meanwhile, numerous African slaves—by 1700, there were 6,000 in the region—escaped and sought refuge with remnant Powhatan.

In 2009, seven tribes that were formerly part of the Powhatan Confederacy were recognized by Virginia. They have 3,000 tribal members, but only the Pamunkey and Mattaponi have retained tribal lands since the 1600s. Both are in King William County. All seven tribes are trying to get federal recognition, but old state records designated citizens only as either white or colored, so proving Indian descent to the satisfaction of the government has been difficult. ■

This watercolor drawing, "Indian Village of Pomeiooc," was done by English colonist John White in 1585 or 1586. The village it shows was somewhere in what is now North Carolina. It provided Europeans with one of the earliest images of a Native American village. The drawing is now held by the British Museum.

PONTIAC

Leader of pan-Indian resistance

O ttawa chief Pontiac (Baandiyaag) was an ingenious statesman. He used an innovation with traditional Great Lakes Indian wampum belts in order to communicate and maintain an alliance of tribes who spoke 15 different languages. Pontiac was primarily concerned with British mistreatment of Great Lakes Indians after the French defeat in the French and Indian War. In 1763, he led a pan-Indian military action against the British.

On June 2, 1763, a large group of Indians supporting Pontiac's rebellion staged a game of lacrosse in front of Fort Michilimackinac. As the game got more intense, it got closer to the fort. British soldiers lined the walls to watch. The ball flew over the wall, and the soldiers opened the gate to allow the Indians to retrieve it. The Indians pulled out weapons and stormed the fort, burning much of it to the ground and killing most of the garrison. Over the summer, Pontiac and his allies captured nine of the 11 British forts in the Great Lakes region and laid siege to the other two.

Pontiac's initial success was reversed by the trials of prolonged conflict. Most of the warriors needed to return home to their families. Pontiac abandoned the sieges and maintained a guerrilla resistance until he was assassinated in 1769 by a Peoria Indian. He didn't force the British out of the region, but he did succeed in altering British policy. As a direct result of his conflict, the British proclaimed that all land west of the Appalachian Mountains was reserved for the Indians. Although that decree proved unenforceable in the long run, it demonstrated the power of pan-Indian resistance and influenced later Indian leaders such as Tecumseh. ■

Pontiac led a federation of Native American tribes against the British settlers.

According to oral tradition, ancestors of today's Ojibwe (Chippewa) began migrating west from the Atlantic Ocean hundreds of years ago. In the late 1600s, the people split into two groups: one moved north into Canada, and the other moved along the south shore of Lake Superior into the northern sections of what is now Wisconsin, Minnesota, and Michigan's Upper Peninsula. By the mid-18th century, the ancestors of the Mille Lacs Ojibwe had established a subsistence lifestyle in the region around Mille Lacs Lake in central Minnesota, hunting the area's abundant bear, moose, deer, and waterfowl. They also relied on fishing, gathering wild rice, berries, and maple sugar, and cultivating small crops.

Everything changed for the Ojibwe with the coming of the French, who were soon followed by a plethora of other Europeans demanding land and natural resources. The band made its first formal land cession to the U.S. government in 1837. In 1855, all remaining land occupied by the Mille Lacs Ojibwe was formally ceded, but tribal members did not relocate. Later treaties signed by Mille Lacs chief Shawbashkung helped to retain a permanent home for the band on the Mille Lacs Reservation as a reward for not having harmed white settlers during a tribal conflict with the government in 1862. The Mille Lacs Ojibwe were pressured to relocate to White Earth. In 1901, their homes were burned, and allotments at Mille Lacs were denied until 1926.

Treaties were soon violated by the federal government, and the band remained in poverty throughout most of the 20th century, as its hunting, fishing, and gathering economy had been virtually destroyed.

The Mille Lacs Band was organized into the Minnesota Chippewa Tribe under the 1934 Indian Reorganization Act, and the tribe's economic growth, while diversified, has been fueled primarily by investment revenues earned from tribal gaming facilities.

Today, there are fewer than 200 fluent Anishnaabemowin speakers on the reservation, but the tribe is working diligently to help preserve and revitalize the language. The band funded a tribal recording project that produced a dictionary of Minnesota Ojibwe, a computerized language database, and a language program that has helped reintroduce Anishnaabemowin into everyday life.

MOHEGAN RESERVATION

Tribe: Mohegan Indian Tribe of Connecticut
Current Location: Connecticut   **Total Area:** 406 acres
Tribal Enrollment: 1,611

Mohegan (Mohican) people are descendants of the Lenni Lenape (Delaware). The name Mohegan is a derivation of the tribal word for wolf, which was one of the tribe's dominant clans. In the late 1500s and early 1600s, the Mohegan began a migratory trek northward through upstate New York and southeastern Connecticut. Under the leadership of Sachem (Chief) Uncas, the Mohegan settled along the Thames River. The tribe's friendship with British settlers created conflict with the local Pequot and Narragansett tribes. With the end of King Philip's War in 1676, the Mohegan lost their stature as military allies of the British colonies, and their socioeconomic livelihood subsequently began to suffer. Colonists encroached on their hunting grounds, forcing the tribe toward an economy reliant on domestic livestock.

In the mid-1700s, Samson Occum became the first ordained Christian Indian minister. He raised the funds to establish an Indian academy, now known as Dartmouth College.

In 1790, the state of Connecticut violated the Federal Trade and Intercourse Act and permitted nontribal, state-appointed overseers to sell Mohegan lands to non-Indians. The tribe was dislocated from its original reservation but maintained a core

MYTH OR FACT?

Indians won't fight to defend America.

MYTH

Indians have fought in every American conflict from the Revolution to Afghanistan. Since World War I, Indians have fought in the U.S. armed services in greater numbers per capita than any other racial group in the nation. Some enlisted for financial reasons and others to honor family military histories. Among the Ojibwe, returning servicemen use the position of *ogichidaa* (warrior) to speak at ceremonies, carry eagle staffs and flags at powwows, and remind people of the proud military heritage of their people.

The seal of the Territory of Wisconsin incorporated an image of Ho-Chunk removal, with the motto *"Civilitas Successit Barbarum"*— "Civilization Succeeds Barbarism."

land base in Uncasville, Connecticut, home of the Mohegan Church, founded in 1831. The church helped in proving the Mohegan's continued presence in the area when they applied for federal recognition more than 150 years later. In 1994, the United States formally recognized the Mohegan tribe as a sovereign entity. A land claims settlement agreement gave the tribe the right to establish an 839-acre reservation in the town of Montville, and the tribe initially reacquired 240 acres of its ancestral homelands in Connecticut. The United States now holds more than 400 acres of land in trust for the Mohegan tribe.

The tribe continues to honor the traditional roles of chief, medicine woman, and pipe carrier. The Ancient Mohegan Village site, a national historic landmark, marks the place where the Mohegan people first settled under the leadership of Sachem Uncas in the 17th century, from which Mohegan people draw their spiritual strength.

NARRAGANSETT INDIAN RESERVATION

Tribe: Narragansett Indian Tribe of Rhode Island
Current Location: Rhode Island   **Total Area:** 1,943 acres
Tribal Enrollment: 2,732

The Narragansett have inhabited the area of present-day Rhode Island for hundreds of years. Giovanni da Verrazano made the first documented European contact during his visit to Narragansett Bay in 1524. He described the Narragansett as a large tribe that practiced horticulture, hunted, and organized under powerful kings *(sachems).* They lived in summer homes (*wetus,* or wigwams made of tree bark) and moved to larger longhouses for the winter, where several families resided together, traveling by foot or using dugout canoes, made from large trees, for water transport.

Rhode Island founder Roger Williams acquired land use rights to Providence from the Narragansett sachems in 1636. During King Philip's War, in

1675, English settlers massacred many Narragansetts and confined remaining survivors to a reservation in southern Rhode Island or sold them into slavery. The Great Swamp Massacre site now comprises most of the tribal reservation lands; however, during the 18th century, most tribal land was lost to non-Indians through real and falsified debt claims.

The Narragansett Indian Tribe incorporated in December 1934 under the Indian Reorganization Act and created a constitution and bylaws. The offices of sachem, medicine man, scribe, prophet, and a nine-member council were sanctioned. The reservation consists of 1,943 noncontiguous, tribally owned acres held in federal trust. The three acres of land on which the Indian Church is located is the only original parcel of tribal land that has never been out of the Narragansett tribe's possession.

With federal recognition, the Narragansett were finally able to work toward economic self-sufficiency. Today, the Narragansett tribe serves members through economic development and social services, while nourishing the tribe's rich culture and heritage.

ONEIDA RESERVATION

Tribe: Oneida Tribe of Indians of Wisconsin
Current Location: Wisconsin   Total Area: 6,645 acres
Tribal Enrollment: 14,745

The Oneida tribe is a member of the Iroquois Confederacy, and its ancestral lands are located in present-day upstate New York. Of the six-million-acre territory, the tribe principally resided in the Oneida Creek and Oneida Lake areas.

The Oneida encountered European explorers in 1609 in upstate New York. The Europeans gradually colonized this region, and the Oneida traded goods and made formal treaties with them. In the Revolutionary War, the Oneida allied with the colonists, while another Iroquois tribe, the Mohawk, supported the British. Following the war, the state of New York usurped Oneida land titles, a bitter betrayal of Oneida loyalty to the colonists.

During the 1820s, a faction of Oneidas voluntarily left their ancestral lands and moved to Wisconsin.

Mohawk (Kanien'keha), Iroquoian language family

"Okariata:ne tahotharatie. Tahsakohroria:ne ne tsi niho:ten. Ne se aonha:a thorihwaka:ion ne se aonha:a thorihwaka:ion"

("The mosquito is bringing a message. He's coming to tell us how poor he is. The truth of the matter is that he is so old-fashioned that he brings the same old message.")

This faction, having converted to Christianity, became known as the First Christian Party. Under the direction of Eleazar Williams, an Episcopalian Mohawk preacher, and Jedidiah Morse, a European-American missionary, the group negotiated a plan with the federal government to relocate all of the New York Iroquois to Wisconsin. The Oneida then purchased eight million acres from the Menominee and Ho-Chunk Nations, only to have the government reduce their acreage to 65,430 by 1838.

In 1845, the territory of Wisconsin requested that the tribe trade its Wisconsin lands for territory west of the Mississippi in order to make Wisconsin available to Euro-American settlers. The tribe refused to move, but in 1887, the Allotment Act divided its lands into 1,527 parcels. By 1929, only a few hundred acres remained in tribal ownership, due to fraud, tax, and foreclosure. Many Oneida tribal members were forced to relocate to Green Bay and Milwaukee.

Water—traveling on it, fishing in it, growing crops with it—has always been central to life in the Northeast.

The government of the Oneida, after the move to Wisconsin, took several forms, but maintained its traditional chief system until the mid-20th century. The tribe accepted the provisions of the Indian Reorganization Act in 1934. The mission of the Oneida Nation is to preserve its heritage through the seventh generation, provide housing, promote education, protect the land, preserve the environment, and provide for a quality of life where the Oneida people come together for the common good.

HO-CHUNK (WINNEBAGO)

The Ho-Chunk (People of the Big Voice) were one of the largest tribes in the Northeast, with an estimated population of 20,000 when French explorer Jean Nicolet first encountered them in 1634. For centuries, the Ho-Chunk dominated most of central Wisconsin from Green Bay to Rock River and Lake Winnebago to Black River Falls. The term "Winnebago"—derived from the Ojibwe term for the tribe, *Wiinibiigoo*—means "People of the Muddy Water." Although that term has dominated government and historical references to the tribe for hundreds of years, the Ho-Chunk Sovereign Nation of Wisconsin employed their own tribal language term of self-reference in 1994 as part of a broad language, culture, and sovereignty initiative, and it has been gaining traction ever since.

Removal

The Ho-Chunk hunted, gathered, harvested wild rice, and also farmed corn, other vegetables, and tobacco. A clan system and complicated kinship network bound each family, community, and the entire people together. Everything from traditional names to religious initiations revolved around kinship and relationships not only with the living but also with deceased family members.

The Ho-Chunk endured tremendous pressure on their land and lives. The tribe signed its first land cession treaty with the U.S. government in 1821. President Andrew Jackson signed the Indian Removal Act in 1830. In 1840, the U.S. government began to aggressively relocate tribal members from Wisconsin to the "Neutral Ground" in Iowa. The Army spent years hunting for Ho-Chunk families that did not cooperate with removal from their ceded lands.

Just a few years later, in 1846, the government decided to close the reservation in Iowa and relocate the Ho-Chunk to central Minnesota at Long Prairie instead. There, the Ho-Chunk found themselves right in the middle of a major ongoing conflict between the Ojibwe and the Dakota. War parties from those tribes constantly went through Ho-Chunk villages, and the land was much more difficult to farm.

A stereoscopic image from the early 1900s shows a Ho-Chunk man posing with his arm on a pony in front of a tent in Kilbourn, Wisconsin.

In 1855, the government relocated the Ho-Chunk again, this time to Blue Earth in southern Minnesota. Although the Ho-Chunk were now confined to much less acreage than before, they industriously farmed the land and adapted to the new environment remarkably well. However, after a conflict between the Dakota and the U.S. government in 1862 resulted in the deaths of several hundred white settlers, all Indians in southern Minnesota were removed to South Dakota. Although the Ho-Chunk did not participate in that conflict, they were treated as if they had. The Ho-Chunk were miserable on the plains, unable to irrigate the land for farming and surrounded by the Dakota. The government moved them yet again, in 1865, to a new reservation in Nebraska. By this time, debilitating waves of disease and warfare had reduced tribal numbers to the hundreds.

War on Culture

The Great Seal of the Territory of Wisconsin incorporated an image of Ho-Chunk removal (with Indians boarding steam-powered barges for relocation while an industrious white farmer plowed the land), with the motto *"Civilitas Successit Barbarum"*—"Civilization Succeeds Barbarism." That image also dominated the Wisconsin State Seal until 1998.

The U.S. government actively suppressed tribal religions and customs through the List of Indian Offenses

In a 1929 photo, three Indians identified as Princess O-Me-Me, a Chippewa; Sun Road, a Pueblo; and Chief Whirling Thunder, a Winnebago, view Chicago's skyline.

(1881) and Circular 1665 (1921–1933). In addition, residential boarding schools were used to assimilate Ho-Chunk tribal members and eradicate the tribal language. The effects were devastating. After attending boarding schools, sometimes for 12 years, many Ho-Chunk children could not recognize their parents and could not speak the same language as they did. Tremendous damage was done to individual lives and the social fabric of communities. But the people were resistant and resilient. Ho-Chunk sovereignty, culture, land, and language would endure.

Revitalization

In spite of incredible hardship, many Ho-Chunk families had continued as squatters on their original homelands in Wisconsin, which had technically been ceded in 1837. It wasn't until the Indian Reorganization Act of 1934 that the sovereign status of the Ho-Chunk in Wisconsin was affirmed, along with that of tribal members who had endured relocation. The Wisconsin Ho-Chunk were scattered across 12 counties and landless in spite of their reaffirmed sovereignty, but since 1934, the tribe has actively purchased land and held it for all members.

Today, the tribal population remains split between the Ho-Chunk Sovereign Nation (Wisconsin), with more than 6,000 members, and the Winnebago Tribe (Nebraska), with more than 3,000 members. The Ho-Chunk language is severely endangered today, with only 230 living fluent speakers, but aggressive efforts to preserve and revitalize it are under way, primarily through Hocąk Wazija Haci Language Division. Day care, Head Start, and school programs conducted exclusively in the tribal language are proliferating, well supported by the tribe. ■

Oneida Indian Nation

Tribe: Oneida Nation of New York   **Current Location:** New York   **Total Area:** 13,731 acres   **Tribal Enrollment:** 1,000

The Onyotaa:ka, or Oneida, were one of the original five nations to join the Iroquois Confederacy. Their ancestral lands encompassed territories from West Canada Creek to Chittenango Creek and from the St. Lawrence River to the Susquehanna River.

The Oneida Nation encountered Europeans in the 1600s and interacted peaceably with the Dutch and British in the fur trade industry. When the colonists set out to gain independence from Great Britain in the Revolutionary War, the Oneida were the first Native nation to forge an alliance with them. Their alliance with the colonists cost the Oneida great

A Nanticoke man dances during an event on Delaware's Eastern Shore. The Nanticoke first came in contact with Europeans in 1608, when the British Capt. John Smith explored the Chesapeake Bay area.

losses. In addition to the hundreds of tribal members lost in battle, in 1779 the Oneida's principal village was destroyed. Many tribal members were forced to seek refuge in other communities, but they eventually returned to reestablish the community in 1784.

In 1794, the Treaty of Canandaigua affirmed special protection of Oneida tribal lands—more than six million acres. However, through a number of illegal agreements with individual tribal members during the 1800s, the state of New York seized almost all of those lands. Throughout the last half of the 19th century and into the 20th, the Oneida fought for restoration of tribal lands. Since 1987, when the Oneida Nation owned 32 acres of unrecognized lands, they have reacquired more than 17,000 acres and greatly improved the tribal economy. With a variety of businesses, including livestock (the second largest herd of Angus in the Northeast), hospitality, tourism, and construction, the Nation is the largest employer in Oneida and Madison Counties. It also owns and operates *Indian Country Today,* the largest American Indian newspaper in the country, as well as the *Oneida,* a monthly newspaper.

The Oneida Nation's traditional tribal government is overseen by the Men's Council and Clan Mothers. The three traditional clans are Turtle (keepers of knowledge), Bear (medicine people), and Wolf (pathfinders). The clans are acknowledged throughout present-day Oneida life, from visual and artistic symbolism to their places in, and contributions to, the tribal council.

ONONDAGA RESERVATION

Tribe: Onondaga Nation of New York   **Current Location:** New York   **Total Area:** 7,300 acres   **Tribal Enrollment:** 1,600

Ancestral Onondaga lands included almost three million acres that extended through the Great Lakes Basin and St. Lawrence River and Seaway. Their way of life utilized deeply forested woodlands, the rugged Adirondacks, and a water system for trade and communication that included the Great Lakes, the Finger Lakes, and innumerable waterfalls and white-water rivers. The Onondagas are the Fire Keepers, Keepers of the Wampum, and the Elder Brothers of the Iroquois Confederacy and, according to its laws, an Onondaga is chief, or *tadodah,* of the Haudenosaunee (Iroquois).

In 1784, Aaron Hill presented the Onondaga Nation's position to the U.S. commissioners, arguing that its members could not be drafted into military service. The United States responded by asking the Nation to be a neutral nation. The Onondaga consider this treaty illegal. Like the Oneida, they have challenged the Selective Service Act and believe that the Indian Citizenship Act is unconstitutional. The Onondaga also resist the state of New York's jurisdiction over their lands and chose not to accept the provisions of the Indian Reorganization Act of 1934.

The Onondaga Nation has a traditional governing system established by the Great Law of Kaianerekowa of the Haudenosaunee. The Grand Council, comprised of 14 chiefs selected by clan mothers and one head chief, oversees tribal operations.

Traditions, native language, and spiritual life are fiercely preserved by the Onandaga. People called faith keepers are responsible for ensuring that the ceremonies are still being performed. These men and women refer to the seasons and the lunar calendar to decide when the many sacred ceremonies will take place in the traditional longhouse. Ceremonies include Midwinter, Maple Sap, Planting, Bean, Green Corn, and Harvest rituals, to name just a few.

THE BATTLE OF SUGAR POINT

In 1898, U.S. officials arrested Leech Lake Ojibwe elder Hole in the Day (Bagone-giizhig) in a bootlegging case. Hole in the Day—not to be confused with the assassinated Ojibwe chief of the same name (see page 22)—opposed many government policies, and some Ojibwe thought the arrest was political. Several helped him escape. Maj. Melville C. Wilkinson, Gen. John M. Bacon, and a hundred U.S. soldiers came to Leech Lake on October 5, 1898, with the intent of arresting Hole in the Day again. When one soldier accidentally discharged his rifle, a group of Ojibwe thought they were being attacked and fired back. Six soldiers, including Major Wilkinson, were killed, as was an Indian police officer. None of the Ojibwe died.

The event was resolved through diplomatic channels. In an astounding comment, Secretary of the Interior Cornelius Newton Bliss wrote: "The Indians were prompted to their outbreak by the wrongs committed against them and chafed under unfair treatment. They now will go back to their homes and live peaceably if the whites will treat them fairly, which is very likely, as the whites were thoroughly impressed with the stand taken by the Indians. In this respect the outbreak has taught them a lesson." The Battle of Sugar Point was the last military conflict between a tribe and the U.S. government. ∎

Hole in the Day poses in 1899 wearing a necklace made from carbine casings collected from the site of the Battle of Sugar Point.

PENOBSCOT RESERVATION

Tribe: Penobscot Tribe of Maine   **Current Location:** Maine   **Total Area:** 65,608 acres   **Tribal Enrollment:** 2,261

The ancestral home of the Penobscot once covered the entire Penobscot River Watershed in eastern Maine. The rich resources of the area amply supplied the early Penobscot people with fish, game, and native plants. Culturally, the Penobscot are one of the four tribes of the original Eastern Abenaki group and a member of the Wabanaki Confederacy. The members of the Penobscot Indian Nation speak an eastern Algonquian language. Beginning in 1615, European diseases ravaged the population of the Eastern Abenaki, reducing their population by three-fourths.

The Penobscot actively supported the rebel colonists during the Revolutionary War, partly on the basis of assurances from the fledgling Provincial Congress of Massachusetts that their territorial rights to the upper Penobscot River drainage would be preserved. The Penobscot joined the Passamaquoddy, Maliseet, and Micmac in securing the town

Abenaki, Algonquian language family

"Enni taolani agaskwikok noesal niona kizosaltoalakws taolawisi maskozisis taolwisi nolka moz sibo ikok pon tekw wobigid sanoba magigwogan n'mahomios chibaio amikimek."

("As long as the deer and moose shall run free and the grass shall grow and the rivers run swiftly, the Abenaki shall survive the white man's wickedness.") Deer Clan Prayer, provided by Chief Edwin "Joe" Pero-Coos

of Machias against British attack in 1777. This victory represented America's first naval success and secured the northern boundary of the colonies for the rest of the Revolutionary War. However, these alliances were abandoned at the end of the war. Massachusetts used a misinterpretation of earlier pledges to wrest most of the middle of the Penobscot River drainage away from the tribe.

When the state of Maine was organized in 1820, the tribe fell under its jurisdiction. In 1833, the state sold about 100,000 acres of Penobscot lands.

The Penobscot did not receive federal recognition until the late 20th century. In 1980, the Penobscot Nation became a sovereign, federally recognized Indian tribe, a municipality under state law, and a business entity. Tribal headquarters are located on Indian Island Reservation near Old Town, Maine. While the tribe has grown dramatically in size since 1995, only around 25 percent of its members live on the reservation.

The tribal economy is supported by the tribe's activity in tourism, manufacturing, gaming, and forestry. The people maintain a strong sense of identity and connection to their ancestral lands and the river.

TECUMSEH

Inspired Shawnee leader, spiritualist, warrior

Tecumseh, a Shawnee chief, worked with his brother to bring several tribes together.

Shawnee chief Tecumseh (1768–1813) used deft diplomacy, inspiring oratory, military action, and knowledge of several languages to unite a coalition of tribes in the southern Great Lakes region to oppose American expansion. He worked with his brother, Tenskwatawa, a prophet who urged Indians to abandon European influences. Many Indians believed the brothers were destined to lead their people to a better place, in part because of events many interpreted as divine intervention. Among those was a challenge from Indiana territorial governor William Henry Harrison in 1806 to Tenskwatawa to demonstrate his spiritual power by making daytime turn to night, which was immediately followed by a dramatic solar eclipse.

The brothers founded multitribe villages in Greeneville, Ohio, and Prophetstown, Indiana. In 1811, Harrison led an attack against Prophetstown while Tecumseh was away. In the ensuing Battle of Tippecanoe, the warriors were forced to retreat and the village was burned. It was a major setback for Tecumseh, who nevertheless continued his work, uniting with the British against the Americans in the War of 1812.

The British agreed to combine with him at the Battle of the Thames, but failed to appear. Tecumseh was killed, and most of his confederacy abandoned the cause. ■

Potawatomi tribe. Chief Leopold Pokagon was able to negotiate with the federal government to keep his band of 280 people in southwestern Michigan throughout the removal era. This group became known as the Pokagon Band of Potawatomi.

"It is clear that for years after the discovery of this country, we stood before the coming strangers as a block of marble before the sculptor, ready to be shaped into a statue of grace and beauty; but in their greed for gold, the block was hacked to pieces and destroyed," said Simon Pokagon, son of Chief Leopold and author of *The Red Man's Rebuke* (1893), *The Red Man's Greeting* (1893), and *O-gi-wam-kwe Mit-i-gwa-ki, Queen of the Woods* (1899).

In the wake of World War I, a number of Pokagon found employment in burgeoning area industries, though the number of band members looking beyond their homegrown rural economy remained quite limited until World War II, after which band members branched out into the region's booming industrial economy.

Present-day Pokagon Indians are highly involved with maintaining their distinct cultural identity, particularly via ceremonies, art, and the use of their tribal language, which embodies the Potawatomi worldview. The sacred longhouse ceremonies, sweat lodges, and powwows have returned to occupy a more central position in the Pokagon culture than they have for many decades.

POKAGON TOWNSHIP RESERVATION

An Ojibwe girl examines figures carved into rock near Nett Lake, Minnesota.

Tribe: Pokagon Band of Potawatomi Indians
Current Location: Michigan and Indiana
Total Area: 4,700 acres   Tribal Enrollment: 3,062

After the American Revolution and the westward migration of white settlers, the Potawatomi were party to 11 treaties with the federal government. The primary land cession treaty was the Treaty of Chicago, signed in 1833 during the Jackson removal era, when all Indians living east of the Mississippi were scheduled for relocation either to Kansas or Oklahoma. In the mid-1800s, the Pokagon and Huron bands refused to leave their Michigan villages and territories for a Kansas reservation that the federal government had arranged for the greater

ST. CROIX CHIPPEWA RESERVATION

Tribe: St. Croix Chippewa Indians of Wisconsin
Current Location: Wisconsin   Total Area: 2,081 acres
Tribal Enrollment: 1,034

The Ojibwe (Chippewa) people are indigenous to the Great Lakes region. They used the products of their woodlands to make shelters, such as wigwams, and to heat their winter lodges. Birchbark and similar materials were fashioned to make baskets, trays, bowls, ladles, spoons, and buckets for gathering sap during maple sugaring. The Ojibwe carried their babies on cradleboards, used snowshoes

OJIBWE (CHIPPEWA)

The Ojibwe are one of the largest tribes in the United States by official population, third only to the Cherokee and Navajo in number of enrolled members. However, there are twice as many self-identified Ojibwe people as enrollees, plus 125 communities in Canada, making the Ojibwe the largest tribe in terms of geographic dispersal, land, and unofficial population. Although their predecessors were in North America for thousands of years, it was just 1,500 years ago that the Ojibwe emerged as one of the largest tribes in the Algonquian language family. They were distinguished from other Algonquian tribes by language and by such customs as writing on birchbark scrolls, using birchbark canoes, and mining and working copper.

Alliances and Enemies

The Ojibwe originally lived along the St. Lawrence Seaway and other parts of the Northeast. Conflict in the Northeast and a series of prophecies by Ojibwe religious leaders convinced many Ojibwe to slowly migrate westward through the Great Lakes. By the time the French arrived in the central Great Lakes region in the 1640s, the Ojibwe had numerous villages located around Sault Ste. Marie and the surrounding area. They formed a powerful trade and military alliance called the Three Fires Confederacy with their cousins the Ottawa and the Potawatomi. It enabled the Ojibwe to leverage a powerful position in the French fur trade and fend off territorial intrusions and attacks from the Iroquois Confederacy to their east.

The Ojibwe relationship with the French was long-lasting and deeply entangled. The French used marriage to cement their relationship with the Ojibwe, and today more than a third of Ojibwe people in the United States and Canada carry French surnames. The Ojibwe population was ravaged by European diseases, but they fared better than many of their Indian neighbors because of an increased standard of

This 19th-century Ojibwe hand drum is decorated with an image of a bird.

living brought about through their preeminent position in trade and technological advantages in warfare (access to guns and the superior birchbark canoe). The Ojibwe actually recovered a significant percentage of their population loss from disease and expanded their territory at the expense of other tribes, multiplying their lands by a factor of 20 after European contact.

Expanding Their Territory

The first major expansion of Ojibwe territory came during the Beaver Wars (also called the Iroquois Wars) from 1641 to 1701. The Iroquois had been pushing west under pressure from their allies, the Dutch and British. The French, however, solidified their military alliance with the Three Fires Confederacy, and over 60 years of intermittent conflict, the Ojibwe and their allies pushed the Iroquois back east. Eventually, the Ojibwe occupied the western edges of Iroquois territory and much of the largely depopulated lands of the Huron in the eastern Great Lakes. That made the Ojibwe the dominant tribal power in the Great Lakes.

The second major Ojibwe expansion was to the west and often has been misunderstood. Ojibwe conflict with the Dakota was significant and long-lived, and did enable the Ojibwe to acquire new lands. However, Ojibwe-Dakota relations were more often peaceful than violent. The Ojibwe shared their primary religious society, the Midewiwin, with the Dakota. The Wakan Dance, as the Dakota called it, dominated their ceremonial life for generations. Similarly, the Dakota gave the Ojibwe the ceremonial Big Drum, which proliferated and remains one of the primary religious and cultural components of Ojibwe life today.

In 1679, the Ojibwe and Dakota made a major peace treaty in which the Dakota gave lands in northern Wisconsin to the Ojibwe in return for Ojibwe people serving as middlemen in Dakota-French trade. By the 1730s, the French had established direct trade with the Dakota, but the alliance endured. However, a series of events catapulted the Dakota into war with the French, and the Ojibwe had to choose between their western tribal alliance and their primary European trade and military alliance. In the end, the Ojibwe decided on their Three Fires Confederacy and French allies, which plunged the Ojibwe and Dakota into a brutal territorial war. By 1800, the Ojibwe occupied most of Ontario, northern Minnesota, and significant parts of North Dakota and Manitoba.

Much Is Lost, Much Remains

The U.S. government sought to divide and isolate pockets of Ojibwe leadership so as to acquire Ojibwe lands piecemeal. As the Ojibwe lost land, the resources they had to supply furs and maintain their standard of living declined. Ultimately, the Ojibwe were forced to sell the land to feed their families. It was a vicious cycle that disempowered the Ojibwe communities. There were several attempts to concentrate and relocate the Ojibwe, including a presidential order in 1850 and a major debacle at Sandy Lake, Minnesota, in which hundreds of people died from spoiled rations provided by the government.

The Ojibwe tenaciously held onto the richest land, and the tribe has rebounded.

Today, the Ojibwe are experiencing a cultural renaissance, as more youths return to traditional culture. Several Ojibwe immersion schools have been developed. Tribal sovereignty and economic power have been fortified through gaming enterprises and the development of court systems and political lobbies. As the political power of the Ojibwe has increased, the battle now rages to revitalize the tribal language, widely considered the critical defining feature of Ojibwe identity. ■

This postcard with a portrait of a Native American man in traditional costume is from about 1906. He is identified as Obtossaway, an Ojibwe chief.

being from St. Croix. Five years later, the same chiefs signed along with Kabemabe and Ayaabens (Little Buck). The original reservation covered 3,145 acres, but all land was formally ceded to the government by 1854. In spite of this, tribal members continued to squat in their traditional villages.

The St. Croix Chippewa Reservation was created on November 28, 1938. The reservation consists of a noncontiguous land base and 11 separate reservation communities scattered throughout three counties in northwestern Wisconsin. The St. Croix Chippewa Indians of Wisconsin is the eastern half of the historic St. Croix Chippewa Indians who lost federal recognition in 1854. The western half of the tribe was incorporated into the legal structure of the Mille Lacs Band of Ojibwe after the Indian Reorganization Act of 1934.

The St. Croix tribe maintains a diverse economic portfolio. Tribal enterprises include a lumber company, fisheries, a supermarket, real estate, a construction company, and a clothing manufacturer. The St. Croix Tribal Historic Preservation Department was established in 2000 for the protection and preservation of cultural and historical resources on the St. Croix Reservation lands.

ST. REGIS MOHAWK RESERVATION

Tribe: Saint Regis Mohawk Tribe   Current Location: New York   Total Area: 22,160 acres   Tribal Enrollment: 11,703

The Akwesasne Mohawk are members of the Haudenosaunee, or Iroquois, Confederacy. They are Elder Brothers and the Eastern Doorkeepers. Their ancestral lands encompassed over 15,000 square miles from the St. Lawrence River to the Delaware River and from the West Canada–Unadilla Creek to the Hudson River along the present-day New York–Canada border.

Around 1755, a small group of Christian Mohawks from the French Mission of Caughnawaga migrated to St. Regis, Quebec, and New York. The French Jesuits had encouraged the migration of this small party because of population pressure at the Caughnawaga Mission and the need to follow the activities of the

and toboggans, and traveled through the woods during long, harsh winters to search for game and check fur trap lines. They made birchbark canoes, harvested wild rice, and fished. The Ojibwe language is known as Anishinaabemowin, and is still spoken by approximately 25 St. Croix tribal members.

The Ojibwe encountered French explorers in the mid-1600s and forged strong economic partnerships with French trappers. In alliance with Pontiac's Rebellion of 1763, the Ojibwe participated in driving the British from all their western outposts. In 1813, the tribe began to enter into treaties with the U.S. government. During the 1837 and 1842 treaties, the St. Croix had a distinct identity. The signature page of the first treaty identifies Chiefs Bizhiki (Buffalo) and Jabenabe (Wet Mouth) along with three warriors as

An ancient Ojibwe pictograph depicting Misshepexhieu, the horned lynx demigod of Lake Superior, is visible at Agawa Rock in Lake Superior Provincial Park in Ontario.

British along the St. Lawrence frontier. The St. Regis Mission is the oldest permanent settlement in northern New York, predating non-Indian settlements by almost 50 years. During the Revolutionary War, while most of the Iroquois Confederacy supported the British, the St. Regis Mohawk were among the minority who supported the colonists.

Prior to the 20th century, the St. Regis Mohawk subsisted primarily through farming, fishing, and trapping. Men worked in the Adirondack lumber camps in late fall and winter; women wove the splint and sweetgrass baskets that gained them international recognition. As farming, fishing, and logging subsided, many Mohawk men found employment in the region's construction and ironworking trades, centered around Montreal and in New York State.

Because the state of New York never ceded any land to the federal government following the ratification of the tribe's constitution, the Mohawk Reservation has never been a federal territory. In the 1930s, the federal government proposed the Indian Reorganization Act, which the St. Regis Mohawk formally rejected in 1935. In 1953, the federal government moved to terminate the reservation, an attempt that the St. Regis Mohawk overturned. Renewed interest in traditional Mohawk culture and language began in the 1960s, exemplified by the establishment of the Akwesasne Freedom School and the restoration of the longhouse teachings. In 2003, the tribe began the development of a judicial program with traditional cultural values. The modern-day economy is based largely around the service industry and tourism.

SAULT STE. MARIE RESERVATION

Tribe: Sault Ste. Marie Tribe of Chippewa Indians of Michigan   **Current Location:** Michigan
Federal Trust Land: 1,608 acres   **Tribal Enrollment:** 30,324

The Sault Ste. Marie Ojibwe have occupied lands along the St. Marys River for hundreds of years, making their homeland the longest continually occupied Ojibwe settlement anywhere. Although the Ojibwe migrated to Sault Ste. Marie from the

POWWOWS

The modern powwow is a thriving cultural form throughout the Northeast. Powwows bring together people from across the region to dance, sing, eat, and visit. Some reservations, such as Leech Lake, sponsor more than a dozen powwows every year. Across the region, there are hundreds of singing groups and many thousands of dancers. Most tribal members have at least attended powwows, even if they do not sing or dance themselves. Powwows offer an opportunity for genuine intergenerational connection, as people of all ages actively participate. Powwow grounds are also consistently drug and alcohol free.

There are two primary variations of the powwow: traditional and contest. The primary distinction is that at contest powwows, dancers and singers compete for money, while at traditional powwows, they do not. Although both types are welcome and popular, they are a new development rather than an ancient tradition. Powwows combine older Dakota-style war dances, Omaha grass dance customs, the jingle dress regalia and dance style (based on an Ojibwe Indian's dream in the early 20th century), and rodeo customs, where Indian warriors who used to parade into soldier forts in war regalia now parade into the dance arbor in dance regalia.

Powwow is a positive development, but it is not a replacement for tribal religions and lifeways. The Ojibwe, Ho-Chunk, Iroquois, and many other tribes actively maintain older traditions and religious societies, but throughout the Northeast, elders worry that the popularity of the powwow is eclipsing their ancient and most sacred beliefs and practices among the younger generations. Money is being valued over respectful generosity, and the money being pumped into powwows motivates people to travel and spend time in the new cultural form rather than in older, sacred ceremonies and rituals. Most tribes spend as much as 20 times more money supporting powwow culture than they do on more traditional culture and tribal language revitalization. Tribes and tribal people have become agents of their own cultural change. ∎

Powwows attract people from all over to watch and participate in a mix of songs, dances, and other social events.

Atlantic coast, the Sault was the launching place for Ojibwe expansion both north and south of Lake Superior, and from Lake Superior all the way to the Rocky Mountains.

In the wake of the Revolutionary War, the U.S. government continued the precedent established by the British and French of dealing with the various bands in the area as one tribal entity. The Sault Ste. Maries were part of the treaty of July 31, 1855, which placed all of the Michigan Ojibwe tribes on several large reservations extending across the eastern portion of the Upper Peninsula.

In the 1930s, the Sault Ste. Marie Band faced tremendous economic challenges. The passage of the 1934 Indian Reorganization Act ultimately did little to reverse the tribe's increasing poverty, but it did enable the confirmation of tribal sovereignty.

During the latter half of the 20th century, the Ojibwe spent a great deal of energy and resources reestablishing their right to self-government. The roots of the tribe's modern government extend to the 1940s, when a group of Sugar Island residents gathered to talk about their common history. Sugar

**Miami,
Algonquian
language
family**

"Aya eeweemilaani.
Tipeewe iišiteehiaanki
keewiihkawiaanki."

("Greetings.
We are glad to have
you visit us.")

Island is located just off the eastern tip of Michigan's Upper Peninsula, between the United States and Ontario. The Sugar Island residents came to understand that while the treaties granted large tracts of land to the federal government, the documents did not end the tribe's sovereignty or terminate their ancestral right to hunt and fish on the ceded lands and waters of the Ojibwe.

Today, both the Bay Mills Indian Community and the Sault Ste. Marie Tribe of Chippewa Indians have interests there and consider the island to be a part of their ancestral homelands.

In 1953, the residents became the Sugar Island Group of Chippewa Indians and Their Descendants. At that time, Sault Ste. Marie and Sugar Island contained no lands for their people, and the federal government considered them members of the Bay Mills Indian Community, located 30 miles west of Sugar Island; however, the Sugar Island Group pushed for recognition as a separate tribe.

It was not until November 1975 that the Sault Ste. Marie's constitution and bylaws were officially approved by the secretary of the interior.

LOUISE ERDRICH

Acclaimed novelist and poet

Louise Erdrich is among the most accomplished Ojibwe authors, having written more than 20 novels, children's books, and poetry collections. Her trilogy *Love Medicine, The Beet Queen*, and *Tracks*, a Native American family saga set in North Dakota, won the hearts of many readers and much critical acclaim, including the National Book Critics Circle Award. Her book *The Plague of Doves* was a finalist for the 2009 Pulitzer Prize. Judges described it as "a haunting novel that explores racial discord, loss of land and changing fortunes in a corner of North Dakota where Native Americans and whites share a tangled history." Erdrich has received many other awards and accolades, including honorary doctorates from the University of North Dakota and Dartmouth College, a fellowship from the John Simon Guggenheim Foundation, and the Pushcart Prize in Poetry.

Erdrich's family comes from the Turtle Mountain Ojibwe reservation in North Dakota. She has spent a great deal of time and energy supporting and promoting other Native authors, especially those who work in the Ojibwe language. She owns and operates Birchbark Books, an independent bookstore in Minneapolis that is an intellectual nexus and launching pad for Native scholars. ■

Louise Erdrich's books treat themes of family and history from an Indian perspective.

SHAKOPEE MDEWAKANTON SIOUX COMMUNITY

Tribe: Shakopee Mdewakanton Sioux Community of Minnesota   Current Location: Minnesota
Total Area: 661 acres   Tribal Enrollment: 391

The Shakopee Mdewakanton Sioux Community is located in southeastern Minnesota, near the Minnesota River. Tribal members prefer the name Mdewakanton or Dakota to Sioux, which is derived from an Ojibwe word for snake. There are fewer than 400 tribal members, which makes the tribe numerically smaller than the Ojibwe communities of northern Minnesota. Prior to 1600, the Dakota inhabited most of Minnesota. Dakota families fished, gathered rice, and hunted game on the prairies and river valley woodlands. Dakota leaders established villages from which the Dakota traveled for hunting, gathering, and meeting with other tribes. As intertribal conflict during the 18th century drove the Mdewakanton Dakota farther south into the Mississippi and Minnesota River Valleys, a large group, led by Chief Shakopee, settled along the south shore of the Minnesota River.

The Mdewakanton participated in the U.S.-Dakota Conflict of 1862. The Dakota were on the verge of starvation, and the government was withholding annuities due to them. Traders refused to give the Dakota food on credit, and one even remarked, "If they are hungry, let them eat grass, or their own dung." In desperation, a small group tried to steal eggs from a local farmer. A brawl ensued, and the Dakota killed the farmer. Afterwards, the conflict escalated into a major war. The Dakota killed 400 to 800 white settlers. The U.S. government killed hundreds of Dakota and imprisoned 1,800 people at Fort Snelling. The government also executed 38 Dakota at Mankato after the conflict, the largest mass execution in U.S. history. Most remaining Dakota were relocated to a reservation at Santee, Nebraska, but a small number returned to Minnesota, including the Mdewakanton in the Prior Lake area, the Lower Sioux Agency at Morton, and the Upper Sioux Agency at Granite Falls.

In this photo from the 1940s, Potawatomi bead artist Josie Green McKinney works outside the bark house she and her husband use in the summer.

The tribe organized under the Indian Reorganization in 1934 and reincorporated with a new constitution in 1969, becoming Minnesota's newest and smallest reservation. The small population on the reservation became an asset when the modern casino gaming era began, making all tribal members wealthy through per capita payments. In addition to supporting tribal programs and services, the community also makes sizable donations to other tribes in the Great Plains and Great Lakes areas for health care, education, infrastructure improvements, and economic development projects, using revenues earned primarily from its gaming facilities.

STOCKBRIDGE-MUNSEE RESERVATION

Tribe: Stockbridge-Munsee Community
Current Location: Wisconsin
Total Area: 16,280 acres   Tribal Enrollment: 1,569

The Stockbridge-Munsee Community is a band of Mohegan (Mohican) Indians, whose ancestors once inhabited the eastern seaboard. Their traditional lands extended from Lake Champlain south nearly all the way to Manhattan Island, extending out on both sides of the Mahicannituck (Hudson River). The Mohegan never forgot that they

FOX (MESQUAKIE)

The history of the Mesquakie Indians is a story of one of the most tenacious efforts at resisting colonization and acculturation in all of the Americas. The Mesquakie (People of the Red Earth), often called Fox, are an Algonquian tribe, closely related to the Kickapoo and Menominee in language. They have a patrilineal clan system; the name Fox as a tribal designation is actually a reflection of the dominance of the Fox Clan among Mesquakie leaders during the period of first contact with Europeans. The Mesquakie had villages along the St. Lawrence Seaway and Lake Huron long before contact with whites, but were primarily located in Michigan and Wisconsin when the French first encountered them at the end of the 17th century.

Fighting the French

The Mesquakie were fewer in number than many of their Indian neighbors, with a population of 10,000 at the time of first contact. Their smaller size was a disadvantage in intertribal warfare, which was endemic with the Huron, Dakota, and Ojibwe for many years prior to French intrusions in the Great Lakes region.

The Fox had primary villages along the Fox River in Wisconsin in the early 1700s. It was a location of critical strategic importance, because it linked the Great Lakes watershed with the Mississippi watershed and served as the primary connection route for French colonies and trading zones in the Great Lakes with New Orleans. The French, however, were never friendly toward the Mesquakie. They had primary trade

This photo from about 1910 shows five men from the Sauk and Fox tribes (now also known as the Mesquakie) in Native dress.

and military alliances with the Ojibwe and the Huron, Mesquakie tribal enemies. The Mesquakie were uncomfortable accommodating French trade and traffic through their territory when the French were arming their enemies with muskets but not offering comparable trade terms or protection to the Mesquakie. A series of brutal wars (sometimes called the Fox Wars) erupted from 1690 to 1742. They devastated the Mesquakie population.

To slow French colonization and arms-dealing with their enemies, the Mesquakie attacked French trade caravans in 1690 along the Fox and Wisconsin Rivers. The French then encouraged the Ojibwe to counterattack the Mesquakie, which they did immediately and in overwhelming numbers. The Mesquakie were formidable and strategic warriors, though, and held their ground, compelling the French to build several new forts in 1692 to protect their trade route. The French ratcheted up pressure on the Mesquakie through successive military campaigns, often through or with other tribes such as the Ojibwe and Dakota.

The Mesquakie forced the French to close portage routes in 1698 and link their colonies in Louisiana and the Great Lakes by sea rather than through Mesquakie territory. It was a costly blow to the French, who were in continual conflict with the British and their much larger navy. The French lost many men and much treasure from their

David Million, of the Sauk and Fox tribes, wears an elaborate outfit at a powwow in Texas.

encounters with the British and disruption in their trade routes during the struggle with the Mesquakie.

Relentless and Deadly Attacks

French fury was soon vented on the Mesquakie, who continued to put up a spirited fight. In 1720, the Fox had to abandon some of their northern villages along the Fox and Wisconsin Rivers, establishing new villages in southern Wisconsin. The French continued to attack the Mesquakie with relentless brutality, killing hundreds of men, women, and children every year in the 1720s. In 1728, the king of France

issued an edict of extermination, directing the government of New France to eradicate the Mesquakie from the face of the Earth. Although there have been many genocidal wars in human history, this was one of the most thorough, calculated, and officially codified efforts ever. In 1733, the Mesquakie wanted to surrender to the French without condition, but the French refused and further directed other tribes not to offer the survivors asylum.

The Mesquakie population was reduced to only 500, who eventually received protection from the Sauk, in spite of French protests. The Sauk and the Fox became a series of merged tribal communities, although cultural and linguistic differences persisted for generations. In 1735, the commingled tribes relocated to the Illinois-Iowa border region because of continued military pressure from the French and their Indian allies. The history of the new people, often called the Sac and Fox, evolved outside of the Northeast throughout later generations, and the Blackhawk War and several removal attempts further eroded the tribal land base and put pressure on tribal members to assimilate.

The Mesquakie survived and adapted. Their culture lives on, and the language is still widely spoken, especially in Tama, Iowa. Other Fox communities are located in Kansas and Oklahoma. Some tribal members took refuge with the Kickapoo as well, and some of their descendants are even located in Mexico. ■

This traditionally carved and painted face was on a wooden pole in a display at the Powhatan Indian Village near the Jamestown Settlement in Virginia.

were relatives of many other tribes who had traveled with them over the centuries. Mohegan leaders often sent warriors to assist their allies when they were in danger of being attacked. But these were temporary alliances and did not result in a powerful confederacy such as that of the Iroquois.

European Christians entered Native villages in order to convert the people to Christianity. First the Dutch, then the English, tried to "civilize" all the Native people in "New England," and the lands that the Mohegans had used for agriculture, hunting, and fishing began to have boundaries and fences and to be shared with non-Indians. Some Native people, noting that the Europeans seemed to be prospering in this new land, agreed to be converted to Christianity. In 1738, John Sergeant started a mission village on Mohegan lands along the Housatonic River, bounded by the Berkshire Mountains in western Massachusetts. In this mission village, a church and school were built, and the Mohegans, as well as other Native people who relocated there, became known as the Stockbridge Indians.

In 1785, at the invitation of Oneida Indians, the tribe founded New Stockbridge in upper New York State. Their new home, however, was on timberland sought after by white settlers, and in 1818 the band resettled briefly in White River, Indiana, only to move again. In 1834, the Stockbridge Indians settled on a large tract of land in Wisconsin negotiated by government officials and missionaries. Two years later they were joined by Munsee (Delaware Indian) families migrating west from Canada and became known as the Stockbridge-Munsee Band. Continued pressure from the government led the tribe to relocate again, eventually coming to a community on the shores of Lake Winnebago, which the tribe named Stockbridge. In the early 1930s, the Stockbridge-Munsee experienced a reawakening of their identity and began reorganizing. Under the provisions of the Indian Reorganization Act, the tribe formed an activist business committee and started reclaiming some of their lost land. They received federal affirmation from the secretary of the interior in 1937.

MYTH OR FACT?

Only Plains Indians hunted buffalo.

MYTH

Buffalo hunts were not limited to the Great Plains. Indians in the Northeast intentionally started fires to burn underbrush, thus generating more arable farmland and artificially extending the range of buffalo east as far as New Jersey. Indians, like all humans, altered their environment to their best interests.

TUSCARORA RESERVATION

Tribe: Tuscarora Nation of New York   Current Location: New York   Total Area: 5,700 acres   Population: 1,138

Members of the Tuscarora Nation originally resided in the southeastern United States. Prior to European contact, their population is estimated at 25,000, but by the beginning of the 19th century, they numbered only 1,700.

In 1722, the Tuscarora living among the Oneida were adopted into the League of Five Nations, becoming the sixth. The Seneca gave the Tuscarora a tract of land on the escarpment overlooking Lake Ontario, which remains in tribal ownership today.

The majority of tribal members moved to the site of the present-day reservation at Niagara Landing following the Revolutionary War. By 1804, most of the members of the Tuscarora Nation that had remained in North Carolina joined the community on the New York reservation. The reservation consists of three tracts: the first is a portion in the northwest corner of the reservation deeded to the tribe by the Seneca Nation in perpetuity; the second is the Holland Land gift to the tribe (the Nation retains the title to that parcel); and the third, and largest, tract of land is held in trust by the federal government.

Traditional tribal culture is very important to the Tuscarora people. The traditional governing, kinship, and spiritual systems remain intact. The Tuscarora language, however, which scholars have recorded since early European contact, is now endangered. With the assistance of the tribe, scholars produced a Tuscarora-English dictionary in 1999.

The Tuscarora Nation has retained its traditional governing system. Each clan is governed by a chief, chosen by the oldest clan mother, who represents the clan on the Tuscarora Council of Chiefs. The council consists of 13 chieftain positions and 7 clan mothers.

As a sovereign tribe, the Tuscarora Nation is committed to self-sufficiency. It accepts virtually no assistance from state or federal agencies. Enterprises owned by individual tribal members serve as the foundation of the tribal economy, and New York state taxes cannot be collected on the reservation.

CHAPTER 2

THE SOUTHEAST

THE SOUTHEAST

I N THE BEGINNING, THERE WAS JUST WATER. ALL THE ANIMALS LIVED ABOVE IT, and the sky was so crowded that they needed more room. They were curious about what was beneath the water, and so Dayuni'si, the water beetle, volunteered to explore. He walked across the surface, but he couldn't find any solid ground. He dove below the surface and found only mud. The mud began to spread outward until it became the Earth. Then one of the animals attached this new land to the sky vault with four strings. The land was flat and soft, so the animals decided to send a bird down to see if it had dried. They sent the great buzzard Galun'lati to prepare it for them. The buzzard flew down, down, a long time. By the time he reached the Cherokee land, he was so tired that his wings hit the ground. Wherever they struck the ground, a valley formed. The Cherokee homeland remains this way, a land of mountains and valleys. (Cherokee creation story)

NATIVE LIFE WAS TRANSFORMED AROUND 800, WITH THE INTRODUCTION OF CORN (MAIZE) THROUGH TRADE.

The southeastern United States has been home to American Indian tribes for more than 18,000 years. The first peoples were hunters. As the climate grew milder, deer and elk claimed the new grasslands and deciduous forests, and migrating fish appeared. The region includes distinctive zones: coastal plain, piedmont, mountain, and grassland areas. These features would later divide tribal homelands.

Native life was transformed around 800, with the introduction of corn (maize) through trade. Local bands adopted agriculture, which tied them to the rivers during the growing season. They caught fish, shellfish, turtles, small game, birds, and deer and gathered a wide variety of indigenous plants. They produced ceramics from local clay tempered with sand, or with finely ground shell or quartz, and they added squash and beans to their cornfields. Populations grew, and ever more distinctive cultural and linguistic patterns emerged.

A variety of pottery forms emerged, along with ceremonial objects of stone, shell, and copper, embellished with designs that reflected an extensive belief system and an understanding of life and death as a timeless sequence of cycles.

The "Mississippian cultures" developed at the same time. These peoples, who proliferated in the Mississippi River Valley, were ruled by a hereditary class of elites, and they flourished from about 800 to 1500. Their trade networks stretched across most of what is now the United States. They constructed pyramid or platform mounds, with houses, temples, and burial buildings on top of them. Their religious beliefs were tied to a ceremonial cycle reinforced with ball games, which served spiritual and political purposes. With the onset of the Little Ice Age, some Mississippian townships were abandoned, and new conflicts developed as tribes from colder areas moved south.

Preceding pages: Seminoles construct thatched huts called chickees in Florida's Everglades. Opposite: Young Shawna Tubby is a Choctaw Indian who lives in Mississippi.

In 1513, the Spaniard Juan Ponce de León explored, and in 1526 Lucas Vázquez de Ayllón established a short-lived colony in what is now South Carolina. Their contact with indigenous peoples was minimal, but they left behind diseases that would soon devastate Native communities: smallpox, chicken pox, measles, and influenza. Pánfilo de Narváez tried to colonize Florida in 1527, leading a disastrous expedition along the Gulf of Mexico to what is now Galveston. Beginning in 1540, Hernando de Soto led 700 Spaniards on a brutal rampage through the Southeast. Repulsed by most of the tribes he encountered, de Soto died of a fever on the west bank of the Mississippi River. More than half of his men died before the expedition reached Mexico City in 1543.

The de Soto expedition's brutality, along with the diseases it introduced, led to reorganization of the remaining Mississippian societies. Confederations emerged or expanded as people of related cultures regrouped. Among these were the Creek (Muscogee), Choctaw, and Chickasaw.

The Spanish had founded St. Augustine in Florida in 1565, and Jesuit priests converted the local Timucua, Guale, and

THE SOUTHEAST

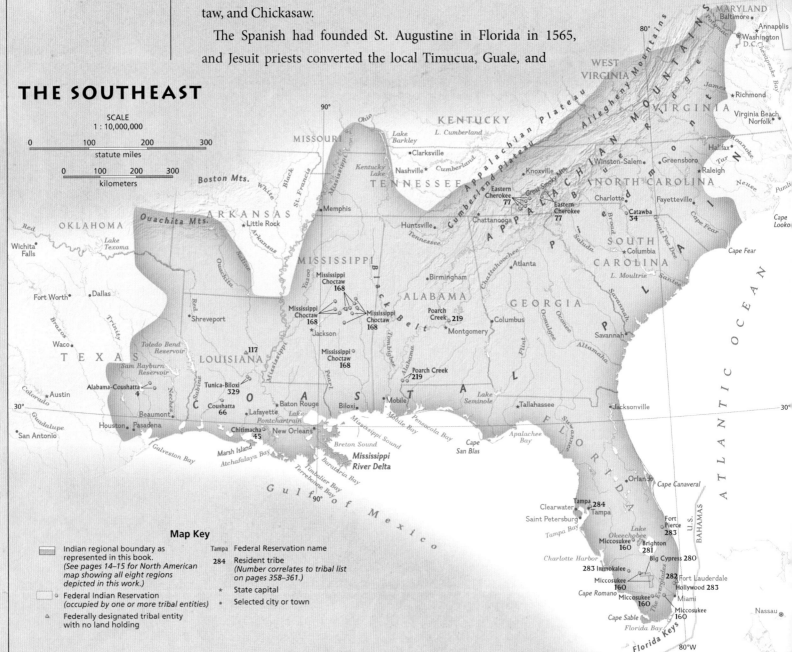

SCALE
1 : 10,000,000

statute miles
0   100   200   300

kilometers
0   100   200   300

Map Key

Indian regional boundary as represented in this book.
(See pages 14–15 for North American map showing all eight regions depicted in this work.)

Federal Indian Reservation
(occupied by one or more tribal entities)

Federally designated tribal entity with no land holding

Tampa Federal Reservation name

284 Resident tribe
(Number correlates to tribal list on pages 358–361.)

★ State capital

• Selected city or town

Appalachee Indians to Christianity, establishing missions in northern Florida and Georgia. These were destroyed by the English, with Muscogee assistance, in the early 1700s. The Indians were killed or sold into slavery.

In 1692, French explorers claimed the Mississippi River watershed for France and established a colony. Pierre LeMoyne, Sieur d'Iberville, visited the coasts of Louisiana, Mississippi, and Alabama in 1699, establishing friendly relations with many tribes. In 1716, the French built Fort Rosalie at Natchez, Mississippi. The fort was destroyed by the Natchez tribe in 1729, and they were in turn decimated by French retaliation.

As European influence grew, southeastern tribes entered a period of turmoil, facing slave raids, war, disease, and eventual starvation as their resources and lands dwindled. Many tribes remained at war for decades, with Euro-American powers and with one another. Tribe after tribe negotiated with colonial leaders, but whether they resisted or not, the result was the same: most lost their homelands, piece by piece.

SOME TRIBES RELOCATED VOLUNTARILY . . . OTHERS WERE FORCIBLY MOVED BY FEDERAL TROOPS DURING DEVASTATING MARCHES SUCH AS THE TRAIL OF TEARS.

After America declared its independence, pressure on the Indians intensified as the new government relentlessly expanded its hold on the continent. Some tribes relocated voluntarily, and many moved repeatedly to escape the settlers. Others were forcibly moved by federal troops during devastating marches such as the Trail of Tears. The Seminole emerged in Florida as a powerful force and refused to surrender.

While most southeastern Indians ended up in Oklahoma, many remained in their homelands, attempting to make new lives and retain their traditions. Those who remained faced state-sanctioned racism, such as the harassment the Choctaw experienced as Mississippi citizens in the mid-1800s. In the mid-1900s, Virginia bureaucrats classified Indians as "colored" on birth certificates and then enforced Jim Crow segregation. In 1958, Lumbee people in North Carolina defended themselves with firearms against the Ku Klux Klan. Indians in the Southeast were regularly denied access to health care and higher education until the 1960s.

The Five Civilized Tribes (the Cherokee, Chickasaw, Choctaw, Muscogee, and Seminole) lobbied successfully against the Dawes Act of 1887, which divided tribally owned lands into individual allotments and opened up millions of acres to American homesteaders. However, those who moved to Oklahoma faced additional challenges, such as federal "termination" policies in the 1950s that threatened to end tribes' relationships with the U.S. government; boarding schools for children; and "relocation" policies that sent families to cities far from home.

Nevertheless, southeastern tribes today are experiencing cultural and economic resurgence. At festivals such as the Cherokee National Holiday, they celebrate the resilience of ancestors and the ties of family and culture. Increasingly, they have assumed control of schools, community services, courts, and business ventures. Colleges offer language classes in Cherokee and Muscogee, as well as tribal history. Despite everything the people have endured, southeastern tribal levels of education and living standards rank among the highest of American Indians. ▪

ALABAMA-COUSHATTA RESERVATION

Tribe: Alabama-Coushatta Tribes of Texas
Current Location: Texas **Total Area:** 5,197 acres
Tribal Enrollment: 1,113

The Alabama and Coushatta tribes, members of the Muscogean linguistic group, are descendants of the ancient mound-building cultures of the Southeast. Their villages were constructed around large central plazas where temple buildings were the center of spiritual and cultural life. They practiced a traditional subsistence lifestyle based on agriculture, gathering, and hunting. They are said to have been the first friendly tribes encountered by Hernando de Soto in 1541.

Both tribes were members of the Upper Creek Confederacy (see Coushatta Reservation, page 84). Fleeing colonial settlements in their aboriginal territory, the Coushatta migrated to eastern Texas sometime around 1795; the Alabama arrived in Tyler

MYTH OR FACT?

Indians were not involved in slavery.

MYTH

Some pre-Columbian southeastern societies enslaved captives. Slavery grew with European arrival. Spanish sailors enslaved Caribbean Indians and captured Native boys during the mid-1500s. Following hostilities, Virginia and Maryland colonists shipped tribes to Caribbean plantations. Some tribes raided one another for captives.

County in 1805. In 1839, Mirabeau B. Lamar, president of the Republic of Texas, issued a proclamation of peace toward the tribes, enjoining Texas residents from engaging in any acts of violence toward them. As a gesture of gratitude for their support of Texas independence, Sam Houston appropriated lands for each tribe in 1854. Because the Coushatta acreage was never deeded, the Alabama shared their land with their neighbors, uniting the two tribes for the first time. They did not engage in conflict with settlers and were therefore allowed to remain in Texas when other tribes were removed to Indian Territory in Oklahoma. After the federal government gave up trusteeship of Alabama-Coushatta lands and other assets in 1954, the state of Texas assumed responsibility for the tribe; the tribe regained federal recognition in 1987.

The Alabama-Coushatta work diligently to maintain distinct cultural values while embracing modern technologies. A majority of tribal members speak the native Alabama-Coushatta language,

John Ross, a planter and business owner, was one of the wealthiest men in northern Georgia.

JOHN ROSS

Elected chief of the Cherokee Nation, 1828–1866

John Ross was born in 1790 in Alabama, the son of a Cherokee/Scots woman and a Scots father. Appointed Indian agent to the western Cherokee, he served in Arkansas and fought against the Creek at the Battle of Horseshoe Bend. He developed a plantation worked by slaves, established a ferry and a trading firm, and became one of the richest men in northern Georgia.

Ross rose to the presidency of the Cherokee National Council through his English-language skills and diplomatic abilities. Convinced of his nation's opposition to removal to Oklahoma Territory, he petitioned Congress with tribal grievances in 1824 and was elevated to principal chief in 1827. After negotiations with the government failed, Ross led the Cherokee to file suit before the U.S. Supreme Court. Its decisions affirmed tribal sovereignty but set the precedent for the "domestic dependent" status of Indian nations. That paved the way for disastrous federal Indian policies to come.

In 1838, those Cherokee who had not voluntarily moved to Oklahoma were forced to do so. Ross led them there. He fought for Cherokee neutrality in the Civil War, but sided with the South when the tribe failed to achieve consensus. The Union Army invaded the Cherokee in 1862, and the Confederates abandoned their Cherokee allies. Ross lived in Washington from 1862 to 1865, advocating for his tribe with minimal success. He died in 1866. ■

In Spencer, Tennessee, a part of the Trail of Tears remains. Thousands of Indians died during forced relocations westward from the Southeast, mostly to Oklahoma. The federal government often moved the tribes on foot, sometimes in freezing weather.

Seminole tribal member Sally Buster demonstrates her beadwork at the Ah-Tah-Thi-Ki Museum on the Big Cypress Indian Reservation in Florida.

practice traditional arts and crafts, and perpetuate the ancient Legend of the Twin Manifestations: a fundamental spiritual teaching of the Alabama-Coushatta people that the Great Spirit has bestowed on humankind the priceless gift of free will so that every individual can make a choice between right and wrong.

The tribal council formed an office of tribal development in 2003 to create "significant and sustainable sources of tribal income, meaningful employment opportunities, and support for entrepreneurship" as the tribe continues to look for ways to ameliorate the cycles of underemployment and poverty. The tribe has its own forestry department to oversee

management of timber on all tribal lands and an oil and gas department to handle the considerable field operations, production, revenues, and compliance issues associated with nine natural gas wells on 3,000 productive acres.

Big Cypress Reservation

Tribe: Seminole Tribe of Florida
Current Location: Florida   Total Area: 52,338 acres
Tribal Enrollment (Statewide): 3,165

The Big Cypress Reservation lies approximately 45 miles west of Fort Lauderdale. Located off I-75, Big Cypress was one of the first three reservations consolidated for the Seminole by the BIA in the 1930s. Tribal members currently occupy less than 2 percent of the reservation; the remainder of the area is home to indigenous plant and animal species, many of them endangered.

In 1957, the Seminole Tribe of Florida adopted a constitution and charter in adherence to the Indian Reorganization Act of 1934, and thus received formal recognition. Reservation lands were first established at Hollywood, Brighton, and Big Cypress, and later at Immokalee, Tampa, and Fort Pierce.

The majority of Seminole tribal lands lie within the swampy regions of the Everglades ecosystem. The Everglades, or River of Grass, has been the heart of Seminole culture for countless years. Characterized by miles of swamplands, it is home to numerous endangered plant and animal species, including the last known remaining Florida panthers. The panther has particular cultural significance to the Seminole people and is represented in the tribe's clan system.

The health and well-being of their surroundings is critical to the well-being of the Seminole people themselves. The tribe has established programs for protecting their natural resources and educating the community, tribal and nontribal members alike, on the Everglades' significance to the larger ecosystem as well as to themselves.

The tribe holds a water rights agreement with the state of Florida and the South Florida Water Management District, allowing the tribe to regulate surface water management, water use, and environmentally sensitive waters on tribal lands.

In the past two decades, the Seminole have grown into a strong sovereign force under an inspired and articulate leadership. The tribe sustains its traditional culture through special events, language, clanship, and arts and crafts.

The tribe publishes a newspaper, the *Seminole Tribune,* every two weeks with a circulation of more than 5,000. In 1989, the *Seminole Tribune* became the first Indian newspaper to win a Robert F. Kennedy Award. It was also nominated for the Pulitzer Prize that same year and has garnered numerous

MYTH OR FACT?

"Federal recognition" of a tribe acknowledges its inherent sovereignty.

FACT

The formal acknowledgment of a government-to-government relationship between a tribe and the U.S. Congress is called "federal recognition." More than 560 tribes are recognized, and more than 200 others intend to petition. Tribes are acknowledged through records and treaties, by an act of Congress, or by a lengthy process within the Bureau of Indian Affairs.

awards presented by the Native American Journalists Association. The newspaper refers to itself as "The Voice of the Unconquered."

The tribe has made great strides in developing its economic base as well, serving as a source of employment for both tribal and nontribal members and becoming an increasingly formidable economic force in the region.

The economy of the Big Cypress Reservation is sustained primarily by the tribe's agricultural enterprises. Citrus groves, for example, cover 1,600 acres and produce a major portion of Florida's lemon crop. In 2003, the grapefruit crop was the earliest-producing in the state, bringing the tribe recognition for its successful practices. The tribe also manages a herd of cattle at Big Cypress. Both the cattle and citrus operations have received state and national recognition.

The reservation suffers from soil pollution because of damaging agricultural practices in the region. In order to address this issue and other environmental concerns throughout the five Seminole reservations, the tribe has implemented programs to limit pollution runoff from pastures, urban areas, and other vulnerable sites.

An aviation department provides safe, efficient, convenient, and cost-effective air transportation for tribal programs and medical travel requests. It also grants helicopter firefighting services to the BIA forestry program and mosquito eradication for the Big Cypress, Brighton, and Immokalee reservations.

The Big Cypress Reservation is home to the Ah-Tah-Thi-Ki Museum, an important repository of artifacts and natural features that educates tribal members and non-Natives about Seminole history and culture. The museum welcomes approximately 2,000 visitors each month. Its exhibits include a full-scale re-creation of a traditional village, a 64-acre cypress dome, and boardwalk nature trails. The museum also houses exhibits on loan from the Smithsonian Institution and a growing collection of military items from the Seminole Wars. Tours are given on a regular basis, and the reservation includes a safari, a rock mine, and an RV resort.

CATAWBA

The Catawba are a Siouan-speaking people whose presence in the southeastern piedmont dates to ancient times. Their Siouan language deviates so markedly from all other forms of Siouan that scholars suspect they may have branched off linguistically as long as 4,000 years ago. Their name, Kadapau (anglicized to Catawba), probably derives from the Choctaw *katápe*, meaning "separate" or "divided," as noted by early historian John Lawson. Among themselves, however, they were known as Esaw (also Iswa or Issa), meaning simply "the people." Once known as one of the fiercest tribes in the Southeast, the Catawba now number about 2,600 people living in their ancestral homeland around Rock Hill, South Carolina.

Traditional Culture

Like other tribes of the region, the Catawba were farmers, skilled also in the arts of pottery and basket weaving, traditions they practice today. They constructed circular, bark-shingled homes and built more elaborate temple structures for religious observances. Men and women worked together in the fields, and their diets included corn, beans, and gathered foods, supplemented by hunting and fishing.

The Catawba traditionally flattened the backs of the heads of male infants, as did several other southeastern tribes. This practice earned them the name "flatheads" among the Iroquois. They placed a pillow of stiff cornhusks under the back of a baby's head while he slept, and the pressure forced the head into a flatter shape that was considered more attractive. Catawba warriors maintained an appearance designed to instill fear. When preparing for war, they painted a black circle around one eye, a white circle surrounded by black around the other, and tied their hair in a ponytail.

Colonial-Era Relations and Warfare

Spanish explorer Hernando de Soto's expedition apparently traveled through

A group of Catawba Indians at the Corn Exposition in Columbia, South Carolina, in 1913

Catawba territory in 1540 but failed to document a corresponding tribal name. When Juan Pardo encountered them in 1567, the Catawba were divided into two powerful groups that may have numbered 10,000 people. They had declined to about 5,000 by 1692, when the English first recorded population estimates.

For centuries preceding European contact, the Catawba had warred with the Lenape (Delaware), Cherokee, Seneca, and other Iroquois (Haudenosaunee) tribes, traveling great distances to attack one another. The Catawba were quick to ally themselves with the English, who entered the Carolinas in the mid-1600s. They supported English interests, protecting the colonies from the French

and Spanish, as well as returning runaway slaves.

With the escalation of the Tuscarora War of 1711—a conflict between the colony of North Carolina and the Tuscarora Nation—the Catawba entered the war as Carolina allies, with their 500 warriors assisting 30 South Carolina militiamen, a force that quickly overcame the Tuscarora. When the colony of North Carolina then refused to pay the South Carolinians' expenses, the South Carolinians seized several hundred Tuscarora prisoners and sold them into slavery. After a second war the next year, hundreds more Tuscarora were sold, while others were tortured to death. Most survivors fled.

Following the war, the Catawba found themselves subjected to the same abuse previously faced by the Tuscarora. English traders seized Catawba women and children, selling them as slaves to cover whiskey debts. Court records document physical abuse at the hands of these traders, who often beat Indian men to death and raped Indian women at will.

Disease, warfare, and alcohol resulted in massive population decline, reducing Catawba numbers to about 1,400 by 1728. A smallpox epidemic in 1738 claimed half of the people, and another in 1760 reduced the population to 400.

Tribal Wars and an American Alliance

Warfare between the Catawba and the Iroquois went on for decades, with treaties and fighting alternating until a peace was negotiated in 1759. The Indian Road through the Great Valley of the Appalachians, later called the Philadelphia Wagon Road, was created by Iroquois warriors as the most direct route to the Carolinas to raid the Catawba.

Meanwhile, the Catawba drove the Yuchi out of their homelands in what is now eastern Tennessee. They also routed the Carolina Shawnee, who joined with the Lenape in present-day Pennsylvania. In 1762, a party of Shawnee killed the Catawba chief, King Haiglar—a blow from which the Catawba never recovered.

A 15-square-mile reservation was confirmed for the Catawba in 1763 near the border between North and South Carolina. Warriors fought on the American side in the Revolutionary War, repudiating their English alliance and earning the gratitude of their neighbors.

Travels, Tribulations, and Today

Even as they incorporated survivors of as many as 20 other devastated tribes, by 1826 only 110 Catawba remained. In desperate poverty, they sold all but one square mile of their land to South Carolina and relocated among the Cherokee in North Carolina, who were themselves facing removal. North Carolina refused to provide land, though, so they returned to South Carolina. In 1853, the Catawba attempted unsuccessfully to relocate among the Choctaw in Oklahoma. As

South Carolina residents, Catawba men joined the Confederate cause.

Although the Catawba were recognized in South Carolina, they did not receive federal acknowledgment until 1941. In 1959, the U.S. government terminated their tribal status. In 1973, the tribe reorganized and filed a claim against South Carolina for lands

illegally appropriated. It received a $50 million settlement and restoration of federal status.

The Catawba now maintain a reservation of about 800 acres, with headquarters in Rock Hill. Membership is around 2,600. The tribe operates a cultural center and numerous social programs and is planning a new bingo hall. ■

Keith Anderson (Catawba, Cherokee) dresses in traditional regalia for a cultural celebration.

BRIGHTON RESERVATION

Tribe: Seminole Tribe of Florida
Current Location: Florida   **Total Area:** 35,805 acres
Tribal Enrollment (Statewide): 3,165

The Brighton Reservation is located northwest of Lake Okeechobee in southern Florida, approximately 90 miles west of West Palm Beach, and encompasses more than 35,000 acres of land held in trust by the federal government.

The Brighton Reservation's economy is supported largely by the tribe's agricultural and aquacultural enterprises. The Brighton Citrus Farm occupies 127 acres, home to almost 19,000 living trees. Groves produce grapefruit, oranges, and tangelos. The

A woman demonstrates how to make cornmeal cakes at the Powhatan Indian Village at the Jamestown Settlement, a living history museum in Virginia.

tribe intends to expand the farm to incorporate an additional 85 acres. Tribal citrus crop sales generate approximately $4 million annually. The tribe has also entered into the aquaculture industry, recently establishing a turtle farm.

There are 42 cattle operators on the reservation who belong to the tribe's cattleman's program, established in the 1960s in cooperation with individual tribal cattle owners. Their cattle are run on more than 12,000 acres of Florida pastures.

The Brighton Reservation is also home to the Seminole Casino, which opened in 1999 and employs approximately 105 individuals.

The Seminole operate their own broadcasting station, the Seminole Broadcasting Department.

Brighton Reservation is one of four station locations (see also page 86).

Tourism and outdoor recreation, which bring important revenue to the tribe as well as cultural awareness of Seminole presence in Florida, are represented at the Brighton Seminole Campground, three miles north of Lake Okeechobee, and the Brighton Rodeo Arena.

CATAWBA RESERVATION

Tribe: **Catawba Indian Nation**   Current Location: **South Carolina**   Total Area: **1,010 acres**   Tribal Enrollment: **2,478**

Linguistic evidence suggests the Yap Ye Iswa, or Catawba, Indian Nation has resided in the region of present-day North and South Carolina for more than a thousand years. The indigenous language belongs to the Siouan family. The Catawba encountered Spanish explorers in 1540 and were devastated by smallpox and other diseases, reducing the population of 5,000 in the early 18th century to only 250 by 1784.

AMOROLECK

Mannahoac/Monacan warrior

While exploring the Rappahannock River near present-day Fredericksburg, Virginia, in 1608, Capt. John Smith encountered warriors who fired arrows at his party. They disappeared when the English returned fire, but a wounded man was left behind. Smith's Powhatan guide attempted to kill the man, declaring him an enemy, but Smith intervened.

With the guide as a translator, the warrior identified himself as Amoroleck, a member of the Mannahoac/Monacan alliance of Siouan-speaking tribes who was hunting in the region. When Smith asked him to describe the societies he knew, he mentioned his own people, then the Powhatan, and a third nation to the northwest—possibly the Haudenosaunee (later known as Iroquois).

Smith asked Amoroleck why his people had reacted with hostility. Amoroleck replied, "We heard that your people came from under the world, to take our world from us."

Amoroleck conducted Smith's party to his hunting camp, where they were welcomed with a feast. Smith later boasted to his Powhatan allies that he had defeated their Mannahoac enemies. Colonial records contain no further mention of Amoroleck's people, and his statement remains the only recorded speech from a Siouan-speaking Indian of that region and that century. ∎

Cherokee, Iroquoian language family

"O-si-yo. Tsa-la-gi-sgo hi-wo-ni-ha? Do-hi-tsu. O-s-da. Wa-do. Do-nv-da-go-hvi."

("Hello. Do you speak Cherokee? How are you? I am fine. Thank you. Until we meet again.")

Monacan school children at Falling Rock Indian Mission in Virginia in 1914.

The tribe has participated in various military efforts throughout U.S. history, and tribal members continue to serve in the armed forces today. Allied with the Carolina settlers, the Catawba fought against the Cherokee and Tuscarora in what became known as the Yamasee War of 1715. They served as scouts for the British during the French and Indian War as well as during the American Revolution, and fought with the Confederates in the Civil War; in 1942, they declared war against Germany and the Axis Powers.

The original reservation occupied more than 15,000 square miles. The present reservation is located within the original establishment in the Pine Tree Hill (1760) and Augusta (1763) treaties. An 1840 treaty was neither ratified by the federal government nor honored by South Carolina, and the tribe remained landless until the state established a 630-acre parcel of land for them in 1943. However, the federal government officially terminated the tribe in 1959, and all its landholdings were dissolved. The state agreed to support the tribe's efforts to regain status if the tribe relinquished its claim to 144,000 acres of ancestral lands. The tribe refused and sought resolution from the federal courts. In 1973, the Catawba Indian Nation reorganized as a nonprofit corporation and began pursuing the land claim with the help of the Native American Rights Fund. In 1993, Congress restored the tribe's federal status and settled the Catawba land claim for $50 million. The tribe was allowed to expand its reservation and intends to continue increasing its land base.

Even though there are no remaining speakers of the language, the Catawba's culture and art are still very much alive. The cultural preservation project received the South Carolina Folk Heritage Advocacy Award (1993) in recognition of its many programs and services designed to protect, preserve, and restore tribal traditions, such as the ancient art of pottery making.

CHITIMACHA RESERVATION

Tribe: Chitimacha Tribe of Louisiana
Current Location: Louisiana   **Total Area:** 445 acres
Tribal Enrollment: 1,102

The Chitimacha tribe once comprised four bands: the Chitimacha, Yagenechito (eastern Chitimacha), Chawasha, and Washa. Archaeological evidence dating back 6,000 years has been unearthed in the ancestral lands, and oral history indicates that the tribe has "always been here." Though vastly diminished in size, the present-day reservation occupies areas that were once part of the Chitimacha's ancestral lands.

The French and their allies regularly forced Chitimacha tribal members into slavery during their occupation of Louisiana. Women in particular were sought to supply troops with female

A mask worn during the Cherokee "Booger" dance

Choctaw, Muscogean language family

"Halito. Chahta imanumpa ish anumpola hinla ho? Chim achukma? Achukma hoke. A. Yokoke. Chee pesa lacheenee."

("Hello. Do you speak Choctaw? Are you well? I am fine. Yes. Thank you. I will see you later.")

"companionship." In the early 1700s, the Chitimacha revolted against the slave trade and killed French missionary Jean-François Buisson de St. Cosme and three other Frenchmen. The French government ordered immediate action against the Chitimacha. Traditional enemies such as the Acolapissa, Bayougoula, Biloxi, Choctaw, Houma, Natchitoches, Pascagoula, and Taensa, and even traditional allies such as the Chawasha, joined the French. This war lasted 12 years, culminating in the eventual defeat of the Chitimacha. The tribe suffered the deaths of numerous warriors and lost many women and children to slavery. The remaining Chawasha joined forces with the Washa and eventually were absorbed into the Chitimacha tribe.

As Euro-American presence in the territory increased, the Chitimacha intermarried with Acadians and converted to Christianity. In time, indigenous spiritual beliefs and cultural traditions were lost, and Cajun French eventually replaced the Native language.

The Spanish sold Louisiana back to France in 1800, and France sold it to the United States in 1803. In 1914, Sarah Avery McIlhenney, a private investor and friend of the women of the Chitimacha tribe, purchased the remaining tribal lands at a sheriff's auction. She then sold the lands to the federal government, and the land was placed in trust for the tribe. In 1916, the Chitimacha became the first Louisiana tribe to receive formal federal recognition. The Chitimacha constitution and bylaws have been in place since 1971.

In addition to the revenue generated by leasing a small portion of land for oil mining, the tribal economy is sustained by enterprises in the agricultural, fishing, and gaming industries. Most notably, the Chitimacha operate a successful casino, the Cypress Bayou Casino, which features slot machines, bingo, and several restaurants.

Currently, the Chitimacha have a school at the center of their reservation. Students are taught the traditional curriculum as well as their Native language.

STICKBALL

Stickball, a game played by the Chero-kee, Chickasaw, Choctaw, Creek, Sem-inole, and Yuchi tribes, evolved as a ritual for settling disputes between commu-nities. Known to some as "the little brother of war," the game is similar to lacrosse.

In earlier times, games took place on a cleared stretch of land, varying in size from 100 yards to a mile in length, involving as few as ten or as many as several hundred players. At each end of the field stood a straight, or V- or H-shaped, goalpost. Players attempted to strike the post with a small ball or to toss it between posts to score a point. Women, who participated only on certain occasions, were permitted to catch the ball with their hands. Men used two hickory sticks, each about two feet long, with small nets of sinew or fiber looped around one end. The ball was made of hide and stuffed with fur.

Participants often spent days preparing for a match, assisted by the most power-ful medicine man, whose job included call-ing on spiritual helpers—swift animals and birds that could assist the players. Ballplayers often incorporated animal parts and feath-ers into their playing attire. Rules governed what could and could not be eaten before a game, and players were required to fast and abstain from sex the preceding night, when a dance would be held. In some tribes, the medicine man placed black beads, repre-senting the opposing players, under a rock, which the women then stepped on, symboli-cally crushing their opponents while singing songs designed to weaken them.

Before the game, the priest exhorted the players with an emotional speech, and each player would be ritually scratched on the arms, legs, chest, and back with a sharpened bone comb. After a cleansing ritual at the river's edge, the medicine man prayed and made offerings to the spirit world to help his team. The host team's medicine man tossed the ball to commence play. Games were rough, and players were sometimes seriously injured.

Stickball is still played among southeast-ern Indian communities and is considered an important intertribal tradition. ■

Four Seminole Indians play stickball, a game that is an ancestor of lacrosse, in a grassy field at the Hollywood Seminole Indian Reservation in Florida.

CHEROKEE

The name Cherokee comes from *Tsalagi*, a Choctaw-derived word meaning "cave people." They call themselves Ani-Yunwiya, "real [or principal] people." Their language is in the Iroquoian family, which suggests that the tribe once lived in the Northeast, an idea supported by its oral history. By the mid-1500s, the Cherokee controlled the southern Allegheny range from southwestern Virginia through the Carolinas and into northern Georgia, eastern Tennessee, and northeastern Alabama. The ancient settlement known as Kituwa in western North Carolina is now part of Qualla Boundary, the Eastern Band of Cherokee Indians' reservation in the Great Smoky Mountains. Cherokee people also live in Oklahoma. Theirs is one of the largest tribes, with more than 280,000 members.

Early Encounters

Hernando de Soto recorded encounters with the tribe, which he called Chalaque, when he crossed through their country in April 1540. The first Cherokee village he found had been abandoned in advance of his arrival. At a second location, west of the Blue Ridge, his men were welcomed, and an alliance was established that permitted Spanish mining and smelting operations on Cherokee homelands for more than a century.

The first Englishmen to enter Cherokee country came from Virginia, intending to establish a trade relationship. James Needham and Gabriel Arthur visited the town of Chota, which Needham described as well fortified and in possession of 150 canoes. Needham's Indian guide killed him on the return trip. Arthur, who had remained in the Cherokee town to learn the language, later accompanied the Chota chief on raids against enemy tribes. In 1674, the chief returned him to Virginia.

Tribal Conflicts, 1700–1800

The colony of South Carolina was established in 1670, and by 1705 its governor had built up an Indian slave trade that involved all area tribes, enflaming old enmities and inciting new conflicts. The Cherokee participated in forcing

Tah-chee, a 19th-century Cherokee chief

the Tuscarora out of North Carolina in 1711–13. In 1715, they joined with other tribes against South Carolina, but failed to defeat the colonists. The next year, they entered the Yamasee War against the Creek, and raids between the two tribes continued as late as 1755.

A smallpox epidemic in 1738–39 took the lives of half of the Cherokee population, some of whom survived the disease but committed suicide due to their disfigurement, according to an English trader in the region. The epidemic caused people to distrust their religious leaders and their ancestral beliefs, and they turned away from their ceremonies.

Following the French and Indian War, the Cherokee were inundated by immigrant settlers who flooded into Virginia's Great Valley, and the Anglo-Cherokee War occurred in 1760. The tribe signed numerous treaties, but was unable to establish a permanent border. In frustration, they sided with the British during the Revolution, and the Chickamauga faction, led by Dragging Canoe, began raiding settlements. Colonial forces retaliated, burning more than 50 towns, seizing Cherokee people and selling them to slave traders or killing them for scalp bounties.

A "Civilized Tribe" and Its Removal

The Cherokee reorganized under Little Turkey, Black Fox, and Pathkiller, three successive principal chiefs, and sided with the United States against the Creek in the Battle of Horseshoe Bend. Leaders developed their own plantations, owned slaves, and educated their sons at mission schools. The tribe divided into factions, one affiliated with the English-speaking elite group of planters, the other a populist group of more traditional tribal members.

In 1825, the tribe named its new Georgia headquarters New Echota and adopted Sequoyah's syllabic alphabet. The legislature appointed John Ross as principal chief. Within a few years, a newspaper was established, and the Bible was translated into Cherokee.

A number of Cherokee people had already voluntarily relocated to Arkansas between 1775 and 1786. In 1829, gold was discovered at Dahlonega, Georgia, and the state demanded that the federal government remove the Cherokee. A tribal faction known as the Ridge Party signed the Treaty of New Echota, which outlined terms for the removal. Even though the majority of the tribe had not agreed to the move, President Martin Van Buren ordered 7,000 troops to evict them.

More than 16,000 Cherokee were forced west during 1838–39. As many as 4,000 died on the way, and the three leaders of the Ridge Party were assassinated by Ross supporters.

Relocated tribal members moved repeatedly. In 1827, Sequoyah represented the Old Settler Cherokee in negotiations with newly arrived Cherokee, and in 1839, he and Ross signed an act reuniting the groups. At the end of the 19th century, the federal government's Curtis Act abolished Cherokee Nation courts and civic institutions as the Oklahoma Territory moved toward securing statehood.

Modern Tribal Communities

Today, the Cherokee Nation is headquartered in Tahlequah, Oklahoma. It operates agricultural interests and businesses, including casinos, and serves as a defense contractor. It has developed health clinics and language immersion programs, publishes a tribal newspaper, and operates a museum. Its Cherokee National Holiday, on Labor Day

weekend, is attended by 80,000 to 90,000 Cherokee citizens each year.

The Oconaluftee people had separated from the Cherokee Nation in 1819 and remained in the Great Smoky Mountains as North Carolina citizens. Some Cherokee groups hid from federal soldiers and avoided removal. Others lived on reserves in Georgia, Tennessee, and Alabama, returning eventually to North Carolina to form the modern tribal communities. Today, the Eastern Band has more than 8,000 members. It operates a casino and other tourist attractions.

In 1934, another group, the United Keetoowah Band of Cherokee, developed its own government under the Indian Reorganization Act, also headquartered in Tahlequah. The tribe, with about 12,000 members today, was federally recognized in 1946. ∎

A Cherokee woman sews a beaded belt as part of a demonstration of traditional crafts at Oconaluftee Indian Village in Cherokee, North Carolina.

COUSHATTA RESERVATION

Tribe: Coushatta Tribe of Louisiana
Current Location: Louisiana   Total Area: 683 acres
Tribal Enrollment: 805

The Coushatta tribe is descended from the Muscogean tribes that once resided in the Southeast. The tribe belonged to the Creek Confederacy and lived a somewhat sedentary lifestyle in the Tennessee River region of Alabama, relying on local agriculture, hunting, fishing, and trade.

The Coushatta encountered Spanish explorers in 1540 and maintained a civil coexistence with Euro-American settlers. In 1783, the Coushatta tribe lost more than 800 square miles to the state of Georgia and set in motion a series of conflicts and treaties that eventually drove the Coushatta out of their ancestral lands and into Georgia, Alabama, Mississippi, Louisiana, and even Texas.

MYTH OR FACT?

Southeastern Indian women held important roles in Native societies.

FACT

European explorers assumed that southeastern Native women traditionally held inferior status to men, because they did the farming. Most societies were matrilineal, however, and women controlled food surpluses, chose marriage partners, governed clans, and served as principal chiefs in some tribes.

Remaining members of the Coushatta tribe participated in the Creek War of 1813. More than 3,000 Native Americans were killed during this conflict, and 22 million acres of ancestral lands were ceded to the federal government. Bands of Coushatta moved south to settle in the lower reaches of the Red River in Louisiana. By 1861, tribal members had begun to settle near Kinder, but continuing encroachment from settlers pushed the Coushatta east of the Calcasieu River. Eventually the tribe purchased land there and established a new community.

In 1898, the United States placed 160 acres of land in trust for the Coushatta, and the BIA provided funding to educate tribal youths. However, in 1953, the tribe was terminated by the federal government.

In 1956, the tribe established the Coushatta Indians of Allen Parish. The group served primarily as a business enterprise that managed the sale and production of tribal arts and crafts. When the tribe received Louisiana state recognition in 1972,

---

Like many other Seminoles, Osceola for years resisted removal to Oklahoma.

OSCEOLA

Seminole resistance leader during the federal Indian removal era

Born in Tallassee, Alabama, in 1804, Billy Powell, later known as Osceola, was the son of a Muscogee/Scots woman. His father is believed to have been William Powell, an English trader. In 1814, Osceola and his mother fled Alabama with other Creek people after Andrew Jackson's victory over the Red Stick Creek at the Battle of Horseshoe Bend. They settled in Florida. There, he rose to prominence as a passionate young leader and orator.

In 1832, several Seminole *micos*, or chiefs, signed the Treaty of Payne's Landing, exchanging their Florida lands for lands west of the Mississippi River. However, five prominent chiefs refused to sign or to move. A series of bloody wars ensued over 40 years as the U.S. Army attempted to round up Seminole people and remove them to Oklahoma. Osceola and his followers ambushed and killed the U.S. Indian agent who had removed the chiefs from their positions. He then led the Seminole through a series of successful battles during the first two Seminole Wars, frustrating a number of U.S. generals.

In 1837, U.S. soldiers deceived and captured Osceola when he arrived for a truce negotiation, and he was imprisoned in St. Augustine. He was transferred to Fort Moultrie in South Carolina, where George Catlin and other well-known portrait artists visited him. In January 1838, less than three months after his capture, Osceola died of malaria. He was 34 years old. ∎

it formed the Coushatta Alliance. In pursuit of federal recognition and assistance, the alliance drafted a constitution and bylaws under the provisions of the Indian Reorganization Act of 1934. The tribe gained federal recognition in 1973.

The tribe utilizes a large portion of its land base for rice farming and cattle grazing and is developing a cattle-raising enterprise. The tribe also operates Coushatta Millworks, producing cabinetry for residential and commercial use. The largest source of revenue for the tribe has become the gaming facilities it owns and operates, which help to fund social services and support the general needs of the reservation population.

Tribal members continue to practice cultural and spiritual traditions. The dialect of the Muskogee parent language still spoken by the Coushatta tribe is considered unique, as it has remained virtually unchanged for several hundred years.

EASTERN BAND OF CHEROKEE INDIANS RESERVATION

Tribe: Eastern Band of Cherokee Indians of North Carolina
Current Location: North Carolina
Total Area: 56,746 acres   Tribal Enrollment: 13,562

Winter Beaver, 2, shows off the turtle-shell shakers used in the stomp dance.

Members of the Eastern Band of Cherokee belong to the Ani-yun-wyia, or Principal People. The Cherokee ancestral homelands encompassed portions of present-day North Carolina, Georgia, Tennessee, Alabama, Kentucky, South Carolina, and Virginia, and the Cherokee are the largest Indian tribe in the United States.

The Cherokee first encountered Europeans in 1540 with the de Soto Expedition. The Cherokee population was severely affected by the arrival of European diseases, warfare, and encroachment upon tribal lands.

In 1835, the Treaty of New Echota ceded the last of the remaining tribal lands east of the Mississippi River to the United States. The North Carolina Band was exempt, but the federal government did not honor the treaty and initiated forced removal of all tribal members to Indian Territory.

The Eastern Band of Cherokee traces its origin to the roughly 1,000 members who eluded forced removal by hiding in the mountains. Approximately 300 individuals were living on tribal lands in 1838 and claimed U.S. citizenship. Other tribal members living in Tennessee and North Carolina were not immediately found and removed to Indian Territory. Though federal agents searched the mountains of North Carolina throughout much of the 1840s, by

1848, Congress agreed to recognize the North Carolina Cherokee's rights if the state recognized them as permanent residents. However, the state did not comply with the policy until nearly 20 years later, following the Civil War.

The reservation covers more than 51,000 acres in the Great Smoky Mountains of western North Carolina. The majority of this land base is known as the Qualla Boundary, and with a few minor changes, these tribal lands remain essentially the same as when they were established in 1876. The area is known for fishing, hiking, biking, and other recreational activities, and each year it hosts numerous cultural festivals, including Cherokee Visitor Appreciation Day and a July Powwow.

The tribe has developed into a prosperous, vibrant community, while maintaining its strong identity and sense of heritage. Approximately 42,000 acres of the Qualla Boundary is forested, and harvesting of pulpwood and hardwoods brings in considerable income. The tribe also operates successful gaming enterprises, a fish hatchery and distribution network for commercial trout fishing (with annual revenues estimated at $200,000), and businesses in construction and manufacturing.

FORT PIERCE RESERVATION

Tribe: Seminole Tribe of Florida   Current Location: Florida
Total Area: 60 acres   Tribal Enrollment (Statewide): 3,165

The Fort Pierce Seminole Reservation lies about three miles southwest of downtown Fort Pierce, on Florida's east coast, and about two miles east of Interstate 95. The reservation was established in 1995; however, it was not populated by tribal members until about 2004. It is the newest and smallest of the six Florida Seminole reservations. There are around 40 tribal families living on the reservation today.

Elaborately carved pendants represent birds' heads.

HOLLYWOOD RESERVATION

Tribe: Seminole Tribe of Florida   Current Location: Florida   Total Area: 497 acres   Tribal Enrollment (Statewide): 3,165

The Hollywood Reservation, home to the headquarters for the Seminole Tribe of Florida, is located south of Fort Lauderdale and just west of Hollywood and the Atlantic Ocean. The reservation's proximity to metropolitan Fort Lauderdale allows residents access to the many services and conveniences of city life and draws large numbers of visitors year-round.

It was during the late 1970s that tribal leadership moved the tribe into its most profitable enterprise: high-stakes bingo, which generates multimillion-dollar revenues annually. This, along with cigarette sales, now underwrites many of the tribe's social services, in addition to providing an annual cash dividend to tribal members. When it opened in 1979, the Seminole Casino was the first high-stakes operation of its kind in the country. The casino employs 770 people and was a crucial factor in opening the industry to Native gaming facilities.

The tribe recently opened the Seminole Hard Rock Café Hotel and Casino, with one site on the Hollywood Reservation and one on the Tampa Reservation—two of very few such franchises located on tribal lands across the nation. Shopping, family events, theaters, and restaurants draw many visitors and promote awareness of the importance of Seminole presence in the area.

The reservation is also home to the Seminole Indian Okalee Village and Museum, a satellite of the Ah-Tah-Thi-Ki Museum on the Big Cypress Reservation (which includes a faithfully reconstructed traditional village).

The Seminole tribe operates a broadcasting department from the Hollywood Reservation. The operation includes a broadcasting station with three sister sites in Big Cypress, Brighton, and Immokalee.

BLACK DRINK

Archaeologists have discovered evidence of "black drink" use dating back to the late Archaic period, through shell cups found in high-status burials of the Hopewell period. Associated artifacts have been found throughout the South and in great quantities from Mississippian sites. Intricately engraved cups of whelk and conch shell display images and figures consistent with the southeastern ceremonial complex.

Throughout the Southeast, from present-day southwestern Virginia to Texas, many tribes still participate in the use of the highly esteemed black drink, often in ceremonies that also feature ritual tobacco, such as the stomp dance and annual Green Corn thanksgiving festival. The Indians' use of black drink, so named by Europeans because of its color, was documented by numerous explorers.

Yaupon holly (*Ilex vomitoria*) plants were carefully gathered, dried, roasted, and stored until needed. The bruised leaves and stems were then boiled to produce dark brown or black tea, which was consumed while hot. The tea contains massive amounts of caffeine. It invigorates mind and body, enhances truthfulness, and stimulates thought. Among many tribes, the tea was served by women to men only, to the highest status man first. Among others, it was used medicinally by both women and men to calm nerves or as an expectorant.

Yaupon is a Catawba word for the plant, which is indigenous to the Southeast. The drink was known by various names among the tribes. The Creek called it *ássi-lupútski,* or *asi.* Personal names associated with the drink were not uncommon among the Creek and Seminole. One notable example is Asi-yahola ("Black-Drink Singer"), a well-known Seminole chief whose name was incorrectly recorded as "Osceola." ∎

Satouriona, a 16th-century Indian chief in northern Florida, conducts a ceremony to prepare himself and his men for battle.

IMMOKALEE RESERVATION

Tribe: Seminole Tribe of Florida
Current Location: Florida **Total Area:** 600 acres
Tribal Enrollment (Statewide): 3,165

The Immokalee Reservation was created in the 1980s when the state of Florida accepted land into trust status for the Seminole tribe. It is located in the Everglades, near the town of Immokalee, approximately 30 miles southeast of Fort Myers. The federal government holds approximately 600 acres of land in trust for the Seminoles.

The reservation's economy is supported in large part by its gaming facilities. The Immokalee Reservation is home to the Seminole Gaming Palace and Casino—a big attraction in southwest Florida.

The tribe also operates two shops to showcase traditional and modern Seminole arts and crafts, and one branch of the Seminole Broadcasting Department transmits from the Immokalee Reservation. The media and telecommunications department provides technical training to its employees and employs 20 members of the Seminole tribe at its four different stations.

JENA BAND OF CHOCTAW RESERVATION

Tribe: Jena Band of Choctaw Indians
Current Location: Louisiana **Total Area:** 62 acres
Tribal Enrollment: 243

The ancestors of the modern Choctaw are believed to have lived in the southeastern region of North America for thousands of years. The aboriginal territory of the Jena Band extended from the east-central region of what is now the state of Mississippi to slightly beyond the Mississippi River to the west.

In 1786, in a peace treaty enacted in Hopewell, South Carolina, the new United States promised the Choctaw protection. Following the Treaty of Doak's Stand in 1820, the Choctaw ceded 5.2 million acres of land in Mississippi in exchange for 13 million

CHOCTAW

The Choctaw homelands, in what is today Mississippi, Alabama, and Louisiana, include Nanih Waiya, an earthwork mound believed to be 2,000 years old, in Winston County, Mississippi. This is the place of Choctaw origin, where they emerged from the ground, according to one story. Another tradition suggests that they and the Chickasaw descend from two brothers, Chata and Chicksah, who came from the west. Of Mississippian descent, the Choctaw speak a Muscogean language closely related to Chickasaw. Hernando de Soto encountered Choctaw ancestors in 1540, when he captured a chief, Tuskaloosa, and demanded laborers and women. When he came to claim his hostages, the Indians feasted with his men, and then attacked, defeating the Spaniards.

Early Alliances

Various groups of Choctaw affiliated with the French and British for trade purposes, including trade in slaves. The alliances led to civil war between Choctaw factions before the American Revolution, and the Choctaw signed treaties with the Spanish following the war.

With George Washington's encouragement, the Choctaw accepted schools, new farming methods, and Christianity. The Treaty of Taboca in 1786 established peace between the U.S. and the Choctaw. When the Shawnee leader Tecumseh tried to persuade the powerful Choctaw chief Pushmataha, in 1811, to join his intertribal alliance against the Americans, he was rebuffed. The Choctaw joined the U.S. Army during the War of 1812, and they fought with Gen. Andrew Jackson against the Muscogee at the Battle of Horseshoe Bend.

Treaties and Removal

In 1820, Jackson arrived in Choctaw country on behalf of the United States. He met with chiefs and headmen, persuading them to exchange part of their lands in Mississippi for lands to the west.

Four years later, the three principal chiefs of the Choctaw visited Washington, D.C., to discuss settlers squatting on their lands. Pushmataha said, "No Choctaw ever drew his bow against the United States . . . My nation has given of their country until it is very small. We are in trouble." Nevertheless, the Treaty of Washington City required even more land of the Choctaw. Before they could return home, Apuckshunubbee and

"No Choctaw ever drew his bow against the United States," Chief Pushmataha said.

Pushmataha died—losses that crippled the Choctaw.

Within six years, Jackson returned, demanding that the Choctaw move beyond the Mississippi and cede their remaining land. The 1830 Treaty of Dancing Rabbit Creek was one of the largest land transfers ever accepted by the U.S. without an act of war. After giving up almost 11 million acres, most of the Choctaw moved to Oklahoma in 1831–32. About 2,500 of the 15,000 tribal members died on the trip.

Although the Choctaw had forfeited their homelands, the treaty provided that nearly 1,300 Choctaw could remain in Mississippi. But those who stayed were subjected to increasing harassment, and removal continued. In 1846, about a thousand Choctaw moved, and in 1903 another 300 followed. A reservation in Mississippi was established in 1918 for those who remained.

As allies of the South in the Civil War, the Choctaw lost more land in the establishment of the Oklahoma Territory, which opened two million acres to white settlement in the Land Run of 1889. In 1894, the Dawes Commission distributed land to individual Indians, ending tribal control of their lands.

The U.S. then proposed dissolving the governments of the Five Civilized Tribes, hoping to admit the territory as a state. The five tribes met at the Sequoyah Convention in 1905 to propose the State of Sequoyah, but President Theodore Roosevelt ruled that the Oklahoma and Indian territories would be admitted as one state, Oklahoma—a Choctaw word meaning "red people."

In a 1930 photograph, the Choctaw woman at left weaves traditional baskets from palmetto leaves at her home near Lacombe, Louisiana.

World War I Code Talkers

Toward the end of World War I, a group of Choctaw soldiers joined the U.S. Army, receiving U.S. citizenship in exchange for military service. They developed a secret communication system for the Americans, using their native language as a code. The code, which could not be broken by the Germans, helped the Allies to win battles in the Meuse-Argonne Campaign. More than 70 years later, the contributions of these first code talkers were recognized when France presented them the Chevalier de l'Ordre National du Mérite. Choctaw code talkers also participated in World War II, along with soldiers from the Navajo and other tribes.

Following World War II, the Choctaw people found themselves destitute, subjects of bigotry and isolation in a segregated society. The Mississippi Choctaw endured more than a century of virulent harassment and discrimination, and the Oklahoma tribe was considered for federal termination in 1959. However, in 1964, the Civil Rights Act brought opportunities for jobs and services.

The Choctaw Today

Under the leadership of Phillip Martin, who served as chief from 1978 to 2007, the Mississippi Band of Choctaw attracted industries such as auto parts, greeting cards, and plastic molding. In 1992, the tribe built a large gaming resort in Choctaw, Mississippi. Today, the tribe operates 19 businesses and employs 7,800 people.

The Choctaw Nation of Oklahoma also operates gaming facilities in Durant, Oklahoma, and runs social service, educational, housing, and health programs. The Jena Band of Choctaw Indians, located in Louisiana, received federal acknowledgment in 1995 and has more than 240 members. Other groups of Choctaw descent claim tribal status in Alabama and Mississippi.

After nearly 200 years, the Choctaw again control their sacred homeland site of Nanih Waiya. Once a state park, it was returned to the Choctaw by the state of Mississippi in 2006. ■

Miccosukee Indian children fish for bream and bass in the Tamiami Canal in Everglades National Park, Florida.

acres in what is now southern Oklahoma, and the U.S. government sought to remove the Choctaw of Louisiana to more western territories. Some Choctaws migrated west on their own, but approximately 5,000 were forcibly removed between 1831 and 1834 and again from 1844 to 1847. Many actively resisted removal.

The first recorded evidence of a settlement at Jena is found in the 1880 U.S. Census, which listed four families living in the area. There was a total of 34 Indians recorded in Catahoula Parish in the 1890 census. These families contributed to Jena's economy—trading skins and cured hides in exchange for products at the local dry goods market. Some

worked as day laborers on farms or lumber mills or as household help to the area's white families.

After incorporation in 1974, the band built a tribal center, which housed various tribal social service programs, community activities, and language and cultural education classes. In 2004, only a few Native speakers remained; consequently, emphasis is now being placed on teaching and maintaining a strong sense of Indian identity and reintroducing the language to daily use. The band's petition for federal recognition was granted in May 1995 and was celebrated with a signing ceremony.

The band has an environmental department funded by a U.S. Environmental Protection Agency General

Assistance Program grant to protect and monitor environmental issues concerning all tribal lands and resources. In addition, the band operates an American Red Cross shelter, open only in disasters declared by the Red Cross, the first of its kind in LaSalle Parish.

MICCOSUKEE RESERVATION

Tribe: Miccosukee Tribe of Indians of Florida
Current Location: Florida **Total Area:** 79,711 acres
Tribal Enrollment: 400

The Miccosukee Indians are descendants of the Creek Nation that once inhabited the regions of present-day Alabama and Georgia. Although the Upper and Lower Creek shared a common heritage, they spoke mutually unintelligible languages and often engaged in war with each other. The direct ancestors of the Miccosukee Tribe were the Lower Creek, who resided at the base of the southernmost Appalachians. Oral history suggests that the Miccosukee originated in northern Florida.

The tribe encountered Euro-Americans in the 1500s as the English, French, and Spanish began to arrive in what would become the southern United States. In the early 1700s, members of the tribe left the area with Spanish forces and settled the Florida peninsula. The tribe established communities in the Apalachee Bay region along the Chattahoochee and Apalachicola Rivers; however, conflicts between the tribe and Euro-American settlers eventually forced the Miccosukee to leave the area and settle in regions around Alachua.

In 1823, the tribe signed the Treaty of Moultrie Creek, agreeing to move to a reservation in central Florida. The tribe then remained undisturbed for a number of years, until the Indian Removal Act of 1830, when a number of Miccosukee sought refuge in the

STOMP DANCE

Perhaps the most important continuing dance tradition among many southeastern tribes is the stomp dance, considered both sacred and social among the tribes that still practice it. "Stomp" is a European name for the dance, describing the rhythmic step performed by the dancers. The Shawnee call it *Nikanikawe,* the dance of friends, while the Creek call it *Opvnkv Haco,* the dance of the altered spirit. Singing takes place in a call-and-response format, with the leader calling out his own version of the many song variations, and a chorus of men responding. Dances can involve several hundred participants.

The stomp dance is practiced today among Cherokee, Chickasaw, Choctaw, Creek, Shawnee, Seminole, and other historically southeastern communities, as well as among the Delaware, the Miami, and the six tribes of the Iroquois Confederacy from New York to parts of Ontario. For many southeastern tribes, the dance is associated with the annual Green Corn thanksgiving festival, a ceremonial occasion held in late summer that dates back to the ancient Mississippian societies. Stomp dance grounds consist of a square platform, known as the Square Ground, with flat sides that face the four cardinal directions, each with an arbor under which the men sit. The center of the stomp dance is the sacred fire, built in a fire pit and kept burning by fire-keepers and their assistants. During the dancing, participants address the fire as a living entity through songs and prayers, inviting the ancestors to dance with the living. Around the Square Ground are clan houses, called camps, where participants prepare the dinner eaten prior to the dance.

The dance is led by a male elder and his assistant, a medicine man, and a speaker. Among the Creek, four head men and four head women also participate. The speaker calls participants to each round of the dance, and a lead singer is chosen, with the remaining men acting as the chorus. The leader uses a rattle, usually made from the shell of a box turtle or, among some tribes, from a gourd. Some tribes employ a handheld water drum.

For each dance, a woman is chosen to carry the rhythm of the song. Women wear turtle shell shakers on their legs to create the rhythm. The shakers are heavy and require endurance as the dance progresses. Each set of shakers requires matched pairs of up to 16 turtle shells filled with river rocks. In modern times, cans have sometimes been substituted for turtle shells because they weigh less and make more sound. Women typically wear dresses and skirts incorporating traditional patterns, and men wear blue jeans with ribbon shirts.

Dancers circle the fire counterclockwise in a spiral or circle pattern, first males, then females, followed by visitors and children, continuing through four songs or rounds, at which point a new lead singer is selected. Dancing begins after dinner and usually continues until dawn. Some participants commit to "touch medicine" during the course of the dance. These dancers abstain from food after midnight; during the night, they touch specific medicine bundles prepared by the medicine man. Touching the medicine brings spiritual well-being to the community and helps to heal physical afflictions. ∎

Women traditionally wear rattles made of turtle shells during the stomp dance. These set the rhythm.

ALEXANDER MCGILLIVRAY

Creek (Muscogee) principal chief and resistance leader

Born in 1750 in the Coushatta community of Little Tallassee, near present-day Montgomery, Alabama, Alexander McGillivray was the son of a loyalist Scots trader and a French/Muscogee mother of the Wind Clan. He was educated in Charleston, South Carolina, and apprenticed in business in Savannah, Georgia.

During the American Revolution, McGillivray, whose Muscogee name was Hoboi-Hili-Miko ("Good Child Chief"), worked for two British superintendents of Indian affairs. He ran a plantation, owned slaves, and was involved in the deerskin trade, while also participating in Creek ceremonies and maintaining his clan obligations.

Following the war, McGillivray resisted Georgia's attempt to confiscate Creek land. In 1782, he became principal chief of the Upper Creek towns, and in 1784, he negotiated a treaty with the Spanish to protect tribal rights in Florida. McGillivray worked to centralize power within the Muscogee Nation, to strengthen tribal sovereignty, and to resist American expansion. His warriors raided American settlers who had moved into their homelands.

When Spain reduced its aid to the Muscogee, McGillivray and 29 other chiefs signed the 1790 Treaty of New York, in which George Washington promised to honor Creek rights and eject illegal settlers, while the Creek promised to return runaway slaves who sought refuge. In 1792, after the United States failed to live up to its obligations, McGillivray repudiated the treaty and negotiated again with the Spanish. He moved to Pensacola and died in 1793. ∎

McGillivray worked with the British and later resisted American expansion.

Everglades. In 1835, the Miccosukee joined other tribes of the Creek Nation in the Second Seminole War, and later they participated in the Third Seminole War. The Miccosukee tribe was identified by the federal government as part of the Seminole Nation. The tribe remained allied with the Seminole until the mid-1900s, when it chose to pursue independent status.

In the early 20th century, the reservation experienced extensive intrusions. Canals cut for drainage of the Everglades and the construction of the Tamiami Trail in 1928 depleted the reservation wetlands, greatly reducing fish and game populations. In 1947, the Department of the Interior declared that most of the Miccosukee ancestral lands were to become part of Everglades National Park.

The tribe has a perpetual lease from the state of Florida for 189,000 acres in southern Florida reserved for the purposes of hunting, fishing, frogging, subsistence agriculture, and traditional

MYTH OR FACT?

In the Trail of Tears march, all southeastern Indians were moved to Oklahoma.

MYTH

Cherokee call the forced removal of their people The Trail Where They Cried. Between 1831 and 1838, the U.S. government relocated Choctaw, Seminole, Creek, Chickasaw, Cherokee, and other tribes to Oklahoma, often on foot in frigid weather. Some Indians, however, escaped detection and remained.

customs. In addition, the Miccosukee share the Florida State Indian Reservation, dedicated in perpetuity to the tribe.

MISSISSIPPI BAND OF CHOCTAW INDIANS RESERVATION

Tribe: Mississippi Band of Choctaw Indians
Current Location: Mississippi
Total Area: 28,402 acres   **Tribal Enrollment:** 9,483

The Choctaw Reservation encompasses nine communities: Pearl River, Bogue Chitto, Tucker, Red Water, Standing Pine, Conehatta, Crystal Ridge, Bogue Homa, and Ocean Springs.

Choctaw people lived throughout the Mississippi and Alabama region, hunting game and farming the area's rich soil for subsistence. The Choctaw's name is an anglicized version of Chahta, the name of a

A burial mound at the Etowah Indian Mounds State Historic Site in Cartersville, Georgia

CREEK (MUSCOGEE)

The Creek descend from Mississippian societies whose homelands encompassed parts of modern-day Alabama, Georgia, and South Carolina, along with small sections of Florida and North Carolina. Their language derives from the Muscogean family. Rumors of Spanish brutality preceded the arrival of Hernando de Soto in 1540, so Creek warriors, led by Tuskaloosa, attacked and crippled that expedition. But by 1559, when Tristan de Luna visited, epidemics had devastated area tribes. The Creek emerged as a loose confederacy of survivors. "Mother towns" developed at Abhika, Coosa, Kasihta, and Coweta along the Alabama River, divided into the Lower Towns and the Upper Towns. Settlers called them the Upper and Lower Creek tribes, and eventually the Creek Indians.

The Ochese Creek Settlement

In 1690, the English established a trading post, called Ochese Creek, on the Ocmulgee River, in present-day South Carolina, and a number of Creek relocated there. Between 1704 and 1706, these tribes, along with the Yamasee, joined colonial militiamen in destroying Spanish missions in Florida, capturing more than 10,000 unarmed Timucua and Apalachee Indians, who were sold into slavery. The English then hired some of the tribes, including the Ochese Creek, to attack the Yamasee, leading to the Yamasee War of 1715–17. The Indian slave trade ended as the Yamasee fled into Florida and the Ochese Creek moved west. In 1718, the Coweta *mico*, or head chief, known as Emperor Brim, organized a council of the Upper and Lower Creek and declared neutrality toward French, English, and Spanish interests.

Brim's sister, Mary, married an English trader, John Musgrove. His trading post later became Savannah, the first English settlement in present-day Georgia. Mary served as translator and used her clan connections to negotiate peace between colonial governor James Oglethorpe and the Creek.

A group of Creek (Muscogee) Indians around 1800

Choosing Sides

Along with Cherokee chiefs, some Lower Creek micos ceded two million acres to Georgia in 1773, sparking Indian discontent and raids against settlers. During the American Revolution, the Upper Creek sided with the British under the Coushatta mico Alexander McGillivray. They fought alongside the Cherokee under Dragging Canoe, raiding American settlements in Tennessee and Virginia. The Lower Creek, initially neutral, sided with the British after they captured Savannah in 1779.

By the end of the war, the Creek population had decreased to around 20,000 people in about 50 towns. In 1790, the Creek and Choctaw disputed boundaries along the Noxubee River and agreed to resolve the matter with a ball game involving thousands of players. When the Creek declared victory, a fight ensued, and nearly 500 people were killed.

The State of Muscogee was established in 1799 by William Bowles, a British-born leader who married a Native woman and inherited a chiefdom. Bowles set up a capital at Miccosuki, near Tallahassee, envisioning an Indian state that would include Cherokee, Creek, Chickasaw, and Choctaw people. He built a small navy, which attacked Spanish ships in the Gulf of Mexico and declared war on Spain in 1800. The next year, he was betrayed by a Lower Creek faction and captured. He died in prison in Cuba.

President George Washington developed a six-point plan to promote the "civilization" of tribes, beginning with the Creek, toward the end of the 18th century. The tribe experienced almost 20 years of peace, but that ended in 1812 when the tribe became embroiled in civil war and then in the war between the British and Americans that followed.

A group of Upper Creek, known as the Red Sticks, joined Tecumseh's intertribal confederation in 1812, resisting the "civilizing projects." They raided white settlers and led attacks at the Battle of Burnt Corn, in southern Alabama, and on Fort Mims, north of Mobile, where nearly 250 settlers were killed.

Enraged militias marched against Upper Creek towns. Joined by a force of Lower Creek known as the White Sticks, they crushed the Red Sticks at the Battle of Horseshoe Bend. Exhausted survivors surrendered to Gen. Andrew Jackson in 1814, and the Creek—including those who had fought with the

Americans—were forced to cede 20 million acres to the United States. Red Stick refugees fled to Florida and joined the Seminole, tripling its population.

The Treaty of Washington, signed in 1826, ceded Creek lands to Georgia but retained the people's right to remain in their homelands. Nevertheless, Georgia's governor mobilized a militia to remove the Indians. Most tribal members were relocated to Oklahoma in 1834.

The Tribes Today

What's now called the Creek (Muscogee) Nation is a federally recognized tribe in Okmulgee, Oklahoma. It encompasses 11 counties and includes more than 69,000 tribal citizens. It operates its own

college, police force, health center, and housing authority.

Three smaller Creek groups in Oklahoma are also federally recognized tribes. Descended from historic Creek towns, the Alabama-Quassarte and Kialegee, both in Wetumka, each enroll about 350 members. The Thlopthlocco, with about 800 members, is headquartered in Clearview and conducts business from Okemah.

In 1984, after a lengthy review, the Poarch Band of Creek Indians, near Atmore, Alabama, was federally acknowledged. The tribe has a 230-acre reservation. The Coushatta Tribe of Louisiana, recognized in 1973, and the Alabama-Coushatta Tribe of Texas, recognized in 1987, also descend from Creek people. ∎

A Creek woman swings a toddler in a hammock hanging beneath a thatched palm frond roof.

BASKETMAKING

For centuries, women wove baskets for beauty as well as utility.
Native American baskets are now prized by collectors.

An enduring tradition among southeastern tribes, basketmaking was traditionally practiced by women. They used native plant materials, primarily river cane, honeysuckle, pine needles, white oak, and hickory. Weavers often used natural dyes to color the materials yellow, brown, red, or black. Some tribes preferred complicated geometric patterns, while others wove images of flowers, vines, and animals into their designs.

A variety of shapes and sizes allowed women to accomplish the many tasks of carrying, sieving, storing, and insulating. Their products included square, round, and curvilinear baskets, with handles, tightly fitting covers, pointed pouches, sieves, or strainers. They also made mats for bedding and for the roofs and walls of dwellings.

The double wall basket, made from river cane, is probably the oldest form of basketry in the region. The Eastern geometric style, common in Creek, Seminole, and Yuchi designs, featured strings of diamonds or *V* shapes. The Western style featured circle motifs.

During the centuries following European contact, basketmaking declined dramatically. Settlers converted natural areas into pastureland and agricultural fields, and basketmakers were unable to locate materials. Modern manufacturing methods decreased the value of handmade goods significantly, and many women died without teaching younger community members their skills.

In recent years, however, basketmaking has reappeared. The growth of cultural tourism and a developing appreciation for Native American arts have created a flourishing market. Some tribes operate cooperatives that help artists sell their works. Rather than functioning solely as utilitarian household items, baskets are also collected today for their beauty. ■

chief. At least 90 percent of the Mississippi Band of Choctaw Indians' tribal members continue to speak the indigenous Muscogean language, while English serves as the second language. Tribal members continue to practice traditional cultural elements.

The Choctaw's first interaction with European explorers occurred in 1540 when the de Soto Expedition marched northwest across the continent—an encounter that resulted in the deaths of 1,500 to 3,000 Choctaw people. In 1786, the Choctaws signed the Treaty of Hopewell, which bestowed federal recognition of their sovereignty, but white settlers continued to settle on Choctaw land.

The historic Treaty of Dancing Rabbit Creek, signed in 1830, deemed removal voluntary and provided land grants and citizenship for those who chose to remain in Mississippi.

Approximately 5,000 Choctaws decided to stay in Mississippi. Seven communities, which coincide with the reservation's current community centers, grew from where they congregated. The band's initial isolation largely accounts for the persistent use of their native language.

Since 1979, the Choctaw have experienced phenomenal economic growth, largely due to lucrative gaming operations. In 2002, the Mississippi Choctaw Tribe was the second largest employer in the state and the single largest employer in Neshoba County.

POARCH CREEK RESERVATION

Tribe: **Poarch Band of Creek Indians**
Current Location: **Alabama**   Total Area: **39 acres**
Tribal Enrollment (Statewide): **156**

The Poarch Band descended from the Creek Nation, whose peoples once occupied a territory covering nearly all of what is now Georgia and Alabama. A small but fiercely vocal group, they have avoided removal for nearly 150 years.

The War of 1812 divided the Creek Nation into two factions. Those Creeks who actively fought alongside the U.S. were rewarded after victory with a land grant of one square mile. With these land

Cherokee dancers perform in their traditional dress at the annual Chehaw National Indian Festival held at Chehaw Park in Albany, Georgia.

A Seminole woman weaves a basket from fronds with help from a boy.

allotments, many Creeks were able to remain in southwestern Alabama after the Creek Removal of 1836. The town of Poarch served as a focal point for the Indian community, and as a result, the Poarch Band remained cohesive and kept its identity through many decades without federal recognition and in spite of overt discrimination and segregation.

The tribe operates gaming enterprises and manufacturing, service, and agricultural businesses. It also publishes the monthly *Poarch Creek News* and, since 1997, runs the Calvin McGee Cultural Center, which is open to the public.

TUNICA-BILOXI INDIAN TRIBE OF LOUISIANA

Tribe: Tunica-Biloxi Indian Tribe of Louisiana
Current Location: Louisiana   Total Area: 1,462 acres
Tribal Enrollment: 1,040

The present-day Tunica-Biloxi reservation in east-central Louisiana, near the town of Marksville and 25 miles west of the Mississippi River, occupies a land base that has belonged to the tribe since the 1780s, when it was given to the Tunica tribe by Spanish colonist and future governor of Louisiana Bernardo Vicente Apolinar de Gálvez.

Although the Tunica and Biloxi speak unrelated languages, both groups are descendants of the ancient Mound People of the area. The tribes have lived on the reservation for the past two centuries, during which they became unified by intermarriages.

The Tunica tribe originated in northern Mississippi and, from their central settlement of Quizquiz—an ancient and highly evolved civilization near the confluence of the Mississippi, Ohio, and Missouri Rivers and close to where de Soto crossed the Mississippi River in 1541—exercised great influence over vast amounts of territory across present-day Arkansas, Oklahoma, Missouri, Tennessee, Louisiana, Alabama, and Florida. The ensuing threat of diseases, famine, and warfare forced the tribe to move southward along the Mississippi River.

The Biloxi tribe originated along the Mississippi Gulf Coast near present-day Biloxi. They encountered French explorers in 1669. The Tunica and Biloxi resided together on the lands granted to the Tunica by the Spanish and united for political reasons during the 1920s.

The tribe was incorporated in 1976 and received state recognition that same year. The U.S. government did not grant federal recognition until 1981. Since the 1960s, the tribe has been particularly active in local and national politics, often forming political coalitions with other Louisiana indigenous groups to further their shared agenda. Tribal members strive to achieve financial self-determination, while at the same time retaining and nourishing their traditional culture and values.

The expansion of tribal enterprises into the gaming industry has bolstered the tribe's economy a great deal and enabled the tribe to provide greater and improved services and facilities to tribal members. The Paragon Casino and Resort in Marksville, for instance, with more than 1,780 employees, has been bringing in revenue since 1994; much of this revenue has been donated to nonprofits.

The Tunica-Biloxi Tribe provides a major source of employment for residents of central Louisiana, abiding by its motto, "Cherishing Our Past, Building for Our Future."

THE SOUTHEAST

WILMA MANKILLER

Principal chief, Cherokee Nation of Oklahoma, 1985–1995

Wilma Pearl Mankiller was born in 1945 in Tahlequah, Oklahoma, the daughter of a Cherokee father and a Dutch/Irish mother. The name "Mankiller" denotes a traditional military rank, *asgaya-dihi* in Cherokee. In 1956, the government relocated her family to San Francisco. She joined the activist American Indian Movement during the occupation of Alcatraz Island in 1969.

In 1977, Mankiller returned with her two daughters to the Cherokee Nation. She was elected deputy chief in 1983 and stepped up to fill a vacancy as principal chief in 1985. She overcame an entrenched faction that was opposed to female leadership, being elected principal chief in 1987 and reelected in 1991. In 1995, she chose not to run again due to health concerns.

Under her leadership, the tribe began community-based development projects and improved the federal-tribal relationship. She has received numerous awards, including the Presidential Medal of Freedom, and she was inducted into the National Women's Hall of Fame in 1993. She wrote an autobiography,

Wilma Mankiller received numerous awards, including the Presidential Medal of Freedom.

Mankiller: A Chief and Her People, and cowrote *Every Day Is a Good Day: Reflections by Contemporary Indigenous Women.* She died in 2010 at her home on her family's ancestral land in Oklahoma. ∎

SEMINOLE

Although most Seminole people descend from Creek Indians who moved into Florida after the War of 1812 and the related Creek War, the tribe also incorporated some of the surviving indigenous Florida Indians, escaped slaves, and Indians fleeing wars and removal elsewhere. The arrival of the Spanish in 1513 began the series of epidemics that killed up to 80 percent of the 200,000 Native Floridians. The English destroyed Spain's missions in the early 1700s, killing or enslaving most mission Indians. But Indians resettled in the state over the years, calling themselves *yat'siminoli,* "free people." Eventually, Americans referred to all Florida Indians as Seminole, although distinct groups developed, some speaking Muscogee and others Hitchiti.

The Creek and Seminole Wars

The Creek War began as a civil war within the Creek Nation spurred by the Red Sticks, who advocated a return to traditional living. Militias from Tennessee, Georgia, and Mississippi were eventually involved in the campaigns, which ended at the Battle of Horseshoe Bend, where Andrew Jackson defeated the beleaguered Red Sticks. They ceded 23 million acres across Alabama and southern Georgia to the United States. Most of the Creek refugees moved into Florida, increasing the Seminole population to about 5,000.

Jackson quickly invaded Florida, crossing into Spanish lands illegally to burn Indian towns and capture escaped African descendants. The First Seminole War, from 1816 to 1818, resulted as the Indians fought back. Through the Treaties of Moultrie Creek (1823) and Payne's Landing (1832), Jackson sought to extinguish Native ownership and convince all the Seminole that their leaders had agreed to move west, to Indian Territory in Oklahoma.

Conflict reignited in 1835, after Jackson became president. For seven years, U.S. forces hunted the Seminole throughout Florida, losing 1,500 soldiers in what came to be called the Second Seminole War. Led by Jumper, Alligator, Micanopy, Osceola, and the powerful medicine man Abiaka, the Seminole resisted fiercely. In 1842, President John Tyler declared the war at an end; the Seminole never surrendered.

Seminole teenagers attend a cultural fair in Davie, Florida.

Another important leader who emerged during the Second Seminole War, Billy Bowlegs, led his people during the skirmishes that constituted the Third Seminole War, from 1855 to 1858. The U.S. government offered him and other chiefs $10,000 each to move to Oklahoma. Initially, Bowlegs refused, but he finally relented. Abiaka, also known as Sam Jones, remained in Florida. He survived five wars and all efforts to remove his people, dying peacefully at his home in Big Cypress Swamp.

More than 3,000 Seminoles were removed to Indian Territory during the wars. They were hunted with dogs and forced onto ships that took them across the Gulf of Mexico and up the Mississippi. Only a few hundred remained in Florida, hiding in the swamps.

Reservations

By the beginning of the 20th century, the Seminole were surviving as hunters, trappers, and traders. Developers, assisted by the U.S. Army Corps of Engineers, began to drain the Everglades, lowering Lake Okeechobee by seven feet, wreaking havoc on the environment and forever altering the Seminole way of life. Most of the people found work as tenant farmers or as curiosities in the tourist attractions. They created an economy for themselves as alligator wrestlers, airboat pilots, and artisans.

By 1913, 18 Seminole reservations had been established, but many of the people refused to live on them. The Miccosukee

In a 1962 photo, five young Seminole men hold alligator mouths under their chins at an alligator wrestling school in Florida.

Tribe of Seminole Indians of Florida resisted reservation life, while a second group, the Seminole Indians of Florida, chose to preserve their traditions on reservation lands. Other families remained independent, living as traditionalists, away from the reservations.

In 1953, the U.S. government passed legislation designed to terminate services to tribes. Florida supported termination for the Seminole, but tribal leaders negotiated successfully to retain their tribal status. In 1962, the Miccosukee received federal acknowledgment as a distinct tribal entity.

In 1977, the Seminole of Florida opened their first "smoke shop," selling discount tobacco, and developed a high-stakes bingo hall, initiating a series of legal challenges that resulted in the Indian Gaming Regulatory Act of 1988. The tribe added two reservations, at Tampa and Immokalee, to its headquarters in Hollywood, near Fort Lauderdale. Business enterprises diversified under Chairman James Billie's leadership to include a hotel in Tampa, a citrus market, a tribal museum, and the Swamp Safari tourist attraction, as well as smoke shops

and gaming enterprises. More than 300 of the 2,000 tribe members work in tribal ventures, and the tribe operates its own Ahfachkee Indian School, legal and law enforcement departments, and social programs.

The Seminole Tribe of Oklahoma consists of more than 9,000 members, with headquarters at Wewoka, Oklahoma. The opening of the Greater Seminole oil field in 1923 brought prosperity to some families. Many members participate in the annual Busk, or Green Corn Ceremony, and traditional stomp dances are held as in times past. ■

CHAPTER 3

THE ARCTIC & SUBARCTIC

THE ARCTIC & SUBARCTIC

A RCHAEOLOGISTS HAVE DEFINED A LONG AND COMPLICATED HISTORY OF THE NORTH Sometime 15,000 to 20,000 years ago, scientists say, people from northeastern Asia began moving across the emerged Bering Land Bridge and around the northern rim of the North Pacific Ocean into Alaska. As the climate warmed and ice barriers melted, Paleo-Indian migrations continued south into the rest of the Americas. Other groups spread east as fishers and hunters through the northern boreal forest, where their descendants became Athabascans and Northern Algonquins. As ice sheets melted, a second trickle of humanity traveled east along the coasts of Alaska into Canada, becoming the ancestors of the modern Inuit.

GEOGRAPHY HAS BEEN BOTH THEIR CURSE AND THEIR SALVATION.

Over time, differences in geography, ecology, and ways of life resulted in different Eskimo and Indian cultures, languages, and adaptations. Alaska has four different Eskimo-Aleut languages, while Inuit from the Bering Strait to Greenland speak dialects of a single language, Inuktitut. Similarly, Indians of the western boreal forest have many different languages, while their eastern relatives speak only a few.

Today's northern Indian and Eskimo people occupy nearly one-third of the continent. Geography has been both their curse and their salvation. It required a subsistence lifestyle as hunters, fishermen, and collectors without agriculture or guaranteed food supplies, which limited population growth and economic development. However, isolation kept them from the worst effects of European contact. Northern forests, tundra, and seas teem with game; its waters are clean and mostly free of pollution; and few animals are endangered or extirpated.

Free from outside competition, northern Native peoples have had a long and relatively stable history. Most suffered less than other Native groups from European diseases. Immigrants were easily absorbed, and the fur trade and religious conversion changed but did not destroy Native life. Their cultures were not ravaged by war or imperialistic neighbors, and few groups were impounded on reservations. Isolation and subsistence economies helped keep their cultures intact and their languages strong.

Even though northern peoples have been in contact with outsiders for hundreds of years, they were never defeated militarily. Isolation conferred a large degree of self-determination. During recent decades, many northern groups attained high levels of education and successfully negotiated land claims agreements that secured economic and political rights. While many social and economic problems persist and the threat of climate change looms, northern people are proud of their cultural and artistic traditions and their continued survival as distinct societies. ∎

Preceding pages: A hunter with sled dog team crosses Greenland's snowy tundra. Opposite: An Alaska Native dances during a ceremony held in Kotzebue, Alaska.

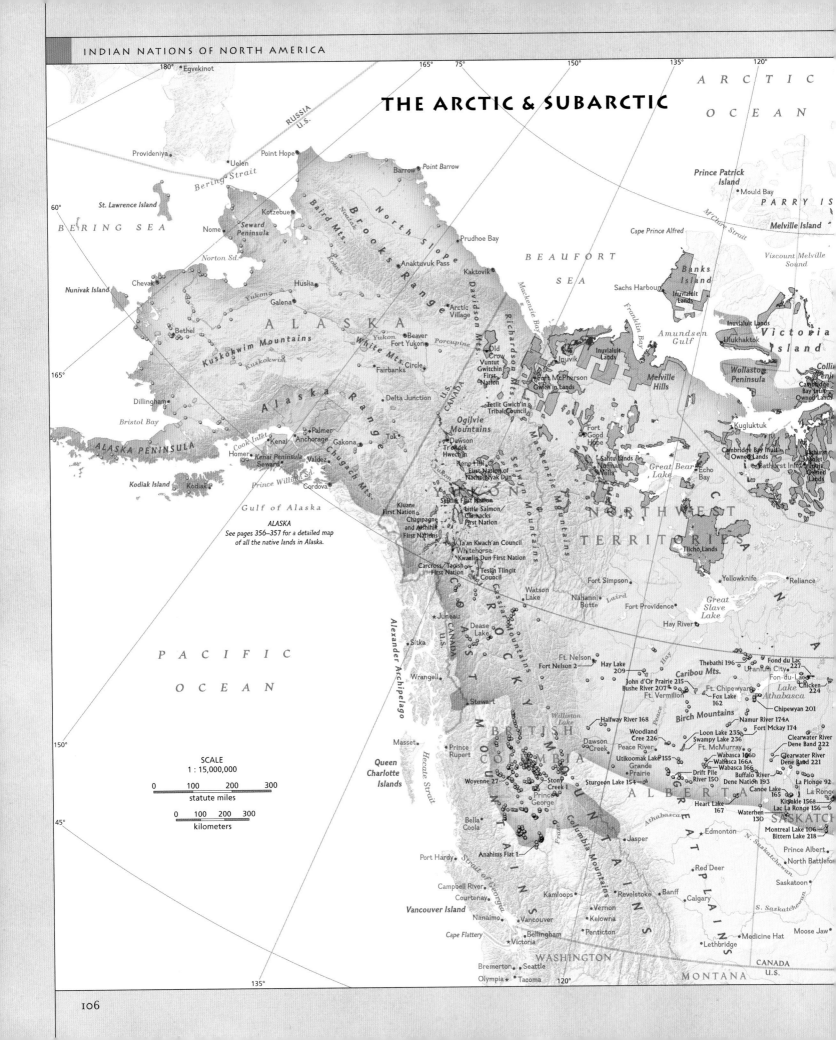

THE ARCTIC & SUBARCTIC

A R C T I C

O C E A N

Prince Patrick Island

PARRY IS

Mould Bay

Melville Island

Viscount Melville Sound

Cape Prince Alfred

Banks Island

Sachs Harbour

Inuvialuit Lands

Amundsen Gulf

Victoria Island

Ulukhaktok

Colli
Peni

Wollaston Peninsula

Cambridge Bay Inuit Owned Lands

Kugluktuk

B E A U F O R T
S E A

Prudhoe Bay

Kaktovik

Mackenzie Bay

Franklin Bay

Inuvik

Inuvialuit Lands

Fort McPherson

Gwich'in Lands

Melville Hills

Great Bear Lake

Echo Bay

Santu Lands

Norman Wells

Fort Good Hope

Bathurst Inlet

Bathurst Inlet Inuit Owned Lands

RUSSIA
U.S.

Egvekinot

Providniya

Uelen

Point Hope

Barrow · Point Barrow

Bering Strait

Kotzebue

St. Lawrence Island

B E R I N G   S E A

Nome

Seward Peninsula

Norton Sd.

Chevak

Nunivak Island

Bethel

Dillingham

Bristol Bay

Kodiak Island

Kodiak

North Slope

Anaktuvuk Pass

Brooks Range

Baird Mts.

Noatak

Kobuk

Arctic Village

Davidson Mts.

Richardson Mts.

A L A S K A

Huslia

Galena

Yukon

Beaver
Fort Yukon

Circle

White Mts.

Porcupine

Fairbanks

Kuskokwim Mountains

Kuskokwim

Old Crow

Vuntut Gwitchin First Nation

Tetlit Gwich'in Tribal Council

Ogilvie Mountains

Dawson
Tr'ondek Hwech'in

Reno Hill
First Nation of Nacho Nyak Dun

Delta Junction

Alaska Range

Palmer

Anchorage

Gakona

Tok

Kenai

Homer

Kenai Peninsula

Seward

Cook Inlet

Valdez

Chugach Mts.

Cordova

Prince William Sd.

Gulf of Alaska

ALASKA
See pages 356–357 for a detailed map
of all the native lands in Alaska.

Selwyn Mountains

Mackenzie Mountains

Y U K O N

Selkirk First Nation

Little Salmon/
Carmacks
First Nation

Kluane
First Nation

Champagne
and Aishihik
First Nations

Ta'an Kwach'an Council

Whitehorse

Kwanlin Dun First Nation

Carcross/Tagish
First Nation

Teslin Tlingit
Council

Fort Simpson

Nahanni
Butte

Laird

Fort Providence

Hay River

N O R T H W E S T
T E R R I T O R I E S

Tlicho Lands

Yellowknife

Reliance

Great Slave Lake

Watson
Lake

Cassiar Mountains

Liard

Juneau

Sitka

P A C I F I C

O C E A N

Alexander Archipelago

Wrangell

Stewart

Dease
Lake

R O C K Y

Williston Lake

Ft. Nelson
Fort Nelson 2

Hay Lake
209

Masset

Prince Rupert

Queen
Charlotte
Islands

Hecate Strait

Bella
Coola

B R I T I S H

C O L U M B I A

M O U N T A I N S

Halfway River 168

Dawson
Creek

Peace River

Woodland
Cree 226

Utikoomak Lake 155

Peace

Grande
Prairie

Sturgeon Lake 154

Woyenne 27

Stony
Creek 1

Prince
George

Anahims Flat 1

Port Hardy

Campbell River

Courtenay

Nanaimo

Vancouver Island

Cape Flattery

Bremerton · Seattle

Olympia ★ · Tacoma

WASHINGTON

Victoria

Bellingham

Strait of Georgia

Vancouver

Kamloops

Fraser

Columbia Mountains

Revelstoke · Banff

Vernon

Kelowna

Penticton

Jasper

Athabasca

Edmonton

Red Deer

Calgary

A L B E R T A

G R E A T

P L A I N S

Lethbridge

Medicine Hat

Moose Jaw

CANADA
U.S.

MONTANA

Caribou Mts.

Thebathi 196

Uranium City

Fond du Lac
227

Fon-du-Lac

John d'Or Prairie 215

Bushe River 207

Ft. Vermilion

Fox Lake

Ft. Chipewyan

Lake Athabasca

Chicken
224

Chipewyan 201

Birch Mountains

Namur River 174A

Fort Mckay 174

Loon Lake 235
Swampy Lake 236

Ft. McMurray

Clearwater River
Dene Band 222

Wabasca 166D

Wabasca 166A

Wabasca 166

Drift Pile
River 150

Buffalo River
Dene Nation 193

Clearwater River
Dene Band 221

La Plonge 92

Canoe Lake
165

La Ronge

Heart Lake
167

Waterhen
130

Kitsakie 156B
Lac La Ronge 156

SASKATCH

Montreal Lake 106
Bittern Lake 218

Prince Albert

North Battlefor

Saskatoon

N. Saskatchewan

S. Saskatchewan

C A N A D A

McClure Strait

165°
75°
150°
135°
120°
180°
60°
165°
150°
45°
135°
120°

SCALE
1 : 15,000,000

0   100   200   300
statute miles

0   100   200   300
kilometers

QUEEN ELIZABETH
Axel
Heiberg
Island
ISLANDS

Eureka

Pond Inlet Inuit
Owned Lands

Grise
Fiord Inuit
Owned
Land

Grise Fiord

Nuussuaq
(Kraulshavn)

Cape York

Qaanaaq (Thule)

Melville
Bay

Upernavik

*Denmark
Strait*

**GREENLAND
(KALAALLIT NUNAAT)
(DENMARK)**

Tasiilaq
(Ammassalik)

GREENLAND
Of Greenland's population of 57,000,
88% are Inuit or part Inuit.
Greenlanders have experienced "home
rule" since 1979, and in 2009 moved to
"self rule", a higher level of autonomy
from Denmark. Prime Minister Kuupik
Kleist is half Danish, half Inuit.

Ilulissat (Jakobshavn)

BAFFIN
GREENLAND
CANADA
BAY

Qeqertarsuaq
Qeqertarsuaq (Godhavn)

Kangerlussuaq

King Frederik VI Coast

Bathurst
Island Resolute Bay Inuit
Owned Lands

Resolute
Bay Inuit
Owned
Lands

Resolute

Cornwallis I.

Lancaster Sound

Somerset
Island

McClintock Channel

*Prince of
Wales
Island*

Gulf of Boothia

Borden
Peninsula
Arctic Bay

Bylot Island

Pond Inlet

Brodeur Peninsula

Arctic Bay Inuit
Owned Lands

Pond Inlet Inuit
Owned Lands

Clyde River

Clyde River Inuit
Owned Lands

Sisimiut
(Holsteinsborg)

Nuuk (Godthåb)

Narsarsuaq

Cape Farewell

Igloolik Inuit Owned Lands

Igloolik

Baffin Island

Qikiqtarjuaq

Qikiqtarjuaq Inuit Owned Lands

Davis Strait

Boothia
Peninsula

Taloyoak Inuit
Owned Lands

Talurjuaq

Hell Beach Inuit
Owned Lands

Kugaaruk Inuit
Owned Lands

*Melville
Peninsula*

Prince
Charles I.

Cumberland
Peninsula

Pangnirtung

Pangnirtung Inuit Owned Lands

Cumberland Sound

Cambridge
Bay

Gjoa Haven

*Queen Maud
Gulf*

Gjoa Haven Inuit
Owned Lands

*Foxe
Basin*

Repulse Bay Inuit
Owned Lands

Repulse Bay

Foxe
Pen.

Cape Dorset Inuit
Owned Lands

Iqaluit Inuit Owned Lands

Iqaluit

Meta Incognita Pen.

Kimmirut Inuit Owned Lands

Kimmirut

Cape Dorset

NUNAVUT

Back

Chesterfield
Inlet Inuit
Owned Lands

Baker Lake

Baker Lake Inuit
Owned Lands

*Dubawnt
Lake*

Theton

Rankin Inlet Inuit
Owned Lands

Whale Cove Inuit Owned Lands

Chesterfield Inlet

Coats I.

Mansel I.

Southampton
Island

Coral Harbour

Coral Harbour
Owned Lands

Jointly
Owned
Land

Hudson Strait

Ivujivik

*Ungava
Peninsula*

Kuujjuaq

*Ungava
Bay*

Torngat Mts.

Natuashish 2

Cape Harrison

Hopedale

Port Hope
Simpson

Whale
Cove

Arviat Inuit
Owned Lands

Arviat

H U D S O N

Churchill

Cape Churchill

Cape Tatnam

B A Y

Many Canadian Indian reserves have a
number as part of their official name.

NUNAVUT
In 1999, after decades of lobbying,
debate, and planning, the new territory
of Nunavut was separated from the
Northwest Territories, giving the mostly
Inuit-populated area its own form of
government within Canada.

Inukjuak

Jointly
Owned
Land

Belcher Islands
Sanikiluaq Inuit
Owned Lands

Whapmagoostui

Leaf

*Réservoir
Caniapiscau*

Caniapiscau

Kawawachikamach
Matimekosh 3

Schefferville

*Smallwood
Reservoir*

Churchill Falls

Happy Valley-
Goose Bay

N E W F O U N D L A N D   A N D   L A B R A D O R

Mealy Mtns.

Laurentide Scarp

Labrador City

**ISLAND OF
NEWFOUNDLAND**

Corner
Brook

Lac Brochet 197A

Wollaston Lake

Lac la Hache 220

Brochet 197

*Reindeer
Lake*

Lynn Lake

Split Lake
171, 171A

Southend 200

Mistahi Wasahk 209

Gillam

Nelson House 170, 170A, 170B

Shamattawa 1

Fort Severn 89

Fort Severn

Chisasibi

Chisasibi

Wemindji

Q U E B E C

Havre-Saint-Pierre

*Réservoir
Manicouagan*

Sept-Îles

Malioténam 27A
Uashat 27

*Gulf of
St. Lawrence*

Channel-
Port aux Basques

Pukatawagan
198

Stanley
157

Thompson

Pelican
Narrows
184B

Cross Lake
19, 19A, 19E

Norway House 17

Wepuskow Ohnikahp

Whitemud Lake

Oxford House 24

God's Lake 23

Winisk 90

Bearskin Lake

Attawapiskat
91

*James
Bay*

Akimiski I.

Eastmain

Nemiscau

Waskaganish

Waskaganish

Mistassini

Betsiamites

Rimouski

**PRINCE
EDWARD
ISLAND**

Charlottetown

Opaskwayak

Cree Nation 21E

The Pas

Waagamack

Garden Hill

Red Sucker
Lake 1976

Kasabonika Lake

Kitchenuhmaykoosib Aaki 84

Wawakapewin

Webequie

Ft. Albany

Ft. Albany 67

Moosonee

Moose
Factory 68

Waswanipi

Chibougamau

*Lac
St-Jean*

Mashteuiatsh

Chicoutimi

Fredericton

Halifax

**NEW
BRUNSWICK**

**NOVA
SCOTIA**

Chemawawin 2

Grand Rapids 33

*Lake
Winnipegosis*

Dauphin

MANITOBA

Sandy Lake 88

Kee-Way-Win

Wunnumin
Lake 87

Deer Lake

Weagamow
Lake 87

Kingfisher 2

St. Theresa Point

Marten Falls 65

Obedjiwan 28

Wemotaci

Rés. Gouin

Waskaganish

Québec

Laurentide Scarp

Sherbrooke

Trois-Rivières

MAINE

Augusta

*Gulf of
Maine*

Poplar River 16

Berens River 13

Little Grand Rapid 14

Bloodvein 12

Fisher River 44

Pikangikum 14

Osnaburgh
63

Ft. Hope 64

Nakina

Hearst

Abitibi 70

*Lake
Abitibi*

Lac Simon
Manawan

Rouyn-Noranda

Timmins

Sudbury

Montréal

Portland

Peguis 1B

Hollow Water 10

Ft. Alexander 3

Lac Seul 28

*Lake
Nipigon*

O N T A R I O

S H I E L D

Abitibi

North Bay

Ottawa

Ottawa

VT.

Montpelier

N.H.

Concord

Regina

Brandon

Roseau River 2

*Trout
Lake*

Winnipeg

Waabaseemoong

Kenora

*Lake of
the Woods*

English River 21

International Falls

Marathon

Thunder Bay

Lake Superior

Sault Sainte Marie

**NEW
YORK**

Boston **MASSACHUSETTS**

N. DAK.

MINNESOTA

CANADA
U.S.

*Lake
Manitoba*

*Lake
Winnipeg*

Saskatchewan River

Map Key

Indian regional boundary as
represented in this book.
(See pages 14–15 for North American
map showing all eight regions
depicted in this work.)

Canadian Aboriginal Land

Alaskan Native Land or
Federal Indian Reservation

Poorman 88 Canadian Indian Reserve name

⊛ Country capital

★ State or provincial capital

• Selected city or town

ADAK VILLAGE

Tribe: Unangan   **Total Area of Entitlement:** 47,271 acres   **Tribal Enrollment:** 316

Adak, in the Aleutian Island chain, lies on the great-circle navigation route halfway between Seattle and Japan, 1,400 miles from eastern Russia and 1,300 miles southwest of Anchorage. It is the southernmost community in Alaska, falling on the same parallel as Vancouver Island in Canada, and the westernmost community in the United States. Before contact, the Unangan, also known as Aleuts, made their living from the sea, using swift kayaks called *baidarkas*. In the early 1800s, Adak—like many Unangan communities—was decimated as Russian fur collectors and their armed crews enslaved Unangan hunters and forced them to leave their families to hunt fur-bearing sea mammals, primarily sea otters. A long famine set in soon after, which, along with newly introduced diseases, reduced the Unangan population from around 20,000 to fewer than 5,000.

However, Adak survived. During World War II, the U.S. used Army installations on Adak to launch a successful offensive against the islands of Kiska and Attu, then held by the Japanese. After the war, Adak was developed as a naval air station, used for submarine surveillance during the Cold War.

The Aleut Corporation exchanged much of its land entitlement granted by the Alaska Native Claims Settlement Act (ANCSA), for the former naval air station on Adak Island in 2004. There is no BIA-recognized tribal council. The Aleut Enterprise Corporation, a subsidiary of the Aleut Corporation, serves some of the same functions as an ANCSA village corporation. Adak's location and existing facilities make it useful as an air and maritime hub. As a former naval air station, it has the complete infrastructure for a community of 6,000, including a modern airport, an ice-free deepwater port, and major fuel storage capabilities. It is already the major marine refueling station for this region of the North Pacific, in the middle of one of the world's richest fishing regions.

Snow goggles carved of driftwood and inlaid with walrus ivory by contemporary Yup'ik craftsman Jack Abraham

Central Alaskan Yup'ik, Eskimo-Aleut language family

"Waqaa"
("Hi! What's up?")

"Piura"
("Good-bye")

"Quyana"
("Thank you")

EKLUTNA NATIVE VILLAGE

Tribe: Tanaina (Dena'ina) Athabascan   **Total Area of Entitlement:** 124,727 acres   **Tribal Enrollment:** 246

The Eklutna area—at the head of Cook Inlet and the mouth of the Eklutna River, 25 miles northeast of Anchorage—was the site of many Athabascan Indian villages as early as 800 years ago. The people lived chiefly in the drainage areas of Cook Inlet and Clark Lake. Tanaina, meaning "the people," was their own name for themselves. Their dwellings were semisubterranean, made of logs and sod for winter warmth, and they built casual shelters for the summer salmon run, which also served as smokehouses. The men hunted and traveled in skin-covered kayaks, while women traveled in larger, open, dory-shaped umiaks, transporting not only themselves but also children, dogs, and household effects.

Russian Orthodox missionaries arrived in the 1840s, and a railroad station was built in 1918. The Russian Orthodox religion is still prevalent, and one of Eklutna's most delightful features is its cemetery, still used today, enlivened with clusters of more than 100 brightly painted "spirit houses" that combine Russian Orthodox and Athabascan practices. Though the Dana'ina Athabascan Indians had been in the habit of cremating their dead (burials at the site date to 1650), the Russian missionaries suggested that they bury their dead in cemeteries. The spirit houses contain items of personal and spiritual significance for the deceased and for the survivors who visit. They stand in rows and feature very colorful paint, the double Orthodox cross, and "crests" along the roofline that reflect clan affiliations.

The Eklutna Native Village is a federally recognized tribe with a traditional village council. Incorporated in 1971, Eklutna Inc., has played a vital role in the economic landscape of the Anchorage area. Eklutna is the largest private landowner in Anchorage, with significant holdings in Mat-Su Valley.

Churchgoers in gaily decorated parkas attend services at an Anglican church in 1968 in what was then the settlement of Coppermine in Canada's Northwest Territories. The village is now known as Kugluktuk and is part of Nunavut, a territory created for the Inuit people as part of a land settlement with Canada.

Inuit boys play basketball on a sunny day in the Canadian Arctic.

EKWOK VILLAGE

Tribe: Yup'ik   Total Area of Entitlement: 93,682 acres
Tribal Enrollment: 242

Ekwok is the oldest continuously occupied Yup'ik village on the Nushagak River in southwest Alaska. It was originally inhabited during the early 1900s, when settlers came to the area to fish and harvest the abundant supply of wood. Initially, the settlement served different purposes, acting as a fish camp in the spring and summer months, and then a base for berry picking in the fall. The name means "beginning of higher ground" or "end of the bluff." In 1930, the BIA established a school, and mail service began in the same year, with a post office that served the entire river and depended on infrequent deliveries by dogsled from Dillingham (43 miles to the southwest). The village continued to grow slowly, drawing residents from coastal communities in the region, officially opening its own post office in 1941, moving to higher ground after severe flooding in the 1960s, and building a high school in 1980.

The main source of income is salmon fishing, and this Yup'ik Eskimo village continues a fishing and subsistence lifestyle. A few residents trap for furs, and many grow gardens in the summer, as fresh produce from elsewhere is extremely hard to obtain. Air transport is most frequently used to reach Ekwok.

The Ekwok Village Council is a federally recognized tribe in the community, with a traditional tribal council headed by a president. Holders of shares in the village corporation are also shareholders in the Bristol Bay Native Corporation, which helps provide economic diversification through mining, construction, oil field services, and civil engineering projects to a region that is perhaps overly dependent on fishing.

GALENA VILLAGE

Tribe: Koyukon Athabascan   Total Area of Entitlement: 115,200 acres   Tribal Enrollment: 652

The Koyukon Athabascans set up four different kinds of camps, one for each of the four seasons, as they followed the migrations of wild game. One of these, a Yukon River fishing camp called Henry's Point, became the village of Galena in 1918 when a mining operation for lead ore increased commerce in the area. It was only 14 miles downriver from another Native village, Louden, and in 1920, Louden's Koyukon Athabascans began moving to Galena to sell wood to steamboats transporting lead ore from the harbor. The busy harbor later saw the construction of two Air Force bases in the 1940s and '50s. Major floods in 1945 and 1971 resulted in a decision to build city offices, a health clinic, schools, and more than 150 homes in New Town, about 1.5 miles east, above Alexander Lake. In 2008, Galena Air Force Base was closed and all its equipment and facilities turned over to the City of Galena and the Galena Interior Learning Academy.

Many of Galena's residents are descendants of Louden Koyukons, and the Louden Tribal Council is a federally recognized tribe in the community as well as a traditional village council headed by a chief. Subsistence foods include salmon, whitefish, moose, and berries. At the same time, Galena serves as the gateway to the western interior and a hub for transportation, government, and commerce, though it is inaccessible by road and relies mostly on river cargo in the brief summer months. In winter, frozen rivers are used for travel to Ruby, Koyukuk, Kallag, and Nulato, as well as the snow trail to Huslia.

KNIK TRIBE

Tribe: Tanaina (Dena'ina) Athabascan   Total Area of Entitlement: 56,497 acres   Tribal Enrollment: 1,144

The Tanaina (Dena'ina) Athabascan Indian name Knik translates to "fire" in English, and the term originally referred to several villages at the head of Cook Inlet. The Knik Tribe, also known

MYTH OR FACT?

Many Alaskan Natives live on reservations, just like Indians in the lower 48 states.

MYTH

The Alaska Native Claims Settlement Act of 1971 dissolved almost all the Indian reserves in the state and allotted land to the Alaska Native regional corporations, whose shareholders are Natives. There is just one federal reservation in the state, the Annette Islands Reserve of the Tsimshian people in Metlakatla.

as Knik-Fairview, resides in the Mat-Su Borough, on the northwest bank of the Knik Arm of Cook Inlet. The Knik's contact with Europeans and Americans came later and was not as cataclysmic as for other groups, due to their geographic isolation.

A Russian Orthodox mission was built in Knik by no later than the mid-1830s. During the 1880s, the local fur trade thrived, and later, gold prospectors came, followed by families and supplies and amenities. Construction of the Iditarod Trail brought mail between Knik and Nome and shipments of gold by dog team to meet boats at Knik. As part of Franklin Roosevelt's New Deal, Camp 13 of the Matanuska Colony, which comprised six farms, was established along Fairview Road in 1935. Within a year, there were enough farmers to form an agricultural cooperative, and over the next few years, about 400 homesteads were applied for. World War II and Korean War veterans also homesteaded the land.

Knik is a checkpoint for the Iditarod Trail Sled Dog Race and has come to be known as the Dog Mushing Center of the World. The Knik Tribal Council is a federally recognized tribe in the community. While little of today's harvest in the watershed represents a true subsistence-based economy, hunting, fishing, and trapping nevertheless are very important considerations in the local culture. Other resource use in the watershed includes agriculture, logging, and mining.

LEVELOCK VILLAGE

Tribes: Yup'ik, Unangan, Athabascan   Total Area of Entitlement: 96,771 acres   Tribal Enrollment: 209

Levelock sits on the west bank of the Kvichak River, 35 miles northwest of King Salmon, in the Bristol Bay region. Within 100 miles of Levelock are the Yukon Delta National Wildlife Refuge, Lake Clark National Park and Preserve, Katmai National Park and Preserve, Becharof National Wildlife Refuge, Kodiak Island National Wildlife Refuge, Aniakchak National Monument and Preserve, and Alaska Peninsula National Wildlife Refuge.

The climate in Levelock is strongly influenced by its proximity to the Bering Sea. The Kvichak River, a

UNANGAN

The Unangan people (previously known as the Aleuts) have long lived in the Aleutian Islands, the 1,300-mile-long chain that stretches from the Alaska Peninsula west almost to Russia. There are more than 160 named islands, and the territory also includes the Pribilof Islands to the north. The Unangan language branched off from the Eskimo-Aleut family about 1000 B.C. Although the weather in the islands is generally temperate, not arctic, the water is cold and fog is common. There are few trees or land-dwelling animals, so the Unangan have always looked to the sea for their livelihood. Traditionally, fishermen paddled among the islands in *baidarka*, animal-skin-covered kayaks. Today, though, most people travel by air between the islands and to the mainland.

A Seafaring People

Unangan settlements before European contact were generally on protected bays, near rich concentrations of the fish, birds, and sea mammals upon which they relied. Permanent winter villages generally consisted of partially subterranean homes, entered through the roof. In some of the eastern islands, people lived in large communal longhouses shared by several families. Societies were hierarchical, with nobles, commoners, and slaves. The women made elaborate, water-resistant, fur and animal-skin clothing, as well as baskets woven from grass. As befits a society that relied on hunting and fishing rather than farming, hunters were highly respected. Increasingly elaborate wooden hunting helmets marked a man's experience and skill, with whale hunters the most honored.

The first Europeans to make contact with the Unangan were the Russians, whose Vitus Bering expedition of 1741 sailed past the islands. At the time, there were an estimated 15,000 Natives in the area. In the decades that followed, the population plummeted because of disease and mistreatment. Russian traders, in quest of lucrative furs, relocated the Unangan for forced hunts of sea mammals and took them as far south as Fort Ross, California. The Russians also brought their religion to the islands in the form of Orthodox Christianity, which is still widely practiced.

A Unangan girl lights devotional candles in a Russian Orthodox church.

The Alaska Purchase

In 1867, the Aleutian Islands, along with the rest of Alaska, were sold to the United States. Under U.S. rule, fur hunting continued, especially for seals and otters, which were hunted almost to extinction. Hunting was somewhat limited by an international treaty in 1911. Then, in 1913, five islands were set aside as a national wildlife refuge. Elsewhere in the chain, Unangan people could still hunt for subsistence as well as to take fox skins. The federal government set aside small reserves of land for schools and a hospital, but unlike in the lower 48, there was no extensive Native reservation system. By 1930, several villages and towns had federal or territorial schools.

One of the darkest periods in Unangan history began in June 1942, when the Japanese bombed Dutch Harbor and invaded elsewhere in the Aleutians. They took a small group of Unangan people off the island of Attu as prisoners of war. The U.S. response to the attack was to remove almost 900 Natives from their villages elsewhere in the islands, transporting them on short notice via cramped ships to internment camps in southeastern Alaska. In the village of Atka, the people watched as U.S. troops set fire to their homes and church so the Japanese could not gain a foothold. Conditions were difficult in the internment camps, called "duration villages," some of which were in abandoned salmon canneries. With almost no medical care in the cold, damp camps, malnutrition and disease were rampant, especially among the

Unangan boys climb a greased pole during a village Fourth of July celebration on St. Paul Island, one of Alaska's Pribilof Islands, a group in the Bering Sea.

elderly. The people were not permitted to return to their homes until after the war with Japan ended in 1945.

The remote location and sometimes-rough weather of the islands continued to shape life. Modern health care was hard to find. Before Alaskan bush planes became common, outside contact was largely via infrequent visits by merchant and military shipping. After World War II, some Unangan students were sent to the Bureau of Indian Affairs boarding school in Sitka or, in later years, schools in Anchorage.

The Unangan People Today

The Aleut Corporation is one of the 12 Alaskan Native corporations formed after the Alaska Native Claims Settlement Act of 1971. As part of that settlement, the Aleut received $19.5 million, 70,789 acres of surface land, and 1.57 million acres of subsurface estate. The Aleut land is on the Aleutian, Pribilof, and Shumagin Islands, with some holdings on the main Alaska Peninsula.

The corporation today has about 3,600 shareholders—that is, tribe members—who share in the corporation's profit, which in 2009 came to more than $43 million. Its businesses include defense contracting, fuel sales, commercial real estate, and resource extraction. It also funds a foundation that supports cultural preservation and provides scholarships.

Artifacts from 9,000 years of Unangan life in the islands are on display in the Museum of the Aleutians, built by the city of Unalaska in 1999. The museum also supports archaeological expeditions and showcases contemporary Native art. ▪

major anadromous fish stream, is frozen over from November until June. Commercial fishing remains the economic focus of village life outside subsistence activities.

Levelock, a village of Yup'ik, Unangan, and Athabascan peoples, retains a high degree of traditionalism. Commercial fishing and subsistence activities are the focus of the community. The people harvest salmon, trout, moose, caribou, and berries and share communally with one another for the benefit of all. Native languages are still spoken.

Early Russian explorers reported the existence of a village named Kvichak at the present-day location of Levelock. Like other 19th-century Native villages, in 1837 the population was reduced to half its number by the smallpox epidemic that swept through what we now refer to as the Bristol Bay region of Alaska. By the 1890 census, the village was mentioned again, but no measure of population was taken at that time. The population was further reduced by the measles epidemic of 1900 but still existed (although renamed Levelock's Mission) as of 1908, when a survey of Russian missions was made.

MYTH OR FACT?

Alaskan Natives still hunt whales.

FACT

While whale hunting around the world is tightly controlled to protect the whale population, the International Whaling Commission sets quotas for aboriginal subsistence whaling. In Alaska, the federal National Oceanic and Atmospheric Administration and the Alaska Eskimo Whaling Commission, which represents Native whalers, jointly allocate the quota for bowhead whales among 11 Eskimo communities.

The 1918–19 worldwide flu epidemic found its way to Levelock, but again the village rebounded and rebuilt. By 1925, a fish cannery had begun operating in Levelock, and after it burned in 1926 (reportedly due to a worker's discarded cigarette butt), a second cannery was built within three years. Many of the village homes were converted to fuel oil heat, and by 1930 the first school was built. A post office was established in 1939, and another cannery was in operation by the 1950s.

The people of Levelock depended on snowshoes and then snowmobiles for transportation until the 1990s, when many village improvements, including year-round roads, a 110-foot unloading dock at the beach area of the Kvichak River, and an airstrip, were added. Now bulk goods can be delivered by river barge and air transport. Economic development initiatives since 1997 have permitted the village to add additional village amenities, upgrade village facilities and infrastructure, build new housing, and improve village streets and access roads.

The five-member traditional Levelock Village Council serves as the local government. The council is recognized by the Bureau of Indian Affairs as the local tribal governing body.

WILLIE HENSLEY

Advocate for Alaska Natives

William L. Iggiagruk Hensley, an Inupiat and lifelong Alaskan, was born in 1941 in a village on Kotzebue Sound, where he was raised by extended family before being sent to boarding school in Tennessee. After graduating from George Washington University in Washington, D.C., Hensley returned to Alaska to become a state legislator and a crusader for Native rights. "For me, Alaska is my identity, my home and my cause," he writes in his 2009 autobiography, *Fifty Miles from Tomorrow: A Memoir of Alaska and the Real People*. Hensley was a founder of the Alaska Federation of Natives and a leader of the fight for the Alaska Native Claims Settlement Act, the landmark legislation that set aside 44 million acres and nearly $1 billion for Alaska Natives. He was also an executive of the NANA Regional Corporation, the Inupiat corporation organized under that law to run the holdings of its nearly 13,000 Native shareholders. There, he writes, "we worked mightily to uplift our people economically by melding our ancient cultural ways with the modern tools of capitalism." He retired in 2008 as manager of federal government relations for Alyeska, the company that operates the Trans-Alaska Pipeline System, and lives in Anchorage. ∎

NATIVE VILLAGE OF ATKA

Tribe: Unangan   Total Area of Entitlement: 102,917 acres
Tribal Enrollment: 174

Until the incorporation of Adak (see page 108), the island of Atka was the westernmost community in the United States. The Unangan presence on the island dates back at least 2,000 years, and archaeological evidence suggests human occupation going back to prehistoric times. The Unangan speak a language that the Russians dubbed Aleut. Atka became an important trade site and harbor for Russians in the mid-1700s. In the 1860s, the site became a settlement, and until the 1920s, fox breeding as well as its copious resources of king crab, black cod, and ocean salmon kept the village solvent. In 1914, reindeer were introduced onto the island, and seals and sea lions are numerous.

During World War II, the people of Atka were evacuated to the Ketchikan area, and the village was burned by the U.S. to prevent advancing Japanese forces from occupying it. After the war, Atkans returned to the community, along with Unangan from Attu who had been prisoners of the Japanese.

Though the village is otherwise a traditional Unangan settlement and the people depend on a subsistence lifestyle, the Unangan language is actually spoken in only about 25 percent of the homes. Much of village life centers on the St. Nicholas Russian Orthodox Church.

Atka is far from the major fishing areas of the southeastern Bering Sea, but it is in the middle of other major fishing grounds. Subsistence living is supplemented by wages earned from the halibut fishery and black cod processing plant and a reindeer herd of more than 2,500.

A portrait of a Native of Nunivak Island, Alaska, the second largest island in the Bering Sea and home to Cup'ik Eskimos.

NATIVE VILLAGE OF BARROW INUPIAT TRADITIONAL GOVERNMENT

Tribe: Inupiat   Total Area of Entitlement: 215,810 acres
Tribal Enrollment: 2,590

Barrow, also known as Ukpeagvik, was named in honor of Sir John Barrow, the second secretary of the British Admiralty and a great promoter of Arctic exploration.

In 1946, exploration of the Naval Petroleum Reserve Number 4 started, and later the Naval Arctic Research Laboratory was built near Barrow. The Navy departed in 1980, and the village corporation acquired it, developed its own research base, and renovated the facility to house a community college and Inupiat Heritage Center.

FISHING AND HUNTING

While many people might think of "subsistence" as "just getting by," in the far north, it has another meaning—it describes a lifestyle of hunting and gathering that allows a family or community to feed itself without buying food or taking handouts. Traditionally, this is how the Native peoples lived; today, many in Alaska and Canada continue with a version of the subsistence lifestyle, although it's governed by more laws now.

The types and availability of food sources shaped a tribe's life. For instance, the Innu of Labrador intercepted caribou herds at water crossings and topographic barriers during their migrations. The myth that hunters "followed the caribou" comes from early, misinformed archaeology in Europe. In fact, caribou move far too fast for humans to follow. Along the coasts, people mostly hunted marine mammals with harpoons and floats from kayaks and caught fish with hooks, spears, or traps. Fish that swam near shores or in rivers, such as the spectacular Pacific salmon migrations, could be taken in large numbers with spears and dip nets. Fish was the most common food of northern peoples, both on the coast and in the interior.

Especially in aboriginal days, these hunts would be accompanied by complex ceremonies. For instance, the captain of a Northern Alaska whaling boat, a respected man known as the *umialik,* had a role akin to that of a priest. There were rituals to greet migrating whales, rituals to lure the whales closer to the hunters, and rituals to butcher an animal and share the carcass. All were meant to honor the spirit of the whale so it might permit itself to be captured, thus feeding a community for months. The number of whales in Alaskan waters plummeted with the rise of commercial whaling by foreigners. Today, whale hunting is controversial and takes place within a complex international legal system. However, Alaska Native villages are still allowed a small quota for subsistence. ∎

A Native woman with fish drying on a rack in Kotzebue, a center of indigenous culture on Kotzebue Sound in Alaska's Northwest Arctic Borough

The Native Village of Barrow is a federally recognized tribe. Shareholders in Barrow's Ukpeagvik Inupiat village corporation are also shareholders in the Arctic Slope Regional Corporation. Some residents continue to rely on subsistence food sources, such as whale, seal, polar bear, caribou, and fish. Barrow is the northernmost community in North America and is on the Chukchi Sea coast. There is no sunset between May 10 and August 2, and no sunrise from November 18 through January 24. Temperatures fall below freezing an average of 324 days of the year. A state-owned airport serves as the regional transportation center for the borough, while marine and land transportation provide seasonal entry to the city.

NATIVE VILLAGE OF DIOMEDE

Tribe: Inupiat   **Total Area of Entitlement:** 105,600 acres
Tribal Enrollment: 248

Diomede, or Inalik, is a traditional Eskimo village with a culture centered on subsistence activities. Sea mammals, polar bears, cod, crab, walrus, seal, and birds are all important subsistence resources. Mainland Eskimos traditionally traveled to Diomede Island to hunt polar bears, while Diomede residents hunted on both sea and ice and traded with Natives in both Asia and Alaska. Diomede Island in present-day Alaska is almost in the center of the narrowest part of the Bering Strait and is sometimes known as Little Diomede, lying only 2.4 miles from Big Diomede, Russia's easternmost point. When the Soviet Union sealed its borders, Big Diomede Island became a military base and all Native residents were moved to the Siberian mainland.

For the Little Diomede Inupiat, employment is limited to jobs with the city and school; seasonal mining, construction, and commercial fishing have declined in recent years. Ivory carving provides supplemental income for a number of village residents, with the city acting as a wholesale agent for the carvings. Steep slopes, rocky terrain, and constant winds from the north hamper accessibility. There is only weekly mail delivery; flights are scheduled from Nome when weather allows, and there is a breakwater and small-boat harbor. Skin boats are still popular for hunting and sea travel. Today, visits to Big Diomede and the Siberian coast are permitted.

NATIVE VILLAGE OF KOTZEBUE

Tribe: Inupiat   Total Area of Entitlement: 164,364 acres   Tribal Enrollment: 2,712

Kotzebue residents are mostly Inupiat, and subsistence is a fundamental part of their lifestyle. The Inupiaq name is Kikiktagruk, meaning "a place that is shaped like a long island" or "almost an island," in reference to their Baldwin Peninsula location in Kotzebue Sound. The native village of Kotzebue lies along a three-mile stretch of land varying in width from 1,100 to 3,600 feet near the ends of the Kobuk, Noatak, and Ssezawick Rivers. The village is 549 miles northwest of Anchorage as the crow flies, and 26 miles above the Arctic Circle.

The site seems to have been inhabited by the Inupiat for at least 600 years. In that period, its location on the coast and proximity to several rivers made it a trading hub in the Arctic region even prior to the arrival of Europeans. Kotzebue Sound was claimed by Russia in 1818 by the German Lt. Otto Von Kotzebue. The community was named for the Kotzebue Sound when a post office was introduced in 1899. During the 20th century, economic growth and expansion has allowed Kotzebue a rapid development.

The city of Kotzebue was incorporated in 1958, under the city manager method of government. It taxes 6 percent on retail, accommodations, and liquor. After the village was incorporated, both an Air Force base and a White Alice Communications System were established. The Bureau of Indian Affairs recognizes Kotzebue as a Native entity, and the village serves on the IRA tribal council and as a tribal government contractor.

A 19th-century Bering Sea Eskimo ceremonial mask of a black bear with a small smiling face on one side

MYTH OR FACT?

No one uses the term "Eskimo" anymore.

MYTH

It depends what area you're talking about. In some areas, "Eskimo" is considered derogatory. In Canada, the term for people who used to be known as Eskimos is Inuit; in Greenland (in English), it's Greenlander, although Inuit is used, too. Alaskans still use the word Eskimo to refer collectively to the Inuit and Yup'ik.

Kotzebue is a service and transportation hub for northwestern villages; because it lies on the confluence of three river drainages, the village is the point of transfer between ocean and inland shipping. It also serves as the region's air transport center. A robust cash economy, an expanding private sector, and a stable public sector ensure the city's continued growth and prosperity. Oil-related activities and mineral exploration and development also contribute to development. The majority of income is in some way tied to government employment, including jobs in the school district, Maniilaq Association, the city, and the borough. In addition, Cominco Alaska Red Dog Mine, a mine of lead and zinc, employs a large number of workers. Most residents supplement their income with subsistence.

In previous decades, commercial fishing for chum salmon had provided ample seasonal employment. In 2003, however, only 2 of 133 commercial fishing permits were used, and only 3 of 131 were used in 2002. In 2004, the state's Department of Commerce, Community, and Economic Development backed a development project in an attempt to restore the industry.

NATIVE VILLAGE OF NIKOLSKI

Tribe: Unangan   Total Area of Entitlement: 77,188 acres   Tribal Enrollment: 85

Nikolski is a traditional Unangan community, whose nearby archaeological sites yielded human remains, funerary objects, masks, fishing tools, household objects, and animal skins as well as fragments of charcoal that indicate habitation for more than 4,000 years and human life on Umnak Island for approximately 8,500 years. Nikolski is located in the Unorganized Borough on Nikolski Bay near the southwest point of Umnak Island in the Fox Islands, one of the southernmost islands in the Aleutian chain. It is a biologically diverse and productive area which has contributed to its long history of habitation. Most of the

NORTHERN ATHABASCAN

Northern Athabascans are not a single tribe. Rather, the term is used to describe a grouping of diverse peoples who speak (or spoke) one of about two dozen Athabascan dialects and lived in a vast subarctic region including the Alaskan interior and large parts of northwestern Canada. Their languages are in the same family as those spoken by the Athabascans of the Pacific Northwest and the Apache and Navajo of the U.S. Southwest. Before contact with Europeans, they considered themselves as small local bands of hunters and gatherers. Their lives were shaped by the resources of the lands, which are snowy and dark in winter and warm during the short summers with their long days. Europeans assigned most tribal names and territories.

Across a Wide Territory

The Northern Athabascan languages were spoken by people who lived in the Mackenzie River Basin area of what's now Canada; the mountainous cordillera that straddles the Alaska-Canada border; the Yukon, Kuskokwim, and Copper River Basins of the Alaskan interior; and the Cook Inlet–Susitna River Basin along the coast near Anchorage and the Kenai Peninsula. These languages are still spoken, but some by such small numbers of people that linguists consider them endangered.

While all these peoples were traditionally hunter-gatherers, their day-to-day life varied depending on the characteristics of the land around them. For instance, the groups that lived in the mountainous highlands hunted mostly big game such as caribou, moving around frequently to intercept the herds at traditional crossing places. Those who lived along the rivers relied heavily on fishing, which provided them with a more stable life, because they didn't have to uproot themselves constantly in search of food; instead, they had winter villages and summer fishing camps. Groups that lived near the coast, such as the Tanaina of the Cook Inlet, hunted aquatic mammals, such as seals,

from seagoing canoes. In the winter, they lived in large log houses.

Belief in Reciprocity

There were also similarities among the groups. For instance, some basic tenets of Athabascan religion were shared around the region, according to Phyllis

Beads and rabbit fur are used to decorate Athabascan dancing boots.

Ann Fast, an Alaskan Athabascan and anthropologist. "The most common of these is that all relations, including those in the spirit world, follow complex rules of reciprocity . . . Notions of reciprocity are pivotal to all northern Athabascan cultures. These include expectations based on certain kinds of family relations (such as uncle to nephew or mother to

daughter), as well as actions, thoughts, and gifts." People also had reciprocal relations with animals and spirits—for instance, people had obligations to the spirits of the animals they hunted.

These beliefs continue today. One of the best known manifestations of reciprocity is the potlatch, a ceremony often connected with a funeral or memorial service. People gather for several days to dance, eat, tell stories, and commemorate the dead. The hosts give generous gifts to their guests. Indians in the Pacific Northwest also hold potlatches. Insufficient food prevented this practice among the peoples of the eastern Arctic and the Canadian forests, although they held communal gatherings during periods of abundance.

Because the areas they lived in were so remote, some Athabascans were among the last North American Indians to come in regular contact with Europeans. For instance, whites did not appear along the Tanana River Valley until about the 1880s, although the Natives had occasionally traveled to trade with the Russians and the Hudson's Bay Company. Nonetheless, fur trading changed the Athabascan subsistence hunting culture, as it did elsewhere in the north. Animals most valuable for their pelts were not the ones

An Alaska Native man plays a mandolin at the Athabascan Fiddlers Festival in Fairbanks, Alaska.

best for food, so the trade changed what the Indians trapped. That meant they had to buy food to survive. The search for gold in the late 19th century and oil in the 20th brought many more fortune seekers north.

Wide Variations Continue

The territory where the Athabascans live is more than 3,000 miles across and in two countries. The people are organized under the differing laws of those lands.

In the United States, that means there are various tribal governments and Alaskan Native corporations, which share the profit from the land and businesses with the Native shareholders in the regions they cover. Doyon, Inc., is the largely

Athabascan Native corporation that covers the Alaskan interior, an area encompassing more than a third of the state. It's the largest private landowner in the state, with more than 12.5 million acres. Doyon's businesses include oil, government contracting, and tourism. Among its properties is the Kantishna Roadhouse, a lodge 100 miles inside Denali National Park, near Mount McKinley, the highest peak on the continent. In Athabascan, the imposing mountain is called Denali, "the Great One." The Tanaka Chief Conference is the nonprofit consortium of 42 villages that operates alongside Doyon. According to the conference, about half the Natives in the region live in Fairbanks, the only urban area. The city is

surrounded by smaller communities, only nine of which are accessible by road.

Other Athabascans live in areas covered by other corporations, including Cook Inlet Region, Inc., which has made highly profitable telecommunications investments. Ahtna, Inc., which covers the Copper River Valley area, owns big chunks of land inside Denali and Wrangell-St. Elias National Parks and runs tourism-related businesses; it is also a sizable federal government contractor, with much of its work outside Alaska.

In Canada, Athabascans are part of numerous self-governing First Nations in the Northwest Territories, the Yukon, British Columbia, Alberta, Saskatchewan, and Manitoba. ■

nearby islands are part of the Aleutian National Wildlife Refuge. The sea in front of the village has dense mats of attached algae which in turn support a wide variety of marine animals, including birds and mammals. Sea otters, harbor seals, sea lions, and whales are concentrated in the area. The village is adjacent to the rich fishing grounds of the Bering Sea and the Alaska/Aleutian shelf, and is within a prime king crab area. There are no large predators on Umnak Island, and the island is home to many ptarmigan, foxes, rabbits, songbirds, eagles, and waterfowl.

Contact with Russian explorers was made in 1741. In the late 1700s, with assistance from Russian explorers, the Umnak Unangan waged war on the people of the Islands of Four Mountains, and that group was substantially destroyed. Survivors of the conflict were incorporated into villages on Umnak.

In 1834, the village was the site of a sea otter hunting camp. In 1920, a boom in fox farming occurred in Nikolski and nearby communities. During World War II, when the Japanese attacked Unalaska and seized Attu and Kiska Islands in the Aleutians, residents were evacuated to the Ketchikan area. A sheep ranch that began in 1926 still operates as part of the Aleutian Livestock Company.

Today, the Unangan language is spoken in most homes. Subsistence activities, including the harvest of salmon, seals, halibut, and waterfowl; sheep and cattle raising; and commercial fishing, sustain the community and form the nucleus of village culture.

Nikolski is unincorporated and is governed by an Indian Reorganization Act council, headed by a president. Most residents support themselves by working outside the village at crab canneries and on fish/seafood processing ships. The Aleutian Livestock Company runs between 4,000 and 7,000 sheep, 300 head of cattle, and 30 horses on Umnak Island. Nikolski has a 3,500-foot unlighted gravel runway, which provides passenger, mail, and cargo service. The airstrip was owned by the U.S. Air Force. Nikolski has no landing or port facilities for ships. Barges deliver cargo once or twice a year. Goods and passengers are lightered three miles to the beach.

MYTH OR FACT?

In the Arctic, Natives eat meat raw.

FACT

North of the tree line, the only wood available is driftwood, so people traditionally ate much of their fish and animal meat uncooked. This practice also maximizes nutrients and fats that can be lost in cooking. Much "country food" is still consumed raw today.

NATIVE VILLAGE OF NUIQSUT

Tribe: Inupiat   Total Area of Entitlement: 137,881 acres   Tribal Enrollment: 349

Prior to the arrival of European explorers in the late 18th and early 19th centuries, Arctic Alaska, stretching from Norton Sound to the Canadian border, was the location of numerous distinct Inupiaq-speaking groups, each associated with a particular territory. For more than 8,000 years, the Colville Delta has been a gathering and trading place

An Inuit elder sits by the cold shore of Kotzebue Bay, Alaska, to drum and chant in the Inupiaq language.

for the Inupiat. Its rivers teem with whitefish, burbot, arctic char, grayling, and an occasional salmon. Bowhead whales and spotted seals, lake trout, caribou, moose, wolves, grizzly bear, wolverine, and fox are all part of the people's livelihood and history.

Today, Nuiqsut is an Inupiat village with a culture continuing to focus on traditional subsistence activities. An older village of Nuiqsut (Itqilippaa) was abandoned in the late 1940s because there was no school. In 1973, with belongings packed on sleds hauled by tractors and snowmobiles, 27 families from Barrow arrived at the present location and lived in a tent village for a year and a half, using snow/ice blocks to help insulate tent walls in the winter months. The Arctic Slope Regional Corporation funded the construction of the village in 1974, including a school and housing, and the city was incorporated in 1975.

Like most North Slope villages, Nuiqsut's economy is based primarily on subsistence hunting and fishing. However, nearly one-third of the workforce is employed in the private sector, mostly by the Kuukpik Corporation (the ANCSA village corporation) and the construction industry that has evolved as a result of projects initiated by the Arctic Slope Regional Corporation.

Nuiqsut sits on the west bank of the Nechelik Channel of the Colville River. It lies about 35 miles from the Beaufort Sea coast, on the extreme North Slope of Arctic Alaska. It is an isolated community at the center of a vast tundra or permafrost region, characterized by low-banked meandering streams, marshy sloughs, and shallow freshwater lakes covering as much as 75 percent of its total surface area. The Colville River Basin is well known for a plethora of birds and other wildlife species. Nesting raptors, arctic peregrine falcons, golden eagles, and rough-legged hawks are numerous. The river also provides an important year-round habitat for brown bears, wolves, and moose and produces a significant number of dinosaur fossils. Frozen most of the year, the Colville River floods each spring.

Nuiqsut lies 50 miles downriver from the site of a $20-million environmental cleanup of PCBs and other toxins that leached into the Colville River at the site of the former Umiat Air Station, a remote military installation south of Prudhoe Bay built during World War II. The post was once a refueling stop for military planes bound for Distant Early Warning radar sites on the continent's northernmost edge. It was also the site of extensive oil exploration. The site was listed as one of the highest cleanup priorities and remains a lingering source of environmental concern for all residents living within the watershed of the Colville River.

Alaskan Yup'ik feather dance fans are used in traditional winter ceremonies. Men hold the fans by the wooden hoops.

Inupiaq, Eskimo-Aleut language family

"Attusigxugu atullakkayaitpigu snauquan?"

("Can I rent a snowmachine [snowmobile]?")

NATIVE VILLAGE OF OUZINKIE

Tribe: Alutiiq **Total Area of Entitlement:** 151,052 acres
Tribal Enrollment: 562

Ouzinkie is mostly Alutiiq, and the majority of residents have lived in the village throughout their entire lives. The Kodiak Archipelago and the surrounding regions of Prince William Sound, the outer Kenai Peninsula, and the Alaska Peninsula are home to the Alutiiq, whose culture and language are most closely related to those of the Yup'ik and Inupiat. Located on Spruce Island and the closest settlement to Kodiak City, Ouzinkie (from the Russian *Uzenkiy,* "Village of Russians and Creoles") was heavily affected by Russian occupation throughout the 1800s. There remain many historical Russian influences in the culture, blending with Alutiiq and global ways of life.

The village was founded in the early 1800s by the Russian American Company as a retirement community, and it was the home of St. Herman of Alaska, the first canonized Russian Orthodox saint in North America. In 1898, the present Russian Orthodox chapel was built, and by 1927, a post office had been established.

The area has been beset by natural disasters in the modern era, including the eruption of Mt. Katmai in 1912 and the 1964 Good Friday earthquake and resulting tsunami, which destroyed the Ouzinkie Packing Company cannery, a major economic force in the community. In the late 1960s, the Ouzinkie Seafoods cannery was built. It burned down in 1976, and as of 2004, no canneries operate in the city. Ouzinkie is accessible only by air and water. The city encompasses 6 square miles of land and 1.7 square miles of water, 20 feet above sea level. Significant coastal erosion has occurred in several places, primarily along the shoreline in the harbor area.

The economy of Ouzinkie relies primarily on commercial salmon fishing. Approximately 25 residents hold commercial fishing permits. The Ouzinkie Native Corporation and Koniag, Inc., the regional Native corporation, have supported economic development. Almost all residents supplement their income (and diets) with subsistence activities for various food sources. Salmon, crab, halibut, shrimp, clams, ducks, deer, and rabbits are harvested. In the 2000 census, the median household income was $52,500, one of the highest in Alaska.

WIFE SHARING

One of the most discussed social practices of Arctic Natives—certainly the one that most shocked Christian missionaries—was wife sharing or spousal exchange. But no matter what the missionaries thought, it was less about sex than about building community ties, according to others who have studied it. Exchanges were also carried out under formal arrangements and with the consent of all parties.

In some form, the practice was common among all traditional Eskimo (Inuit and Yup'ik) societies. Sometimes, a hunter whose wife could not accompany him on a trip because she was ill might trade spouses with a friend who was remaining at home; in a culture in which women and men so heavily relied on each other's skills the hunter would have help, while his wife

would have protection. In other situations, a swap was a sign of friendship or political alliance between two men. Sometimes, an exchange was initiated out of hospitality toward a stranger, but it wasn't a casual gesture; such an exchange linked two families in a lifelong partnership. Family members always needed allies, even when they visited different regions.

Technically, these exchanges were always initiated by the men. But women had a respected voice in these societies and were not considered the property of their husbands. Thus, it's generally believed that a woman could initiate an exchange if she desired. Logistically, the arrangements were certainly easier on the women: Usually, the women remained in their homes while the men did any needed traveling. In a region

of such extreme and forbidding weather, travel carried no insignificant level of risk. Although spousal exchange was an important part of social relationships, adultery without a spouse's consent was not acceptable and, indeed, could result in serious repercussions and even lead to deadly feuds.

Interestingly, the prevailing belief about spousal exchange was that it was impossible that it would result in conception. No party in the exchange would ever have felt that they were stuck raising someone else's child. In fact, the alliances created by the exchanges also extended to the children, bonding offspring to both sets of parents.

In most areas, missionaries succeeded in wiping out the practice of wife sharing by the 1890s, but in isolated areas of the central Arctic, it persisted into the mid-20th century. ∎

The Ouzinkie Tribal Council, headed by a president, is a federally recognized tribe. In 2001, the president of the tribal council was also the vice mayor of the city.

NATIVE VILLAGE OF POINT HOPE

Tribe: Tikeraqmuit Inupiat   Total Area of Entitlement: 138,240 acres   Tribal Enrollment: 873

The Point Hope Peninsula is one of the longest continually inhabited areas in North America. Some of the earliest residents came to hunt bowhead whales more than 2,000 years ago. The remains of Old Tigara Village, a prehistoric site with the remains of sod houses and an abundance of archaeological evidence scattered throughout the area attest to the longevity and richness of Inupiaq culture in the area, though the rising sea level is a new threat to the people. An even earlier site with about 800 house pits, known as Ipiutak, was occupied from around 500 B.C. to A.D. 100. Ipiutak and the surrounding archaeological district are on the

National Register of Historic Places. In addition to the prehistoric village sites, there are burial grounds in the area, including a cemetery marked by large whalebones standing on end, where ceremonies are still held at the end of whaling season.

Today, Point Hope is a culturally intact Tikeraqmuit Inupiat village with a culture and economy based largely on marine subsistence activities. The Native people historically exercised dominion over a vast region extending from the Utukok to Kivalin Rivers and to areas far inland. The peninsula on which the village is located, Point Hope, or Tikerq Peninsula/Promontory, forms the westernmost extension of the northwest Alaska coast. Commercial whaling activities brought Westerners to the area. By the late 1880s, shore-based whaling stations such as Jabbertown had been established, but these disappeared with the demise of commercial whaling in the early 1900s. Point Hope's government was incorporated in 1966, and in the early 1970s the village was moved to the present location because of erosion and periodic storm flooding from the Chukchi Sea. There has been no flooding at the new town site.

INNU

The Innu people, formerly referred to as the Montagnais-Naskapi, live in eastern Quebec and Labrador, a land they call Nitassinan. Traditionally, they were hunters and fishers who moved around a vast, sparsely populated territory using canoes, snowshoes, and toboggans. They hunted caribou, which provided them not only with meat but also hides for clothing and bone and antler for tools. Small groups of three or four families lived together in winter, often sharing a lodge. In the short summers, many bands would gather together on lakeshores or riverbanks to socialize, trade, hold ceremonies, and escape the insects in the woods. After Europeans arrived, trapping became important, and some families settled near trading posts, but many continued their nomadic life.

Always on the Move

Because the Innu traveled so widely, it is difficult to determine how many of them there were at the time of European contact, but some scholars estimate there were about 4,000 people in a territory of 300,000 square miles. That population crashed because of disease, especially the Spanish influenza in 1916–18, and other stresses on resources that came with colonization. However, their numbers rebounded in the second half of the 20th century with the increasing availability of medical care and food. Today, there are about 17,000 Innu who live in 12 settlements in Quebec and Labrador.

In 1633–34, Jesuit priest Paul Le Jeune spent the winter with a band of Innu, and his detailed written account of that time provides a window into everyday life. Between November and April, the band of 19 people broke camp 23 times to follow the caribou herds, according to a summary of Le Jeune's account by 20th-century anthropologist Eleanor Leacock. The band shared a lodge and generally traveled with two other bands, of 10 and 16 people. Le Jeune describes a social system as freewheeling as the

At dusk in the forest in southern Labrador, Canada, light shines through a tent at an Innu autumn hunting camp.

travel schedule. There were no chiefs; rather, informal leaders were followed because they were articulate. The people constantly joked and laughed, even when times were bad, because they believed that sadness weakened them. They routinely shared food and hospitality with other groups who were in need. Men could have multiple wives. Work was generally divided by the sexes, with men doing the hunting. Women had a voice in group decisions and were nowhere near as obedient to men as the Jesuit would have liked. Children were treasured and never physically punished or scolded, according to Le Jeune, although they began work very young.

The large lodges—many were conical, but other shapes were common, too—were made of wooden poles covered with bark or skins. Fires were built inside for heating and cooking. Traditional clothing was made of tanned hides, with fur for warmth. In spring and summer, when lakes and rivers were passable, birchbark canoes were a common way to travel. The women sat in the stern and steered, according to Leacock, while the men sat toward the front. In the winter, when the bands tracked caribou through the snow, they wore snowshoes and dragged toboggans. In the early 20th century, some Innu adopted the Inuit practice of using sled dogs, which have now generally been replaced by snowmobiles.

As the years went on, fur trading became an important element of what was once a subsistence economy. Some families settled near trading posts, and the men headed out to trap fox and beaver. Numerous times, the Hudson's Bay Company moved bands from post to post to meet its needs. Traditional bands had never owned land, but the fur trade fostered a system of hunting territories. Still, up until the 1950s, many families remained migratory.

"The oldest Tshishennuat (Elders) remember the days when caribou were speared from canoes as they crossed the Mushuau-shipu (George River). They recall living in shaputuans (multi-family dwellings) that were heated by open fires, hunting partridge with bow and arrow, and wearing caribou-hide clothing," according to "Tipatshimuna" ("Innu stories from the land"), a website about Innu culture prepared by a group of Canadian museums.

Contemporary Life

The majority of the Innu speak Innu-aimun, their traditional language, a sub-group of the Cree language, as well as French or English. Most call themselves Innu rather than Montagnais, the French term. Others, who generally live in the north, refer to themselves as Naskapi.

Current Innu settlements are far from the urbanized portions of Canada, and often far from each other. The economies of many of the Innu First Nations depend on logging and tourism.

In Labrador, the Innu Nation represents two settlements, in Sheshatsiu and Natuashish. The latter is a planned community built in 2002 to replace the old community of Davis Inlet, whose squalid conditions were notorious.

The Innu in Labrador were greatly affected by the flooding of a huge area in 1970 when the Churchill River was dammed to create Smallwood Reservoir and the Upper Churchill Falls hydroelectric project. The nation negotiated with the provincial government for reparations and a stake in the proposed Lower Churchill hydroelectric project. That 2008 deal, called the New Dawn Agreement, upset some Quebec Innu, however, who say that it draws boundaries and assigns territories that curb their ancestral rights. ∎

At an Innu hunting camp in Labrador, a tribal member threads caribou skin lacing onto a new pair of snowshoes.

A Yup'ik artist teaches traditional dances to children in a longhouse, a traditional dwelling place for men. The Yup'ik are the largest group of Alaska Natives, and they keep their language and other traditions alive.

Aqqaluk Lynge

Global voice of the Inuit

Aqqaluk Lynge, a Greenland Inuit poet, politician, and activist, has been an advocate for indigenous rights around the world and also a prominent voice warning against the dangers of global climate change. He has pointed out to audiences around the world that the Inuit live daily with the shrinking of polar ice, so warming is more than an academic concern. "In the Inuit language, we use the word sila for ice," he told one group in 2009. "But sila also means much more than ice. It also means weather, climate, environment, sky, and indeed, the universe. So when Inuit experience changes to the ice, as we are now due to the first effects of climate change, this is more than 'just' a change in ice conditions and climate, it is a change in our basic environment and indeed, our universe."

Lynge, born in 1947, has been a member of Greenland's Home Rule Parliament, a government minister, and a member of the United Nations Permanent Forum on Indigenous Issues. He is also a leader of the Inuit Circumpolar Council, a group that unites U.S., Canadian, Russian, and Greenland Inuit, the peoples that live closest to the North Pole. He was the international president of the group from 1997 to 2002 and afterwards president of the Greenland council. Lynge has written in Danish and English as well as Greenlandic. His poetry, much of it political, has largely been written in Greenlandic, but a collection of 35 years of poems has been translated into English and published as *The Veins of the Heart to the Pinnacle of the Mind.* ■

Greenlander Aqqaluk Lynge warns people around the world of the perils of climate change.

Point Hope is located in the North Slope Borough near the end of a triangular spit that juts 15 miles into the Chukchi Sea, on the North Slope of Alaska. It is the westernmost village in the North Slope Borough. The village area encompasses 6.3 square miles of land at an elevation of 40 feet above sea level. Point Hope lies within 100 miles of the northern border of the Cape Krusenstern National Monument and is approximately 100 miles from the westernmost border of the Noatak National Preserve. The Chukchi Sea is ice free from late June until mid-September.

Point Hope is the second largest city on the North Slope, with an economy largely based on subsistence hunting and fishing. The North Slope Borough employs more than 40 percent of the working population, and the school district employs another 28 percent. Close to one-fourth of the labor force works in the private sector. The median household income surveyed in the 2000 census was $63,125,

MYTH OR FACT?

Indigenous languages are extinct in the north.

MYTH

Many of the traditional languages of the north are endangered, but others are still widely spoken. In eastern Canada and Greenland, most Inuit children learn their traditional language. In Alaska, by contrast, only two of the 20 indigenous languages are spoken by children in the home. The state does have bilingual education programs, though, and there are still adult speakers, especially of Central Yup'ik.

the highest in Alaska. The Arctic Slope Regional Corporation is largely responsible for the high levels of economic development initiatives and construction projects in the area.

Residents produce a wide array of arts and crafts, including carved ivory, Eskimo clothing and parkas, baleen baskets, whalebone masks, caribou-skin masks, etched baleen, ivory-tipped harpoons, and bird spears. These are marketed through the Chukchi Sea Trading Company, a Native arts and crafts cooperative.

Native Village of Tatitlek

Tribe: Chugachigmuit Alutiiq   Total Area of Entitlement: 137,246 acres   Tribal Enrollment: 90

Tatitlek, or Tátitláq, is a coastal Alutiiq village. The name means "windy place" in Alutiiq. Nestled between mountains and sea among spruce and hemlock trees along the northeast shore of Tatitlek Narrows, it sustains its people in a fishing and subsistence-based culture. The blue dome of the Russian Orthodox church graces the horizon near the waterfront. Like many Alutiiq villages, it has moved several times. In 1910 the U.S. Geological Survey indicated that the village originally stood at the head of Gladhaugh Bay before it was moved to its present site.

Beginning in the 19th century, its residents began trading furs for European goods. Hunters traded sea otter pelts first with the Russians at Nuchek and, by the 1890s, with American traders at the Alaska Commercial Company store at Tatitlek. Many new people came to the region in the early 1900s as prospectors passed through the village on their way to mines on the Copper River. A copper mine opened at nearby Ellamar in 1898, and a cannery at Ellamar (in operation from 1940 to 1954) provided jobs for people from Tatitlek. In 1989, the *Exxon Valdez* ran aground not far from Tatitlek and spilled millions of gallons of crude oil into the waters of Prince William Sound. Although currents carried most of the oil away from the village, the harvest of subsistence species decreased that year by 89 percent.

Commercial fishing, fish processing, and oyster farming are the primary sources of employment in Tatitlek, and subsistence activities provide the majority of food items for residents. A coho salmon hatchery at Boulder Bay is nearing completion for subsistence use. Many Tatitlek families participate in commercial fishing for salmon and halibut. All through the year, they also hunt, fish, and gather plants and beach foods for their own use. Seals, salmon, and herring are some of the most important wild foods. Each spring, Tatitlek hosts a heritage festival, where students from Alaska schools spend a week learning traditional crafts and activities.

Tatitlek has an Indian Reorganization Act village council, the Native Village of Tatitlek, headed by a president and federally recognized. The council serves as the governing body for the community.

RESIDENTIAL/BOARDING SCHOOL

"Boarding school taught me that everything I knew about my culture, language, and world view were evil and must be pushed away. Wrangell Institute Elementary school did its best to eradicate everything I identified with as an Inupiaq . . . There was emotional abuse, psychological abuse, physical abuse, and sexual abuse."

—Jim La Belle, "Boarding School: Historical Trauma among Alaska's Native People"

In the late 19th century, U.S. policy toward Native people shifted from one of annihilation and relocation to one of assimilation. One manifestation was the Indian boarding school.

Alaska schools were racially segregated for many years. White children usually went through 12th grade; Natives stopped at eighth grade. Indian children of high school age, and sometimes younger, went to faraway government boarding schools. .

Boarding school could be traumatic, especially for young children. Jim La Belle, who spent ten school years at such schools, narrates a searing account of violence, dehumanization, and cultural eradication in a 2006 paper published under the auspices of the University of Alaska–Anchorage, where he has been on the faculty. "The moral impacts of those bygone educational policies are evident today," writes La Belle. "There are many boarding school-era students who have faced a loss of cultural identity, language, and tradition. They suffer from post-traumatic stress disorder due to the indignities and traumas of years in boarding school. Since the mid-1970s, these individuals have made up the high percentages of alcohol-fueled statistics: accidents, domestic violence, murder, and suicide."

Two other University of Alaska researchers, Diane Hirshberg and Suzanne Sharp, in 2004 and 2005 interviewed 61 adults who had attended these schools. They spoke of good teachers and good friends but also of abuse and loss of their culture.

In 1972, Natives sued the state in what became known as the Molly Hootch case, contending that the situation discriminated against Native children. Renamed *Tobeluk* v. *Lind*, the case was settled in 1976 via a consent decree under which the state agreed to build local schools. ∎

A group of Eskimo children pose outside a federally run public school near Cape Prince of Wales, Alaska, sometime between 1900 and 1930.

NATIVE VILLAGE OF TUNUNAK

Tribe: Yup'ik   Total Area of Entitlement: 115,200 acres
Tribal Enrollment: 350

Tununak is a traditional Eskimo village. The first detailed outside exploration of the area was made in the winter of 1878–79 by E. W. Nelson, a Smithsonian naturalist, whose records indicate that six people were living in Tununak at that time. In 1889, the Jesuits sent a missionary to the village, and a small chapel and school were built. However, by 1892 the school had closed because of the migratory nature of the people and their close ties with their own traditions. In 1925, a government school was built in Tununak, and a general store was opened four years later. Residents continued to retain traditional customs and lifestyle; as late as 1936, some people continued to live in indigenous sod homes.

In 1934, the Jesuit mission was reopened by a locally renowned missionary named Father Deshout, but the 1950s brought the greatest lifestyle changes to the people of Tununak. Many villagers experienced their first sustained exposure to outsiders through their involvement with the Alaska Territorial Guard, working in fish canneries, and seeking health care treatment. By the 1970s, snowmobiles were replacing dogsled teams, and Native architecture—in spite of its environmental superiority—had given way to more contemporary housing.

Tununak is situated in a small bay on the northwest coast of Nelson Island, where there are relatively warm winters and cool summers. The school district, village corporation, stores, and commercial fishing industry are the primary employers. Trapping and Native crafts also generate cash. Subsistence activities are an important contributor to villagers' diets. Seal meat, seal oil, and herring are staples. Beluga whale and walrus also are hunted. A lottery to hunt muskox on Nelson or Nunivak Island is available to residents. Coastal Villages Seafood processes halibut and salmon in Tununak.

A Yup'ik doll, dressed like a young female

NATIVE VILLAGE OF UNALAKLEET

Tribe: Inupiat   Total Area of Entitlement: 180,374 acres
Tribal Enrollment: 1,185

Unalakleet, on Norton Sound in the Bering Strait, has a history of diverse cultures and flourishing trade activity. It is known as the "place where the east wind blows" and means "the most southerly point" in the Inupiaq language. It also lies on the border between the Inupiat to the north and Yup'ik territory to the south and has served as a major trade center between the Athabascans and the Inupiaq peoples. Archaeologists have dated house remains along the beach ridge to approximately 2,000 years ago. Unalakleet is the terminus for the Kaltag Portage, an important winter travel route connecting to the Yukon River. Indians on the upper river were considered "professional" traders, who had a monopoly on the Indian-Eskimo trade across the Kaltag Portage.

In the 1830s, an important trading post was opened up by the Russian-American Company. Lapland reindeer herders arrived in 1898 to teach herding to the Unalakleet locals. In 1901, the U.S. Army Signal Corps built a telegraph line between St. Michael and Unalakleet. And since the beginning of the yearly Iditarod Trail Sled Dog Race, which runs from Anchorage in south-central Alaska to Nome in the northwest, Unalakleet has been the first checkpoint on the Norton Sound.

Unalakleet's economy is the most active and diverse in Norton Sound and takes place alongside a traditional Inupiat subsistence lifestyle. Fish, seal, caribou, moose, and bear are utilized. Employment in government organizations and village schools is relatively plentiful in Unalakleet. A herd of muskoxen is maintained near the village, and the underwool (*qiviut*) is hand-knit by village residents. Both commercial fishing for herring and herring roe and subsistence activities are major components of Unalakleet's economy. The Norton Sound Economic Development Council

INUIT/INUPIAT

"Inuit" is an umbrella term used to describe all the indigenous peoples who traditionally spoke the Inuit/Inupiaq language, part of the Eskimo-Aleut linguistic family. These people live in the polar regions of northern Alaska, where they call themselves Inupiat; Canada, where Inuit is the preferred term; and Greenland, where they use Greenlander or Inuit. They share elements of a culture shaped by the icy region where they live, which traditionally revolved around hunting whales and other animals that shared their world. Although communities in all three places have embraced elements of modern life as diverse as satellite television and snowmobiles, they continue to live a life influenced by their harsh environment.

Arctic Pioneers

What archaeologists and other scholars call the Thule culture originated in the Bering Strait and northern Alaska about a thousand years ago. These nomadic hunters pursued baleen whales, such as bowhead or right whales, using harpoons and large skin-covered boats. On land, they traveled over ice and snow in dogsleds. In summer, they lived in tents in their hunting camps; in winter, they stayed in place in large villages. From Alaska, these peoples spread east along the northern coast of Canada and onward to Greenland, overrunning earlier Dorset culture inhabitants and, in Greenland, the Norse.

Over time, the Thule culture adapted to the local ecologies. While outsiders might think of the Arctic as one vast white wasteland, there are notable variations. For instance, in Alaska in the winter the Inupiat lived in partially underground homes made of sod, stone, and driftwood because there's very little wood in this region, which is generally north of the tree line. The earth acted as insulation and kept the house warm.

In Canada and Greenland there's another abundant building material: snow. Throughout the Arctic east of Alaska, Inuit constructed snowhouses for temporary shelter, and in some places,

An Inuit-carved narwhal tusk, from Nunavut, Canada's Inuit territory

they lived all winter in these structures—the iconic igloo, although the word *iglu* actually means any kind of house. A man built a snowhouse for his family by carving big blocks of snow and stacking them, spiral fashion, in the shape of a dome. He worked from the inside, which means the living space was sunken below the surface of the snow. To warm and light the space, families used lamps that burned whale, walrus, or seal oil. Snow is a good insulator, so the inside of a snowhouse was warm enough that the inhabitants could strip down to the waist.

Staying Warm and Well-Fed

Staying warm is important in this cold climate, and the Inupiat traditionally relied on fur clothing for that. Women spent much of their time preparing animal hides and sewing them into parkas, fur pants, socks, and boots. Because the Inuit generally did not tan animal skins, women chewed them to keep them soft. Women were in charge of the domestic sphere, including food preparation and child rearing.

A man's big job was hunting. Although the Inuit hunted for all types of animals—their diet included almost no plants, because little grows that far north—the whale shaped their society. Baleen whales migrated along the north coast. A crew of hunters in a skin-covered boat pursued the whales, harpooning them and bringing them to shore, where women butchered them. These huge beasts fed whole communities, including large numbers of sled dogs; their oil kept the people warm.

The whales also lured outsiders to a region many viewed as hostile. Beginning in the 1500s, European explorers occasionally visited Inuit settlements, introducing trade goods such as metal tools. But continued contact didn't come until the 19th century, when demand for whale products soared around the world. In 1880, the introduction of the steam-powered whaling boat meant the hunt could begin in spring, before the ice broke up, and American whaling crews became a constant presence along the Alaska coast.

Degrees of Self-Determination

The Inuit Circumpolar Council, which includes Native peoples in the Arctic regions of the U.S., Canada, Greenland, and Russia, claims to represent about 160,000 Inuit people. The Alaska Native Language Center, using narrower definitions, counts 15,700 Inupiat in Alaska, 30,500 Inuit in Canada, and 47,000 Greenlanders. The societies these people live in today are shaped in good part by the different approaches these nations take toward their indigenous peoples.

In Alaska, life changed dramatically for all peoples, indigenous and not, with the discovery of oil on the Arctic shore and North Slope in 1968, near the ancestral lands of the Inupiat. In 1971, the aboriginal claims of Native Alaskans were resolved under the Alaska Native Claims Settlement Act, which gave land and money to the indigenous people via Native-owned corporations. The majority of the Inupiat are shareholders in either the Arctic Slope Regional Corporation or the NANA Regional Corporation. More than 80 percent of the people who live in the northern Alaska areas covered by these two corporations are Natives. Much of the income in these regions comes from oil and mining, but the people also still embrace subsistence hunting.

In Canada, the Inuit struggled for much of the 20th century for a degree of political self-determination. Inuit communities across the nation negotiated with federal and provincial governments to settle land claims. The biggest of these settlements created Nunavut, a territory carved out of the Northwest Territories in 1999.

Nunavut, which means "Our Land," covers more than two million square kilometers (772,000 square miles); it has its own legislature and self-government powers, the same as other Canadian territories.

Greenland, where most of the inhabitants are of Inuit descent, is part of Denmark. However, it was granted home rule in 1979 and increasingly has taken over government functions. ▪

An Inuit hunter armed with a spear stands poised on an ice floe near Baffin Island, Nunavut, waiting for a ringed seal to appear.

operates a fish-processing plant. Tourism is becoming increasingly important, and there is world-class silver salmon fishing in the area.

NENANA NATIVE ASSOCIATION

Tribe: Tanana Athabascan   Total Area of Entitlement: 138,240 acres   Tribal Enrollment: 717

Home to several Iditarod Trail Sled Dog Race competitors and former champions, Nenana is in interior Alaska, 40 air miles southwest of Fairbanks, or 55 miles by road, on the south bank of the Tanana River and just east of the mouth of the Nenana River. It was incorporated as a home-rule city in 1921, with a mayor and city council. The BIA-recognized Nenana Native Association has a traditional village council, headed by a chief. Nenana has a strong seasonal private-sector economy, serving as a rail-to-river transportation hub for the interior region of Alaska. The majority of Native households rely on subsistence foods, such as salmon, moose, caribou (by permit), bear, waterfowl, and berries, but the traditional subsistence lifestyle of the residents is now supplemented by occasional, seasonal, or full-time employment. Many residents hold commercial fishing permits.

Nenana is in the westernmost portion of traditional Tanana Athabascan territory. The present population of Nenana is diverse, a mixture of Athabascans, Inupiat, Yup'ik, Alutiiq, and non-Natives. The majority of these residents maintain a culture centered on subsistence activities. The Tanana Athabascan language has fallen out of use, now spoken only at Nenana and Minto. The Athabascan population of those two villages totals about 380, of whom only about 30 people—the youngest around 60 years old—speak the language.

The community now called Nenana was first known as Tortella, the transliteration of *toghotthele*, a Native word meaning "mountain that parallels the river." Long accustomed to trade with Europeans, the Tanana people made trading journeys to the

A 19th-century Yup'ik mask, worn during ceremonial dances

village, where Russian traders bartered for durable and manufactured goods. Gold was discovered in Fairbanks in 1902 and brought increased trading activity and settlement with it. To resupply river travelers and miners, a trading post and roadhouse was established in 1903, and an Episcopal mission was built upriver in 1905. A post office opened in 1908. Native children from other communities attended school in Nenana, and by 1915 construction projects, including work on the Alaska Railroad, doubled Nenana's population. In 1917, surveyors for the Alaska Railroad and local residents created a tradition of guessing the date and time of the ice breakup on the Tanana River. That event became the Nenana Ice Classic, now a popular annual competition.

The community incorporated in 1921, and a railroad depot was completed in 1923, just after President Warren Harding drove the final (golden) spike at the north end of the 700-foot steel bridge over the Tanana River to celebrate the completion and official opening of the railroad. Nenana's 5,000 people now had transportation to Fairbanks and Seward, and many of the newly arrived were quick to leave. The population during the 1930 census was only 291, and the community fell into an economic slump, but the construction of an Air Force base in Clear, Alaska, in 1961 breathed new vitality into the local economy and resulted in a year-round road south to Clear and, to the north, a bridge that opened easier travel to Fairbanks. In 1967, the community was devastated by one of the largest floods ever recorded in the valley. The George Parks Highway was completed in 1971, providing a shorter, more direct route to Anchorage.

NEWTOK VILLAGE

Tribe: Yup'ik   Total Area of Entitlement: 92,160 acres   Tribal Enrollment: 429

The people of Newtok, a traditional Yup'ik village, share a strong cultural heritage with the communities of Tununak, Nightmute, Toksook Bay, and Chefornak on nearby Nelson Island in southwestern Alaska. Together the five villages make up the Qualuyaarmiut, or "Dip Net People," whose ancestors have lived on the Bering Sea coast for at least 2,000 years. Being relatively isolated, the village had only intermittent outside contact until the 1920s.

Around 1949, the village was relocated from Old Kealavik, ten miles away, to its present position on higher ground. A school was built in 1958, although many high school students traveled to Bethel, St. Mary's, Sitka, or Anchorage to complete their education. This was often their first exposure to life outside the village; they returned with command of the English language and modern American culture, as well as a high rate of tuberculosis, resulting in many residents being sent away for treatment.

As recently as the 1960s, the villagers made an annual journey by dogsled, before the spring ice breakup, to their traditional summer fishing camp at Nilikhrguk, on the north coast of Nelson Island, where they lived in tents through the summer. After the herring run, men traveled to the Bristol Bay area to work in the canneries. The 1970s saw the abandonment of the last *qasgiq*, the traditional men's community house. Housing projects were built, and a high school was constructed in Newtok in the 1980s.

Newtok is governed by a traditional village council headed by a president. Employment opportunities in Newtok are primarily in commercial fishing, the school, government offices, the health clinic, and other village services.

Newtok maintains an active subsistence lifestyle with a relatively high degree of adherence to historic cultural practice and customs. Its observance of tradition is perhaps stronger than in other parts of Alaska due to its isolation in extreme southwest coastal Alaska, on the Ninglick River, north of Nelson Island, in the Yukon-Kuskokwim Delta region. The village area encompasses one square mile of land, approximately 20 miles inland from the Bering Sea. The present village site is experiencing severe erosion along the banks of the Ninglick River. The average annual erosion rate is 90 feet per year, and it is expected that the land under Newtok will erode by

SOCIAL STRUCTURE

An Inuit couple sit outside an igloo in northwestern Greenland. About 88 percent of Greenland's population are Inuit or part Inuit.

Among the Inuit, the Arctic people of Canada, the roles of men and women were sharply defined in traditional nomadic society. Men were the hunters. They tracked and killed the caribou and seals. Women ran the home, butchered meat, cooked, and produced the clothing that made survival possible.

Life required both sets of skills, so marriage was the basis of society. A married woman was close to her man's equal. She could own property and had a voice in family decisions. The couple and their children moved with the seasons. They would band with a few other families for a few months, then with different ones. The intricate hierarchies so common among people who lived in gentler environments weren't important.

In the parts of Canada and Alaska where food was more plentiful, social groups were more complex. Villages were frequently located in one place through the year. Nuclear families existed, but larger kin groups and clans were dominant. For instance, among the Yup'ik of southwestern Alaska, women and children lived in separate family houses, while the men and older boys of a clan lived in a large men's house, called a *qasgi*, where the young men were taught to make kayaks and weapons. A large village might have several such groupings and a population of several hundred people. ■

2011. In an exchange with the federal government, the people of Newtok will relocate their village across the Ninglick River to an upland area in the Yukon Delta National Wildlife Refuge on Nelson Island. The Newtok Corporation will give up approximately 11,105 acres on the mainland and relinquish selection rights to approximately 996 acres on Baird Inlet Island. Both locations are important wildlife habitats. In exchange, the corporation will receive title to approximately 10,943 acres.

Inuit hunters face challenges on the broken ice of Lancaster Sound, in Canada's Baffin Bay.

SHEILA WATT-CLOUTIER

Nobel Prize nominee

Sheila Watt-Cloutier, a Canadian Inuit who has worked to raise global awareness of climate change and human rights, was born in 1953 in Kuujjuaq, a village in the far northern Nunavik portion of Quebec. She had a traditional childhood, she has said, traveling only by foot and dogsled for the first ten years of her life.

Watt-Cloutier argues that greenhouse gas emissions and the resulting global climate change violate the cultural and environmental rights of the Inuit, who live so close to the shrinking polar ice. She has also campaigned against persistent organic pollutants, chemicals such as pesticides that enter the Arctic food chain. "We must now speak environment, economy, foreign policy, health, and human rights in the same breath. Everything is connected," she tells audiences.

From 1995 to 2002, Watt-Cloutier was the Canadian president of the Inuit Circumpolar Council, a group that combines U.S., Canadian, Russian, and Greenland peoples to advocate for their shared interests. From 2002 until 2006, she was the international chair of that group. She was nominated for a Nobel Peace Prize in 2007 for her climate change advocacy, the year that former U.S. vice president Al Gore won the prize for his work in the same field. ■

Sheila Watt-Cloutier has worked internationally to raise consciousness about climate change.

NIKOLAI VILLAGE

Tribe: Upper Kuskokwim Athabascan   **Total Area of Entitlement:** 69,120 acres   **Tribal Enrollment:** 167

Nikolai is historically an Upper Kuskokwim Athabascan village centered on subsistence activities. It became the site of a trading post and roadhouse during the gold rush of the late 19th century. Situated on the Rainy Pass Trail, it connected the Ophir mining district to Cook Inlet and had a population of six in 1899. It later became a winter trail station along the Nenana-McGrath Trail, which was used until 1926. By 1927, the St. Nicholas Orthodox Church was constructed. In 1948, a private school was established, and in 1949 a post office opened.

The community was first opened to year-round accessibility in 1962, when residents cleared an airstrip. The city was incorporated in 1970. The present site was established around 1918 and serves as a checkpoint during the Iditarod dogsled race from Anchorage to Nome, held annually in March. Winter weather is highly conducive to winter sports,

Central Alaskan Yup'ik, Eskimo-Aleut language family

"Niicuynissuun"

("Radio"—literally, "instrument for listening")

with temperatures ranging from minus 62 degrees Fahrenheit to zero degrees. However, days are short in winter, with December having only about four hours of daylight.

Upper Kuskokwim Athabascan is spoken in the villages of Nikolai, Telida, and McGrath in the Upper Kuskokwim River drainage. Of a total population of about 160 people, about 40 still speak the language.

Nikolai is on the south fork of the Kuskokwim River, 46 miles east of McGrath, within 60 miles of Denali National Park and Preserve and the Nowitna National Wildlife Refuge, and approximately 100 miles from the eastern border of the Innoko National Wildlife Refuge and 100 miles north of the Lake Clark National Park and Preserve. The city encompasses 4.5 square miles of land and 0.3 square mile of water at an average elevation of approximately 1,500 feet above sea level. The Kuskokwim River is frozen over from October through June, and the region experiences approximately 21 hours of daylight in June.

Nikolai was incorporated as a second-class city in 1970, with a mayor and city council. It is located

YUP'IK

The Yup'ik are the peoples of Alaska and Siberia who spoke one of the languages in the Yup'ik family. "Yup'ik," with an apostrophe to denote a hard p, refers to the people who speak Central Alaskan Yup'ik; without the apostrophe, "Yupik" refers to a smaller group that lives on St. Lawrence Island, speaks the related Siberian Yupik language, and shares roots with their Russian kin. Alaskans still use the term "Eskimo" to refer collectively to the state's Inuit and Yup'ik peoples—two groups that are linguistically and historically different, although the icy climate where they all live means they share many cultural similarities.

The Yup'ik live in the southwestern part of the state, along the Bering Sea and along the rivers of the Yukon-Kuskokwim Delta, from Bristol Bay in the south to Norton Sound in the north. They were one of the last of the Native peoples to come in regular contact with outsiders. Children in a number of villages still learn their languages at home as a mother tongue, a rarity in Alaska.

Culture Shaped by Climate

Their homeland's climate can be one of the harshest on the planet, but the Yup'ik adapted to it and did much more than survive. They developed complex artistic forms, especially along the Bering Sea, that celebrated nature and their connection to it. Utilitarian objects necessary for survival, such as clothing, hunting tools, and food vessels, were elaborately decorated. They carved ivory, adorned garments with fur and feathers, and weaved geometric and nature-inspired patterns into their baskets.

Especially in the late winter, when hunting and gathering were difficult and stored food was available, there was time for ceremonies and dancing as well as for decorative carving and other crafts. Powerful shamans—usually male, but

A Yup'ik woman in Togiak, Alaska, fillets red salmon to prepare for winter.

sometimes female—connected people with the spirits. The masks some tribes used for ceremonial purposes evoked animal spirits and the natural world.

Moving with the Seasons

The Yup'ik (and the related Cup'ik) traditionally traveled with the seasons, moving from their winter villages to summer camps along the coast and rivers to access the fish, animals, and plants upon which they relied—although they were more stable than other precontact peoples who relied on more migratory game such as caribou. In some communities, once they were old enough to leave their mothers, men lived in the winter in *qasgiq*, or men's community

center. These were often centers for singing, dancing, and ceremonies. Women brought the food and firewood the men used at the house. Women and little children lived in smaller communal buildings called *ena*. Winter dwellings were usually partly underground, to conserve warmth.

Those who lived close to the southwestern Alaska coast hunted walrus, seals, and small whales, but not large whales, which seldom came to this shallow coastal region. That also meant foreign whalers seldom came, keeping European contact with these people to a minimum, at least compared with most other northern peoples. Interior groups hunted birds and fish as well as land animals such as caribou and bears. Again, outsiders weren't very interested in their resources in the 18th and 19th centuries, except for the fur trade.

Social organization was generally informal, not hierarchical. Labor was divided according to the sexes, with women preparing food, making clothing, and rearing children, and men hunting. Successful hunters often became community leaders.

In Alaska, the Siberian Yupik live on St. Lawrence Island, which is about 50 miles from Russia. Until the late 19th century, their ties were with their Russian kin, rather than with Alaska. But the 20th-century Cold War divided them. It was not until the collapse of the Soviet Union that ties were renewed.

The Tribes Today

The Central Yup'ik are the most numerous of Alaska's Native population groups. The Alaska Native Language Center estimates there are 25,000, with more than 10,000 speaking the Yup'ik language—the largest group of speakers of any of the Alaskan Native languages. There are about 1,400 Siberian Yupik in Alaska (1,000 speaking the language) and another 900 in Russia. Many still practice a degree of subsistence hunting and harvesting, although they now use powerboats and snowmobiles instead of traditional tools.

These people are shareholders in one of several different Alaska Native corporations, depending on where they live. The Bering Straits Native Corporation includes Central Yup'ik and Siberian Yupik as well as Inupiat who live on the northern coast.

The Calista Corporation—the name comes from the Yup'ik for "work" or "worker"—is made up of those people who live in the Yukon-Kuskokwim Delta, including Yup'ik, Cup'ik, and Athabascans. Nearly all the settlements are close to water and originated as fishing villages. The corporation says that its shareholders have the most intact traditional culture in the state, with most of them speaking Native languages.

Shareholders of the Bristol Bay Corporation include Yup'ik as well as other groups. The Yup'ik there traditionally subsisted on caribou, moose, bear, waterfowl, ptarmigan, salmon, and other fish. Brown bears still outnumber people in the Bristol Bay region. ■

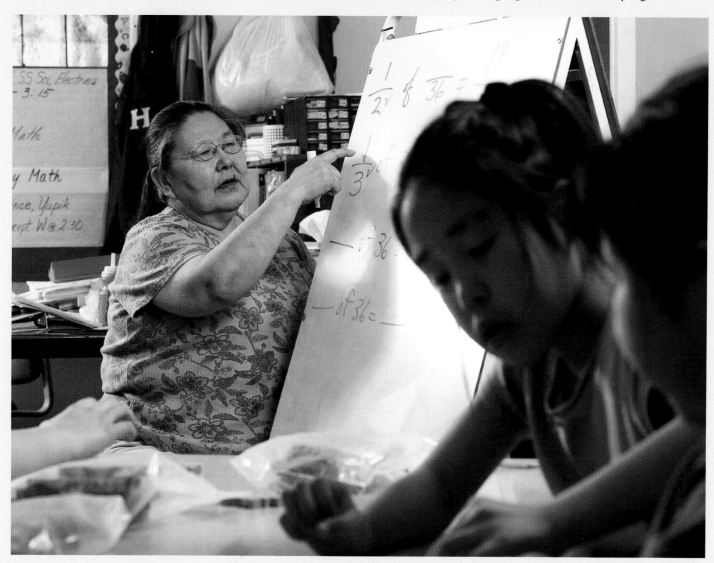

A Native woman teaches math to children in a classroom in Akiachak, Alaska, a Yup'ik village in the western part of the state.

in the Unorganized Borough. Nikolai Village, also known as Nikolai Edzeno' Village Council, is a BIA-recognized Native entity with a traditional council headed by a first chief.

Access to Nikolai is by air or water only, and the economy depends to a large extent on seasonal cash jobs and year-round subsistence activities. Residents harvest salmon, bear, moose, caribou, and rabbits. Some tend gardens during the short growing season, and others depend upon trapping (both for commercial and personal purposes) and production and sales of Native handicrafts. Village employment peaks during the summer months, when construction gets under way. Governments provide all year-round employment opportunities in the village.

PRIBILOF ISLANDS ALEUT COMMUNITIES OF ST. PAUL AND ST. GEORGE ISLANDS

Tribe: Unangan   **Total Areas of Entitlement:** St. George 129,082 acres; St. Paul 154,413 acres   **Tribal Enrollments:** St. George 131; St. Paul 653

A carved ivory handle, shaped like a wolf's head, is used for pulling dead seals back from the hunt.

The St. Paul and St. George Islands communities are actually a single Alaskan Native entity with two cities, St. George and St. Paul. They are located on the Pribilof Islands, in the south-central Bering Sea, 300 miles west of the Alaska mainland. The islands are predominantly Unangan communities, with small Inupiat and Indian populations.

The Pribilof Islands were discovered in 1786 by Russian fur traders searching for the famed northern fur seal breeding grounds. During the height of the fur trade, the Russian American Company enslaved and relocated the Unangan from Atka and Unalaska to the islands to hunt fur seals; their descendants live there today. Between 1870 and 1910, the U.S. government leased the Pribilof Islands to private companies, which provided housing, food, and medical care to the Unangan in exchange for work in the fur

seal plant. In 1910, the U.S. Bureau of Fisheries took control of the islands, but poverty conditions ensued due to overharvesting the seals. During World War II, residents were moved to southeast Alaska as part of the area-wide evacuation.

In 1979, the Pribilof Unangan received $8.5 million in partial compensation for the unjust treatment to which they had been subjected under federal administration between 1870 and 1946. After formally ending the commercial seal harvest and federal oversight in 1983, the U.S. government provided $8 million and $12 million, respectively, to help develop and diversify the economies of St. George and St. Paul. This left residents to develop an economy based on commercial fishing, which lasted until the opilio crab decline in 2000, when tourism joined commercial fishing as the community's main economic forces.

The islands are in the most diverse biological region in the Northern Hemisphere, providing nesting and breeding grounds for thousands of migratory marine mammals and birds.

QAWALANGIN TRIBE OF UNALASKA

Tribe: Unangan   **Total Area of Entitlement:** 115,200 acres   **Tribal Enrollment:** 657

Unalaska, where Dutch Harbor is located, began as an Unangan village influenced by early Russian explorers and the fur seal industry. The community is now primarily non-Native and culturally diverse, but subsistence activities remain central to the culture of the Unangan community.

During the late 18th-century fur trade, hunters were enslaved and relocated to the area by the Russian American Company to work in the fur seal harvest. In 1820, the Russian Orthodox Church of the Holy Ascension was built, and the first priest of Unalaska, Ivan Veniaminov, composed the first Unangan writing system with local assistance in order to translate scripture into Unangan. Since the Unangan were not forced to give up their language or culture by the Russian Orthodox priests, the church remained strong in the community.

Dutch Harbor provides natural protection for fishing vessels, and its rich resources have allowed Unalaska to develop rapidly. The great-circle shipping route from major West Coast ports to the

Pacific Rim nations passes within just 50 miles of the town.

The Qawalangin Native residents today work with the Alaska Rural Systemic Initiative in hosting Camp Qungaayu, which brings together Unangan elders, mentors, and outside biologists to train the younger generation in traditional subsistence techniques and cultural practices.

CLOTHING

In the far north, it's usually cold and often wet. Today, Native people generally wear the same types of clothing as other Alaskans or Canadians. But before Gore-Tex and other technically advanced fabrics, staying warm and dry meant dressing in the skins and furs of animals. Making clothing—women's domain—began with scraping and dressing the skins, sometimes by tanning them in urine and scraping off the hair. Thread was made from animal sinew, which swelled when wet and helped keep garments waterproof.

Tailoring was the key to producing warm Eskimo winter clothing, often made from caribou fur, which has hair that is hollow, light, and insulating. Where caribou were not available, winter clothes were sewn from duck, goose, or auklet skins. Cormorant garments were desirable for their light weight and iridescent sheen and were used in ceremonies. Ground squirrel was prized by Yup'ik people for light summer garments. Sealskin, which is waterproof, was commonly used for tough summer work clothing. Rain jackets were made from the guts of sea mammals, sewn in horizontal strips in southern and southwestern Alaska and in vertical strips on St. Lawrence Island. These jackets, called *kamleika* by the Sugpiaq (Alutiiq) and Unangan, were waterproof, strong, and light.

In the coldest areas, people dressed in parkas of bird skins, polar bear hide, or caribou fur fitted with hoods trimmed with a fringe of wolverine, wolf, or dog fur. In the Kotzebue Sound area of northwestern Alaska, people wore inner parkas, with the

fur on the inside; outer parkas, with the fur side out; inner and outer pants; and socks and boots. Greenlanders usually made their pants from polar bear fur. Sealskin was used by most Eskimo peoples for boots, and socks were made from rabbit fur or woven grass. Fancy ceremonial parkas were fashioned from patterns of brightly contrasting furs and were edged with embroidery, dyed strips of hairless pelt, and tassels. Western Alaskan garments often were fitted with bright wedge-shaped gores on either side of the neck that made the wearer look like a walrus. Headgear was produced from a

variety of furs and bird skins and was often decorated with strings of glass beads and colorful fur strips.

Northern Natives had fewer materials to make clothing from and wore long tunic-like garments of tanned and dehaired deer or elk skin. Outer garments were made from caribou, moose, or deer fur. Leggings and moccasins, or boots in the winter, completed the attire. Before European contact, Indian outer garments were often decorated with patterns of dyed porcupine quill; afterward, floral patterns made from brightly colored trade beads were common. ■

Coats made from the guts of sea mammals are lightweight and waterproof, just right for staying comfortable in wet weather.

VILLAGE OF
ANAKTUVUK PASS

Tribe: Nunamiut   **Total Area of Entitlement:** 92,160 acres
Tribal Enrollment: 348

Inuit men, women, and children near Barrow, Alaska, gather around a captured bowhead whale before it is stripped of its skin and blubber.

T he Village of Anaktuvuk Pass, or "The Place of Caribou Droppings," is the last remaining settlement of the Nunamiut—inland northern Inupiat. Though today's villagers now live a more sedentary lifestyle than their nomadic predecessors,

Nunamiut residents continue to rely on subsistence activities. Anaktuvuk Pass is the only noncoastal community in the borough, and the Nunamiut are the only people in the borough dependent on caribou rather than fish and marine mammals or employment in the petroleum industry.

Cultural changes in response to Western civilization and the dearth of caribou in the mid-1920s forced the Nunamiut to leave the Brooks Range. In 1938, many coastal Nunamiuts returned to the of the Arctic National Park and Preserve, on the divide between the Anaktuvuk and John Rivers in the central Brooks Range. It is treeless, at 2,200 feet in elevation, and much of the land is subject to flooding.

VILLAGE OF OLD HARBOR

Tribe: Alutiiq   **Total Area of Entitlement: 115,200 acres**
Tribal Enrollment: 606

Before the Russian conquest, there had been about 10,000 Alutiiq people spread among the numerous villages in the Kodiak Archipelago. People lived in dozens of large villages under the leadership of hereditary chiefs. Alutiiq people traded and intermarried with the Unangan of the Aleutian Islands, the Central Yupiit and Dena'ina Athabascans to the north, and the Tlingit to the east. Oral histories also tell of battles over territory and resources. Old Harbor is a traditional Koniag Alutiiq village with a subsistence-centered culture, settled more than 5,000 years ago.

In 1784, Russians led by Grigorii Shelikhov massacred several hundred Alutiiq men, women, and children at Refuge Rock, a small islet by Sitkalidik Island. The Russians held Alutiiq hostages at Three Saints Harbor before moving to their new headquarters at Paul's Harbor (Kodiak) in 1793. The settlement they left behind at Three Saints became known as the "old harbor." Its Alutiiq residents labored for the Russians by hunting sea otters and producing foods such as dried fish, whale meat, and berries. This colony was devastated by a tsunami, and the people relocated to the northeast coast and did not return until 1884. Eighty years later, the Good Friday earthquake and resulting tsunami destroyed the community; only two homes and the church remained standing. The community has since been rebuilt in the same location.

Old Harbor's economy is centered around commercial salmon fishing. Most residents depend to some extent on subsistence activities to supplement their incomes. Salmon, halibut, crab, deer, seal, rabbit, and bear are harvested.

MYTH OR FACT?

Eskimos kiss by rubbing noses.

MYTH

The traditional Inuit greeting of rubbing noses, known as a *kunik*, is not a romantic kiss. It's a sign of affection and welcome, often exchanged among family members.

mountains, taking up residence at Killik River and Chandler Lake. Then, in 1949, a new migration began as families from Chandler Lake made their way to Anaktuvuk Pass. The settlement grew as the Killik River group joined them, and later, Nunamiuts from other areas.

The Village of Anaktuvuk Pass is a federally recognized tribe and traditional tribal council, which is also known as the Nasragmiut Tribal Council. The community is located within the Gates

THE PLAINS

THE PLAINS

THE PLAINS AREA EXTENDS FROM MID-SASKATCHEWAN IN THE NORTH TO mid-Texas in the south, with the Mississippi River to the east and the deserts to the west. The many tribes who inhabited this vast region depended on the buffalo for their sustenance, and everything in their world reflected this association. They became migratory peoples who followed the herds and developed into mighty warriors and hunters.

Most civilizations organize a form of government, moral standards, a religious belief system, and other such necessities. Foremost, a society must place a high value on its children, for through children there is a future and a degree of immortality.

Plains Indian children traditionally learned in several ways, but the main one was oral tradition. The elders shared a lifetime of knowledge with them, not in crowded classrooms but often around a flickering campfire. With the canopy of stars high above, the children were taught the origins of their tribe. They could learn why dog is man's best friend, why the chipmunk has spots, and why the bear must live alone.

As teenagers, boys on the Plains would join the first of the age-graded tribal societies, where they would come together with other youths to pray, hold ceremonies, hunt, and practice to be warriors. When older, they could enter the next society and learn more about the ways of a hunter and warrior, primary skills to ensure the continuity of the tribes.

A girl's world centered around the home. Her relatives taught her how to gather and prepare food, how to tan hides, and how to fashion clothing. Most of the attractively decorated moccasins, shirts, dresses, leggings, and other traditional artworks were created by women.

Indians of the Plains believed in a Supreme Being, but one without human form. He is sometimes called the Great Spirit, the One Above, or simply Grandfather. He is an all-powerful force, an essence. He is in the sweet spring rain that falls upon the people's faces or the bright flowers that color the meadows. He teaches that all things have power and deserve respect. Birds, trees, and even rocks have this essence and deserve a place on Mother Earth. Everyone must take care of this Mother if we are to survive. These beliefs and formal ceremonies, such as a Sun Dance, united the tribe.

Life changed with European contact. The foreigners came from a world that placed the highest value on wealth. They subdued the Native people in their search for riches. Missionaries campaigned to erase Native traditions and replace them with Christianity. The people who

> PLAINS INDIAN CHILDREN TRADITIONALLY LEARNED IN SEVERAL WAYS, BUT THE MAIN ONE WAS ORAL TRADITION. THE ELDERS SHARED A LIFETIME OF KNOWLEDGE WITH THEM.

Preceding pages: With the sun just below the horizon, a South Dakota Native American holds a buffalo skull up toward the sky while on a spirit quest. A deep connection to nature is a hallmark of Native spirituality. Opposite: A Native American dances in traditional costume at a powwow being held in Browning, Montana.

120°   110°   100°

Many Canadian Indian reserves have a number as part of their official name.

Cold Lake 149
Onion Lake 119-1
Ministikwan 161
Big River 118
Kehiwin 123
Ahtahkakoop 104
White Fish Lake 128
Thunderchild First Nation 115B
Mistawasis 103
Alexander 134
Saddle Lake 125
Little Red River 106C
Alexis 133
Sturgeon Lake 101
Wabamun 133A
Edmonton
Puskiakiwenin 122
Stony Plain 135
Unipouheos 121
Louis Bull 138b
Seekaskootch 119
O'Chiese 203
Ermineskin 138
Prince Albert
Samson 137
Little Pine 116
James Smith 100
Sweet Grass 111
Muskoday First Nation
North Battleford
Beardy's 97 and Okemasis 96
Red Pheasant 108
Pine Creek 66A

BRITISH COLUMBIA
ALBERTA
SASKATCHEWAN
MANITOBA
ONTARIO

Saskatoon

Lake Winnipeg

Stoney 142, 143, 144
Calgary
Tsuu T'ina Nation 145
Siksika 146
Medicine Hat
Regina
Poorman 88
Cote 64
Waywayseecappo First Nation
Ebb and Flow 52
Gordon 86
Dog Creek 46
Peepeekisis 81
Ochapowace 71
Sandy Bay 5
Cowessess 73
Waywayseecappo
Assiniboine 76
Sioux Valley Dakota Nation
Brandon
White Bear 70

Lake Manitoba

Piikani 147
Lethbridge
Blood 148
Blackfeet 20
Turtle Mountain 331
Turtle Mountain 331
Turtle Mountain 331
Turtle Mountain 331
White Bear 70
Winnipeg
Lake of the Woods

Turtle Mt. 331
44 Rocky Boy's
Fort Belknap
Turtle Mt. 331
Fort Peck 10
Turtle Mt. 331
Turtle Mt. 331
Turtle Mt. 331
Turtle Mt. 331
Turtle Mt. 331
Spirit Lake 303
Grand Forks
Upper Red L.
Lower Red L.

Great Falls
87
Fort Berthold 321
Minot
Turtle Mt. 331
WASH.
ROCKY
MONTANA
NORTH DAKOTA
Fargo
MINNESOTA
IDAHO
Missoula
Helena
Bismarck
Lake Sakakawea
St. Croix
Billings
Crow 71
Crow 71
Turtle Mt. 331
Standing Rock
St. Paul
WIS.
Crow 71
Northern Cheyenne 181
Turtle Mt. 331
Cheyenne River 41
Lake Traverse 295
Minneapolis
SOUTH DAKOTA
Upper Sioux 336
Northern Cheyenne 181
Cheyenne River 41
Pierre
Lower Sioux 146
Rapid City
Lower Brule 143
Crow Creek 70
Flandreau 85
Sioux Falls
Wind River 8
Pine Ridge 185
Rosebud 259
Yankton 355
Sac & Fox, Meskwaki Settlement 263
WYOMING
222 Ponca
Santee 275
Sioux City
Casper
IOWA
Winnebago 351
Des Moines
Omaha 187
NEBRASKA
Winnebago 351
Omaha
Lincoln
Cheyenne
Iowa 112
Denver
Sac & Fox 262
Kickapoo 128
COLORADO
Prairie Band of Potawatomi 225
Topeka
Kansas City
St. Louis
Jefferson City
Colorado Springs
KANSAS
MISSOURI
Pueblo
193
Springfield
159, 210, 245, 285, 288
Dodge City
Wichita
170
78
221
123
74
354
324
Osage 191
NEW MEXICO
192
207
Tulsa
39
113
335
Santa Fe
40
261
175
OKLA.
129
320
126
Oklahoma City
27 7 1
279
5
130
349
ARKANSAS
73
93
42
Little Rock
53
Memphis
46
TENN.
Amarillo
Wichita Falls
MISS.
Lubbock
Roswell
Llano Estacado
Fort Worth
Dallas
Shreveport
Odessa
Waco
LOUISIANA
Baton Rouge
Del Rio
Austin
San Antonio
Houston
Galveston
Gulf of Mexico

30°N

50°
40°
30°N

THE PLAINS

SCALE
1 : 13,000,000

0   200   400
statute miles

0   200   400
kilometers

Map Key

Indian regional boundary as represented in this book.
(See pages 14–15 for North American map showing all eight regions depicted in this work.)

Canadian Aboriginal Land

Federal Indian Reservation (occupied by one or more tribal entities)

△ Tribe receiving federal recognition but without a designated reservation

Poorman 88   Canadian Indian Reserve name

Omaha   Federal Reservation name

187   Resident tribe
(Number correlates to tribal list on pages 358–361.)

★ State or provincial capital

• Selected city or town

were not killed by the foreigners and their deadly new diseases were removed westward so the newcomers could take their land.

Treaties were at first negotiated between the tribes and England or France, then the United States and Canada, promising "the utmost good faith" and peace while they defined the Indian land holdings. But almost as soon as the treaties were made, they were broken.

Over the years, the Indian people rose up in arms to resist the invasion. There were some victories—such as at Little Big Horn, in what is now Montana, in 1876 when the Sioux and Cheyenne wiped out Gen. George Armstrong Custer's forces—but not enough. For many, resistance ended on a bitter, frozen day at Wounded Knee, South Dakota, where on December 29, 1890, the U.S. Army massacred Sioux men, women, and children.

IN SURVIVAL THERE IS VICTORY, AND THE INDIAN PEOPLE SOMEHOW HUNG ON, EVEN IN THEIR POVERTY.

A more insidious "removal" movement surged in the 1900s. Realizing that adults were usually set in their ways, the promoters of "Christianity and Civilization" began to take Indian children from their parents and culture, often sending them to government-backed boarding schools. After their long hair was shorn, they were forced to don uniforms. Traditional foods were unavailable. They were forbidden to practice their spiritual ways and were punished if they spoke their Native language. Horror stories of these schools are still told on the reservations.

The profession of anthropology developed at the same time extermination threatened the tribes. Anthropologists, who for the most part worked for museums, decided that even if they could not save the Indian people, they could preserve elements of their culture. Wave after wave of anthropologists descended upon Indian Country to record stories, collect ethnographic materials, establish theories, write books, and become famous.

In the early 20th century, the pressure began to ease. The Indian people were not seen as a threat anymore. Their numbers had been drastically lowered, they held title to only 2 percent of what had been their land, their culture was nearly destroyed, and their children were in distant schools.

But in survival there is victory, and the Indian people somehow hung on, even in their poverty. The exiled students came home and over time combined their new skills and knowledge with the culture of those who had been fortunate enough to remain.

American Indians are still under siege from those who want to abrogate the treaties. Farmers, ranchers, and mining companies want the remaining water rights, land, and minerals. Every day, the tribes do battle with them and the politicians who depend upon them for reelection. Nonetheless, in the past few decades, the Indian world has experienced a cultural renaissance as the population has increased and some young people have embraced tradition while working for economic and social betterment. Indian people can be found in most professions as they pursue their chosen way, enrolling in college like never before, but now by choice, not compulsion. ■

ABSENTEE SHAWNEE RESERVATION

Tribe: Absentee-Shawnee Tribe of Indians of Oklahoma   Current Location: Oklahoma
Total Area: 11,680 acres   Tribal Enrollment: 3,029

The Shawnee are an Algonquian tribe who controlled a vast swath of territory from Pennsylvania to the southern Appalachians prior to the 17th century. "Shawnee" is derived from the Algonquian term *Shawun* (South) or *Shawunogi* (Southerners). The Shawnee were village dwellers with a sophisticated material culture. They farmed, hunted, and maintained complex trade networks.

In 1872, nearly three decades after the Absentee Shawnee had abandoned Kansas for Indian Territory, the tribe received title to a portion of a reservation between the north and south forks of the Canadian River near present-day Shawnee, Oklahoma. The other portion of the reservation went to the Citizen Band of Potawatomi.

The tribe includes two bands that occupy two geographically distinct communities; the Big Jim Band is in Cleveland County, and the White Turkey Band is in Pottawatomie County near the city of Shawnee. The tribe's ancestral homeland lies in the region of Ohio and Kentucky. During the 19th century, the U.S. government removed the tribe to what is now the state of Kansas. The tribe absented itself from the reservation in Kansas in 1845 (thus the name), relocating to Indian Territory (in Oklahoma). The Big Jim Band settled along the Deep Fork River, while the White Turkey Band settled in its present site near Shawnee, Oklahoma. In 1886, the U.S. Army uprooted the Big Jim Band again, moving them to the site of its present community in Cleveland County. There are 12,002 acres in federal trust, most of which are allotted, forming a checkerboard pattern.

After the passage of the Dawes Act of 1887, most tribal members accepted individual allotments,

A pair of Cree children's moccasins decorated with a beadwork flower motif. Nature frequently provides inspiration to Native artists.

and by 1900 most of the tribe had been more or less assimilated into mainstream American culture. The Absentee Shawnees following this path were of the White Turkey Band, named for their assimilationist chief. The Big Jim Band, on the other hand, fiercely opposed assimilation and even considered moving to Mexico, where they hoped to find the freedom to maintain their communal traditions. Hard feelings passed between the two bands, though they were finally organized as one tribe under the Oklahoma Indian Welfare Act of 1936.

The tribe maintains a number of cultural traditions, such as the Big Jim Band's tribal thanksgiving dances in the fall, the Green Corn Dances held during both the spring and fall, and the ceremonial War Dance that takes place in August near Little Axe. The Absentee Shawnee Tribe has the largest number of members of any of the three Shawnee bands in Oklahoma who continue to speak the Native language.

ALABAMA-QUASSARTE TRIBAL TOWN

Tribe: Alabama-Quassarte Tribal Town   Current Location: Oklahoma   Total Area: 80 acres   Tribal Enrollment: 336

The Alabama-Quassarte (Coushattas or "weed gatherers") are descendants of the Alabama people, a Muscogean-speaking tribe of the southeastern United States. Early Euro-American settlers in the region, beginning in the 18th century, referred to them as "Alabama" or "Creek." The Alabama lived in riverfront or coastal villages in the area of present-day Alabama, Louisiana, and western Florida, practicing a subsistence lifestyle based on hunting, fishing, and horticulture. These people demonstrated a cultural link to the prehistoric Caddoan and Mississippi cultures and were linguistically and culturally related to the Yamasee, Seminole, Apalachee, Choctaw, and Chickasaw.

Hernando de Soto led the first party of Europeans into Alabama/Creek territory in 1539; over the next two centuries, the lower southeastern portion of the continent became an economic and military battleground for the competing European powers. The Creek allied with the English against the Spanish during the 18th century but eventually became embroiled in warfare with other tribes competing for English trade items. As a subgroup of the Creek, the Alabama formed part of the Five Civilized Tribes, a name applied to the Choctaw, Chickasaw, Creek, Cherokee, and Seminole by English settlers because of their rapid adoption of many Euro-American cultural practices. Warfare between Creeks arose during the War of 1812, as different bands declared allegiance to either the British or the United States.

A massive influx of American settlers into the Southeast during the early 19th century led President Andrew Jackson to sign the Removal Bill in 1830, giving him the power to exchange land west of the Mississippi for lands held by southeastern tribes. In 1836, the U.S. Army forced the Creek to relocate to Indian

Wichita, Caddoan Language Family

"Ná꞉sa꞉khí'nnih"
(Sunday—"when it is his day")

"Kíriwaré꞉sa꞉kh'innih"
(Monday—"when it is no longer his day")

"Wicha kínné꞉sa꞉khí'innih"
(Tuesday—"twice it's not his day")

"Nackháti꞉kih"
(Wednesday—"the middle day")

"Ní꞉c'arhi'irhé꞉sishah"
(Thursday—"the day they go to stay overnight")

"Acs nasa꞉khaskhírih"
(Friday—"when a good day is going by")

"Wa꞉khácsa꞉khir'a"
(Saturday—"cow day")

Territory. In eastern Oklahoma, the Creek became relatively prosperous farmers. The area's topography is typical of the southern Great Plains, with gently rolling grass-covered hills; trees and other relatively dense vegetation are found only in riparian areas.

They eventually lost most of their tribal lands through allotment, however. Fortunately, despite the devastating effects of relocation and allotment, the tribe has succeeded in maintaining its tribal culture; the Muscogean language continues to be spoken by tribal youths.

APACHE TRIBE OF OKLAHOMA RESERVATION

Tribe: Apache Tribe of Oklahoma
Current Location: Oklahoma   Total Area (jointly held): 189,263 acres   Tribal Enrollment: 1,860

Known historically as the Ka-ta-ka, the members of the Apache Tribe of Oklahoma are descendants of the Athabascan-speaking Eastern Apache groups who have inhabited the Plains since the 15th century. However, because of their alliance

D'ARCY MCNICKLE

Scholar of his people

D'Arcy McNickle was a scholar, author, and voice for Indians. He was born in 1904 on the Flathead Indian Reservation in St. Ignatius, Montana, of mixed Cree Métis and Irish heritage.

McNickle left for a federal boarding school in 1914. His commitment to the Indian cause was shaped there, where he was shocked by the constant attempts to undermine Native culture. He attended the University of Montana and then in 1925 sold his land allotment to go to the University of Oxford in England.

He worked in New York as an editor and a writer; his 1936 novel *The Surrounded* was set on the Flathead Reservation and examined cultural identity. That year, he joined the Bureau of Indian Affairs under New Deal reformer John Collier, and he held many posts there over 16 years. He quit the bureau in 1952 because of the U.S. policy of terminating recognition of tribes as sovereign nations.

McNickle went on to spend years as an educator and advocate. In 1944, he had co-founded the National Congress of the American Indian, which worked for tribal sovereignty and treaty rights. In 1972, he helped found the Center for the History of the American Indian at the Newberry Library in Chicago, now the D'Arcy McNickle Center. He was active there until his death in 1977. ∎

D'Arcy McNickle at the Newberry Library, where he founded a center for Indian history.

THE PLAINS

with the more numerous Kiowa tribe, the Plains Apache were commonly referred to as the Kiowa Apache. They were hunters, following the great southern bison herd across the grasslands of western Texas, Oklahoma, and eastern New Mexico. Buffalo represented the centerpiece of Apache life, providing meat, clothing, tools, weapons, and shelter, and the Plains Apache also traded buffalo meat and hides to the Pueblos of the Rio Grande Valley, in exchange for corn, beans, blankets, turquoise, and ceramics.

The arrival of the horse around 1660 transformed the Plains Apache into highly mobile hunters and raiders. During the 18th century, French and Spanish traders arrived, bringing with them guns, horses, and disease. The latter drastically reduced the tribe's population. During the mid-19th century, the United States made a number of treaties with the Southern Plains tribes. In 1865, the unratified Treaty of the Little Arkansas assigned the Plains Apache, Cheyenne, and Arapaho to a common reservation. However, settlers continued to pour into tribal lands, and the Medicine Lodge Treaty of 1867 placed the Apache on a reservation with the Comanche and Kiowa tribes. Reservation lands were opened for allotment during the late 19th century, with most passing into non-Indian hands.

This reservation land is jointly held by the Comanche Nation and the Kiowa Indian Tribe of Oklahoma. Today, tribal members work in a variety of professions in the Anadarko and Fort Cobb areas, and tribal identity and tradition continue to flourish.

NAMES IN THE INDIAN WORLD

Names for people in the Plains Indian world are more meaningful and dynamic than in most other places. Sometimes the name can be the same as that of an ancestor, whether notable or not. My grandfather presented me, his first grandson, with the name of his younger brother, Spotted Otter, who died as a young man. At other times, if something prominent occurred around the time of birth, it could become a name. My daughter is named Daylight, after her maternal great-great-grandmother Coming Daylight, who may have been born just before dawn.

The names of my sons came easily because they are named after their ancestors. The oldest carries the same tribal name as Horse Capture, his great-great-grandfather, even though no one knows the exact meaning of the term. His brother Joseph bears the tribal name for Catcher, a relative who disappeared in the early 1900s.

A time-honored way to determine a baby's name is through dreams or visions. When my oldest son's wife had a baby girl, he was unable to come up with something suitable. I worried about this. Finally, after several restless nights, I had a dream where I saw many birds flying in the willows near a bridge where we played as children. I awoke knowing I was sent a message, but didn't know what it meant. Before falling asleep again, I asked the One Above to be more specific. When the dream returned, one large, white bird emerged from the rest and perched among the willows. I jerked awake, called my son, and told him he could interpret the dream. Since then, the girl's name has been White Bird. ∎

— *George P. Horse Capture, Sr.*

CADDO RESERVATION

Tribe: Caddo Nation of Oklahoma **Current Location:** Oklahoma **Total Area (jointly held):** 55,199 acres **Tribal Enrollment:** 4,911

The Caddo Nation of Oklahoma descends from the Caddoan-speaking people of the lower Red River Valley. For more than 2,000 years, the Caddo lived in villages, practiced horticulture, and built large temple mounds throughout an area now part of southeastern Oklahoma, southwestern Arkansas, northeastern Texas, and northwestern Louisiana. The Spanish explorer Hernando de Soto made contact with the Caddo in the early 1540s. In the 17th century, the French ventured south on the Mississippi River into Caddo territory. Being good traders, bartering furs and salt for European finished goods, the Caddo were able to maintain relative stability despite these early encroachments.

Contact with American settlers migrating westward following the Louisiana Purchase in 1803 brought conflict. During the 1830s, Texans dispossessed the Caddo of their lands, which lay within the Texas Republic. The Caddo were removed to Indian Territory, and they were settled in 1859 at the Wichita Agency and Reservation north of the Washita River. This reservation was dissolved following the Jerome Agreement of 1890, and tribal lands were allotted to individual members. In 1936, the tribal constitution was approved under the Oklahoma Indian Welfare Act. The people were incorporated as the Caddo Tribe of Oklahoma in 1938. In 1963, federal trust lands were restored to the Caddo, Delaware, and Wichita tribes; the lands are presently held in common.

Despite dislocation and relocation, the Caddo retain much of their culture, particularly ceremonial songs and dances. The Nation holds an annual Turkey Dance and Indian Exposition and maintains the Caddo Nation Heritage Museum. The American Indian Hall of Fame and Indian City USA are located in nearby Anadarko.

The Caddo Nation works jointly with the Delaware and Wichita tribes to provide economic opportunity for tribal members in the three-county area that makes up the tribal statistical area. The jointly owned WCD Enterprises raises revenue through leasing land and buildings. The Nation fosters cultural awareness through the cultural center and a traditional language program for Head Start children.

CHEROKEE NATION RESERVATION

Tribe: Cherokee Nation **Current Location:** Oklahoma
Total Area: 91,449 acres **Tribal Enrollment:** 257,824

The Cherokee Nation is the second largest tribe in the United States and the largest in the state of Oklahoma. Prior to European contact, the Cherokee people lived for almost 1,000 years in the southeastern part of North America (see also pages 82–83), with a traditional territory spanning approximately 126,000 square miles. Through a succession of treaties between 1721 and 1819, this vast territory was reduced to the mountainous areas of North Carolina, Tennessee, Georgia, and Alabama.

Football Hall of Famer Jim Thorpe, perhaps the most famous professional athlete of the early 20th century, was of mixed European and Indian heritage. He was born in Oklahoma and his Native name, Wa-Tho-Huk, means "Bright Path."

An extremely progressive, democratic people, the Cherokee often intermarried with white settlers. They had their own educational system throughout the region, improved in part by the Cherokee linguist Sequoyah. Born in 1770 in Taskigi, Tennessee, he codified a syllabary, or alphabet, for the Cherokee people in 1821, providing a written language that the Nation quickly adopted. Today the Cherokee language is spoken by more than 10,000 Cherokees residing in northeastern Oklahoma, and by at least 1,000 Cherokees living in the vicinity of Cherokee, North Carolina.

Although a group of Cherokee people began to migrate west during the early 1800s to avoid the encroachment of European descendants on their

ARAPAHO

I t is said that during one successful hunt by one of the large tribal groups on the Great Plains, after the hunters brought down some buffalo, the women rushed forward to butcher the beasts. Two women began to fight over the innards of one animal. Soon their families joined in. Before matters got out of hand, the men stepped in to talk about what happened. They agreed that the tribe was getting too large and there might be competition over food. One group, the A'aninin (Gros Ventre), therefore broke off from the main body and moved into modern-day Canada. The main group, the Inunaina (Arapaho), moved west. According to tribal beliefs, which are shared among several groups from the immense Algonquian-language stock, this major split happened about 1700.

Northern and Southern Groups

The main body of the Arapaho then seems to have slowly divided again into a northern group that lived along the mountains near the headwaters of the Platte River in Colorado, and the southern branch, which moved toward the Arkansas River. The nomadic tribe finally made peace with the Dakota around 1840; they became long-term allies. The Kiowa and Comanche were their friends, too, but not the Pawnee, Ute, or Shoshone.

The divisions were independent of each other, with the Northern Arapaho living in the sparsely populated northern plains, where for a while hunting remained possible, and the Southern Arapaho living in Kansas and Colorado. But both bands were on or near the routes the settlers took west. Conflicts increased as the buffalo herds became smaller and more Indian land was occupied by the newcomers.

In the north, the Arapaho were in danger as their allies, the Sioux and the

An Arapaho porcupine-quill pouch dating from the late 19th or early 20th century. Encircling the pouch is a fringe of quill-wrapped leather strips and carved deer hooves.

Northern Cheyenne, increasingly conflicted with civilians and federal troops. In the 1850s and '60s, it is estimated that the U.S. took part in almost a thousand battles against the Indian tribes, who waged a gallant resistance. But after years of war, hunger, and deprivation, the Arapaho wanted a treaty that would give them a new secure homeland.

The agreement they finally had thrust upon them, however, was likely not what any of them desired. The Fort Laramie Treaty of 1851 assigned the Arapaho and Cheyenne much of Colorado west to the foothills of the Rockies, plus parts of nearby states. Yet despite the treaty, settlers soon arrived on their land. The Northern Arapaho withdrew to the north and attempted to hold onto part of Wyoming.

Treaties Signed and Broken

The Medicine Lodge Treaty of 1867 is important because it affects much land and many tribes today. It is a set of three agreements signed between the U.S. and the Kiowa, Comanche, Plains Apache, Southern Cheyenne, and Southern Arapaho. The primary goal was to make peace by removing tribes from the westward routes of expansion, to make some provisions for the tribes, and to put the tribes on reservations.

The previous Treaty of the Little Arkansas in 1865 assigned a reservation to the Southern Cheyenne and Arapaho in portions of Kansas and Oklahoma.

The Medicine Lodge Treaty cut their previously assigned territory in half, but they were allowed to hunt as long as there were buffalo. They were to stay away from the whites.

The package of treaties was controversial, and the tribes refused to ratify them. The pacts remained inactive until the Kiowa chief Lone Wolf sued the U.S. government on behalf of some of the tribes. The case, *Lone Wolf* v. *Hitchcock,* was decided by the Supreme Court in 1903. The Court said that the Indians did not merit the protection of the Bill of Rights and that they were "wards of the nation . . . Dependent [on the United States] for their daily food." This precedent, which has never been overturned, holds that Congress has the "power to abrogate the provisions of an Indian treaty," which meant the government was legally allowed to take back land it had previously assigned to the tribes.

On the Reservations

However, the free days of the Arapaho had ended years before the Court ruled. The Northern Arapaho eventually were placed on the 2.3-million-acre Wind River Reservation in west-central Wyoming in 1867, along with their traditional enemies the Shoshone. The tribes now share the reservation; there are about 5,000 Arapaho there and about 2,500 Shoshone.

The Southern Arapaho were settled with the Southern Cheyenne at the Darlington Agency on the North Canadian River in 1847. After 1891, the lands of the Arapaho and Cheyenne were taken away. Each tribal member received 160 acres as an allotment, and the remainder, 3.5 million acres, was opened to non-Indians. The Southern Arapaho united with the Southern Cheyenne in 1935 to form the federally recognized Cheyenne and Arapaho Tribes, based in Concho, Oklahoma.

The Arapaho Indian people are blessed in spite of the loss of their traditional homelands. The source of their tenacity and strength is their unwavering belief in the Creator, the Sun Dance, and their sacred Pipe, all of which survive today. ■

Arapaho teenagers wear the traditional powwow regalia of a jingle dancer and a fancy shawl dancer during the Gift of the Waters pageant in Wyoming.

THE PLAINS

A costumed participant in the Red Earth Festival of Native culture, held annually in Oklahoma City, Oklahoma

territory, the history of the Cherokee people was permanently altered by their forced removal to Indian Territory from their ancestral lands in the Southeast. The discovery of gold in Georgia fueled anti-Cherokee resentment and a thirst for expansion on the part of the new settlers. Upon the recommendation of President James Monroe in his final address to Congress in 1825, the succeeding President, Andrew Jackson, authorized the Indian Removal Act of 1830. Many political and religious leaders such as Senators Daniel Webster and Henry Clay and the Reverend Samuel Worcester, a missionary to the Cherokee, opposed the displacement of the Indians. Worcester even took the matter all the way to the Supreme Court, winning a case against Georgia's attempt to extinguish Indian title to land in the state.

Cherokee Nation v. *Georgia* (1831) and *Worcester* v. *Georgia* (1832), considered two of the most influential decisions in Indian law, challenged the constitutionality of the Removal Act and the U.S. government precedent for unapplied Indian-federal law. The U.S. government used the Treaty of New Echota in 1835 to justify the removal. The treaty, signed by 20 Cherokees, whose supporters numbered only between 5 and 10 percent of the Cherokee population and were known as the Treaty Party, relinquished all lands east of the Mississippi River in exchange for land in Indian Territory and the promise of money, livestock, and various provisions and tools. Opposition to the removal was led by Chief John Ross, of mixed Scottish and Cherokee descent. The Ross Party and most Cherokees opposed the New Echota Treaty, but

Georgia and the U.S. government prevailed, using it as justification to force almost all of the 17,000 Cherokees from their southeastern homeland. An estimated 2,000 to 2,500 Cherokees died from hunger, exposure, and disease during their forced exodus. The journey became memorialized as the Trail of Tears.

After the significant suffering caused by their removal, the Cherokee people settled into their new home and a new age of progress and prosperity that lasted until the American Civil War. The *Cherokee Advocate,* printed in both English and Cherokee, became the first newspaper in the state of Oklahoma, and the *Cherokee Messenger* was its first periodical. By the time of Oklahoma's statehood in 1907, the Cherokee Nation had established an advanced education system. The tribe's 144 elementary schools as well as the Cherokee National Male and Female Seminaries (two higher education institutions) provided learning opportunities to a broad community. With the Cherokee syllabary, the tribe was able to achieve a higher rate of literacy than their white counterparts.

After the war, more Cherokee land was taken to accommodate other tribes displaced by U.S. government policy. The social and economic isolation experienced by the Oklahoma Cherokee after statehood was compounded by the Great Depression and Dust Bowl era of the 1930s. It is estimated that more than a third of the residents of Oklahoma left the state during this time, including many Cherokees. Presidents of the United States appointed various principal chiefs in the 65 years following statehood, with little authority or responsibility, as there was no formalized Cherokee government. Since reorganization in the 1970s, the Cherokee Nation has become a leader in education, health care, housing, vocational training, and economic development in northeastern Oklahoma. An annual three-day Cherokee National Holiday, celebrated since 1953, commemorates the signing of the 1839 Cherokee Constitution each Labor Day weekend. The event has grown into one of the largest in Oklahoma, attracting more than 70,000 people from across the world.

Arapaho, Algonquian language family

"hébes"
("beaver")

"néb, nówo'"
("fish")

"ho'óowu'"
("house")

"wo'ów"
("ice")

"hi' i"
("snow")

Under the indomitable leadership of Principal Chief Wilma P. Mankiller (see page 99), the first elected female chief of any major tribe, the Nation negotiated a PL-638 Self-Governance Agreement with Congress on February 10, 1990. This agreement authorizes the tribe to plan, conduct, consolidate, and administer programs and receive direct funding to deliver services to tribal members.

The Cherokee Family Research Center, located in the Museum Building of the tribe's Heritage Center houses a research library of genealogy materials. The Cherokee National Historical Society, established in 1963, is a tribally sponsored nonprofit organization dedicated to preserving Cherokee history and promoting Cherokee culture and the education of all people. Both Natives and non-Natives are welcome as members of the Cherokee National Historical Society.

CHICKASAW NATION RESERVATION

Tribe: Chickasaw Nation   Current Location: Oklahoma
Total Area: 73,079 acres   Tribal Enrollment: 38,740

One of the so-called Five Civilized Tribes, the Chickasaw Nation today is one of the largest federally recognized tribes.

Before European contact, the Chickasaw tribe, known to its people as "unconquered and unconquerable," lived in stable, sophisticated town sites in a region spread out across present-day Mississippi, Alabama, Tennessee, and Kentucky. In 1540, they encountered Europeans for the first time when Hernando de Soto passed through the area.

During the French and Indian War, the Chickasaw, who were fierce warriors, aided the British in defeating French and Spanish forces and gaining control of what is now the southeastern United States. Because of this, many historians now acknowledge the impact the Chickasaw had upon the emergence of the United States as an English-speaking country. Before their removal from the region in the 1830s, the Chickasaw controlled the waters of the Mississippi River. Although their reputation as warriors led early historians to refer to them as "Spartans of the Mississippi," the Chickasaw maintained a brisk trade with other tribes as well as with the French and the Spanish.

In the 1830s under President Andrew Jackson, the Chickasaw were forcibly removed from their homelands to Indian Territory in what is now Oklahoma. They were assigned to live as part of the Choctaw Nation, with whom they shared a similar language that descended from the Muscogean linguistic family. An 1855 treaty formally severed this relationship, and on March 4, 1856, the Chickasaw Nation was officially reestablished as a tribal government in Tishomingo, Indian Territory. Following the Civil War, the Chickasaw people wrote a new constitution that was adopted on August 16, 1867.

The 1897 Atoka Agreement forced both the Chickasaw and Choctaw into an allotment experiment initiated by the 1887 Dawes Act. In 1902, Congress subsequently enacted a series of measures that effectively terminated tribal existence and fueled an unparalleled exploitation of Indian lands, all of which culminated within a decade in Oklahoma statehood.

By 1920, an estimated 75 percent of all Chickasaw lands, over 4.7 million acres, had passed out of tribal hands by either sale or lease. Virtually all community tribal lands had disappeared. Efforts by the federal government to terminate the Chickasaw Nation by way of the Dawes Act and other legislation in the 1890s and early 1900s failed, however, as did later efforts in the 1950s.

Despite removal from their homeland in the southeastern United States to Indian Territory and subsequent efforts to abolish the Chickasaw Nation, the tribe not only survived but flourished, and has become a valuable asset to the state.

The community is marked by a strong governmental infrastructure and diverse educational, vocational, and social services. A significant portion of the population still speaks the Native language, and from the 1970s onward a strong revival of interest in traditional heritage and cultural practices has emerged.

MYTH OR FACT?
Indians don't have to pay taxes.

MYTH
U.S. Indians pay federal and state taxes just like everyone else.

CHOCTAW NATION OF OKLAHOMA RESERVATION

Tribe: Choctaw Nation of Oklahoma
Current Location: Oklahoma   Total Area: 135,745 acres
Tribal Enrollment: 174,681

The Choctaw originated in what is now Mississippi and areas of Alabama. Under provisions of the Treaty of Dancing Rabbit Creek, the Nation

became the first of the five great southern U.S. tribes to be moved to the Oklahoma area. The entire tribe, minus those able to elude troops, was forced to relocate. Of the more than 20,000 Choctaws forced onto this Trail of Tears, about 12,500 survived to reach their new homeland.

By the 1880s, white settlers, along with the federal government, had their collective eye on Indian Territory. The federal government enforced the General

Native veterans established the All Indian American Legion Post 38, also called the Buffalo American Legion Post after Ponca Tribe veteran Alfred Little Standing Buffalo, in Ponca City, Oklahoma, in 1927.

Allotment Act of 1887 and was met with overt resistance by the Choctaw and the other members of the Five Civilized Tribes (which also included the relocated Cherokee, Chickasaw, Creek, and Seminole). Nevertheless, the tribes had little choice but to acquiesce by signing the Atoka Agreement in 1897, and allotment proceeded in a manner that ultimately removed most reservation land from their collective ownership and allowed it to pass into

BLACKFEET

I t is said that one time, long ago, a tribe was traveling and could not find enough food; they were all hungry. The chiefs agreed that the tribe should temporarily divide into groups to make it easier to find food. Later in the summer, they regrouped. The faces and hands of one northern group were stained red because they ate mostly berries: They became known as Bloods or Kainai. Another group had to walk across a large burned-out area, and their moccasins and leggings were black: They are now known as the Blackfeet in the United States and Blackfoot in Canada, where there are three groups, the Northern Piegan, the Kainai Nation, and the Siksika Nation. They share origins, culture, and their native language, which has its roots in the Algonquian language stock.

At First, Far from White Expansion

The traditional territory of the Northern Blackfeet extended from the North Saskatchewan River in Canada to the Missouri River headwaters in Montana. It is theorized that they moved into the Plains area from the lake regions in the Northeast and lived in southwestern Canada before contact with Europeans. These locations far to the northwest of the American western expansion would, for a time, keep them out of harm's way.

Sometime after 1730, the Blackfeet obtained the "elk dog"—the horse—through the Shoshone, who moved up from the south. Soon the gun made its way to the Plains, brought by the eastern Cree trappers. Then the horrible diseases came, even before the white men appeared in person.

As the tribes were pushed west, the Assiniboine tribe divided from the Yanktonai Sioux tribe, moved north and formed a lasting alliance with the Plains Cree. Both groups were trappers, and they aligned themselves with the Canadian fur traders, who gave them guns. That made them a formidable power

against tribes that had only bows and arrows. Over time, the coalition moved up to the rivers and lakes, pushing other tribes farther west.

An unidentified Blackfeet chief sits astride a horse that drinks from the Bow River in Alberta, Canada, in the late 1800s or early 1900s.

Like dominoes, when one tribe was displaced and forced to move, they displaced another tribe. Movement by the Shoshone and Gros Ventre cornered the Blackfeet against the Rocky Mountains. Conflicts erupted among the groups in the early 19th century, until all of them obtained horses and guns and a sort of balance developed.

The tribes were organized into bands, with each band having its own structure and rules. They would come together in the spring or early summer and camp together as a tribe for sacred ceremonies. Each lodge had its special space in the giant circle of tepees.

Drastic change began in 1853 when Isaac I. Stevens was appointed the first territorial governor of Washington and the Superintendent of Indian Affairs. Stevens, who was first in his class at West Point, also spent some time in the Corps of Engineers. On his way to his new post, the ambitious soldier volunteered to survey the northern route for a railroad from Minneapolis to the West Coast. Moving slowly across the prairie, he met most of the tribes and their headmen and had them sign many long-lasting treaties in 1855. His methods were stern and intimidating; some negotiations even involved killings. Most of those treaties, however, are still in effect today.

The tribes that signed surrendered their rights to their regions. They promised to live in peace, allow outsiders to

Blackfeet Indian tepees, circa 1950, lined up in Glacier National Park, Montana

travel in peace, and permit the construction of roads and telegraph lines. In turn, the Blackfeet received a huge Montana reservation that still holds great beauty. A decade later, though, the government reduced these holdings, and clashes ensued. In January 1870, forces under Maj. Eugene Baker attacked the peaceful camp of the Blackfeet chief Heavy Runner, killing 173 people, mostly women and children.

The Buffalo Disappear

The closest steamboat port to the Blackfeet was Fort Benton, Montana, on the Missouri. The usual scalawags piled ashore there in hopes of finding their fortune. Many went on to Helena and Butte, but others stayed to peddle alcohol to the Indians and to cheat them whenever possible. The Blackfeet, somewhat isolated to the northwest, avoided much of the turmoil, but the unsuccessful buffalo hunts of 1883 and 1884 made them more dependent upon the government to keep from starving. As the conflicts with the whites subsided and the intertribal struggles began to fade after the reservation was established in 1887, commerce flourished.

In 1935, the Blackfeet tribe in the United States was organized under the Indian Reorganization Act, and today it exists as a political entity and a business corporation, with an elected tribal council. Browning, Montana, is its largest town, the tribal headquarters, and the gateway to Glacier National Park. The reservation is just a small part of the tribe's ancestral lands, but it includes the portion of those lands that was traditionally most sacred. Its 3,000 square miles are studded with rivers and lakes, with the Rocky Mountains to the west and a rolling prairie to the east. There are about 10,000 people on the reservation, with another 7,500 enrolled tribe members around the world. Some main attractions are the Museum of the Plains Indians and the North American Indian Days powwow in the summer. ■

the hands of settlers. It was in this manner that the state of Oklahoma was born in 1907 (the Curtis Act of 1898 having provided for the termination of the Choctaw Tribal Government by 1906). All Choctaw educational institutions and policy passed to the U.S. government, and the following year all tribal courts were abolished.

In subsequent decades, the tribe made numerous attempts to reestablish its institutions so as to gain some control over its internal affairs. At a convention in 1934, the tribe endorsed the Indian Reorganization Act. This act excluded Oklahoma from its provisions, however, leading to the BIA-administered Oklahoma Indian Welfare Act, which the tribe refused to recognize. By the 1950s and 1960s, the Choctaw were engaged in a serious effort to establish a sovereign tribal government and to avert termination. By the 1970s, this movement had gathered momentum, and finally, in 1983, the tribe ratified a new constitution and the U.S. government formally recognized it.

Since then, the Choctaw Nation has steadily gained economic independence and tribal sovereignty. By the mid-1980s, it had assumed control of

MYTH OR FACT?

Indians of the Plains lived in tepees.

FACT

Plains Indians built tepees (also spelled "teepees" or "tipis"). The word is originally from the Sioux, meaning "used to live in."

all BIA programs administered on tribal lands. The tribe funds almost 85 percent of all tribal programs, depending on the federal government for less than 20 percent.

In 2000, the Choctaw Nation reached a landmark agreement with the state of Oklahoma. Together with the Chickasaw Nation, the Choctaw signed an agreement to unite Indian water rights with existing state water laws. The agreement affects issues in nearly 25 Oklahoma counties and the area along the Kiamichi River Basin. It will assist the state in paying the $40 million it owes the federal government, defines tribal water rights, provides a system to administer water rights, institutes water quality standards, and addresses issues of development in southeastern Oklahoma.

In addition to economic independence, the tribe has made great strides in developing tribal programs that preserve and enhance Choctaw culture, language, and everyday life. Tribal language, social, housing, and health programs provide the community with valuable quality services. Interest in traditional culture and practices remains strong, with many younger Choctaws expressing the desire to learn the language, dances, and ceremonies of their ancestors. Baptist missionaries long ago gained a foothold in the tribe's culture, and today that faith is still fairly widespread among tribal members, albeit in hybrid form; many elders pray and sing Baptist hymns in the Choctaw language.

NORMAN HARRY HOLLOW

Longtime leader of the Fort Peck Tribes

Norman Harry Hollow (1919–1996) was for decades a leader of the Fort Peck Reservation in the northeastern part of Montana, which is home to members of the Assiniboine and Sioux tribes. Hollow, a Sioux, was born and reared in the Fort Kipp portion of the reservation. During the Great Depression, he worked with the Civilian Conservation Corps job program to help build the Fort Peck Dam. Afterward, he became a farmer and rancher. He also worked with local youth as a basketball coach and 4-H leader, activities that made him well known in the community.

In 1947, Hollow was elected to the Tribal Executive Board, where he served until 1973, when he became chairman of the Fort Peck Tribes. During his years as chairman, the tribe negotiated with the state to secure water rights, the first time such a deal had been reached in the state through discussion rather than lawsuits. He held that post until 1985, then again became a member of the executive board, a position he held the rest of his years. During his life, he received numerous awards, including a 1982 award from the Department of the Interior as an outstanding Indian leader. He was named Montana's Small Businessman of the Year in 1986 and received an honorary doctorate in business from Montana State University in 1991. ■

CITIZEN POTAWATOMI RESERVATION

Tribe: Citizen Potawatomi Nation
Current Location: Oklahoma   Total Area: 5,284.68 acres
Tribal Enrollment: 25,980

The name of the Potawatomi means "People of the Place of the Fire" in the Algonquian language. The Citizen Potawatomi call themselves Nishnabec, meaning "True People," and early records confirm that Potawatomi as a distinct tribe inhabited Michigan 500 years ago. The first Potawatomi encountered by Europeans were hunters, fishermen,

An unidentified chief of the Blackfeet Indians dressed in full tribal regalia sings tribal war songs into a gramophone
at the Smithsonian Institution in Washington in 1916. Smithsonian anthropologist Frances Densmore is operating the recording device.

and farmers living near what is now Green Bay, Wisconsin. During French incursions, many Potawatomis intermarried with Creole settlers, and the tribe spread south across present-day Michigan, Indiana, and Illinois. They began to hire other local tribesmen to collect and trap the furs that they had once procured. In turn, they would sell or trade the furs to the French, thus expanding their tribal control and estate over a vast area.

In 1832, the tribe ceded more than 780,000 acres in these areas to the U.S. government in exchange for an annuity and manufactured goods, and some members accepted a new reservation in what is now east-central Kansas. From September to November 1838, the Mission Band (today known as the Citizen Band) of Potawatomi was forced to march across four states to the new reserve in Kansas. In Potawatomi history, the event is now known as the Potawatomi Trail of Death.

Tepees arrayed at the Fort Union Trading Post National Historic Site in Williston, North Dakota. The trading post was built in 1828 by the American Fur Company to do business with Northern Plains tribes.

The Citizen Band Potawatomi are descended from one of the two major groups of Kansas Potawatomis, which divided as a result of pressure from land speculators in the 1860s. The members who agreed to sell their land, become U.S. citizens, and buy new land for an Oklahoma reservation became known as the Citizen Band, while those who refused and were removed by U.S. soldiers to a smaller Kansas reservation became known as the Prairie Band. In 1890, the Oklahoma reservation was in turn broken up into smaller parcels by the U.S. government, with plots given to individual tribal members constituting a "reservational area." It is estimated that approximately half of the 900-square-mile reservation was simply given away by the government to settlers, and during the desperate Dust Bowl era, many tribal members followed other Oklahomans to California and other states, where they formed loose-knit communities.

By the early 1970s, the tribe's holdings had shrunk to just two acres of trust land and $550. Today the Citizen Potawatomi Nation is the largest of the eight federally recognized Potawatomi tribes and the ninth largest tribe in the United States. Tribal members adopted a constitution in 1985, giving a vote to all tribal members, regardless of their place of residence. Tribal members staff the regional offices, thus providing members who do not live in Oklahoma an opportunity to access tribal services. The administration holds council meetings within each specified region each year. This arrangement allows members who live outside Oklahoma to receive the tribe's services. The Nation, with a portfolio of varied business operations, is the largest employer in the city of Shawnee, with a significant impact on central Oklahoma's economic life.

CROW CREEK RESERVATION

Tribe: Crow Creek Sioux Tribe of the Crow Creek
Reservation   Current Location: South Dakota
Total Area: 151,512 acres   Tribal Enrollment: 3,507

The Crow Creek Sioux are members of the Great Sioux Nation. They call themselves Lakota or Dakota, meaning "friend" or "ally." The word "Sioux" comes from *nadowesioux,* a Chippewa (Ojibwe) word that means "little snake" or "enemy." French fur trappers in the area now known as Minnesota were the first to call them Sioux. Crow Creek Sioux are descendants of two divisions of Dakota and Nakota people: the Ihanktowan (Yankton and Yanktonais), or Middle Sioux; and the Isanti (Dakota), comprising four bands that lived on the eastern side of the Dakota Nation. The groups speak the Nakota dialect of the Siouan language, and they were farmers in the river plains who supplemented their diet with extensive hunting, especially of buffalo. They maintain a strong oral tradition, passing along history from elders to youth in a centuries-old cultural custom.

Shortly after encountering white explorers about the end of the 17th century in north-central Minnesota, the Lakota (also called Western Sioux) moved west in pursuit of buffalo into what is now South

**Wichita,
Northern
Caddoan
language
family**

"assé'hah"
("all")

"nikwa'c'a"
("arrow")

"ti'k'ac'iya'?"
("bark [tree] 'pole
shell' ")

"ichiri"
("bird")

"né'rhir'a"
("male buffalo")

"ta'rha"
("female buffalo")

Dakota, Montana, Wyoming, and Nebraska. They did not actively resist white immigration until the whites began to decimate the buffalo herds. Eventually, following Little Crow's War in Minnesota, a treaty with the United States was signed in 1863, designating western lands along the Missouri River as a reservation. Although the Lakota originally had a woodland economy based on hunting, fishing, and gathering, they had to change radically to survive. The Lakota became classic Plains Indians, skilled horsemen and buffalo hunters, and they often allied with the Cheyenne and Arapaho. Their territory extended at one time from the Big Horn Mountains in the west to Minnesota in the east, and from Canada in the north to the Platte River in the south in what is now Nebraska.

Sioux fame was established by the Red Cloud Wars of the 1860s, distinguished as the only victory of American Indians in war against the U.S. government. In a direct violation of the 1868 Treaty of Fort Laramie, Gen. George A. Custer and his Seventh Cavalry entered the Black Hills in 1874 and found gold there, starting a gold rush of white settlers and miners. When the Sioux resisted all attempts by the federal government to buy or rent their sacred Black Hills, Custer's cavalry was ordered to "round up" all warring Sioux and place them on the reservation. The famous Battle of the Little Big Horn took place on June 25, 1876, at Greasy Grass, Montana. It was a stunning defeat for the Seventh Cavalry. Nonetheless, many Sioux fled to Canada; many others surrendered to the reservation. Still determined to obtain access to the gold in the Black Hills, the U.S. government passed the Agreement of 1877, which illegally took the Black Hills from the Great Sioux Nation. The Allotment of 1887 divided Indian lands into 160-acre lots—one per household—or 80-acre lots for single adult males. This partition further divided Sioux lands.

An act in 1889 broke up the Great Sioux Nation into smaller reservations. The Crow Creek Reservation, or Wiciyela Sioux Division, formally established on March 2, 1889, was one of only three parcels of land the Sioux retained, and it serves as

CHEYENNE

The earliest written reference to the people that became known as the Cheyenne was in a letter from the French explorer La Salle in 1680. He wrote that some Cheyenne visited him after traveling from their homeland on the headwaters of the Mississippi River in what is now Minnesota to the Illinois River in southwest Illinois. Like many tribes of that day, the Tsethasetas, as the Cheyenne called themselves, once lived in bark tepees and grew corn, beans, and squash. However, they left their agricultural life by the close of the 17th century and began moving west to the Plains to seek the buffalo. Early traditions of the Algonquian-speaking Cheyenne say they were driven out of the north by a powerful enemy and settled after crossing a large body of water.

Life Was Never Peaceful

Pressure from their enemies—the Assiniboine and Cree, who were armed with guns—and the hope of an easier life as buffalo hunters probably weighed in on the tribe's move to the Plains. Wary of the more powerful Sioux, the Cheyenne moved to North Dakota, then South Dakota. Life was never peaceful for too long for these travelers, as they searched for a homeland, adapted to a new lifestyle, forged alliances, and encountered foreigners and their unfamiliar materials.

The situation was in just this state of flux when the Sioux, facing pressure from the Chippewa, acquired guns in 1708. The Cheyenne left the Black Hills, again seeking the buffalo. Eventually, the Tsethasetas turned south toward the headwaters of the North Platte River in Wyoming. In 1833, Col. William Bent persuaded many Cheyenne people to live on the Arkansas River in southeast Colorado around Bent's Fort, while others stayed in Wyoming.

They had no central home base and roamed the beautiful open plains. They became close allies to the Arapaho through peace and warfare, but

A 19th-century Southern Cheyenne warrior's shirt, adorned with quillwork, paint, and hair

were strident enemies of the Sioux and Assiniboine. Nevertheless, because alliances were essential to survival, in 1840 the Cheyenne and Sioux made permanent peace and fought enemies together. With the addition of the Arapaho, they made a formidable trio.

The Fort Laramie Treaty of 1851 laid out territory for many tribes, including the Cheyenne. The treaty provided a reservation that encompassed approximately half of Colorado and some of Wyoming, Kansas, and Nebraska.

Unfortunately, the area was in the route of westward expansion, settlement, and mining. Therefore, conflict was inevitable.

In 1857, troops were sent to control the Cheyenne, who fought as fervent patriots for their land. Col. Edwin V. Sumner and his men killed a number of chiefs and destroyed 200 lodges, causing outrage and retaliation from the Cheyenne. As the fighting spread, the government called a treaty meeting in 1861 at Fort Wise, Colorado. The Cheyenne were now skeptical about such deals, and only six tribe members signed the treaty that took away most of the land designated for them earlier, leaving the tribe with an insignificant tract in Colorado. And settlers immediately wanted that land, too.

Massacre at Sand Creek

The government asked the Tsethasetas and some Arapahos to take part in a meeting on November 24, 1864, under Army protection at a place that will live in infamy—Sand Creek, Colorado. More than 500 tribe members attended. The Indian leader, the respected Chief Black Kettle, flew the U.S. Stars and Stripes from his tepee, as well as a white flag of truce. Despite the pledges of safety, Col. John M. Chivington ordered his troops to attack, even though some of his men begged him not to assault friendly Indians. The attack was bloody, with atrocities committed upon Indian men, women, and even babies.

The indiscriminate slaughter did not break the Cheyenne, but instead inflamed their thirst for revenge. Less than six weeks later, warriors attacked a military stage and burned the town of Julesburg, Colorado. After a peaceful few months, on October 14, 1865, a treaty council gave the Cheyenne a small reservation partly in Kansas and Oklahoma, but the wording in the treaty rendered it almost meaningless. The armed

conflicts continued for more than a decade of bloody confrontations, broken promises, and repeated betrayals.

Although the Cheyenne fought hard, they were outnumbered, and in the summer of 1877, many of them were moved to Oklahoma. On September 9, 1878, about 300 Cheyenne escaped and headed north. In spite of many battles along the way, the group was soon captured and taken to Fort Robinson, Nebraska. At that point, they numbered less than 150. Freezing and starving, they managed to briefly escape again, but many were killed. On January 22, 1879, surrounded by four companies of cavalry, 19 brave warriors with their women and children refused to surrender, and 23 people were

killed. Fewer than 15 got away. On March 25, the last band was taken prisoner. They were placed at Fort Keogh, Montana, and then in 1884 were given a tiny reservation on the Tongue River in Montana.

Today about 4,000 tribe members live on the Northern Cheyenne Indian Reservation, with headquarters in Lame Deer, Montana, and another 5,000 live elsewhere. Several prominent people have come from their ranks, including Senator Ben Nighthorse Campbell and W. Richard West, Jr., founding director of the National Museum of the American Indian, along with numerous state legislators, college presidents, veterans, and many beautiful children who still ride their horses. ▪

Three Cheyenne Indians survey the rolling plains in about 1905.

Cherokee cheerleaders at Sequoyah High School in Tahlequah, Oklahoma, rally support for their homecoming.

the home to Lakota people from several areas. It was administratively separated from the Lower Brule Reservation on the other side of the Missouri River in 1971. Replacing 80 percent unemployment rates with relative prosperity has been a decades-long battle. Most employment on the reservation is provided by the tribe via its many initiatives and through the BIA and the Indian Health Service. The major economic activities are cattle ranching and farming.

DELAWARE RESERVATION

Tribe: Delaware Tribe of Indians [Delaware, Wichita, Caddo]   Current Location: Oklahoma   Total Area: 487 acres   Tribal Enrollment (BIA, 2001): 1,302

The Delaware Tribe of Oklahoma descends from the eastern woodland Delaware Indians, an Algonquian-speaking tribe of the Delaware and Hudson River Valleys in what is now southern New York and northern New Jersey. They called themselves Lenni Lenape, or "original people,"

and were called "grandfathers" by other tribes, most likely because of their longtime existence prior to European contact and for their reputation as peacekeepers.

The Delaware were forced into what is now Pennsylvania by waves of European immigrants seeking new lives and land in the emerging colonies. By the time of the American Revolution, the Delaware were residing as far west as present-day Ohio. American colonists referred to the Delaware as "friendly" Indians because of their cooperation in treaty negotiations; loyal to the fledgling United States, the Delaware served as scouts and soldiers.

One band of Delawares branched off in 1793 and settled in present-day Missouri. Referred to as the Absentee Delaware, this band became the ancestors of the modern Delaware Tribe of Oklahoma. The Absentee Delaware received a land grant from the Spanish government in 1820 and relocated to what is now East Texas. In 1854, Texas settlers drove them off their land. Five years later, several Delaware families settled at the Wichita Agency in Indian Territory (Oklahoma). The Wichita Agency was largely allotted following the Jerome Agreement of 1890, and the Absentee Delaware were allotted as either Caddo or Wichita. Since members were not designated as Delaware on any census between 1895 and 1930, organization under the 1934 Indian Reorganization Act presented a struggle for the tribe. They eventually organized under the Oklahoma Indian Welfare Act in 1936. Thereafter, the tribe worked to rebuild after centuries of cultural dislocation and forced relocation. During the 1950s, the tribe filed joint claims with the Indian Claims Commission and received a small settlement in 1977. The tribe also gained joint ownership of trust lands with the Caddo and Wichita tribes.

The Delaware also participate in the Four Tribes Consortium of Oklahoma, an employment and training program designed to provide tribal members in Caddo County with the skills, work experience, and support necessary to become employable. The legal status of the Delaware Tribe of Oklahoma will almost certainly remain in flux until the

Blackfeet, Algonquian language family

"ksisskstakiwa" ("beaver")

"mamí'wa" ("fish")

"moyisi" ("house")

"kokotoyi" ("ice")

"kona" ("snow")

federal law reflects the reality of this tribe, which has endured since their ancestors entered into the very first Indian treaty with the U.S. government in 1778.

EASTERN SHAWNEE RESERVATION

Tribe: Eastern Shawnee Tribe of Oklahoma
Current Location: Oklahoma **Total Area:** 1,195.09 acres
Tribal Enrollment: 2,367

In 1669, the Shawnee were living in two groups a considerable distance apart. Those living west of the Appalachians migrated south to present-day Tennessee near Cherokee territory, as well as into South Carolina. Beginning in 1690, the Shawnee entered a protracted conflict with English settlers and southern tribes. The Shawnee in Tennessee were driven northward into the Ohio Valley by the Cherokee, while the Shawnee of South Carolina returned to Pennsylvania. During the French and Indian War, the Shawnee of Ohio engaged in constant conflict with British forces. Those in Pennsylvania remained neutral, but joined the Ohio band

THE PLAINS

PLAINS INDIAN CHILDREN

In the buffalo days, a Plains Indian mother didn't have much time to recuperate from birth. There was too much work to be done.

On a typical day, a baby would wake from a night asleep on soft furs, eat, and be bathed. The mother would then put the baby on a soft hide that was covered with an absorbent plant material such as burst cattail down or moss. The baby's arms were placed by his sides, and he was snugly wrapped with only his head protruding. He was then laced into a baby carrier. The mother kept the baby in his carrier in her sight as she worked.

At the end of the day, after they returned to the tepee, the baby was removed from the carrier, and the cattail or moss diaper was discarded. When the baby was clean

and fed, he was again free to crawl around naked and play.

Older children were taught in many ways. There were few classrooms where a teacher lectured. An Indian child was instead free to learn as the opportunity arose. For instance, when an experienced horseman rode, the children would watch. Through observation, they learned how to mount, to lean into a turn, and to stop. When they felt they were ready, they would tell a relative and then ride.

When children misbehaved, they were never spanked. Indian people wanted their children to be active and energetic to best cope with the world. Hitting them would cause pain and perhaps break their spirit.

The relationships among Plains Indian people and their children were very close.

Like the parallel layers of the earth, they extended horizontally across the culture. In addition to the biological mother and father, all the siblings of those parents were also considered mothers and fathers to a child. In other words, there was no concept of aunts and uncles, only additional mothers and fathers. So, if her mother had one sister and her father had two, a child would have four mothers.

The children of these "extra" parents were one's brothers and sisters, not cousins. The adults had duties to the children. For instance, a father would teach a boy how to make a bow and arrows and how to hunt. A girl would learn how to prepare hides from one of her mothers. Grandparents often helped raise children, too, and taught them the old ways. ■

in 1755. Following the American Revolution, the Shawnee allied with other midwestern tribes to prevent further Euro-American incursion into the Ohio Valley.

The Shawnee war chief Bluejacket led 1,400 warriors in a siege of Fort Miami in 1793. During the early 19th century, Shawnee Chief Tecumseh attempted to forge a pan-tribal alliance in the Ohio and Mississippi River Valleys. William Henry Harrison's American forces defeated the Shawnee at Tippecanoe in 1811. Those Shawnee remaining in Ohio signed a treaty in 1831 ceding their lands to the United States. In 1832, they were removed to a reservation in present-day Ottawa County, Oklahoma. These Shawnee refugees united with a small band of Seneca to form the United Nation of Senecas and Shawnees. They were widely referred to as the Loyal Shawnees because of their loyalty to the Union during the Civil War.

Shawnee tribal lands were largely allotted during the early 20th century. In 1934, the tribe reincorporated under the Oklahoma Indian Welfare Act as the

Blackfeet or Cheyenne doll from the early 20th century

Eastern Shawnee Tribe of Oklahoma; it adopted a constitution and bylaws in 1937 in accordance with the Indian Reorganization Act.

The principal governing body of the Eastern Shawnee Tribe is the General Council, consisting of all enrolled members 18 years of age or older. A committee governs matters of tribal business, including housing, educational assistance, community services, child and family protection services, law enforcement, environmental concerns, employment assistance, communication, and social services. The Eastern Shawnee Tribe adopted a constitution and bylaws in 1937. A new constitution was ratified in April 1994. The reservation's economy is supported by federal funding for tribal programs and infrastructure, and by revenues from their gaming and other business enterprises.

FORT BERTHOLD RESERVATION

Tribe: Three Affiliated Tribes of the Fort Berthold Reservation [Arikara, Mandan, and Hidatsa]
Current Location: North Dakota   Total Area: 423,974 acres
Tribal Enrollment: 11,897

The Arikara call themselves Sahnish, or "original people from whom all other tribes sprang." The Mandan, once divided into distinct bands, were known among one another by their band names: Is'tope, Nup'tadi, Ma'nana'r, and Awi'kaxa. The Hidatsa, also divided into linguistically distinct clan or band groupings, were known by the other groups as "well-dressed men" or "people of the water." The name they used for themselves means "willows." Geographically and linguistically independent at the time of initial contact with Euro-American culture, these three tribes lived along the Missouri River, hunting buffalo and growing squash, corn, and beans. Meriwether Lewis and William Clark passed through this territory during their cross-country voyage and explorations of the continent in 1804–05, and spent their first winter in 1804 at Fort Clark near the Mandan, Hidatsa, and Arikara villages.

RUNNING FISHER

Gros Ventre warrior chief

Running Fisher (1846–1910) was born in southwestern Montana, where his father of the same name was a chief of the Gros Ventre tribe. They were named for the fisher, a fast, aggressive, carnivorous relative of the weasel. During the winter of 1872, when he was only 16 years old, he went on his first war party against an enemy to the west. During the many tribal conflicts of this time, he proved himself again and again on the battlefield. Running Fisher fought the Sioux, the Blackfeet, the Nez Perce, the Shoshone, and others. His military accomplishments can be seen in paintings in museums across the country.

He became chief in 1890 and devoted the rest of his life to the welfare of the tribe. As the reservation became settled, he was selected to be the first tribal chief of police and served in that capacity for many years. He later became known as Jerry Running Fisher. The esteemed photographer of the Indian way of life Edward S. Curtis selected him as one of his subjects. He was one of many chiefs from numerous tribes who attended a gathering in the Little Big Horn Valley in 1909, styled as the "last great Indian council." According to records of that meeting, for 40 years of his life, he "had averaged a battle for every other year," and, he said, "I have 20 shots in my body received in battle." ■

An 1884 portrait of Sitting Bull (Tatanka Yotaka), a Hunkpapa Lakota Sioux spiritual leader who led his tribe in resistance to the white settlers, including the defeat of George Armstrong Custer at Little Bighorn in 1876. He was assassinated in 1890.

mid-1860s. The U.S. government built a new village for them, known as Fort Stephenson, 17 miles farther east, near the modern community of Garrison, North Dakota. Between 1866 and 1870, many more tribal members died as crops failed, promised annuities were never delivered, and another wave of smallpox struck the Plains. By 1888, Like-a-Fishhook was virtually deserted.

Though the Treaty of Fort Laramie had granted the three tribes more than 12 million acres, subsequent executive orders and the General Allotment Act of 1887 eventually reduced the reservation's size to less than a million acres. Fraudulent land deals in the first and second decades of the 20th century resulted in further losses of acreage.

During 1954, the tribes lost another 156,000 acres, along with innumerable natural resources, due to the inundation of the Missouri River to form Garrison Reservoir, now known as Lake Sakakawea. The flooding destroyed natural resources and long-established Indian population centers, such as Elbowoods, the central Indian business community. Families who had supported themselves by ranching and farming along fertile Missouri River bottomlands were forced to relocate to dry, windy uplands. The tribal administrative center was moved to New Town, which was not officially on the reservation at that time. Although the tribes received $12 million in compensation for their flooded land, an independent evaluator placed the loss at more than $20 million. By the end of 1959, tribal lands had dwindled to just over 426,000 acres, of which only 21,308 acres were tribally owned and 60 percent were utilized by non-Indians.

Traditional culture has been revived and encouraged in recent years, with Native American Church ceremonies, sweat lodges, and the use of Native languages. The tribes maintain discrete tribal identities through the preservation of their languages, crafts, and cultures. The reservation continues to support limited farming and ranching, but the tribes have been more successful in establishing or attracting businesses in electronics manufacturing, construction, and gaming.

Contact with the new arrivals brought predictable consequences: skirmishes with the U.S. Army, conflicts with white settlers, losses of land via cession treaties, and, most notably, a devastating smallpox epidemic in June 1837, which served as a catalyst for tribal consolidation as a means of economic and social survival. To escape the disease, a group of Hidatsas moved up the Missouri River in 1845 and established the village of Like-a-Fishhook; the Fort Berthold Reservation was established for the Three Affiliated Tribes by the Fort Laramie Treaty of 1851. Euro-Americans were not the only threat however; a rival tribe inflicted a major setback when a structure built to house the Indians at Fort Berthold was burned to the ground by a Sioux raiding party in the

MÉTIS

As French fur trappers spread across Canada, beginning before 1600, many married Cree or Chippewa women. Their offspring intermarried over the years, producing a self-sustaining new people, the Métis (pronounced MAY-tee). The Canadian government formally recognizes them as an aboriginal group equal in standing to the First Nations—as Canada calls Indian tribes—and the Inuit. They are also known as Me'tsis or Michif, or sometimes mixed-bloods or half-breeds. Their homeland reaches across Canada and into parts of Montana, North Dakota, and northwestern Minnesota. Their historical language is either Métis French or a mixed language called Michif, but today they predominantly speak English, with French as a second language, as well as many Indian tongues.

Children of Trappers

The name Métis originally referred only to the children of a French man and an Indian woman. As the fur trade moved west, more Métis were born in the new areas. The term later expanded to include children of other foreign trappers, such as the English and Scottish.

Although many of them assimilated into the general population, the Métis realized that they were considered neither Native by the Indian people nor white by the white people, so they chose elements of the lives of each group and fashioned their own aggregate lifestyle. For example, instead of transporting their material on an A-frame pole travois as the Indians did, they constructed two-wheeled wooden oxcarts for the same purpose. Their music featured the fiddle and the jig dance, instead of the drum and chants of the Indian people. Although their clothing styles were similar to others of the north, their finely made beadwork designs were unique, and they favored half-leggings over their trousers.

Métis Resistance

The Hudson's Bay Company and other trapping enterprises moved from the eastern waterways to the interior with great success over the years. In 1812, farmers, mostly Scots, arrived in large numbers in the Red River Valley in Manitoba, and Hudson's Bay, the titular owner, assigned land to them. That obstructed the open way to the west that the trappers, Indians,

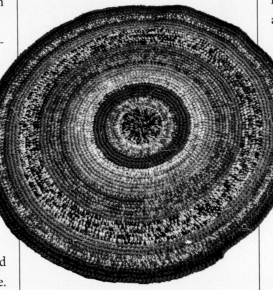

A handwoven Métis rug from about the 1890s

and others used, however, which created friction. To assert its influence over the country, the Canadian government in the mid-1800s set up a treaty process that forced the First Nations to sign treaties. As in the United States, the Indian tribes were compelled to give up their land in the west in exchange for promised assistance, resulting in increased tension among groups.

Hudson's Bay sold the land it claimed, called Rupert's Land, to the Canadian government in 1869. Louis Riel, an educated Métis leader, agitated for representation for his people. To permanently establish a Métis homeland in Manitoba, in 1870 he created a provisional government made up of the Métis and others, with some limited success.

But conflicts between the Métis and the Canadian government increased, culminating in what is known as the Red River Rebellion, which ended when the government sent in troops. Riel was formally exiled from Canada for five years.

In 1875, while in church in Washington, D.C., Riel experienced a vision that God had anointed him as "the prophet of the new world," rather than just a failed political leader. His mental health seemingly declined thereafter; he often removed his clothes in public. He lived in several places, including Fort Benton, Montana, where he married and had children.

In 1884, a Métis delegation from Canada pleaded for Riel to return from Montana to assist his people. He went north and made several unsuccessful attempts to help; soon, his ragtag

Cree and Métis women prepare whitefish in a dimly lit workroom in Saskatchewan.

bunch of sympathizers, including Cree chiefs Poundmaker and Big Bear, took up arms. They killed some mounted police, prompting the government to send additional troops to the conflict, which became known as the North-West Rebellion. Riel fled the final battle near Batoche, surrendering on May 15, 1885. He was tried and executed, and the chiefs were imprisoned.

Thousands of Métis and Indian people fled the turmoil in Canada. Many took up residence with tribes that had previously lived up north, including the Chippewa people of what would be the Tuttle Mountain Reservation in North Dakota, and the Chippewa/Cree people of what is now the Rocky Boy Reservation in Montana.

At this unstable time, most of the Canadian tribes in Montana and North Dakota were landless and destitute. They wandered from reservation to reservation and from town to town, not really welcome anywhere, but their names and blood lines are spread throughout the West. Today, the Métis people in Montana are organized into two groups and have been recognized by the state, but they are struggling among themselves as they strive for federal recognition.

Although their Canadian population is more than 300,000, there is no formal definition of a Métis. Whether they have treaty rights is still a sensitive issue, but in 2003, the Canadian Supreme Court ruled that the Métis are a distinct people with significant rights. ▪

KAW NATION OF OKLAHOMA RESERVATION

Tribe: Kaw Nation [Kaw, Kanza, Kansa]
Current Location: Oklahoma   Total Area: 1,146.98 acres
Tribal Enrollment: 2,821

The Kanza (People of the Wind, South Wind) or Kaw tribe traditionally occupied the lower Ohio Valley. The tribe belongs to the Dhegiha-Sioux division of the Hopewell cultures, along with the Osage, Ponca, Omaha, and Quapaw, who lived together in communities in the Ohio Valley well into the late 15th century. Traditional homes included bark- or earth-covered lodges in permanent settlements and tepees in transitional communities. Around 1750, tribal members began to migrate westward, toward the mouth of the Ohio River. Eventually, the Kaw tribe assumed control over most of present-day eastern and northern Kansas, western Missouri, and portions of Iowa and Nebraska.

But by 1800, epidemics had reduced the Kaw population to about 1,500. Even so, the Kaw presented a formidable obstacle to American expansion into the Louisiana Purchase. From their villages and small vegetable farms in northeastern Kansas and later along the Kansas River west of present-day Topeka, Kaw warriors maintained control of the lower Kansas Valley against both white settlers from the east and alien tribes to the west. Kaw hunters also engaged in semiannual hunting expeditions onto the plains of western Kansas, as far west as Colorado.

All of this changed dramatically after the Indian Removal Act of 1830, which provided for the removal of nearly 100,000 members of the Shawnee, Delaware, Wyandot, Kickapoo, Miami, Sac and Fox, Ottawa, Peoria, and Potawatomi tribes from their tribal lands to those of the Kaw and Osage tribes. The Kaw were then forced to cede vast amounts of land to the government, accepting promises of annuities and assistance in return.

The first and perhaps most devastating Kaw treaty was negotiated in 1825, when the Kaw ceded more than 18 million acres of their aboriginal territory and in return received a reservation 30 miles wide and $70,000, or a third of a cent per acre, to be paid at a rate of $3,500 per annum for 20 years in money,

N. SCOTT MOMADAY

Pulitzer Prize–winning author

Navarre Scott Momaday, an esteemed Kiowa educator, writer, and artist, won the Pulitzer Prize for fiction in 1969 for his first novel, *House Made of Dawn*. Born of a Kiowa father and an English/Cherokee mother in Lawton, Oklahoma, in 1934, he spent his first year at his grandparents' home in a Kiowa community. With his parents working as teachers in Indian communities, Momaday was exposed to the richness of his father's Native traditions, as well as to academic traditions. He graduated from the University of New Mexico, won a poetry fellowship in creative writing at Stanford University, and earned his doctorate in English literature in 1963.

In addition to his Pulitzer-winning novel, which explores the harsh forces of society on a young Indian man, he wrote *The Way to Rainy Mountain* (1969), a collection of Kiowa stories illustrated by his father, Al Momaday; the essay "The American Land Ethic" (1971); *Angle of Geese, and Other Poems* (1974); *The Names* (1976); and *The Gourd Dancer* (1976). He has taught at the University of California, Berkeley; Stanford; and the University of Arizona. President George W. Bush presented him the National Medal of Arts in 2007 "for his writings and his work that celebrate and preserve Native American art and tradition."

N. Scott Momaday's literary work examines the connection of humankind to the natural world.

merchandise, provisions, or domestic animals. The Kaw also ceded 36 parcels of good lands on the Big Blue River to be sold, with the proceeds to be deposited in a school fund for the education of Kaw children.

Poverty-stricken by the effects of the 1825 treaty and weakened by continuous government (and private) pressure for yet another land cession—this time to accommodate railroad, town, and land speculators—the Kaw leadership went to the treaty table in 1846 and again in 1860. Each time yielded disastrous terms for the Kaw.

Finally, on May 27, 1872, in a measure strongly opposed by Chief Allegawaho and most of his people, a federal act was passed that provided for the removal of the Wind People from Kansas to a site in present-day Kay County, Oklahoma, that had been carved out of former Cherokee/Osage land.

The tribal culture began to suffer after the tribe's removal from their traditional lands in Kansas. Tribal youth were forced to attend schools, where they were punished for speaking the indigenous language, wearing traditional clothing, or practicing traditional spirituality. Tribal members nevertheless made a concerted effort to retain cultural elements and maintain their relationships with members of other tribes.

In 1902, a new agreement was reached. However, before any lands could be allotted, the Kaw agreed to set aside and cede 160 acres of land to the United States to maintain a school for the education of Indian children. In addition, the Kaw set aside and reserved 20 acres of land for the tribal cemetery and 80 acres for a town site to be known as Washunga, which had been located in the area inundated by the Kaw Reservoir. After years of negotiations with various federal and local officials, the tribal cemetery was relocated to Newkirk, Oklahoma, and the tribal council house was relocated to a 15-acre tract a few miles northwest of its former location. By subsequent congressional action, 132.5 acres of land located in Kay County just west of the former Washunga town site was placed in trust for the Kaw Nation.

The Kaw Nation has managed to survive its many hardships since the arrival of Euro-Americans. Tribal members continue to revive traditional

MYTH OR FACT?
So as not to be wasteful, Plains Indians ate every part of the animals they killed.

MYTH
They did not eat the hooves, hair, horns, or bones. However, they used these to make tools, clothing, ornaments, rope, and other items.

practices, including the powwow. Reintroduced in the community in 1977, the event is now celebrated annually at the powwow grounds at Washunga Bay.

Kanza, the Siouan language of the Kaw Nation, is closely related to the Osage, Ponca, Omaha, and Quapaw tribal languages. In order to support the survival of this language, a Kaw language coordinator serves on the tribal staff, and a website promotes its study.

KICKAPOO TRIBE OF OKLAHOMA RESERVATION

Tribe: Kickapoo Tribe of Oklahoma
Current Location: Oklahoma   Total Area: 6,821 acres
Tribal Enrollment: 1,654

The Kickapoo Tribe of Oklahoma is descended from the Algonquian-speaking Kickapoo people of the Great Lakes region. The name "Kickapoo" is derived from "Kiwigapawa," meaning "standing now here, now there." The name is fitting, given the Kickapoo's history. They lived in established settlements and maintained close ties with the Sac and Fox tribes within their aboriginal territory. Like the Shawnee, the Kickapoo were skilled farmers. They constructed longhouses and lived in fixed villages throughout the summer months, separating into smaller communities after the autumn harvest and communal buffalo hunts. They enjoyed a subsistence lifestyle with a diet consisting of beans, corn, and squash, supplemented by meat. Early Indian agents in the territory now known as Illinois reported the Kickapoo using horses for buffalo hunts before contact with western Plains tribes had been made.

Catholic missionaries were the first to come into contact with the Kickapoo, in 1667, and were met with fierce resistance. In the early 1700s, the Kickapoo, estimated to have numbered between 2,000 and 4,000, were pushed out of their aboriginal territory throughout the St. Lawrence River Valley into Wisconsin, and by the 1800s they occupied southern Wisconsin and Illinois. They signed their first treaty with the U.S. government at Greenville, Ohio, in 1795. In 1809 and 1819, they ceded lands in Illinois to

Gros Ventre (A'aninin), Algonquian language family

"Wah-hay"
("Hello")

"wass-wah-hawn"
("peppermint plant")

"nay-kaa-nay"
("spotted otter")

Milky Way, a Penateka Comanche chief, was also known as Asa Havi or Bird Chief. He holds a bow in this 1872 photo.

the United States and relocated near the Osage River in Missouri. During the War of 1812, the Kickapoo allied with the Shawnee chief Tecumseh against the United States. White encroachment on their Missouri lands caused them to petition the government for lands in Kansas in the 1830s, but these, too, were ceded to the U.S. for 768,000 acres in northeastern Kansas. Among the treaty signers were the famous Kickapoo prophet Kennakuk, or Kanakuk, who established a tribal religion and advocated virtuous living, and Pa-shacha-hah (Jumping Fish).

In 1852, a number of Kickapoos moved to Mexico and have become known as the Mexican Kickapoo. By 1873, many had returned to the United States, to Oklahoma and the Kansas Reservation; others remained in or near the Santa Rosa Mountains of eastern Chihuahua and western Coahuila. A reservation was assigned to the Kickapoo who returned from Mexico in 1883, but in the interim, nearly all of the land located near McCloud, Oklahoma, had been absorbed by non-Indians. The government bought the rest of the Kickapoo reservation and held a land run in May 1895. This acreage became part

of Lincoln, Oklahoma, and Pottawatomie Counties, where most Oklahoma Kickapoos still reside. Despite losing their land base, most Kickapoos adhere to tribal customs and traditions in religion, arts and crafts, and ceremonies.

LAKE TRAVERSE RESERVATION

Tribe: Sisseton-Wahpeton Oyate of the Lake Traverse Reservation **Current Location:** South and North Dakota
Total Area: 107,902 acres **Tribal Enrollment:** 11,763

The "D" dialect of the Siouan tongue was spoken by the Isanti people, the ancestors of the Sisseton-Wahpeton Sioux Tribe. For about a century after the appearance of white explorers, all of the Sioux occupied village sites along the Minnesota-Wisconsin border, an excellent spot for hunting, fishing, and planting. Most of these bands were Dakota speaking. When the settlers began to put down roots, a series of treaties was imposed upon the Indians; in 1851, the Sisseton accepted the terms of the Traverse des Sioux Treaty. In the wake of the 1862 Minnesota Sioux War (also known as Little Crow's War), federal officials placed subdivisions of Sissetons on both Lake Traverse and Devils Lake Reservations.

Between 1865 and 1868, several treaties between the Great Sioux Nation and the U.S. government defined the Nation's land base, which once stretched from Wisconsin to the Bighorn Mountains. After defeating Gen. George A. Custer and his Seventh Cavalry at the Battle of the Little Big Horn in Montana in 1876, large numbers of Sioux dispersed to reservations or to Canada. Over time, reservation lands were allotted or otherwise reduced in size. Residents of the Lake Traverse Reservation endured land loss, financial hardship, and federal paternalism. The approximately 2,700 tribal members were allotted just over 300,000 acres, with the remainder purchased for non-Indian settlement. Over the years, tribal members sold off their allotments for survival, and by 1952 they retained only about 117,000 acres.

During the Depression, tribal members survived through subsistence farming, trapping, hunting,

A Lakota Sioux man performs a tribal dance at a powwow—a gathering of people, often from several tribes, to celebrate Native American traditions.

GROS VENTRE (A'ANININ)

A common Indian origin story entails the tribe crossing a large body of water in the frozen winter; the ice is broken and a water monster emerges, destroying those on the ice. Those who had already crossed continue forward, while those still on the home shore go back. Many tribes believe that across that large body of water they still have relatives. After the glaciers receded across much of North America, the weather became warmer and drier, and people lived mostly in the high mountains or near large lakes. There is evidence that about 1200 the Great Plains were very dry and mostly barren of human beings. Eventually the rains returned, bringing forth plants, then animals, and then the hunters who followed them.

The Canadian Years

Before 1600, the Gros Ventre lived south of Winnipeg Lake. They moved west in the early 1800s, out of the Parklands to the Cyprus Hills in southern Canada, where they eventually settled between the branches of the Saskatchewan River. The tribe's traditional name is A'aninin, meaning "the white clay people." Gros Ventre is French for "large belly." There are several stories about the origin of the name, including one that says it stems from a misinterpretation of a sign language gesture that meant "waterfall people," because the white traders first noted the tribe near the rapids of the Saskatchewan. This Algonquian-speaking group separated from the Arapaho tribe

In 1908, a Gros Ventre party surveys a small Native American encampment in Montana.

around 1700, and long have been hunters and agriculturists.

The Canadian years were both tough and exciting as the tribe struggled to survive as a distinct group. During this period of transition, they and other tribes encountered several new threats. The most deadly were the new foreign diseases that came up the Missouri River with Europeans and spread across the prairie. Smallpox took the greatest toll, killing thousands. The epidemics came in waves beginning in 1780, often reducing the tribal population by half.

The Gros Ventre also had to protect themselves from a new weapon, the guns wielded by the Assiniboine and Cree. Without guns, the tribe was unable to defeat this coalition in combat. Instead, the tribe attacked their sources of supply, burning three forts near the Saskatchewan River— South Branch House in 1793, Manchester House the next year, and Chesterfield House in 1826. But the tribe made little progress against its enemies and was forced to move south into Montana.

Fighting, Then Treaties

The Gros Ventre battled Mexican troops near the Cimarron River in 1829, trappers at Pierre's Hole in Wyoming in 1832 (one of the worst encounters between Indians and trappers in the West), and other tribes for various reasons over the years. They were considered fierce warriors, but joined the several tribes who signed the Fort Laramie Treaty in 1851, guaranteeing peace and safe passage to settlers in return for land and money.

The treaty, which was quickly broken, began a series of land deals that resulted in ever-shrinking territories for the Gros Ventre and others. As the tribes competed for the dwindling resources and government rations, conflicts among them increased. Forts initially

A Gros Ventre buffalo robe from North Dakota, circa 1833, is painted with elaborate depictions of mounted warriors.

constructed for protection and control became the sources of rations to fend off starvation. Access became critical.

After several forts proved unsatisfactory, the government purchased an existing trading post built in 1871, called old Fort Belknap, near Chinook in north-central Montana, approximately 50 miles from the Canadian border. The agency shifted 24 miles east in 1888, to near Harlem, but kept the name (after William W. Belknap, President Ulysses S. Grant's secretary of war who was impeached in 1876 for accepting bribes and resigned in disgrace to avoid trial). The reservation was further reduced in 1895 when the government sent three

envoys who threatened the tribes with starvation if they didn't "sell" a seven-mile strip of land on the south side of the mountains so miners could search for gold. The tribes probably never received any funds, and today the mountains are severely damaged, with two of them destroyed and the groundwater still poisoned by mining chemicals.

Fort Belknap Today

The 675,000-acre Fort Belknap Reservation measures about 25 miles across and 40 miles long. The northern boundary is the Milk River, and the Little Rocky Mountains are to the south. The center is filled with buttes, prairie, wheat fields, antelope, meadowlarks, and eagles. Among the resources on the reservation is a tribal community college, Fort Belknap College.

Even on the reservation, the Gros Ventre maintained many of their spiritual traditions, including the ritual of the Sacred Flat Pipe bundle. Through these ceremonies, knowledge is shared among the generations. Today, respected men in the tribe remain guardians of the pipe.

About 5,000 people live on the reservation. They come from several tribes, most of them traditional antagonists at one time or another. A division of the Assiniboine eventually settled on the Fort Peck and Fort Belknap Reservations in Montana, as well as on several reserves in Canada. A number of Cree and Métis with historical connections to the Assiniboine people also settled at Fort Belknap, but they are not recognized as a tribe by the U.S. government. ■

fishing, and federal trust fund payments until New Deal programs came along. The Civilian Conservation Corps was especially helpful in providing employment to the reservation. By the 1960s, cultural renewal had generated changes in tribal education and government. Congress funded two new schools, one in Sisseton and one in Peever, to provide integrated instruction. In 1975, tribal councilors chartered the Sisseton-Wahpeton Community College and the Tiospa Zina High School to furnish education with an emphasis on tribal values. Tribal elders continue to teach the oral tradition to the younger generation.

The region's economy, based primarily on agriculture and cattle grazing, has long supported substantial numbers of tribal members through fieldwork. By the 1980s, however, the tribe had successfully established a manufacturing base on the reservation, and by the early 1990s it had developed a highly lucrative gaming industry. In addition, the tribe controls all rights-of-way, waterways, watercourses, and streams that flow through any portion of the reservation and to other lands later appended to the reservation under U.S. statutes.

LOWER BRULE RESERVATION

Tribe: Lower Brule Sioux Tribe of the Lower Brule Reservation   Current Location: South Dakota
Total Area: 144,588 acres   Tribal Enrollment: 3,036

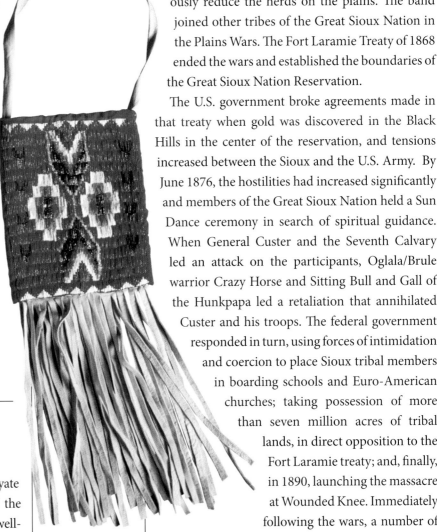

Beaded Sioux bag from South Dakota

The Lower Brule Sioux, Kul Wicasa Oyate ("Lower Men Nation"), are a subband of the Sicangu (Burnt Thigh) Teton/Tituwan (Dwellers on the Plains), and a constituent band of the Sioux Nation. The Teton/Tituwan Band subdivided into the Oglala, Sicangu, Minneconjou, Sihasapa, Oohenunpa, Hunkpapa, and Itazipco groups. The Lower Brules became a further subband in the late 1700s when they split from the Heyata Wicasa/Upper Brule, who currently reside on the Rosebud Sioux Reservation. The Brules speak an "L" dialect of the Siouan language.

The Sicangu were named "Brule" by French fur traders in the late 1600s, and the Kul Wicasa Oyate were originally designated "far western" reservation lands along the Missouri River by a treaty with the United States on October 14, 1865. The 1851 Fort Laramie Treaty included these lands in its definition of the Great Sioux Reservation. The Teton/Tituwan bands did not actively resist settlers to the Dakotas until Euro-American buffalo hunting began to seriously reduce the herds on the plains. The band joined other tribes of the Great Sioux Nation in the Plains Wars. The Fort Laramie Treaty of 1868 ended the wars and established the boundaries of the Great Sioux Nation Reservation.

The U.S. government broke agreements made in that treaty when gold was discovered in the Black Hills in the center of the reservation, and tensions increased between the Sioux and the U.S. Army. By June 1876, the hostilities had increased significantly and members of the Great Sioux Nation held a Sun Dance ceremony in search of spiritual guidance. When General Custer and the Seventh Calvary led an attack on the participants, Oglala/Brule warrior Crazy Horse and Sitting Bull and Gall of the Hunkpapa led a retaliation that annihilated Custer and his troops. The federal government responded in turn, using forces of intimidation and coercion to place Sioux tribal members in boarding schools and Euro-American churches; taking possession of more than seven million acres of tribal lands, in direct opposition to the Fort Laramie treaty; and, finally, in 1890, launching the massacre at Wounded Knee. Immediately following the wars, a number of tribal members relocated to Canada, where many remain today. Still others were relegated to reservations within the United States. The Lower Brule were confined to their reservation lands along the Missouri River, in central South Dakota.

Often referred to as the Big Bend, or Grand Detour, the Little Bend area of tribal lands is one of the longest inland peninsulas in the world. The area is very fertile

SATANTA (WHITE BEAR)

Kiowa raider

After the Medicine Lodge Treaty of 1867 failed, the U.S. government continued to subjugate the Southern Plains tribes. Rather than acquiesce, brave warriors such as Satanta, Big Tree, and Lone Wolf of the Kiowa fought for their land. Although he had been involved in earlier raids and confrontations, Satanta (ca 1816–1878) came to notoriety because of the Warren Wagon Train Raid on May 18, 1871, when wagons hauling supplies to West Texas was ambushed and seven teamsters were killed. Satanta boasted about being responsible for the killing and was arrested, along with Satank and Big Tree. Satank gnawed his wrist to the bone to get free, then stabbed a trooper and was shot. Satanta and the other Kiowas were convicted and sentenced to death. However, their sentence was later commuted to life imprisonment, and they were subsequently paroled after promising to follow the path of peace.

Eventually Satanta was accused of violating his parole and returned to prison. On October 11, 1878, he slashed his wrists and, while being taken to the second floor of the prison hospital, dove out a window, killing himself. In his last act as a Kiowa, he deprived the whites of victory by taking his own life. Satanta is buried on Chief's Knoll in the Fort Sill Cemetery in Fort Sill, Oklahoma. ■

This portrait of Kiowa warrior Satanta was probably taken around 1870.

and holds numerous culturally significant resources. The Lewis and Clark expedition traveled through the Little Bend during their explorations.

Reservation boundaries were redefined after the Great Act of March 1889. In the late 1890s, the entire reservation was moved north 20 miles to a 440,000-acre parcel of land. This reservation was located well within the Lower Brule's traditional territory. Approximately 442 tribal members refused to relocate and were instead added to the Rosebud Sioux tribal rolls, along with 195,000 acres originally belonging to the Lower Brule. Many members of this group remain today, feeling that they are not fully served by either tribe.

During the 1950s and '60s, the tribe was forced to sell more than 29,000 acres of prime river bottomlands to the federal government under the Fort Randall Taking Act and the Big Bend Taking Act, in order to create the Fort Randall and Big Bend Dams, which subsequently caused flooding and loss of further tribal lands and physical improvements. Sixty-nine percent of the reservation's families were forced to abandon their homes, and several culturally significant areas, including worship and gathering sites and cemeteries, were lost in the flooding. The tribe has established an aggressive land repurchase and consolidation program to restore traditional Lower Brule lands to tribal ownership. Since the 1950s, the tribe has regained approximately 20 percent of its lands, about 29,000 acres, both on- and off-reservation.

MIAMI RESERVATION

Tribe: Miami Tribe of Oklahoma   Current Location: Oklahoma   Total Area: 321 acres   Tribal Enrollment: 3,321

Myaamias, or the Miami people, originated in the modern state of Indiana and held the Great Lakes regions of Indiana, Illinois, Ohio, southern Wisconsin, and southern Michigan as their homelands. They also count regions within Kentucky, Iowa, and Missouri as areas of importance. Miami presence in these areas was largely due to war and hunting. The Miami Tribe of Oklahoma, the federally recognized sovereign Miami Nation, owns lands in the Great Lakes area, Kansas, and Oklahoma.

The Myaamia are of the Central Algonquian linguistic group. Their relatives are the Weas and Piankashaw. The great Nation of the Myaamia is well documented in the history of the United States, in large part due to the leadership of the great war chief Mihsihkinaahkwa, who was also known as Little Turtle. Little Turtle led the Miami and their allied forces in major victories over U.S. troops in the late 1700s. The Indian victories over Gen. Josiah Harmar and his troops in 1790 and the most notable defeat over Gen. Arthur St. Clair in 1791 are viewed as the worst defeats suffered by the U.S. Army during the Indian Wars.

Following the allied tribes' victories, the 1794 Battle of Fallen Timbers took place in the area around what is now Maumee, Ohio. U.S. troops, led by Gen. "Mad" Anthony Wayne, defeated their allied enemies, led by the Shawnee chief Bluejacket. This defeat led to the signing of the Greenville Treaty in 1795, in which lands were ceded and boundary lines drawn for the Myaamia as well as their relations. Land loss did not stop there. Continued white encroachment into Miami country, the signing of the Indian Removal Act in 1830, and an 1840 treaty led to the forced removal of the Myaamia from their homelands to land reserved for them west of the Mississippi near present-day La Cygne, Kansas. The Nation resided on the Kansas reserve until the signing of an 1867 treaty, which called for yet another removal, this time to Indian Country.

The Miami Tribe of Oklahoma adopted a constitution and bylaws on August 16, 1939, in accordance with the Oklahoma Indian Welfare Act of June 26, 1936. That constitution was revised and adopted on February 22, 1996, and remains in effect. The Nation's Office of Cultural Preservation restores important tribal buildings and structures, maintains the Nation's cemeteries and burial grounds, supports language reclamation, publishes a quarterly newspaper, and oversees the Nation's Heritage Archive. The Nation owns and operates Tahway Farms, which oversees approximately 1,000 acres of farmland, pasture, and pecan groves and raises grass-fed black and red Angus, Hereford, and Devon cattle.

Cree, Algonquian language family

"Ghees-guy-yoo" ("Bobbed tail" [as on a dog])

"Aush-tum" ("Come here")

MODOC RESERVATION

Tribe: Modoc Tribe of Oklahoma   Current Location: Oklahoma   Total Area: 86 acres   Tribal Enrollment: 181

Members of the Modoc Tribe of Oklahoma are descendants of Modoc warriors and their families, who were exiled from their homelands and led to the Quapaw Agency in Indian Territory in 1873, in what is now southern Oregon and northern California. A small tribe, the Modoc were divided into three groups: the Gumbatwa, or "people of the west"; the Kokiwa, or "people of the far out country"; and the Paskanwa, or "river people." The Modoc called themselves Mqlaq, which meant "the people." Their ancestral home consisted of some 5,000 square miles along both sides of what is now the California-Oregon border, encompassing portions of the beautiful and rugged Cascade Range, the alkali flats to the east, and the lava beds to the south. The Modoc were migratory hunters, fishers, and gatherers, moving with the seasons to follow their food sources. However, their lives changed drastically with the arrival of outsiders. An influx of non-Indians during the mid-19th century had a dramatic impact on Modoc culture. The Modoc readily adopted non-Indian clothing, and many took non-Indian names.

In 1864, the Modoc ceded their lands along with the Klamath and Paiute and agreed to go to the newly established Klamath reservation. Abysmally unhealthy conditions on the reservation spurred the Modoc chief Captain Jack to lead his tribe off the reservation and back to the Lost River. Attempts to return the band to the reservation led to the explosive Modoc War. Captain Jack and his band were returned to the reservation by 1865, but they then retreated to the lava beds and held off the Army until 1873. Following the band's surrender, the Modoc leaders were hanged, and the survivors were exiled to the Quapaw Agency in Indian Territory.

Four thousand acres were purchased for the Modoc in 1874, but the people languished in Indian Territory due to a lack of food and clothing. Reservation lands were allotted to the 68 remaining tribal

members in 1891. Following allotment, they became successful farmers in northeastern Oklahoma, but their Native language and customs were lost. Since the Modoc who wanted to return to Oklahoma from Oregon were on Klamath rolls and had no jurisdiction in Oklahoma during the 1950s, the Eisenhower Administration terminated federal supervision of the Modoc tribe along with the Klamath. In 1967, the Modoc in Oklahoma banded together to form an unofficial tribal government, and the tribe regained federal recognition in 1978.

Today, tribal members are involved in ranching, teaching, small business, and other professions. The tribe is working to reestablish a land base, and tribal members strive to preserve their heritage and culture.

John Tarness, a Shoshone medicine man, shown here in the Little Wind River, Wind River Reservation, Wyoming

MUSCOGEE

Tribe: Muscogee (Creek) Nation
Current Location: Oklahoma   Total Area: 133,811 acres
Tribal Enrollment: 55,955

The Muscogee tribe descends from a Mississippian culture that spanned virtually the entire southeastern United States before 1500. Prior to contact, the people lived a subsistence lifestyle in large, permanent, stockaded villages of earth lodge houses with small gardens, surrounding a centrally located earthen temple and plaza. One of Oklahoma's Five Civilized Tribes, the Muscogee Creek's aboriginal homeland included the region that later became Alabama, Georgia, Florida, and South Carolina.

First contact was made during Spaniard Hernando de Soto's exploratory journey into the interior of North America, which destroyed local food supplies and brought European diseases. Entire villages perished. By the 1600s, the English had established permanent colonies along the eastern seaboard, and trade with settlers developed into a flourishing economy for the Creek, as they exchanged food items, pelts, baskets, and pottery for finished goods, such as iron pots, steel knives, guns, and cotton cloth.

In 1715, the Yamasee War erupted against fraudulent British trade practices, including the capture and shipment of Indian slaves to work on sugar plantations in the Caribbean. The original Ocmulgee Town, located on Ochese Creek (Georgia), was burned to the ground. The Creeks withdrew to the Chattahoochee River, taking their Yuchi neighbors with them. These people became known as the Lower Creek. The Upper Creek were centered on the Coosa and Tallapoosa Rivers to the northeast. As a way of decreasing hostilities, the Creek entered into treaties with the British crown, and in 1773 ceded much of their land to the British government. Following the close of the war, in 1783, England returned control of Florida to Spain, and Spain ceded control of the Creek Territory to the new United States, bringing new waves of settlers into the area.

THE PLAINS

KIOWA

Little is known of the prehistoric origin of the Kiowa, but they have a story that tells how a trickster led the people out of a dark lower world into this one by climbing up a hollow cottonwood log. A pregnant woman got stuck and could not get out, though, blocking the way for the rest; they say this is why there are not many people in the tribe. Scholars disagree whether they migrated south to the Montana mountains sometime after the glaciers melted or moved north in more recent times. Over the years, they moved to southwestern Oklahoma. Spanish sources note that the Kiowa were on the Plains in 1732. They may have become mounted buffalo hunters a few years earlier, obtaining horses from other tribes. Linguistically, they are related to Tanoan language stock.

Alliances on the Plains

Horses changed the culture of the Plains Indians, allowing them to cover more ground and hunt buffalo more effectively. In 1806, the Kiowa and Comanche became allies and shared a common territory. They became close friends with the Cheyenne and Arapaho in 1840.

The Kiowa and Comanche inhabited an area where the land claims of the United States and Mexico overlapped; they constantly raided the Mexicans as far south as Durango. Horses and women were the main prizes, but other valuables were welcome. When the rains came, the buffalo were plentiful, the annual Sun Dances took place as scheduled, and life was ideal.

As early as 1802, the Kiowa had contact with traders. Over the years, though, they came to hate the encroaching Americans because of a history of battles and broken promises. The Kiowa became some of the fiercest warriors of the West, raiding and fighting in defense of their homes.

Trading posts developed beginning in the late 1820s. In 1837, a treaty established peace among the Kiowa, the Comanche, the Creek, the Osage, and the U.S. government. The Kiowa and Comanche agreed to peace with Mexico as well, but continued to raid Mexico, Texas, and New Mexico until after the Civil War.

In the 1867 Treaty of Medicine Lodge with the Plains Apache, Kiowa, Coman-

Vanessa Paukeigope Morgan, a Kiowa regalia-maker, fashions buckskin dresses and other garb.

che, Cheyenne, and Arapaho, the government forbade white hunters from invading reservations and promised the tribes annuities and schools. In return, the tribes ended hostilities, granted right of way, and agreed to settle on a smaller reservation. When the treaty was broken in 1868, the tribes began raiding for food, but after the Washita Massacre, when troops led by Gen. George Custer attacked an Indian village, the tribes capitulated. The Kiowa, along with the Comanche and Kiowa Apache, were placed on a reservation in southwestern Oklahoma, although they lost most of that land when it was opened to white settlers. In the 1870s, raids continued into Texas, as did the government's violations of treaties. The winter of 1873 was a particularly hard one, and horses had to be killed for food.

Power from Prayer

Realizing their power was fading, the Kiowa sought sources of new strength. One of these main sources was prayer. The Sun Dance was forbidden by the government in 1887, and Christian evangelists began to pour in, but many Kiowa began to look at Indian beliefs such as the peyote movement around 1880 and the Ghost Dance in 1890.

The Ghost Dance, which involved invoking an apocalypse that would obliterate the white invaders and create a new Earth for the Indians and their ancestors, inspired resistance among some Plains Indians but soon faded out. The peyote movement grew, however, and developed into the Native American Church. Another contemporary movement, the

Delwin Fiddler (center) of the Lakota Sioux tribe and Toni Tsatooke (left) of the Kiowa tribe lead dancers into the circle for the "grand entry" start of a powwow.

powwow, took hold and continues today. The Kiowa played a prominent part in the dissemination of these powerful unifying movements.

Among the distinctive accomplishments of the Kiowa is their traditional decorative artwork, much of which is enhanced by glass trade beads manufactured in Venice, Italy. The larger "pony beads" were available by the mid-19th century. Then came the smaller "seed beads," which became popular because they offered more colors and had greater availability.

Most of the Plains people prefer certain bead colors, patterns, and methods of application. The beadwork is accomplished by the women using either the appliqué or lazy-stitch method for their geometric patterns. On many items, they use beads sparingly. For example, a Kiowa moccasin might have only thin strips of beading. The long fringes on the top of women's leggings are often beaded, as are the insteps of men's footwear. The yoke of a woman's dress is seldom beaded; instead, it is decorated with elk teeth or shells. The artisans often dye their deer hide base and even twist the fringes on some of the items for that extra bit of class.

The most stunning of their utilitarian creations are their imaginative hooded baby carriers. They are larger than average and somewhat rigid. These are beaded, and the entire exterior design is divided lengthwise, with each half decorated totally differently, often with abstract floral shapes in deep reds, browns, and blues.

The Kiowa Today

The Kiowa Tribe of Oklahoma, a federally recognized tribe, has about 12,000 members. Most of them live near the tribe's headquarters in Carnegie, Oklahoma. The tribal complex there includes social support programs for tribe members, as well as a museum with displays of history, artifacts, and art. The tribe owns a casino in Devol, Oklahoma, and planned to open a second one in 2010 in Verden. The Kiowa live near Comanche and Apache reservations, and jointly with those tribes own about 7,600 acres of scattered federal trust land, much of which is leased out to cattle ranchers and farmers. ▪

By the early 19th century, U.S. Indian policy began pressuring for the removal of the Muscogee and other southeastern tribes to areas west of the Mississippi River. The Muscogee resisted removal, but finally, in 1832, they exchanged the last of their ancestral homelands for new lands in Indian Territory. While some of the confederacy resettled on its own, the U.S. Army had to forcibly remove the majority of the Muscogee people between 1836 and 1837. The Nation, which had been categorized as the Lower and Upper Muscogee tribes, soon reestablished its farms and plantations—even its ancient towns—in its new homeland, but prosperity and peace were disrupted by the Civil War, when a Confederate force attacked a large group of neutral Muscogees within their territory.

Eventually, Indian lands became part of the new state of Oklahoma. The Muscogee determinedly resisted these attempts by the federal government to terminate their nation and culture, and throughout this dark period, the tribe was able to maintain its cultural identity, along with a cursory form of tribal leadership. Despite their vigilance and determination during this period, however, the Muscogee witnessed the removal of approximately $50 billion in oil from their territory by outsiders who had fraudulently secured leases or ownership of allotted lands.

In the 1970s, the tribe adopted a new constitution, revitalized its National Council, and made strides toward political strength and economic development. During the 1980s, Muscogee leadership built a tribal complex and created a set of social services that the BIA has referred to as "the best in the nation."

INDIAN TREATIES

Treaties are written agreements negotiated between sovereign nations to settle a contentious situation. They can end wars, establish commerce, create alliances, or transfer land. After the Europeans arrived in America, some debated whether the Natives were truly human beings. In 1537, Pope Paul III issued a papal bull—a formal decree—that stated that Indians were indeed humans, rational beings with souls who could not morally be enslaved. The Spanish and others were bound to treat them as sovereign nations.

After U.S. independence, treaties with Indian tribes were common, but cultural and legal difficulties arose. For instance, U.S. negotiators usually provided the translator, recorded specifics, and were pragmatic. Indian leaders valued ceremony, oratory, and honor. Nonetheless, several hundred treaties were signed. In 1871, Congress abolished tribal treatymaking, probably because it became too complex, and the government declared that it didn't view Indian sovereignty as valid anymore; a year later, the government began making "agreements" with the tribes in lieu of treaties. Today, tribes are again viewed as sovereign nations that retain some treaty rights. ■

An 1806 treaty between the U.S. government and six tribes, bearing the signature of President Thomas Jefferson

OTTAWA RESERVATION

Tribe: Ottawa Tribe of Oklahoma Current Location: Oklahoma Total Area: 26 acres Tribal Enrollment: 2,536

The Algonquian-speaking Ottawa people of the Northeast consisted of five clans: Otter, Fork People, Bear, Gray Squirrel, and Fish. The Ottawa Indian Tribe of Oklahoma descended from the Otter and Fork People clans. The name Ottawa derives from the Algonquian *adawa*, meaning "to trade or barter." The Ojibwe and Potawatomi are their close tribal relatives. The Ottawa were a migratory tribe that traveled great distances to hunt, trade, and make war. They lived in villages and practiced some horticulture, but were best known as far-ranging intertribal middlemen who traversed the rivers of the northeastern United States and the Great Lakes and traded in tobacco, cornmeal, herbs, furs, and skins. They also traveled along the "Moccasin Trail" into Florida.

Recorded history of the Ottawa dates from 1615 when an Ottawa trading party encountered French explorer Samuel de Champlain near the mouth of

Georgian Bay on the Atlantic coast of Canada. A quarter century later, pressured by the Iroquois, the Ottawa moved to Green Bay in present-day Wisconsin, and from there they spread into northwestern Illinois and southern Wisconsin.

The tribe signed treaties with the British and French during their periods of occupation. However, the tribe allied primarily with the French. During the French and Indian War, the Ottawa supported the French, and later, under the commanding leadership of Ottawa war chief Pontiac, they strongly resisted British power in the Great Lakes region. In 1763, Pontiac led the Ottawa, Potawatomi, and Ojibwe to besiege Fort Detroit; his forces captured a series of fortified posts, but in 1769, three years after a peace treaty with the British, a member of the Peoria tribe assassinated Chief Pontiac. His assassination initiated a fierce war between the Ottawa and Peoria tribes, which resulted in the near annihilation of the Peoria people. Pontiac remains one of the most famous and revered leaders among the Ottawa people.

During the American Revolutionary War, the Ottawa sided with the British, but they were able to control most of Ohio after the war. Euro-American encroachment upon tribal lands following the war forced the tribe to move westward. In 1832, they were moved to Kansas, and remained there until 1868, when the tribe was forced to relocate to a 14,863-acre reservation in present-day Ottawa County, Oklahoma. Remaining lands were opened to white settlement in 1908. Though they lost most of their land, the Ottawa continued to farm and raise livestock in Ottawa County.

The tribe reorganized under the Oklahoma Indian Welfare Act in 1938, but federal recognition was terminated in 1955. On May 15, 1978, the Ottawa were reinstated as a federally recognized tribe. Today, the tribe is working to rebuild its land base, while providing economic opportunities for its members and preserving Ottawa culture and heritage. The tribal

A hide vest for a Sioux child, made in the late 19th or early 20th century, is beaded in geometric patterns in red, green, and blue on a white background.

MATO'-TOPE (FOUR BEARS)

Leader of the Mandan of North Dakota

The mighty Missouri River was the easiest route to the High Plains and Indian Country. From St. Louis, the ancient route crosses several states to Fort Benton, Montana, and beyond. In North Dakota, there are earth lodge villages that always welcomed travelers. Mato'-Tope, or Four Bears (ca 1795–1837), a second Mandan chief, was honored by his name because he fought the Assiniboine with the fury of four bears. He befriended most visitors to his lands and became a favorite of traveling artists. George Catlin, who visited in 1832, admired him for his honesty and demeanor and viewed him as a pure Native man unchanged from his natural state. He painted him whenever possible. So did the Swiss painter Karl Bodmer, who recorded some of the greatest visuals of the Upper Missouri tribes.

Around 1836, Mato'-Tope became chief. Then a smallpox epidemic killed most of his tribe, leaving only 125 survivors. Having already lost his wife and children to the disease, he contracted it as well. Gallant to the end, in his final speech he denounced the whites, whom he had always treated as brothers, for bringing this horrible disease. He said that, in death, his scarred face would be so ugly even the wolves would turn away. ■

economy is supported primarily from revenue earned by the tribe's activities in the tourism industry.

PEORIA INDIAN RESERVATION

Tribe: Peoria Tribe of Indians of Oklahoma
Current Location: Oklahoma
Total Area: 870 acres   **Tribal Enrollment:** 2,761

The Algonquian-speaking Peoria were members of the Illinois Confederacy in the Old Northwest. While exploring the Mississippi River in 1673, Jacques Marquette found the tribe living near present-day Peoria, Illinois. The name Peoria derives from the French form of the personal name Piwarea, meaning "He comes carrying a pack on his back." During the 18th century, the Peoria traded extensively with French outfits moving up and down the Mississippi River, but later they were among the many tribes of the Ohio Valley and Old Northwest displaced by the onslaught of white settlers pouring over the Appalachians.

In 1832, the Peoria, together with a small number of the Kaskaskia (one of the other tribal groups of the Illinois Confederacy), made a new home for themselves when they emigrated to a recently established reservation located on the Osage River in what is now eastern Kansas. The two tribes were joined by two bands of the Miami, the Wea and Piankshaw, in 1854, and the group formed a cohesive whole. In 1857, these newly united tribes moved to the Quapaw Reservation in present-day Ottawa County, Oklahoma. The Peoria Tribe organized under the Oklahoma Indian Welfare Act of 1936, adopting a constitution in 1939; a second constitution was ratified in 1981. The tribe's economy is mainly supported by the tribal government and by the gaming, retail, and tourism industries.

SAC AND FOX RESERVATION

Tribe: Sac and Fox Nation   Current Location: Oklahoma
Total Area: 26,715 acres   Tribal Enrollment: 3,356

Members of the Sac and Fox Nation are descendants of the Sauk and Fox, two Algonquian-speaking peoples of the Great Lakes region. The name Sauk is derived from the tribe's own name, "Osa'kiwug," meaning "People of the Yellow Earth." The Fox people called themselves Meshkwa kihug, meaning "People of the Red Earth." The two tribes were independent, though closely related in culture and language. Both tribes were semi-sedentary village dwellers who subsisted primarily on hunting and fishing. Pressure from the French and other tribes during the late 17th century forced the Sac and Fox into an alliance. Pushed west, the tribes settled in present-day Wisconsin, Iowa, Illinois, and Missouri, mainly along the Mississippi River. During the American Revolution, some Sac and Fox allied with the British.

When the Missouri Band ceded all their lands east of the Mississippi to the United States in 1832, Sauk war chief Black Hawk rebelled. The short, bloody Black Hawk War ended with the massacre of Black Hawk's people at Bad Axe, Wisconsin, by

Mandan, Siouan language family

"Wráp" ("Beaver")

"tíʔ, otíʔ" ("house")

"xóre" ("ice")

"pó" ("fish")

"waʔhi" ("snow")

regular troops and militia on August 3, 1832. The tribe bought a reservation in Kansas in 1842; in 1867, it exchanged this land for a larger reservation in Indian Territory. The Sac and Fox Nation constitution, with a court system and centralized government, was approved in 1885. In 1891, the reservation was opened for allotment.

The Sac and Fox Nation retains a strong government, having reestablished the first complete tribal court, police, and taxation system in Oklahoma, and it preserves and celebrates its rich cultural heritage through learning and enrichment programs.

THLOPTHLOCCO TRIBAL TOWN RESERVATION

Tribe: Thlopthlocco Tribal Town [Creek (Muscogee)]
Current Location: Oklahoma
Federal Trust: 2,500 acres   Population: 638

The members of the Thlopthlocco Tribal Town are descendants of the Muscogee (or Mvskoke), also known as Creek, people of the southeastern United States. These peoples originally lived in riverfront or coastal villages in the areas of present-day Alabama, Louisiana, Mississippi, and western Florida. They practiced a subsistence lifestyle based on hunting, fishing, and horticulture, significantly influenced by the prehistoric Caddoan and Mississippi cultures. They are related linguistically and culturally to the Yamasee, Seminole, Apalachee, Choctaw, and Chickasaw tribes.

The Muscogee term *tvlwv* is translated as "tribal town." However, this word carries a much deeper connotation. Thlopthlocco, a Creek tribal town, has figured prominently in Oklahoma's Creek history and traditions. It was the site of religious happenings, public events, and the Sacred Fire. Each town functioned independently but shared ties of language and kinship.

Throughout the 17th and 18th centuries, the lower Southeast was an economic and military battleground for competing European powers as they tried to gain land in the New World. The Creek, caught in the middle of this power struggle taking

A wild horse stands on a ridge late one afternoon in the Badlands of western North Dakota. Horses were and are integral to Native culture on the Plains.

place on their own homelands, first allied with the English against the Spanish, but they eventually became embroiled in war with other tribes competing for English trade items.

The Creek formed part of the Five Civilized Tribes. The conflicts raging around them eventually ignited conflicts between the Creeks themselves. Warfare between Creeks arose during the War of 1812 as different bands declared allegiance to either the British trying to regain its colonies or the fledgling United States. In 1836, the U.S. Army forced the Creek to relocate to Indian Territory in present-day Oklahoma. Once settled in their new homeland in eastern Oklahoma, the Creek became relatively prosperous farmers. However, they eventually lost most of their tribal lands through allotment. The tribe adopted a constitution in accordance with the Oklahoma Indian Welfare Act on November 17, 1938. The Thlopthlocco Tribal Town is part of the Creek Nation of Oklahoma.

Turtle Mountain Reservation

Tribe: Turtle Mountain Band of Chippewa Indians
Current Location: North Dakota **Total Area:** 77,619 acres
Tribal Enrollment: 28,823

Members of the Turtle Mountain Band of Chippewa belong primarily to the Pembina Band of the Chippewa (Ojibwe) Nation. The Anishinaabe, the "Original People," or the Ojibwe have resided in North America since approximately 900. The people originated on the Island of La Pointe in the Great Lakes region and migrated in various directions as the bands dispersed. Members of the Ojibwe Nation include the present-day Ojibwe, Ottawa, and Potawatomi tribes of Canada, Michigan, Minnesota, Wisconsin, North Dakota, and Montana. The Ojibwe language is a member of the Algonquian linguistic family. The Ojibwe encountered Jesuit missionaries and French traders in 1640 along the shores

MANDAN

The Mandan call themselves Me'tutahanke, after their old village. They speak a dialect of the Siouan linguistic stock, and "Mandan" is a corruption of a Sioux word. Early traditions point to an eastern origin, from near the Winnebago people or the southern Great Lakes country, but they eventually moved near the Heart River, around where Bismarck, North Dakota, is now. The first recorded white man to visit them was Sieur de La Verendrye, a Frenchman from Canada, who was exploring the area in 1738. White artists who visited in the 1800s regarded the Mandan as men in their noble natural state and captured their images in some of the best known art of the Old West. But contact with whites inevitably led to tragedy, as disease nearly obliterated the tribe.

Earth Lodges and Buffalo Hunts

Unlike their neighbors farther west, the Mandan lived in close-knit villages. Their earth lodges were partially underground and were covered with a framework and soil so they looked like mounds. Several families lived in each lodge, and animals such as horses were kept there, too. Bringing some of their old lifestyles from the past, the Mandan people grew corn and other vegetables. In autumn, they hunted buffalo farther west, drying much of the meat for the cold winters. Surplus dry meat and dried produce, as well as the beautiful painted robes and other leather clothes they created, attracted other tribes to the trade center that developed beginning around 1700.

Whenever the Mandan tribe is mentioned, two other closely related tribes should be discussed, because they have lived together and intermarried for an extended period: the Siouan-speaking Hidatsa tribe and the Caddoan-speaking Arikara tribe. The Hidatsa, whose traditional name for themselves means "willow," are said to have emerged from near Spirit Lake, North Dakota. They then

A Mandan woman invokes spirits of the sun and the moon in an engraving based on a watercolor by Karl Bodmer, who traveled the West from 1832 to 1834.

moved west to the Missouri River and settled near the Mandan, who taught them farming. They are closely related to the Crow tribe of Montana and are often confused with the Gros Ventre people of Montana because they share several

names. The Arikara are related to the Pawnee of the lower Missouri Valley. Under pressure from settlers and other tribes, they moved upriver to become neighbors with the Mandan and Hidatsa. Together, the Mandan, Hidatsa, and Arikara are now known as the Three Affiliated Tribes and live on the Fort Berthold Indian Reservation in North Dakota.

Europeans and Disease

Before planes, trains, and automobiles, the main thoroughfare to the northern plains from St. Louis was the Missouri River. Travelers boarded a keelboat of some type and journeyed into Indian Country, usually stopping and visiting the hospitable Three Affiliated Tribes in their earthen mound villages in North Dakota. The best known of these adventurers was the Lewis and Clark expedition, which stopped on its way to the Pacific Ocean in 1804. Twenty-eight years later, painter George Catlin made his way west and visited the Mandan people, whom he painted in groups and as individuals in some of his most famous works. Soon after, in 1834, the German scientist and adventurer Prince Maximilian zu Wied and his talented watercolorist Karl Bodmer spent time with the Mandan, interviewing people and collecting scientific and ethnographic materials.

American Indians had no immunity to many of the diseases of the Old World. In 1837, the steamboat *St. Peter* arrived at Fort Clark, adjacent to the Mandan villages, and brought smallpox to the tribes. The two villages that had assisted Lewis and Clark were devastated. Of the estimated 1,600 residents, only 31 survived. The disease soon spread to most of the tribes of the Upper Missouri, with a 98 percent death rate among the infected. Estimates of fatalities during the four-year epidemic range from 60,000 to 150,000. Mandan chief Mato'-Tope (Four Bears), a favorite subject of artists Catlin and Bodmer, died cursing the whites who brought the disease that killed his people.

The Three Affiliated Tribes

After the epidemic, the Mandan, Hidatsa, and Arikara banded together for survival. They kept their own cultures, including ceremonies and clan systems. There's a story that, back in the 1960s, several Indian students were enrolled in the same class at Harvard University, when the professor stated that the Mandan Indian tribe was extinct. One of the Indian students from North Dakota raised his hand, and said, "I don't think so. Outside the window there, walking across campus, is my cousin Robert. He's from Fort Berthold, North Dakota, and as we can see he is alive and he has always been a proud Mandan."

Nonetheless, very few full-blood Mandan remain among the people of the Three Affiliated Tribes living on the Fort Berthold Reservation. The construction of the Garrison Dam on the Missouri in the years after World War II flooded more than a quarter of the land on the reservation and dislocated 325 families, or about 80 percent of tribal membership. Negotiations with the U.S. government about reparations continued for years, although the resulting settlement left many people unhappy. Families and tribal functions were moved in 1954 to the area around New Town, North Dakota. The tribes today run several health, welfare, educational, and business operations, including the Four Bears Casino, Lodge, and Recreational Park. ∎

A Mandan man in a round feather headdress and other traditional regalia of his tribe participates in a celebration at the Fort Berthold Indian Reservation in North Dakota.

THE PLAINS

A group of American bison, also known as buffalo, graze beneath Grand Teton in Wyoming. Buffalo hunting once supported many tribes.

of Lake Superior and became heavily involved in trade; their interactions with Cree and French traders forged strong relationships among those groups. Near the end of the 1700s, the Mikinakwastsha-Anishinaabe Band of the Ojibwe separated from the tribe and established a community in the Turtle Mountains of North Dakota. The separation was primarily an economic move, as well as an attempt to find refuge from encroaching Euro-American settlement in Wisconsin. In North Dakota, the Ojibwe engaged in conflict with members of the Dakota tribe. Skirmishes over territorial rights continued for about 50 years, until the 1858 Sweet Corn Treaty defined tribal lands for both groups and mandated numerous resolutions for the tribes.

In 1882, the Turtle Mountain Reservation was formally established on a 24-by-32-mile tract. The government wanted to allot the land into individual parcels, but the Ojibwe refused, and the land remained in communal property. Though the initial reservation agreement encompassed about ten million acres, in 1884 its size was dramatically reduced when the government decided that most of the mixed-blood population was Canadian in origin. After ongoing legal battles, the federal government finally agreed to compensate the tribe one million dollars and to allot land from the public domain as distant as Montana and South Dakota once reservation lands were exhausted.

During the 1950s, the Turtle Mountain Chippewa were targeted for termination, though Congress did not authorize the termination. During the 1970s, enhanced tribal sovereignty, along with federal help in attracting business investment and housing construction, allowed the tribe to realize a degree of success and self-sufficiency. During the late 1980s, the federal government recognized the unfairness of the so-called Ten Cent Treaty and began a reparations process.

Currently, the traditional Chippewa and Mitchell languages are still spoken on the reservation and vicinity, as is Mitchif, a Creole language. Moreover, while the majority of tribal members are Roman Catholic, a small but growing percentage practices

MYTH OR FACT?
Indians invented scalping.

MYTH
Scalping—the removal of the top of an enemy's head after or for the purpose of killing the enemy—has been used on other continents throughout the ages as a way to mark victories and count the defeated.

traditional religious customs. The tribe also operates the Anishinaubag Intercultural Center, which includes a Plains Indian village as well as Mandan earth lodges, log cabins, and other historic recreations that demonstrate the Native American history of the area.

WINNEBAGO INDIAN RESERVATION

Tribe: Winnebago Tribe of Nebraska
Current Location: Nebraska   Total Area: 28,167 acres
Tribal Enrollment: 4,321

The Ho-Chunk, "People of the Parent Speech" or "People of the Big Voice," constitute the Winnebago Tribe of Nebraska. The Winnebago are part of the Chiwere Siouan linguistic family. In the region of present-day Kentucky, the Winnebago's presence in North America has been traced as far back as 500 B.C. They arrived in Wisconsin by A.D. 500 and identify this region as their ancestral homeland.

During the 17th century, Algonquin refugees from the Beaver Wars moved into present-day Wisconsin, igniting intertribal warfare. More devastating, though, was the arrival of foreign illnesses, which nearly wiped out both the Winnebago and Menominee tribes. By 1665, when French explorers returned to the area now known as Wisconsin, the Winnebago numbered approximately 500.

A series of treaties signed with the United States beginning in 1816 resulted in their removal to a series of reservations in Iowa, Minnesota, and South Dakota. They remained near Blue Earth County, Minnesota, until after the Sioux uprising of 1862. Since their war chief Little Priest participated with the Sioux in two battles, the United States removed the Winnebago to a reservation established for the Yankton Sioux in South Dakota. Many rebelled and returned to their land; others traveled the Missouri River to the Omaha Reservation in Nebraska. The 40,000-acre Winnebago Indian Reservation was established by treaties in 1865 and 1874.

During the 1880s, half of the tribe moved back to Wisconsin. The tribe lost two-thirds of its Nebraska

THE PLAINS

reservation land due to the General Allotment Act of 1887. In 1975, the Indian Claims Commission awarded the tribe $4.6 million for the land lost in 1837; the tribe decided to use some of the award monies for per capita payments and a wake and burial program. In 1986, the tribe reestablished its sovereignty via the legal system, and the tribal court system now has jurisdiction over misdemeanor criminal and concurrent civil matters within tribal boundaries.

The region surrounding the Winnebago Indian Reservation has traditionally supported agriculture, and it remains a significant source of tribal income today. Otherwise, tribal businesses, particularly the casino, provide for much of the employment among members. Traditional culture remains relatively vital, with many members belonging to the Native American Church and approximately 10 percent continuing to use the language.

HUNTING PARTIES

Plains Indians had several types of "hunting parties." These depended upon the quarry: buffalo, horses, or human enemies.

Until the early 1700s, the Indians of the Northern Plains had no horses. The primary styles of mass hunting involved driving a buffalo herd into an alcove or a corral and then killing the animals with spears or bow and arrow, or organizing the tribe to drive the herd off a low cliff where the fall would immobilize the beasts but not ruin the meat. After the kill, the women butchered and dried the meat. By the mid-1700s, many tribes had firearms and horses, which eliminated the need for the earlier tactics.

Hunting for enemies and horses could be considered overlapping, because they often were found together. It would begin with a warrior letting it be known that he was going horse raiding. The next morning, a small group of volunteers would assemble with food and extra moccasins because they often walked to their raid—why take a horse on a horse raid? They would arrive at the enemy's camp in darkness, sneak in, untie the animals' tethers, and depart with their booty. If they were discovered, conflict followed. Horses became a symbol of wealth and prestige. For many years, there was no other currency. ■

Plains Indians as they would have appeared on a buffalo hunt, shown in a photograph probably taken between 1910 and 1915

WYANDOTTE RESERVATION

Tribe: Wyandotte Nation   **Current Location:** Oklahoma   **Total Area:** 218 acres   **Tribal Enrollment:** 4,279

The Wyandotte Nation, composed of members of the Wendat (Huron) Confederacy, the Attignawantan Nation, and the Khionontateronon (Petun) Nation, occupied the forests of the present Canadian provinces of Quebec and Ontario. The Wyandotte Nation originally consisted of 12 tribal bands, though many no longer exist. While "Wyandot" is the accepted ethnological spelling, the tribe goes by Wyandotte. The definition of the word "Wyandot" is not completely understood but it may mean "Island Dweller" or "Inhabitant of a Peninsula."

At the time of initial contact with French trappers and missionaries in the 17th century, the Wyandotte practiced a subsistence pattern based on hunting and fishing. Migration out of traditional homelands led tribal members to accept a more agricultural lifestyle, spurring the small-scale cultivation of crops such as corn, beans, squash, sunflowers, peas, pumpkins, melons, and tobacco. After falling to the Iroquois Confederacy in 1649, the Wyandotte and their Huron allies fled to present-day Mackinac Island, Michigan. Many later migrated to the northeastern corner of Wisconsin, then to the Ohio Valley. The Wyandotte continued to flee from the Iroquois forces until 1700, when they made an appeal to establish peace with that confederacy.

A large segment of the tribe settled at the French outpost in Detroit in 1701. The Wyandotte loosely allied themselves with the British during the American Revolution and were later defeated in 1794 by the American general Anthony Wayne at the Battle of Fallen Timbers. The Wyandotte were forced to cede much of their territory to the United States at the Treaty of Greenville in 1795. The tribe subsequently lost the remainder of its land in Michigan and Ohio at the Fort Meigs Treaty of 1817.

In 1843, the Wyandotte were relocated to what is now eastern Kansas. An 1855 treaty terminated the tribe and most tribal lands. While the majority of tribal members accepted the conditions of the treaty,

Replica of a Native American painting done on buffalo hide, from the Knife River Indian Villages National Historic Site, North Dakota

a small band fled to Oklahoma in 1857. An 1867 treaty confirmed the tribe's legal existence and gave the Wyandotte title to 20,000 acres of former Seneca land in northeastern Oklahoma. Much of this land was later lost through allotment.

The tribe persevered and reorganized as the Wyandotte Tribe of Oklahoma in 1937. The Wyandotte are rightfully proud of their ability to weather the numerous obstacles that have threatened their existence. A small number of tribal members live on the reservation at Wyandotte, Oklahoma, while other tribal members and descendants of the Wyandotte tribe continue to live throughout the Great Lakes region.

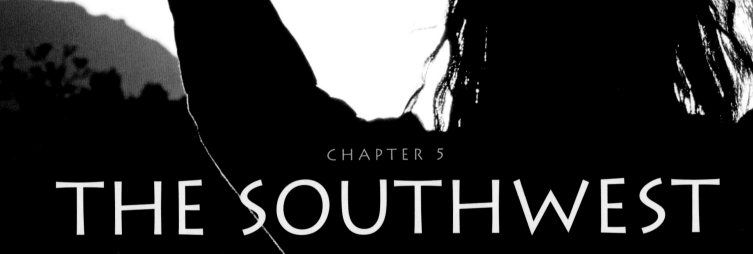

THE SOUTHWEST

THE SOUTHWEST

AMERICAN SOUTHWEST, THE AREA THAT INCLUDES MOST OF MODERN NEW Mexico and Arizona, as well as parts of adjoining states, is a region where the Native American influence is pervasive. Modern visitors can see the well-preserved ruins of sophisticated ancient dwellings at places such as Mesa Verde National Park in Colorado. They can buy southwestern jewelry, rugs, and pottery from people who still use the artistic techniques they learned from their ancestors. They can also glimpse contemporary Native life on huge reservations, such as that of the Navajo Nation, or smaller settlements, such as those of the 20 Pueblo tribes—places where today's Indians still live on their ancestral homelands, albeit with much smaller territories than they controlled in centuries past. These cultures have been shaped by their adaptation to the often harsh environment of the Southwest, a place where life-giving water is never abundant.

IN THE DESERT, SURVIVAL REQUIRES MAKING THE BEST OF SCARCE WATER SUPPLIES.

PREHISTORIC CIVILIZATIONS

ARCHAEOLOGISTS CLASSIFY THE PREHISTORIC PEOPLES OF THE Southwest into three great farming civilizations: the ancestral Puebloans (also called Anasazi) in the Four Corners region; the Mogollon of mountainous southwestern New Mexico; and the Hohokam, who used irrigation to farm in southern Arizona and northern Mexico. Other cultures have also played major roles over time, especially the semi-nomadic Southern Athabascan peoples now known as the Navajo and Apache.

The three civilizations developed about A.D. 100 or 200, overtaking the Paleo-Indian and Archaic civilizations that had inhabited the region for thousands of years. They became more complex over time, with cultures that peaked between about 700 and 1300, depending on location. Notably, the ancestral Puebloans built massive masonry structures of multiple stories, some with hundreds of rooms; there are dozens of such "great houses" at Chaco Canyon in New Mexico.

These civilizations collapsed in the period from 1200 to 1400, probably from interrelated reasons that include drought and warfare. But just because the people abandoned their old settlements doesn't mean they abandoned the land. The ancestral Puebloans are the likely ancestors of today's Pueblo people, as the Hohokam are of today's O'odham.

Preceding pages: A spiritual guide greets the sun with prayer feathers in Arizona. Opposite: Eldon Owens, a Navajo, performs the grass dance in Gallup, New Mexico, in 2003.

SPANIARDS, MEXICANS, AMERICANS

THE SPANISH WERE THE FIRST EUROPEANS TO VISIT THE SOUTHWEST. LURED BY TALES OF gold, explorer Francisco Vasquez de Coronado led an expedition from Mexico to what is now New Mexico in 1540. The search for gold was fruitless, but that trip began 140 years of

heavy-handed Spanish domination of the region. Eventually, Spanish oppression in the name of the Catholic Church became too much for the Pueblo people. In 1680, tribes and villages in New Mexico and Arizona united in a successful revolution against Europeans on American soil, known as the Pueblo Revolt.

The goal of the revolt was to drive the Spaniards from their land, and it succeeded. The victory came with the destruction of many Spanish churches and the death of many Franciscan priests. The Spanish retreated to what's now El Paso, Texas, and made a few abortive attempts

SOUTHWEST

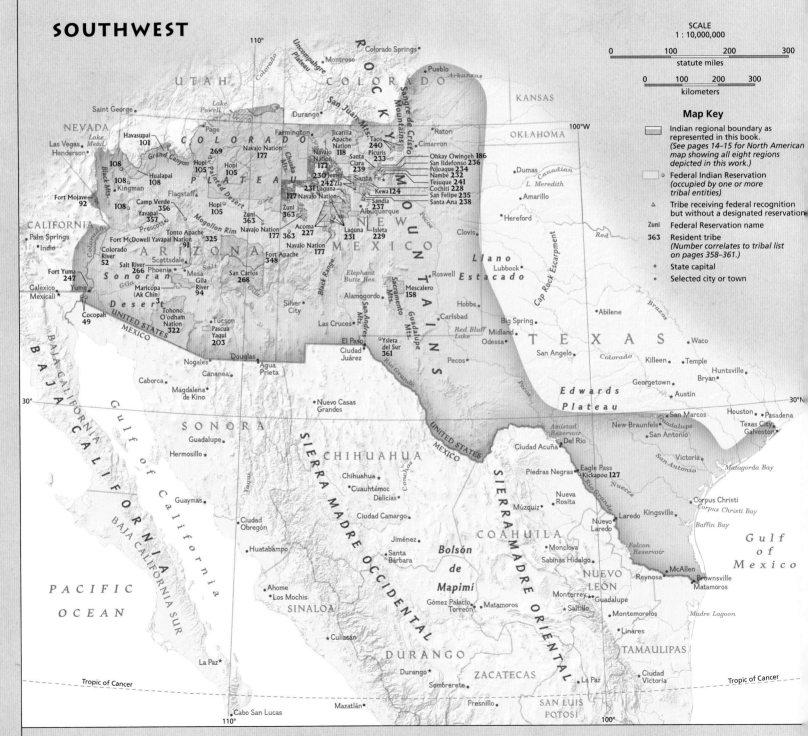

SCALE
1 : 10,000,000

statute miles

kilometers

Map Key

Indian regional boundary as represented in this book.
(See pages 14–15 for North American map showing all eight regions depicted in this work.)

Federal Indian Reservation (occupied by one or more tribal entities)

Tribe receiving federal recognition but without a designated reservation

Zuni — Federal Reservation name

363 — Resident tribe
(Number correlates to tribal list on pages 358–361.)

★ State capital

• Selected city or town

to reclaim the land. Finally, in 1692, Don Diego de Vargas arrived in the Rio Grande Valley for what became known as the Spanish Reconquest. De Vargas took the lands back for New Spain in a more peaceful manner than his predecessors.

The Southwest passed into Mexican control in 1821 when Mexico became independent from Spain. It eventually came under U.S. control in two pieces: the majority with the 1848 Treaty of Guadalupe Hidalgo, which ended the Mexican-American War, and the southernmost chunks of Arizona and New Mexico with the 1854 Gadsden Purchase.

American interaction with the Indians of the Southwest in the latter half of the 19th century was often violent. The Apache and Navajo, in particular, resisted the incursions of the white man onto their homelands. These Southern Athabascan people had long lived as seminomads, doing some farming but relying heavily on hunting and gathering to support themselves. Such a lifestyle by necessity requires access to vast areas of land.

> INDIANS IN ARIZONA AND NEW MEXICO DID NOT WIN THE RIGHT TO VOTE UNTIL 1948, AND THEN ONLY AFTER LAWSUITS.

The Americans, with superior firepower and numbers, eventually won. They pushed the Indians onto reservations that were much smaller than the land they had lived on before. In many cases, the history of these reservations is one of forced relocations and broken promises, extending well into the 20th century. For decades, the federal government embraced assimilationist policies that affected Indians in the Southwest as they did tribes elsewhere in the country. These included shifting land-ownership laws and the forced attendance of children at often far-off boarding schools. In the mid-20th century, federal programs supported the relocation of Indians from reservations to cities. Even as some government policies tried to absorb Indians into the broader culture, others explicitly discriminated against them—for instance, Indians in Arizona and New Mexico did not win the right to vote until 1948, and then only after lawsuits.

TRADITIONAL CULTURES IN THE MODERN WORLD

THROUGHOUT THE SOUTHWEST, THE TRIBES THROUGH THE CENTURIES HAVE CLUNG TO many elements of their traditional cultures. Their religions, origin stories, and languages are still passed down from elders to children. These spiritual traditions explain how humans interact with the natural and supernatural worlds as well as with each other. The tribes and villages regularly conduct often elaborate ceremonies involving traditional dances and songs. Some are open to non-Indians, who visit to witness such events as the colorful kachina dances. Other ceremonies are private religious rituals, open only to believers.

Throughout the Southwest, one reason that Indians have held onto as much of their land as they have is likely that it didn't appeal to other people. With so little water, farming remains difficult, as does much else, and legal fights over water rights are contentious. Many of the reservations are poor and far from any source of employment. However, over the years, numerous tribes have strived to make the best of available natural resources that lie below the land, including metals, oil, and gas. Since the 1990s, many have also taken advantage of another avenue to economic development: their right to run casinos on that ancestral land. ■

MANUELITO

Navajo leader in war and peace

Manuelito (1818–1893) led Navajo fighters in the Navajo Wars of 1863–66. His followers were the last to surrender after Kit Carson's scorched-earth campaign to force them to relocate to the Bosque Redondo Reservation near Fort Sumner, New Mexico.

Manuelito was born in southeastern Utah. He rose to prominence among his people during years of attacks against Mexicans, U.S. troops, and neighboring Indian tribes. In 1858, Maj. William T. H. Brooks ordered Manuelito to move his livestock from the land where his father and grandfather had grazed their herds. He refused, so the Army killed 60 of his horses and more than 100 of his sheep.

In the late 1860s, after the Navajo Wars, Manuelito traveled to Washington, D.C., to petition for the return of his people to their homeland. On June 18, 1868, some 7,000 Navajo people began a six-week journey home from exile. Manuelito was one of two men in charge of leading the people safely home to their native land along the Arizona–New Mexico border.

He is famous for advising his people: "The white men have many things we Navajo need, but we cannot get them unless we change our ways. My children, education is the ladder to all our needs. Tell our people to take it." ■

This photograph of Navajo war chief Manuelito was taken in 1874.

ACOMA

Tribe: Pueblo of Acoma   Current Location: New Mexico
Total Area: 378,262 acres   Tribal Enrollment: 4,819

Haaku is among the oldest inhabited sites in the United States. The Spanish title "Kingdom of Acu" originated during encounters with the Spanish in the 16th century. Early descriptions supported the Pueblo of Acoma's claims to traditional lands comprising some 1.5 million acres and numerous villages throughout the Acoma province. The vast majority of the Pueblo of Acoma's aboriginal lands were taken from them. The pueblo's 100-year land recovery program began in 1877, when the United States measured off the Acoma grant erroneously, and the Spanish land grant was all Acoma had in its legal possession until 1928. Today, the pueblo's land base has grown by almost 400 percent.

The reservation includes the villages of Acomita, McCartys, Shutivaville, Anzac, and Old Acoma. Old Acoma, or Haaku, often referred to as "Sky City" by Americans, lies atop a 365-foot mesa above the surrounding valley.

MYTH OR FACT?
Indian pueblos are closed to outsiders.

MYTH
Many pueblos welcome visitors, as long as those visitors are respectful and follow rules about such things as taking pictures. Some pueblos close during ceremonies or at other designated times.

In 1863, President Abraham Lincoln presented a silver-headed cane to Acoma and several other Pueblo groups in New Mexico in recognition of their political and legal right to land and self-government. Traditionally, the governors of each pueblo keep their cane as a symbol of their authority during their terms of office. Although the tribe is organized under the Indian Reorganization Act of 1934, the Pueblo of Acoma chose not to adopt a constitution or charter. Acoma's traditional government serves as a stabilizing force for the community.

The Pueblo of Acoma maintain a tribal court system with an independent and separate trial court.

COCHITI

Tribe: Pueblo of Cochiti   Current Location: New Mexico
Total Area: 50,681 acres   Tribal Enrollment: 1,180

It is generally agreed that the Cochiti lived at Frijoles Canyon until a few centuries before the beginning of the Spanish colonial era in the 1590s. The band has occupied the site of the present-day pueblo for at least 700 years. The present Cochiti village lies

A Mexican fisherman, most likely a Cucapá Indian, cleans his nets. The Cucapá, spelled Cocopah in the United States, are the Mexican portion of a tribe that straddles the border along the Colorado River. The Cocopah, long known as the River People, have a U.S. reservation about 13 miles south of Yuma, Arizona.

A girl hugs her great-aunt after the fancy dress competition at a powwow. Such competitions are a colorful part of these popular gatherings.

near the center of the reservation, a tract of land situated along the Rio Grande.

Cochiti lies west of the Rio Grande and away from the primary Spanish routes, and as a result, outsiders didn't regularly visit the pueblo until after 1581. In 1680, the Pueblo Revolt resulted in the expulsion of the Spanish colonists from the area north of the Rio Grande. The Pueblo Indians maintained their independence, and in 1689 the Spanish crown established the original pueblo land grant. Cochiti Pueblo enjoyed independence until 1821, when the Mexican government gained control over New Mexico. In 1846, the United States gained control, and the 1848 Treaty of Guadalupe Hidalgo confirmed the traditional Indian land grants. In 1864, the U.S. Congress patented the original Cochiti land grant from the Spanish crown.

The Cochiti are a member of the Eastern Keresan language group and part of an anthropological grouping known as the Keresan Bridge Pueblos, which include Acoma, Cochiti, Laguna, Santa Ana, Santo Domingo, San Felipe, and Zia—characterized partly by the power vested in the medicine societies. In addition to their usual duties related to curing disease and performing rites of exorcism, medicine societies among the Keresan Bridge Pueblos play a much greater role than elsewhere by exerting a powerful influence in preserving traditional ways as well as by assuming governmental and ceremonial functions. The village chief, or *cacique*, and his assistants are medicine men in Keresan pueblos.

Cochiti is the northernmost Keresan pueblo in New Mexico. The tribe is governed under a traditional system. Each year, the tribal cacique appoints a war chief, lieutenant war chief, governor, lieutenant governor, major fiscale, and lieutenant fiscale. The pueblo also maintains its own tribal court system. The tribal economy is supported in large part by enterprises in the retail, tourism, and agricultural industries, of which the largest source of revenue is the tribally owned Cochiti Lake, a man-made lake on tribal lands.

COCOPAH INDIAN RESERVATION

Tribe: Cocopah Tribe of Arizona   Current Location: Arizona   Total Area: 7,772 acres   Tribal Enrollment: 940

The Cocopah Indians are one of the Yuman tribes—expert farmers of the Colorado River flatlands with a language belonging to the Hokan family, spoken by peoples from southern Oregon all the way south into Mexico. Around 1760, the Yuma, Maricopa, and Cocopah formed one tribe, known as the Coco-Maricopa, living around the Gulf of California, near the mouth of the Colorado River. Sometime after that, they migrated northward and settled along the Colorado River.

The ancestors of the Cocopah may have been among the first Native Americans in the Southwest to encounter Europeans. Hernando de Alarcón made contact with the river people in 1540, and in that same year Melchior Diaz visited the river people and wrote of semisubterranean houses covered with straw and of long structures that could shelter 100 people at a time.

In the 1850s, Cocopah weapons, food, and agriculture were virtually unchanged from those mentioned by Alarcón 300 years earlier, but the 1850s saw the beginning of more intensive contact and communication between the Cocopah and the non-Indian people who settled along the lower Colorado River. When ethnologist W. J. McGee visited the Cocopah in 1900, he wrote that they were divided into seven groups, each one identified by its leader.

Leadership of the people was and is determined by ability and experience; figures of importance were believed to derive their powers from dreams. The ability to speak well and to serve as a consultant and adviser to the people bears even more weight today. Funeral orators, singers, and, until the 1950s, healing shamans were traditional figures of importance in Cocopah society.

In 1917, a U.S. government decree gave the American Cocopahs legal title to three small areas of land as a reservation under the jurisdiction of the Yuma

MYTH OR FACT?

Some Indians speak languages no one else speaks.

FACT

Some tribes, such as the Zuni, speak languages unlike those of any other group on the planet. Some tribes speak languages that are related to others within their language family but are so foreign to outsiders that they can serve as secret codes, as was the case with the Navajo and other Indian code talkers of World War II.

Agency of the BIA. In 1961, the Cocopahs in Arizona began to organize to improve housing, introduce electricity, and complete their first tribal building. They revised their constitution in 1968 with advice from the Navajo Nation.

COLORADO RIVER INDIAN RESERVATION

Tribe: Colorado River Indian Tribes (Chemehuevi, Hopi, Mohave, and Navajo)   Current Location: Arizona and California   Total Area: 269,920 acres   Tribal Enrollment: 3,705

The Colorado River Indian Tribes Reservation straddles the border of Arizona and California, with the majority of its land base falling in Arizona. The reservation is home to four tribes. The original inhabitants were the Mohave and the Chemehuevi, who have farmed on the lower Colorado River since before recorded history. After World War II, they were joined by relocated Navajos and Hopis. The Chemehuevi traditionally lived

Two children play at the Gila River Indian Community south of Phoenix, home to the Akimel O'odham (Pima) and Pee Posh (Maricopa) peoples.

APACHE

The Apache are a group of Southern Athabascan–speaking peoples, part of the same language family as the Navajo. Historically, they occupied a huge swath of the American Southwest, including parts of what are now Arizona, New Mexico, Colorado, Oklahoma, and Texas, as well as northern Mexico. General usage as of the late 20th century separates the Apache into six main tribal groups: Chiricahua, Jicarilla, Lipan, Mescalero, Plains Apache, and Western Apache. However, the way U.S. policies toward Indian tribes have been carried out over time means that they have been split and moved around into a patchwork of reservations, allotment land, and nations. Some of the most famous Indian battle leaders of the 19th-century West were Apache: Mangas Coloradas, Cochise, and Geronimo.

Many Peoples, Similar Cultures

Although the different groups of Apache developed different dialects and cultural attributes, they also shared numerous unifying traits. Their basic social grouping was the extended family. When young men married, they left their parents to live with the family of their wife's mother. Several extended families that lived near each other would come together as a local group. These groups would be led by a chief, but this was not a hereditary title; rather, the chief was a man acknowledged for his outstanding abilities and charisma. Population density was low; the often-arid lands where the Apache lived did not support large settlements.

The religious/ceremonial and mythical beliefs of the Apache were complex, but they generally revolved around the idea that there was a supernatural force in the universe that could be drawn upon by humans, for good or evil. Sickness and other troubles were often blamed on witchcraft.

The Apache were essentially hunters and gatherers, although by the 19th century, farming and raising sheep were increasingly important. Like other Indians, they had acquired horses by the early 17th century and relied on them for hunting and warfare.

Mescalero Apache Indians in New Mexico perform the Dance of the Mountain Gods.

Guerrilla Resistance

Contact between Europeans and the Apache dates back to the first Spanish incursions into New Mexico and Arizona in the 1500s. In many areas, it was marked by Apache raids on white settlements and white military campaigns against the Apache.

The bulk of Apache land came under U.S. control in 1848, at the end of the Mexican-American War. The Americans wanted to use the land for mining and farming, but the Apache, expert guerrilla fighters, resisted the settlers for years. The U.S. Army, violently enforcing the government policy of subduing the Indians, considered the Apache among its greatest enemies. These decades of conflict are often lumped together as the Apache Wars and have been fictionalized in many movies and novels.

These years produced some of the most famous leaders among the Chiricahua Apache, whose territory was in southeastern Arizona, southwestern New Mexico, and across the Mexican border. One was Mangas Coloradas, who had fought the Spanish. When the Americans took over, miners flooded into Apache land, and Mangas Coloradas was reportedly captured and flogged by a group of miners, inflaming his hatred of the new white men. While some historians say there's not much evidence of that incident, it's obvious that he was a declared enemy of the settlers. In 1861, he joined with his son-in-law Cochise to relentlessly fight the Americans. With promises of treaty talks, the older chief was lured to his death at the hands of U.S. soldiers in 1863. Cochise fought on for another decade, until he surrendered and joined many of his people on a reservation, where he died in 1874.

Geronimo, a spiritual leader and medicine man, famously held out the longest against the whites, leading raids and revolts after thousands of his people were confined to the San Carlos Reservation in Arizona. He and a small band of supporters finally surrendered in 1886. Along with several hundred other Apaches, he was sent to Fort Marion, Florida. Eventually, Geronimo and others were transferred to Fort Sill, Oklahoma, where he died in 1909.

Relocation to Reservations

By the 1880s, the Apache were largely spread among reservations in the Southwest. Although some of these reservations seem geographically large, they are much, much smaller than the territories these tribes once roamed.

Each tribe had its own often convoluted trail of relocations. For instance, the Mescalero Apache Reservation in south-central New Mexico includes subtribes of Mescalero, Lipan, and Chiricahua Apache. In Camp Verde, in the Verde River Valley of Arizona, a group of Western Apache historically lived on one side of the river, and a group of Yavapai—a completely different family of Indians— lived on the other. After gold was found nearby in 1863, the tribes were under almost continual attack. In 1871, the Camp Verde Reserve was established for the Apache; the Yavapai were moved there two years later. In 1875, 1,500 people of the two tribes were forced to move 180 miles to the Indian Agency at San Carlos, Arizona, along with Apache from numerous other locales. They

were not allowed to return until 1900, at which time only about 200 made it back.

There are eight federally recognized tribes with "Apache" in their names: the Fort Sill Apache Tribe of Oklahoma, the Apache Tribe of Oklahoma, the Jicarilla Apache Nation, the Mescalero Apache Tribe of the Mescalero Reservation, the San Carlos Apache Tribe of the San Carlos Reservation, the Tonto Apache Tribe of Arizona, the White Mountain Apache Tribe of the Fort Apache Reservation, and the Yavapai-Apache Nation of the Camp Verde Indian Reservation. These tribes generally have embraced gaming as a way to enhance their economies. ■

Apache people line up for a sacred Sunrise Dance at the Fort Apache Reservation, Arizona.

The Taos pueblo in New Mexico, a UNESCO World Heritage site and national historic landmark, has been continuously occupied for more than 1,000 years.

between the Mohave and the Quechan, who lived farther to the south.

Initially, the Mohave welcomed Spanish explorers. The first Spaniard known to have contacted the Mohave was Juan de Oñate, in 1604. Later, Father Francisco Garces arrived in the Mohave Valley in 1776 and estimated the population to be 3,000 souls. However, no missions or Spanish settlements were established in Mohave territory, and the people maintained their independence. This changed with the arrival of the Americans and the 1857 defeat of the Quechan-Mohave allies at the hands of an alliance of Pima and Maricopa warriors. Weakened in numbers and hostile to the American imposition of a new lifestyle, in 1858 the Mohave attacked a wagon train bound for California. This led to the establishment of Fort Mohave in the Mohave Valley. The resistance of the Mohave ended after they lost a battle with U.S. forces in 1859.

The reservation was formed in 1865. The development of a reliable irrigation system has played an important role.

Tohono O'odham, Uto-Aztecan language family

"Hascu 'o cem 'e-ga:g?"

("What are you searching for?")

FORT APACHE RESERVATION

Tribe: White Mountain Apache Tribe
Current Location: Arizona   **Total Area:** 1,684,225 acres
Tribal Enrollment: 13,230

The White Mountain Apache traditionally roamed the wilds between the Pinaleño Mountains to the south and the White Mountains to the north. When the horse was introduced, they expanded their reach, raiding and trading with neighboring tribes and the Spanish.

In reaction to raids and attacks on Spanish settlements beginning in the mid-18th century, the Spanish government attempted to defeat and control the Apache by military means, but by 1786, it had become clear that the Spanish goal of extermination was unrealistic. In response, the Spanish viceroy of a new Indian policy, designed to placate the Apache by settling them in villages near the Spanish military encampments, offering them supplies and, most significantly, alcohol as enticements to keep them peaceful. For nearly 25 years this

POPÉ

Medicine man and military strategist

The leader of the successful revolt against the 14-decade Spanish occupation of New Mexico was born in the San Juan pueblo and given the name Popé, a Tewa word meaning "Ripe Squash." Popé (ca 1630–1688) became a medicine man, learning that what a Tewa thinks and what he does should never contradict each other.

In 1675, Popé was one of 47 medicine men taken captive by the Spaniards in an attempt to quash unrest. Instead, the Pueblo marched to the capital in Santa Fe to demand the release of their spiritual leaders, and the Spanish relented.

As he made the 20-mile trek home, Popé decided to advocate for unity against the Spaniards, whom he called the "metal people." He moved to Taos pueblo so his tribe would not be endangered by the

Pueblo revolutionary Popé, as envisioned by modern Jemez Pueblo sculptor Cliff Fragua

threats against him. From there, he trained traders and medicine men to spread the word.

The medicine man watched the weather. He determined that heavy winter snows would cause the waters of the Rio Grande to rise in the spring of 1680, delaying Spanish supply wagons from Mexico until late summer and leaving the Spaniards vulnerable. The goal was clear: All the metal people north of Santa Fe had to die. All vestiges of Catholicism had to be wiped out—all the churches, the statues, the priests.

The Pueblos rose up the morning of August 10. In Santa Fe, survivors clustered under siege. On August 21, some 2,000 hungry and humiliated Spaniards marched south out of the city and out of Native lands. The conquistadors would not take back New Mexico for 12 years.

Throughout the revolt, Popé remained in Taos. He lived eight more years, and never again encountered any of the metal people. ■

PUEBLO REVOLT

The arrival of the Spanish in what is now New Mexico changed life for all the indigenous people of the Southwest; the brutality and oppression that followed lasted 140 years. Finally, in 1680, the Natives of New Mexico rebelled; they drove the Spanish out of New Mexico for 12 years, the most successful revolt of Natives in what is now the United States.

Under the leadership of Tewa medicine man Popé, chiefs from around the region met secretly over time to plan a coordinated, multifaceted military action. The central element of the plan was to cut off the smaller Spanish settlements from the capital in Santa Fe. The key was acting together. Runners were sent out to each of the villages with knotted yucca cords. As the sun rose each day, a knot was untied. When the last knot was untied, it would be time to act.

The attacks came at sunrise on August 10, 1680. The rebels destroyed all the outlying settlements, with very few escapees. Most of those who survived gathered in Los Cerrillos and at a settlement called La Cañada. Soon the refugees made their way to Santa Fe with the horrible news of the attacks, crowding into the buildings at the governor's residence.

As another part of the plan, Puebloans pretended to side with the Spanish so that rumors could credibly be spread in Santa Fe about other attacks taking place to the south, especially along the Rio Grande in the village of Isleta. Isleta was a pueblo that had always sided with the Spaniards and was also the headquarters of the lieutenant governor. When Governor Antonio de Otermin did not hear word from his lieutenant, he assumed that the village had fallen to the rebels; the governor did not know the messengers had been stopped before they could reach him. The rebels also sent runners to inform Isleta that the areas to the north had come under control of Popé and his forces. Thus, the two groups of Spaniards each thought the other was vanquished, confusing and weakening them.

In Santa Fe, the rebels cut off the water supply to the government buildings. After two days in the summer heat, animals started to die, and people started to get sick. Governor Otermin decided to counterattack. As the Spaniards charged out of the government buildings, they surprised and killed many Indians. They continued on to a Pueblo stronghold nearby, killed Indians, gathered water, and returned to the capital buildings with 47 rebel captives.

But they had not broken the Indian resistance. The 2,000 Spanish refugees, hungry, sick, and humiliated, finally left Santa Fe on August 21. They simply marched out of the city, and the rebels let them go. ■

policy worked with moderate success, but when the Mexican government could no longer subsidize the Apache, the people left to regroup in their traditional territories. After U.S. acquisition of the Gadsden Purchase in 1853, it became clear that the new American settlers sought to control the Apache and usurp their territory. The Indians responded with open hostility, resulting in a dramatic 40-year war, ending with the defeat of the Apache, who were relocated to reservations.

In July 1869, Maj. John Green of the U.S. First Cavalry led a scouting expedition of more than 120 troops into the White Mountains, giving explicit instructions to kill or capture any Apache people they encountered. The expedition headed north up the San Carlos River, across the Black River, and to the White River in the vicinity of the future site of Fort Apache, the most isolated of the U.S. Army outposts. A large tract of land was marked off around Fort Apache for the Cibecue and the northern bands of the White Mountain Division, but in 1874 the Department of the Interior embarked upon a removal campaign designed to concentrate all the White Mountain Apache, Chiricahua, and Yavapai on the San Carlos Apache Reservation. During this unrest, the U.S. Army under Gen. George Crook led a group of White Mountain Apaches deep into Sonora's Sierra Madre mountains to enter into negotiations with Geronimo. In 1884, several groups of Apaches, including Geronimo and a small band of dissident Chiricahuas, were returned to Fort Apache. Here, under strict military supervision, they worked to construct irrigation dams and to plant crops.

Currently, the reservation supports numerous thriving White Mountain Apache enterprises, including forestry, agriculture, ranching, fisheries, and manufacture, along with a sustained vision for economic development, stewardship of the land, and cultural preservation.

FORT McDOWELL RESERVATION

Tribe: Fort McDowell Yavapai Nation **Current Location:** Arizona **Total Area:** 24,000 acres **Tribal Enrollment:** 927

Residents of the Fort McDowell Reservation, located in south-central Arizona, are descended from bands of Apache, Mojave, and Yavapai people. The fates of these previously separate groups became entwined when they were assigned to the Fort McDowell Military Reservation at the end of the Indian Wars during the second half of the 19th century.

The aboriginal homelands of these peoples once included all of the Mogollon Rim country as well as the greater part of what is now the state of Arizona. The Nation was created by executive order on September 15, 1903, for the Kwevikopaya (Southeastern Yavapai) who lived in the Mazatzal, Four Peaks, and Superstition Mountain region, one of the most important outposts in the Southwest during the Apache Wars of 1865 through 1891.

In November 1981, Native community members voted against the sale of their land to the federal government for construction of the Orme Dam, which was to be built at the confluence of the Verde and Salt Rivers and would have flooded the entire area, forcing residents from their ancestral homelands. Their victory was a monumental historical landmark in reaffirming tribal sovereignty.

The Fort McDowell Yavapai Nation claims the famous historical personage of Dr. Carlos Montezuma, a Yavapai man stolen by Pima Indians and sold to an Italian photographer, who took him to Chicago to be educated. In 1889, Dr. Montezuma, or Wassaja, was one of the first Native Americans to receive a degree in medicine. Later he fought for Native American rights and became an important human rights activist leading the struggle to regain Yavapai-Apache homelands.

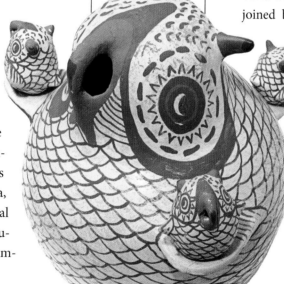

A clay Zuni owl, made in the early 20th century. The owl is a frequent subject of Zuni art.

GILA RIVER INDIAN RESERVATION

Tribe: Gila River Indian Community
Current Location: Arizona **Total Area:** 371,822 acres
Tribal Enrollment: 20,479

Some 6,000 years ago, various cultural groups that are collectively labeled the Archaic people wandered into the surprisingly fertile Sonoran Desert. Over the years, they transformed the desert into a formidable agricultural empire, complete with extensive irrigation systems, that provided all their needs and enabled them to settle into large, sophisticated population centers. The Pima identify themselves as Akimel O'odham, or "People of the River," in recognition of the Gila River's life-giving presence in their territorial homeland. The Spanish gave them the name Pima, by which they are known today.

Around 300 B.C., these early inhabitants were joined by peoples from central Mexico. The migratory Maricopa, or Pee Posh ("The People"), arrived from the southern Colorado River area and became allies with the agricultural Akimel O'odham, who taught them irrigation practices and farming. For unknown reasons—perhaps extended drought or competition from the fierce nomadic Apache—the once-thriving Akimel O'odham settlements were reduced to small villages by the late 1600s, the time of European contact.

In the 19th century, when settlers diverted the entire flow of the Gila River for their own lands, the Pima and Maricopa Indians confederated to fight the encroachment. By 1859, a reservation was established by an act of Congress. The people had yet to be mortally threatened by famine and poverty between the late 1800s and the 1920s as their lifeblood, the Gila River, was subjected to diversions and dams and their lands were in continuous dispute with the new state of Arizona.

HOPI

The Hopi live in northeastern Arizona, on a dry, stark high-desert plateau surrounded by the much larger Navajo Reservation. Their 12 villages include what is probably the oldest continually inhabited community in the United States, Old Oraibi, which dates back to 1150. The villages are high on First Mesa, Second Mesa, and Third Mesa, with farming in the valleys below. The villages are the focus of elaborate religious ceremonies that involve dances by colorful masked figures of the kachinas, the spirits of nature and dead ancestors. The traditional Hopi language of most of the villages is in the Uto-Aztecan family, different from that of the other Pueblo peoples. One village belongs to a group of Tewa speakers, the Hopi-Tewa, who have been there since about 1700.

Centuries on the Mesas

Prior to European contact, the Hopi had developed a civilization notable for its successful agriculture and mining, as well as its distinctive art and religion. They mined abundant local coal for cooking, heating, and firing pottery. Their pottery was striking, painted with stylized black-on-orange, black-on-yellow, or polychrome designs.

Despite the lack of rain, the Hopi grew high-yielding beans and corn, using dry-farming techniques—practices that rely solely on the scarce precipitation—in the valleys and washes, and irrigation on terraces up near the villages. Some of those terraces have been gardened since 1200. There's archaeological evidence of agriculture even earlier, and according to Hopi legend, farming goes back to the beginning of time. The Hopi believe that humans are now living in the Fourth Way or Fourth World, having left behind earlier, corrupt worlds. According to their creation stories, the Hopi people emerged out of the Third World and into the Fourth with ears of corn.

The Spanish missionaries who arrived in the 16th century made little headway in converting the Hopi to Christianity, except in one village, Awatovi,

which is now in ruins. Instead, the Hopi clung tenaciously to their kachina religion, which involves an annual cycle of ceremonies in the villages. At winter solstice, a ceremony asks the kachinas—

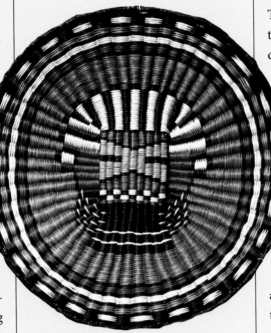

A modern Hopi Indian wicker plaque, decorated with colorful geometric and kachina designs

powerful benevolent spirits, most of them dead ancestors, who act as messengers to the spirit world—to appear and to bring with them rain and fertility. The masked dancers who personify the kachinas arrive in the villages each January or February. They participate in various ceremonies, including the initiation

of children into religious societies, and depart in midsummer. The second half of the year includes a roster of unmasked ceremonies. Painted wooden kachina dolls that represent these spirits are used to teach children about their religion. They are also collected; authentic contemporary ones can cost hundreds of dollars, antiques much more.

The Hopi took part in the Pueblo Revolt against the Spanish in 1680, which forced the conquerors out of New Mexico for a time. When the Spaniards returned to reassert control in 1692, the Hopi were some of the strongest resisters. Their territory was so far from the main Spanish strongholds that they by and large succeeded. There were few Spanish settlers in their region, and the few military attempts to subdue the Hopi in the 18th century failed.

The Land and Its Uses

In the traditional Hopi view, their homeland stretches down to the Grand Canyon and through much of the rest of northern Arizona—a vast definition accepted by neither the neighboring Navajo nor the U.S. government that eventually controlled Arizona. In 1882, the government set aside a formal Hopi reservation, a rectangle of 55 miles by 70 miles, including the mesa villages, surrounded by the vast Navajo reservation. Those boundaries and subsequent government actions set off a long, complicated land dispute between the Hopi and Navajo. In 1958, the Hopi sued; a court in 1962 converted a 1.8-million-acre area to joint use. But the two tribes continued to fight, with many Navajo living on what the Hopi considered their land. In 1966, the government froze development while the tribes worked things out; a number of land laws and settlements came in the ensuing years. Since then, many of the families living on the other tribe's land have been relocated; the development freeze was lifted in 2009,

signifying the official end to the dispute.

The Hopi stopped mining coal sometime after the Spanish arrived, but there's still coal in the region, some of it in the long-disputed land. Peabody Energy ran coal operations in the area for several decades before shutting its mine in 2005. The effort to reopen it has been highly controversial, and as of early 2010, the federal government was blocking that reopening.

Today's Hopi still live in their ancestral adobe villages, although many people leave the reservation to find work. Their religious ceremonies continue. Some of them are open to the public, although the Hopi are adamant that visitors not

photograph or record anything in their villages without a special permit, or enter any areas that are not specifically designated as public.

Unlike many other Indian tribes, the Hopi don't run a casino. Gambling goes against their traditional values, and tribal members have repeatedly voted down such a venture. However, they have made other attempts to develop tourist businesses. The Moenkopi Legacy Inn and Suites, the first hotel built on Hopi tribal land in 50 years and only the second hotel on the reservation, opened in 2010. It's in Moenkopi, a Hopi village about 40 miles away from the concentration of villages on the three mesas. ■

A young Hopi wears a traditional feather headdress for a ceremonial dance.

THE SOUTHWEST

Conditions began to improve in the 1930s with the completion of Coolidge Dam and the creation of the San Carlos Reservoir. The project included an irrigation system to the reservation and enabled the tribe to restore some farming. Since the late 1990s, successful agricultural, industrial, and recreational economic development projects have allowed the tribes to move from federal dependence to increasing self-reliance and prosperity.

Hualapai dancers gather in 2007 for the opening ceremonies at the Grand Canyon Skywalk, an Arizona tourist attraction owned by their tribe.

HAVASUPAI RESERVATION

Tribe: Havasupai Tribe **Current Location:** Arizona
Total Area: 188,077 acres **Tribal Enrollment:** 679

The Havasupai are a Yuman-speaking tribe, related by language to peoples occupying land in present-day southern Oregon and south into central Mexico. They call themselves the Havasuw 'Baaja ("People of the Blue-Green Water"), and they

are probably direct descendants of the Cohonina people who inhabited the plateau region south of the Grand Canyon around A.D. 600. Centuries later, between 1050 and 1200, some left the Coconino Plateau for the safety and rich agricultural lands of Cataract Creek Canyon below.

In winter, the Havasupai hunted antelope, deer, mountain sheep, and rabbits living on the Coconino Plateau. Between April and September, the tribe

Chiricahua Apache, Southern Athabascan language family

" 'Iłk'idą, k ǫǫ
yá'édįná'a.

'Ákoo Tł'ízhe hooghéí
dá'áíná bikǫ' 'óliná'a.

'Ákoo Tł'ízheí gotál
yiis'ąná'a.

'Ákoo Mai'áee
hiłghoná'a.

Gotál jiis'ąí 'áee,

Mai tsíbąąee
naaná'azhishná'a.

'Ákoo bitseeí
tsínáiłgoná'a."

("Long ago, there
was no fire.

Then only those
who are called Flies
had fire.

Then the Flies held
a ceremony.

And Coyote came
there.

At that place where
they held the
ceremony,

Coyote danced around
and around at the
edge of the fire.

And he continually
poked his tail in
the fire.")

From "Coyote
Obtains Fire," by
Lawrence Mithlo

harvested corn, beans, and squash, irrigating their crops and storing food for the winter—duties shared by the entire family.

Havasupai houses reflected their lifestyle and the variation in seasons. Winter homes were well insulated, while summer homes had thatched walls and dirt-covered roofs and were used only for sleeping.

In later years, as whites began to migrate westward, cattle, mining activities, and general misuse destroyed the natural habitat. The encroachment of miners and cattle ranchers into Havasupai territory led to the establishment of the 518-acre reservation at the bottom of the canyon in 1880, and the tribe's economic viability was threatened as over 90 percent of its aboriginal lands were lost. From 1880 to 1939, the tribe's economic independence was completely destroyed. By the 1940s, the tribe's seasonal migration from the canyon to the plateau had ceased, and the Havasupai cultivated more land in the canyon to offset the loss of plateau grazing and hunting lands.

In 1974, Congress established a 160,000-acre reservation and designated 95,300 additional acres within Grand Canyon National Park as a traditional-use area for the Havasupai people. The tribal members live in Supai Village at the base of Havasu Canyon, between Havasu and Moony Falls.

HOPI RESERVATION

Tribe: Hopi Tribe of Arizona   Current Location: Arizona
Total Area: 1,621,044 acres   Tribal Enrollment: 12,213

Hopi people refer to their ancestors as Hisatsinom ("People of Long Ago"), while archaeologists refer to them as Anasazi or San Juan basketmakers. They formed small settlements in a region stretching from the Grand Canyon to Toko'navi (Navajo Mountain) in present-day Utah, eastward to the Lukachukai Mountains near the New Mexico–Arizona border, and south to the Mogollon Rim. Small masonry villages were built between 900 and 1100, but a severe, long-lasting drought forced the abandonment of 36 of the 47 mesa-top villages. Following the drought, the 11 remaining villages grew in size, and three more were developed. Thus,

THE SOUTHWEST

the modern-day Hopi have lived in the Black Mesa region of the Colorado Plateau for nearly 1,000 years. The Hopi village of Old Oraibi is considered one of the oldest continuously occupied cities in the United States.

The Spanish visited the region several times between 1540 and the Pueblo Revolt in 1680. During the revolt, the Hopi moved many of their villages to mesa tops for defensive purposes and sheltered refugees from other pueblos. Contact with whites was sporadic prior to 1848, increasing during the 1850s and '60s as U.S. government surveyors, investigators, missionaries, and BIA employees streamed into the area. In 1882, President Chester Arthur established the Hopi Reservation through an executive order, with 2.5 million acres. A policy of forced assimilation followed, and attempts to eradicate remaining vestiges of Hopi culture and religion accompanied legalized efforts to take their land through the allotment system. Tension between those who accepted white ways and those who resisted culminated in a split in the village of Oraibi in 1906. The Indian Reorganization Act of 1934 codified the U.S. government's obligations to protect the rights of all Native Americans, and soon thereafter the Hopi formed a tribal council to establish a single representative body.

The Hopi currently live in 13 villages on three thin mesas projecting south from Black Mesa and to the west along Moencopi Wash. Their homeland is called Tutsqua. Every village is relatively autonomous, but only one has adopted a constitution and established a westernized government—the 11 other villages operate with some degree of adherence to the traditional Hopi form of governance. Oraibi remains traditional. Central to their cultural heritage, the Hopi carefully guard tribal traditional knowledge such as the Emergence Story (the origin of people), passed on via the interactive method of storytelling. Together, the Hopi practice a variety of annual dances and ceremonies, among them, the Kachina Dance, Snake Dance, and Flute

MYTH OR FACT?
Indians of the Southwest grew food in the desert.

FACT
Some tribes thrived in arid deserts that seldom receive more than a few inches of rain a year. They developed farming methods that took advantage of every available drop of water.

Kokopelli, the flute-playing trickster, is found in legends and old petroglyphs in the Southwest.

Ceremony. The Hopi celebrate the summer solstice and hold seasonal ceremonies to honor nature and the people's role as caretakers of the earth.

HUALAPAI INDIAN RESERVATION

Tribe: Hualapai Indian Tribe   **Current Location:** Arizona
Total Area: 992,462 acres   **Tribal Enrollment:** 2,004

Hualapai Indians (Hwal'bay means "People of the Tall Pine") are descendants of a group known archaeologically as the Cerbat and, together with the Havasupai and the Yavapai, comprise the Upland Yuman language group in the Yuman linguistic family. The Hualapai and Havasupai have occupied northwest central Arizona for thousands of years, with aboriginal territory spanning more than five million acres along the middle corridor of the Colorado River and Grand Canyon area. The people refer to this region as Hakataya, "The Backbone of the River."

Significant numbers of white fur trappers and prospectors began entering Hualapai territory during the 1820s and dramatically increased by the late 1840s. Though their presence provoked occasional attacks by the Hualapai, most were accommodated, to the extent that the Hualapai soon became a reliable source of easily exploited labor for the prospectors. This continued until 1874, when the U.S. Army forcefully removed the tribe to the Colorado River Reservation in an arduous journey that many Hualapais did not survive. One year later, most escaped the encampment and fled back to the traditional homeland. A few others fled south; thus the Paipai in Mexico are considered brothers and sisters. The miners supported the Hualapai's return two years later from the encampment because it meant a continued source of cheap labor and freed up the majority of the tribe's ancestral lands for grazing.

During the Depression, many Hualapais were employed on the reservation through New Deal programs like the Civilian Conservation Corps.

After the corps was terminated, a number of tribal members took up cattle raising. Colorado River rafting tours began during the 1980s, providing some much-needed economic diversification. The tribal economy is based on tourism, river rafting, hunting expeditions, individual cattle ranching, and traditional and modern folk arts.

A Zuni woman wears heirloom turquoise and silver rings and bracelets. Families in the Zuni pueblo still craft this famous jewelry.

ISLETA

Tribe: Pueblo of Isleta   **Current Location:** New Mexico
Total Area: 301,102 acres   **Tribal Enrollment:** 3,980

Isleta pueblo has occupied its present site for at least 450 years. Members of the Tue-i, or Isleta, tribe resided at the Isleta pueblo in its present location when Francisco de Coronado first explored the area in the 1540s. Isletans speak Tiwa, a dialect of Tanoan, and are considered part of the Eastern Pueblo group anthropologically. Traditionally an agricultural society, the tribe's principal crop was corn. Irrigation systems were developed using water from the Rio Grande. Spanish colonists returned in 1598, led by Juan de Oñate, and harsh Spanish rule devastated pueblo life over the next 80 years. The Mission of San Antonio, constructed in 1613 in the village of Isleta, was part of the Spanish colonists' system of forced religious conversion. Though the Isletans did not actively participate in the Pueblo Revolt of 1680, the Spaniards took hundreds prisoner, and the remaining population was forced to flee westward to Hopi territory. The pueblo was repopulated, incorporating quite a few Hopis, in the early 1700s.

During the 1800s, members of the Laguna and Acoma pueblos relocated to the Isleta community. Despite differences in language, the Pueblo of Isleta share many cultural similarities with the Acoma and Laguna Pueblo due to prolonged periods of

PUEBLO OF ISLETA

When the Spanish conquistadors encountered them, the Isleta Pueblo people were living on islands along New Mexico's longest and largest river, the Rio Grande—*isleta* is a Spanish word meaning "little island." They remain in the same area today, on 211,000 acres about 12 miles south of Albuquerque. Roughly 4,000 people live in the village at the main site of Isleta Pueblo and the satellite villages of Oraibi and Chicale. Many tribal members still farm along the banks of the Rio Grande; traditional arts and crafts such as pottery, weaving, embroidery, and jewelrymaking are practiced, as are the old songs and dances.

Apart from the Other Pueblos

The Isleta Pueblo has an eventful and troubled history. When the Pueblo Revolt of August 1680 began, Isleta did not join in the uprising. "Whether this was because of sympathy with the Spaniards, fear of retaliation, or hesitation in the unusual step of allying themselves with other Pueblos is unknown," explains Florence Hawley Ellis, a University of New Mexico archaeologist and anthropologist who wrote about Isleta.

Spanish refugees from the revolt came to Isleta, and many tribal members retreated with them to El Paso del Norte, in what is now Texas. Some Isleta Pueblo members went west to present-day Arizona, to the Hopi Pueblo.

Spanish governor Antonio de Otermin and his people, fleeing after the fall of Santa Fe to the rebels, reached Isleta Pueblo in September 1680 and found it all but deserted. The church and convent of San Augustin de la Isleta mission, begun around 1612, had been burned and ruined. Upon leaving the village in January, the Spanish took with them 385 Isleta villagers and burned the rest of the town. A pueblo near El Paso was established for the prisoners that they named San Antonio de Isleta.

Rebuilding After the Revolt

Although Isleta pueblo was burned twice, it was not completely destroyed. When Spaniard Diego de Vargas reached

Children play outside an adobe building at the pueblo of Isleta in New Mexico.

the village site in October 1692, intent on the reconquest of New Mexico, he found the nave of the church still standing among the ruins.

The bulk of the historical and archaeological evidence indicates that Isleta was refounded at its present site around 1710. With extensive renovation and repairs, the adobe San Augustin de la Isleta church is one of the oldest mission churches in New Mexico. It stands on the main plaza of the pueblo, looking over the space where many traditional dances still take place.

When the dispersed Pueblo members moved back, some came with their new Hopi families. Another cultural strain was added to the mix in the late 19th century, when the people of Isleta offered sanctuary to a group of Laguna Pueblo people in return for the Laguna promise to contribute their religious kachina masks to Isleta. Friction over religion and ritual in the years that followed led to the establishment of the satellite villages.

As in New Mexico's other pueblos, the traditional economy was essentially agricultural. Because they were so close to the river, irrigating crops was not difficult, even before European contact. The Isletans also traded with nearby pueblos as well as with the many Spaniards who came to the region.

Although the Catholic Church has a prominent place in the village, the people of Isleta, like those of other pueblos, clung to their traditional social and religious structures, albeit often secretively. One level of tribal structure involves corn groups, which connect with traditional colors and the four cardinal directions. These groups are responsible for a number of rituals and blessings. Parents "give" a child to a corn group, usually that of at least one parent. A child is also made a member of a moiety, a system that separates the tribal members into winter and summer groups. The traditional language of Isleta Pueblo is Tiwa, a dialect of the Tanoan language group. English and Spanish are also widely spoken.

Even though the Isleta people today continue to live with much of their ancient culture, they also run successful modern businesses. The Isleta Casino and Resort, one of the premier gaming sites in the Southwest, is home to a casino, a motel, and the championship Isleta Eagle 27-hole golf course. In late 2009, the pueblo struck a deal under which its casino will expand and become the first in the state to operate under the Hard Rock Hotel and Casino name. There's a state-of-the-art bowling alley, laser tag, billiards, and arcade games. There's also year-round fishing and camping, and the big cottonwood trees along the Rio Grande shade wonderful summer picnic spots. ■

In a 1924 photograph, Maria Chiwiwi carries a clay jar on her head as she leaves her adobe home at the Isleta pueblo.

A young Hopi man wears ceremonial makeup, headdress, and jewelry.

JEMEZ

Tribe: Pueblo of Jemez   **Current Location:** New Mexico
Total Area: 89,619 acres   **Tribal Enrollment:** 3,628

The pueblo of Jemez is the only remaining village of the Towa-speaking Pueblos in New Mexico. Oral history holds that ancestors of the present-day Jemez people migrated to the Cañon de San Diego region of New Mexico from a place they called Hua-na-tota (in the Four Corners area) in the 14th century and became one of the largest and most powerful of the Pueblo cultures by the time of European contact in 1541. Coronado's men found the Tano in large, fortresslike villages made of stone on top of mesas, with buildings up to four stories high that could contain 3,000 rooms. The people were successful hunters, farmers, and warriors. The villages included barriers to protect their religious sites, monitor trails, and ward off invaders. The Coronado expedition must have wisely decided not to disturb the tribe, because they came and went in a day, and the tribe was left alone for 40 years, until the next wave of Spanish explorers arrived.

In the next 80 years, the Jemez people carried out numerous revolts and uprisings in response to Spanish attempts to forcibly Christianize them, culminating in the Pueblo Revolt of 1680. By 1688, the Spanish had begun their reconquest, and in 1696 they finally succeeded in subduing the Jemez Nation and concentrating the tribe into the village of Walatowa, where they reside today. The original Spanish land grant to the Pueblo was made on September 20, 1689. In 1838, the Towa-speaking people from the pueblo of Pecos (east of Santa Fe) requested to be taken in by Jemez and to resettle at the Jemez pueblo in order to escape harassment by the Spanish and Comanche. In 1936, the two tribes were merged by an act of Congress.

Traditional culture remains vital at Jemez, with many dances and ceremonies held throughout the year, most of which remain closed to the public. The tribe's traditional law makes it illegal to make Towa a written language, and thus it is preserved entirely by the speakers at Jemez pueblo. Many tribal members

contact. Isleta is one of the largest pueblos in New Mexico, covering more than 329 square miles. Its terrain is diverse, extending from the forested Manzano Mountains in the east to the mesa lands of the Rio Puerco in the west. In 1855, the U.S. Congress confirmed the Spanish land grant to Isleta's inhabitants, which was reconfirmed and patented in 1864. The main communities within the pueblo today are Oraibe, Chicale, and Isleta.

The Pueblo of Isleta have five corn groups. In addition, tribal members belong to one of two moieties, or kinship groups: the Shifun (Black Eye) and the Shure (Red Eye). Each is responsible for executing one major ceremonial dance per year. These types of ceremonial gatherings are an integral part of the lives of Isleta's people.

now work in the region's timber industry and in the reservation's thriving and internationally renowned arts and crafts cottage industry.

JICARILLA APACHE RESERVATION

Tribe: Jicarilla Apache Nation   **Current Location:** New Mexico
Total Area: 879,917 acres   **Tribal Enrollment:** 3,578

Apache people were among six Athabascan groups that migrated from Arctic regions of western Canada to the desert Southwest of the United States between the late 13th and 16th centuries and became a dominant force throughout portions of Texas, Colorado, and New Mexico. Jicarilla, or "little basket," is a Mexican name, honoring one of the tribe's most renowned products.

The Apache people, including those on the Jicarilla Apache Reservation, are linguistically related to the greater Na-Dene language family, and their clans are matrilineal. The Jicarilla were first mentioned by this name early in the 18th century. Later, their different bands were designated Carlanes, Calchufine, Quartelejo, and so on, after their habitat or chieftains. Their traditional lands spanned more than 50 million acres, bounded by four sacred rivers.

The Apache vehemently resisted the encroachment upon their traditional lands by Spanish, Mexican, and American settlers and military forces and were the single band that refused to cooperate with the U.S. military in trying to locate Geronimo. But by the mid-1880s, the Apache were consolidated on various southwestern Indian reservations, and the Jicarillas were sent to the Mescalero Apache Reservation in southeastern New Mexico.

Jicarilla tribal leadership, stepping outside the bounds of traditional channels, sought to win the support of New Mexico territorial governor Edmund Ross in 1886 in an attempt to regain their northern reservation. Ross's influential coalition persuaded the President to sign the Executive Order of February 8, 1887, which created the permanent site of the Jicarilla Apache Reservation.

Navajo, Southern Athabascan language family

"Diné bizaad yee Atah naayéé' yik'eh deesdlii'."

("The Navajo language assisted the military forces to defeat the enemy.")

The reservation's ample natural resources have proven to be the tribe's greatest economic asset, and protecting these assets continues to be the Jicarilla people's greatest challenge. The tribe has been very active in preserving and restoring natural resources on tribal lands. The Harvard University Honoring Nations Program recognized the tribe's wildlife and fisheries program in 1999.

LAGUNA

Tribe: Pueblo of Laguna   **Current Location:** New Mexico
Total Area: 495,442.66 acres   **Tribal Enrollment:** 8,092

The pueblo of Laguna is one of the largest of the Keresan-speaking villages. Its people are closely related to the Acoma, Zuni, and the Western Pueblo group, characterized by a matrilineal clan structure, female ownership of house and garden plots, and a strong Katsina (or kachina) cult. Katsinam are ancestral beings who have the power to bring rain and well-being. In an environment where the success or failure of crops is never certain from year to year, ceremonies place an emphasis on weather control and rainmaking. A bountiful harvest is believed to be the result of the successful observance of religious retreats and rituals.

Laguna ancestors migrated from the north, eventually settling in their present location. Living in villages, the Laguna cultivated small areas of land around their villages and collected clay from the surrounding areas. The first contact with European settlers came during the 16th century, when Spaniards arrived in the Rio Grande Valley. Until this time, the Laguna people had relied primarily on farming, but with the Spanish introduction of livestock, many became herders.

The Laguna's status, as it existed under Spanish domination, was retained under Mexican law. At the end of the Mexican-American War, the Southwest came under the sovereignty of the United States. However, the U.S. failed to adequately define Pueblo rights and the status of their land claims, thereby creating an ongoing source of contention. Then, in 1876, a U.S. Supreme Court ruling deprived the

Pueblo of federal land protection and allowed thousands of non-Indians to settle on Pueblo lands.

The Laguna, poor in resources (particularly water) and impoverished by lack of federal recognition, did not accept the Indian Reorganization Act until 1949. Since that time, the tribe has made steady progress on both the economic and social fronts. Culturally, the Laguna maintain a rich tradition of ceremonies and customs. Ancient dances and village feast days are held as part of an ongoing celebration of life.

MARICOPA (AK-CHIN) INDIAN RESERVATION

Tribe: Ak-Chin Indian Community
Current Location: Arizona **Total Area:** 21,840 acres
Tribal Enrollment: 730

The Ak-Chin Indian Community, residing on the Maricopa Indian Reservation, is comprised of Tohono O'odham Indians whose ancestors migrated away from the Tohono O'odham Nation (see pages 234–35, 237) and settled just outside the present-day city of Maricopa, Arizona.

From the early 18th century onward, O'odham lands were occupied by foreign governments. With the independence of the Republic of Mexico, the O'odham fell under Mexican rule. In 1853, through the Gadsden Purchase, or Treaty of La Mesilla, O'odham land was divided almost in half between the United States and Mexico. In 1874, a small band of Tohono O'odham people moved to the present-day site of the Ak-Chin Indian Community to farm at the end of Vekol Wash. In later years, members of the Gila River Pimas assisted with the harvest. The two tribes came together to form the Ak-Chin Indian Community. Ak-Chin is an O'odham word meaning "mouth of the wash" and refers to a type of farming that relies on washes—seasonal flood plains created by winter snows and summer rains.

On the U.S. side of the border, the transfer of the Gadsden Purchase had little effect on the O'odham initially because they were not informed that a purchase of their land had been made, and the new

Hopi, Uto-Aztecan language family

"Itam Hopiit hapi pas kyaahisatngaqw yep yeesiwqey pan sinomatsiwata. Itam yep pu' Arizona tutskwat ep haqe' yesqey naat pang yeskyangw haqami ahoy tsivot sunatsikis naanangk qatsivaptsit ang qatsikuyvayaqat pangsoqhaqami nga' yyungwa yep itaatutskway epe'."

("We Hopi are known for having lived here as a people continuously from ancient time. Where we are located today in present-day Arizona is where we have always lived, with roots back in time to some 100 generations in our land. Our culture, therefore, is one of the first [oldest] on the continent.")

border between the United States and Mexico was not strictly enforced. In recent years, however, the border has come to affect the O'odham in many ways. Immigration laws prevent the O'odham from crossing freely and, on occasion, from transporting goods and raw materials such as feathers of common birds and sweet grasses, essential components used for maintaining practices of spirituality, economy, and traditional culture.

O'odham bands are now broken up into four federally recognized tribes: the Tohono O'odham Nation, the Gila River Indian Community, the Ak-Chin Indian Community, and the Salt River (Pima-Maricopa) Indian Community. Each band is now politically and geographically distinct and separate. The remaining band, the Hia-C'ed O'odham, is not federally recognized, but resides throughout southwestern Arizona. All of the groups still speak the O'odham language, derived from the Uto-Aztecan language group, although each has its own dialects.

MESCALERO RESERVATION

Tribe: Mescalero Apache Tribe **Current Location:** New Mexico **Total Area:** 460,769 acres **Population:** 3,156

Mescalero (Spanish for "Eater of Mescal") applies to one branch of the Eastern Apache people or culture. The Mescalero Apache Reservation is home to three Apache bands—the Mescalero, Lipan, and Chiricahua Apache—which collectively organized in 1936 under the Indian Reorganization Act as the Mescalero Apache Tribe.

From before European contact through the mid-19th century, the Mescalero and Lipan Apache hunted and gathered in a vast area stretching from present-day Santa Fe, New Mexico, in the north to Chihuahua City, Mexico, in the south. Primarily desert dwellers, the Chiricahua and Lipan subsisted on buffalo, antelope, and various desert flora, while the Mescalero resided in the mountainous and plains areas. They made frequent forays into several mountain ranges, including the Sacramento, to hunt game and cut tepee lodge poles.

A written record of the Mescalero begins around 1540, at the time of the Spanish conquest of northern New Spain. Accounts of early Spanish exploration reference *indios vaqueros, teluges, querechos,* and *faraones*—Spanish names for the tribe. Neither the Spanish nor the Mexicans succeeded in subordinating them. During the Spanish and Mexican periods of occupation, the Mescalero and Lipan managed to retain self-governance.

Establishment of the New Mexico Territory in 1850 brought them into increasing conflict with the U.S. Army and Euro-American settlers encroaching upon their domain. Following hostilities, the Mescalero signed a treaty in 1852, which confined them to the Bosque Redondo. The addition of exiled Navajos to the territory in 1863, now known as the Long Walk, placed the Mescalero in dire straits. They left slowly, and on the night of November 3, 1865, the remaining able-bodied residents vacated. When things settled, the Mescalero reappeared in their traditional homeland, and after 1880 the territory became fairly stable. Subsequent executive orders expanded the reservation's boundaries, and in 1889 the U.S. Army relocated several bands of Lipan Apache and some of Geronimo's Chiricahua to the Mescalero Reservation.

The Mescalero, Lipan, and Chiricahua languished throughout the early 20th century under Indian Service pressure to become farmers. After incorporation in 1936, the Mescalero Apache Tribe initiated a long-term program of development and diversification. In recent decades, the tribe has become known as one of the most ambitious in the United States, with a diverse tribal economy.

NAMBÉ

Tribe: Pueblo of Nambé   Current Location: New Mexico
Total Area: 19,093.83 acres   Tribal Enrollment: 643

Nambé is a Tewa pueblo in the region of the northern Rio Grande. The name is a Spanish version of the Tewa word *nanbé,* meaning "earth roundness." Before the Spaniards arrived, Nambé pueblo served as a religious and cultural mecca for New Mexican Pueblo communities, and because of this, it became a target for Spanish plans to destroy the indigenous New Mexico cultures.

In 1620, the King of Spain ordered the New Mexico Pueblo to choose civil officials by popular vote to govern each pueblo. The tribes adopted the new form of government and integrated it into the traditional systems. The right of each pueblo to self-governance was subsequently recognized by the crown and later by Mexico and the United States.

The state of New Mexico and the federal government have repeatedly recognized the status of the Pueblos as sovereign nations. Over the years, the Pueblo have become largely Hispanicized, though there has been a resurgence of interest in the indigenous culture within the Pueblo community. The Nambé pueblo is now registered as a national historic landmark. Tribal housing continues to comprise traditional homes, some several hundred years old, as well as contemporary structures.

The tribal government, as in a number of the other northern pueblos, is fairly traditional in structure. In August 1994, the Nambé Pueblo were

DIEGO DE VARGAS

Leader of Spain's second conquest of New Mexico

In 1673, Don Diego de Vargas Zapata Lujan Ponce de Leon y Contreras (ca 1643–1704) left Spain to become a judge in Mexico. He then advanced through the colonial ranks and gained the title Governor of New Mexico. On August 10, 1692, 12 years after the Pueblo Revolt drove the Spaniards from New Mexico, he proclaimed that he would reconquer that territory. With about 40 soldiers, a few civilians, 50 natives, and a few friars, he marched to Santa Fe.

To his surprise, 1,000 or more Pueblo Indians were occupying the Palace of the Governors. Using the same siege strategy the Pueblos had once used to defeat the Spanish, de Vargas and his soldiers cut off the water, surrounded the palace, and placed their cannon at the gate. De Vargas offered peace to anyone who renewed allegiance to God, the Church, and Spain. He proclaimed Spanish sovereignty and returned south for supplies.

When he came back the next year with 70 families, the Indians had still not surrendered their stronghold. On December 29, 1693, the Spaniards finally set fire to the palace's main gate and took it by storm. Some Pueblo leaders took their own lives, and 70 of the holdouts were executed. De Vargas turned over 400 women and children to the colonists for ten years of servitude, cementing the Spanish hold on New Mexico. ∎

NAVAJO

The people of the Navajo Nation call themselves Diné and their homeland Diné Bikéyah, or sometimes Dinétah (Navajoland). The modern reservation, still bounded by the four sacred mountains, covers 27,000 square miles in Arizona, New Mexico, and Utah. It's the largest U.S. Indian reservation, a place of astoundingly beautiful desert and mountain landscapes and occasional great poverty, with an estimated 250,000 residents. There are various ways of counting members of an Indian tribe, but by any of them, the Navajo are one of the largest. The tribe's traditional language, which is still widely spoken, is part of the Athabascan language family, closely related to the other Apachean languages of the Southwest.

Seminomads and Sheepherders

About the time of European contact, the Navajo not only farmed part of the year but also moved around to hunt, a lifestyle more similar to that of other Athabascan-speaking peoples in the region than to that of the more settled Pueblo peoples who also lived there. Many families herded sheep, cattle, and horses as well. The Spaniards dubbed them Apache de Nabajó, after the region where they lived. Like the other Apacheans, they supported the Pueblo Revolt of 1680, which forced the Spanish out of New Mexico. When the Spaniards returned in 1692 for the reconquest, many Pueblo refugees fled to Navajo territory and were absorbed into the tribe, their culture mixing into that of the Navajo.

The United States took control of this part of the West in 1848. The tribe and the U.S. fought for decades, until, in 1864, the Army quashed resistance and forced thousands of Navajo to walk 300 to 450 miles from their homes to a reservation in eastern New Mexico. Their miserable exile ended in 1868, when a treaty granted them some of their old territory back. Gradual increases in that territory over the years created the current

reservation, which is larger than West Virginia and nine other states. For decades, the Navajo were in an acrimonious land dispute with the Hopi, whose

A Navajo pictorial rug, likely from about 1890, depicts horses and cattle.

reservation is surrounded by the Navajo Reservation. As of 2010, that dispute appeared to be resolved.

Seeking Harmony

The traditional dwelling of the Navajo is the hogan, a six- or eight-sided house of

wood and mud, with a domed roof and a door that opens to the east, toward the rising sun. Many Navajo on the reservation still have hogans on their land.

If they live in houses or trailers, the doors usually face to the east. They still retell legends of how First Man and First Woman came into the world and shaped Navajoland, then produced Changing Woman, who created the Navajo people.

There are also legends that say Spider Woman, in the earliest days, taught the Navajo to weave. Anthropologists say it's more likely that when Puebloan Indians mixed with the Navajo in the 17th century, they brought the craft. Either way, Navajo women are celebrated for their textiles, making and selling the geometrically styled wool blankets that are an intrinsic part of the look of the Southwest today. In the 19th century, the Navajo developed into expert silversmiths, as well, producing intricate turquoise and silver jewelry.

Many Navajo still follow their traditional spiritual ways. These begin with a belief that the universe is a grand system of interrelated elements, some good, some evil. When the harmony of this system is disrupted, bad things happen, including sickness and death.

Sometimes, those evil forces are stirred by malevolent witchcraft. To heal, harmony must be restored, using one of the more than 50 ceremonies that are part of what is known as the Blessing Way. A person or family engages a traditional singer—someone with years of training—to perform what is often an elaborate, multiday ceremony.

Land of Red Rock and Desert

The reservation includes iconic locations recognizable throughout the world, including Monument Valley, which is tribally owned and run parkland that has been the scenic backdrop for many movies and television shows. Canyon de Chelly National Monument, on tribal land but run by the U.S. Park Service, contains the ruins of cliff dwellings built by people who lived there from roughly 350 to 1300. It also shelters the homes of Navajo families on the cool, shaded canyon floor.

The reservation has rich natural resources, including coal, uranium, oil, and natural gas, but determining how to best extract them and profit from them has often put the tribe at odds with energy companies. Water rights have also been the subject of long battles. The construction of the Navajo-Gallup Water Supply Project, started in 2010, will finally bring running water to some 10,000 families.

Economic development is a continuing concern on the reservation, where unemployment has run as high as 55 percent. Many Navajo move away to work, even though the tribe has several businesses. The Navajo were latecomers to gaming, rejecting the idea in two elections before eventually approving it. The first Navajo casino opened in Gallup, New Mexico, in 2008; a second is planned for Flagstaff, Arizona, with construction scheduled for late 2010. ■

A Navajo boy displays his crop of shiitake mushrooms.

THE SOUTHWEST

granted a federal charter and formed the Nambé Pueblo Development Corporation. The tribe is a member of the Eight Northern Indian Pueblos Council, a nonprofit organization that provides community-based services to Nambé, Taos, Picurís, Ohkay Owingeh, Santa Clara, San Ildefonso, Pojoaque, and Tesuque Pueblos. The tribal economy is supported in large part from the tribe's agricultural enterprises.

NAVAJO NATION RESERVATION

Tribe: Navajo Nation   **Current Location:** Arizona, New Mexico, and Utah   **Total Area:** 17,028,026 acres
Tribal Enrollment: 273,872

The Navajo have been in the Southwest since at least 1300, after migrating from western Canada. Today, they call themselves Diné, "The People." The Navajo people are most closely related by language and culture to the Apache peoples of the Southwest, but Navajo religion shares many elements with the religions of nearby Pueblo peoples. It was also the Tewa Indians who first called them Navahu.

During the 1600s, the Navajo acquired horses and sheep from the Spaniards, along with the knowledge of working with metal and wool. The Navajo resisted Spanish domination during the late 18th and 19th centuries, also fighting against colonization after 1846, when the Americans took over the southwestern territory once owned by Mexico. After the infamous Long Walk to Fort Sumner, Americans attempted to teach them a sedentary, agricultural lifestyle. However, the people failed to thrive, and by 1868 the project was abandoned. A new treaty then established the Navajo Reservation, and the Navajo resettled part of their original lands. There they practiced a mixed subsistence economy of agriculture and herding. The discovery of oil and gas on the reservation in 1921 and the later discovery of uranium provided the stimulus for modern economic development.

This 15-inch-high pottery figure, credited to the ancestral Puebloans, was likely made between 900 and 1200.

The Navajo now occupy four different locations: the main Navajo Reservation plus three areas in New Mexico: Cañoncito Reservation, Alamo Reservation, and Ramah Reservation.

OHKAY OWINGEH RESERVATION

Tribe: Ohkay Owingeh   **Current Location:** New Mexico
Total Area: 12,236 acres   **Tribal Enrollment:** 2,791

Ohkay Owingeh, meaning "Mother Village of the Tewa Nation" and formerly known as the pueblo of San Juan, is the largest of the six Tewa-speaking villages. The Spanish named it San Juan Bautista (St. John the Baptist) in 1598; in the same year they established the first Spanish capital in New Mexico at the site of the old Tewa Pueblo on Ohkay Owingeh land. In 1689, the Spanish officially confirmed the pueblo by designating 17,544 acres as the San Juan Pueblo Land Grant.

Though the Treaty of Guadalupe Hidalgo guaranteed the tribe's title to this land in 1848, the land base steadily decreased through the late 19th and early 20th centuries due to encroachment by outsiders. The Pueblo Lands Act of 1924 reduced it further, to 12,234 acres. Though all the land is considered trust land, individual Pueblo families were assigned pieces of land during the 1930s, which could be left to descendants or sold or traded to other Pueblo residents of the village. Some of the pueblo lands were left as common grazing lands.

The Ohkay Owingeh Reservation sits in the Rio Grande Valley, along the river, and features an abundance of relatively flat farmland. Until World War II, farming, raising cattle, and trade had served as the backbone of the Ohkay Owingeh tribal economy. By the 1960s, wage work, mostly in Santa Fe, Española, or Los Alamos, had become dominant. In 1965, the Eight Northern Pueblos Community Action Program was created, by which the Ohkay Owingeh obtained various grants for construction projects. A federal grant funded the Eight Northern Pueblos Artisans Guild at San Juan from 1972 to 1982. Many tribal members support themselves as independent artists and craftspeople, partly through the Ohkay Owingeh Cooperative, a self-sustaining arts and crafts collective.

The tribe continues to host traditional ceremonies, some open to the public and some reserved for pueblo members only, and many members speak primarily Tewa, with English as a second language. Ohkay Owingeh tribal culture, as a whole, follows this pattern, with the members maintaining the most meaningful parts of their traditional culture while adapting aspects of American culture that enhance their ability to survive and prosper.

PICURÍS

Tribe: Pueblo of Picurís **Current Location:** New Mexico
Total Area: 15,034 acres **Tribal Enrollment:** 302

Native peoples of Tigua have occupied their remote pueblo, now known by its Spanish name, high in the Sangre de Cristo Mountains for at least 750 years. They originated in the Pot Creek area (the largest known prehistoric adobe pueblo north of Santa Fe) and migrated to their current site around 1250. Tiwa is spoken by the people of Picurís, Taos, Sandia, and Isleta.

Currently the smallest of New Mexico's northern pueblos, Picurís is believed to have been the largest at the time of Spanish contact. Even today, the Pueblo of Picurís often refer to themselves as the People of the Hidden Valley. Due to its geographical isolation, the pueblo was missed entirely by explorers, including the Coronado expedition of 1540, and remained undisturbed until Gaspar Castaño de Sosa's 1591 expedition. De Sosa found the province of Tiguex, on the Rio Grande, containing 12 pueblos along the river, and people possessing corn, beans, melons, skins, and long robes of feathers and cotton. In 1680, the year of the Pueblo Revolt, the population was estimated at around 3,000. Further revolts against the Spanish led to

the evacuation of the pueblo in 1696. In 1706, the Spanish returned about 300 Picurís people to the reservation from the plains.

The tribe traditionally relied on farming, raising stock, and hunting for subsistence but were forced to almost entirely abandon those activities. During the 1940s and '50s, the Picurís suffered desperately, both culturally and economically. During the 1960s, the Pueblo's fortunes began to turn, due to the tribal council's avid pursuit of federal aid and other

THE NAVAJO LONG WALK

After many years of bloody fighting between the Navajo and the U.S. Army, Brig. Gen. James Henry Carleton thought he had a solution: Subjugate the Indians and move them from their land in the Four Corners area. He set up a military post and reservation in eastern New Mexico called Fort Sumner and Bosque Redondo. In 1863, he ordered frontiersman and military officer Kit Carson to round up the Indians. The Navajo fought back, but the Army destroyed their farms, homes, and livestock.

In January 1864, amid snow and bitter cold, Carson clashed in Arizona's Canyon de Chelly with a band led

by Navajo leader Barboncito. More than 200 Navajo eventually surrendered there. In the ensuing months, across Navajoland, thousands more turned themselves in, hoping for food, shelter, and peace. They were marched on foot to Fort Sumner, a journey of 300 to 450 miles. Along the way, many died of starvation, disease, or exhaustion. Eventually, as many as 9,000 Navajo, along with about 500 Mescalero Apache, were at Bosque Redondo—far more than Carleton had planned for. (Perhaps 2,000 or more remained hidden in their old territory and elsewhere.) Conditions were miserable. Crops failed, and people starved. Hundreds escaped, but nearly a third died. Carleton was removed from his post in 1866.

"Bringing us here has made many of us die, also a great number of our animals," said Barboncito, pleading for the release of his people from Bosque Redondo. "Our grandfathers had no idea of living in any other place except our own land, and I don't think it is right for us to do what we were taught not to do." In 1868, the U.S. and the Navajo negotiated a treaty that allowed the Indians to return home, although to a smaller territory than they once claimed. ■

Kit Carson rounded up the Navajo for the Long Walk from their lands.

BIGOTES

Guide to the Pueblos

Tales of gold drew Spanish conquistadors from Mexico to what is now New Mexico. In 1540, an expedition led by Francisco Vasquez de Coronado set out in search of the seven golden cities of Cibola. What they found instead was a cluster of Zuni pueblos. They set up headquarters in one, Hawikuh.

There they were visited by a group from another pueblo, Cicuye, later called Pecos. It was led by a young man the Spaniards called Bigotes because of his mustache, rare among the Indians. He spoke of his home pueblo and others, and told the Spaniards about the buffalo of the Great Plains. He then acted as a guide for a detachment of Spaniards under Capt. Hernando de Alvarado, bringing them on a generally peaceful tour of several pueblos. At the Acoma pueblo, which Alvarado wrote "was one of the strongest ever seen," Bigotes performed a ritual to demonstrate the group's peaceful intentions. The people came down from their fortress to trade with the newcomers. When the group reached Cicuye, another Indian, called El Turco, took over as guide. He spoke of yet another glittering city, Quivira, which of course was nothing of the kind. And he told them Bigotes had a golden armband. Alvarado returned to Cicuye, kidnapped Bigotes, and tortured him. Bigotes was released; sometime afterward, the Spaniards killed El Turco. ■

assistance programs, and the tribe continues to pursue avenues for growth and development.

The sale of their traditional micaceous pottery, coupled with federal aid and assistance programs, now serves as the primary source of tribal revenue. Picurís artisans are internationally known for their pottery. Tribal members have traditionally gathered the clay used for potting from a sacred site located approximately four miles from the community and the center of a legal suit that the tribe filed in its attempt to regain ownership of the land.

The community center of Picurís is defined by a clustering of adobe houses around a church; a *placita*, or plaza; and a cemetery. An excavation project undertaken at the old village site uncovered an ancient kiva and many artifacts that will aid in the study of the people. The tribe also operates a museum, which offers exhibits of prehistoric artifacts, photographs, and art produced by regional artists. The museum maintains the pueblo ruins.

MYTH OR FACT?
Some Indians believe witchcraft causes illness.

FACT
Some tribes, including the Navajo, believe that the forces of the world, which should be in harmony, can be maliciously pulled out of balance by people intent on creating evil. These people can cause others to become ill, and healing requires putting the victim back into harmony through special ceremonies. The Navajo words for these bad people and their damaging actions best translate in English to witches and witchcraft.

POJOAQUE

Tribe: **Pueblo of Pojoaque**   Current Location: **New Mexico**
Total Area: **12,004 acres**   Tribal Enrollment: **367**

The Pojoaque pueblo was inhabited long before the area's occupation by the Spanish, which began during the 1500s. Archaeological studies of the area have dated inhabitation of the historic Tewa-speaking Pojoaque pueblo area to as early as A.D. 500, with a sizable prehistoric community in the late 15th and early 16th centuries. The Pueblo of Pojoaque have managed to retain a strong cultural identity. Tewa (also known as Tano) is one of five Kiowa-Tanoan languages spoken by the Pueblo people of New Mexico. Though the five languages are similar, speakers of one often struggle to comprehend speakers of another.

Oppression by the Spanish colonists led to the 1680 Pueblo Revolt, which successfully, if temporarily, removed the Spanish from the Rio Grande Valley. When Spanish rule was reestablished during the early 1690s, the Pojoaque people scattered to escape retribution for their participation in the revolt. By 1712, Pojoaque pueblo's population had declined to 79, and by 1890 the pueblo had only 40 residents, a small fraction of its precontact population. During the 19th century, Pojoaque was further devastated by a smallpox epidemic, lack of water, and a drastically diminished agricultural base due to encroachment by non-Indians. The pueblo virtually disappeared as an organized entity during the early 20th century, but in 1934, after a tenacious struggle by tribal member Antonio Jose Tapia, the commissioner of Indian affairs called for all tribal members to return to the reservation. Under that year's Indian Reorganization Act, 14 members of tribal families were awarded lands that had passed into the hands of Mexican families.

Since that time, particularly over the past 25 years, the tribe's reliance on agriculture has diminished as the Pojoaque have focused on developing a long-term land-use plan and innovative ways to merge growth with traditional tribal culture. The tribe's official tourist center and its Poeh Cultural Center and Museum are two successful examples.

SALT RIVER RESERVATION

Tribe: Salt River Pima-Maricopa Indian Community
Current Location: New Mexico   Total Area: 54,483 acres
Tribal Enrollment: 8,217

The Salt River Pima-Maricopa Indian Community comprises two distinct tribes: the Pima—or Akimel Au-Authm ("River People")—and the Maricopa—or Xalychidom Piipaash ("People Who Live Toward the Water"). Both groups have traditionally been river-basin desert farmers in the area, providing protection for one another against invasion by Yuman and Apache tribes; thus, their histories are intertwined. The Pima believe they descend from the ancient Hoo-hoogam, or Hohokam, who created an elaborate irrigation system to farm the arid desert land. Remnants of those ancient canals

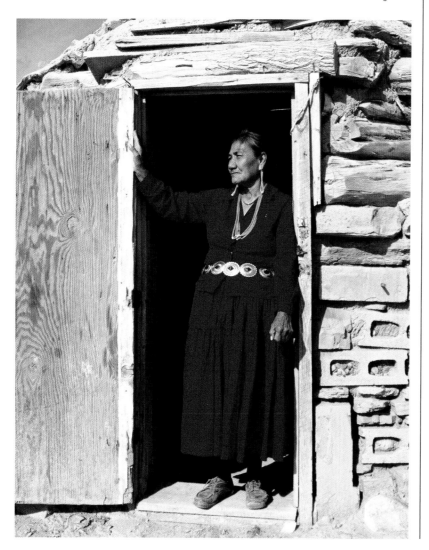

A Navajo woman standing in her doorway. The doors of Navajo homes traditionally face east, toward the rising sun.

can still be found, although they are now modernized. The Maricopa, living in small bands along the lower Colorado and Gila Rivers, were less sedentary than the Pima. They were driven toward the Pima settlements by shortages of water and the pressure of warfare with other tribes.

The earliest mention of the Pima was made by the Spaniard Marcos de Niza in 1589. Padre Eusebio Francisco Kino, a Jesuit, made several trips into the Gila River area between 1694 and 1699. Agricultural production increased after the Pima received wheat from the Spanish, possibly from Father Kino.

Increasing production and trading success led to more cooperation and to more economic specialization, with men concentrating on farming and women on producing crafts for trade. Pima people are known for watertight, intricately woven basketry. Maricopa women specialized in pottery, typically made of red clay. The California gold rush caused a great increase in demand for Pima wheat, leading to a boom economy and an enormous expansion of production between 1848 and 1854.

The decline of the Pima economy began in earnest at the end of the Civil War, when immigrants, settling in the area that would become the city of Phoenix, constructed a dam on the Gila River upriver from the Pima and Maricopa villages. The resulting shortages of water led a number of Pimas to move south to a new location on the Salt River. On June 14, 1879, this new settlement was recognized and established as the Salt River Indian Reservation.

SANDIA

Tribe: Pueblo of Sandia   Current Location: New Mexico
Total Area: 22,890 acres   Tribal Enrollment: 487

The Sandia people have resided at T'uf Shu Tu' ("Green Reed Place") since at least 1300. Originally, the Sandia were one of approximately 20 Pueblo cultures stretching south along the Rio Grande in the province that Spanish explorer Coronado called Tiguex. Sandia pueblo was not identified by its current name until the 17th century, when

ZUNI

The Pueblo of Zuni, situated in the Zuni River Valley of New Mexico about 35 miles south of Gallup and 150 miles west of Albuquerque, is the largest of the 20 Pueblo tribes in the Southwest, with about 10,000 people. In some ways the A:shiwi, as they call themselves, are the most traditional of the Pueblo tribes. The Zuni language, which is still spoken and taught, is what linguists call an isolate—that is, it's not closely related to any other language. They maintain their religion and culture, including ceremonies that are kept secret from outsiders. The Zuni continue to farm and herd livestock where their ancestors lived thousands of years ago and have also developed a thriving culture of family-based artists' workshops.

The Ancestral Pueblo

The Zuni River Valley, like other parts of the Southwest, is dotted with abandoned ancient settlements. People lived there at first in pit houses, and then in dense multistory masonry villages made up of living spaces and kivas, ceremonial rooms that are always entered through a hole in the roof. Archaeologists in the early 20th century called these people the Anasazi, but some Indians prefer to describe them as the ancestral Puebloans.

By the late 1300s, the old settlements in the eastern end of the Zuni Valley were deserted, probably because of a mix of environmental and social disasters. Those in the western end, around the current Zuni home, were growing.

In 1539, an expedition led by the Spanish Franciscan Fray Marcos de Niza came to the Zuni Valley. One of de Niza's companions, a black slave named Estevan, was killed by the Zunis. De Niza himself did not visit, but instead returned to Mexico to tell one of the great untruths of history—that in the north, there were seven golden cities called Cibola. The next year, an expedition led by Francisco Vasquez de Coronado reached the valley but found no gold. He captured the Zuni town of Hawikuh, but left shortly afterward.

In the years soon after the Pueblo Revolt of 1680 and the Spanish Reconquest of 1692, the Zuni abandoned their other settlements and consolidated at what's now the old part of Zuni, also known as Halona Idiwan'a, or the Middle Place. They farmed in the land surrounding the village. Because of their remote location, there were no Spanish settlements in their region, so they were relatively isolated from European influences.

Zuni dragonfly pin, circa 1950, made from silver, turquoise, spiny oyster, and jet

However, in the 19th and 20th centuries, repeated contact was unavoidable and change inexorable. Anthropologists, missionaries, and traders visited. The federal government imposed rules about land use, governance, and education. The population expanded beyond the bounds of Halona Idiwan'a, and people built modern homes outside the old walls.

Raw People and Cooked People

Nonetheless, the ancient traditions continue. Many of them revolve around a worldview that seems confusing and mysterious to modern Westerners. In part, that's because the Zuni consider their spiritual system private, not something to be shared with outsiders.

For the individual Zuni, the system rests on a web of kinship, clan, and religious affiliations. A child belongs to his or her mother's household and clan, but he or she is also a "child of" the father's household and clan—a relationship with two-way responsibilities. A man belongs to one of several kivas, or ceremonial organizations. Both men and women may also belong to medicine societies and priesthoods. The groups that an individual belongs to shape behavior, marriage possibilities, and spiritual roles.

In the Zuni worldview, there are "raw people" and "cooked people." "The cooked or daylight people depend on cooked food, while the raw people eat food that is either raw or has been sacrificed to them by daylight people," explains Dennis Tedlock, an anthropologist who has written about Zuni religion and legends. "They are 'people' in the sense that one of their potential forms is anthropomorphic, and in the sense that they and the daylight people [humans] should behave as kinsmen toward one another."

The raw people include the Earth, the Sun Father, and the Moon Mother. There are many other raw people, including the kachinas, who wear masks and dance; they live in the Kachina Village, located "at the bottom of a lake two days' walk from Zuni; there they sing and pray for rain and the growth of crops," according to Tedlock. Among them are the *koyemshi,* also known as mudheads, silly and capricious clowns who have a disruptive role in ceremonies. The land around the Zuni reservation holds many sites and shrines sacred to various figures in this cosmology.

Ceremonies Survive

The Zuni have a yearlong calendar of ceremonies, many of them involving dances by masked kachina society members. The best known and most elaborate is the Sha'lak'o, a winter solstice dance that bids farewell to the old and asks for blessings in the new year.

Some Zuni ceremonies are open to non-Zuni visitors, although photography is discouraged. The Zuni also have a museum and cultural center and encourage tours of both Halona

Zuni girls, probably carrying water, were photographed by Edward S. Curtis, who documented Indian life in the early 20th century.

Idiwan'a, which is still occupied, and of the sites of some of the abandoned villages, including the Village of the Great Kivas, a ruin known for its petroglyphs and pictographs.

Zuni tribal members farm the land around their village, but the biggest industry in town is the manufacture of

traditional crafts at home. An estimated 80 percent of families make and sell such items, which are among the most recognizable of southwestern indigenous arts. These include fine silver jewelry, often inlaid with turquoise and other stones; carved stone animal fetishes; kachina dolls; pottery; and more. ■

Spanish settlers dubbed it Sandia ("watermelon"), a reference to the deep red color of the sacred mountains at sunset.

The many villages of the Tiguex Province, Sandia being the largest, suffered under Spanish occupation, with many sites becoming depopulated and reduced in geographical extent. In response to their mistreatment, the Pueblo of Sandia participated in the Pueblo Revolt of 1680. The Spanish burned the pueblo as they retreated, and Governor Antonio de Otermin burned it again during early attempts at reconquest. The people of Sandia sought refuge with the Hopi, and they temporarily settled in the village of Payupki on Second Mesa. The Sandia people were finally granted their petition to resettle in their traditional territory in 1748, when a land grant established the boundaries of the pueblo.

The pueblo's old village has a central plaza. The original site of the 17th-century San Francisco de Sandia mission now serves as the pueblo's cemetery. The second mission church, Nuestra Señora de Los Dolores y San Antonio de Sandia, is located at the northern end of the old pueblo. A third church, San Antonio de Padua, built in 2001, has received architectural awards. Traditional practices are maintained, and the Tiwa language is taught to tribal youths. The reservation's location has led some tribal members to embrace multiple languages, becoming trilingual in Tiwa, English, and Spanish.

The Pueblo of Sandia continue to honor traditional governing roles. The tribe is governed by a governor, a lieutenant governor, and governing staff. A war chief and lieutenant war chief also exercise authority within the pueblo and are responsible for all religious and ceremonial activities. The tribal economy is supported by leasing tribal lands, by tribal retail enterprises, and most significantly by tribal gaming facilities. Agriculture and livestock continue to be major sources of income for some tribal families as well.

A basket made of dyed yucca fiber and galleta grass made about 1970 by Bessie Polengyouma of the Hopi Pueblo

Zuni, not a member of any other language family

"Keshi, Hom á-hói, Ko'don la:k'yadinapkya?"

("Hello, my people, how are all of you today?")

In the past several decades, the Rio Grande has become one of the most endangered rivers in the country, a major concern to the Pueblo of Sandia. The tribe's water quality program is all-encompassing, involving the tribe's environmental department, community members, and tribal youths in protecting and restoring the water supply. The John F. Kennedy School of Government at Harvard University and the Environmental Protection Agency have both honored the program.

SAN FELIPE

Tribe: Pueblo of San Felipe
Current Location: New Mexico
Total Area: 48,929 acres   Tribal Enrollment: 3,377

Katishtya, or the San Felipe pueblo, was established at its current site in northern New Mexico in 1706. Tradition has it that enemies drove the people of San Felipe to the banks of the Rio Grande from their home on the Pajarito Plateau. Previously, their ancestors and those of the Cochiti Pueblo were one tribe that spoke a single dialect, but because their neighbors to the north, the Tewa, remained hostile, the tribe was divided in two, with one branch heading south, where they established the Katishtya (later San Felipe) pueblo, while the other formed Cochiti.

The people of San Felipe pueblo speak an eastern dialect of Keres. Their identity as a people is very strong, and they consider their privacy integral to maintaining their traditional lifestyle. Ceremonial dances are held throughout the year, and the Native language is still spoken.

Under the provisions of the 1848 Treaty of Guadalupe Hidalgo, the United States ratified the San Felipe Pueblo as Mexican citizens. In 1864, Congress confirmed and patented Spain's original land grant to the tribe of 30,000 acres. The tribe organized in 1934 under the Indian Reorganization Act, but still considers itself a traditional entity. President Lincoln presented the San Felipe Pueblo with

INTER-TRIBAL INDIAN CEREMONIAL

Each August, tribal members from around the Southwest gather in Gallup, New Mexico, for a multiday celebration of all things Indian called the Inter-Tribal Indian Ceremonial, or simply the Ceremonial. The event welcomes non-Indian tourists. It combines parades, rodeos, art, food, and cultural demonstrations. There's a contest pow-wow, where dancers and drummers compete for cash. Throughout the gathering, there are public dance performances. Even tribes that seldom allow outsiders to view their ceremonies adapt religious or nonreligious dances for the occasion.

The Ceremonial has been held since 1922. Tobe Turpen, Jr., who joined his family's trading post in Gallup in 1946, reminisced in the late 1990s with a historian from Northern Arizona University about the old days. "The Ceremonial was the biggest thing in our life," said Turpen, a non-Indian who was on the board of the Ceremonial for years, and its president for a time. "We did as much business in four days as we did any other month. First, that monetarily was a great thing. But it was a great thing for the town. The people that put the Ceremonial together, put it together for the Indians. They didn't put it together for themselves. They didn't put it together to make money. They put it together as a celebration for the Indian . . . When it first started, the Indians came in to the dances, they started bringin' different dance teams in. They like to see each other dance.

"And then [organizers] became aware that this would be a good place to show arts and crafts . . . And the traders from the reservation and the traders from town would come in and show their wares and make beautiful exhibits. So it was really, really authentic. The public learned about it, the people overseas learned about it, and all of a sudden it became a pretty good-sized event for a little town.

"We had a parade every morning at 10 o'clock for the three or four days of the show; a rodeo in the afternoon; and the dances at night. And the dances were wonderful. All the Indian groups would come out on the field, and they'd have about six or eight big campfires all built. It was dark, there was no lighting, there was no cameras. It was just as authentic as it could be. And then each team stepped out and danced.

"It has changed dramatically, as times have changed, as everything changes." ∎

Native American dancers perform at a ceremony during the 83rd Annual Inter-tribal Indian Ceremonial at Red Rock Park in Gallup, New Mexico, in 2004.

SAN ILDEFONSO

Tribe: Pueblo of San Ildefonso   Current Location: New Mexico   Total Area: 28,179 acres   Tribal Enrollment: 672

The Tewa Indians of San Ildefonso settled near the site of the present-day pueblo around 1300, occupying villages known today as the ruins of Sankewi, Otowi, and Potsuwi. After the 1694 attack by the Spanish general Don Diego de Vargas, the tribe sought refuge atop Black Mesa, where it heroically repelled repeated attacks and withstood captivity. After two years, the tribe surrendered and resettled just north of its previous home, but European contact brought diseases that decimated its numbers.

Like most of the other New Mexican Pueblo tribes, the San Ildefonso Tewa's rights were recognized and confirmed under the Treaty of Guadalupe Hidalgo between the United States and Mexico in 1848. The grant was patented in 1864. Since that time, additions to the reservation have been made by congressional acts.

By 1864, census figures showed only 161 remaining pueblo residents. By the early 20th century, factionalism between the tribe's summer and winter clans resulted in partitioning the tribe into the North and South Plaza People, each group maintaining its own secular and religious officers.

Prior to 1848 and the Treaty of Guadalupe Hidalgo, the tribe subsisted on agriculture and hunting, with the barter system serving as the primary method of exchange. In the wake of the treaty, the entire Southwest experienced a great influx of traders and merchants, who introduced a cash and wage economy. This trend continued, and by World War II many tribal members sought work off the reservation, with a number employed at the laboratories in nearby Los Alamos or in Santa Fe. This remains the case today, though the emergence of a pueblo-based arts and crafts cottage industry has arrested the trend to a degree.

Pottery, the backbone of the tribe's arts and crafts market, has held great significance for the tribe for many centuries. By the 1920s, tribal members Maria

Nellie Martin weaves a rug out of wool sheared from her sheep on her Navajo Reservation farm near Navajo, New Mexico.

a silver-headed cane as a gesture of governmental recognition. The governor keeps the cane throughout his term.

The pueblo hosts numerous ceremonies and dances throughout the year, which reflect both its Native and mission heritage, often entwining the two strands, as in the Green Corn Dance, which is held on St. Philip's feast day in May. The San Felipe Church is an outstanding example of early Franciscan mission architecture, and the town's unique sunken plaza provides an unusual setting for dances.

and Julian Martinez developed a strain of pottery inspired by ancient shards excavated by archaeologists at a nearby ruin. This new highly polished black or red ware has become a lucrative source of income today for many tribal craftspeople, as well as a source of community pride.

SANTA CLARA

Tribe: Pueblo of Santa Clara   Current Location: New Mexico   Total Area: 53,437 acres   Tribal Enrollment: 2,200

The Tewa people have lived at Kha P'o (the Valley of the Wild Roses), or the Santa Clara pueblo, for several hundred years. The historical focus of the Santa Clara pueblo is the Puye cliff dwellings, which are a registered national historic landmark. For more than three centuries, this spectacular plateau was home to the more than 1,500 Puye people who lived, farmed, and hunted game. The first dwellings were caves hollowed in the volcanic cliffs. Later, adobe structures were built along the slopes and on top of the mesa. The Tewa abandoned the Puye area more than 400 years ago, after severe drought caused them to settle in the lowlands of the Rio Grande Valley, the site of the current pueblo. Archaeologists believe that the early dwellings of Puye Cliffs were last occupied about 1680.

The Pueblo of Santa Clara received their initial land grant under the Spanish and were pronounced citizens of Mexico when that country gained its independence from Spain. The United States confirmed the tribe's land grant in 1858 and patented it in 1909.

A protracted schism between factions within the traditional governing body during the early 20th century led the tribe to accept the terms of the 1934 Indian Reorganization Act and base a new constitution on it. The tribe was the first of the Pueblos to adopt a written constitution. A major result of the 1935 constitution's adoption was the separation of religious and secular matters, which transformed tribal religious ceremonies into voluntary affairs. The pueblo of Santa Clara is the second largest of the six Tewa-speaking pueblos in New Mexico and a member of the Eight Northern Indian Pueblos Council, whose headquarters are at Ohkay Owingeh pueblo.

IRA HAYES

Hero of Iwo Jima

Ira Hayes (1923–1955) was a Pima Indian, born on the Gila Indian Reservation in Sacaton, Arizona. He grew up to be a dedicated Marine who was admired by those who fought alongside him in three major Pacific battles of World War II.

On February 19, 1945, when he was 23, Hayes took part in the landing on Iwo Jima. He was among the Marines who took Mount Suribachi. On February 23, his life changed. On a hilltop above the Pacific island, a small group of Marines struggled to raise the American flag to claim victory over the Japanese occupiers. Hayes rushed to help his comrades. The image of the raising of that second American flag on Mount Suribachi by five Marines and a Navy corpsman was immortalized by photographer Joe Rosenthal. It became an icon of the war and of the Marine Corps.

Overnight, Hayes (in the middle of the photograph, entertaining Dean Martin's kids) became a national hero, along with the two other survivors. Hayes's story drew particular attention because he was Native American. After the war, he toured the country, but never became comfortable with the acclaim surrounding him. In his last years, he returned home to the reservation, where he drank heavily and died one night of exposure. ■

TOHONO O'ODHAM

The Tohono O'odham, or Desert People, live in the dry Sonoran Desert region of southern Arizona and northern Mexico. Until 1986, the tribe was known as the Papago, a corruption of a Spanish phrase meaning "bean eaters." They are closely related to the Akimel O'odham tribes, or River People, sometimes known as the Pima. Both groups speak dialects of the same O'odham language, part of the Uto-Aztecan family, and claim descent from the Hohokam, an archaeological classification of the prehistoric farming peoples who lived in the same region of the Southwest prior to the disappearance of their civilization about 1400. The traditional Tohono O'odham life meant adapting to the harsh environment—where modern people might see a spiny, foreboding saguaro cactus, they saw food.

Life with Little Water

In the arid desert, a successful life is one that makes the best of the little water available. At the time of European contact, the Tohono O'odham lived what anthropologists describe as a "two village" lifestyle, spending the winter in the foothills, where there were natural springs, then moving down to the valleys for the summer. There, they set up their brush houses in spots near the desert washes that would allow them to take advantage of the occasional torrential summer rain to raise their crops of corn, beans, and squash. They gathered plants, including saguaro fruit, cholla buds, and mesquite bean pods, and hunted the small animals with which they shared the desert, including rabbit and javelina.

Although Spanish explorers passed through Tohono O'odham territory in the 16th century on the way from Mexico to New Mexico, they didn't take much notice of the people until Jesuit missionary Father Eusebio Kino arrived in 1687. He brought with him not only European religion but also cattle, horses, and new foods, including wheat. Kino and the Jesuits founded about two dozen missions and converted most of the Tohono O'odham to Catholicism. The northernmost of those missions

A teenage pageant winner prepares for the parade before the O'odham Tash powwow, held in Casa Grande, Arizona.

was at San Xavier, south of Tucson on part of what is now the Tohono O'odham Reservation. In 1783, another group of priests began construction there of the San Xavier del Bac mission church, now the national historic landmark known as the White Dove of the Desert.

Mexico controlled this part of Arizona from 1821, when it became independent from Spain, until 1854, when the southern part of what's now New Mexico and Arizona was sold to the United States. That sale split the Tohono O'odham land with an artificial national border. The people for many years considered the border little more than a formality, crossing it repeatedly to gather food, see family, and visit sacred sites. However, the border also meant Indians on the two sides received different treatment from the two governments. In Mexico, many Indians were largely assimilated into the population, although, in 1927, the government set up small reserves of land for the Tohono O'odham. There are now nine small communities on the Mexican side of the border. On the American side, the government set aside the San Xavier Reservation in 1874, the Gila Bend Reservation in 1882, and the main Tohono O'odham Reservation in 1917, with its capital in the town of Sells, Arizona. The 20-acre Florence Village tract was added in 1978.

Building in the Desert

With 2.8 million acres and 28,000 members, the tribe is the second largest in Arizona in both land size and population, after the Navajo. About half the enrolled members live on the

The traditional diet of the Tohono O'odham includes the drought-resistant tepary bean, cultivated on their Arizona reservation.

reservation, where there are government programs, recreation centers, a health center, schools, and a tribal community college. The traditional culture, called the Tohono O'odham Himdag, is fostered in the Cultural Center and Museum; the community college requires all graduates to take two culture classes. For some, returning to that culture is vitally important. The Tohono O'odham have one of the highest rates of adult-onset diabetes in the world, with half the adults on the reservation suffering from the disease. Health educators say greater reliance on traditional crops rather than processed foods would reduce the incidence of diabetes.

One food-related tradition is the harvest of the saguaro fruit. The saguaro, the towering many-armed cactus that is an icon of the Southwest, grows throughout the Tohono O'odham lands. The fruit is harvested in the spring, using long poles. It's then made into jams, jellies, and saguaro wine. The wine is central to the Nawait I'i, or Rain Ceremony, which celebrates the coming of summer storms.

The tribe's location on 75 miles of the U.S.-Mexico border is a constant issue, particularly in times of heightened concern about security and illegal immigration. People who live on both sides of the border complain that Border Patrol members harass them on their many routine crossings, which are permitted by tribal membership. The Tohono O'odham also cope daily with the smuggling of people and drugs across their land and the violence that is a result of the Mexican drug wars.

Many tribal members live in poverty, and despite attempts to diversify the economy, the biggest business remains gaming. The tribe runs three casinos and, as of 2010, was caught up in a controversy over whether it could open a fourth casino west of Phoenix in Glendale. The West Valley Resort, which would be the largest casino-resort in the state, is proposed for land the tribe acquired under federal provisions that compensate it for land it lost in the 1970s because of flooding from the Painted River Dam. The local government opposes the project, and the tribe went to court to force the federal government to act in its favor. ■

TAOS

Tribe: Pueblo of Taos   **Current Location:** New Mexico
Total Area: 96,106 acres   **Tribal Enrollment:** 2,410

The Tiwa-speaking community of Taos pueblo has inhabited the Taos Valley since about 900. It is believed that the tribe is descended from the Chico or ancestral Puebloans and that the pueblo may have been one of the fabled golden cities of Cibola that drove Coronado's obsession. The Taos pueblo is the oldest continuously inhabited community in the United States. The original structure

Al Dean Joe Nastacio of the Zuni Pueblo, a member of the Cellicion Traditional Dancers, performs the White Buffalo Dance, which pays respect to that rare albino animal.

consists of two houses, the Hlauuma (north house) and the Hlaukwima (south house), both believed to have been constructed between 1000 and 1450. The pueblo has been recognized as a national historic landmark and was included in the World Heritage List as one of the most significant cultural landmarks in the world.

The people encountered Europeans when Spanish explorers arrived in the region in 1540. The Taos people were typically at the forefront of Pueblo revolts against domination by the Spanish, and in 1847 they joined the Mexican settlers in their fight against the U.S. government. In 1680, the Taos residents spearheaded the Pueblo Revolt. These altercations set the tone for the tribe's determination to protect its water rights, political sovereignty, and land base.

Perhaps the most dramatic of their battles has been for Blue Lake, the tribe's most important religious shrine, lying 20 miles from the pueblo behind Taos Mountain. When Blue Lake and 48,000 acres of surrounding aboriginal-use area were incorporated into the Carson National Forest in 1906, the tribe took the government to court, finally winning its case for restoration in 1970. This marked the first time that land instead of money was returned to an American Indian tribe upon completion of a land claims case.

The tribe's worldview stresses a powerful sense of spiritual tradition, community, and loyalty to one's extended kin, and it remains a commanding anchor within the pueblo. The Taos tribal culture remains active and vibrant. Extended family ties appear as strong as ever, and since the 1970s, many of the tribe's younger members have shown a renewed commitment to their identity as Taos Indians. In addition, the kiva-based religion maintains the tribe's rich ceremonial life. The six active subterranean kivas together with their constituent societies are Big Earring, Day, and Knife on the north side, Water, Old Axe, and Feather on the south. The tribe also practices an extended and rigorous male initiation between the ages of seven and ten that culminates in, and is tribally validated by, the annual August pilgrimage to Blue Lake.

Tohono O'odham Reservation

Tribe: Tohono O'odham Nation of Arizona
Current Location: Arizona   **Total Area:** 2,846,409 acres
Tribal Enrollment: 26,673

Members of the Tohono O'odham Nation are also known by the names the Spanish gave them, but originally they were Tohono O'odham ("Desert People" and "the Papago") and Akimel O'odham ("River People" and "the Pima"). Expert irrigation farmers, both the Pima and the Papago lived a seminomadic lifestyle in many parts of the desert Southwest and parts of northern Mexico. Some became cattle ranchers after the Spanish introduced cattle to the area.

Struggles with surrounding groups led to conflict. Beginning around 1821, immigrant farmers, ranchers, and miners began encroaching upon O'odham lands and water supplies. The Indians successfully defended themselves, only to be confronted by Mexicans 19 years later. That struggle lasted for three years, at the end of which the Tohono O'odham negotiated a surrender. The Gadsden Purchase, closely following the end of the Mexican-American War in 1848, added an international boundary that cut through traditional O'odham lands. By 1898, many of the remaining Pimas and Papagos had left Mexico as a result of local hostility and greater job opportunities in Arizona.

Tohono O'odham culture remains vibrant, practiced by young and old alike, as evidenced by the regular occurrence of tribal rituals and the performances of traditional music known as chicken scratch, or *waila* (a Mexican adaptation of "polka"). Public ceremonies continue to be held for the celebration of nature as well as human achievements, including rain, farming, hunting, war, and other activities. There are also elaborate, albeit private, ritual cures for sicknesses engendered by violations of taboo. The O'odham knowledge of herbal medicines is extensive. The language continues to thrive as well, both in private homes and in public schools.

Navajo, Southern Athabascan language family

"Dá níla' ísh táásíngiz?" "Aoó, shíla' tááségiz."

("Did you wash your hands?" "Yes, I washed my hands.")

Ysleta del Sur

Tribe: Ysleta del Sur Pueblo of Texas   **Current Location:** Texas   **Total Area:** 530 acres   **Tribal Enrollment:** 1,324

The Tigua of Ysleta del Sur pueblo near El Paso, Texas, are descendents of Isleta Pueblo refugees from the middle Rio Grande Valley in what is now the state of New Mexico, and the only Pueblo tribe in Texas. They speak the Tiwa language, a dialect similar to that spoken by Isleta, Sandia, Taos, and Picurís Pueblos. During the Pueblo Revolt of 1680, many Isleta Pueblo people fled the war-torn *norte;* some were taken to the *sur,* becoming the first true community within what are now the boundaries of the state of Texas, and they named their new settlement Ysleta del Sur. By 1682, they had built a church, La Misión de Corpus Christi de la Ysleta, which became the focal point for community life. In 1751, King Charles V of Spain made a 36-square-mile grant of land to these Christian Indians, and they were subsequently protected by the Spanish and Mexican governments until Ysleta del Sur pueblo came under Texas rule in 1848 with the Treaty of Guadalupe Hidalgo. Within 30 years, the Texas legislature allowed towns to give public lands to homesteaders, and settlers quickly seized much of the tribe's fertile farmlands.

The state of Texas recognized the Ysleta del Sur Pueblo grant in the 1854 Ysleta Relief Act, but the people were not officially recognized as a tribe by the state until May 1967, when they were placed under the jurisdiction of the Commission of Indian Affairs. Meanwhile, in the 1950s the City of El Paso had annexed large areas of the lower valley, including Ysleta del Sur pueblo, and it enforced a new set of tax codes on land the Indians had always owned. Many lost their homes as a result. The tribe was late in obtaining federal recognition due to its physical isolation from other pueblos, but the federal government finally recognized it in 1987.

The mission church is still the religious focal point of the Tigua Indian community. When the Catholic Church banned Indian dances as devil worship, the Tigua tribe changed some feast days and accommodated the Catholic calendar in order to keep its traditional Butterfly Dance, Round Dance, Turtle Dance, and Pueblo Two-Step. The Sacred Drum, a dance of special spiritual significance, was carefully preserved in private practice and is now performed as a community once again. The Tigua practice many unique customs that cannot be found in any other pueblo.

ZIA

Tribe: Pueblo of Zia   **Current Location:** New Mexico
Total Area: 121,613 acres   **Tribal Enrollment:** 832

The Zia's early ancestors are thought to be the eastern ancestral Puebloans who lived in the Chaco Canyon area of western New Mexico prior to A.D. 400. At the end of the 12th century, these people began migrating southeast, likely motivated by a 25-year drought in the beginning of the 13th century. The present site of Zia pueblo was settled and has been continuously occupied since around 1250. The pueblo's sophisticated dry farming methods and ditch irrigation made successful cultivation by large populations possible in a desert climate. Traditional crops include corn, beans, squash, and melons.

The tribe's first contact with the Spanish was in 1541 with the Coronado expedition. Spanish records from the time describe Zia pueblo as containing more than 1,000 well-kept two- and three-story houses and a society that included 4,000 adult males, as well as women and children. Spanish interference with the Pueblo's spiritual traditions led the Zia to join in the Pueblo Revolt of 1680, which ultimately resulted in the pueblo's decimation by a bloody assault during the 1688 reconquest by the Spanish.

A Spanish land grant to the Zia people was enacted in 1689. Mexico recognized the grant after Mexican independence in 1821, and the United States honored it as well, following the Treaty of Guadalupe Hidalgo in 1848. Purchases and executive orders since then have increased the reservation to its present size. Today the tribe's main income comes from wage jobs in the nearby cities of Albuquerque and Rio Rancho, and from farming and ranching.

NAVAJO CODE TALKERS

Two U.S. Marine Navajo code talkers, signalmen who used a version of their Native language, send a radio signal during the Battle of Bougainville in 1943.

In 1942, a group of 29 young Navajo men answered the call of duty for the U.S. Marine Corps. Their unit, the Navajo Code Talkers, devised a World War II code that Japanese intelligence experts couldn't break.

The idea was proposed to the Marines by civilian Philip Johnston, who grew up in a missionary family on a Navajo reservation and spoke the Navajo language. The code was perfected by the Navajo men who used it on active duty. They began with 200 terms, which eventually grew to more than 600. By the end of the war, about 400 Navajo men had trained as code talkers.

The code used both military and Navajo terms. In a very simple way, the military terms resembled the things with which they were associated. The Navajo word *chay-da-gahi*, which means "tortoise," was used for a tank. *Gini*, the Navajo word for a chicken hawk, meant a dive-bomber, because chicken hawks dive for their prey. To supplement these, words would be spelled out using Navajo terms assigned to individual letters—the Navajo term was based on the first letter of the Navajo word's English meaning. For example, *wo-la-chee means* "ant" and would sometimes represent the letter *A*. Other *A* words would be substituted so no single word would be repeated too often, which might have led to the code being broken.

The code talkers could communicate with each other in a way that even uninitiated Navajos could not understand and even the best cryptologists could not decode. Their code was not written down, so these soldiers became living coding machines. And what took coding machines 30 minutes to accomplish the code talkers could do in 20 seconds. In battle, these soldiers were instrumental in every major Pacific engagement from Guadalcanal to Okinawa. ■

In 1692, the Zia accepted mass baptism and became nominal Roman Catholics. This action did not erase the old ways, however, and the Zia Pueblo maintain their elaborate, centuries-old cultural and religious traditions. The tribe is organized under the rules of the 1934 Indian Reorganization Act, though its members also consider themselves a traditionally organized tribe. The Zia Tribal Council runs the tribal government. The general council, or Zia Secular Council, is composed of male tribal members over the age of 18. The tribe maintains its own tribal court system as well, with the governor serving as chief judge.

ZUNI RESERVATION

Tribe: Zuni Tribe   Current Location: New Mexico
Total Area: 588,093 acres   Tribal Enrollment: 10,258

The Zuni and their ancestors have occupied the Zuni and Little Colorado River Valleys for more than 2,000 years. The Spanish established their first mission there in 1629. After the 1848 Treaty of Guadalupe Hidalgo, the United States came into possession of the 16 million acres of Zuni aboriginal territory and traditional-use areas, which include parts of New Mexico, Arizona, Utah, and Colorado. At that time, the Zuni tribe was arguably the wealthiest and most secure political force in that region of the Southwest. During the mid-19th century, the Zuni cultivated between 10,000 and 12,000 acres of crops, primarily corn, and grazed thousands of sheep on the grasslands within a two-million-acre area. They also harvested salt from the Zuni Salt Lake, which provided an important resource for their consumption and religious icons.

Between 1846 and 1876, non-Indian settlement of the West resulted in the Zuni losing approximately nine million acres. Still, the tribe maintained control over most of its grazing land and almost all of its upper watershed area until the U.S. Congress, having determined that a southern transcontinental railroad would greatly benefit the nation, set aside a small tract of land for a Zuni reservation and authorized Atlantic & Pacific to begin building. The railroad cut a swath through the former Zuni territory, harvesting tens of millions of board feet of lumber from the once-pristine watershed area in the process. At least 11,000 acres of prime irrigable land have been lost to Zuni agricultural use since the coming of the railroad in 1881.

Petitions from the tribe in 1917, 1935, and 1949 led to reservation expansion. Over the years, the tribe has been involved in nearly continuous litigation over land claims and water rights. For example, in 1978 the tribe was awarded the return of its Salt Lake property, but in the 1980s the New Mexico courts dismissed claims for damages to their remaining lands.

A girl poses in traditional clothing at the Tesuque pueblo, just north of Santa Fe, New Mexico.

THE SOUTHWEST

THE GREAT BASIN
& PLATEAU

THE GREAT BASIN & PLATEAU

THE GEOGRAPHY OF THE GREAT BASIN AND COLUMBIA RIVER PLATEAU regions is characterized by the high subalpine forests of the Cascade, Rocky, and Uintah Mountains; the high desert sage- and rabbitbrush-covered foothills; and the Columbia, Snake, and Colorado Rivers. The tribes of these regions spoke dialects from several different language families. They were all known as accomplished hunters and gatherers, taking only what was needed, using fishing and hunting equipment that was made from local resources. Today, language revitalization, economic development, and cultural self-determination are major concerns for each of the tribes as they attempt to ensure and protect their sovereign rights for future generations.

Tribal lands included in this chapter span ten U.S. states. Features will focus on four select tribes in Washington, Idaho, Utah, and Oregon—the Yakama, Shoshone-Bannock, Ute, and Warm Springs—following the story line of their cultural similarities and diversity.

TRIBES OF THE GREAT BASIN AND PLATEAU HISTORICALLY WERE HUNTERS AND GATHERERS.

HUNTING, FISHING, GATHERING

THESE TRIBES HISTORICALLY WERE HUNTER-GATHERERS. THEY hunted deer, elk, bison, antelope, moose, and on occasion caribou for both food and clothes made from the tanned hides. The nearby rivers, lakes, and streams provided salmon, trout, and sturgeon. A variety of food roots, berries, and nuts also supplied a great deal of necessary nutrients. The people would gather these foods during the spring and summer, then prepare, dry, and store them for use throughout the year.

The traditional foods essential to the diet of the people from the Columbia River Plateau, still gathered today, were salmon, deer, food roots, huckleberries, and chokecherries. While the women gathered the plants, the men hunted and fished for the deer and salmon. A variety of tools were made and used to gather these resources, such as fish weirs made of willow branches, long-handled dip nets, hooks made of carved bone or wood securely fastened to line, and bow and arrows for fishing and hunting. Women used digging sticks, called *kapns,* made of small-handled sharp-pointed sticks, to dig for and gather the edible roots. To hold the roots and berries, they created two different types of baskets: a soft-sided twined bag, or *wapas,* made of Indian hemp and rye grass, and a coiled cedar-root basket decorated with an intricate pattern of bear grass.

Traditional men's and women's clothing is still made from deer and elk hides and decorated with elk teeth, bone, stone, natural paints, and shells. By 1805, the Shoshone-Bannock and other Plateau people had acquired a wide variety of materials through trade routes, including

Preceding pages: A rancher rounds up horses for branding on the Confederated Tribes of the Warm Springs Reservation of Oregon. Opposite: A Shoshone-Bannock man in traditional warrior dress holds a coup stick while astride a horse painted with traditional war symbols.

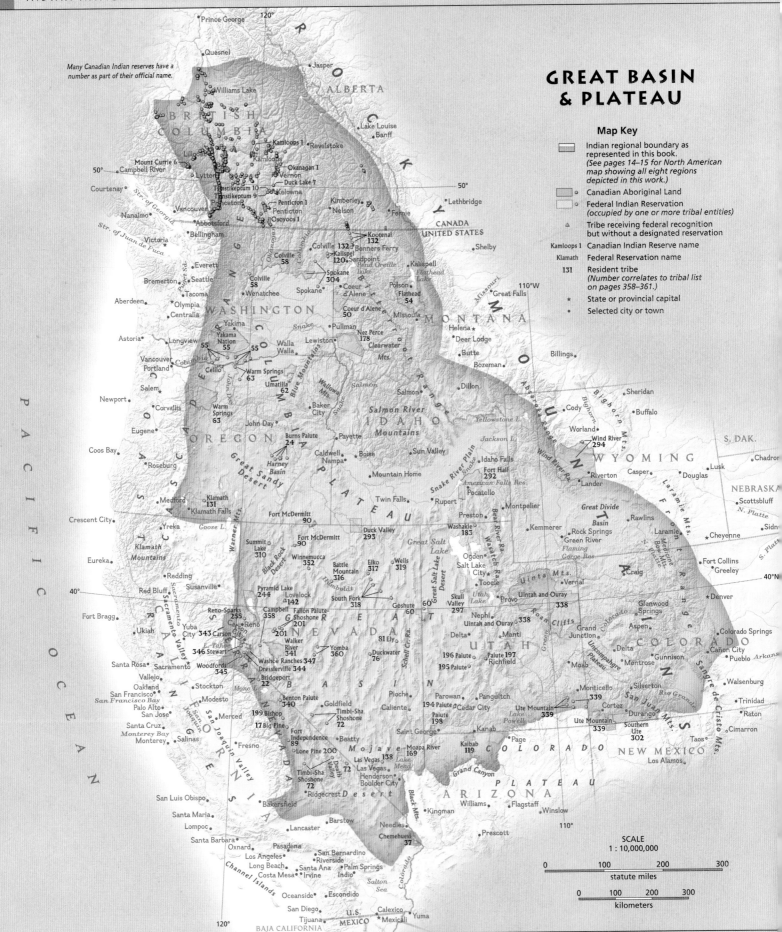

GREAT BASIN & PLATEAU

Map Key

Indian regional boundary as represented in this book.
(See pages 14–15 for North American map showing all eight regions depicted in this work.)

Canadian Aboriginal Land

Federal Indian Reservation
(occupied by one or more tribal entities)

Tribe receiving federal recognition but without a designated reservation

Kamloops 1   Canadian Indian Reserve name

Klamath   Federal Reservation name

131   Resident tribe
(Number correlates to tribal list on pages 358–361.)

★   State or provincial capital

•   Selected city or town

Many Canadian Indian reserves have a number as part of their official name.

SCALE
1 : 10,000,000

0   100   200   300
statute miles

0   100   200   300
kilometers

glass beads, cotton thread, and needles; wool, cotton, and velvet fabrics; and silk and velvet ribbon. The women's cloth dresses worn today are variations of the older hide dresses, and men's ribbon shirts are adaptations of the hide shirts. Tribal members who are accomplished beadwork artists have created modern interpretations of early utilitarian works of art.

Before the Plains-style tepee was adopted, the tribes of the Plateau and Great Basin made lodges using resources common to their areas. The Plateau tribes lived in earth lodges and longhouse-style accommodations constructed of tule mats tied to pine poles. The Ute of the Great Basin lived in conical, pole-framed shelters known as wickiups, which were covered with juniper bark or tule.

NATIVE AMERICAN SPIRITUAL BELIEFS ARE NATURE BASED, TEACHING THAT ALL THINGS IN NATURE HAVE A SPIRIT.

In the Great Basin region, ringed by the Sierra Nevada and Wasatch ranges, the Washoe who lived in the mountains near Lake Tahoe spoke a Hokan language related to languages spoken by Indians elsewhere in California. Others spoke languages in the Numic subfamily of the Uto-Aztecan language family, sometimes called Plateau Shoshonean. In the Plateau region, that area between the Rocky Mountains and the coastal mountains, most of the tribes spoke languages in the broad Salishan and Penutian language families. Today, though, after many of these tribes have been shuffled among various reservations shared with tribes from different backgrounds, multiple traditional languages can be present on the same reservation. In many of these places, the old languages are endangered, with few if any fluent young speakers. The tribes are taking various steps to bring these languages back.

WHAT HAS SURVIVED

THE TRADITIONAL WAY OF LIFE OF ALL THESE PEOPLE WAS OVERTURNED BY THE WAVES of American immigrants from the east heading to the west—explorers, gold miners, settlers, missionaries, and early military companies. These immigrants brought with them goods the Indian people found useful, such as cotton fabric, blankets, and beads. They also brought livestock and disease, however, both of which devastated the land as well as the people. Missionaries introduced education and a new form of religion.

Native American traditional spiritual beliefs in these regions are nature based, teaching that all things in nature have a spirit. Each tribe performs its own form of ceremony to bless the food with the return of each new season. The Yakama and Warm Springs peoples both have two major first-foods feasts: the Salmon Feast in spring and the Huckleberry Feast in summer. Both tribes believe that long before people were upon the land, salmon, deer, food roots, chokecherries, and huckleberries presented themselves one by one to the Creator to sacrifice themselves as food, clothing, and shelter for the people. Also in line was a small bird, which said, "I am too small for food, but I can lead the salmon on their way upriver." Today, this bird is a sign of spring. The sacrifice by the animals and plants is still honored by the Yakama people with annual thanksgiving feasts held at their longhouses. ▪

Big Pine Reservation

Tribe: Big Pine Band of Owens Valley Paiute Shoshone Indians of the Big Pine Reservation **Current Location:** California **Total Area:** 279 acres **Tribal Enrollment:** 398

Members of the Big Pine Band of Owens Valley are descendants of the Owen Valley Paiute and Panamint Shoshone tribes. The Shoshone language spoken by tribal members is related to the larger Uto-Aztecan language group spoken by many peoples across the Great Basin and down into central Mexico. The tribe originally controlled a vast territory along the Owens River. However, today the Owens Valley Paiute Shoshone occupy four land tracts that represent only a small fraction of that original area.

Traditionally the Paiutes practiced hunting and gathering for subsistence, with some production of wild seed and root crops. By employing an innovative

Members of the tribes of the Warm Springs Reservation of Oregon pose in front of tepees at the Kah-Nee-Ta Resort in 1967. The resort has added a casino, a spa, golf, and more, but guests still can choose to camp in tepees.

irrigation system composed of an extensive network of ditches, the Paiute were able to channel water to various places in the valley.

The Paiute, including those of Big Pine, were not settled on reservations until after 1900. In 1902, a portion of what had been Camp or Fort Independence, a military post, was officially set aside for use by local Indians.

The greatest impact on the livelihood of the Owens Valley Paiute occurred after the 1937 congressional act that ceded all previously owned Indian land to the City of Los Angeles in exchange for 1,391 acres of city-owned property. This transfer ultimately ended the ranching and farming economies that Big Pine residents had depended on for wage labor. Today the reservation spans just 279 acres, about a quarter of which is used for growing alfalfa or grain hay, along with some small-scale corn cultivation for personal use.

CHEMEHUEVI RESERVATION

Tribe: Chemehuevi Indian Tribe of the Chemehuevi
Reservation   Current Location: California   Total Area:
30,653 acres   Tribal Enrollment: 928

The Chemehuevi people are considered to be the most southern group of the Southern Paiute Indians, who are linguistically related to the greater Uto-Aztecan language family. The Chemehuevi are a division of the Southern Paiute tribe, and members of the Great Basin cultural region.

Nuwu ("The People"), or the Chemehuevi ("Those Who Play with Fish"), have always resided in the Mojave Desert. Their homelands included the mountains and canyons of the Mojave, as well as the shoreline of the Colorado River. The Chemehuevi gathered seeds for subsistence and, after the coming of the Spanish, planted wheat along the Colorado River.

While originally occupying a territory that extended from the Tehachapi Mountains to the Colorado River and from southern Nevada to the vicinity of Parker, Arizona, the Chemehuevi dispersed after 1900, as non-Indians moved onto their traditional lands. Because the Chemehuevi tribe was not yet organized, the federal government considered them illegal occupants of government property along the Colorado River. Those residing along the river in the Chemehuevi Valley were ultimately forced to move when their lands were flooded for the California Parker Dam project in 1930. Many of the farm families living in this region scattered throughout the United States; some sought wage employment, while others settled on the nearby Colorado River Reservation.

In 1951, the Chemehuevi Business Committee joined other Southern Paiute people in an Indian Claims Commission case. Eventually the Chemehuevi were awarded $82,000 to compensate for the land used by the Metropolitan Water District; however, this money was not disbursed until the 1960s, after a congressional Special Committee on Chemehuevi Affairs decided which of the contesting parties

Ute, Uto-Aztecan language family

"Tograyock. Pooneekay Vatsoom Ahdtui."

("Thank you. I'll see you again.")

should receive the compensation. In 1970, the tribe was officially recognized, and the Chemehuevi Indian Reservation was set aside the following year.

The Chemehuevi culture has a rich legacy of storytelling, song, and dance. The Chemehuevi Salt Song is of particular importance as it celebrates the cycles of life and death and distinguishes the tribe from other indigenous groups in the region. Chemehuevi artisans are known worldwide for their coil baskets woven of willow and devil's claw. Unfortunately, the art is in danger of extinction as cultural knowledge wanes among tribal members.

COLVILLE INDIAN RESERVATION

Tribe: Confederated Tribes of the Colville
Reservation   Current Location: Washington   Total Area:
1,130,082 acres   Tribal Enrollment: 9,171

The Confederated Tribes of the Colville Reservation comprise members of 12 different tribal groups: the Colville, Wenatchee, Entiate, Chelan, Methow, Okanogan, Nespelem, San Poil, Lakes, Moses Columbia, and Palus bands (which traditionally occupied territories in eastern Washington) and the Nez Perce (which originated in northeastern Oregon). The traditional dwellings of these tribes were often located near waterways, including the Columbia, San Poil, Okanogan, Snake, and Wallowa Rivers, and sustenance for the bands included hunting, fishing, and trading furs.

During the 1820s, the Hudson's Bay Company conducted business in the region, operating out of Kettle Falls, a well-known and frequented trading center. It was at this site that Fort Colville was constructed, and the indigenous groups in the area were then confederated as the Colville tribes. The fort provided steady business opportunities for the tribe members. Between 1826 and 1887, tribes traded beaver, bear, muskrat, fisher, fox, lynx, martin, mink, otter, raccoon,

Yakama imbricated coiled basket, circa 1906. Similar baskets, commonly referred to as Klickitat baskets, are made throughout the Plateau region and used to gather berries.

wolverine, badger, and wolf pelts at the fort. There was great demand for these furs, with as many as 20,000 pelts traded into the mainstream market each year.

Outsiders often called the Colville tribes Scheulpi or Chualpay; the French traders called them Les Chaudières (The Kettles), in reference to Kettle Falls. Though the fort became a stable business hub for the Colville peoples, fur trading did not have a settling effect on the migratory tribes. Until the mid-19th century, members of the Colville tribes continued to practice their nomadic lifestyles. However, the arrival of settlers, and the eventual establishment of the Canadian border, forced tribal members to put an end to their migratory patterns. While many members eventually settled in the United States, a number of Colville peoples remained in Canada. The reservation was originally established in 1872 through an executive order by President Ulysses S. Grant. Later additions of the Chief Moses and Chief Joseph bands, among others, helped to create a reservation of unparalleled cultural and political complexity, due in part to the different languages spoken by the confederated tribes.

The Colville tribes were not without their share of troubles in terms of their reservation land. In 1938, the U.S. government engineered the Grand Coulee Dam, which flooded the tribes' salmon spawning areas and ruined orchard and agricultural lands. The Colville tribal government has won a series of claims against the federal government for lands appropriated improperly and/or at fraudulent prices, including a case against the government for the mismanagement of tribal resources that were decimated by federal hydroelectric projects like the Grand Coulee Dam.

Despite the conversion of the Colville Indians to Catholicism and various Protestant faiths during the last century, traditional cultural and religious practices abound today. One example is the Seven Drum Religion, which was introduced by the Chief Joseph Band of Nez Perce. The tribe supports many efforts to retain the indigenous languages and continues to host various cultural events and activities.

MYTH OR FACT?

The image of the current U.S. dollar coin is a depiction of Sacagawea.

MYTH

The image on the $1 coin is a visual interpretation in honor of Sacagawea. The model used to create the likeness is Randy'L He-Dow Teton, a Shoshone-Bannock tribal member.

Duck Valley Reservation

Tribe: Shoshone-Paiute Tribes of the Duck Valley Reservation   Current Location: Nevada and Idaho
Total Area: 297,786 acres   Tribal Enrollment: 2,516

The federally recognized Duck Valley Reservation is home to the Shoshone (Newe) people and to the Paiute (Numa). The Duck Valley Reservation dates back to the 1863 Treaty of Ruby Valley, signed by the United States and the Western Shoshone tribes. Ancestral lands of the Western Shoshone and Northern Paiute tribes make up the present-day Duck Valley Reservation.

In the 1800s, encroaching Euro-Americans prompted a Shoshone leader named Captain Sam to look for a new home for his people. He inspected the Duck Valley region in 1870 and recommended to the federal government that they be allowed to settle there. The government granted his request, establishing the reservation by executive order in 1877; the few white settlers who lived on the land were ordered to vacate. Shoshones occupied the land but soon faced a severe winter, forcing many to leave Duck Valley. In 1884, a special Indian agent called the remaining Indians together to request they move to Idaho. Captain Sam and other Indians argued earnestly against removal, and the government acquiesced.

The Shoshone were soon to have company in their new homeland. In 1885, a band of about 60 Paiutes arrived at Duck Valley with a letter from an Indian agent recommending that they be allowed to settle there. The addition of these new tribe members stretched the land resources of the existing boundaries, but this was soon remedied; in 1886, President Grover Cleveland issued an executive order adding land to the Duck Valley Reservation for the use of the Paiutes. President William Howard Taft then added additional acreage to the reservation in 1910. The two tribes share the reservation to this day.

The tribes receive a small but steady income from the sale of fishing permits as well as a marina and store. Business leases, land leases, and livestock grazing permits also provide income, but cattle and agriculture remain the mainstay of the economy.

FALLON RESERVATION AND COLONY

Tribe: Paiute-Shoshone Tribe of the Fallon Reservation and Colony   Current Location: Nevada
Total Area: 8,218 acres   Tribal Enrollment: 1,002

Ancestors of present-day Fallon Paiute-Shoshone tribal members were primarily Northern Paiutes (Numa) of the Toi Ticutta (Tule Eater; tule is a fibrous water plant) and Koosi Pah Ticutta (Muddy Water Eater) bands who roamed the marshy lakebeds of the Carson and Humboldt Sinks from prehistoric times into the 19th century, subsisting on a diet of fish, pine nuts, waterfowl eggs, and small game. The benevolent marshes also provided the Numa with materials for shelters, clothing, and tools. A short growing season prevented them from practicing horticulture.

The blazing of the California Trail during the 1840s brought the Northern Paiute into increasing contact with Euro-American settlers. The Toi Ticutta clashed with a force of U.S. Army volunteers in 1860 near Pyramid Lake. Following the conflict, the Army responded by increasing its presence in the area, establishing Fort Churchill, 35 miles southwest of present-day Fallon. Numerous small conflicts arose between the Army and the Toi Ticutta. Simultaneously, Euro-American farmers moving into the Lahontan Valley permanently displaced the Koosi Pah. Both bands of Numas fled to the marshes and joined together.

In the early 1890s, the U.S. government moved individual Numa families to a reservation divided into 160-acre plots near present-day Fallon. As settlers began moving into the area, they realized that the Numa land was valuable for agriculture, and in 1902 the federal government asked the Numa people to relinquish their 160-acre allotments in exchange for 10-acre allotments and water rights, with the underlying threat that those who didn't relinquish their acreage would not receive water from the new dam. Lacking irrigation ditches, most landowners had to acquiesce to the Newland Project of 1906. Many of these families were pressured off their land by white farmers, and they moved nearer to the town of Fallon. In 1908, the Indian Service established an Indian school 10 miles east of Fallon and built 30 homes for the Toi Ticutta, who also received additional irrigable land from the federal government.

In 1958, the Toi Ticutta and Shoshone in the Stillwater area incorporated as the Fallon Paiute-Shoshone Tribe, adopting a constitution and bylaws. Today, individual tribe members own 4,640 acres of allotted land. Some 865 acres remain as tribal trust land, divided between the Fallon Reservation and the Fallon Colony, outside the town of Fallon.

FLATHEAD RESERVATION

Tribe: Confederated Salish and Kootenai Tribes of the Flathead Reservation   Current Location: Montana
Total Area: 817,631 acres   Tribal Enrollment: 7,083

The Confederated Salish and Kootenai Tribes comprise the Bitterroot Salish, Pend d'Oreille, and Kootenai tribes. Their ancestors lived in the territory now divided into western Montana and parts of Idaho, British Columbia, and Wyoming.

A group of Ute Indians in Salt Lake City in 1867

YAKAMA

The Confederated Tribes and Bands of the Yakama Nation, a conglomeration of 14 Indian groups, was created by the Treaty of 1855. These groups historically lived throughout what is now central Washington. Each band spoke its own dialect and had its own council of leaders. Before 1855, their land covered 10.8 million acres along the eastern slope of the Cascade mountain range. Today their descendants live around the open rolling hills and mountains of the 1.4-million-acre Yakama Indian Reservation. Its defining features are the Yakima River and Mount Adams, a snowcapped peak within the Cascade Range known to the Yakama as Pahto. Although the people once spelled their name the same as the river, they changed the accepted spelling to Yakama in the 1990s to reflect historical use.

Life in the Columbia River Basin

The tribes and bands that the Yakama Nation now comprises—the Yakama, Palouse, Pisquouse, Wenatshapam, Klikatat, Klinquit, Kow-was-say-ee, Li-ay-was, Skin pah, Wish-ham, Shyiks, Ochechotes, Kah-milt-pah, and Se-ap-cat—were seminomadic hunters and gatherers. They had temporary and semipermanent villages located throughout the Columbia River Basin.

Before European contact, the people lived in earthen lodges and tule lodges. The earthen lodge, which came into use as a permanent home thousands of years ago, was a dome-shaped structure built from willow branches, reeds, grasses, and mud. These were replaced by tule lodges, summer homes used during the food-gathering seasons. They were built with mats of tule reeds wrapped around a frame of pine poles and tied with Indian hemp rope or rawhide. Nowadays, the people live in modern homes built by the Yakama Nation Housing Authority.

The Yakama people, like other American Indian tribes, follow an animistic belief system that holds that all things have a spirit. Many Yakama people are

Wearing colorful dresses and headgear, a pair of twin girls prepares to perform in a Yakama dance competition in White Swan, Washington, in 1994.

members of the traditional Washat religion, which holds services at longhouses throughout the region. This religion was revived in the 19th century by Smohalla, a Wanapum prophet from the Priest Rapids area along the Columbia River.

Other Yakama belong to denominations that were introduced by European immigrant missionaries or to the Indian Shaker Church. That church, founded by John Slocum from Mud Bay on the Puget Sound, found its way to the Yakima Valley in 1899. On or nearby the Yakama Reservation there are seven longhouses and three Indian Shaker churches.

Following Their Food

The traditional diet of the Yakama people consists of salmon, deer, roots, chokecherries, and huckleberries. They moved with the seasons. In the spring, they gathered with tribes from throughout the Plateau region at Celilo Falls, a major fishing and trade center along what is now the Oregon-Washington border. That historic site is now inundated by the waters behind The Dalles Dam, built on the Columbia in 1957.

After enough fish was caught and preserved, the Yakama would move to the foothills in order to dig roots. Then, in late summer, they traveled to their favorite chokecherry gathering sights and up into the mountains to pick huckleberries.

Catching the fish, digging the roots, and picking the berries required long hours of work. Then, because these were all seasonal and perishable items, to ensure there would be food for the whole year, many hours were spent cleaning and cutting the fish to dry, and cleaning, peeling, and drying the roots. The berries needed to be cleaned and dried, too (today, the berries are cleaned and canned or frozen). Once all this work was done, the people would move to the Yakima Valley, Kittitas Valley, or Tygh Valley for celebrations such as family reunions, wedding trades, stick games, and horse racing.

Language and Economy

The traditional Yakama language is classified as a dialect of Sahaptin, part of the Penutian language family spoken around the western Plateau. The Yakama people refer to their language as Ichishki'in. Tribal efforts to encourage Yakama youth to understand their tradition, heritage, and culture have been under way since the early 1970s. Scholars have written several books documenting the language and legends, including the extensive *Ichishki'in Siinwit Yakama/Yakima Sahaptin Dictionary,* published in 2010.

Today, there are about 12,200 enrolled Yakama Indians living on or near the Yakama Reservation. They operate their own government, with tribal headquarters located at Toppenish, Washington. The tribe's businesses include the Yakama Nation Legends Casino, Yakama Forest Products, Yakama Nation Land Enterprise, Yakama Nation Cultural Center, Yakama Nation Fish and Wildlife, Yakama Nation Credit Enterprise, and an energy company called Yakama Power. To ensure cultural resources management on the eastern portion of its ceded territory, the Yakama Nation works with the Department of Energy at the Hanford nuclear site. ■

THE GREAT BASIN

A Yakama woman tends to salmon hanging in the drying shed. Salmon is also canned or frozen for use throughout the year.

Unlike most other tribes in Montana, the Bitterroot Salish migrated from the west. After acquiring horses in the early 1700s, they moved east, changing from a lifestyle based on salmon fishing to one more dependent on native plants and buffalo.

The Kootenai descended from peoples who inhabited Montana more than 14,000 years ago, in the mountainous terrain west of the Continental Divide, venturing seasonally to the east for buffalo hunts. One northeastern band had a lifestyle based on hunting (primarily buffalo), while the other lived in the mountains of the west and sought sustenance in the rivers and lakes there. During the 1700s, the Salish and the Kootenai shared both hunting and gathering locations.

On September 4, 1805, Sgt. Patrick Gass of the Lewis and Clark team recorded in the official journal, "It is of no very great importance, at present, to know by what names the several tribes and bands are distinguished; and . . . without an interpreter it was very difficult to ascertain them with any degree of certainty." Communication was passed through Salishan and Shoshone, Hidatsa, French, and English, aided by a Shoshone boy among the Flatheads and,

accompanying the expedition, Sacagawea and Jean-Baptiste Charbonneau.

The Hellgate Treaty of 1855 was yet another example of poor communication and imperfect cross-cultural understanding with serious consequences. Representatives of the Salish, Kootenai, and Pend d'Oreille, misunderstanding both the language and the spirit of what they were signing, ceded some 20 million acres of ancestral land to the U.S. government, retaining title to only about 1.3 million acres as their homeland. Since the 1940s, the resident tribes have been buying back reservation lands; over 65 percent was tribally owned by 2000.

FORT MCDERMITT INDIAN RESERVATION

Tribe: Fort McDermitt Paiute and Shoshone Tribes of the Fort McDermitt Indian Reservation   **Current Location:** Nevada and Oregon   **Total Area:** 34,604 acres   **Tribal Enrollment:** 844

Descendants of the people known as the Numa now inhabit the Fort McDermitt Paiute-Shoshone Reservation. Fort McDermitt was originally set up as a camp to protect white settlers and travelers in the midst of Indians and Euro-American hostilities. After the Bannock and Paiute War of 1878, many Numas of the Paiute and Shoshone tribes were rounded up and forced to march more than 400 miles to the Yakama Indian Agency in northern Washington. After several years of adverse conditions at Yakama and petitioning the authorities to allow them to leave, the Indians vacated the area in 1883 without permission, but the government did not appear to offer any opposition.

Some of the Indian families who left settled at Fort McDermitt, where they were assigned land parcels by federal allotment, drawing numbers from an Indian agent's hat. The land proved inadequate for subsistence farming, and in 1934, under the Indian Reorganization Act, the federal government purchased neighboring farmland and transferred it to the tribe. Land transfers from the federal government have continued, to bring the

KA-MI-AKIN

Yakama head chief

By 1853, Ka-mi-akin, head chief of the Yakama, knew about the federal government's desire to purchase Indian land in the Northwest and push Indians onto reservations. To rally other chiefs to join him in opposition, he said, "We wish to be left alone in the lands of our forefathers, whose bones lie in the sand hills and along the trails, but a pale-face stranger has come from a distant land and sends word to us that we must give up our country, as he wants it for the white man." Nonetheless, on June 9, 1855, at the Walla Walla Treaty Council, Ka-mi-akin reluctantly signed the treaty.

But by October, promises were already being broken, and the Yakama War began, with Ka-mi-akin fighting to protect the lands of his people. Despite some victories in early battles, the Indians lost, although Ka-mi-akin refused to surrender. The chief, who lived from 1800 to 1877, spent most of his life in present-day central Washington; he also traveled to the Great Plains, where he distinguished himself as a warrior and hunter. Later, as a cattleman and farmer, he was known as a businessman of good judgment. Throughout the Northwest, people respected him as a counselor, orator, and peaceful man who loved his people and native land. ■

reservation to its present size. Today, along with the continuing use of the Paiute language, the consolidated tribe maintains a distinct, thriving culture at Fort McDermitt.

GOSHUTE RESERVATION

Tribe: Confederated Tribes of the Goshute Reservation   Current Location: Utah and Nevada   Total Area: 113,349 acres   Tribal Enrollment: 457

Goshute comes from the Native word *ku'tsip* or *gu'tsip,* meaning "ashes," "desert," or "dry earth and people." In Utah, the Numic- (or Shoshonean) speaking peoples of the Uto-Aztecan language family evolved into four distinct groups: the Northern Shoshone, Goshute or Western Shoshone, Southern Paiute, and Ute. The Goshute (Kusiutta) inhabited the inhospitable western deserts of Utah. Derogatorily labeled "Digger Indians" by early white observers for their tuber-gathering, the Goshute were supremely adaptive hunter-gatherers living in small nomadic family bands. Prior to contact, they wintered in the Deep Creek Valley in wickiups built of willow poles and earth. They hunted small game in the mountains and dug for wild onions, carrots, and potatoes. They exemplified the historic Great Basin desert way of life, using at least 81 species of wild vegetable foods, including seeds, berries, roots, and greens. One of the most important foods was nuts from the piñon tree, which were gathered annually.

In the 1850s, Mormon missionaries entered Goshute territory, followed by U.S. Army troops. Depredations against the tribe spurred them to sign the Shoshoni-Goship peace treaty in 1863. The Goshute people incorporated as the Confederated Tribes of the Goshute Reservation on November 24, 1940.

The Goshute have maintained traditional arts and crafts, weaving willow, winnowing baskets, carving cradleboards, crafting beaded jewelry, and tanning deerskin for buckskin trade items. Many tribal members are active in the Native American Church, while others have become members of the Church of Jesus Christ of Latter-day Saints, commonly referred to as the Mormon Church.

In this 1899 portrait, a Yakama woman wears abalone disk earrings, silver bracelets, bead necklaces, and a beaded belt, along with a beaded and decorated overshirt.

KAIBAB PAIUTE INDIAN RESERVATION

Tribe: Kaibab Band of Paiute Indians of the Kaibab Indian Reservation   Current Location: Arizona   Total Area: 120,797 acres   Tribal Enrollment: 288

The Kaibab Paiute band belongs to the larger Southern Paiute Nation, which has historically occupied the region that is now southern Utah, northern Arizona, and the Great Basin of southeastern Nevada. For at least 1,000 years, ancestral Kaibab Paiutes gathered grass seeds, hunted animals, and raised crops near the springs for which Pipe Spring National Monument, on the northern border of Arizona, is named. Mormon immigrants brought cattle to the area in the 1860s, and by 1872 a fortified ranch house, which came to be called Winsor Castle, was built over the main spring, and a large cattle ranching

A Yakama fisherman at Celilo Falls on the Columbia River in eastern Oregon hauls in his catch using a dip net, circa 1950. The falls were inundated in 1957 with the construction of The Dalles Dam.

operation was established. The outpost became a way station for travelers on the Arizona Strip—the region of the state north of the Grand Canyon. The area is semidesert, with piñon-juniper woodland giving way to sagebrush and prickly pear cactus, and high temperatures reaching 115°F in the summer. Travelers found cool waters at the springs, which are fed by the Navajo Sandstone aquifer. The Paiute stayed in the area, and by 1907 the Kaibab Paiute Indian Reservation was established. Pipe Spring and the ranch remained in private hands. In 1923, the U.S. government purchased the ranch and established it as a national monument.

Between 1900 and 1940, Paiute children were often sent away to government boarding schools and the Paiute suffered tragic losses due to infectious diseases. In 1965, the U.S. Indian Claims Commission awarded them more than $7 million in compensation for illegally taken aboriginal lands, which Kaibab has used to fund economic and social development.

KALISPEL RESERVATION

Tribe: Kalispel Indian Community of the Kalispel
Reservation **Current Location:** Washington
Total Area: 7,614 acres **Tribal Enrollment:** 380

The Kalispel, or Pend d'Oreille, Indians, known as "river and lake paddlers" or "camas people" by other native tribes, were seminomadic hunter-gatherers and fishermen. A staple of the Kalispel diet was the camas, a relative of the onion that grows in abundance along the Pend Oreille River. The Kalispel

**Yakama,
Penutian
language
family**

"Shix mayts'ki.
Mishpamwa?"

("Good morning.
How are you?")

were given the name Pend d'Oreille ("earring") by the French because of the shell earrings they wore. The Lower Kalispel occupied a 200-mile-long territory along the Pend Oreille River from present-day Newport, Washington, to across the Canadian border. This is the band from which the present-day Kalispel descend.

The Kalispel Indians have a rich culture derived primarily from their relationship with nature. The Pend Oreille River is a natural element of great significance for the tribe, and one on which all aspects of traditional tribal life are centered. They used it for commerce and social purposes, built their villages beside it, and dug camas roots in its floodplain. Their historic culture was similar to that of the Spokane and other tribes of the Plateau area. Their language belongs to the Salishan branch of the Algonquian-Wakashan linguistic stock.

In an attempt to assimilate the Indians and convert them to Catholicism, Roman Catholic priests began working with the Kalispel in 1844. In 1855, the Upper Kalispel gave up their lands and moved to a reservation in Montana. In contrast, the Lower Kalispel resisted outside interference, avoiding participation in various treaties with the federal government that were intended to relocate them to established reservations. This strategy ultimately backfired. Without a treaty, the tribe had no legal protection for its land, and it saw the land taken by non-Indian settlers under state and federal homestead laws. The tribe's membership dropped from an estimate of 3,000 to fewer than 400 by 1875 and to just 100 by 1911. In 1914, the tribe was granted its reservation. In 1960, the tribe received approximately $3 million for loss of its aboriginal lands. In 1977, the tribe began a program of land acquisition to enhance its prospects for economic development.

The tribe is highly concerned about pollution in the Pend Oreille River, particularly the impact of area dams on water quality and the preservation of habitat. Remnant populations of bull trout and west-slope cutthroat trout live in tributaries of the Pend Oreille River. Both species are historically important to the tribe.

SHOSHONE-BANNOCK

The traditional territory of the Shoshone and Paiute peoples, which included the Bannocks, encompassed the wide-ranging lands known as the Great Basin and stretched into the southern Columbia Plateau and the western face of the Rocky Mountains of east-central Idaho, southern Montana, and western Wyoming. Four of the many bands of Shoshone, plus a band of Bannock, now live on the Fort Hall Reservation in southeastern Idaho. Historically, the Shoshone and Paiute were not structured as tribes; they lived and worked together in bands or groups of related families whose villages were within a distinct territory.

Similar Cultures, Different Tongues

The Shoshone and Bannock are culturally similar—they each constructed the same types of houses, used similar tools, gathered similar foods, and occupied similar lands. However, they have distinct traditional languages. The Bannock language is a dialect of Northern Paiute. The Shoshone of Fort Hall speak a variety of dialects, indicating their origins among different Shoshone bands. However, the various Shoshone dialects are similar enough to one another that Shoshone from one region can understand those who come from another.

Given that the variety of supplies available within the various bands' regions differed, their food, hunting methods, and tools varied as well. The bands identified themselves in a number of ways—by the major food supply in their traditional territory, for instance, as Tuka Dika ("Sheep-Eaters"); after their

A late 19th-century Shoshone dance at Fort Washakie Reservation, Wyoming, now the Wind River Reservation. Standing at left, with arm outstretched, is Chief Washakie.

leader, as "Pocatello's band," for instance; or by locality.

Before the coming of the white man, the Shoshone and Bannock were hunter-gatherers, moving with the seasons as food became available. Each band had its winter village near a river or in the area indicated by the band name. Recurring camps include salmon-fishing sites along the forks of the Salmon and Snake Rivers and their tributaries below Shoshone Falls; Camas Prairie in the vicinity of present-day Fairfield, Idaho, where bands gathered camas roots; and the pine groves near the City of Rocks region, where they gathered pine nuts. They also made infrequent expeditions to distant locations, such as the falls at The Dalles, Oregon, for salmon.

Early Spanish explorers introduced the horse to the American West, and the Shoshone were the first group to obtain horses. That greatly increased their mobility, even allowing buffalo-hunting trips onto the Great Plains. Horses provided the Shoshone a clear advantage over neighboring tribes. Their territory expanded far to the north, into what is now Canada.

From a Wide Territory to a Shrinking Reservation

The Fort Bridger Treaty of 1868 established the 1.8-million-acre Fort Hall Reservation. Between 1868 and 1932, however, the reservation was reduced by more than two-thirds due to non-Indian infringement on the land. Today, the reservation is 544,000 acres, situated about eight miles from Pocatello, Idaho. It's divided into five districts: Fort Hall, Lincoln Creek, Ross Fork, Gibson, and Bannock Creek.

More than 70 percent of the approximately 5,300 enrolled Shoshone-

Sunglasses are a necessary accessory for summer powwows on the Shoshone-Bannock Reservation in Fort Hall, Idaho.

Bannock tribal members still live on the Fort Hall Reservation. The diverse traditional dialects and the strong ties to specific locales have shaped strong group identity among the people of Fort Hall. Today families trace their lineage by whether they are Shoshone or Bannock and by the particular bands from which they descend.

Nonetheless, they also act as a single people, with a unified tribal government and numerous tribal businesses. Each summer since the early 1960s, they have held a multiday Shoshone-Bannock Festival, with a parade, rodeo, dancing, art show, and feast of salmon and buffalo. The Fort Hall Indians are well known for their beadwork, which frequently incorporates floral designs. Individual artists sell and exhibit their own works, but the tribe also sells beadwork through stores on the reservation and via the Internet.

The tribe employs nearly 1,000 Native and non-Native people in a range of businesses: the Bannock Ecological, *Sho-Ban News*, Clothes Horse, Trading Post Grocery, Trading Post Gas Station, Sage Hill Travel Center and Casino, and Shoshone-Bannock Tribal Museum. ■

KLAMATH RESERVATION

Tribe: Klamath Tribes [Klamath, Modoc, and
Yahooskin]   Current Location: Oregon
Total Area: 556 acres   Tribal Enrollment: 3,579

The Klamath Tribes are composed of the Klamath tribe, Modoc tribe, and the Yahooskin Band of Snake River Indian tribe. The tribes' ancestral lands covered approximately 22 million acres in south-central Oregon, north-central California, and parts of Nevada and Idaho. It was because of their location in the interior of the state that the tribes managed to avoid the region's white settlers until fairly late in the contact period, escaping the devastating waves of disease brought on by Europeans. The tribe also managed to evade the typical pattern of violent confrontations with white settlers—their first contact with settlers occurred in 1826 with Hudson's Bay Company traders, who declared them "a happy people." Eventually the tribe acquired guns and horses, but for the most part the people relied on fishing, hunting, and gathering.

On October 14, 1864, the Klamath, Modoc, and Yahooskin tribes signed a treaty that ceded to the U.S. government 19.5 million acres of high, semiarid land east of the Cascade Range. In return, the Klamaths retained rights to approximately 1.2 million acres to establish their reservation and became collectively known as the Klamath Tribes. Disputes over land rights and government surveys marked much of the tribe's subsequent history. Unlike other tribes, the Klamaths were allowed to retain rights to nonallotted or "tribal surplus" lands; this allowed them to retain large stands of valuable timber, which later became an important source of tribal income.

By the mid-1950s, the Klamath Tribes had become the second wealthiest tribal entity in the United States. However, the tribe was formally terminated in 1954, resulting in the loss of tribal land.

The artist of this beaded bag, circa 1930, meticulously captured the image of a mountain goat defending itself against the attack of a bear.

Then, in 1958, the vast majority of the Klamath Tribes' members voted to withdraw from the tribe. In order to pay each of them their shares, the federal government sold most of the remaining 880,000 acres of land.

Nevertheless, the Klamath Tribes' identity remained vital. Despite having been terminated, the tribes maintained their hunting, fishing, and gathering rights as agreed upon in the treaty of 1864. However, the state of Oregon refused to recognize these rights, and tribal members were harassed and often arrested. In 1972, five tribal members filed suit against the state. A federal circuit court upheld their rights. In 1986, the Klamath Tribes regained their federally recognized status under the provisions of the Klamath Restoration Act.

During the 20th century, the region's economy has been based largely on timber, grazing, and agriculture. Reinstatement has brought about a revitalization of traditional practices, including the translation of books into the Penutian language and a renewed emphasis on traditional crafts, ceremonies, and religion.

MOAPA RIVER INDIAN RESERVATION

Tribe: Moapa Band of Paiute Indians of the Moapa River Indian Reservation   Current Location: Nevada   Total Area: 70,587 acres   Tribal Enrollment: 304

The Moapa Band of Paiutes, or Nuwuvi, are part of the Southern Paiute Nation, whose traditional territory covered much of present southern Nevada, northern Arizona, and southern Utah. The Moapa Band hunted small game and gathered plant foods in southern Nevada's Moapa Valley; this is the prehistoric floodplain of the Muddy River, which today flows southward through the valley and drains into Lake Mead. The Moapa Paiute's first contact with Euro-Americans occurred after the blazing of the Old Spanish Trail through their territory in 1830. Until the Mexican-American War, this trade route between the Mexican provinces of New Mexico and California afforded Mexican slaveowners the opportunity to raid Paiute settlements for slaves. American explorer John C. Frémont encountered a Moapa war party during his passage through the Moapa Valley in 1844. The Moapa Paiute were subsequently regarded as the most hostile Nuwuvi band. However, Mormon missionaries entered the Moapa Valley during the 1850s and found the Moapa people friendly and courteous. Prior to the arrival of Mormon settlers, New Mexicans, and other emigrants, the Moapa had adapted to hunting and gathering with great ingenuity. They were skilled in using the land's natural resources, like animal skins and plants. Plants were used for medicinal purposes and basketry, and leather was used for shoes.

Under pressure to open Paiute lands for white settlement, the federal government confined the Moapa Band to a 70,566-acre reservation in 1873. Two years later, the reservation was reduced in size to 1,000 acres. This reduction was followed by 60 years of Indian Service neglect and white theft from the reservation. By the early 1900s, the cultural disruption caused by foreigners in the area had all but destroyed the Moapa's observances, driving legends, songs, and dances that had once been routine parts of daily life into near extinction. Furthermore, individual allotments were too small to support economically effective farms. As a result, many people fled the reservation or began to live on low-wage farming for others. Tuberculosis and whooping cough wracked the remaining population during the 1920s and '30s.

The Southern Paiute decided to try to reclaim their land. In 1951, the tribe filed a claim with the Indian Claims Commission and won a settlement in 1965 of $7,253,165.19. In 1981, Congress restored 70,565 acres to the Moapa Reservation. The Moapa Band's mission statement—"To advance the Moapa Bands of Paiutes and preserve our homeland by building an independent and self-governing community that provides an opportunity for all peoples

LAVINA WASHINES

Traditionally trained Yakama leader

Lavina Washines, a member of the Kah-milt-pah (Rock Creek band) of the Yakama Nation, was nurtured in a traditional Yakama upbringing. She used what she was taught by the Rock Creek elders to work as a Yakama language teacher, a cultural specialist, and later as a judge in the tribal court system. Washines believes firmly in God's unwritten laws and still practices her traditional way of life as a food gatherer. In her religious upbringing, she was taught that the Indian peoples originated on the North American continent, rather than descending from ancestors who crossed the Bering Strait from Asia, as some scientists hypothesize. She said, "I wish that all the tribes would come together to challenge the Bering Strait theory." She was also taught to safeguard the sovereign rights guaranteed under the Treaty of 1855. That means guarding the right to fish on the Columbia River, protecting landmarks of cultural significance, improving health care, and ensuring a better education for all tribe members. Washines worked with the Yakama Nation Code of Ethics committee as its executive secretary, and in 2007 she was elected to the Yakama Nation Tribal Council, becoming the first tribal councilwoman. ∎

who have made a commitment to this mission. Traditional, Contemporary, Progressive"—epitomizes its outlook. Today, the tribe strives to improve the well-being of members through social services and economic development while maintaining a firm grasp on Paiute culture and heritage.

**Paiute,
Uto-Aztecan
language
family**

"sumu'yoo"
("one")

"waha'yoo"
("two")

"pahe'yoo"
("three")

"watsuggwe'yoo"
("four")

"manage'yoo"
("five")

PAIUTE INDIAN RESERVATION

Tribe: Paiute Indian Tribe of Utah   Current Location: Utah   Total Area: 43,566 acres   Tribal Enrollment: 841

The Paiute Indian Tribe of Utah includes five distinct bands: Shivwits Band of Paiutes, Cedar City Band of Paiutes, Koosharem Band of Paiutes, Kanosh Band of Paiutes, and Indian Peaks Band of Paiutes. All are Southern Paiute peoples who once occupied a broad territory extending across southern Utah and southern Nevada and, following the sharp bend in the Colorado River, southward into California. The Southern Paiute language is one of the northern Numic dialects of the Uto-Aztecan language family. The Paiute are thought to have entered Utah between 1100 and 1200.

COLVILLE ART

Joe Feddersen is a prolific contemporary artist from the Confederated Tribes of the Colville Reservation (Okanogan Band) in north-central Washington. His work analyzes the landscape of the Inland Plateau of the Columbia Basin, intertwining basic elements of designs from his ancestral home with urban imagery to create a visual dialogue articulating changing views of the environment.

His monumental prints, fiber arts, and glassworks are inspired by ephemeral images, an assortment of man-made structures, and the geometric designs of historic flat twined bags. The artists who made those bags honored their surroundings by borrowing their designs from nature, combining geometric patterns that represented animals, birds, people, and the land. Each work told significant stories from the weaver's life. These meticulous flat twined bags, also called corn husk bags, are still woven today.

Created in 2002, Feddersen's "Okanagan II" is a monumental siligraph relief print—84 panels, each of which is 15½ by 15½ inches, or 93 by 127 inches overall. It seemed to be a rite of passage from Feddersen's early mixed-media print work, not in scale from small to large, but rather in the absolute quality and mastery of printmaking depicting the extensive landscape of the Inland Plateau region.

"The Rainscapes" series he created in the mid-1980s suggests the short-lived moments of a passing storm, possibly erosion, or the fine line of a Colville tribal member beginning to create modern art from traditional ideas.

Known to be a soft-spoken man of few words, Feddersen said of his art, "My print work builds from a dialogue with traditional basket designs. The prints typically build complexity through layering signs. Carrying segments of patterns, the plates become the linear structures of the compositions. Each layer printed on top of another entwines in a labyrinth of a modernist aesthetic. These signs tenuously dissolve into an overall field while still maintaining direct ties to my native heritage."

Feddersen retired from Evergreen State College in Olympia, Washington, where he taught printmaking for more than 18 years. His work, which has been exhibited in museums around the country, is held in both private and public collections. ■

"Brick Mountain" is a 2004 work in blown and sandblasted glass by Joe Feddersen, whose art explores the visual dialogue between traditional interpretations of nature and modern urban life.

Each of the bands maintained an economically self-sufficient aboriginal territory. Members relied on varied sources for food: Small game provided the Southern Paiute with their chief source of protein, but plant foods, including seeds, roots, berries, agave, and pine nuts, were the mainstay of their diet. The introduction of irrigable agriculture a few decades before Euro-American occupation bolstered the Southern Paiute economy; they raised corn, squash, melons, gourds, and sunflowers.

The first direct Spanish contact with the Southern Paiute came in 1776. By the early 19th century, Spanish colonies in present-day northern New Mexico and southern California had institutionalized slavery, and slave raiding on the Southern Paiute did not end until soon after the Mormons came into northern Utah in 1847. In the 1850s, several Mormon communities sprang up in Southern Paiute territory, displacing the Indians from their most fertile lands; starvation and diseases drastically reduced the Paiute population. Traditional food supplies were further depleted by livestock grazing, timbering, and other activities, but Mormon missionaries among the bands prevented major confrontations with settlers.

The Shivwits Reservation was established in 1903 and was expanded in 1916 and 1937. The other reservations were established as follows: Indian Peaks in 1915, Koosharem in 1928, and Kanosh in 1929. None of these had agricultural land bases sufficient to support the population. Federal funds were appropriated in 1899 and 1925 to purchase land for the Cedar City band; however, the funds were never expended for that purpose because the Mormon Church had already purchased 10 acres on the outskirts of Cedar City and established the band there. Due to insufficient land base and irregular, inadequate assistance, none of the reservations could achieve economic self-sufficiency, and many Paiutes moved off the reservations to nearby towns, while others remained on the reservations but sought outside wage work.

The Shivwits, Indian Peaks, Koosharem, and Kanosh reservations were terminated from federal

Yakama religious leaders pose with hand drums in this photo taken about 1910 at the old tule-mat long-house in Wapato near present-day Parker, Washington.

control in 1954. In 1957, the Southern Paiute filed suit with the Indian Claims Commission (ICC) for compensation for their aboriginal lands. In 1965, the commission awarded the Southern Paiute $8.25 million, or approximately 27 cents per acre, for 29,935,000 acres; the funds were not distributed until 1971.

On April 3, 1980, the Paiute Indian Tribe of Utah Restoration Act was passed. The Kanosh and Koosharem bands in central Utah, and the Shivwits and Indian Peaks bands in southwestern Utah were restored to federal trust relationships. The Cedar City band, also residing in southwestern Utah and whose status had long been uncertain, was confirmed as being under trust. By 1984, approximately 4,470 acres of the more than 15,000 acres that had been lost were returned to the Koosharem, Kanosh, Indian Peaks, and Cedar City bands, along with a $2.5 million irrevocable trust fund from which they could develop tribal services and economic development initiatives.

MYTH OR FACT?

Each tribe lives on its own reservation.

MYTH

Many tribes have been displaced due to reasons beyond their control to areas far from their original homeland, and they often have been forced to share reservations.

PYRAMID LAKE RESERVATION

Tribe: Pyramid Lake Paiute Tribe of the Pyramid Lake Reservation   Current Location: Nevada   Total Area: 479,741 acres   Tribal Enrollment: 2,263

The people inhabiting Pyramid Lake Reservation are known as Cu-Yui Ticutta, or Kuyuidokado, "Eaters of Cui-ui," a species of lake suckerfish that inhabits Pyramid Lake and is found nowhere else in the world. The tribe is a subdivision of the ancient Numa people who once roamed northern Nevada and southern Oregon. In January 1854, explorer John C. Frémont arrived at Pyramid Lake, where the Cu-Yui Ticutta gave him food and hospitality, but hostilities soon ensued. In 1859, the General Land Office ordered the establishment of the reservation, and the area was withdrawn from sale and settlement in 1861. President Grant issued an executive order confirming the Pyramid Lake Reservation in 1874. A school for children was established

UTE

The traditional territory of the Ute Indians stretched across 150,000 square miles of the Colorado Plateau, an area they roamed for thousands of years before the arrival of the white man. The original seven Ute tribes—the Capote, Grand River, Mouache, Tabaguache, Uintah, Weeminuche, and Yampa—lived in villages in and around the Rocky Mountains. The Ute, whose traditional language is in the Shoshonean family, called themselves Noochew, or "The People." They were hunters and gatherers who lived on wild game and fish. Before the Spanish introduced the horse, they moved on foot from season to season. But soon, they were raising and trading horses, as well as cattle and sheep, and using horses to hunt bison. By 1830, the bison had nearly disappeared from Ute territory.

Descendants of the Bear

The Ute historically lived in conical, pole-framed shelters known as wicki-ups, which were covered with juniper bark or tule, a wetlands plant. Later they adapted the hide-covered, easily transportable tepee. They hunted with bows made of cedar, chokecherry, and sheep horn. Knives were made from flint. Their clothing and blankets were made from deer hide, mink, and jackrabbit fur. When the men were out hunting, the women gathered seed grasses, nuts, berries, roots, and greens.

The Ute's spiritual beliefs revolved around nature, with animals serving as their central divine beings. They say they are close descendants of the bear, a prominent figure in Ute legends. Their spiritual calendar includes two core ceremonies: the Momaqui Mowat, also known as the Bear Dance, is held each spring, and the Sun Dance is held in the middle of summer. The Bear Dance was given to the Noochew as a time to gather together after the long hard winter to celebrate life, to see who made it through the winter, and to commemorate births, marriages, and deaths. They use rasps and tin boxes to make rumbling sounds that resemble the first thunder of spring as well as the awakening bear.

Three generations of Ute women, circa 1900. A baby can be seen wrapped in a hide cradleboard.

The Momaqui Mowat is a lady's choice dance. The women line up first and select their partners by flipping their shawl fringe at the man. The dancers form two lines. The women face the west; the men face the women, looking east. The dancers each hold hands with the persons next to them, and both lines dance back and forth in time to the music. The dance lasts four days and is maintained by the Cat Man. During the last two days, the lines form into couples. The dance ends with one final song that continues until a couple falls or the singers get tired. The Bear Dance chief blesses the fallen couple, in turn blessing the whole tribe.

Split among Reservations

Today, the seven Ute bands have been spread onto three reservations: the Northern Ute are on Uintah and Ouray Reservation, headquartered at Fort Duchesne in northeastern Utah; the Southern Ute reservation is headquartered at Ignacio in southwestern Colorado; and the Ute Mountain Reservation is in the Four Corners area of Colorado, Utah, and New Mexico, with headquarters at Towaoc, Colorado.

When the Mormons came west in the 19th century, they introduced an agricultural lifestyle and put pressure on the Ute to adopt a similar life. The Northern Ute in particular resisted the change, feeling that it was imprudent to stay in one place.

The Mormons continued to settle on more and more Ute land. A series of raids against Mormon settlers led to the Walker War of 1853–54. By 1869,

the Northern Ute were forced onto the Uintah Valley Reservation, leaving their beloved, beautiful Provo Valley. The Uncompahgre Reservation was established adjacent to the Uintah Reservation in the 1880s, and two other bands from Colorado were removed to the combined reservation in Utah. The three-county area known as the Uintah Basin is now home to the Uintah and Ouray Reservation, the second largest reservation in the United States, at more than 4.5 million acres. There are about 3,000 enrolled members of this Ute nation, and about half live on the reservation.

The Southern Ute Agency was established in Colorado in 1877 for the Capote, Mouache, and Weeminuche; treaties in the 1880s then forced them into southwestern Colorado. The bands divided over the years as land was shuffled, reserved, and allotted. There are now about 2,000 enrolled members of the Ute Mountain Ute, once known as the Weeminuche, and about 1,400 enrolled members of the Southern Ute, made up of the two other bands.

The Ute on all three reservations have a variety of sources for their income, including energy companies, agriculture, and casinos. ■

THE GREAT BASIN

Two Ute girls on a horse at sunset, in Ouray, Utah

NELSON WALLULATUM

Protector of the culture

As chief of the Wasco, one of the Confederated Tribes of Warm Springs in Oregon, Nelson Wallulatum has worked tirelessly for 50 years advocating for tribal sovereignty, campaigning for the protection and recovery of Columbia River salmon, and encouraging tribal economic development. Wallulatum, a lifetime member of the Tribal Council of the Confederated Tribes of the Warm Springs Reservation, said he was 12 years old when his tribe started opposing construction of the dams in the early 1930s. "Our very existence depends on the respectful enjoyment of the Columbia Basin's land and water resources," he has said.

Wallulatum is a founder of the Middle Oregon Indian Historical Society, now known as the Museum at Warm Springs, and an advocate for the protection of cultural resources. His testimony on behalf of the protection, preservation, and safekeeping of Native American material culture helped lead to the passage of the Native American Graves Protection and Repatriation Act of 1990. He continues to work to get ancestral remains, religious artifacts, and other objects of cultural patrimony held in museums throughout the country returned home. ∎

Nelson Wallulatum has spent decades working to protect his people and their river.

at the reservation as early as 1879, and a sawmill was built in late 1884.

The tribe, which has never signed a treaty with the U.S. government, is incorporated and owns its reservation land. Fishing was long the major income-producing activity for the Cu-Yui Ticutta, but by the early 1940s fish were nearly extinct in Pyramid Lake, largely due to federal water projects upstream. Three fish hatcheries still exist.

In the band's cosmogony, the Mother cried over the loss of her other Paiute children (bands) and sat near a mountain where she could look toward Pitt River country. Her tears formed a great pool beneath her. This became Pyramid Lake—the terminal desert lake recognized as the state's largest natural body of water. She sat so long that she turned to stone, and so is called Stone Mother. There she remains to this day, on the eastern shore of Pyramid Lake, with her basket by her side.

The Pyramid Lake Paiute Tribe is actively involved in environmental issues pertaining to the lake and habitat. Since 2003, the environment department has managed a breeding program for the northern leopard frog, a threatened species now found only in the reservation's portions of the wetlands along the Truckee River, as well as spadefoot toads, western toads, and Pacific tree frogs. It also works to reconstruct and preserve the oxbow lakes and ponds suitable for breeding and living habitats.

RENO-SPARKS INDIAN COLONY

Tribe: Reno-Sparks Indian Colony [Washoe, Paiute, and Shoshone]   Current Location: Nevada   Total Area: 1,836 acres   Tribal Enrollment: 854

The Reno-Sparks Indian Colony is composed of three tribal groups: the Washoe, the Paiute, and the Shoshone. The people that inhabited the Great Basin prior to the European invasion were the Numu and Nuwuvi (Southern and Northern Paiute), Washeshu (Washoe), and Newe (Shoshone). All these names meant "The People." Each group evolved in such a manner as to provide an efficient social and economic unit that could comfortably inhabit and live off the land.

Though each group spoke a different language—the Washoe a Hokoan derivative; the others, dialects of Uto-Aztecan origin—they understood and respected the lifestyles of the other groups and tribes with whom they came in contact, and much trade and commerce occurred among the original inhabitants of the North American continent; however, war occurred when a group was forced to raid or confiscate the resources of another group out of economic necessity.

Pushed out of their aboriginal homelands, denied access to most sources of water, and facing starvation, the Native peoples of Nevada had to develop adaptive strategies. One important strategy was to attach themselves to ranches that were developing where many of them had lived. These settlements became colonies (the term "colony" for a type of Indian trust territory came into use during the 19th century and is apparently unique to Nevada). Only in the 20th century did these "camps" sometimes actually become trust territory. The Reno-Sparks Colony was established in 1917. The colony has operated for nearly a century as an urban tribe.

SKULL VALLEY RESERVATION

Tribe: Skull Valley Band of Goshute Indians   Current Location: Utah   Total Area: 18,126.65 acres
Tribal Enrollment: 118

The Goshute exemplified the Great Basin Desert way of life perhaps better than any other group. The Great Basin is one of the most arid regions of the continent, as well as one of the most varied in climate, topography, animals, and plants. In aboriginal times, the people based their subsistence on growing cycles, variations in climate, and animal distribution patterns. Family groups hunted and gathered, often in conjunction with other large family groups. Men typically hunted the large game, while women and children collected plants, seeds, and insects. A hunter would share large game with other village members, but families were able to

Wasco-Wishram, Penutian Language Family
(a Chinookan language)

"Aga ya'xt' itc!i'nôn gali'kim: 'Aga na'it!a demî' 4nua lxli'wix anxu'xwa; k!ā2y' aqxangelgla'ya, aic qa'ma ɛï'x aqenge'lgela.' Alugwagi'ma ide'lxam, 'Itc!i'nôn igidi'mam, dā'2uyax iu'gwat itc!i'nôn, qxadaga'tci itc!i'nôn p' atcixcga'ma ia' xan iqwô'qwô; k!wa'c tci'uxt.' "

("And that Eagle said: 'Now I for my part shall be in the mountains for ever and ever. I shall not be seen at all, only once in a great, great while will anyone see me.' The people will say, 'Eagle has come; here is Eagle flying about, in order that Eagle may take from the grizzly bear his son—he fills him with dread.' ")

provide for themselves without help. At their peak the Goshute numbered about 20,000.

The Skull Valley Goshute's first Euro-American encounter was in 1827, when Jedediah Smith traveled through Western Shoshone territory. The Goshute were heavily impacted by the establishment of the Church of Jesus Christ of Latter-day Saints in their territory as early as 1847. The numbers of Euro-Americans traveling into and through Goshute territory increased substantially with the discovery of gold in California in 1848 and at Gold Canyon in 1849. The discovery of the Comstock Lode in 1857 was the greatest single impetus for Euro-American settlement of Nevada. U.S. government depredations among the Goshute spurred the tribe to sign the Treaty of Tooele Valley on October 12, 1863, but no land was set aside for the Skull Valley Goshute until 1912.

The reservation is currently beset by environmental concerns: to the east is the world's largest nerve gas incinerator; to the northwest is a low-level radioactive disposal site responsible for burying the radioactive waste for the entire country; and to the north is the most polluting magnesium production plant in the United States, as identified by the U.S. Environmental Protection Agency. In the 21st century, reclaiming the health of the land has become a definitive mission for the Skull Valley Band.

SOUTHERN UTE RESERVATION

Tribe: Southern Ute Indian Tribe of the Southern Ute Reservation   Current Location: Colorado
Total Area: 314,995 acres   Tribal Enrollment: 1,420

Members of the Southern Ute tribe belong to the Mouache and Capote bands of the Ute Nation. The Southern Ute Reservation was created in the late 1800s on a strip of land 15 miles wide and 110 miles long that once belonged to the larger, original Ute Reservation but was designated for the Mouache and Capote bands in 1895. During the allotment process in the late 1800s, tribal lands were opened to the public. Tribal lands are now checkerboarded with non-Indian landholdings. In 1937, about half of the original reservation was restored to the tribe. These restored lands turned out to be energy rich, providing the contemporary Southern Ute with a valuable source of income. The tribe is growing rapidly, with over half of the population under the age of 25.

SPOKANE RESERVATION

Tribe: Spokane Tribe of the Spokane Reservation
Current Location: Washington   Total Area: 133,399 acres
Tribal Enrollment: 2,305

The Spokane ("Children of the Sun") are modern descendents of the Interior Salish people who inhabited the areas now known as northeastern Washington, northern Idaho, and western Montana for centuries prior to first contact. The Spokane are part of the Salishan linguistic family—a language they shared with the neighboring Flathead, Coeur d'Alene, and Kalispel tribes.

Traditionally the Spokane relied heavily on the plentiful salmon in fresh-flowing rivers of the area for their subsistence. Ever resourceful, over time the Spokane developed a specialized fishing technology using basic materials available to them. Their communities were further characterized by semisubterranean pit houses, widespread gathering and storage of plant and root crops, and consensus of opinion among the three bands of the tribe. The pit house typically consisted of an excavated pit protected by a conical roof of poles covered with brush and earth.

Contact with whites, first documented in 1807, resulted in the tribe's division into three bands: Upper, Middle, and Lower, according to their location on the Spokane River. Each band had a chief and several subchiefs.

During the early portion of the 20th century, the Spokane economy and way of life suffered dramatically as a result of the construction of two dams: first, the Little Falls Dam (1908) at the traditional site of a major salmon fishery and trading spot with other tribes, and later the Grand Coulee Dam, a structure

This beaded bag, from Yakama or Warm Springs, circa 1925, depicts a man and woman in traditional clothing standing next to an American flag, the pole decorated with eagle feathers.

that ultimately stopped all salmon migration. In 1946, the Spokane brought a claim for redress of the 32 cents per acre they had accepted under duress in 1887, and voted to accept $6.7 million in compensation, to be held in trust.

In 1954, uranium was discovered on the reservation, leading to the creation of two Indian companies that mined the ore until the Three Mile Island disaster in 1979. The success of the discovery soon led to disappointment, however, as tribal factionalism erupted over disagreements regarding distribution of uranium proceeds. The Spokane Indian Association was formed to deal with the conflict, which escalated to the point the BIA recommended termination of the tribe in December 1955.

Tribal leadership was able to successfully focus the disparate energies of its membership and fend off termination.

Traditional culture remains viable, with a number of members, mostly elders, continuing to speak the language, use the sweat lodges, and practice traditional religions. Traditional arts are still practiced, and the tribe is now teaching its language to children in an effort to revive its everyday use. Each January, the tribe celebrates the creation of its reservation.

UINTAH AND OURAY RESERVATION

Tribe: Ute Indian Tribe of the Uintah and Ouray Reservation **Current Location:** Utah
Total Area: 1,021,597 acres   **Tribal Enrollment:** 3,174

The Uintah Valley Reservation was established in 1861, after nearly 15 years of conflict with the newly arrived Mormon settlers. By 1879, in the face of the ever growing number of settlers, almost all members of the Tumpanuwac, San Pitch, Pahvant, Sheberetch, Cumumba, and Uinta-at bands (collectively known as the Uintah band) had been relocated onto the reservation land. In 1881, the federal government moved members of the Yamparka and Parinuc bands (Whiteriver Utes) of Colorado to the reservation. The Taviwac were assigned to the Ouray Reservation on the Tavaputs Plateau, immediately south of the Uintah Reservation. The reservations maintained separate agencies until 1886, when they merged.

In 1888, the federal government claimed a 7,004-acre portion of lands from the eastern end of the Uintah Reservation. Valuable gilsonite deposits were discovered on these lands. By 1909, tribal lands within the Uintah and Ouray Reservation had been reduced from nearly four million acres to 250,000 acres of jointly owned grazing lands and 103,265 acres of individual allotments. In addition to a decrease in tribal lands, the Ute suffered as Euro-Americans established control over the region. Starvation and disease eventually cut tribal numbers in half.

The shrinking tribe accepted the provisions of the Indian Reorganization Act of 1936, and its fortunes began to marginally improve. In 1948, it regained 726,000 acres of traditional lands, and in the 1950s the government found that the tribe was entitled to repatriation payment for lands lost in Colorado and Utah. In 1986, the U.S. Supreme Court upheld a

HOVIA EDWARDS

Native American flute player

Next to the drum, the Native American flute is the sound most associated with Indian music—it's the sweet note of the wind. Hovia Edwards, a member of the Shoshone-Bannock Tribes of the Fort Hall Indian Reservation in Idaho, has been playing the instrument since she was a toddler. Her name comes from the Shoshone word for song; her father, Herman, is a flutemaker and player. Hovia was still a teenager when she released her first professional recording in 2001, *Morning Star,* on Canyon Records, a Native label. She has also released an album with Robert Tree Cody, her mentor and one of the best known players of the instrument. Edwards performed in the opening ceremonies of the 2002 Olympics in Salt Lake City when she was 18 and was featured in a PBS documentary about young Indian musicians. Her music has appeared on soundtracks to documentaries and television programs, including the PBS production of *A Thief of Time,* set on the Navajo Reservation. She regularly plays at Indian events, takes part in dances, and speaks to youth groups. ∎

Hovia Edwards, a Shoshone who plays the Native American flute, toured internationally as a teenager.

WARM SPRINGS

The people that live on the Warm Springs Reservation in Oregon are a confederation of three tribes known individually as the Warm Springs, the Wasco, and the Paiute. Historically, the Warm Springs and Wasco lived along the Columbia River and its tributaries long before European contact. They were nomadic hunting and gathering people who lived seasonally in various village sites from the high forests of the Cascade Range to the high deserts of central Oregon. Trade between neighboring tribes supplied various foods that were not readily available to them from their own lands. The Paiute on the reservation are descended from people who lived in southeastern Oregon; many other tribes around the country are also Paiute.

The Three Tribes

The Warm Springs bands spoke a dialect of Sahaptin. They moved between winter and summer villages and primarily ate fish, game, roots, and berries. They built scaffolding over waterfalls and basalt cliffs along the Columbia River. By this means they were able to fish with long-handled dip nets. Even though they were culturally and linguistically distinct from the Wasco, they crossed paths and traded frequently.

The Wasco bands, the easternmost group of Chinookan-speaking Indians, lived on the Columbia River in the area now known as The Dalles. Although they were principally fishermen, they also traded biscuit root, ground salmon, and bear grass with other tribes nearby. The Clackamas, also a Chinookan-speaking band, provided roots and beads. The neighboring Warm Springs bands and the more distant Nez Perce supplied game, clothing, and horses.

The Paiute came from southeastern Oregon and spoke a Shoshonean dialect. They lived a considerably different lifestyle from that of the Wasco and Warm Springs bands. Their high-plains survival required that they migrate farther and more frequently for game. The

Paiute were foreign to the Wasco and Warm Springs bands, and commerce was rare. In 1879, 38 Paiutes moved to Warm Springs from the Yakama Reser-

A 19th-century Warm Springs buckskin dress, called a deer tail dress, is made of two hides with the tail turned down to form the yoke of the dress.

vation. These 38 people, along with many other Paiutes, were forced to move to the Yakama Reservation and Fort Vancouver after joining the Bannocks in a war against the U.S. Army. In time, more of them arrived, becoming a permanent part of the Warm Springs Reservation.

Waves of settlers from the east upset the old way of life in Oregon in the 1800s. In 1843, a thousand immigrants passed through The Dalles, considered the end of the Oregon Trail that took settlers west. In 1847, that number had grown to 4,000, and by 1852, up to 12,000 settlers were displacing Wasco and Warm Springs people from their territories each year. In 1855, Joel Palmer, superintendent for the Oregon Territory, established the Warm Springs Reservation well south of the Columbia River, on the eastern side of the Cascades along the Deschutes and Warm Springs Rivers. Under the treaty, the Warm Springs and Wasco tribes relinquished approximately 10 million acres of land, but reserved the Warm Springs Reservation for their use. They kept their rights to gather fish, game, and other foods from the reservation in their usual and accustomed places.

Life on the Shared Reservation

Once the tribes were clustered onto the reservation, life changed for them. Salmon wasn't as plentiful as it was on the Columbia, and the harsher climate and poor soil conditions made farming more challenging. They quickly found that their former economic system was

Boys at the Warm Springs Indian Reservation, Oregon, are ready to dance, wearing beaded yokes with traditional geometric images. The headdress is made of porcupine hair.

no longer workable. In addition, federal assimilation policies forced them to abandon many of their customary ways in favor of modern schools, sawmills, and other unfamiliar institutions.

Nonetheless, gathering and preparing food was a substantial part of daily life, and the methods used became as much a part of the tribal culture as the foods themselves. They caught fish from the Columbia River using long-handled dip nets. Roots were dug and pulled from the ground with *kapns* (digging sticks). Berries were picked and gathered in coiled cedar-root baskets. These foods and the methods of obtaining them are still part of life on the reservation. Annually, the Warm Springs Indians observe three religious feasts of thanksgiving based on important native foods: the spring Root Feast, then the Salmon Feast, and in late summer the Huckleberry Feast.

The three languages that were spoken by the Confederated Tribes of Warm Springs—Ichishki'in (Sahaptin), Kiksht (Wasco), and Numu (Paiute)—are in danger of extinction. As of 2010, there were only about 60 speakers of the three languages, all of them elders. The tribe has established a program to attempt to revive the languages. The tribe's investment arm, which has run timber, hydroelectric, and other resource-oriented businesses for decades, pushed to diversify in the 1990s, opening a museum and a casino. ■

CHIEF OURAY

Chief of the Utes, respected and diplomatic leader

Ouray (1833–1880) is revered as one of the greatest leaders of the Ute. He was raised as an Apache, his mother's tribe, although his father was a Ute. He grew up near Taos, New Mexico, mastering the Spanish and English languages and attending Catholic Mass regularly. His broad education in English, Spanish, Ute, and Apache prepared him for later life. His intellect would impress the great white leaders of Washington, D.C., as well as his own people. In 1859, Ouray married Chipeta, a Tabequache Ute woman. Chipeta was a smart woman who spoke little English, preferring the Indian way of life.

By 1860, Ouray was chief of the Ute Indians, including the Uncompahgre band. His character and ability to lead gained him respect among the Ute and proved to be useful in dealing with whites. Ouray saw the increasing hordes of gold prospectors heading over the Continental Divide into Ute territory and knew the newcomers would push for land. The chief chose to work with the whites in a diplomatic fashion rather than risk an unnecessary war. He said,

This portrait of Chief Ouray of the Uncompahgre Ute was taken in the 1870s.

"We do not want to sell a foot of our land, that is the opinion of our people. The whites can go and take the land and come out again. We do not want them to build houses here." ∎

decision acknowledging the tribe's legal jurisdiction over three million acres of reservation lands. Currently, the Ute people are involved in a number of complex negotiations with state and county governments over hunting and mineral rights and right-of-way access.

UMATILLA RESERVATION

Tribe: Confederated Tribes of the Umatilla Reservation
Current Location: Oregon   **Total Area:** 86,784 acres
Tribal Enrollment: 2,542

The Confederated Tribes of the Umatilla Reservation comprises the Cayuse, Umatilla, and Walla Walla tribes, which traditionally resided in the areas of northeastern Oregon and southeastern Washington. The Umatilla lived along the lower reaches of the Umatilla River in what is now northeastern Oregon, and along the banks of the Columbia River over to the mouth of the Walla Walla River in southeastern Washington. Before acquiring horses in the early 1700s, they depended largely on salmon and other fish as their primary food source. After the

MYTH OR FACT?

The Indian languages of the Plateau and Great Basin are extinct.

MYTH

The languages of these regions are endangered, but not yet extinct; some elders speak them, and some youths are learning them.

introduction of the horse, they became more mobile and often joined the Nez Perce and other bands to hunt bison on the western plains.

In 1848, the Umatilla joined their Cayuse neighbors in fighting a volunteer army of Willamette Valley white settlers avenging the Whitman Massacre. This became known as the Cayuse War, the result of an increasing wave of white immigrants spilling off the Oregon Trail into the area. In 1855, the Walla Walla Treaty combined the Umatilla, Cayuse, and Walla Walla into a confederation and relocated them to a newly proposed reservation—the current reservation site.

Prior to the cultivation of wheat on the reservation, the tribes used their lush grasslands primarily as a range for their horses. During the late 19th and early 20th centuries, settlers rounded up many of those horses for slaughter as food or for pulling trolleys in eastern cities. Partly in response to this repeated encroachment, Congress passed the Slater Act of March 3, 1885. While further reducing the reservation, it did allot a limited amount of land to Indian people. Other Acts of Congress in 1888, 1902, and 1917 allotted additional land to tribal members.

The region today is still agricultural; tribal members lease out much of the reservation's tillable land for farming and the McNary Dam town site for manufacturing. Though Catholic and Presbyterian missionaries have had a major impact on the reservation—their influence helped to weaken traditional Native language and culture—a revitalization has been under way, manifesting in a renewed interest in the Seven Drum Religion and other traditional practices.

WALKER RIVER RESERVATION

Tribe: Walker River Paiute Tribe of the Walker River Reservation   Current Location: Nevada
Total Area: 323,386 acres   Tribal Enrollment: 2,979

The Agai Dicutta Yadua, or "Trout-Eater Speakers," have lived on the eastern side of the Sierra Nevada mountain range for thousands of years. They are a band of the Northern Paiute Nation, a group that traveled extensively throughout the Pacific Northwest prior to European contact. Walker Lake was known in the Numa language as Agai Pah, Trout Lake. The Agai Dicutta tribes traditionally lived on the north end.

The Northern Paiute first encountered Euro-Americans during the early 1800s, but contact was relatively minimal until gold was discovered in California in 1848, spurring vast numbers of American settlers to travel through Nevada, establishing communities on tribal territory. The entire region was highly desired by generations of settlers for many uses, and Indian claim to the land was hotly contested. An 1859 land office order established the reservation, which President Grant's 1874 executive order formally recognized.

In 1890, tribal member Wovoka initiated the Ghost Dance religion and called for indigenous people across the continent to rally for the revitalization of Native languages, cultures, and spiritual beliefs and for the restoration of tribal lands and rights. The force of its following propelled the

In this 1894 photo, taken near Parker, Washington, a circle of Indians greets visitors. In the center of the circle are a chief identified as Umtash, an interpreter called Chat Ike, and a woman labeled as "white lady reporter."

federal government to outlaw all Native religious practices and ceremonies. Wovoka died in 1932 and is buried on the Walker River Reservation. A small number of tribal members continue to practice the Ghost Dance religion.

Water issues became troublesome to Indian farming efforts. Though a dam completed at Weber in 1937 helped alleviate the problem, legal action had to be taken to assure Walker River Reservation's water rights. During the 1990s, the federal government opened the dam, which drained the reservoir and cut off the water supply the tribe used to irrigate crops and water cattle. In 2002, the tribe began a series of appeals through the Department of the Interior to reverse the decision to drain the Weber Reservoir and regain water rights for the Walker River Basin.

WASHAKIE INDIAN RESERVATION

Tribe: Northwestern Band of Shoshone Nation
Current Location: Utah   **Total Area:** 217 acres
Tribal Enrollment: 466

Until the middle of the 19th century, the Northwestern Band of Shoshones moved throughout a large territory from northern Utah to southern Idaho, and from western Wyoming to eastern Nevada. Their livelihood depended on the rich grasslands that provided wild grains for themselves and their horses. There were originally ten Northwestern bands. The size of the bands varied depending on their needs; small groups were favored where resources were widely scattered, and larger ones in times of plenty or warfare. Band membership was fluid, with each family deciding whom they wanted to follow. Members of the current Northwestern Band of Shoshone Indians are descendants of families who followed Bear Hunter, Lehi, and Sagwitch.

Beginning in the 1840s, members of the Church of Jesus Christ of Latter-day Saints

began moving into areas that the Shoshone used as their livelihood. Shoshone grasslands were plowed, and the Natives had to compete with the new settlers for game animals. In the 1850s, there was mass migration of Euro-Americans to the Oregon Territory. These immigrants increasingly competed with the Shoshone for natural resources. The discovery

BEADWORK

The Plateau people historically created—and continue to make—beautifully delicate abstract and realistic images using small glass seed beads. Early designs of this type were broad rectangular bands of color, typically blue, red, and white beads sewn to the curvilinear yokes of dresses or the beaded strips of hide shirts and leggings. As the sparsely populated tribes came into greater contact with one another as well as with outsiders, they had increased opportunities to acquire materials with which to

create beaded designs. With more colors and sizes of beads secured through trade, artists were able to make increasingly detailed floral and pictorial images which continued to be inspired by the older geometric designs of twined bags.

The beadwork created in this manner expresses the rich and vibrant cultural continuity of the Plateau people. It also demonstrates how the artists see, understand, and represent their families, their homes, and their world. Each of us perceives the concept of home in the Plateau region differently. It can be represented by the gathering of natural foods, the ability to speak and understand our native language, or the way we see our land—from the sagebrush-covered hills to the high alpine forests to the banks of the Columbia River.

For thousands of years, Plateau artists incorporated geometric designs into stone carvings and rock wall paintings, recording how they experienced and understood nature—especially the relationship between humans and the natural world. Today, these patterns continue to hold great significance, as symbols of place that still connect the Plateau people to their culture, history, environment, knowledge, and values. ∎

With tiny beads, Plateau artists created lovely geometric, floral, or pictorial images such as the one on this bag, circa 1920.

of silver in Montana and gold in California brought additional people seeking their fortunes. The Shoshone were displaced from their traditional gathering and hunting lands. Misunderstandings led to conflicts, culminating in the Bear River Massacre on January 29, 1863, when federal troops from Camp Douglas in Salt Lake City massacred a village of Shoshone.

While a series of treaties and agreements in 1863 left southern Idaho and northern Utah as Shoshone country, the second Treaty of Fort Bridger in 1868 ceded those lands to the U.S. government. Some members of the original ten Northwestern bands settled on the reservations created in 1868 at Wind River, Wyoming, and Fort Hall, Idaho.

The Northwestern Band of Shoshone Indians is largely descended from survivors of the Bear River Massacre who chose not to relocate to a reservation, remaining in their traditional homelands in northern Utah and southern Idaho. The Northwestern Band received very few services from the federal government until the early 1980s. The group gained official recognition in 1987, and today the Northwestern Shoshone are developing their tribal holdings in Idaho and Utah.

A basketwork baby carrier, circa 1920

WIND RIVER RESERVATION

Tribes: Arapahoe Tribe of the Wind River Reservation and Shoshone Tribe of the Wind River Reservation **Current Location:** Wyoming **Total Area:** 2,268,008 acres **Tribal Enrollments:** Arapaho Tribe: 7,417; Shoshone Tribe: 3,724

The Wind River Reservation is the third largest in the nation and the only Native American reservation in the state of Wyoming. The reservation is unique as the only reservation in the United States that encompasses lands chosen by the tribe compelled to live there, in the traditional territory of the Eastern Shoshone people. Both the Eastern Shoshone and Northern Arapaho (also sometimes spelled Arapahoe) tribes now occupy the Wind River Reservation. The Eastern Shoshone formerly roamed freely between their summer homes in eastern Idaho and their ancestral hunting grounds in the Wind River Valley in Wyoming. The tribe was influenced by the diversity of its home territories and demonstrated cultural attributes associated with Plains Indians—the use of horses, reliance on bison, tepees for housing, and so on—as well as the influence of their Great Basin and Colorado Plateau kin. As pressure from white settlement began to push tribes out of their traditional homelands, Chief Washakie determined that a permanent move into Wind River Country would be best for his people. The area was known for its mild winters, abundant game, and plentiful mountain-fed streams.

The Arapaho are a southwestern extension of the Algonquin people. Sharing cultural ties with the Plains tribes, the Arapaho are distinguished from others in the region by their language, a variation of Algonquian. In 1851, the Arapaho and Cheyenne cosigned a treaty with the United States. Unfortunately, pressure from whites—particularly gold prospectors—soon caused tensions, and the tribes found themselves in conflict with the government. In 1864, a band of several hundred Cheyennes and Arapahos, led by Black Kettle, camped on the banks of Sand Creek, near Lyons, Colorado. When the young men had left to hunt, Col. John Chivington ordered a surprise attack on the encampment. Between 150 and 200 Indians—mostly women, old men, and children—were shot in spite of their white flag of surrender.

War continued for several years, forcing the Arapaho to follow what is now known as the Sand Creek Massacre Trail from southeastern Wyoming to the Wind River Reservation, where the Eastern Shoshone allowed them temporary residence. It was a difficult alliance—the tribes had formerly been enemies. To this day, there remains some ambivalence about their forced arrangement. However, the Arapaho and the Shoshone have jointly ruled the Wind River Reservation while managing to retain their respective identities, cultures, and tribal governments.

THE NORTHWEST COAST

THE NORTHWEST COAST

A**ND SO RAVEN FILLED HIS BEAK WITH AS MUCH WATER AS HE COULD HOLD.** As he flew back to his home, drops and dribbles of water spilled on to the land. These spilled drops created the oceans, lakes, and streams of the world. In these bodies of water, the water animals flourished, providing food, clothing, and adornments for the people. (Tlingit legend)

For countless generations, the Tlingit people of southeastern Alaska and other native peoples of the Northwest Coast have lived close to the water and drawn from it sustenance and strength. Their bountiful marine environment, extending for more than 1,500 miles from Alaska to Oregon, was first occupied more than 10,000 years ago as glaciers that sealed off the coast during the Ice Age receded. Migratory bands may have entered the region from the interior along rivers like the Columbia, Fraser, Skeena, and Stikine, which provided corridors through coastal mountain ranges.

The first people here settled along inlets teeming with salmon and other fish and piled up mounds of discarded shells called middens as they harvested clams by the thousands. They were blessed with plenty of timber, including towering Sitka spruce and red cedar, which flourished in coastal areas receiving more than 100 inches of rain a year in some spots. From those great trees, they built houses up to 60 feet long that accommodated several families and carved canoes in which they hunted seals and whales or traveled to the many islands along the Northwest Coast, which formed a protected waterway known as the Inside Passage from Puget Sound to Glacier Bay.

> THEY WERE BLESSED WITH PLENTY OF TIMBER, INCLUDING TOWERING SITKA SPRUCE AND RED CEDAR, WHICH FLOURISHED IN COASTAL AREAS RECEIVING MORE THAN 100 INCHES OF RAIN A YEAR.

CULTURAL FOUNDATIONS

BY 3000 B.C., NORTHWEST COAST NATIVES WERE LIVING IN PERMANENT VILLAGES AND had a variety of tools for fishing, hunting, and working wood. Exposed to the elements, their ancient wooden houses have not survived. However, a landslide that occurred around 500 years ago at Ozette on Washington's Olympic Peninsula buried a village of the Makah and preserved many wooden artifacts crafted there, including a cedar canoe used to hunt whales or trade with tribes on Vancouver Island.

The Makah were one of many tribal groups encountered by Europeans when they explored the Northwest Coast in the 1700s. Others who had long inhabited the region when those first contacts occurred included the Tlingit in Alaska, the Haida on the Queen Charlotte Islands and nearby, the Tsimshian along the lower Nass and Skeena Rivers, the Kwakwaka'wakw (Kwakiutl) on northern Vancouver Island and the mainland across from it, the Nuu-chah-nulth (Nootka) on

Preceding pages: A carver of the Kwakwaka'wakw (Kwakiutl) stands beside historic totem poles at Alert Bay on Vancouver Island. Opposite: Totem poles like these at Alert Bay were carved by Native people of the Northwest Coast to display clan or household crests.

the west coast of Vancouver Island, the Coast Salish around Puget Sound, the Chinook along the lower Columbia River, and the Tillamook on the Oregon coast. Each of those tribal groups consisted of various communities or subtribes. The Coast Salish, for example, included the Lummi, Swinomish, Tulalip, Puyallup, Suquamish, Quinault, and Skokomish, which have separate reservations in Washington today.

Tribal groups of the Northwest Coast traditionally lived in large, multifamily houses and subsisted mainly on fish and marine mammals, but also hunted game and gathered plants. The climate and soil did not favor agriculture, and they grew only tobacco before Europeans introduced potatoes. Most tribal societies here were divided into three classes: slaves, many of them seized in raids; commoners; and nobles. People of all classes lived together in the large houses, with slaves usually residing near the entrance, nobles or chiefs at the far end, and commoners in between. Partitions along the walls divided the sleeping quarters of the various families, situated around a central fireplace.

Nobles acquired wealth and distributed goods freely to guests at potlatches, held on special occasions, such as funerals or when one chief succeeded another. Nobles traced their high status to ancestral spirits, who often took the form of animals—raven, wolf, salmon, eagle, killer whale—and bestowed healing powers and property rights such as ownership of fishing or hunting grounds. People honored those ancestors by carving crests on totem poles, which displayed their distinguished heritage.

In the warmer months, many people left their villages and moved to fishing camps. Some men ventured far in their canoes to attack distant tribes or trade with them. The Haida had to cross the often-turbulent Queen Charlotte Sound to do so and crafted sturdy, seaworthy canoes that were highly valued by the Tlingit and others with whom they traded. By late fall, people were back in their villages and spent the winter in their big houses, where they performed ceremonies and told creation stories of Raven and other beings.

NORTHWEST COAST

SCALE
1 : 10,500,000

statute miles
0   100   200   300

kilometers
0   100   200   300

Map Key

▭ Indian regional boundary as represented in this book.
(See pages 14–15 for North American map showing all eight regions depicted in this work.)

▭ Canadian Aboriginal Land

▭ Federal Indian Reservation or Alaskan native land
(occupied by one or more tribal entities)

△ Federally designated tribal entity with no land holding

Cowichan 1 Canadian Indian Reserve name

Siletz Federal Reservation name

56 Resident tribe
(Number correlates to tribal list on pages 358–361.)

164 Alaska resident tribe
(Number correlates to tribal list on pages 361–363.)

★ State or provincial capital

• Selected city or town

Many Canadian Indian reserves have a number as part of their official name.

CHALLENGES FROM ABROAD

THE FIRST EUROPEANS TO VISIT THE NORTHWEST COAST WERE RUSSIANS, WHO EXPLORED Tlingit territory in 1741 and returned in the late 1700s to settle at Sitka. The Tlingit welcomed trade with foreigners but opposed Russian colonists, who forced Native hunters from Kodiak Island and the Aleutians to work for them taking sea otters in Tlingit waters. The sea otter trade expanded in 1778 when the British explorer Capt. James Cook entered Nootka Sound and obtained from the Nuu-chah-nulth some sea otter pelts that his crew later sold in China for a princely sum. Among the items Natives received in exchange for those pelts was iron, which enhanced their skills as carvers and builders.

By the 1800s, sea otters had been overhunted. British and American traders sought new sources of wealth by building forts along the coast and obtaining beaver pelts and other furs from Natives, some of whom settled around those posts. Many Tsimshian moved to the vicinity of Fort Simpson, constructed by the Hudson's Bay Company in 1834 near the mouth of the Skeena River. Some Chinook gathered at trading posts on the lower Columbia River and devised a pidgin language called Chinook Jargon, combining English phrases with their own terms and those of other tribes.

Here, as elsewhere in North America, contact with white men exposed Natives to devastating diseases such as smallpox. Those who endured lost much of their territory when Americans and Canadians began settling along the coast in the mid-1800s, followed by fortune hunters seeking gold. Christian missionaries offered their services to tribes in distress, but insisted that they abandon traditional ceremonies like the potlatch, which was outlawed as wasteful by the Canadian government in 1885.

IN RECENT TIMES, TRIBES OF THE NORTHWEST COAST HAVE REVIVED SUCH CUSTOMS AS POTLATCHES AND THE CARVING OF CANOES AND TOTEM POLES.

A TIME OF RENEWAL

BY THE EARLY 1900S, NATIVES OF THE NORTHWEST COAST WERE PROTESTING INFRINGEMENTS on their rights and property. The Alaska Native Brotherhood, founded in 1912, went to court and overturned an Alaska statute that allowed Native Americans to vote only if they severed ties with their tribe and were endorsed by five white residents. Other legal victories in decades to come, such as the Boldt Decision in Washington in 1974, restored to tribes ancestral lands and treaty-protected fishing rights, providing some with new economic opportunities.

In recent times, tribes of the Northwest Coast have revived such customs as potlatches and the carving of canoes and totem poles and have won recognition for their past and present accomplishments. Like other Native peoples around the world, they are reasserting their identity through programs designed to preserve the unique languages, art forms, and ceremonies that distinguish their enduring cultures and are living modern lives while honoring ancient traditions. ■

CHEHALIS RESERVATION

Tribe: Confederated Tribes of the Chehalis
Reservation Current Location: Oregon
Total Area: 2,124 acres Tribal Enrollment: 728

The two principal tribes now living on the Chehalis Reservation are the Lower Chehalis and the Upper Chehalis, also known as the qyaya. They speak related Salish languages and traditionally maintained close ties through trade, intermarriage, and shared spiritual beliefs. The Upper Chehalis people lived from Cloquallum Creek to the Chehalis River waterways and tributaries. While the Lower Chehalis primarily relied on ocean resources for their sustenance ("Chehalis" means "sand"), the Upper Chehalis, in their shovel-nose canoes, depended on a river-based economy along the Chehalis and Cowlitz River systems. This canoe highway with its negotiable portages was utilized well into the 1900s, not only by tribes but also increasingly by non-Natives. The people lived in cedar longhouses with one end open to the water, the bounty of salmon, and other river-based sustenance.

Tlingit, Athabaskan language family

"Wáa sá i yatee?"
("How are you?")

Though the Chehalis people were affiliated with the 1855 Treaty Council held by Governor Isaac Stevens, they never signed a treaty; their rights as affiliates have, to this day, never been formally recognized. In 1864, the secretary of the interior approved an executive order setting aside 4,215 acres for the Chehalis Reservation, and it was expected that the Cowlitz, Chinook, and Shoalwater Bay peoples would settle there. However, few besides the Chehalis did so.

In 1906, the combined Chehalis tribe began a series of petitions to the federal government to compensate for lands the government had appropriated. Over more than half a century, their claims were denied. In the late 1950s, however, after numerous appeals, the Indian Claims Commission concluded that the Chehalis held aboriginal title to approximately 840,000 acres, and they were compensated at about 90 cents per acre.

Today, subsistence and ceremonial fishing remain central to tribal culture. The tribe has entered into water settlement negotiations to plan for the future use of "reserved water" rights and oversees more than

Elizabeth Peratrovich helped end discrimination against her fellow Tlingit and other Native Alaskans.

ELIZABETH PERATROVICH

Alaska Native civil rights pioneer

"Whites Only. No Indians Allowed." Such signs once hung in shops and restaurants throughout Alaska, segregating Natives from whites. When Elizabeth and Roy Peratrovich moved back to Alaska from the lower 48 in 1941, that segregation angered them. They became the presidents of the Alaska Native Sisterhood and the Alaska Native Brotherhood, two civic groups that actively lobbied the legislature to outlaw segregation. Roy was also a territorial senator. Elizabeth, a member of the Tlingit nation, delivered compelling testimony before the legislature on the harmful effects of segregation and other forms of discrimination. When asked if laws would stop racism, she replied, "Do your laws against larceny and even murder prevent those crimes? No law will eliminate crimes, but at least you as legislators can assert to the world that you recognize the evil of the present situation and speak your intent to help us overcome discrimination." On February 16, 1945, the Alaska Anti-Discrimination Bill was signed into law, forbidding segregation. In 1988, the legislature established February 16 as Elizabeth Peratrovich Day to honor her efforts to achieve equal rights for Native Alaskans. ∎

one million dollars to monitor, clean up, restore, and maintain the Chehalis River. As responsible keepers of the river, the tribe educates people about environmental stewardship.

Programs have been developed to preserve the Chehalis language. Basket weaving, drummaking, regalia, and storytelling classes allow members share their culture with future generations.

CONFEDERATED TRIBES OF COOS, LOWER UMPQUA, AND SIUSLAW INDIAN RESERVATION

Tribe: Confederated Tribes of Coos, Lower Umpqua, and Siuslaw Indians of Oregon **Current Location:** Oregon
Total Area: 130 acres **Tribal Enrollment:** 813

The Confederated Tribes of Coos, Lower Umpqua, and Siuslaw Indians are the aboriginal inhabitants of the central and south-central coast of Oregon. The tribes have struggled for years to keep their history, land, and culture intact. Regular association with settlers began in 1826 when the Hudson's Bay Company came searching for beaver hides. The tribes placed little value on the hides and offered assistance in pointing out the streams with plenty of beaver. In the 1850s, entrepreneurs and pioneers viewed Coos Bay and the Umpqua Valley as excellent places to settle. In 1855, a treaty was negotiated with all the tribes along the Oregon coast. From that point, the Confederated Tribes began their uphill struggle.

In 1856, the Rogue River Wars broke out between various tribes of southwestern Oregon and white settlers. Fearing that the Coos and Lower Umpqua Indians would join in the war, the white settlers gathered the Coos and Lower Umpqua, held them at an encampment at Fort Umpqua for four years, and then removed them to Yachats. The tribes recall the 80-mile forced march to Yachats as their Trail of

Masks like this one, representing a man-killing monster that took the form of a dragonfly, were crafted by Northwest Coast tribes for use in ceremonies.

Tears. Many died of hunger, starvation, exposure, mistreatment, and exhaustion. However, the reservation life at Yachats was worse. The people were often chained, whipped, and left without food, blankets, or clothing. The tribe dwindled from 700 to fewer than 300 members.

In 1876, white settlers again wanted to remove the Indians. Many returned to their original homelands, after being forcefully removed from Yachats without payment for the 21 years of forced labor there, and found that their land had been taken over by white settlers. Although disheartened by the promises broken by the federal government, many assimilated to white life, but they also continued to fight for what was their own by banding together to pursue payment of land claims, which paved the way for many other Oregon tribes.

Just as things seemed to be improving, in 1956 federal Indian policy terminated the Confederated Tribes. As they stood their ground before, the Coos, Lower Umpqua, and Siuslaw tribes fought to reverse the termination. Eventually the federal policy was disavowed, and in 1984 the Confederated Tribes were restored to federal recognition. They are now one of the ten federally recognized tribes in the state of Oregon.

COQUILLE INDIAN RESERVATION

Tribe: Coquille Tribe of Oregon **Current Location:** Oregon
Total Area: 6,481 acres **Tribal Enrollment:** 842

Members of the Coquille tribe have resided on the southern Oregon coast, along the Coquille River and inland toward the area of Coos Bay, for at least several thousand years. The original Coquille Indians were an Athabascan band called Mishikhwutmetunne, "People Living on the Stream Called Mishi," and their languages were Clatskanie, Umpqua, and Coquille-Tolowa. Over

time, the indigenous language of the Coquille people has been almost entirely replaced by the pidgin Chinook language.

In 1855, the tribe entered into treaty agreements with the United States. They ceded their ancestral lands in exchange for federal services and protection within a designated reservation. Despite the treaty, the tribe eventually began to suffer the effects of the influx of explorers, trappers, and missionaries.

Many Coquille bands and villages were nearly obliterated in the Rogue River Wars of 1856, and the survivors were forcibly relocated to reservations such as Siletz. In the early 20th century, George Bundy Watson began investigating Coquille land claims based on the 1855 treaty. Convinced of fraud perpetrated against the tribe, he took the Coquille's case before the Court of Claims, which decided in favor of the tribe in 1945 and awarded a monetary judgment.

A totem pole erected near Juneau, Alaska, overlooks Gastineau Channel, one of many protected waterways that facilitated trade between the Tlingit and other tribes.

In 1954, however, the tribe was terminated along with 42 other western Oregon tribes.

It took intense lobbying by tribal leaders to finally regain federal recognition in 1989. The restoration of tribal governmental powers included full eligibility for federal benefits and services similar to other tribes and provisions for establishing a government and acquiring a land base.

COWLITZ RESERVATION

Tribe: Cowlitz Indian Tribe   Current Location: Washington
Total Area: 72 acres   Tribal Enrollment: 3,824

The name Cowlitz is derived from "seeker," referring to the tribe's spirituality. The Cowlitz tribe includes two groups, the Upper and Lower Cowlitz. The tribe's original territory, centered on the Cowlitz River (named after the tribe), included some 3,750 square miles. The more numerous Salish-speaking Lower Cowlitz lived in 30 villages along the river, from about a mile above the Columbia River to 45 miles or so upstream. The Sahaptin-speaking Upper Cowlitz (Taidnapam) wintered along the Cowlitz River east of the Lower Cowlitz, then moved up into the Cascades during warm weather. Both groups had highly evolved social organizations, were skilled negotiators as well as warlike when necessary, and maintained trading and kinship alliances throughout what is now southwest Washington and northwest Oregon. They were a regional power until influenza epidemics in the early 1830s killed perhaps seven-eighths of the tribe.

The Cowlitz became disillusioned as settlers began to occupy more and more of the valley. Throughout the 20th century, the Cowlitz people struggled with both state and federal governments for land and subsistence rights. In 1951, Cowlitz leadership filed a land-claims petition with the federal Indian Claims Commission. Twenty-two years later, the commission found in favor of the tribe. Through the 1980s and '90s, the Cowlitz pressed for federal recognition, and they were recognized in January 2002.

The modern Cowlitz Indians have been able to maintain many traditional tribal observances in child rearing, religion, food, and kinship networks. Cowlitz baskets are renowned for their intricate construction, very close stitching (indeed, they are watertight), and striking designs.

GRAND RONDE RESERVATION

Tribe: Confederated Tribes of the Grand Ronde Community of Oregon [Kalapuya, Clackamas, Molalla, Rogue River, Chasta/Shasta, Umpqua, Salmon River, and Nehalem Band of Tillamook]   Current Location: Oregon
Total Area: 10,678 acres   Tribal Enrollment: 4,985

The Confederated Tribes of the Grand Ronde is composed of more than 20 tribes and bands whose traditional lands included regions throughout western Oregon and some parts of northern California. The various tribes that live on the Grand Ronde Reservation initially spoke

numerous languages and dialects, not all related or mutually intelligible. The Chinook (Chinuk) language, which was a shared common language among many tribes as a trade language along the Columbia River, later became the primary language of the reservation tribes and today is being actively revitalized through cultural programs and instruction.

The Grand Ronde Reservation was established by treaties in 1854 and 1855 and an executive order in 1857. From 1855 to 1856, many of the

CANOES

Living close to the water, tribes of the Northwest Coast relied mightily on their canoes, which they carved out of massive cedar or spruce trees that had been growing in their forests for hundreds of years. Some canoes were more than 40 feet long and weighed more than half a ton. After they were carved, shaped, and smoothed, designs associated with the owner's tribe, clan, and family were etched, carved, or painted on the surface.

Navigating the straits and inlets of the Northwest Coast required an intimate knowledge of currents, tides, and geography, developed over thousands of years and passed from one generation to the next. Canoes were used for trade, warfare, migrations, seasonal travel between summer and winter residences, and subsistence activities such as fishing, whaling, and hunting. Broad, flat paddles were used for propelling and

steering the vessel, while slimmer, tapered paddles were used as decoration, in dances, and as weapons.

In recent times, Northwest Coast tribes have revived the art of building canoes for ceremonies honoring their maritime traditions. In 1989, Natives from several communities on the Olympic Peninsula paddled canoes they had crafted to Seattle, where they gathered with people of other tribes arriving by canoe. That marked the beginning of Tribal Journeys, an annual event that observed its 20th anniversary in 2009. Members of more than 30 tribal communities from the United States, Canada, and New Zealand paddled to a celebration of coastal canoe culture hosted by the Suquamish of Puget Sound. Each group had a chance to share its songs, dances, and stories with others during the weeklong gathering. ■

A model canoe of the Makah shows how the dugouts were decorated.

HAIDA

The Haida live mainly on the Queen Charlotte Islands, known to them as Haida Gwaii, and on nearby islands in southeastern Alaska. Like their northern neighbors the Tlingit and other tribes, their name derives from a term in their own language meaning simply "The People." Their population is about 4,000, residing largely in the Canadian towns of Masset and Skidegate and the Alaskan town of Hydaburg. Of all the Northwest Coast tribes, their homelands lay farthest from the mainland. Long renowned for their skills as canoe builders and long-distance traders, they remain a venturesome people.

From Forest to Ocean

The Haida environment is rich in timber and marine resources. No asset meant more to their culture than the great cedar trees that grew in their forests. From the cedar, they built towering totem poles and canoes that measured up to 40 feet long, with upward-sloping bows and sterns to break the waves of open waters. Those canoes allowed them to troll for deepwater halibut, using large, V-shaped hooks baited with octopus.

What the Haida could not obtain close to home they secured through trade, crossing Queen Charlotte Sound in canoes using paddles or an advancement they adopted soon after encountering Europeans in the late 1700s: sails. Among the goods they obtained from the Tsimshian to their east was grease from the eulachon, or candlefish, which spawned in rivers on the mainland. Its oil was used as a condiment on foods such as dried fish. From the Tlingit to the north, the Haida acquired precious Chilkat blankets, woven from the hair of mountain goats and cedar bark—an art taught to the Tlingit by the Tsimshian.

Master builders, the Haida excavated pits before erecting their big wooden houses, which had tiers that rose in

Tlingit/Haida master carver Nathan Jackson carves a traditional mask at Saxman, Alaska.

stair-step fashion from the central fireplace. The chief of the household resided on the top tier at the rear of the building and presided over dances, potlatches, and other ceremonies. At the entrance stood a house post that served as a kind of family tree, displaying the crests associated with the lineage or extended family residing within. A household could acquire crests through various means, including marriage, heroic deeds, warfare, or purchase from another lineage that lost its fortune. On the other hand, if a chief displayed a crest to which his lineage did not have legitimate claim, the rightful owner might demand payment for the transgression or shame the chief by hosting a potlatch and giving away more goods than the pretender could afford to offer.

Dealing with the Iron People

In 1774, a Spanish ship exploring the Northwest Coast reached the Queen Charlotte Islands and was well received by the Haida, who paddled out in canoes and scattered eagle down on the water to signal that the visitors were welcome. This was the first recorded encounter between the tribe and the foreigners they called Yets-Haida, or "Iron People," for the metal merchants offered in exchange for sea otters and other coveted items. Haida soon learned to forge iron and craft iron tools, with which they honed their skills as builders and carvers.

When sea otters were depleted and trade shifted to the mainland, the Haida offered the occupants of Fort Simpson dried halibut, potatoes, and other goods in exchange for manufactured items like blankets and cloth. That led to new forms of handiwork and artistry, as women of the Haida and other Northwest Coast tribes embroidered trade blankets with buttons, beads, and shells to form alluring designs. The Haida became well known for intricate carvings in argillite, a soft black stone found on Haida Gwaii, that were purchased by traders, travelers, and explorers.

The Haida were quick to adapt to the new materials and modes of commerce introduced by Europeans. But they could not contend with the devastating diseases they were exposed to in the process, which reduced their population on the Queen Charlotte Islands from nearly 7,000 in 1840 to less than 600 in 1915. As their numbers dwindled, they had little choice but to accept the small reserves the Canadian government set aside for them there, amounting to less than 4,000 acres.

The Haida in southeastern Alaska had difficulty maintaining their old villages. Many of them relocated in 1911 to the new town of Hydaburg, established with federal support after their representatives signed a document stating that they had abandoned their tribal customs. That was a requirement for those seeking U.S. citizenship in Alaska until 1922, when the Alaska Native Brotherhood went to court and overturned the law. Privately, however, Haida here and in Canada carried on ancient traditions that government authorities discouraged or outlawed.

Recent decades have seen a cultural resurgence by the Haida, who are preserving and perpetuating their language and arts, including carving, painting, jewelrymaking, textile weaving, and basketmaking. They have joined with their neighbors to form the Tlingit and Haida Central Council, a tribal governing body that represents and advocates for the Native peoples of southeastern Alaska. There are Haida living around the globe, but Haida Gwaii remains the center of their world, a source of cultural strength, pride, and solidarity for the Haida people. ▪

Haida Natives in Alaska paddle a canoe like those once used by tribal traders to obtain materials for button blankets like the one worn here.

tribes were relocated to the reservation, with the exception of the Nehalem Band of Tillamook and the Salmon River Band. During this period, the government attempted to force Euro-American traditions upon them, banning Native religions, dress, and ceremonies and imposing the English language and Christian religion on the community. For subsistence, tribal members worked as servants, farmers, or loggers and sold baskets and other handmade goods.

DALE JOHNSON

Makah leader and conservationist

Dale Johnson, former chairman of the Makah Tribal Council, has long been active in his community at Neah Bay as a skilled fisherman, canoe skipper, and conservationist, working to ensure that the natural resources sustaining his people today will be available in years to come. He advocated for the Boldt Decision, which upheld tribal rights to traditional fishing grounds. In the late 1970s, Johnson helped win support among the Makah for the difficult decision to close rivers during fishing seasons to allow salmon and other fish to restore their populations. He pointed out that the Makah should protect and preserve their fishery as a legacy for future generations. His political efforts and personal financial resources helped create one of the largest and most successful tribally run fisheries and fishing fleets in the U.S. The Makah fishing program seeks to maintain an ecological balance between the needs and traditions of the people and the resources that sustain them. Johnson is highly regarded in Neah Bay and other Native communities for his commitment to the well-being of his people. ■

Dale Johnson has done much to develop and preserve the natural resources of the Makah.

In 1901, the tribes lost a total of 27,791 acres. Though much of the former reservation had been sold or taken from tribal ownership, many of the tribal members remained in Grand Ronde and supported the 1934 Indian Reorganization Act, as it provided many jobs and allowed them to purchase land.

In 1954, the tribes entered perhaps their most difficult period as the federal government declared the Grand Ronde terminated. A large percentage of tribal members were forced to leave the area and seek work in Portland and elsewhere. In 1983, the persistence and dedication of those who had continued to lobby against termination paid off in the form of the Grand Ronde Restoration Act, which allowed the tribes to function as one tribal unit, restored most of their previous rights, and transferred nearly 10,000 acres of former reservation lands back to the tribe.

JAMESTOWN S'KLALLAM TRIBE OF WASHINGTON RESERVATION

Tribe: Jamestown S'Klallam Tribe of Washington
Current Location: Washington   Total Area: 72 acres
Tribal Enrollment: 526

S'Klallam derives from the original name nuxsklai'yem, meaning "Strong People." In addition to the Jamestown Reservation, S'Klallams reside in two other nearby communities, Lower Elwha and Port Gamble.

The S'Klallam possessed a rich social and religious culture based on the abundant natural resources of the Northwest Coast. They were considered one of the most aggressive tribes in the area, and in the 1800s they expanded their territory to the areas of Vancouver Island and Hood Canal.

S'Klallam contact with Europeans began in the 1700s and increased in the 1800s, after the establishment of Hudson's Bay Company trading posts. The S'Klallam tribe entered into the Point No Point Treaty with the United States in 1855 but resisted removal to the reservation of the Twana people at Skokomish. They remained in most of their

The killer whale was much admired by Native people of the Northwest Coast and inspired carvings like this one displayed at Old Kasaan, a Haida historic site in Alaska.

traditional areas, and in 1874 the S'Klallam from the village at Dungeness privately purchased 210 acres of land, establishing Jamestown.

In the 1930s, the tribe was given the choice of moving to the reservations purchased for the other two S'Klallam tribes or remaining where they were, unrecognized. They chose to stay on the land they had bought themselves. Tribal members received services from the federal government until 1953, when the government ceased recognition. Beginning in the 1950s, the three S'Klallam tribes combined to litigate land claims and fishing rights. In cases that went to the U.S. Supreme Court, the S'Klallam ultimately regained the fishing rights they had been granted in the Point No Point Treaty. Facing increasing problems in the areas of fishing rights, health care, and education, the tribe began

an intensive effort to obtain recognition in 1974 and adopted a constitution in 1975. It received federal recognition in 1981.

LUMMI RESERVATION

Tribe: Lummi Tribe of the Lummi Reservation
Current Location: Washington
Total Area: 8,011 acres   Tribal Enrollment: 4,096

Before the 1855 Treaty of Point Elliott, the Lummi occupied the northern San Juan Islands and the adjacent mainland from Bellingham Bay to Point Roberts. Salmon served as the primary source of food and the center of many tribal ceremonies, beliefs, and community activities. The western red cedar also played a significant role in the tribe's material and spiritual life.

The tribe's history during the 20th century is inexorably tied to its fishing-centered economy and treaty fishing rights issues. After 1855, the federal government expected the tribe to adopt agriculture as its primary means of subsistence. The Lummi, however, continued to travel off-reservation for fishing and gathering, particularly to their traditional reef-net locations. As it turned out, the tribe's reef-net fishing territory placed it at the epicenter of the region's budding commercial salmon industry. Organized commercial interests squeezed the Lummi out of the business by appropriating their prime net locations, which led to a series of lawsuits by the tribe. The government was finally ordered to pay $57,000 in 1970, a settlement the Lummi rejected as totally inadequate. In 1974, they participated in another lawsuit over treaty fishing rights, this time against the state of Washington. The suit culminated in a court-ordered allocation of the state's commercial salmon harvest.

Historically, the Lummi have been opposed to expansion that would be harmful for the environment. However, they realize they must find a balance between environmental stewardship and economic growth. One solution being considered is designating specific areas for development and agreeing on activities that will be allowed there.

MUCKLESHOOT RESERVATION

Tribe: Muckleshoot Indian Tribe of the Muckleshoot Reservation [Coast Salish]
Current Location: Washington   Total Area: 1,125 acres
Tribal Enrollment: 1,712

The Muckleshoot are descendants of the Coast Salish peoples and have lived in the Northwest for thousands of years. Ancestral homelands include areas along the eastern and southern reaches of Puget Sound and the western slope of the Cascade Range. The Coast Salish tribes had intricate social structures and a hereditary nobility.

Adorned with copper, this haunting wooden mask was worn by a Tlingit shaman credited with supernatural powers.

**Haida,
Not a member
of any other
language
family**

*"Sánuu dáng
gíidang?"*

("How are you?")

They depended on the abundance of natural resources in the Pacific Northwest coastal region, especially salmon and red cedar, and were very prosperous.

The treaties of Point Elliott and Medicine Creek established the Muckleshoot Indian Reservation. Members from the Stkamish, Yilalkoamish, Smulkamish, Tkwakwamish, Duwuamish, Snoqualmie, Tulalip, and Suquamish clans of Coast Salish relocated to the reservation and became the Muckleshoot Indian Tribe.

In the 1960s and '70s, the Muckleshoot tribe became involved in what have been called the Fish Wars, actively pressuring the government to recognize and implement the tribe's fishing and hunting rights guaranteed in the original treaties. The Boldt Decision of 1974 upheld the tribe's rights. The tribe has been designated legal comanager of the King County Watershed, which recognizes the tribe's ancestral fishing and hunting rights to the land and permits them to control those environments. The tribe has initiated efforts to restore the White River salmon passages into Jones Creek, Blocks Creek, and Charlie Jones Creek on the reservation.

Each year, according to the customs of an ancient ceremony, the first salmon to return from the sea to the freshwater streams is caught and brought to the village as an honored guest. The flesh is removed and shared by all members of the community. Afterward, the skeleton is returned to the river and asked to tell its brother and sister salmon of the Muckleshoot's hospitality.

PORT MADISON INDIAN RESERVATION

Tribal Entity: Suquamish Indian Tribe
Current Location: Washington   Total Area: 7,486 acres
Tribal Enrollment: 950

The Port Madison Indian Reservation covers more than 7,400 acres on the Kitsap Peninsula. Five miles west of Seattle, the reservation is composed of two separate areas: the northern end has the village of Indianola, and the southwestern end includes the village of Suquamish. The 1855 Treaty of Point Elliott placed the Suquamish people on their present-day reservation. Sealth, chief of the Suquamish in the mid-1800s, is Seattle's namesake.

The Suquamish people and their ancestors have lived, hunted, and fished in the heavily populated Puget Sound area for several thousand years. In the late 1700s, Capt. George Vancouver sailed into Puget Sound, bringing trade items as well as small-pox, measles, and other European diseases. Missionaries arrived during the 1830s and '40s to establish schools and churches. Today, Suquamish people practice a variety of religions, including traditional, Indian Shaker, Catholic, and Christian. Lushoot-seed, or Puget Sound Salish, is the Suquamish Native language and has largely been replaced by English,

SPIRITUALITY

Tribes of the Northwest Coast are blessed with a bountiful environment. Today, as in the past, thanks is given for all the gifts that nourish and sustain the people in their prayers, songs, and dances. Failing to do so might anger the spirits who cause rain to fall, trees to grow, rivers to run, and salmon to spawn. Many tribes honored the first salmon they caught each year to show their appreciation for its offerings and ensure that it would come again the following year. Among the Nuu-chah-nulth (Nootka), the first catch was treated as an honored guest and sprinkled with eagle down, a gesture of peace and goodwill. After a formal welcome made by the village chief, a celebratory feast would take place. Afterward, the bones of the fish were returned to the water so that its spirit would endure and find its way back to the village the following year.

Some tribal clans trace their origins to ancestors who encountered animal spirits and received gifts or special powers from them. In some cases, when an animal was responsible for a person's death, the loss was repaid by the family of the deceased having the right to use that animal or its spirit as a crest, which then became property of their clan.

Like other indigenous groups, members of Northwest Coast tribes sometimes meditated in isolation, away from their communities. Young people around the age of puberty often went off alone for long periods, eating little or nothing. The intense concentration and fasting sometimes brought people in touch with spirits who could take various forms, either human or animal. These spirits would instruct them about powers they could acquire or already possessed but were unaware of.

Both men and women obtained gifts in this way, including the power to heal the sick and foresee the future, and were highly regarded in their communities. These people, known as *shamans,* performed healing ceremonies and other rituals wearing headdresses, masks, or other regalia honoring the spirits to whom they attributed their gifts. Native people blessed with healing and prophetic powers are still greatly respected among tribes of the Northwest Coast and undergo lifelong preparation and training to fulfill their calling. ■

A shaman's rattle portrays land otters—animals thought to cause insanity—perched on the back of a shorebird.

TLINGIT

The Tlingit live in and around southeastern Alaska and have a population of more than 20,000. There are coastal and inland Tlingit. The inland Tlingit's traditional territory lies eastward of the mountains along the Alaska–British Columbia border. Coastal Tlingit live west of those mountains on inlets and islands along the Pacific and have much in common culturally with the neighboring Haida and other tribes of the Northwest Coast. In Tlingit society, everyone belongs to one of two groups, or moieties. One is called Raven, and the other is called Eagle in some places, Wolf in others. All traditional Tlingit marriages united a member of one group with a member of the other. Each moiety consists of numerous clans. Children are born into their mother's group and clan. Relatives on the mother's side often share in raising the children, providing them with a wide circle of elders to guide them.

Clan members are not necessarily related by blood, but consider themselves descendants of a common ancestor or spirit, who bequeathed to the clan its crest. Tlingit clans are identified by the crests of animals, natural wonders, or supernatural beings, including Salmon, Bear, Ocean, Moon, and Thunderbird. Clans also have names, which are different from the titles of their crests. Clan crests are carved or painted on totem poles, house posts, screens, drums, bowls, spoons, and hats. The Tlingit refer to their crests and other clan keepsakes as *at.óow,* meaning "our belongings." Those belongings include songs, stories, and regalia. Some forms of clan belongings can be sold or exchanged.

The Tlingit and other Natives of the Northwest Coast likened the many species of fish and game they pursued to clans, which were sometimes friendly and sometimes hostile. The killing of a Tlingit by a grizzly bear might be avenged in much the same way as an attack by a rival clan. The various species of salmon are viewed as friendly clans, who kindly arrive at different times to allow more fish to be harvested.

Conflict and Accommodation

The Russians who intruded on Tlingit territory in the late 1700s met with strong opposition. Tlingit warriors wore wooden body armor and helmets and

A Tlingit wears traditional regalia at a modern potlatch in Haines, Alaska.

were acquiring firearms from coastal traders of other nationalities when Russians settled with Aleut hunters in Sitka in 1799. Three years later, the Tlingit destroyed that colony. Anticipating retaliation, they felled spruce trees and built a massive fort. In 1804, the Russians returned with warships and pounded that fort, but it proved so strong that cannonballs could not penetrate it. After repulsing an attack by Russian and Aleut forces, however, the Tlingit ran out of gunpowder and had to withdraw. The Russians then dismantled the fort and rebuilt their settlement.

In time, the Tlingit reached an accommodation with the settlers and began trading with them. Russian Orthodox priests, like Ivan Veniaminov, who came to Sitka in 1834, were more tolerant of tribal traditions than some other missionaries and converted a number of Tlingits to their faith. Veniaminov vaccinated Natives against smallpox, which was taking a heavy toll here as elsewhere along the Northwest Coast.

Sold to America

When the U.S. bought Alaska from Russia in 1867, the Tlingit objected that it was not Russia's to sell. They never entered into a treaty ceding any part of their land or establishing tribal reservations. The act organizing Alaska as U.S. territory stated that Natives should not be disturbed in possession of lands "now actually in their

Tlingit clan members assemble at Klukwan, Alaska, in 1895 for a potlatch at the Whale House, which was filled with splendid carvings, including a sculpted human head.

use or occupation or now claimed by them." But that did not give them legal title to their lands, which were often encroached on by settlers or claimed as government property.

Tlingit activists founded the Alaska Native Brotherhood in 1912 and the Alaska Native Sisterhood in 1923 to assert their rights as Americans, including voting and property rights. Other tribes in British Columbia and the U.S.

formed similar civic organizations during this period, which saw increasing intertribal cooperation. The Central Council of the Tlingit and Haida, established in 1935, worked to secure their joint title to Alaskan lands.

In 1971, the Alaska Native Claims Settlement Act granted ten tribal communities and a corporation formed by the Tlingit and Haida title to more than 400,000 acres, increasing their

involvement in Alaska's fishing, logging, and tourist industries. Today, the Tlingit are organizing new businesses and developing their cultural resources by sponsoring the biannual tribal gathering "Celebrate!" and Tlingit language courses for people at all levels, from preschool up through graduate studies at the University of Alaska. Such efforts are opening a new chapter in the life of the Tlingit. ∎

Carver Doug Cranmer of the Kwakwaka'wakw (Kwakiutl) works on a totem pole in his studio at Alert Bay.

but in recent times, Lushootseed has experienced a revival.

The tribe lost much land due to taxation policies and the appropriation of land for military use by the government. Villagers were forcibly relocated to individual allotments across the reservation. Although encouraged to become farmers, most retained their hunting and fishing lifestyles. By 1920, commercial fishing had depleted the salmon runs that had always been central to Suquamish lifeways. Federal assimilation policies removed tribal children from their homes, placed them in boarding schools, and severed contact with their families, languages, religious ceremonies, and homelands. The tribe continues to repair the damage caused by removal and actively promotes cultural practices, believing its members and the natural systems that sustain them are its greatest resources.

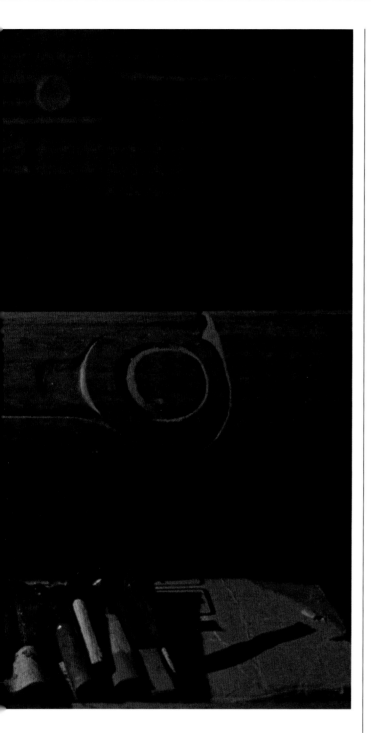

MYTH OR FACT?

Northwest Coast tribes worship totem poles.

MYTH

Northwest Coastal tribes never worshipped totem poles. There are several varieties of carved poles found along the Pacific coast, including house posts, totem poles, and mortuary poles. House posts adorn and structurally support houses; totem poles relate clan or family histories; and mortuary poles commemorate the lives of political and spiritual leaders.

PUYALLUP RESERVATION

Tribe: Puyallup Tribe of the Puyallup Reservation
Current Location: Washington
Total Area: 103 acres   Tribal Enrollment: 3,547

The S'Puyalupubsh (meaning "generous and welcoming behavior to all people who enter our lands"), or Puyallup, have resided in the Pacific Northwest for thousands of years. Tribal lands encompassed regions between the foothills of Mount Tacoma and Puget Sound. The Puyallup speak the Lushootseed dialect of the Salish language.

The Puyallup encountered European explorers as early as 1792, when the British entered the area. As settlers moved into the region over the next 50 years, the Puyallup were steadily pushed out of their traditional territory. In 1854, the tribe agreed to the Medicine Creek Treaty, which created reservations for the Puyallup, Nisqually, and Squaxin Island tribes. The reservations were not sufficient for the tribes, though, and a war ensued. In 1856, the treaty was renegotiated and the Puyallup Reservation expanded. In 1886, it was divided into 178 individual allotments. One small area, known as Indian Addition, was the only tract of land to remain in tribal ownership. Encroachments by whites resulted in losses of lands and rights, especially with regard to fishing.

In the 1960s and '70s, the Puyallups played a pivotal role in the return of treaty-protected fishing rights to Washington tribes. Since the turn of the 20th century, the state of Washington had ignored federal treaties, intent on eliminating Indian gill net fishing outside reservation borders. Nets were seized and tribal members were assaulted and repeatedly arrested, with cases appealed to higher and higher levels of the state and federal courts. Members of the general public, including many non-Indian supporters, joined in demonstrations, referred to as "fish-ins," which attracted state and national news coverage. A succession of state and federal court cases was overturned, as language in the treaty and subsequent state laws seemed contradictory.

Suits filed under the 1951 Indian Claims Commission Act began to bear fruit in the mid-1970s. In order to coordinate efforts among the various Northwestern coastal tribes with respect to the fishing struggles, the Puyallup Tribal Council was pivotal in developing the Inter-Tribal Planning Consortium.

In 1990, the tribe signed the Puyallup Tribe of Indians Settlement Act of 1989 in resolution of their long-standing land claims. Throughout the 1990s, the Puyallup built a tribal infrastructure and assumed leadership on key intergovernmental boards to protect cultural resources for the future benefit of all tribal members, draft ecology and wildlife protection policies based on sound watershed quality analyses, and develop air quality standards.

QUILEUTE RESERVATION

Tribe: Quileute Tribe of the Quileute Reservation
Current Location: Washington   Total Area: 880 acres
Tribal Enrollment: 706

Archaeological finds along the coast of Washington indicate that the area has been inhabited for many thousands of years. Quileute tribal genealogy is linked to people who lived during the Ice Age, making them possibly the oldest inhabitants of the Pacific Northwest. The people practiced a hunting, fishing, and gathering subsistence lifestyle, dominated by the widespread use of whale and seal oil, which were also valuable trading commodities. Traditional homes were constructed of cedar, and cedar canoes were used for hunting and fishing. The last whaling days were held in 1910; the last seal hunts were in 1955.

Land-hungry white settlers began arriving in 1830. The Quileute were party to the Quinault Treaty of 1855 and the Treaty of Olympia, signed in 1856, wherein the U.S. government demanded that they move to Taholah, on the Quinault Reservation, in exchange for 800,000 acres of ceded aboriginal territory. The demands were never enforced, however, and in an executive order of 1889, President William H. Harrison established a one-square-mile reservation for the 252-member Quileute tribe. The original village site of La Push burned later that same year while tribal members were in the neighboring village of Puyallup harvesting hops. The fire consumed 26 buildings and the last remaining carved masks, baskets, hunting equipment, and sacred regalia from precontact days.

The Quileute language is from the Chimakuan family of languages, one of a few polysyllabic languages with no nasal sounds, such as *m* or *n*. In 1971, the Quileute Cultural Committee created a Quileute

FOOD

The Northwest Coast tribes derive much of their food from the sea and the rivers flowing into it. Among the fish they rely on are five species of salmon: coho, sockeye, chinook (king), pink (humpback), and chum (dog salmon). Some salmon are caught with hook and line early in the year as they gather in bays or inlets. Most, however, are taken in late summer or fall as they surge up rivers and streams to spawn.

Traditionally, many tribes moved seasonally in anticipation of those salmon runs and maintained summer homes at their fishing camps. Among the traditional devices used to snare salmon were basket traps and weirs, which guided fish to enclosures where they could be speared or netted. Much of the catch was dried or smoked to provide food through the winter. These winter preparations of the salmon are still practiced today.

Other fish caught in coastal waters included steelhead trout, sturgeon, and halibut, as well as herring, which could be raked in as they spawned in shallow water in early spring. Clams and other mollusks were gathered at low tide with digging sticks. Game made up a smaller part of the diet, but deer and elk were hunted by many tribes, as were waterfowl and marine mammals, such as whales, seals, and sea otters. Native peoples also harvested hundreds of wild plants, including ferns, bulbs, nuts, lichen, mushrooms, and berries.

Traditional subsistence activities remain important to tribes of the Northwest Coast, who have recently reclaimed fishing or hunting rights infringed on by settlers or government authorities. Among those who benefited from the Boldt Decision in 1974 restoring fishing rights to tribes in Washington are the Lummi, who operate one of the nation's most productive salmon hatcheries at their reservation on Puget Sound. ∎

Makahs at Neah Bay on Washington's Olympic Peninsula carve up a whale, a rich source of meat, bone, and oil for coastal tribes that hunted the marine mammal in their canoes.

dictionary and established a language teaching program. In 1996, according to the tribe, there were only five fluent speakers left; However, children attending the Quileute Tribal School are learning the language, along with traditional arts and crafts. In the 1990s, there was a revival of interest in canoe carving, and many people raise a special breed of woolly-haired dogs whose hair is cut and spun into highly prized blankets.

QUINAULT RESERVATION

Tribe: Quinault Tribe of the Quinault Reservation [Hoh, Quileute, Chehalis, Chinook, and Cowlitz]
Current Location: Washington
Total Area: 208,105 acres **Tribal Enrollment:** 2,454

Membership of the modern Quinault Indian Nation includes the Quinault themselves and descendants of five additional coastal tribes: Hoh, Quileute, Chehalis, Chinook, and Cowlitz. They speak a Lower Chehalis dialect of the Quinault language, part of the coastal division of the Salish linguistic family. Prior to first contact, the Quinault ("Canoe People" or "People of the Cedar Tree") lived in large longhouses, practicing a subsistence lifestyle.

The first recorded contact between the Quinault and Europeans occurred in 1775, when a Spanish vessel came ashore, provoking a hostile response from the Quinault and resulting in several deaths on both sides. For the next 80 years, the tribe attempted unsuccessfully to distance itself from the region's growing non-Indian settlements. On July 1, 1855, under pressure from the U.S. government, the Quinault, along with the Quileute and the Hoh, signed the Quinault River Treaty, giving up vast amounts of territory, while reserving economically and ceremonially vital lands for their own use. Treaties in 1855 and 1856 established a 10,000-acre reservation at Taholah in exchange for all lands north of Gray's Harbor, expanded to 20,000 acres on November 4, 1873, when an executive order formally established the reservation's boundaries.

As shown here, the traditional fishing gear of the Makah included long hooks used to catch halibut and other large deepwater fish and a sinker to submerge those hooks.

The 1887 General Allotment Act divided the reservation into individual allotments. By 1933, virtually no commonly held tribal lands remained. The allotment process, along with corrupt and irresponsible BIA management of lands leased to the timber companies, ultimately resulted in vast areas of clear-cut hillsides, decimated river valleys, and the displacement of tribal members. In the 2000 census, nearly 50 percent of all Quinaults lived off-reservation. Even more tragic is the loss of Native speakers of the Quinault language. In 1990, when the entire reservation population numbered approximately 1,500, there were only six speakers of Quinault.

The Quinault Indian Nation restored some traditional cultural practices in the latter decades of the 20th century. In 1989, it formed the Quinault Canoe Society and revived the long-standing custom of the Canoe Journey, and its members continue to practice potlatch and other ceremonies.

SKOKOMISH RESERVATION

Tribe: Skokomish Indian Tribe of the Skokomish Reservation [Twana] **Current Location:** Washington
Total Area: 5,169 acres **Tribal Enrollment:** 750

The Twana, or Skokomish, people originally resided in the Hood Canal drainage basin in present-day Washington. The Twana subsisted on hunting, fishing, and gathering. Extended families served as the key social groups in the Twana culture. Tribal members lived in communities of one or more households, or with related tribal members in other Twana villages within or outside the tribe's traditional territory. The communities were self-sufficient.

A portion of tribal lands located between the west and main channels at the mouth of the Skokomish River were seized around 1900. Subsequent dikes and farming on the lands caused the depletion of a number of plant species, including the sweet grass variety tribal members used in their weaving. Between 1926 and 1930, the City of Tacoma constructed two dams

MAKAH

The Makah make their home on Cape Flattery in Washington, at the northwestern tip of the continental United States. They call themselves Qwiqwidicciat ("People of the Cape") and have a population of more than 1,500, most of whom live in the town of Neah Bay, within their reservation. They have long been a fishing and whaling people, drawing on the resources of the Strait of Juan de Fuca and the Pacific Ocean. The ancestral territory of the Makah was much larger than the reservation they occupy today and extended as far south as Ozette Lake, beyond which lay the territory of the Quileute. Their neighbors to the east were the Klallam, a Coast Salish tribe with whom they traded and sometimes intermarried.

The Makah resided in five permanent villages, including Neah Bay and Ozette, now an important archaeological site. In summer, many people moved to fishing or hunting grounds situated elsewhere on the mainland or on islands like Tatoosh, off Cape Flattery.

Wealth from the Whale

The most prestigious subsistence activity of the Makah was the whale hunt, reserved for men of high rank, who performed rituals beforehand to ensure that whales would offer themselves to the hunters. The whale meat and oil was evenly distributed among villagers after the hunters had taken their share. Like other tribes of the Northwest Coast, the Makah developed a social hierarchy as chiefs and heads of households amassed wealth and prestige through lucrative activities like whaling and bequeathed their possessions and privileges to their heirs.

Leaders of the Makah displayed their wealth and generosity by hosting potlatches on important occasions, such as births and marriages or the death of a leader and the subsequent transfer of his rights and property to his heir. That inheritance included songs, dances, and

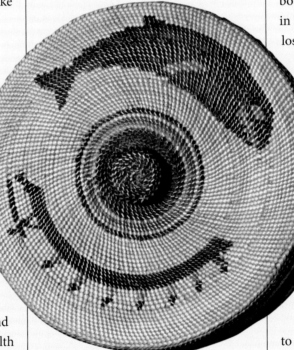

A basket cover depicts Native whalers in a canoe, pursuing their prey.

stories, passed down from one generation to the next and shared by hosts with their guests at potlatches. This cherished tradition was threatened when the Makah came under the authority of the U.S. government, which, like Canada, tried to eradicate potlatches and other tribal ceremonies.

Trials and Treaties

The Makah were forced to come to terms with the government after they were decimated by smallpox, measles, and other diseases acquired from Europeans and Americans, who began arriving here in the 1790s. By the time the Strait of Juan de Fuca was designated as a boundary between the U.S. and Canada in 1845, the Makah were suffering severe losses to epidemics. In 1852, they abandoned one of their villages, Biheda, because there were too few people left to maintain that community.

The Makah risked losing everything to incoming American settlers unless they entered into a treaty reserving to them part of their land and resources. Thus, in 1855 they signed the Treaty of Neah Bay, ceding more than 300,000 acres of territory to the United States. In exchange, the government agreed to recognize their right to hunt whales and catch salmon and other fish in their "usual and accustomed grounds" and pledged to provide health services and education to the Makah on their newly created reservation. Government instructors, though, in teaching children English and American customs, discouraged the use of the Makah language and tried to suppress their traditions. Although the Makah continued to fish and hunt seals and whales along the coast, they had to compete with other tribes and commercial fisherman for the limited resources.

By the early 1900s, commercial hunting had reduced the gray whales found in Makah waters to near extinction. They voluntarily ceased whaling in the 1920s, with the understanding that they could resume hunts in the future. Fishing then became increasingly important to them. In 1974, the Makah and other tribes in Washington won a major victory in court known as the Boldt Decision that affirmed their traditional fishing rights, as recognized in treaties, and significantly boosted their share of the commercial salmon harvest.

A Return to Tradition

By the 1990s, the population of gray whales, protected as an endangered species since 1972, had rebounded. The Makah obtained permission from the government and the International Whaling Commission to resume hunts on a limited basis. In 1999, amid intense media scrutiny, they took their first whale in 70 years. Critics protested the hunt, but indigenous peoples from around the world supported their right to resume an age-old practice guaranteed to them by treaty and joined in celebrating their return to whaling.

Recently, the Makah have again faced legal challenges to their right to hunt whales. But other efforts to uphold their traditions have been notably successful. Potlatches, once held secretly in defiance of government restrictions, are now openly celebrated. Through the efforts of the Makah Cultural and Research Center, they have preserved their language by incorporating it into their educational system along with English, beginning in preschool.

The archaeological discoveries at Ozette, where more than 50,000 tribal artifacts have been unearthed, affirm Makah oral tradition stating that they have occupied their lands for thousands of years. Some of those artifacts are on display at the Makah Museum in Neah Bay, revealing the historical roots from which Makah culture continues to grow. ∎

A Makah artist paints a ceremonial mask at his doorstep around 1900. The Makah preserved such traditions despite efforts by reservation agents to root out tribal customs.

on the North Fork of the Skokomish River, destroying important cultural sites, ravaging salmon and fish resources, and creating increased restrictions on the tribe's saltwater access and shellfish gathering. Further resources were lost when Potlatch State Park was created along the shoreline in 1960.

The 1974 Boldt Decision allowed the tribe to harvest 50 percent of each run of salmon returning to traditional Indian fishing areas and to comanage, with the state, the important fishery and other natural resources on and adjacent to the reservation and in its traditional (pretreaty) areas.

The Skokomish people are actively restoring traditional cultural elements. While a number of traditional ceremonies and practices had been largely unused for nearly a century, by the late 1970s, tribal members were beginning to revitalize traditional basketry, carving, weaving, spiritual ceremonies, and dances.

SNOQUAIMIE RESERVATION

Tribe: Snoqualmie Tribe
Current Location: Washington   Total Area: 56 acres
Tribal Enrollment: 1,000

The Snoqualmie tribe lived in the Puget Sound region, hunting deer, elk, and other game animals, fishing for salmon, and gathering berries and wild plants. Historically, tribal members lived in an area that now contains the communities of Monroe, Carnation, Fall City, Snoqualmie, North Bend, Mercer Island, and Issaquah. Snoqualmie means "People of the Moon Transformer." Snoqualm, the Changer or Transformer, is an important figure in Puget Sound Salish legend and spirituality.

Patkanim was the principal chief of the Snoqualmie during the treaty negotiations and armed conflicts of the 1850s. Patkanim was initially hostile toward white settlers, but after traveling to San Francisco in 1850 and seeing the masses of Europeans

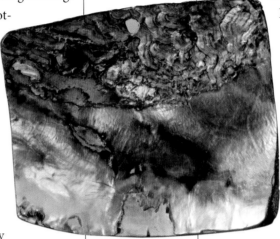

Polished shells like this abalone plaque were prized as ornaments by coastal tribes. Others served as currency, like the tooth-shaped dentalium shell.

and Americans flooding west, he decided that cooperating with white settlers offered his people a better chance of survival. When other Native leaders rose up against white settlements in the Puget Sound area, Patkanim's people became scouts and fought alongside the settlers and the government against neighboring tribes. In 1855, the Snoqualmie signed the Point Elliott Treaty. Despite the help that Patkanim and his people had offered to the settlers, the treaty negotiations left them with no reservation of their own. In legal limbo for many years, tribe members were scattered around the area, though some stayed in the valley of their ancestors.

The efforts of Chief Patkanim's nephew, Chief Jerry Kanim, helped preserve the identity of the Snoqualmie tribe into the late 20th century and laid the groundwork for successful federal recognition efforts in the 1990s. After a struggle of nearly 47 years, in October 1999 the BIA once again granted the Snoqualmie tribal status based on evidence that the tribe had maintained a continuous community from historical times to the present.

SQUAXIN ISLAND RESERVATION

Tribe: Squaxin Island Tribe of the Squaxin Island Reservation [Noo-Seh-Chatl, Steh Chass, Squi-Aitl, Sawamish/T'Peeksin, Sa-Heh-Wa-Mish, Squawksin, S'Hotle-Ma-Mish]
Current Location: Washington   Total Area: 2,054 acres
Tribal Enrollment: 782

Like many tribes of the Pacific Northwest, the Squaxin Island Tribe, People of the Water, is made up of descendants of the original maritime inhabitants of the seven inlets of South Puget Sound.

The people of Squaxin Island were signatories to the Treaty of Medicine Creek of 1854, along with the Puyallup and the Nisqually, wherein the tribes ceded 2.56 million acres of aboriginal territory to the federal government. Following the war of 1856–57 that erupted after the tribes realized the extent of the government's duplicity, hundreds of people from the various tribes were confined for a time on the island. Out of thousands of square miles of land ceded to the U.S. government, the tiny island was retained as the main reservation area.

This community became a headquarters for the Indian agency and a school; a blacksmith shop and a church were established. Many fled the island after failed attempts at farming left them in poverty, becoming loggers or working in the hop and berry fields of the mainland. By 1862, the number of island residents had dwindled to 50, and the Indian agency headquarters was moved to Puyallup. By 1959, only four year-round residents continued to live on Squaxin Island, and currently there are none. However, the island is still a place of great spiritual significance to the tribe.

Many tribal members belong to the Indian Shaker Church founded by Squaxin tribal member John Slocum in the late 1880s. The original church was established on a place now known as Church Point. The Squaxin have also revived many cultural practices in recent decades. From trees that were alive prior to the New World arrival of Christopher Columbus, the tribe initiated the Canoe Project, carving a huge canoe in the old way, to be utilized during an annual flotilla reminiscent of the ancestors' travel upon the waters of Puget Sound.

STILLAGUAMISH RESERVATION

Tribe: Stillaguamish Tribe of Washington
Current Location: Washington
Total Area: 265 acres   **Tribal Enrollment:** 182

Members of the Stillaguamish Tribe are descendants of the Stoluckwamish River Tribe. At its peak, the tribe's total population is estimated to have been nearly 3,000.

After contact, the tribe traded with settlers, and tribal members were often employed to clear land and harvest crops. As more settlers arrived in the region, the Stillaguamish were forced to cede their lands. The Treaty of Point Elliott in 1855 called for the tribe to relinquish its lands in exchange for federal assistance and designated lands for participating

CLOTHING

The traditional garments and shoes of people along the Northwest Coast were made from the skins of animals or woven from local plant fibers, such as cedar bark. In cold weather, people wore cloaks or blankets made of fur or leather. Most hats were made from grasses, cedar bark, or spruce roots and were so tightly woven that they were water repellent. During ceremonies, clan leaders wore hats sculpted of wood and painted to represent the clan's crest. Garments were sewn with sinew or thread made of plant fiber and decorated with shells, shell beads, and animal pelts or parts, such as claws and teeth. Personal adornments included earrings, lip rings or labrets, tattoos, necklaces, and masks worn by dancers or healers to represent spirits, animals, and ancestors.

When tribes began trading with Europeans, they acquired cloth, thread made of cotton or silk, glass beads, and other items. By combining those new materials with their customary materials, they fashioned button blankets and robes, tunics modeled after military uniforms, and other garments now considered traditional. Native people of the Northwest Coast have long worn European-style clothing for everyday purposes and dress traditionally only during potlatches and other special occasions. ■

Animal bones and teeth adorn a necklace belonging to a Haida shaman.

tribes. A separate reservation was not established for the Stillaguamish people; instead, the tribe was required to relocate to the Tulalip Reservation, originally located on Whidbey Island. While a number of tribal members did remain on the Tulalip Reservation, a number returned to their ancestral lands along the Stillaguamish River. Because the majority of the tribe refused to leave their homelands and reside on a reservation, the federal government rescinded recognition of the tribe in 1870.

By the 1900s, the tribe had become very dispersed. In 1920, the population was only 29. That year, under the guidance of tribal member Esther Ross, the Stillaguamish began their quest for federal recognition, and in 1953 they adopted a tribal constitution. In 1970, the Indian Claims Commission awarded the tribe a $64,460 judgment for the former 58,600 acres of tribal lands. In the 1974 Boldt Decision, the tribe was granted fishing rights based on treaty guarantees. The tribe petitioned for federal recognition in 1974, and in 1976 it was granted status.

SWINOMISH RESERVATION

Tribe: Swinomish Indians of the Swinomish Reservation [Swinomish, Kikiallus, Lower Skagit, and Samish] Current Location: Washington
Total Area: 3,630 acres Tribal Enrollment: 787

The modern Swinomish Reservation is occupied by descendants of aboriginal Swinomish, Kikiallus, Lower Skagit, and Samish tribes, who lived in the region for thousands of years. First contact came with white explorers in the 1500s; however, the tribes remained relatively unaffected until large numbers of permanent settlers entered aboriginal hunting and gathering areas.

The reservation was formed by executive order in 1873 following the 1855 Treaty of Point Elliott. Through the provisions of the General Allotment Act of 1887, reservation lands passed largely from communal to individual ownership as part of a strategy to "civilize" the Indians, opening the door to the eventual alienation of nearly half of the reservation lands from the hands of tribal members.

MYTH OR FACT?
All Indians in Alaska are Eskimos.

MYTH
Native people in Alaska are not known as Indians. They are called Alaska Natives. There are many different tribal groups in Alaska, each with their own name, language, customs, and traditions.

In 1892, the commissioner of Indian affairs prohibited the traditional Spirit Dance, Indian medicine, and plural marriage; however, dancing and other ceremonies continued underground at various locations throughout the region. By the 1920s, conditions for the Swinomish were dire: housing and health conditions were poor, Indian agents had actively undermined the tribe's political autonomy, and the BIA Tulalip School overtly rejected traditional values and the use or teaching of Salish dialects.

Through inspired leadership, the circumstances of the Swinomish people improved somewhat during the 1930s. The tribe established its constitution in 1936 under the Indian Reorganization Act and created a tribal senate. The reactionary Tulalip School was closed, and Swinomish children began attending public schools in La Conner. Economically, the tribe made some progress during this period as well.

Restrictions on practices like the Winter Spirit Dance were removed in the 1930s, and today interest in traditional culture and language is strong. A traditional longhouse replica was dedicated in 1996, and there is increasing involvement in Seowyn practice and the rituals of the smokehouse, spiritual traditions integral to the tribe's cultural identity. By 2004, about 1,100 acres of reservation land had been recouped. The tribe is a Harvard Tribal Governance Awards Program Honoring Nations honoree (2000) for its innovative Cooperative Land Use Program.

A Makah wearing a mask and cape performs the Wolf Dance, one of many ceremonies preserved and performed by Natives of the Northwest Coast today.

CHAPTER 8

CALIFORNIA

CALIFORNIA

BEFORE EUROPEANS ARRIVED, ROUGHLY 300,000 TO A MILLION INDIGENOUS people from more than 500 nations lived in what is now California. This area is large and geographically diverse with a correspondingly diverse indigenous population.

In today's society, Native Americans live in homes that are like the homes that any American lives in, and wear the types of clothing that most non-Natives wear. However, many of them go to dance lodges or other sacred spaces for events or ceremonies for which they change from their street clothes into traditional clothing. They may practice both their traditional religion and Christianity. They may work 9-to-5 jobs and then spend their weekends gathering traditional materials to make baskets or attending language classes on their reservation or rancheria. There is a balance that Native people have to develop to carry their histories with them yet still function in contemporary America.

Among California Indians, there are large differences in indigenous languages, lifeways, clothing, beliefs, and ceremonies. There are at least six language groups and more than a hundred federally recognized tribes in the state's 58 counties. There are also a number of tribes without federal recognition; a list of these is maintained by the Native American Heritage Commission. Additionally, many tribes may not currently occupy or may have limited access to their cultural lands due to forced relocation by Spain, Mexico, or the United States.

> THERE IS A BALANCE THAT NATIVE PEOPLE HAVE TO DEVELOP TO CARRY THEIR HISTORIES WITH THEM YET STILL FUNCTION IN CONTEMPORARY AMERICA.

GENOCIDE, RELIGION, AND SLAVERY

THESE DAYS, WE ACKNOWLEDGE THAT SCHOOLS HAVE GROSSLY MISINFORMED STUDENTS about Native American history. This happened because colonizing powers always interpret events from their own perspective. It is hard for a colonial power that is still occupying territory to be objective about how it achieved dominance. At the time of contact, Native people were already familiar with issues of cross-cultural identities, economies, slavery, war, and competition for resources; these were not new and were not introduced by Europeans. However, the introduction of Europeans increased these complexities, and the subjugation of indigenous peoples made it possible to silence their voices.

It is a hard and painful truth that many atrocities were committed against Native Californians, and these often have been left out of our historical, social, and political narrative. If one reads anthropological, sociological, and linguistic data collected by scientists from the early 1900s, their arrogance and ethnocentric bias is apparent. Those people with Eurocentric values

Preceding pages: Karuk fishermen use dip nets at Ishi Pishi Falls on the Klamath River. Opposite: Butch Marks, a Yurok tribal member, holds freshly caught salmon.

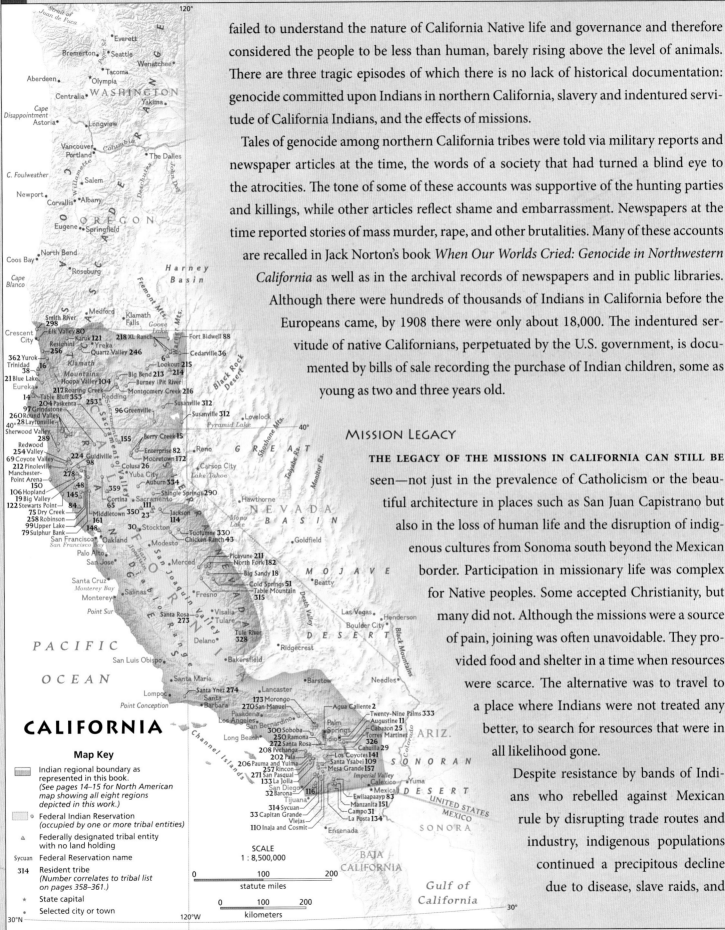

CALIFORNIA

Map Key

- Indian regional boundary as represented in this book. *(See pages 14–15 for North American map showing all eight regions depicted in this work.)*
- Federal Indian Reservation *(occupied by one or more tribal entities)*
- Federally designated tribal entity with no land holding
- Sycuan   Federal Reservation name
- 314   Resident tribe *(Number correlates to tribal list on pages 358–361.)*
- ★   State capital
- •   Selected city or town

SCALE
1 : 8,500,000

0   100   200
statute miles

0   100   200
kilometers

failed to understand the nature of California Native life and governance and therefore considered the people to be less than human, barely rising above the level of animals. There are three tragic episodes of which there is no lack of historical documentation: genocide committed upon Indians in northern California, slavery and indentured servitude of California Indians, and the effects of missions.

Tales of genocide among northern California tribes were told via military reports and newspaper articles at the time, the words of a society that had turned a blind eye to the atrocities. The tone of some of these accounts was supportive of the hunting parties and killings, while other articles reflect shame and embarrassment. Newspapers at the time reported stories of mass murder, rape, and other brutalities. Many of these accounts are recalled in Jack Norton's book *When Our Worlds Cried: Genocide in Northwestern California* as well as in the archival records of newspapers and in public libraries. Although there were hundreds of thousands of Indians in California before the Europeans came, by 1908 there were only about 18,000. The indentured servitude of native Californians, perpetuated by the U.S. government, is documented by bills of sale recording the purchase of Indian children, some as young as two and three years old.

MISSION LEGACY

THE LEGACY OF THE MISSIONS IN CALIFORNIA CAN STILL BE seen—not just in the prevalence of Catholicism or the beautiful architecture in places such as San Juan Capistrano but also in the loss of human life and the disruption of indigenous cultures from Sonoma south beyond the Mexican border. Participation in missionary life was complex for Native peoples. Some accepted Christianity, but many did not. Although the missions were a source of pain, joining was often unavoidable. They provided food and shelter in a time when resources were scarce. The alternative was to travel to a place where Indians were not treated any better, to search for resources that were in all likelihood gone.

Despite resistance by bands of Indians who rebelled against Mexican rule by disrupting trade routes and industry, indigenous populations continued a precipitous decline due to disease, slave raids, and murder; some reports put the loss of life at more than 50 percent. In some regards, the Indians were very successful, but they had no immunity to foreign diseases, which turned Indian villages into graveyards.

In 1848, the signing of the Treaty of Guadalupe Hidalgo marked the end of Mexican rule over California. Survival was even more difficult under U.S. control. The first governor of California, Peter Burnett, said in his 1849 inaugural speech, "That a war of extermination will continue to be waged between the two races until the Indian race becomes extinct, must be expected."

> AMONG CALIFORNIA INDIANS . . . THERE ARE MORE THAN A HUNDRED FEDERALLY RECOGNIZED TRIBES.

RANCHERIAS AND RESERVATIONS

MOST OF US ARE FAMILIAR WITH RESERVATIONS, LAND THAT WAS set aside in the 19th century as places for Native Americans to live separately from other Americans. Many California Indians now live in settlements called rancherias. There is no difference between a reservation and a rancheria. In California, "rancheria" is used north of the Los Angeles area and "reservation" to the south. The use of the term rancheria, which is unique to California, may be due to the Spanish and Mexican influences in the state.

If you can, imagine that you and scores of your neighbors are ordered to move to a city that is about a hundred miles away. You, or your parents, don't have jobs or much food, and there are no jobs in the new city, either. Still, some of your neighbors decide to stay there because they are afraid to go back home or because their mother or little sister can't walk that far. But others of you decide to risk everything just to go home. You and your family walk all the way back—only to find strangers living in your home. So, you are left to live in the woods or camp in a park. Eventually the government decides that you are a problem, so it buys one or two square miles of land near where you used to live and gives that to you. This is what a rancheria, or reservation, is. This is the system devised by the U.S. government to "handle" the Indians who were forcibly removed from their land and homes.

CONTEMPORARY INDIGENOUS CALIFORNIA

TODAY, NATIVE CALIFORNIANS FIGHT HOSTILE RACISM AND AN EDUCATIONAL SYSTEM THAT historically has not promoted or sustained indigenous cultures. They also fight the loss of indigenous languages; struggle with poverty, drug abuse, alcoholism, diabetes, and the bureaucracy surrounding access to resources; and contend with the pervasiveness of popular culture, for example, when young Native people identify with other cultures instead of their own.

Nevertheless, there are some bright spots. For example, the California Indian Basketweavers Association continues to grow and to promote traditional artistic techniques. There are many others who are working at a grassroots level to sustain their lifeways and to stand up to local, state, and federal governments for what is in their tribe's best interests, such as water and fishing rights. ■

AGUA CALIENTE INDIAN RESERVATION

Tribe: Agua Caliente Band of Cahuilla Indians
Total Area: 31,500 acres   **Tribal Enrollment:** 418

The Agua Caliente Band of Cahuilla Indians is composed of several small groups who have lived in the area of present-day Palm Springs for centuries. They named the area Se-Khi, or "Boiling Water," and the Mexicans later renamed it Agua Caliente, meaning "Hot Water." The tribe established complex communities in the Palm, Murray, Andreas, Tahquitz, and Chino Canyons. With abundant water and plant and animal life, the Cahuilla Indians thrived and grew crops; gathered plants and seeds for food, medicines, and basket weaving; and hunted animals. They harvested piñon nuts, acorns, mesquite beans, and the dates of the *Washingtonia filifera,* the only palm native to California. They also ate agaves, which, in addition to food, provided fiber for making nets, slings, sandals, and other items.

Commander José María Estudillo wrote the first recorded history of the tribe in 1822, when the

Chemehuevi, Uto-Aztecan language family

"'suu"
("one")

"wa'ha"
("two")

"pa'hi"
("three")

"waciw"
("four")

"ma'nig"
("five")

Mexicans were seeking a route from Sonora, Mexico, to California. Cahuilla ceremonial life was rich and varied, and the people had a reputation for integrity, peace, and independence. Relatively isolated from the active centers of Spanish colonization and travel, they were initially spared many of the abuses and diseases of Spanish and Mexican immigration. This prosperity and peace ended in the 1860s, when many tribal members died from measles, smallpox, dietary changes, and harassment by whites.

Legacies of the Cahuilla society can still be seen in the Andreas, Murray, Palm, and Tahquitz Canyons that the people traditionally inhabited: There are numerous examples of rock art, cave paintings, house pits and foundations, food preparation areas, irrigation ditches, dams, reservoirs, and ancient trails, as well as the natural features sacred to the people.

Today approximately 10,700 acres of the reservation lie within the city limits of Palm Springs, and the Agua Caliente Band is the city's largest single landowner. The tribal government oversees tribal activities; protects and preserves tribal property, such as wildlife and natural resources; repairs and maintains

Loren Me'-lash-ne Bommelyn has worked to guard the language and traditions of the Tolowa people.

LOREN ME'-LASH-NE BOMMELYN

Tolowa tradition bearer

Loren Bommelyn, also known as Me'-lash-ne, is of Tolowa and Karuk ancestry. He was born in 1956 and grew up between Smith River and Crescent City, small towns near the Oregon border. Smith River is the center of government for the principal population of the Tolowa Dee-ni' at the Smith River Rancheria. As a youth, Bommelyn was often singled out by tribal elders who saw in him a desire and ability to learn Tolowa Dee-ni' culture and language. He has studied basketry, songs, dance ceremony, and oral tradition with the elders.

Bommelyn, who graduated from the University of Oregon with a master's degree in linguistics, credits his parents with instilling in him an awareness of his people's theology and the fortitude to fight for their right to be accurately represented in the state curriculum and in state and federal policy. He assisted with the writing of the Tolowa Dee-ni' language for the first time, a community effort that began in 1969. Until then, the language had been orally transmitted. In 1997, following years of work with Native speakers, he developed the Tolowa Dee-ni' alphabet to meet the computer age. In 2002, the National Endowment for the Arts honored him with a National Heritage Fellowship for his life's work. ∎

Ancient petroglyphs are chipped into the volcanic rock throughout the Owens Valley near Bishop, California, at the foot of the eastern Sierra Nevada mountains.

facilities; cultivates tribal arts and culture; and works with other local governments to foster harmonious relationships. The Agua Caliente Development Authority, formed in 1989, is an economic development subsidiary consisting of tribal and community members and is designed to increase tribal assets.

The mineral springs at Agua Caliente were an ancient gathering place for Cahuilla Indians. The hot springs were traditionally used for curative purposes and bathing. Public bathhouses have been in operation since 1870. The Spa Resort Casino, located in downtown Palm Springs, was purchased by the tribe in 1992 and is an internationally renowned resort. Tribal lands also include Tahquitz, Andreas, Murray, and Palm Canyons, which are located to the southwest of Palm Springs; collectively they are known as Indian Canyons. Listed on the National Register of Historic Places, they offer a vast network of hiking and equestrian trails and are home to the greatest concentration of wild desert palm trees in the world. There are also several streams fed by spring runoff from Mount San Jacinto. The lands of Indian Canyons are operated by the tribe.

The Cahuilla tribe seeks to protect and preserve the natural vegetation, wildlife (the bighorn sheep in particular), and cultural heritage found in their ancestral lands and has drafted a multispecies habitat conservation plan. The Cahuilla were also a founder of the Santa Rosa and San Jacinto Mountains National Monument.

BARONA RESERVATION

Tribe: Barona Group of Capitan Grande Band of Mission Indians [Kumeyaay-Diegueño Nation]
Total Area: 6,295 acres   **Tribal Enrollment:** 455

The residents of the Barona Reservation, located in traditional Kumeyaay-Diegueño territory, speak a Hokan language, an ancient language group found throughout California and into southern Mexico. The coastal country and the Salton Sea

A Karuk spiritual leader performs a traditional welcome dance. The Karuk tribe has long lived on the Klamath River in northern California.

Yurok, Algonquian language family

"Nue-mee noo-rew' kue chee-shep."

("These flowers are beautiful.")

margins contain archaeological evidence suggesting that they are some of the oldest known Indian-inhabited areas in the United States; middens, or refuse heaps, have been found that date back some 20,000 years.

Before 1875, the U.S. government issued permits for Indians to occupy certain areas; no reservations existed. That changed in 1875, when President Ulysses S. Grant's executive order established the Capitan Grande Reservation on 15,573 acres. There are only 12 Kumeyaay reservations today; most of these were set up by Grant's executive order.

In 1932, the Barona group purchased a former ranch situated in traditional Kumeyaay-Diegueño homelands—the original Spanish land grant named La Cañada de San Vicente y el Mesa del Padre Barona. The group resettled there in 1932, bringing with them the remains of their ancestors from the Capitan Grande cemetery. While the Viejas and Barona bands continue to share a joint-trust patent for the Capitan Grande Reservation, no tribal members reside there. Currently living on the Barona Reservation are 'Iipay speakers, formerly residing east of La Jolla, and Tipai speakers, formerly residing in the San Diego area.

Historically, the Kumeyaay people have been politically active in their support for the authority of their tribal leadership. By the late 1800s, many Kumeyaay leaders were forced underground, in response to a BIA order forcing tribal leaders to unequivocally obey local agents. In response, Kumeyaay leaders created organizations that opposed the BIA. Today, however, the tribal government determines its own sovereign rights.

In 1984, the gaming industry began to transform this community into the thriving economic success it is today. The Barona Cultural Center and Museum opened in 2000. It is the only museum in San Diego County dedicated to the area's indigenous populations and features artifacts, dioramas, and exhibits that are a testament to the tribe's presence in the region for

BASKETRY AND PESTICIDES

Basketry is integral to the continuation of the cultural and medicinal traditions of California Indians. The art form embodies stories, family histories, oral traditions, and cultural knowledge.

Traditionally, the basket weaver had access to land to cultivate the necessary plants, to harvest them, and to burn or thatch certain areas so that the plants could grow again.

What happened to disrupt this tradition is well documented. With the takeover of the California territory from Mexico by the U.S. government, there was an unyielding tide of newcomers, shrinking the Indians' land base. These settlers brought with them industry, domesticated animals, and pollution. While the destruction of the lands proved to be cataclysmic, the art and necessity of basketry has continued.

There are continuing threats to this tradition, however. Today, the land base of California Indians is as small as it ever was. Their lands are owned by the government or by individuals who are very reluctant to allow access to areas where traditional plants grow. The basket weavers have to apply and pay a fee for a permit to gain access to these lands; if they are caught without one, they can be and have been jailed.

Additionally, the wide use of herbicides and pesticides by individuals, the National Park Service, and the state of California has contaminated traditional gathering areas. Before European contact, the people contained unwanted or invasive plants through natural measures such as burning. The modern use of pesticides and herbicides raises health issues because while preparing basketmaking materials, weavers run the pieces through their mouths, directly exposing them to dangerous chemicals. Also, the contaminated materials are woven into baby baskets and rattles, thereby exposing children whose immune systems are not fully mature.

Nonetheless, the basketry tradition continues. Notably, in 1992, California Indians banded together to form the California Indian Basketweavers Association to advocate for and provide support to basket weavers and to protect traditional lands and lifeways. Their baskets are highly prized by collectors and can sell for thousands of dollars. ∎

CALIFORNIA

Farmers spray fields to control pests, but the use of chemicals has upset the ecological balance in areas where Native Americans have traditionally gathered basketry materials.

CHEMEHUEVI

Chemehuevi are most often identified as Great Basin Indians. Their name comes from a Mohave term meaning "Those Who Play with Fish." The Chemehuevi's name for themselves is Nuwu, or "The People." Tribes that are Chemehuevi are the Mokwat, Yagat, Howait, Tumplsagavatsit, Kauyaichit, and Moviat. Historically, their high desert ancestral territory spanned Arizona, California, and Nevada, from the Colorado River on the east to the Tehachapi Mountains on the west and from the Las Vegas area and Death Valley in the north to the San Bernardino and San Gabriel Mountains in the south. Today their reservation is made up of 32,000 acres of land in and around Lake Havasu, California, and includes Colorado River frontage.

Losing the Land

In 1853, the Chemehuevi lost their traditional lands when the federal government declared them public domain. Authorities established the Chemehuevi Valley Reservation in 1907, but the people were relocated to the Parker, Arizona, area and their status as a tribe was taken away. In 1935, Congress authorized the acquisition of much of the reservation for the Parker Dam project. By 1940, 8,000 acres of traditional Nuwuvi lands were underwater. After many years of persistence, the Chemehuevi were federally acknowledged in 1970.

The Chemehuevi split from the Southern Paiute in the Las Vegas area before the early 19th century and moved toward what is now called the Chemehuevi Valley and the area south of it on the Colorado River. They lived in relative harmony with local tribes, sharing the Mojave Desert's resources and living just far enough apart that they would not encounter each other.

Their material culture reflected the resources around them. The Chemehuevi were skilled basketmakers, using a coiling technique that was distinctive from others in the area because their baskets had constricted necks. Their caps, carrying baskets, and other materials were diagonally twined, and they usually painted designs on them, as opposed to weaving them into the basket. They also used local materials such as cane, willow, or, in special cases, sinew-backed hickory or willow to create bow and arrows.

Johnny Hill, Jr., one of the last speakers of the Chemehuevi language, at age 53 in 2008

They had four different kinds of houses. One was a flat or shade house, built for ceremonies. Another was a flat house built to store goods that would be brought to a Cry, a time of mourning where the goods would be burned or given away. The other two types had sloping roofs.

The Chemehuevi food sources were seeds, hearts of mescal, meat, melons, and squashes, which would be dried and stored in pots or baskets within caves. Food was scarce enough that if goods were stolen, it was cause for war.

The most complete ethnography of the Chemehuevi was written by Carobeth Laird, the wife of George Laird, a Chemehuevi tribal member. In an article entitled "Chemehuevi Religious Beliefs and Practices," she recounts many stories told to her by her husband in the early years of the 20th century. She describes Chemehuevi origins, shamans, a shaman's familiar, and the rules and reasons for a Cry, which is a Gathering but can also be a burial. In earlier times there was a difference between a Gathering, where chief would address the people, and a Cry, but there have been times where the two were blended.

Stories and Songs

There are at least two variations of the Chemehuevi creation story. Both start when there was nothing but water. The four main beings were Ocean Woman, Mountain Lion, Wolf, and Coyote; these four maintain a strong presence throughout Chemehuevi storytelling. Additionally, in 1889 and 1890,

A coiled basket with curved sides made by the Chemehuevi between 1905 and 1910

the Ghost Dance was a presence in Chemehuevi religious life. They called it Nekap, which was the old name for a circle dance. Although this may have contributed to a disruption in the transmission of traditional culture, other factors such as the disappearance of hunting ranges, displacement, and indoctrination into Christianity played more significant roles.

Socially, the Chemehuevi were divided into two groups that were roughly defined by their hereditary songs: the Mountain Sheep Song and the Deer Song, each of which describes trips through the mountains and valleys along the Colorado River. Rights to sing the song were established by heredity. If someone owned a Deer Song, he could not hunt in an area belonging to those who owned the Mountain Sheep Song, and vice versa. Marriage could not occur between two people who owned the same song.

The Chemehuevi have had a long history of displacement. Even today, while some of them live on the Chemehuevi Reservation, others live on the Colorado River Indian Reservation or other reservations in the area. Historically, some would set up small sites of three or four families and try to maintain their lifeways, but settlers, other tribes, or federal agents would either forcibly remove them or ignore them and leave them to survive with no assistance.

Today, the tribe has a strong government and a strengthened economic base founded on a casino operation. The Chemehuevi have opened a cultural center and provide language instruction. During the first week of June, the tribe holds Nuwuvi Days, which are geared specifically toward tribal members to honor their ancestors and to provide a forum for showing pride in culture, identity, and survival. ■

Image of Chemehuevi Indians by Heinrich Balduin Mollhausen, a German artist who traveled the West in the mid-19th century

KINTPUASH

Modoc leader and warrior

Kintpuash, the famous California Indian warrior known as Captain Jack, was a leader of the Modoc nation from about 1864 until his death by hanging at the hands of the U.S. Army in 1873. The U.S. forced the Modoc out of their ancestral lands around Tule Lake and onto the Klamath Reservation in southwestern Oregon. Conditions were so bad, however, that many of the Modoc returned to California, but in 1869, the Army rounded them up and returned them to the reservation. Captain Jack then led them back to the Tule Lake area in 1870.

Two years later, the Army tried to return them once again, but the Indians fought back in the Battle of Lost River. Afterward, Captain Jack led his band into what is now called Lava Beds National Monument, where old lava flows created hiding places in a landscape of caves and hills. The band settled into what is now called Captain Jack's Stronghold. Kintpuash and the U.S. entered into peace negotiations, but he seized the opportunity to shoot and kill the negotiators. He continued to fight and elude capture until he was tracked down in June 1873 and was hanged for murder. In 1898, his skull was sent to the Smithsonian Institution. In the 1970s, his descendants learned it was there, and his skull was finally returned to his community in 1984. ∎

Kintpuash, also known as Captain Jack, was hanged by the U.S. Army in 1873.

more than 10,000 years. Traditional classes are offered to both tribal members and the public and include basket weaving, pottery, stories, and the construction of a Kumeyaay style house, called an *'ewaa*. It has partnerships with most of the museums, universities, and colleges in the San Diego area. Agua Caliente Cultural Center is a Smithsonian Institution affiliate.

CABAZON RESERVATION

Tribe: Cabazon Band of Mission Indians [Cahuilla]
Total Area: 1,376 acres   **Tribal Enrollment:** 30

The Cabazon Band takes its name from Chief Cabazon, leader of the Desert Cahuilla during the mid-1830s, but the Cahuilla have resided in southern California for at least 2,500 years, locating their villages in areas where native plants and wild game were abundant. The Cahuilla language belongs to the Uto-Aztecan language family, which includes languages spoken by peoples from the Great Basin south to central Mexico. Linguistic evidence suggests that by 1000 B.C., the Cahuilla became a separate linguistic, and somewhat culturally independent, tribe.

The Cahuilla people encountered Euro-Americans in the late 1700s when the Spanish began to settle California. Foreign diseases greatly reduced the Cahuilla population in the mid-1800s, and the arrival of the Southern Pacific Railroad brought widespread encroachment upon tribal lands, forcing the Cahuilla to relocate from their traditional territories. The Cabazon band was living near Indio in 1876 when an executive order established the Cabazon Reservation there. It originally included three parcels of land totaling 2,400 acres. The railroad claimed 700 acres to create a railroad system and for interstate right-of-way.

None of the several Cahuilla reservations located in southern California accepted the terms of the Indian Reorganization Act of 1934, which was intended to grant more autonomy to tribes and stipulated the development of tribal constitutions. The Cahuilla remained politically active, filing Indian Claims Commission cases for traditional lands taken by non-Indians and the government and suing the government for damages resulting from the loss of water rights.

CAHUILLA RESERVATION

Tribe: Cahuilla Band of Mission Indians
Total Area: 18,884 acres   Tribal Enrollment: 307

Members of the Cahuilla tribe have long resided in the area of southern California where the present reservation exists. In fact, the present-day reservation is located within the ancestral lands of the tribe on the site of an ancient community called Paui. Elders continue to speak their ancestral language, which belongs to the Takic branch of the greater Uto-Aztecan linguistic family. Like most southern California tribes, some forms of traditional music, such as Bird Songs and Peon Songs, remain important and are performed regularly on social occasions.

The Cahuilla bands were assigned to reservations during the mid-1800s. The Cahuilla Reservation was created by an executive order in 1875. The Cahuillas were able to maintain their traditional subsistence patterns of hunting native game and gathering piñon nuts and mesquite beans.

During the first part of the 20th century, the Cahuilla derived their income from wage labor, farming, and raising livestock on reservation lands. At that time, Cahuilla reservations retrieved some of the land that had been returned to the public domain by the 1891 Act for the Relief of Mission Indians. None of the Cahuilla reservations participated in the Indian Reorganization Act of 1934. Cahuilla reservations joined other southern California Indian groups in the Indian Claims Commission cases of the 1940s and '50s, and some have sued the government for determination of damages in respect to the loss of water rights. Cahuilla Creek Casino is one of the tribe's major sources of income. The economy is also sustained by leasing tribal lands.

The Cahuilla Reservation is located between Mount Palomar and Mount San Jacinto, 4,000 feet above sea level. The terrain largely consists of rolling hills, dry washes, giant boulders, and desert brush, and the reservation's water supply is limited. Although the on-reservation population is small, land ownership is under the control of individual tribal members.

Central Miwok, Penutian language family

"nana" ("man")

"assa" ("woman")

"hiema" ("sun")

"kome" ("moon")

CAMPO INDIAN RESERVATION

Tribe: Campo Band of Diegueño Mission Indians [Kumeyaay-Diegueño Nation]   Total Area: 15,480 acres
Tribal Enrollment: 302

The historic territory of the Kumeyaay people reached from northern San Diego County out to the Salton Sea and south 50 miles into Baja California. Property was generally passed from father to son, while females as well as males served as spiritual and religious leaders and healers. Creation stories and rituals were tied to specific locations—such as Tecate Peak (Kuuchamaa) and Signal Mountain (Wee-ishpa)—and celebrated through songs and dances.

The Kumeyaay first encountered Spanish explorers in 1542. Over the next 200 years, the Spanish continued to arrive along the Pacific coast and venture inland, subjugating the Kumeyaay. In 1769, a mission was established in San Diego, and the Kumeyaay began a series of revolts against the Franciscans and Spaniards living there. They were subsequently rounded up, brought in as forced laborers, and made to convert to Catholicism. Small skirmishes continued to flare up between the Kumeyaay and the settlers, and in 1775 the Kumeyaay attacked the mission. The battle resulted in the destruction of the mission and the deaths of many residents. Spanish and Mexican soldiers eventually managed to achieve dominance in the coastal area of San Diego County, with the Kumeyaay laboring at the missions as cattle ranchers, subject to Mexican hacienda owners. They were continuously pushed farther east by landowners and settlers.

In 1875, the Kumeyaay clans were excluded from an executive order that created reservations throughout present-day San Diego County. The Campo Indian Reservation was established in 1893. As a result of the government's failure to ratify the treaty of 1850, many of the Kumeyaay bands refused to acknowledge the authority of the federal government. Some Kumeyaays continued to live off-reservation in mountain areas until the

A dancer displays elaborate feathered garb at a Chumash powwow in Oak Park, California.

expansion of Campo in 1911. Tensions grew until 1929 when an altercation between tribal members and BIA police resulted in several deaths at Campo. Campo people continued to maintain their independence whenever possible, refusing to participate in the Indian Reorganization Act of 1934. In 1950, the BIA closed its Campo offices. Tribal members responded by burning all BIA structures on the reservation. Finally, in 1975, the Campo people established a constitution to formalize governmental operations.

Chico Rancheria

Tribe: Mechoopda Indian Tribe
Total Area: 690 acres   Tribal Enrollment: 442

The Mechoopda encountered Euro-Americans perhaps as early as 1828, when members of the Hudson's Bay Company were trapping in the area's waterways. In 1850, John Bidwell acquired the Spanish land grant of Rancho Arroyo Chico. The tribe relocated to a former summer campsite south of Chico Creek, and later moved downstream nearer the Bidwells' residence. It is believed that Bidwell and a tribal member named Nuppani were married, thus establishing the foundation of a long-lasting relationship between the settler and the tribe. Tribal members participated in the agriculture, livestock, and mining industries as laborers for Bidwell. In return, they were paid wages equal to their non-Native counterparts, and Bidwell extended his protection against federal intervention to the community.

In 1851, after some negotiation, the Mechoopda reached a treaty agreement with the federal government. However, the U.S. government did not actually ratify the treaty, nor did it ratify others that had been negotiated with 18 California tribes. Policies of forced removal were subsequently initiated. Unlike the other tribes, though, the Mechoopda likely did not face removal from tribal lands since Bidwell continued to provide protection. For this reason, during this period many Native peoples sought and received refuge with the Mechoopda tribe at Bidwell's ranch. In 1868, the tribe established a community just to the west of its present-day location, and members of many tribes and Native communities joined the Mechoopda there.

The fate of Bidwell's marriage to Nuppani is unclear, but Bidwell married his second wife, Annie Kennedy, in 1868. She established a Christian church within the Mechoopda village, as well as a small school. Annie Bidwell was an outspoken

Bird Songs

In southern California, bird songs are one of a number of specialized song cycles. Others include funerary songs, salt songs, and wildcat songs. Many of the songs were lost when local Indians were under the control of the Spanish Catholic missions from about 1769 to 1832, but the bird songs survived.

They are sung by men from the Kumeyaay-Diegueno and Cahuilla Nations, as well as other tribes in the area and into the Southwest. A gourd filled with native palm seeds is used to keep rhythm. In olden times, the gourds were painted to signify association with a clan.

The songs are used for many occasions, especially traditional gatherings where neighboring nations visit one host nation. They also are performed at powwows and other intertribal gatherings, but not in their entirety. According to singer Ron Christmas, the presentation has little "flash," so that it does not detract from the beauty of the song or its intent.

The origins of the bird song cycle names vary by nation, but the Kumeyaay say they were given to the people by a beautiful bird as a gift from the Creator. The songs are allegorical and provide instruction on the way to live. They can have up to 300 pieces, and to sing them all takes all night or longer. According to an interview with Paul Apodaca (a Cahuilla/Navajo/Mexicano) in *Studies in American Indian Literatures,* the entrance songs come as the sun goes down. The cycle is sung until, as the sun rises, the men sing the final song. ■

Bird dancers at a traditional gathering and powwow at the Sycuan Indian Reservation near San Diego

CALIFORNIA

CHUMASH

Chumash Indians traditionally occupied one of the most beautiful regions of southern California. Prior to contact with Spain, they lived in portions of modern Los Angeles, Ventura, Santa Barbara, and San Luis Obispo and on three of the Channel Islands: Santa Cruz, Santa Rosa, and San Miguel. There was an abundance of plants for food as well as for making homes, clothing, and baskets. There were also many animals on land and in the sea to hunt and fish. They were fine boat builders, using redwood that came down the coast from the north. At the time of contact with early European coastal explorers, the Chumash were thriving and had complex sociopolitical and socioeconomic structures, but they suffered under the mission system the Spaniards imposed.

Society before the Spaniards

The Spanish likely weren't the first outsiders to come in contact with California coastal groups. For example, it has been suggested that the Chumash may have borrowed their method for creating seafaring plank canoes from Polynesian visitors. Archaeological records do not support this theory, but the presence of the hypothesis suggests that scholars have considered the possible presence of undocumented visitors prior to the mission-based expeditions.

Information on Chumash life at the time of contact has been gleaned from such sources as oral histories, tribal elders, and tribal historians as well as the papers of explorers and missionaries. Later authors gained access to the community via tribal members. One of the earliest was John P. Harrington, an ethnologist and linguist who worked for the Smithsonian beginning in 1915. His studies influenced others whose works provide much of the following information.

Chumash political roles were mostly hereditary, with commoners, elites, and chiefs, who could be male or female. When a couple married, they moved in with the wife's mother and lived with her family. According to author and anthropologist Lynn H. Gamble: "Chiefs, their

A Chumash Indian pictograph above a cave entrance in the San Emigdio Mountains, Kern County, California

family members and other highly ranked individuals were members of the 'antap society who performed dances and rituals at ceremonies. Each Chumash settlement had an 'antap society consisting of 12 members who were initiated into the group as children. Other people who were not chiefs had roles and duties assigned to them according to their status in the community. For example, one person was responsible for making mortar, another responsible for singing at ceremonies, another responsible for predicting the weather."

The Mission Era

The lives of the Chumash changed with the influx of Europeans, notably with the arrival in 1542 of Juan Cabrillo, a Portuguese explorer working for Spain. He died, but the Spanish laid claim to what's now California. Nevertheless, they did not return until 1769, when an expedition led by Gaspar de Portola, along with soldiers and missionaries, arrived in the area. They built a mission and presidio in San Diego, beginning California's mission era. At that point, there were about 310,000 indigenous people in California, historian James Sandos estimates, with about 65,000 in or adjacent to the coastal areas from San Diego to north of San Francisco, the area of mission influence. An estimated 22,000 were Chumash. At the end of the mission period, there were 2,788 Chumash registered within the missions.

The first mission built on Chumash lands was San Luis Obispo; five others were built by 1817. The missions provided the Spanish crown with free labor and the Catholic Church with converts. The padres considered Indians inferior people, merely superstitious pagans who needed their help to become civilized.

Living conditions contributed to the spread of smallpox and other diseases, and there was never enough medical care, food, or water. Even the youngest children were forced to work.

Given the dehumanizing conditions, why would Indians live in a mission? One theory is that, because adults were harder to convert than children, families were torn apart and children forcibly taken into the mission. In addition, Indians who were not forced into the missions may have been pushed there by harsh environmental conditions.

Chumash life was disrupted by the European insistence that they shift from hunting and gathering to farming. Introduced livestock destroyed native plants. Irrigation systems disrupted water flow. Given the depleted population and resources, the missions became the only option for survival.

The Chumash staged a dramatic month-long rebellion in 1824. Spain sent a battalion to hunt down the participants, who had scattered. The rebels were captured and killed or jailed.

The Chumash Today

It is important to note the diversity within the Chumash. There is not a single Chumash tribe or nation, but several. However, the only federally recognized band at present is the Santa Ynez Band of Chumash. The Coastal Band of the Chumash Nation and the Barbareño/Ventureño tribal groups are in the process of gaining federal recognition. There are at least three other tribal groups.

Today, about 5,000 people identify as Chumash. There is interest in maintaining languages, songs, and stories; documenting oral histories; continuing cultural practices such as canoeing and basketry; and protecting cultural and land resources. The Santa Ynez Band of Chumash Indians Foundation has invested $13 million in philanthropic efforts. In addition, contemporary Chumash authors, artists, and educators, such as Ernestine de Soto, Frank Dominguez, Mike Khus, Alan Salazar, Georgiana Sanchez, Julie Tumamait, Tharon P. Weighill, Sr., and Lihui Whitebear, are teaching young and old about Chumash culture. ■

A Chumash dancer performs at a powwow in Oak Park, California.

GEORGE BLAKE

Hupa-Yurok artist

George Blake was born in 1944 on the Hoopa Indian Reservation in Humboldt County in northern California. After three years in the Army, Blake returned home and attended the College of the Redwoods; he later transferred to the University of California, where he majored in fine arts and Native American art. He is known for his beautiful elkhorn carvings and for his devotion to learning traditional methods and art forms to perpetuate cultural lifeways. Blake taught himself featherwork and regaliamaking. He also studied with two tribal elders to learn the way to make a redwood dugout canoe. He is passing that knowledge on by teaching a variety of traditional crafts to local youths.

Blake, who was a curator at the Hupa Tribal Museum in the 1980s, won the National Endowment for the Arts Heritage Fellowship in 1991. He is also a successful contemporary artist who uses dark humor and irony to combat social stereotypes of American Indians. His work has been featured in many museums, including the Los Angeles County Museum of Art, the Brooklyn Museum, the Smithsonian's National Museum of the American Indian, the Indian Craft Shop at the U.S. Department of the Interior, and the Phoebe Hearst Museum. ■

Renowned artist and museum curator George Blake

---

supporter of Native rights and continued to support the Mechoopda community following her husband's death in 1910. Upon her death, the Bidwell lands were deeded to the Board of Home Missions of the Presbyterian Church to serve as trustee for the Native residents. The lands were held in trust until 1939, when the government conveyed the land into federal trust. However, all of the lands were later lost or sold through unscrupulous land transactions.

The tribe was terminated in 1958, under the California Rancheria Act. In 1986, along with three other California rancherias, the Mechoopda tribe challenged the unlawful termination in *Scotts Valley* v. *United States*. The tribe was rewarded for its efforts, receiving federal recognition in 1992. The current location of the rancheria is in Chico, California, within the traditional territories of the Mechoopda tribe. Since the date it received its federal recognition, the tribe has successfully purchased a number of parcels of land. The tribal economy is supported by agricultural enterprise—specifically 40 acres of almond groves—and by leasing homes owned by the tribe.

MYTH OR FACT?

California Indians traditionally held powwows.

MYTH

While many California Indians participate in powwows today, such gatherings are traditionally part of Plains Indian cultures. The dances performed include the Fancy Dance, the Shawl Dance, the Traditional Dance, and the Grass Dance. None of these are traditional to cultures in what is now California. They came to California as a result of intermarriage or as a way to provide fellowship.

COLUSA RANCHERIA

Tribe: Cachil DeHe Band of Wintun Indians of the Colusa Indian Community   **Total Area:** 573 acres
Tribal Enrollment: 69

The Wintun Indians originated in the regions around the Sacramento River. The Sacramento River holds historic importance as a provider of salmon and as a meeting ground for exchange and trade. The Cachil DeHe Band is still guaranteed the right to hunt and fish along the Sacramento River. The Wintun were a numerous and prosperous people, benefiting from the resources around Mount Shasta and the Sacramento River until European arrival in California destroyed areas that were rich in plants and bulbs vital to the people's diet. Damage to streams and vegetation from copper-processing plants, and the inundation of lands by dams, dramatically decreased the Wintun's ability to continue traditional subsistence practices.

Tribal lands are located in central California and consist of two parcels: the rancheria and the reservation, located four miles apart in the valley of the Sierras, approximately 200 miles inland from the Pacific coast. Farming serves as an important source of tribal revenue and employment for the Colusa community.

The Wintun's devout concern for protecting burial grounds and other sacred places is continually being challenged by developers of new subdivisions and highways and by general construction. The protection of Mount Shasta as a viable sacred place is a major issue for the Wintun. Environmentalists have joined them in this concern to protect the mountain from development.

Tribal members continue to practice numerous cultural traditions, annual ceremonies, the use of the roundhouse and sweat lodge on the reservation, healing ceremonies, and ceremonial dances. They also participate in other celebrations with the Wintun peoples of the Cortina, Rumsey, Grindstone, and Wintun rancherias.

CORTINA INDIAN RANCHERIA

Tribe: Cortina Indian Rancheria of Wintun Indians   Total Area: 640 acres   Tribal Enrollment: 152

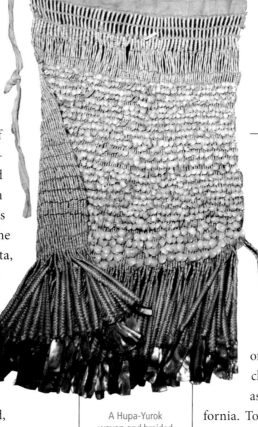

A Hupa-Yurok woven and braided grass skirt is decorated with tiny clam and abalone shells.

The Wintun—the ancestors of Cortina Rancheria tribal members—traditionally inhabited a long narrow stretch of the western Sacramento Valley north of what is now known as San Francisco Bay. The Wintun, along with the Pit River, Shasta, and Modoc peoples, consider Mount Shasta sacred ground, a potent symbol of power and divinity.

As elsewhere, the imposition of European culture inflicted extremely negative results upon the Native people of the region. In the early days of California statehood, Congress attempted to herd all the Indians onto four major reservations, against the wishes of the various tribes who had profound attachments to their traditional areas.

Since the early 1970s, the Wintun have undergone an incredible revitalization. While the tribe continues to strive for its own economic independence and development, it has managed to overturn the termination proceedings that were previously under way and organize to meet the 21st-century challenges of environmental issues, tribal reorganization and recognition, and the continuance of traditional and religious activities.

The Cortina Indian Rancheria was established in 1907, with 160 acres set aside for the exclusive use of this band of Wintun Indians. This action was pursuant to the Act of Congress of January 12, 1881, creating a Mission Indian Commission, which was charged with selecting a reservation for each band of Mission Indians residing in California. Subsequently, Cortina acquired an additional 480 acres. A trust patent was issued on June 6, 1958, authorizing the U.S. government to hold the aggregate 640 acres in trust for the Cortina Band of Indians.

ELK VALLEY RANCHERIA

Tribe: Elk Valley Rancheria [Tolowa]   Total Area: 21 acres   Tribal Enrollment: 98

Members of the Elk Valley rancheria are Tolowas, whose ancestral homelands span the coastal redwood forest region of what is now northern California and southern Oregon. They were on the southern end of the trade in dentalia, or tusk shells (the shells of the mollusk *Dentalia hexagonum* and closely related species), which were used as money from British Columbia to California. Tolowa villages had separate locations for living, working, and burials.

Before Euro-American contact, Tolowa numbered about 4,000; by 1906 only 254 remained, having survived massacres by settlers, military destruction, diseases, and removal to the Siletz and Hoopa reservations during the mid-1800s. Traditional Tolowa culture, long repressed by white society, found religious expression in the Indian Shaker Church, imported from the Siletz Reservation in Oregon in 1929. The Tolowa found great solace in the healing and culturally inclusive practices of the "Shake," eventually adapting and hybridizing it. During the late 1960s, language preservation became a high priority, with Tolowa elders offering formal classes in the region's public schools. The late 1980s ushered in a period of optimism for the Tolowa, as accomplishments in the arenas of culture and health inspired confidence in the tribe's ability to meet economic and political challenges.

The Tolowas currently number about 1,000, and the rancheria population consists of Tolowa, Yurok, and Karuk tribal members. During the 1970s, fellow tribesmen in the historic Tolowa fishing village of Nelechundun created the Nelechundun Business Council, a move that helped build momentum for restoration of federal recognition.

Elk Valley Enterprises supports a diversified array of small businesses and gaming. The economy of the surrounding region has historically been based on the fishing industry. Today, commercial fishing remains a vital part of the region's economic base, providing considerable revenues and employment for many tribal members. The timber industry also remains fundamental to the tribe and to the area.

MYTH OR FACT?

California Indians paint their faces and bodies for important occasions.

FACT

California Indians have long used plants to create pigments to put on their faces and bodies. Patterns denote social and economic status. They are also known for their tattooing. Many women in the north had their chins tattooed when they came of age, and the men tattooed their arms to demonstrate their wealth.

EWIIAAPAAYP
INDIAN RESERVATION

Tribe: Ewiiaapaayp Band of Kumeyaay Indians [Kumeyaay-Diegueño Nation]   Total Area: 5,464 acres
Tribal Enrollment: 7

The tribal affiliation of the Ewiiaapaayp (formerly the Cuyapaipe) is Kumeyaay, and it is one of the 12 Kumeyaay bands in San Diego County. Ewiiaapaayp means "leaning rock," referring to a sacred rock on a high ridge on the Ewiiaapaayp Reservation, where it served as the touchstone and site marker in the Kumeyaay's travels from the coast to the mountains and the desert beyond. Archaeological evidence suggests that the Kumeyaay Indians have lived in the greater San Diego and northern Baja California area for some 12,000 years. The inland Kumeyaay bands were centered on the lands now part of the present-day Ewiiaapaayp Reservation. The bounty of the area's resources ensured that the people lived well. But all that was to change with the influx of the Spanish and later white settlers.

The Mission Indian Relief Act of 1891 enacted recommendations of the Jackson-Kinney Report, stating: "The history of the Mission Indians for a century may be written in four words: conversion, civilization, neglect, outrage . . . Justice and humanity alike demand the immediate action of Government to preserve for their occupation the fragments of land not already taken from them."

The late Tony J. Pinto, Ewiiaapaayp tribal chairman from 1967 to 2001, and his family worked to preserve the cultural traditions of the Kumeyaay,

Pictographs (drawn or painted images) and petroglyphs (carved images) cover the walls of volcanic caves in the Cascade Range, last used by Modoc Indians in the 19th century.

including the Peon Games and Bird Songs. As a part of the Mission Indian Federation, they opposed policies of the BIA, which the traditional leaders believed would damage their people. Pinto participated in the Mission Indians Claims case and the water claims settlement, worked to protect sacred places from desecration, encouraged younger Kumeyaays to become tribal cultural and political leaders, and apprised the Mexican government of the needs of the Paipai and Kumeyaay Indians of northern Baja California.

CUPEÑO

The Cupeño are often called one of the smallest nations in California, although small tribes are more the rule than the exception there. Today they have roughly 920 members who live at Pala, a 12,273-acre reservation in northern San Diego County. It is home to the Cupeño as well as the Luiseño Band of Mission Indians. There are also Cupeño Indians on the Los Coyotes Band of Cahuilla and Cupeño Indian Reservation near Warner Springs. They originally lived in two villages. One village is called Kupa; due to the Spanish influence of the region, -eño was appended and they came to be called Cupeño ("the people of Kupa"), Cupa, or Kupa. The other village was called Wilakal. However, in their language they called themselves Kuupangaxwichem or "People Who Slept Here."

Conflict with Newcomers

The Cupeño lived near the hot sulfur springs on Warner Springs Ranch, close to the headwaters of the San Luis Rey River. They had little contact with outsiders before 1810, when they began interacting with the Spanish, and then the U.S. settlers coming west in search of land and opportunity. The hot springs, which had been a source of healing waters for the Cupeño, became quite popular and attracted visitors. The Indians were slowly and painfully displaced; by the late 1840s, they were pushed to the brink. Cupeño leader Antonio Garra headed up an 1851 revolt, fed by people from many southern California nations. But as key stakeholders fell away, the revolt lost its power. Garra was captured and executed within days, and the village of Kupa was burned.

A series of attempts by the Mexican and U.S. governments to take over their land or to sell it to private owners eroded the tenuous legal rights of the Cupeño. By effectively ignoring their presence, governments marginalized them within the legal systems and eventually pushed them off their land and onto reservations.

A Cupeño woman, as depicted in a 1924 photograph

Forced Removal Strains Ties with the Land

At first, only Luiseño people lived on the reservation. On May 12, 1903, armed U.S. government forces began evicting the Cupeño from their homes, and their belongings were piled into carts or left behind as they were marched to the reservation, a 40-mile journey that took three days. There were no houses on the new reservation, and the new residents were forced to sleep out in the open.

Today, the tribe has a yearly observance of the displacement, known as Kupa Days, during the first weekend of May. By removing the people, the government also took away their religious associations with the land, thereby limiting the way in which religious knowledge and practices were passed down to future generations.

Many of the southern California nations are called Mission Indians, because they lived in the mission establishments or were under the authority of the Franciscan priests during the mission period, which lasted from 1769 until approximately 1834. Although some of the Cupeño were baptized into the Catholic Church around 1816, there were many who were unconverted and remained on tribal lands, just outside of the mission grounds.

Federal relocation and urbanization policies instituted in the 1950s spurred the mass migration of American Indians into cities, especially San Diego and Los Angeles, where a large number of

Indians from Southern California live today. Many Cupeño live in Los Angeles, but others remain close to their original land.

The Cupeño Today

The Cupeño continue to be strong cultural and environmental resource managers who closely monitor their land, water, and air. They have long resisted constructing a landfill in culturally significant Gregory Canyon, which is just two miles off the reservation. They manage many successful businesses, including a 90-acre avocado grove, a spa, a resort, and a casino. The Cupeño have a strong philanthropic record, supporting not only their local schools and housing programs but also universities, colleges, and youth programs off-reservation as well as other American Indian relief programs.

Cupa Cultural Center was founded in 1974 through the efforts of Pala community members like Cupeño elder Rosinda Nolasquez, a survivor of the move to the reservation. It aims to preserve, perpetuate, and enhance traditional cultural practices and continue research and documentation of Pala's past and present. In the center, people practice basketmaking and beading and preserve and teach the Cupeño language. ■

Hoop dancer at a Cupeño powwow in Oceanside, California. Some Native American hoop dancing competitions draw thousands of spectators.

Due to the inaccessibility of the Cuyapaipe Reservation, the U.S. government established an Indian school (since closed) on the more accessible Campo Reservation. Ewiiaapaayp Band families with school-age children were relocated from the Ewiiaapaayp Reservation to the other reservations of Campo, La Posta, Laguna (terminated), and Manzanita in order for children to attend the school. This relocation and the subsequent disenrollments due to the lack of utilities, adequate roads, and any kind of employment opportunity is why the Ewiiaapaayp Band has only seven enrolled members.

GREENVILLE RANCHERIA

Tribe: Greenville Rancheria of Maidu Indians of California   Total Area: 1.8 acres   Tribal Enrollment: 103

Tribal members of the Greenville Rancheria belong to the mountain Maidu tribe, which consists of three bands in Plumas, Shasta, Tehama, and Lassen Counties. The three groups are closely related culturally and linguistically. Ancestors of Greenville Rancheria tribal members resided in northern California as early as 1000. Spanish explorers arrived in California in the late 1500s. During the Spanish, and later Mexican, dominance of the territory, lands were seized from the Native populations and held in trust for the Spanish crown. Indigenous people were displaced, enslaved, and often murdered. Americans arrived in California in the mid-1800s and initiated a war with Mexico for rights to the California region. The Mexicans were defeated, and in 1848 the Treaty of Guadalupe Hidalgo ended the Mexican-American War.

Between 1851 and 1853, Indian commissioners negotiated 18 treaties between the government and multiple Native groups. They agreed to reserve over 7.5 million acres for various tribes across the state, but the Senate did not ratify these treaties. The tribes were not informed of this decision until the 20th century, though, so they proceeded to live in agreement with the mandates outlined by the treaties. They ceded millions of acres of land to the government and were confined to the rancherias designated by

INDIAN SHAKER CHURCH

The Indian Shaker Church came into existence in 1882 via John Slocum, a Nisqually Indian from Puget Sound, outside Seattle. The church combines Christianity and traditional Indian religious practices. The name "Shaker" comes from the feeling of shaking and lightness that Slocum's wife, Mary, felt upon seeing her husband's revival from seeming death. The shaking resembled what healers experience and is interpreted to be a source of spirituality and healing. (It's not related to the Protestant Shaker sect known for its furniture.)

The Shaker Church is a syncretic religion, one that combines elements of multiple faiths. One example of the way this religion combines Christian and Indian beliefs is in the use of the Bible. Some early congregations argued that the Bible is just for white people and not for Indians, who receive the Holy Spirit directly through the shake, which is the Native aspect of the religion. The association of the shake with traditional healers but also with Christianity was seen by some as an authentic continuation of the old ways. Others strongly believe that the Christian element annuls the Indian character of the Shaker Church. The presence of this religion is a source of intense discussion and conflict, particularly in northern California among those who see Christianity as a threat to cultural survival.

The church continues to have followers today, but is marginalized from the larger Indian population. Traditionalists who participate in the big dances largely reject the church; Shakers became tolerant over the years, allowing members to participate in the dances. One thing that can be said of the Indian Shaker Church is that it is an example of a timeless phenomenon: the evolution of religious practices. ∎

A group of Clallam Indians inside the Indian Shaker church, Jamestown, Washington, about 1903. The sect originated in that region.

the Barbour Treaties. Local, state, and federal agencies condoned what was in effect genocide against the Native people of California. The Mexican government finally interceded, and some tribes escaped total annihilation. The population of the Greenville tribe in the early 1800s was about 4,000. By the end of the century, there were fewer than 500 tribal members.

The original rancheria land was in Greenville and was called the Indian Mission. The rancheria was terminated from federal status in 1958; tribal lands were allotted and many allotments sold. As with the Elk Valley Rancheria, recognition was restored in 1983 pursuant to the *Tillie Hardwick* decision (see page 343). The tribe is not organized under the Indian Reorganization Act of 1934. In 1995, a new constitution was drafted. A five-member tribal council, elected by general membership, governs the tribe.

The forestry industry is a major contributor to the rancheria's economy. Although the tribe does not own or operate any facilities, many tribal members are employed with local companies, and the tribe also provides jobs in the community.

Chumash grinding stones were used against large rocks like a mortar and pestle to grind acorns into flour.

GRINDSTONE INDIAN RANCHERIA OF WINTUN-WAILAKI INDIANS

Tribes: Grindstone Indian Rancheria of Wintun-Wailaki Indians [Nomlaki and Wintun]
Total Area: 100 acres   Tribal Enrollment: 137

The Nomlaki and Wintun people resided in the greater Sacramento Valley, the Nomlaki people specifically in parts of what are now Tehama and Glenn Counties. White contact in the early and mid-19th century spread diseases that devastated the Nomlaki and reduced their population by at least 75 percent. The settlement process, with tribal lands confiscated and gathering areas of traditional

foods and materials destroyed, also contributed to the disruption of tribal unity, as did the introduction of domesticated hogs, cattle, and sheep and the damaging by-products of copper processing plants during the 1880s and '90s.

In 1854, a 25,000-acre Nome Lackee Reservation was established for several related peoples, but in 1863 the reservation was dissolved and the land was taken over by white immigrants. The Nomlaki people were then brutally removed to the Round Valley Reservation.

After the turn of the 20th century, the Grindstone Indian Rancheria finally offered a sanctuary, which stabilized the group. A sacred roundhouse, which still exists, was built on the rancheria; it is perhaps the oldest in use in California today. During the 1970s, the rancheria was able to rebuff a California water project, known as the Peripheral Canal Project, which planned to purchase rancheria property for a dam site.

Agriculture serves as the area's primary source of revenue, and the tribe is planning to expand its own agricultural activities. At present, Grindstone Rancheria members find seasonal employment by harvesting walnuts, pears, and prunes, often involving whole families. The rancheria is considering a number of economic development projects that would utilize local resources, such as a gravel-processing plant that would use gravel culled from the creek running through the rancheria and a wood-processing enterprise.

KARUK RESERVATION

Tribe: Karuk Tribe   Total Area: 596 acres
Tribal Enrollment: 3,427

Archaeological and anthropological evidence supports the fact that ancestors of the Karuk occupied northwestern California by around 10,000 B.C. and perhaps much earlier. The traditional boundary of Karuk territory followed the watersheds bordering the Klamath River. Living in scattered villages along or near rivers and streams, the Karuk fished the river for salmon and hunted the surrounding richly forested woodlands for such large game as elk, bear, and deer as well as smaller animals such as beaver.

The General Allotment Act of 1887 declared all unallotted land to be available for homesteading. With virtually all of their land now declared public, most Karuks were forced to move from the river in search of wage-earning employment in the agricultural valleys to the east or shipping centers on the coast to the west. In addition, many Karuk children were removed for long periods and sent to government boarding schools far away.

During the 1850s, the tribe signed a treaty with the federal government, but it was never ratified by Congress. In the 1950s and '60s, nonprofit organizations, chartered by the state of California, represented the Karuk people's interests. Functioning in place of a tribal council, these organizations administered programs, purchased land, and operated under democratically elected boards of

directors. Until 1979, the tribe remained unrecognized by the federal government and had no formal reservation, though tribal members continued to reside on portions of their ancestral homelands throughout California.

Although it is one of the largest tribes in California, the Karuk have a small land base. Federal recognition occurred only after a group of elders purchased a 6.6-acre parcel of land and placed it into trust status. This sequence of events qualified the tribe for establishment under the Indian Reorganization Act of 1934.

Various ceremonies remain an important aspect of the Karuk lifestyle; the Pick-ya-wish (World Renewal Ritual), the Jump Dance Ceremony, and the White Deerskin Ceremonies reiterate the Karuk's relationship with and appreciation for the natural world and serve as a means of regulating social relations.

In 1994, the tribe entered into a partnership with the National Forest Service for the protection and restoration of the forests located within its ancestral lands. The tribe has secured more than $1 million to assist efforts to revitalize the area and has

ISHI

The last Yahi Indian

"Ishi"—his real name will never be known—was the last Yahi Indian, who emerged from the wilderness in 1911, emaciated and frightened. He was taken to jail by the white men who found him and then sent to San Francisco and on to the Museum of Anthropology at the University of California at Berkeley (now the Phoebe Hearst Museum), where he lived the rest of his life in relative comfort. Alfred Kroeber, an anthropologist at the museum, named him Ishi, which means "man" in the Yana dialect. His story has changed from one that focused on how he was "helped" to a cautionary tale that gives museum professionals, anthropologists, and other social scientists a chance to reflect on how ethnocentric values can lead well-meaning people astray. The story raises numerous questions: What role did Ishi play at the museum? Was he used as a human display, as an example of a primitive and disappearing culture? Was he there as a willing participant? Did he understand what he was representing to the public? Why was his wish that his body not be autopsied ignored? Why was his brain separated from his remains and kept at the Smithsonian Institution until the 1990s? Such questions give us a chance to consider our roles in the past and to learn from them. ■

A 1914 photo of the man known as Ishi. What can he teach us today?

developed a comprehensive watershed restoration training and implementation program. In 2004, a number of representatives from the Karuk, Yurok, Hoopa, and Klamath tribes traveled to Glasgow, Scotland, to address environmental concerns at the headquarters of a company responsible for damming the Klamath River and for the effects on the salmon population.

LA JOLLA RESERVATION

Tribe: La Jolla Band of Luiseño Indians
Total Area: 8,541 acres   **Tribal Enrollment:** 604

The Luiseño tribe has resided for thousands of years in a territory that originally covered roughly 1,500 miles of southern California to the north of the Kumeyaay's land, including most of the San Luis Rey and Santa Margarita drainages. The term Luiseño is derived from the San Luis Rey mission and has been used in southern California to refer to the Takic-speaking people associated with the mission.

The Luiseño people first met European settlers when Gaspar de Portola's expedition arrived in 1796. The Mission San Luis Rey was founded two years later. Members of the La Jolla, Pala, Pauma, Rincon, and San Pasqual bands of the Luiseño Indians have resided in the San Luis Rey River Basin since the late 1800s. Historically, they relied on agriculture for subsistence, using sophisticated farming techniques to manage the area's natural resources.

The Luiseño people continued their reliance upon agriculture until early in the 20th century, when the City of Escondido built a dam above La Jolla, effectively diverting all their water. Many Native people were forced to leave the reservation and seek work in the wage economy.

In 1951, the tribe filed a claim for the stolen reservation water, adding it to the Mission Indian Land Claim case. After a 1973 hearing, the Federal Power Commission required Escondido to regularly release six miner's inches from the dam. In 1988, a settlement was reached in the form of the San Luis Rey Indian Water Rights Settlement Act, authorizing

MYTH OR FACT?
California Indians lived in tepees.

MYTH

California Indians did not live in tepees. There is an enormous diversity in the styles of homes in which the tribes lived before contact with Europeans, but they did not use the tepee that was common in the Great Plains. Today, they live in typical modern homes.

$30 million to be awarded to the Luiseño bands in compensation for the loss of water rights. In addition, the act also mandates the delivery of water to tribal territories. The funds are used to promote economic development and to support the San Luis Rey Indian Water Authority.

LAYTONVILLE RANCHERIA

Tribe: Cahto Indian Tribe   **Total Area:** 202 acres
Tribal Enrollment: 81

The Cahto traditionally resided on lands now part of northern California. The region's varied plant-food sources, primarily acorns, have served as the tribe's dietary staple. A nomadic culture, they traveled where the food was plentiful, taking yearly treks to the Mendocino coast to harvest seaweed and fish.

There were an estimated 1,100 Cahto Indians residing in about 50 different villages in the Laytonville area during the early 18th century. Concern over the welfare of the "landless" Cahto propelled the area's missionaries to purchase land for the rancheria; a variety of title problems persuaded the federal government to take over the purchase by 1908. The confines of rancheria life, and the usurpation of their traditional lands, forced the Cahto into the wage economy in the 20th century. The hilly terrain of Mendocino County offered opportunities for employment in the cattle- and sheep-ranching industries. Later in the century, the timber industry provided jobs.

The Cahto tribe living on and near the Laytonville rancheria remains a small, cohesive group. They have preserved many of their stories and legends, and since the 1950s the rancheria's population has dramatically increased. A cedar roundhouse stands in the center of the residential area and serves as a dance and meeting hall for the tribe.

The tribe is working in cooperation with other tribes and the county to develop a tribal court system. Tribal members participate in both the organization Multi-Indian Tribes as well as its subsidiary, EARTH, which stands for Economic Advancement

YOKUT

The Yokut of central California included at least 60 tribes that lived in the San Joaquin Valley, from the mouth of the San Joaquin River to the foot of Tehachapi Pass. Most Yokuts would not want to be called Yokut, but rather want to be identified by their tribal names. Contemporary tribes include the Choinumni, who may have been the most populous before the arrival of Europeans; the Chukchansi; the Tachi (or Tache); and the Wukchumni. There are about 2,000 Yokut people living on the Picayune Rancheria of Chukchansi Indians, the Santa Rosa Rancheria, the Table Mountain Rancheria, and the Tule River Indian Tribe of the Tule River Reservation. There are about 600 more in two tribes that are not federally recognized or that are living off-reservation.

Yokut Lands and Diversity

In the early 18th century, the Yokut numbered between 18,000 and 50,000, which is believed to be one of the highest populations of Native Californians. They were well situated to be central players in trade between coastal tribes and their neighbors to the east.

Three divisions or classifications of the Yokut were created by early ethnographers, anthropologists, and linguists —the Northern Valley Yokut, the Southern Valley Yokut, and the Foothill Yokut. Each division included tribes with their own dialects and customs. These people were probably multilingual to facilitate trade, marriages, and travel. In the Foothill division, the Tulamni lived around Buena Vista Lake; the Hometwoli, or Humetwadi, lived on Kern Lake; and the Tuhohi, Tohohai, or Tuhohayi lived along the channels of the lower Kern River. In the Poso Creek group of the Foothill division were the Paleuyami, Padeuyami, or Peieuyi, who lived beside Poso Creek but also in Poso Flat and Holmiu in Linn's Valley. They lived alongside Shoshonean nations. Other tribes in the Foothill division

The Indians who lived near Tulare Lake were just some of the many Yokut tribes of central California.

lived at King's River, in the central region where they lived alongside the Mono. The Yokut also stated to researchers that Tulare Lake belonged to three tribes only: the Wowol, the Chunut, and the Tachi. The term Tachi is often used when referring to Yokut who lived in the central region, Chukchansi when referring to northern Yokut, and Yaudanchi and Yauelmani when referring to southern Yokut.

Societal Structures

While social customs varied, there were some similarities. For example, they had

(and may still have) totems, a representative animal that gives strength and wisdom to a group. Eagle, falcon, magpie, bear, cougar, and blue jay are examples. The Central Foothill Yokut of the Kaweah and Tule River areas and the Southern Foothill Yokut of the Kern River had lineages; other tribes are believed to have used moieties. A moiety is a division into two halves. For those who followed the moiety system, the animal world was divided between the "western, downhill, downstream" and the "eastern, uphill, upstream." Each moiety had its own chiefly lineage, and a chief could be a man or a woman. Politically, chiefs were prominent within each tribe, with no single tribe's chief being superior to the others. Their responsibilities might have included helping feed the poor, greeting and hosting visitors, and participating in ceremonies by gathering and paying for dancers.

As was common among California Indians, the girls were tattooed when they came of age. An obsidian blade or flint was typically used to make cuts and then charcoal ash was rubbed into the cut to make the coloring. The tattoos were most frequently on their chins, but some Chukchansi women would have tattoos across their chests, abdomen, arms, and legs.

Given the diversity of the tribes and their living conditions, the food they ate and homes they built varied. Some used tule reeds for clothing and housing as well as to build watercraft, such as rafts. Other groups used bark or brush to build homes.

Destruction and Life Today

The populations of the Yokut tribes were fatally impacted with the coming of the missions. Worse, in 1856, according to the Tachi-Yokut tribal website, the state of California issued a bounty of 25 cents per Indian scalp, increasing the bounty in 1860 to five dollars per scalp. The authorization to form "militias," basically hunting parties that could kill at will and profit from the death of Indians, caused the extinction of many populations of Yokut. European settlers not only were encouraged to kill Indians and turn their scalps in for money but also were permitted to take children, if needed, as servants in a form of indentured servitude.

Given the distance between California and Washington, D.C., the federal government chose to leave the welfare of California Indians up to the state government. However, the state's treatment of the Indians was so appalling that during the 1860s—likely after the Civil War—the U.S. military was finally called in as intermediaries and the federal government took more control. The solution, predictably, was to create rancherias and reservations. Few, if any, of those who murdered, raped, and kidnapped Indians were ever brought to justice.

Today, the remaining descendants of the Yokut work to retain their cultural legacy through basket weaving, language survival, and storytelling. Most important, they fight to retain their sovereignty through education and economic independence. ■

Robert "Junior" Villegas, a Tule River Yokut tribal member, is among the Indians who belong to the Golden Eagles Hotshots, troops of California Native wilderness firefighters.

for Rural Tribal Habitats. EARTH's planning component has helped the members of the tribe to further many aspects of their economic development program, including such projects as proposal writing, grant writing and control, and project assistance, as well as administrative tasks such as accounting and bookkeeping.

A tribally owned casino generates income for the Cahto. Tribal members continue to seek employment in the timber and agricultural sectors. While the timber industry has been in decline, the majority of employed Cahto men still work in wood processing and related fields. Seasonal employment is also plentiful during harvest season for pears, grapes, prunes, and walnuts.

Clapper sticks, percussion instruments typical of California Indians. They are made from a split stick that creates a clapping noise when waved and slapped in the palm.

LOOKOUT RANCHERIA

Tribe: Pit River Tribe   Total Area: 40 acres
Tribal Enrollment: 2,381

The traditional territory of the Pit River tribe spanned what are now Lassen, Shasta, and Modoc Counties of northern California. The Pit River tribe is composed of 11 distinct bands whose contemporary tribal lands include the Alturas, Big Bend, Likely, Lookout, Montgomery Creek, and Roaring Creek Rancherias, and the XL Reservation, as well as some allotted lands and 79 acres in the northern California town of Burney. These bands (Ajumawi, Aporidge, Astariwi, Atsuge, Atwamsini, Hammawi, Hewisedawi, Illmawi, Isatawi, Kosalektawi, and Madesi) traditionally spoke the Achumawi and Atsugewi languages, closely related members of the Palaihnihan branch of the greater Hokan linguistic family, whose languages are, in turn, spoken by peoples from southern Oregon to southern Mexico.

The Pit River tribe's post-contact history is characterized by a continued struggle for a permanent land base. Many of the Pit River people were forced to the Round Valley Reservation during the 19th century, while others were able to resist

Chumash, Hokan language family

"Haku tikali'?"

("Hello, how's it going?")

this move and continued to live in marginalized groups along the fringes of their ancestral territory. It was not until the passage of the Dawes Act in 1887 that some members of the tribe were actually able to acquire land as individual allotments that geographically resembled their traditional band divisions. The ability to live in more customary groupings reinforced band relationships and allowed the Pit River people to continue traditional subsistence practices.

Unfortunately, the Pit River people, like many Native peoples, found that they were unable to retain ownership of their allotted lands. By 1950, few of the former allotments remained. A congressional act calling for the investigation of the status of California's "landless" Indians at the beginning of the 20th century led to the establishment of seven small rancherias in Pit River territory, though none of these was suitable for intensive agriculture, and one of the bands—the Atsuge—received no rancheria land at all.

Beginning in 1919, the Pit River tribe attempted to gain compensation for land "ceded" to the U.S. government under unratified treaties. Eventually, political activism instigated by younger members of the Pit River tribe during the 1960s resulted in renewed cohesion among the different bands. Their activities focused on issues of tribal sovereignty, the free practice of Indian religion, and self-determination.

The Pit River Tribe's Cultural Resource Representatives Committee consists of members from each of the 11 autonomous bands who are chosen by the band because of their knowledge and connection to the environment and its cultural resources. The cultural committee communicates closely with the Environmental and Natural Resources and Roads Department on a variety of issues. The mission of the committee is to promote protection and restoration of traditional environmental values and prevention of environmental degradation on tribal ancestral lands.

LOS COYOTES RESERVATION

Tribe: Los Coyotes Band of Cahuilla and Cupeño
Indians   Total Area: 25,049 acres   Tribal Enrollment: 288

Members of the Los Coyotes Band of Indians are descendants of the Cahuilla and Cupeño tribes. Ancestors of these groups originally occupied two village sites in the vicinity of the area's hot springs. Although from distinct tribes, both groups spoke a language belonging to the Takic branch of the larger Uto-Aztecan linguistic family. While the Cupeño lived along what came to be known as Warner's Hot Springs, the Cahuillas resided in the hills to the immediate east, the present site of the Los Coyotes Reservation.

The area's hot springs have played a significant role in the history of the Los Coyotes people. Until the establishment of the San Luis Rey and San Diego missions, the hot springs and the adjacent lands served as the center of Cupeño life. Jonathan Trumbull (also known as Juan José Warner) acquired the springs and established a ranch there in 1844. The hot mineral waters offered restorative powers to passing visitors on the east-west Butterfield stagecoaches. Throughout this period, the indigenous people continued to live nearby, practicing a somewhat diminished version of their traditional subsistence patterns.

Bowing to commercial interests, however, the California Supreme Court decided in 1903 that the Cupeño had to leave their ancestral territory and move to the Pala Reservation. While the majority of the people were forced to relocate, some remained in their traditional territory, coexisting with the neighboring Cahuilla tribe. After their exile, a resort was built at the springs, and today the San Diego community uses these waters as a resource.

After joining the wage economy in the early part of the 20th century, the region's Native people primarily sought income by working on ranches and farms and in other employment in communities adjacent to their reservations. In addition, a number of tribe members farmed and raised stock on their reservation lands. The labor trend at Los Coyotes reflects this employment pattern.

The tribe is a PL-638 tribe, which essentially means that it contracts for tribal government, roads, natural resources, and water resources services. The tribal economy is supported in large part by revenue generated from such entrepreneurial activities as collecting camping fees and selling Christmas trees. Pear and apple orchards, introduced by the Spanish, thrive on much of the prime land on the Los Coyotes Reservation. The climate and terrain has proved ideal, yielding healthy crops with little maintenance.

GHOST DANCE IN CALIFORNIA

Followers of the spiritual practice and religion known as the Ghost Dance believed that performing certain dances and songs would bring about the revival of dead ancestors, the destruction of the white invaders, and a return to life as it was before whites and others came to the continent. In California, the Ghost Dance appeared in 1870 and faded out around 1872. The Ghost Dance in California was most prominent among the Hill Patwin, Lake and Coast Miwok, Wintu, Shasta, Pomo, Sinkyone, Coast Yuki, Wappo, Achumawi, Yurok, Tolowa, and Nomlaki.

When the Ghost Dance came through a particular area, it usually took on elements of the local religious beliefs and reflected culturally appropriate tenets. For example, the Earth Lodge religion, which passed from the Hill Patwin to the Pomo, was similar to the Ghost Dance in that its followers danced to see the dead; however, when the end of the Earth came, it proclaimed, only those who were in the subterranean lodges would survive the catastrophe. Other forms of the Ghost Dance in California were the Bole-Maru and the Big Head religions. ■

This old photograph depicts men in traditional headdresses, with the prophet Wewoka (Wovoka) seated. He was the mystic whose religious pronouncements spread the Ghost Dance among tribes across the West.

Mooretown Rancheria

Tribe: Mooretown Rancheria of Maidu Indians
Total Area: 365 acres   **Tribal Enrollment:** 1,149

The Concow-Maidu of Mooretown Rancheria are descendants of the ancient Northwestern Maidu, who migrated to the area of today's Butte County about 1200 B.C. and settled on a ridge between the Middle Fork and South Fork of the Feather River.

They practiced a subsistence lifestyle, practiced horticulture, and traded extensively with coastal tribes. The aboriginal hunting territory for the Maidu extended roughly from Mount Lassen and Honey Lake on the north to the Cosumnes River on the south, between the Sacramento River and the Sierra Nevada.

Despite persistent stories of European contact having been recorded in a Spanish document of the 1500s, the earliest verifiable contact occurred in 1800. The railroads brought timber interests and agricultural and commercial development, and the Concow-Maidu were dispossessed of their homelands. During one removal to a reservation, in

Indians on the Hoopa Valley Reservation gather ferns for use in traditional basketmaking.

September 1863, 461 Concows left Chico, but only 277 survived the two-week trip to Round Valley.

A widespread public outcry over the mistreatment of Indians led to the Rancheria Act of 1884; in June 1894, one citizen, James T. Grubbs, gave 80 acres of his own land for the use and benefit of some Indian families. Their settlement consisted of four small cabins in the middle of about eight usable acres. The remaining 72 acres were of very poor quality, but these original settlement families lived there for the next 50 years, planting fruit trees and cultivating gardens.

MYTH OR FACT?

All healers or medicine people in California are men.

MYTH

Traditionally, both men and women could be medicine people or healers. There are many women today who practice traditional medicine.

The BIA purchased an additional 80 acres for the 53-member Frank Taylor Band of Indians, as they were named on a previous census document, in 1915. Mooretown Rancheria was created for one of three tribes that eventually received compensation for lost lands, but it was not distributed until 1972. Furthermore, payment was made based upon the 1853 land value of 47 cents per acre. Federal recognition was restored in 1983. The tribe purchased 203 acres in 1990, near the historic Pence Ranch in Mesilla Valley, notorious as the gathering point for the Maidu Trail of Tears of 1853; an additional 35 acres of land was purchased near Oroville in 1992.

The tribe is working diligently to restore traces of its cultural heritage via the Mooretown Heritage Project, an initiative involving the collection of documents and photographs related to Mooretown, its members' ancestors, and the original founders. The tribe is also developing a Cultural Preservation Ordinance and a Concow-Maidu language program.

PALA RESERVATION

Tribe: Pala Band of Luiseño Mission Indians [Cupeño]
Total Area: 12,273 acres   Tribal Enrollment: 906

Members of the Pala Band belong to the Kuupangaxwichem—or Cupeño, as the Spanish called them—and Luiseño tribes. The Pala Reservation represents one of the communities of Indians forced together by Spanish Franciscan missionaries during the 1800s. Although Cupeño descendants form the majority, there has been much cultural integration between the tribes.

The Luiseño people occupied about 1,500 square miles of southern coastal California, including the San Luis Rey River area where the Pala Reservation is now. They were farmers who used advanced agricultural techniques such as controlled burning, water and erosion management, and plant husbandry. In 1875, through the initiative of Chief Oligario Calac, the Luiseño petitioned the federal government to have their ancestral lands granted reservation status. The 1891 Act for the Relief of Mission Indians

MIWOK

The name Miwok (also spelled Miwuk, Mi-wuk, or Me-wuk) refers to any one of several linguistically related peoples who lived in north-central California, from the coast to the plains to the western slope, foothills, and ranges of the Sierra Nevada. As with many other California Indians, the Miwok were mainly hunter-gatherers who lived in small bands or villages and operated under a form of governance that was not easily understood by outsiders. Disputes were resolved using a system of repayment, and there was no particular person who stood out as a chief. To simplify and understand the diversity of Miwok cultures, early scientists divided them into four ethnic subgroups: Coast Miwok, Plains and Sierra Miwok, Lake Miwok, and Bay Miwok.

Coast Miwok

Little is known of contact between the Coast Miwok and outsiders until the latter part of the 16th century, although there was probably contact via the sea. It is thought that Sir Francis Drake visited around 1576. A variety of historical documentation exists between the Coast Miwok and the Spanish and Russians between 1595 and 1808. Their territory stretched from Bodega Bay in the north, east to present-day Sonoma and down into Marin County. More than 600 village sites have been uncovered. They were in contact with the most southerly of the Wintun and the most northerly of the Costanoan.

The Coast Miwok ate food from the bays, lagoons, rivers, and ocean as well as from the land. They dried their fish and meat, and harvested clover and buckeye nuts. In the spring, they gathered sweet sap from oaks and wild honey. They made fishing nets and traps and constructed beautiful baskets for capturing small game. Today the Coast Miwok have a Spring Festival to celebrate spring and its first fruit, and a Fall Festival, celebrating the acorn. Active trading relationships with area tribes are showcased at the "Big Time" Festival at Kule Loklo.

The Sierra Miwok lived in cedar-bark cabins like this reproduction on display in the Yosemite Valley.

They continue the tradition of making handmade clamshell beads, which were used as money. Owning many beads was a sign of wealth.

Plains and Sierra Miwok

The Miwok of the Plains and Sierra are most closely associated with the beautiful Yosemite region of California, which was part of their traditional lands. They had a clan or moiety kinship system. Divisions within the moieties included frog people, blue jay people, bear people, bee people, butterfly people, and others.

Again, food was abundant. They hunted small game, along with the usual food staple for that area—acorns from black oaks—from which they made soup and bread. The Southern and Central Sierra Miwok fished for deepwater sturgeon from the Stanislaus and Merced Rivers. Mushrooms and berries were collected, crushed, and dried and made into cider. Interestingly, they roasted yellow jackets and grasshoppers.

In 1848, gold was discovered in Woods Creek near Jamestown in Tuolumne County, which is in the territory of the Central Sierra Miwok. The discovery and the gold rush that followed ended their traditional life. During the Mariposa Indian War of 1850–51, U.S.-sanctioned troops made repeated raids on settlements. Villages were burned to the ground. The people were left with no shelter or food and eventually forced into submission.

Lake Miwok

The Lake Miwok spoke their own language, in the Penutian dialect, and lived in the Clear Lake Basin of Lake County. They were surrounded by the Pomo, the Wappo, and the Wintun. Before contact, the Lake Miwok population was around 500. They were particularly hard-hit by the smallpox epidemic in 1837 that emanated from Fort Ross, a Russian settlement established as a hub for fur trading. Other diseases brought by the Spanish also contributed to a massive loss of human life. In addition, villages of the Lake Miwok and other Miwok groups were often raided by Mexicans and others looking for slaves or cheap labor.

Bay Miwok

The Bay Miwok occupied many areas, following seasonal food availabilities. They lived in areas that are now the eastern portions of Contra Costa County, extending from the town of Walnut Creek eastward to the Sacramento-San Joaquin delta. They also encompassed the southeastern portion of the Montezuma Hills near Rio Vista and the spiritually significant Mount Diablo. The Bay Miwok were among the first to undergo missionization by the Spanish. Indeed, much of the written record about the Bay Miwok comes from the ecclesiastical records of the times. We know from baptismal records that there were seven Bay Miwok-speaking nations. They suffered catastrophic depopulation from contact with the missionaries and disease. However, there are descendants alive today.

The Miwok Today

Many bands of Miwok survive. They have only small land bases left, due to the influx of settlers and constant displacement at the hands of the U.S. government. There is strength in the continuation of their ceremonial lives, their basketmaking, and their language revitalization attempts.

There are several federally recognized tribes: the Buena Vista Rancheria, California Valley Miwok Tribe, Chicken Ranch Rancheria, Ione Band of Miwok Indians, Jackson Rancheria, Shingle Springs Band, Tuolumne Band, United Auburn Indian Community of the Auburn Rancheria, Federated Indians of the Graton Rancheria, Middletown Rancheria (made up of members of Pomo, Lake Miwok, and Wintun descent), and Wilton Rancheria Indian Tribe. There are also several unrecognized groups, including the Miwok Tribe of the El Dorado Rancheria, Nashville-Eldorado Miwok Tribe, Colfax-Todds Valley Consolidated Tribe of the Colfax Rancheria, Southern Sierra Miwuk Nation, and Calaveras Band of Mi-Wuk Indians. ∎

A Miwok warrior poses for a 1927 photo.

created five Luiseño reservations, including Pala. Immediately after its creation, as decreed by the act, the reservation was divided into allotments.

In 1903, the Cupeño people joined the Luiseño on the reservation. Occupying two villages near Warner Springs, the Cupeño were forcibly moved from their farmland to Luiseño territory. In an attempt to retain their traditional land, the Cupeño, along with another band, fought their expulsion all the way to the U.S. Supreme Court. After they lost their case, the government purchased additional land and added it to Pala to accommodate relocated tribal members. In addition to this acreage, the government promised to provide these displaced people with homes and infrastructural improvements. But the Cupeño received only temporary clapboard shacks and lean-tos. While the majority of the Cupeño refugees remained at the Pala Reservation, a significant number moved early in the 20th century to the Morongo Indian Reservation. Both groups continued their agricultural traditions, raising fruit trees, market and subsistence crops, cattle, horses, chickens, and bees. Many Pala residents participated in the wage economy as ranch and farm laborers. By 1910, the average annual income of Pala residents either matched or exceeded that of the area's non-Indian farmers.

Water issues have plagued Pala residents. Beginning in 1894, via a number of dishonest maneuvers, water has been consistently diverted from the Pala Reservation. In 1951, a claim for the stolen water was added to the Mission Indian Land Claim. Finally in 1985, when the Pala and other area reservations brought forth the San Luis Rey case, an out-of-court settlement compensated these groups for water damages, and the federal government promised that 16,000 acre-feet of other water would be made available to these groups.

People on the Pala Reservation continue to observe traditional cultural practices, such as rituals for the dead and Peon games. Their settlement pattern, of a central-village type, reflects the housing arrangement of the Cupeño homeland at Warner Springs.

Indian tribes along the California coast carved fishing hooks from seashells.

PAUMA AND YUIMA RESERVATION

Tribe: Pauma Band of Luiseño Mission Indians
Total Area: 5,877 acres   Tribal Enrollment: 189

The Pauma and Yuima Reservation is one of the homes of the Luiseño tribe, which originally occupied about 1,500 square miles of coastal southern California. In the last 100 years, the history of the reservation has been closely linked to the water-use policies within the area. In 1916, the owner of the land surrounding the Pauma and Yuima Reservation subdivided the land and sold the orchards. Subsequently, non-Native orchardists appropriated a majority of the reservation's water supply, and the Pauma's prosperous orchards died.

By 1955, a lack of water forced most Pauma residents to seek employment off the reservation. In 1951, a claim for the stolen water was added to the docket of the Mission Indian Land Claim case. After a 1973 hearing, the Federal Power Commission required the city of Escondido to regularly release water from its dam for use by several reservations downstream. There was also some monetary compensation for the tribes involved, and the federal government promised 16,000 acre-feet of water to the reservations and rancherias involved in the lawsuit. The settlement led to a small revitalization on the reservation, as a number of tribal members returned to live there. The tribes involved in the water rights battle formed the San Luis Rey Indian Water Authority to manage water, approve developments, and distribute benefits from the settlement for past damages.

The fertile soil in the Pauma Valley and the band's rights to Pauma Creek's surface water make the reservation land valuable for agricultural, commercial, and residential uses. Twenty-five percent of the tribe's acreage has been devoted to growing lemons, oranges, and avocados. As the city of San Diego continues to expand in the direction of the Pauma Reservation, the land and its resources will correspondingly continue to become more valuable.

PECHANGA RESERVATION

Tribe: Pechanga Band of Luiseño Mission Indians
Total Area: 5,371 acres   **Tribal Enrollment:** 1,342

The Pechanga Band has resided in the Temecula Valley for thousands of years. It is one of six bands of the Payomkawichum, or Luiseño, tribe, comprising the indigenous groups that once inhabited the villages near the Mission San Luis Rey de Francia. The mission was founded in 1798 and served the ranchos of the Temecula Valley. These ranchos were established within boundaries of Native communities, and ranchers forced the indigenous residents into servitude for the mission.

In 1869, local ranchers petitioned the district court of California in San Francisco for a Decree of Ejection of Indians living in Temecula Valley. The court granted the decree in 1873, and in 1875 the tribe was forcibly removed from their ancestral lands, to which they held title. The band was moved to the hills south of the Temecula River.

The Pechanga Reservation is located 20 miles inland from the Pacific Ocean in the Temecula Valley near the city of Temecula. President Chester Arthur's executive order established the Pechanga Indian Reservation in 1882. Under provisions of the General Allotment Act, 1,233 acres of the reservation were allotted in 1891, which increased the reservation's land base. The allotments were not suitable for farming, and in 1907, tribal members petitioned the government for more suitable lands. More than 500 acres were added in 1988 under two separate acts. In 2001, the tribe purchased 700 acres of its ancestral homelands. The BIA placed the lands into federal trust in 2003.

A symbol of pride for the Pechanga is the Great Oak Tree, an ancient tree standing on the tribe's reservation land. This tree is thought to be the oldest living coast live oak (*Quercus agrifolia*) in North America, estimated to be more than 1,500 years old. An evergreen with thick, leathery leaves, the tree stands more than 96 feet tall, with a trunk 26 feet in diameter and sturdy crooked branches. The Great Oak Tree is now under the tribe's protection.

TAKEOVER OF ALCATRAZ ISLAND

In 1969, protesting American Indians took over Alcatraz Island in San Francisco Bay, site of an unused federal prison. The occupation lasted for about 19 months. At its height, as many as 400 people were living on the island.

At the height of the civil rights movement in the United States, American Indians came together in one of the most successful protest actions in Native history. On November 20, 1969, a group of Indian students who called themselves Indians of All Tribes broke into the famous prison on Alcatraz Island in San Francisco Bay, which had been abandoned by the federal government since 1963. Left to decay, the prison had no working plumbing and, for part of the time, no electricity.

The students wanted to reclaim Alcatraz as Indian land and build Indian-focused institutions such as a center for Native American studies, a spiritual center, and a museum. They also wanted to raise awareness of the history of broken treaties and the failed government policy of the termination of tribes. At the height of the occupation, there were around 400 people living on the island. Locals, both Native and non-Native, ignored the blockade surrounding the island and brought food and other needed supplies to the occupiers.

Although the FBI wanted to remove the occupiers forcibly, President Richard M. Nixon, who was at times sympathetic to American Indian concerns, sent a representative to negotiate instead. After the occupation, Nixon increased the budget of the Bureau of Indian Affairs dramatically, doubled funds for Indian health care, and increased scholarship funds, among other federal policy and budget changes.

After visiting the occupiers, members of the American Indian Movement began a series of national protests using the occupation as a model, although none of them would be as effective. The occupation lasted for about 19 months and ended peacefully when police and federal agents invaded the prison and removed the last 15 occupiers. ■

ROUND VALLEY
RESERVATION

Tribe: Round Valley Indian Tribes [Yuki, Concow-Maidu, Little Lake, Pomo, Nomlaki, Cahto, Wailaki, and Pit River]   Total Area: 31,751 acres   Tribal Enrollment: 3,785

The Round Valley Reservation was created in 1856 as the Nome Cult Farm. It was originally designated for occupation by the Yuki tribe of California, which had lived in Round Valley for thousands of years. The reservation itself represents one of the oldest reservations in California. The large Nome Lackee Reservation was established in 1854 on the eastern foothills of the Coast Range, and the vestiges of many cultural groups living around the Central Valley were removed to it. When Euro-American settlers

Tongva tribal dancers perform a blessing ceremony on Catalina Island in 2004. Their ancestors historically occupied the Los Angeles Basin and several offshore islands.

claimed this land in 1863, these people were herded over the mountains to Round Valley, with considerable loss of life over the course of a two-week journey.

During the late 19th century, as Euro-American encroachment on tribal lands in California burgeoned, the federal government began to relocate members of other tribes to the reservation. Although many of the tribes were traditional rivals, eventually they created a nation of confederated tribes that share a common experience and land base. Members of the Round Valley Indian Tribes are descended from the Yuki, Concow-Maidu, Little Lake, Pomo, Nomlaki, Cahto, Wailaki, and Pit River groups of California. The tribe was initially referred to as the Covelo Indian Community but later evolved into the Round Valley Indian Tribes.

The reservation is located in an isolated and geographically round valley in Mendocino County. It is the second largest reservation in California. Today ownership of the land base is a mosaic divided between tribal lands under individual Indian family ownership and trust lands.

The potential for economic development on the Round Valley Indian Reservation lies in its rich natural resources. Within the valley, untapped reserves of fertile soil, water, and timber tracts provide potential areas of economic growth. Employment opportunities for tribal members are in the timber industry, tourism and recreation, agricultural projects, and the tribal government.

The reservation has a small fruit orchard and approximately 1,000 acres suitable for agricultural uses. Three percent of tribal members are employed in the agricultural industry. Approximately 750 acres of reservation land have been leased for cattle grazing. In addition, individual tribal members own cattle ranches on the reservation. Logging and milling serve as the primary source of employment for tribal members.

SAN MANUEL RESERVATION

Tribe: San Manuel Band of Mission Indians [Serrano]
Total Area: 814 acres   **Tribal Enrollment:** 178

San Manuel Reservation residents are primarily people of the Serrano tribe. The term *serrano*, meaning "mountaineer," was initially used by Spanish settlers as a generic term of designation for otherwise "unnamed" Indians in the mountainous areas of southern California. Later the name came to refer only to one band, whose territory extended roughly from Mount San Antonio in the San Gabriel Mountains to Cottonwood Springs in the Little San Bernardino Mountains. The Serrano originally occupied much of the Mojave Desert and the San Bernardino Mountains but had largely disappeared from both sectors by the 20th century. The other Serrano base is the Morongo Reservation, about 30 miles to the east.

The Serrano, trained in agriculture at the Catholic missions in the area, have made agriculture—especially citrus—the region's ongoing economic mainstay.

CALIFORNIA

SUSAN MASTEN

Contemporary Native leader

Susan Masten works to support female leadership among Native tribes.

Susan Masten, a Yurok tribal member from northern California, has been a pioneer and role model for female leadership in contemporary Indian tribes. She was the chair of her tribe from 1997 to 2004 and served on the front lines of what were called the "salmon wars," a series of often-violent clashes with the federal government over natural resources and traditional fishing rights. Masten was elected president of the National Congress of American Indians in 1999, the first Californian and second woman in that position. She has held a long list of other posts, including an appointment by the secretary of the interior to serve as a Yurok transition team member to implement the Hoopa-Yurok Settlement Act; vice chair of the Intertribal Monitoring Association on the Indian Trust Funds; and cochair of the Department of the Interior Trust Reform Task Force. She has also been chair of the board of directors of the Indian Law Resource Center, president of the Klamath Chamber of Commerce, and leader of a group defending traditional fishing rights. In 2004, Masten was among the founders of Women Empowering Women for Indian Nations (WEWIN), a group of Native women that aims to support the next generation of female leaders. ∎

POMO

Pomo peoples historically lived along the northern California coast, in a large territory extending east to the main range of the Coast Range, north to the town of Cleone, and south to Duncans Point; there was another small group northeast of there. The population, estimated at about 8,000 in 1700, had fallen to between 800 and 1,200 by 1910. The word Pomo seems to be a combination of the Northern Pomo words for "at red earth hole" and "reside," suggesting "Those Who Live at Red Earth Hole." However, referring to the Pomo as one tribe vastly oversimplifies the linguistic, sociopolitical, and socioeconomic system. Now there are about 20 federally recognized Pomo groups who live in Mendocino, Sonoma, and Lake Counties, with about 4,900 members.

Roundhouses and Social Structure

The Pomo village systems were confounding to white settlers and to the U.S. government. Because they didn't see a system of government they could relate to, they found it hard to negotiate and communicate with the Pomo. The Pomo had decentralized systems in place to work out issues around trade, for example. Villages governed themselves and did not want interference. People had everyday and seasonal homes and traveled to the coast for fish and other resources.

Social and political structures were based on a kinship system and a concentric village structure. At the center of the village were a roundhouse and a sweat lodge, and these were surrounded by homes for women and children where chores were done. The roundhouse, sweat lodge, and wilderness outside the village were the men's world. Roundhouses, which are generally partly underground and hold many people, are still central to community life. They are used for ceremonies that are dictated by a dreamer, a spiritual person who has visions.

Russians and Other Settlers

In the early 19th century, while many Indians in southern California were suffering from contact with Spain and Mexico, Natives in the north were contending with arrivals from Russia. The Russians attempted to establish merchant colonies and trade relations. Indians from several tribes, including the Pomo, were hired to work long hours in dangerous conditions. When they were paid at

Pomo baskets are made of natural materials using traditional techniques such as coiling, twining, and plaiting.

all, it wasn't much, and it was usually with tobacco, beads, or sometimes food.

In 1822, Mexico secured control of California from the Spanish. This was followed by a marked increase in disease and slave raids. In 1848, at the end of the Mexican-American War, Mexico ceded California to the United States.

Then came the California Gold Rush, an era that has been romanticized in American history. But for indigenous Californians, this was a time of war, genocide, and great human and cultural loss. The U.S. government removed Pomo Indians to reservations in other areas of California. But the overcrowded reserves failed, and when the Pomo returned, they found white farmers on their land. They had to work as cheap labor in return for being allowed to live on their own lands.

Settlers considered Indians to be less than human. According to many sources, in 1850, what has become known as the Bloody Island Massacre started when a number of Pomo exacted revenge upon settlers Andrew Kelsey and Charles Stone for crimes against Pomo who had been pressed into forced labor and for the rape of the chief's wife.

It is said that the two men had forced 50 Pomo men to work as laborers on a gold expedition. Having sold their food rations, Kelsey and Stone allowed all the Pomo men who had gone on the expedition to starve, except for one or two who survived. In retaliation, warriors attacked the house of the two men and killed them. The U.S. Army cavalry, in reprisal, found a group of Pomo on an island called Bonopoti (later known as Bloody Island), where they slaughtered

Pomo chief Little John and his great-grandson, Little Eagle Feather, work with a bag that sports the eagle logo of the New Deal's National Recovery Administration, 1933.

anywhere from 60 to 400 Pomo, including women and children. Then the army killed 75 more Indians along the Russian River. One of the few survivors was Ni'ka, or Lucy Moore, whose descendants have created the Lucy Moore Foundation to improve relations between the Pomo and other Californians.

Modern Pomo

By the beginning of the 20th century, the Pomo had been uprooted and moved and uprooted again, only to return to their ancestral lands. Leadership within the tribes may have changed at times from being hereditary to being based upon education, that is, who could best communicate with the government and the Bureau of Indian Affairs.

There are several surviving Pomo communities. The landmark 1983 case of *Tillie Hardwick et al.* v. *United States* reinstated federal recognition for many tribes in northern California, including some Pomo groups. Others remain unrecognized by the federal government but own land in the Ukiah Valley; they simply operate as a tribal community without the usual government services. The Pomo are revitalizing their languages and lifeways. People who have worked with tribal youths on language, singing, and dancing, such as Cynthia Daniels and the late Ira Campbell, exemplify the life and strength within the community today.

The Pomo continue to make some of the most remarkable baskets by anyone's standards. Their materials—sedge root, willow shoots, redbud, black ash—and techniques—coiling, twining, plaiting—make them distinctive. They are decorated with feathers and clamshell beads. Baskets were utilitarian or medicinal in older times, but beginning in the late 1880s, they were made for sale. Great care is taken when preparing to harvest the roots to provide for the spirits of both person and plant. Well-known basketmakers such as Julia Parker (a Kashia Pomo) still work today. ■

Today few people remain who speak the Serrano language and few ancestral rituals survive, although some people continue to sing traditional Bird Songs on special social occasions. Most of the few remaining Serranos today live on or near the reservation. Through the tribe's Cultural Awareness Program, the language and culture is being revived. The San Manuel Band has also been instrumental in shaping the school curriculum at both the local and statewide level to include lessons on tribes indigenous to California, and it annually hosts a conference for students at California State University, San Bernardino.

SANTA ROSA RANCHERIA

Tribe: Santa Rosa Indian Community [Yokut]
Total Area: 587 acres   Tribal Enrollment: 738

The descendants of the Tachi, Wowol, and Chunut bands of the Yokut tribe currently live on the Santa Rosa Rancheria. Out of what was once approximately 60 Yokut tribes, only a few still remain, and there are only three federally recognized rancherias and one reservation comprised of Yokut descendants.

Following the passage of the General Allotment Act in 1887, many Yokut people were displaced from their traditional tribal lands. Primary sources of employment for many Yokuts during this period and into the early 20th century included logging, working for livestock ranchers as ranch hands, and working as farm laborers in the fruit, vegetable, and cotton fields of the San Joaquin Valley.

Until the 1950s, many Yokut children were sent to Indian boarding schools. During the 1960s, political activism took hold within the greater Native American community. One prominent manifestation of this activism was the Sierra Indian Center. It involved people from many area tribes and was pivotal in establishing other organizations, both local and statewide, that still exist today. The Sierra Indian Center's agenda was, in part, focused on the revitalization of tribal culture and traditional practices. The center's mission stemmed largely from the recognition that Native adaptation to Euro-American

Luiseño, Uto-Aztecan language family

"kiicha" ("house")

"tawwilash" ("chair")

"kupu"ilash" ("bed")

culture, as well as the intrusion of non-Indian schools and religion, had altered or reduced many aspects of indigenous culture.

The March 1 Celebration stands as just one example of the continuing of the tribe's traditional and cultural practices; it constitutes the Santa Rosa Rancheria's main tribal activity and is a time dedicated to spiritual renewal and future prosperity.

TABLE BLUFF RESERVATION

Tribe: Wiyot Tribe   Total Area: 88 acres
Tribal Enrollment: 526

The Wiyot have resided along the northern California coast for thousands of years. Their ancestral lands include Indian Island and extend from the Little River to the Bear River and inland to the first range of mountains.

Tragedy struck on February 26, 1860, when a group of settlers massacred at least 100 tribal members on Indian Island, killing women, children, and elders. Only one infant survived the slaughter. On that same evening, Wiyot villages on the mainland, Eel River and South Spit, were attacked, and 100 more tribal members were murdered. The surviving Wiyot people were relocated to Fort Humboldt for their protection, and many were later dispersed to reservations throughout California, including the Klamath River Reservation. When floodwaters inundated the reservation, residents were relocated to the Smith River, Hoopa, and Round Valley Reservations. Precontact, the Wiyot population is estimated to have ranged in size from 1,500 to 2,000 people. Their numbers dropped sharply and by 1860, there were only around 200 tribal members. In 1910, fewer than 100 full-blood Wiyot people remained within the tribe's traditional territory.

The Wiyot continually attempted to return to their homelands, particularly Indian Island. The island had served as a ceremonial site for countless years and is of great cultural significance to the Wiyot people. Tuluwat Village, on the island, contains a clamshell mound that measures over six acres in size. It is estimated to be at least 1,000 years old and

is known to contain cultural artifacts as well as burial sites. In addition to natural erosion, Euro-American encroachment upon the mound resulted in the desecration of many grave sites and the destruction of significant areas. In 2004, the City of Eureka returned portions of Indian Island, including Tuluwat Village and the shell mound, to the Wiyot people. It was the first time in California that a city restored a sacred site to a tribe.

Years of racism and genocidal tactics have taken their toll on the Wiyot. In addition to reducing the tribal population, there has been a stifling of traditional culture that members are struggling to reverse. The 1860 massacre on Indian Island halted the annual renewal celebrations held there, an important facet of Wiyot spiritual practices and cultural beliefs. Tribal members hope the return of their sacred sites on Indian Island will mark the beginning of renewal of Wiyot traditions.

A brightly colored Chumash pictograph, found in the San Emigdio Mountains of southern California

TORRES MARTINEZ RESERVATION

Tribe: Torres Martinez Desert Cahuilla Indians
Total Area: 23,842 acres   **Tribal Enrollment:** 573

The Cahuilla, meaning "masters" or "powerful ones," are usually divided into three groups by geographic location: the Pass Cahuilla of the San Gorgonio Pass and Palm Springs, the Mountain Cahuilla of the San Jacinto and Santa Rosa Mountains, and the Desert Cahuilla of the eastern Coachella Valley. The Desert Cahuilla were the first known inhabitants of the Coachella Valley and are ancestors of the Torres Martinez tribe. Tribal members are active in preserving their language and customs, through songs, dances, and educational and oral tradition. The annual Su-Kutt Menyil Fiesta brings together neighboring tribes and local communities to share in the Torres Martinez culture.

The Karuk Indians of Northern California still fish the Klamath River using traditional-style dip nets.

one of them and serves as a center for tribal activities. The tribe recently received a grant to restore the structure. This site was one of the stopping points of the Bradshaw Wagon Company, the Pony Express, and other travelers.

TRINIDAD RANCHERIA

Tribes: Cher-Ae Heights Indian Community
Total Area: 83 acres   Tribal Enrollment: 171

Members of the Cher-Ae Heights Indian Community descend from the Wiyot, Yurok, and Tolowa tribes, which share some aspects of cultural heritage. Traditionally, these groups lived throughout the coastal region of what is now northern California and southern Oregon. An abundance of native plants, including acorns and wild herbs, marine resources, and game provided a comfortable living. Though these tribes engaged in commerce and lived peaceably nearby one another for at least 1,000 years, the Wiyot also share characteristics of more inland groups; for example, they did not practice a First Salmon ceremony. The Tolowa, sedentary coastal hunter-gatherers who relied heavily on a diet of salmon, smelt, and sea lion, did observe the ceremony for the first salmon, as did the Yurok.

The first land contact between the Wiyot tribe and Euro-Americans occurred in 1849, when the indigenous people of the region provided shelter and sustenance for the Josiah Gregg exploration party. After lending their hospitality, the local people showed the Gregg party the trail to Humboldt Bay. The Wiyot and Tolowa were nearly annihilated by subsequent immigrants. The present rancheria site is located near one of the largest precontact Yurok villages on the coast, called Tsurai, which was reduced to a single person by 1916. Some rancheria members can trace their descent from former Tsurai residents.

Since the mid-1970s, the tribe has accomplished an enormous revitalization. After nearly having its federal status terminated, the tribe has focused on improving its infrastructure, particularly inadequate water supply; developing housing facilities; and creating a stable economy to serve its members.

Between 1905 and 1907, more than 11,000 reservation acres were flooded when a Colorado River irrigation aqueduct broke, forming the Salton Sea. The remaining 13,800 acres are agricultural lands. In 2002, after 90 years of litigation, the government agreed to compensate the tribe for the lost land.

The Martinez Historic District has three buildings that are the oldest standing Indian Agency buildings in the state. The BIA schoolhouse, built in 1907, is

TULE RIVER RESERVATION

Tribe: Tule River Indian Tribe [Yokut]
Total Area: 55,396 acres   Tribal Enrollment: 1,555

Members of the Tule River Tribe are descendants of the Tule-Kaweah band of the Yokut tribe, composed of the Bokinuwas, Kawia, Wuchamni, Yausanchi, and Yokod groups. The Yokut tribe comprises 50 separate bands. The tribe's traditional homelands span central California, from the foothills of the Tehachapi Mountains to the Sierra Nevada and the San Joaquin River. Many Yokut groups were forced together on the Tule River Reservation when it was established by executive order in 1873. The majority of tribal members live on or within five miles of the reservation.

Beginning in the 20th century, the region's indigenous people joined the wage economy, working in the logging industry and on the area's ranches and farms. Many Tule River residents worked as ranch hands or as farm laborers in the fruit, vegetable, and cotton fields of the San Joaquin Valley.

In the 1900s, the region's Yokut people pushed to revitalize some of their traditional cultural practices. Toward this end, several Yokut bands founded the Sierra Indian Center, which serves as a hub for both political and cultural activism. The Wukchumni tribe, many of whose members reside on the Tule River Reservation, have their own tribal council, which is intensely involved in preserving traditional village sacred sites.

The 14,000 acres of conifers on the reservation provide the tribe with its principal source of income. The tribe employs a timber management plan to actively protect and develop the forest area.

YOCHA DEHE RESERVATION

Tribe: Yocha Dehe Wintun Nation
Total Area: 269 acres   Tribal Enrollment: 44

The Yocha Dehe Wintun Nation comprises just one part of the Wintun tribe, a band numbering about 12,000 in the early 1800s. Given the range of Wintun territory, their language (Wintu)

MYTH OR FACT?

The staple of the California Indian diet was the corn tortilla, the same as in Mexico.

MYTH

Indigenous people ate the plants and animals available locally. That meant the diets of California Indians varied greatly, depending on where they lived.

evolved into a number of dialects. There are three divisions of the Wintun people: the Wintu, Nomlaki, and Patwin. Their traditional lands are located in the greater Sacramento Valley, following the Sacramento River from the Wintu Mountain rivers in the north, through the Nomlaki plains, to the marshes, valleys, and hills of the Patwin. For food, the Wintun depended on the semiannual runs of king salmon as well as on acorns, with secondary use of other vegetable foods and game. Today there are approximately 2,500 people of Wintun descent; apart from the Yocha Dehe, many live on the Colusa, Cortina, Grindstone, and Redding rancherias as well as on the Round Valley Reservation.

In an all too familiar pattern, tribal unity was destroyed by the usurpation of land and resulting destruction of traditional food- and materials-gathering areas. As Congress attempted to isolate all the state's Indians in four major reservations, against their wishes, the Wintun struggled to return to their aboriginal lands. Finally, in 1909, a reserve was set aside east of present-day Rumsey. The reservation was moved in 1940 to a 60-acre tract 15 miles south of Rumsey, part of the current site. By 1970 the rancheria had dwindled to only three members and was on the verge of termination. In 1982, 118 acres were added to the rancheria as it began acquiring new members. Later the tribe obtained financing for the construction of Cache Creek Indian Bingo and Casino.

Agriculture remains the primary land use of the Wintun Reservation, and it has passed historically through several distinct phases. Fruit colonies established around 1900 gradually declined because local climate and soils do not favor commercial fruit production. Around 1920, farmers planted almond orchards and then shifted to the cultivation of walnuts. Other farmers continue to grow field crops, while ranchers graze livestock in the hills. The reservation has become a hub for organic produce cultivation. The Wintun continue to practice their traditional culture even as they succeed within mainstream society. Many still harvest traditional foods, most significantly acorns and salmon.

YUROK

The Yurok Indian Reservation is located in parts of Del Norte and Humboldt Counties on a 44-mile stretch of the Klamath River in northern California. The reservation covers about 87 square miles. With more than 5,500 enrolled members, the Yurok tribe is the largest in California. For countless generations, the Yurok have depended upon the river for subsistence. It is a source of strength and identity and something to be protected at all costs. They have a strong relationship with their lands and rivers and a deep knowledge of how to sustain them. The Yurok have often clashed, sometimes violently, with federal agencies and commercial fishing enterprises over their environment, in particular over salmon fishing rights.

The People and the River

Since the early 20th century, the Klamath has been dammed, against the wishes of the Yurok. The tribe has strived to maintain free access to the river, fighting for cultural and traditional rights to fish. Their success is exemplified in the Klamath Basin Restoration Agreement and the accompanying Klamath Hydroelectric Settlement Agreement, which will bring about the largest dam removal project in the history of the world as well as landscape-scale restoration. Those agreements include PacifiCorp, which owns the four dams that will be removed, as well as the federal government and the states of California and Oregon. They also involve 25 other diverse stakeholders, such as farmers and Indian tribes. This effort will restore more than 350 miles of salmon habitat and thousands of acres of wetlands, improve river flows and water quality, and revitalize programs for tribal communities, according to an article in *Indian Country Today*.

Such an ambitious agreement is not without controversy. The Hoopa Valley Tribe has decided not to sign, asserting that it could get better results through litigation or legislation. In addition, a

A six-inch-long purse made of elk horn and leather was used by 18th-century Yurok Indians from the lower Klamath River Valley.

few environmental groups complain that the agreement does not go far enough in restoring flows or protecting national wildlife refuges.

Contact and the Gold Rush

Up until about 1828, there was comparatively little contact between the Yurok and non-Native people. Their interactions were with other indigenous peoples in the area, including the Tolowa, Karuk, Wiyot, and Hupa as well as tribes from central California, Oregon, Washington, and farther east. In 1828, Jedediah Smith, a trapper and expedition leader, guided a team of trappers into the area. Reports of what Smith saw and found eventually led to an increase in non-Indian settlement. Then in 1849, the news of the discovery of gold set off the overwhelming surge of non-Indians into the area.

There were several years of resistance, notably by the group called the Red Cap Indians, who are believed to have consisted of a mix of tribes. By 1855, the federal government had quelled the rebellion, though, and the reservation era began. The Yurok, along with other Indians in the area, were shuffled from reservations within their territory, up to Smith River in Tolowa lands, and to the Hupa reservation. None of these succeeded, and the Yurok came back to their lands, where they watched as outsiders took their land and they were considered squatters. They were eventually removed by military force.

Many Yurok at this time were also being forcibly removed from their families and sent to boarding schools in California and Oregon. California's boarding schools were at Riverside in the south and Chemawa in the north. The goal of boarding schools was to "kill the Indian, but leave the man," rather than to educate Indians in a particular discipline. Native students were forced to use English and to change their clothing and hair styles. Boys were taught menial trades, and girls were taught domestic work. Eventually the use of boarding schools declined and the government established day schools on the reservation, but students were still pressured to assimilate into American society.

The Modern Tribe

Almost 75 percent of the Yurok people died in the years following contact and the Gold Rush. The loss of the people who transmitted culture through language, dance, and storytelling was catastrophic. The community has seen resurgence in recent years, though. The era of the civil rights movement ushered in a similar push for the rights of American Indians and a desire by the younger generations to regain some of what was lost. Consequently, in the late 1970s and '80s, the religious aspect of Yurok culture was slowly making its way back to contemporary life. Many of the ceremonial dances were reintroduced, including the Brush Dance, the White Deerskin Dance, and the Jump Dance. When the tribe surveyed their language, it found that, as of 1996, there were only 20 fluent and 12 semifluent speakers; more recently, the tribe counted just 11 fluent speakers, but 37 advanced, 60 intermediate, and approximately 311 basic speakers.

Today the Yurok work toward continued self-sustaining businesses, strong language revitalization programs, a cultural center, housing and health services, and educational programs.

The primary tribal government's administrative office and community center is in the town of Klamath, on the reservation's northern end, with a community center and administration office on the eastern portion of the reservation in Weitchpec. The tribe also operates a satellite office in Eureka. ■

The rivers of northern California have long sustained the Yurok Indians. This photo from about 1923 shows a Yurok canoe on the Trinity River.

CHEROKEE

THE STORY OF TSALI

As troops commanded by Gen. Winfield Scott gathered people of the Cherokee Nation for removal in 1838, they searched for those who tried to hide. Most Cherokee cooperated—and spent their final days back East in the stockades—but 1,000 or more either hid from the troops or hoped their relative isolation would protect them. Tsali and his family were among these people. By the time the troops finished rounding up all of the stragglers they could ferret out, those remaining behind—the first of the Eastern Band—would number about 1,000.

As a farmer and provider, Tsali was more concerned with the weather and his crops. Tribal factions struggled. Politicians argued. Tsali's brother-in-law, Lowney, brought word of companies of soldiers searching the valleys and the thousands of Cherokee people herded in stockades. The whites were preparing for a great march to the west, to a new Cherokee home in Oklahoma. Tsali returned to his fields. As he worked, Tsali imagined his people remaining in the mountains and carrying on the traditions and wisdom of their ancestors.

Federal scouts discovered Tsali's family and ordered them to join the other Cherokee in the stockade at Bushnell. Like the rest of the Nation, Tsali and his family were given little time to prepare. Taking only the belongings they could carry, Tsali, his wife, sons, and brother-in-law left their home, guarded by two soldiers. When Tsali's wife stumbled and a soldier prodded her with his bayonet, Tsali spoke to his kinsmen in their Native tongue. "When we reach the turn in the trail," he said, "I will fall and complain of my ankle. When the soldiers stop, leap on them and take their guns. Then we'll escape into the hills."

Tsali's Fate Is Sealed An accidental discharge during the ensuing struggle left one soldier dead and turned Tsali, Lowney, and their sons, Ridges and Wasituna, into wanted men. Tsali's family fled to a concealed cave under Clingman's Dome, now a part of the Great Smoky Mountains National Park, where the Army troops would be at a marked disadvantaged if they discovered the fugitives. Tsali was committed to fighting to the death rather than letting his family become prisoners. The fugitives weren't aware that more than a thousand other Cherokee were also hiding out in remote areas of the Great Smokies. They had banded together under the leadership of Utsali ("Lichen"), who had sworn never to leave their mountain homeland. Tsali's family and Utsali's band eluded capture during the summer of 1838. By fall, the final group of soldiers and Cherokee detainees began the long trip west.

General Scott's Proposal Faced with the nearly impossible task of capturing the fugitives, General Scott came up with an idea for ending the campaign and revenging the death of his soldier. He sent for Will Thomas, a white trader who had been adopted by the great chief Yonaguska. "If Tsali and his kin will come in and give up," he told Thomas, "I won't hunt down the others. If Tsali will voluntarily pay the penalty, I will intercede with the government to grant the fugitives permission to remain. But if Tsali refuses, I'll turn my soldiers loose to hunt every one of them." When Thomas delivered the message under Clingman's Dome, Tsali agreed to turn himself in. Tsali, Ridges, and Lowney were sentenced to death, while the younger Wasituna and his mother were spared.

A Legend Is Born In a field next to the stockade at Bushnell, the condemned men were stood against three trees. The colonel in charge asked the prisoners for their customary final words. Tsali spoke up: "If I must be killed, I would like to be shot by my own people." Three Cherokee men were selected to be the executioners. Tsali and his kin waved aside the blindfolds they were offered. A volley rang out in the valley, and the men slumped to the earth. Tsali, Lowney, and Ridges were buried near the stockade. A little over 100 years later, the valley was flooded, and today the graves are covered by the waters of Fontana Lake.
(Adapted from "Tsali," appearing on the Cherokee North Carolina website: http://www.cherokee-nc.com/index.php?page=60. Used with permission.)

OJIBWE

GOOKOOKO'OO OTAWAGAANG
(IN THE EAR OF THE OWL)

This is what must have happened long ago, as children are kept [in] here for a reason so that they don't play when it starts to get dark. Their mothers and fathers chased everyone inside so that they wouldn't do this. Then they were told, "If you play out there in the night, he will have you. He'll steal you away. That owl will take you." That's what they were told. They tried to scare them.

But no, that one boy didn't listen. So he hid, playing in the night. Well, in the meantime they thought their boy had gone to bed. But the boy must have been out there playing when he was taken by that owl. He was brought there into its ear.

In the morning all the Indians must have gotten up. Now they were missing their boy. He wasn't there. Now they were worried about him, wherever their son had gone. Now they started asking others if they had seen their son. Nope. Then they saw that owl over there sitting in that tree. But they didn't think anything of that owl. Well, truly the Indians kept it in their minds how their son was lost. He meant so much to them.

And they hired someone. An old man spoke, having a big ceremony now. They must have gone over and hired that old man to have a ceremony. Then that old man had a shake tent ceremony and told his spirits to look for their boy wherever he had gone. Now that one spirit must have went and found him. And it was there that retrieved him from the owl's ear where their son had been held captive. The spirit retrieved him from that place he was held there to where the ceremony was taking place.

So now they are told to be very fearful of owls. Well, children are always told now, "Don't play late at night. The owl will get a hold of you. You'll be put in his ear." That's how the children were frightened. That's what happened long ago.
(Told by Thomas J. Stillday of Ponemah, Minnesota, of the Red Lake Reservation. Originally published in the Oshkaabewis Native Journal; *reprinted with permission from the editor.)*

RAVEN MYTH

It was the time when there were no people on the earth. For four days the first man lay coiled up in the pod of a beach pea. On the fifth, he burst forth, falling to the ground, and stood up, a full-grown man. Feeling unpleasant, he stooped and drank from a pool of water, then felt better. Looking up, he saw a dark object approaching with a waving motion until it stopped just in front of him. It was a raven. Raven stared intently at man, raised one wing and pushed up its beak, like a mask, to the top of its head, and changed immediately into a man. Still staring and cocking its head from side to side for a better view, Raven said at last: "What are you? Whence did you come? I have never seen the likes of you." And Raven looked at Man, surprised to see that this stranger was so much like himself in shape.

Then Raven told Man to walk a few steps, again marveling: "Whence did you come?" To this the Man replied: "I came from the pea-pod," pointing to the plant nearby. "Ah!" exclaimed Raven, "I made that vine, but did not know anything would come from it." Then Raven asked Man if he had eaten anything, to which man replied he had taken soft stuff into him at a pool. "Well," said Raven, "you drank some water. Now wait for me here."

He drew down the mask over his face, changing again into a bird, and flew far up into the sky, where he disappeared. Again Man waited four days, when the Raven returned, bringing four berries in his claws. Pushing up his mask, Raven became a man again and held out two salmonberries and two heathberries, saying, "Here is what I have made for you. Eat them." Then Raven led Man to a creek where he took clay and formed two mountain sheep, which Man thought were very pretty. Telling Man to close his eyes, Raven drew down his mask and waved his wings four times over the images, which became endowed with life and bounded away. When Man saw the sheep moving away, full of life, he cried out in pleasure. Next Raven formed two other animals of clay, but because they were not fully dry when they were given life, they remained brown and white. Thus originated the tame reindeer. Raven told Man they would be very scarce. In the same way a pair of wild reindeer, or caribou, were made, being permitted to dry and turn white only on their bellies before being given life. These, Raven said, would be more common, and people could kill many of them.

"You will be very lonely by yourself," said Raven. "I will make you a companion." Going to a more distant spot and looking now and again at Man, he made an image very much like him, fastening a lot of fine water grass on the back of its head. After the clay dried, he waved his wings over it as before, and a beautiful young woman arose and stood beside Man. "There," cried Raven, "is a companion for you."

In those days there were no mountains far or near, and the sun never ceased shining; neither did rain fall or winds blow. Raven showed them how to make a warm bed of moss where they slept, while Raven lay nearby in the form of a bird. Waking before the others, Raven went to the creek and made pairs of sticklebacks, graylings, and blackfish. When Man arose and came to see them, Raven explained that the graylings would be found in the mountain streams and sticklebacks along the coast, and both would be good to eat. Next the shrewmouse was made, Raven saying that it would not be good for food but would enliven the ground and prevent it from seeming barren and cheerless.

(Yup'ik creation story adapted by William Fitzhugh from Edward W. Nelson's monograph, "Eskimos about Bering Strait," 1899, in William W. Fitzhugh and Susan A. Kaplan, Inua: Spirit World of the Bering Sea Eskimo, *Smithsonian Institution Press, 1982.)*

ARAPAHO

HOW THE EARTH AND MEN WERE MADE

It is said that long ago it rained and rained until there was nothing but water everywhere. In the midst of the water, the sacred Flat Pipe was floating. He was all alone but realized he was a Creator and he had the power to do wonderful things.

Man-Above, who was everywhere but could not be seen, said to Flat Pipe, "You should call on your helpers and ask them to help you make a world different than this." Flat Pipe thought that this was a good idea and called on the water people because they were on the water. Ducks first came to mind because they were water birds, and they quickly appeared, floating on the water in front of him. This took place when the animals could still talk with each other.

The mallard said, "Brothers, why are the water people here? Do you want us to do something?"

"Be strong and dive to the very bottom of the water, and bring whatever is there back to me," Flat Pipe told the ducks.

"Are the waters very deep?" the mallard asked.

"No one knows how deep or shallow the waters may be because no one has been there before," said Flat Pipe.

"Let the smallest water bird try first, then," the ducks decided, and they chose the little teal to dive first into the murky waters. The teal eagerly jumped in but was not seen for the longest time, and when he finally surfaced he was coughing and gasping for breath and very tired. "I tried but couldn't do it, the bottom is too far away for me to reach."

Next the mallard himself tried the long dive, but he, too, barely made it back from the depths.

"You ducks did the best you could," Flat Pipe said, "but we have to keep trying. Let us ask the great wild geese from the north."

"Why did you ask for us? What do you want us to do?" the geese asked.

"We want you to dive into the deep water and find out what is down there so we can make a world," answered Flat Pipe. "Many of the other animals have tried to do this but cannot reach the bottom."

So the great wild geese stood at their tallest and dived into the dark depths, and after a long time they too came up, wet and tired. Flat Pipe thought that perhaps even the larger birds could make it, and he thought of the handsome swans.

"Be careful," Man-Above warned Flat Pipe, "you have created three kinds of water being. You can make only one more."

"I will be careful," Flat Pipe said, and sent the swans down, too, but when they returned without anything he began to get discouraged.

"Perhaps you should make something that can live in the water and on land, but is not a bird," Man-Above advised.

Flat Pipe sat and thought for a long time, while he and the birds floated around in the water. "Land," he remembered. "What is land? Perhaps it is something the opposite of water on which beings walk and not fly, and there must be beings without wings." Then he thought of many beings and settled on the turtle, and it came swimming to him.

"Sister, dive to the bottom of the waters, and bring up whatever is beneath them," Flat Pipe instructed her.

"Yes, I will try," the turtle said, and she disappeared in a splash.

She was gone for so long that Flat Pipe and the birds began to worry, but Man-Above knew better than they did.

"Just wait and see," he said. "Flat Pipe has done everything correctly, so the turtle will soon be back."

Before too much longer, they heard the turtle's leg splashing in the water as she swam to Flat Pipe and spat out a small piece of the earth.

"You did it," Flat Pipe said, and all the birds cheered with him. "Now we will make a world." And the piece of earth that Flat Pipe held between the palms of his hands began to grow and grow until it became the world, and the birds sat on it and the turtle walked around on it, and they were all pleased with their new home.

Then Flat Pipe reached down and took more earth, and made a man and a woman and a buffalo. Now they could all be together for the rest of time. He made other animals, too: deer, antelope, and even rabbits—everything that could walk and run. He made the war birds of the sky and the sacred birds, first the eagles and hawks, then the flycatchers, and then the songbirds.

"That is a lot of creatures," Flat Pipe observed.

"There may be too many," Man-Above warned. "They are filling up much of the space around you."

So Flat Pipe decided to divide the land, so he made another ocean, but not as big as the one on which they had first floated. He made some new different people that had light-colored skin and placed them on the other side of the second ocean. "Always stay there," Flat Pipe ordered them. "Do not bother my people on the buffalo path."

But the light-colored people did not obey him, as we all know.

(Told by Lillian Toahty [Arapaho] to A. Marriott and Carol Rachlin, Smithsonian Institution, National Museum of the American Indian)

NEZ PERCE
OUR ALA

Lydia Moses was one of many Nez Perce women who suffered hardships placed upon them by a military group, but she held on by her faith that one day she would come home. She told me stories about being cold, tired, and hungry, then patted me on my head and said, "I hope your grandchildren will never feel the cold that stings and hunger that holds you on and on and the wetness of your clothes from the rain and heat."

Grandmother Lydia was taken to Fort Leavenworth, along with 410 other people. They were camped along the Missouri River bottom, two miles above the fort between a lagoon and the river. It was the worst possible place; the humidity and the heat were unbearable. The climate killed many people. All the newborn babies died. Old people suffered; everything was different from our old home place. No mountains, no springs, no clear running water. We called where we were held Eeikishpah ("Hot Place"). All the time, night and day, we suffered from the climate. Mothers would dig shallow holes in the sand to keep their babies cool.

After being held prisoner for two years, grandmother and her sister Ahtims decided they couldn't stay any longer—it was just too much to bear. They saved as many rations as they could. They decided to take only what they could pack on their backs, along with extra clothing, a blanket, and food. They waited until it was dark so the soldiers wouldn't see them leave.

They told only a few relatives of their plans. Among the group there was a baby, Ahtims's niece (a girl of about eight), Lydia and her sister, two men (Ilaskulata and Utska), and Ahtims's husband, John Cook. It took them two years to come home to Lapwai. They would stay with friendly Indians along the way, and at times they walked only at nights because some Indian tribes weren't friendly.

In the beginning when they had been traveling through unfriendly territory, the little girl became sick. She would cry from pain and hunger. The other man became worried that she would attract attention, and he warned Ahtims if she didn't keep her quiet, he would. The mother and Lydia tried as best they could. Lydia carried her on her back; Ahtims carried the baby. Each had small bundles. It was the girl who decided that she would go no further. She told her aunt early in the morning, "I can go no further. I want to stay here; I want you to leave me. You must go on. I'll never see our mountains again, see another sunrise." In those days, people—even the children—were very strong, and when a decision was made, it was carried through. So the two women combed the girl's hair, then Lydia braided it. The men found a large rock and rolled it over. It made a depression. The men dug some more dirt away and they laid the little girl in it and rolled the stone back.

(Told by Rosalie K. Bassett about her grandmother, Lydia Moses; National Museum of the American Indian)

TLINGIT
THE EAST AND NORTH WINDS

A high-caste man married the daughter of East-wind (Sâ'nAxet). After a time he heard of a very pretty high-caste girl, the daughter of North-wind (Xûn), so he left his first wife, came north, and married her. Then he took her back to the village where his first wife lived.

Now the people said to his first wife, "There is a very pretty woman here. Her clothes are very valuable and sparkle all over. They make a noise like bells." East-wind's daughter was at once jealous and said, "I will soon be able to fix that pretty girl you boys are talking about." Quite a while afterward it began to grow cloudy and warm, and sure enough the daughter of North-wind lost all of her beautiful clothing. It was icicles and frost that were so pretty, and when she lost these she lost her beauty with them.

(From "Tlingit Myths and Texts," collected by John R. Swanton, Bureau of American Ethnology Bulletin, 1909

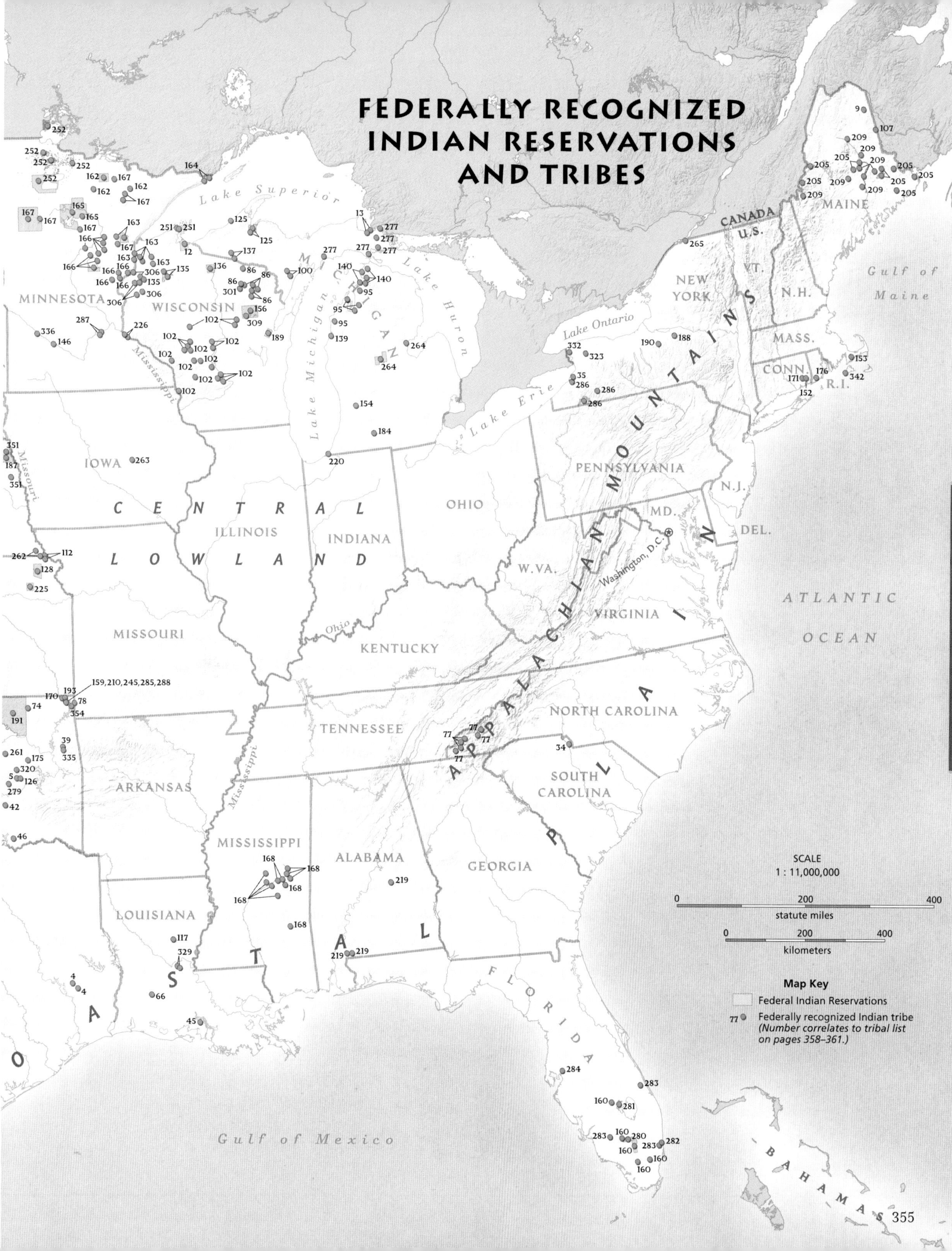

FEDERALLY RECOGNIZED INDIAN RESERVATIONS AND TRIBES

SCALE
1 : 11,000,000

0	200	400

statute miles

0	200	400

kilometers

Map Key

Federal Indian Reservations

77 ● Federally recognized Indian tribe
(*Number correlates to tribal list
on pages 358–361.*)

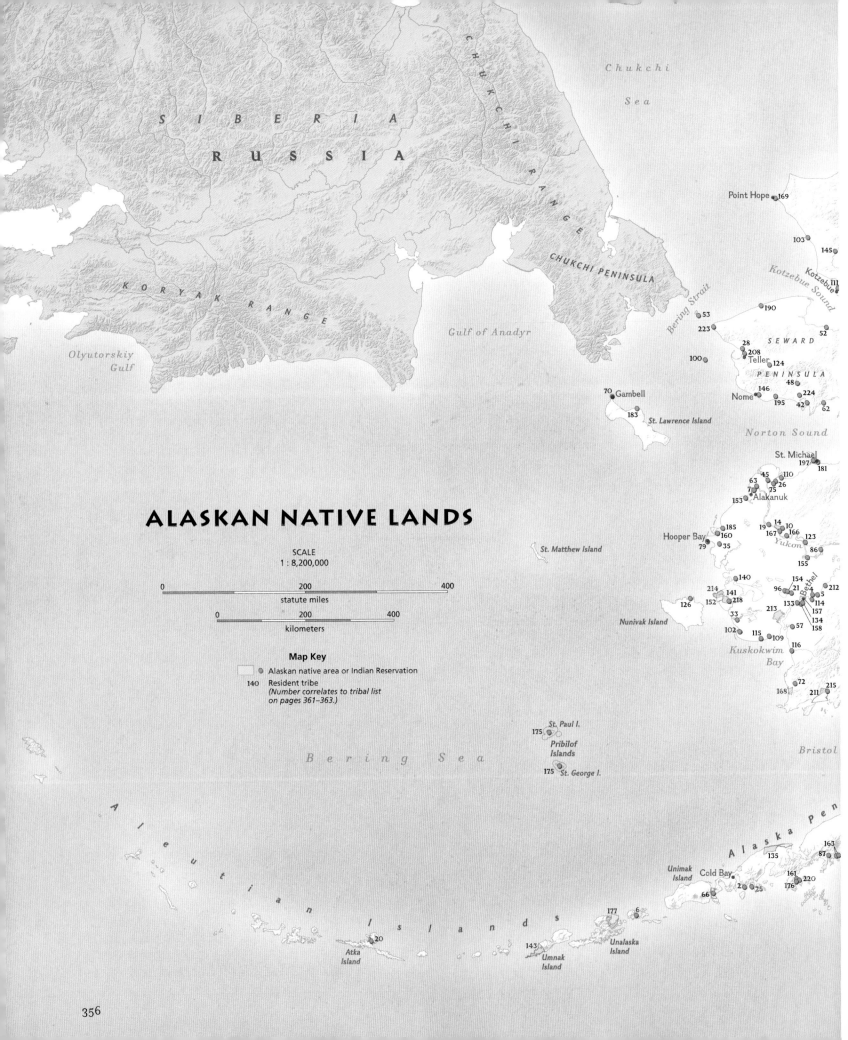

ALASKAN NATIVE LANDS

SCALE
1 : 8,200,000

statute miles
0   200   400

kilometers
0   200   400

Map Key

Alaskan native area or Indian Reservation

140   Resident tribe
(Number correlates to tribal list
on pages 361–363.)

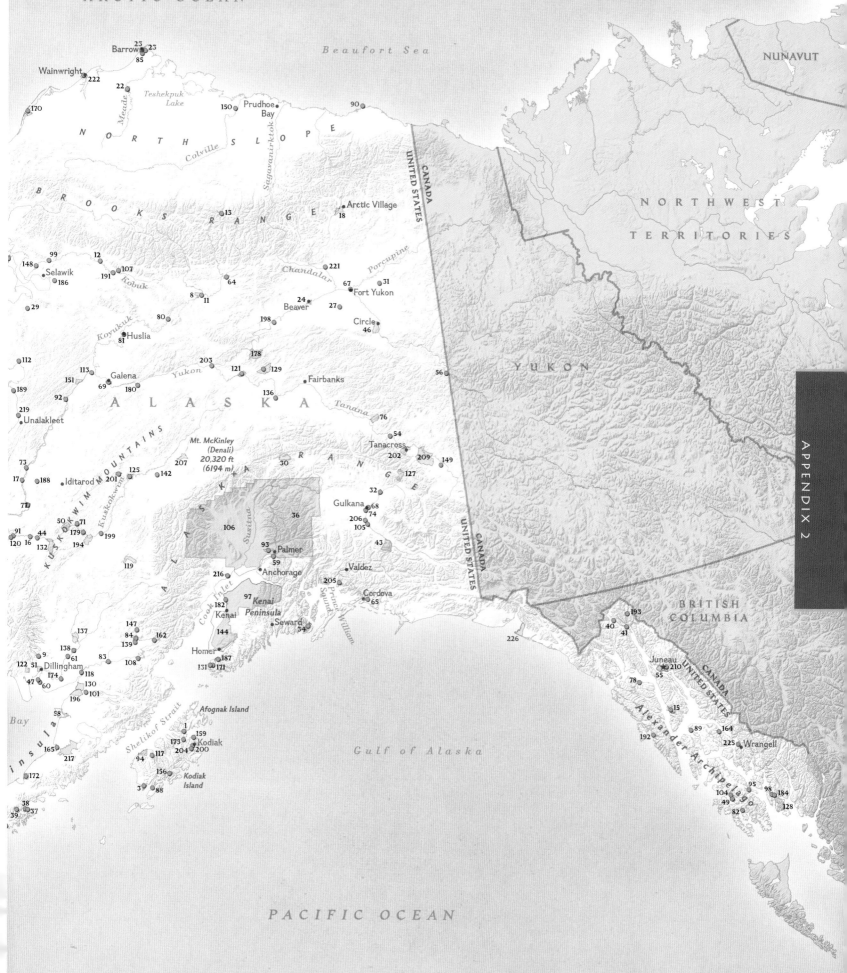

ARCTIC OCEAN

Beaufort Sea

NUNAVUT

Barrow 23 23
85

Wainwright 222
22
Meade

170

Teshekpuk
Lake

150 Prudhoe
Bay

90

NORTH SLOPE

Colville

Sagavanirktok

NORTHWEST

TERRITORIES

UNITED STATES
CANADA

BROOKS   RANGE

13

Arctic Village
18

Chandalar

Porcupine

99
148   12
Selawik   191 107
186   Kobuk

29

221
64
67 31
Fort Yukon

YUKON

8 11
80   Beaver
Koyukuk
81 Huslia

24
198   27
Circle
46

112
151   113
189   Galena 69
92   180

203
121 129
178

Fairbanks

56

Unalakleet
219

Yukon

136

Tanana
76

54
Tanacross
202 209 149
127

73
17   188
Iditarod 201 207
125 142
71

Mt. McKinley
(Denali)
20,320 ft
(6194 m)

30

A   L   A   S   K   A

R   A   N   G   E

32

Gulkana
68
206 74
105

APPENDIX 2

50 71
91 44 179
120 16 132 194
119

ALASKA

Susitna

106

36

43

93
59 Palmer
216   Anchorage

205
Valdez

Cordova
65

97 Kenai
182 Peninsula
Kenai

Cook Inlet

Prince William Sound

226

BRITISH
COLUMBIA

147
137 84
138 162
61
122 51 9 83
Dillingham 118 108
174
47 130
60 196 101

144

Homer
131 187
171

Seward
34

193
40 41

Juneau 210
55

78

Bay

58

Afognak Island

Shelikof Strait

1
159
173 Kodiak
204 200
94 117
156
3   88   Kodiak
Island

Gulf of Alaska

15

89 164
192   225 Wrangell

Alexander Archipelago

95
104 98 184
49
82 128

insula
165
217

172

PACIFIC OCEAN

357

1 Absentee-Shawnee Tribe of Indians of Oklahoma PLAINS

2 Agua Caliente Band of Cahuilla Indians of the Agua Caliente Indian Reservation, California CALIFORNIA

3 Ak Chin Indian Community of the Maricopa (Ak Chin) Indian Reservation, Arizona SOUTHWEST

4 Alabama-Coushatta Tribes of Texas SOUTHEAST

5 Alabama-Quassarte Tribal Town, Oklahoma PLAINS

6 Alturas Indian Rancheria, California CALIFORNIA

7 Apache Tribe of Oklahoma PLAINS

8 Arapahoe Tribe of the Wind River Reservation, Wyoming PLAINS

9 Aroostook Band of Micmac Indians of Maine NORTHEAST

10 Assiniboine and Sioux Tribes of the Fort Peck Indian Reservation, Montana PLAINS

11 Augustine Band of Cahuilla Indians, California (formerly the Augustine Band of Cahuilla Mission Indians of the Augustine Reservation) CALIFORNIA

12 Bad River Band of the Lake Superior Tribe of Chippewa Indians of the Bad River Reservation, Wisconsin NORTHEAST

13 Bay Mills Indian Community, Michigan NORTHEAST

14 Bear River Band of the Rohnerville Rancheria, California CALIFORNIA

15 Berry Creek Rancheria of Maidu Indians of California CALIFORNIA

16 Big Lagoon Rancheria, California CALIFORNIA

17 Big Pine Band of Owens Valley Paiute Shoshone Indians of the Big Pine Reservation, California GREAT BASIN

18 Big Sandy Rancheria of Mono Indians of California CALIFORNIA

19 Big Valley Band of Pomo Indians of the Big Valley Rancheria, California CALIFORNIA

20 Blackfeet Tribe of the Blackfeet Indian Reservation of Montana PLAINS

21 Blue Lake Rancheria, California CALIFORNIA

22 Bridgeport Paiute Indian Colony of California GREAT BASIN

23 Buena Vista Rancheria of Me-Wuk Indians of California CALIFORNIA

24 Burns Paiute Tribe of the Burns Paiute Indian Colony of Oregon GREAT BASIN

25 Cabazon Band of Mission Indians, California CALIFORNIA

26 Cachil DeHe Band of Wintun Indians of the Colusa Indian Community of the Colusa Rancheria, California CALIFORNIA

27 Caddo Nation of Oklahoma PLAINS

28 Cahto Indian Tribe of the Laytonville Rancheria, California CALIFORNIA

29 Cahuilla Band of Mission Indians of the Cahuilla Reservation, California CALIFORNIA

30 California Valley Miwok Tribe, California CALIFORNIA

31 Campo Band of Diegueño Mission Indians of the Campo Indian Reservation, California CALIFORNIA

32 Capitan Grande Band of Diegueño Mission Indians of California: Barona Group of Capitan Grande Band of Mission Indians of the Barona Reservation CALIFORNIA

33 Capitan Grande Band of Diegueño Mission Indians of California: Viejas (Baron Long) Group of Capitan Grande Band of Mission Indians of the Viejas Reservation CALIFORNIA

34 Catawba Indian Nation (aka Catawba Tribe of South Carolina) SOUTHEAST

35 Cayuga Nation of New York NORTHEAST

36 Cedarville Rancheria, California CALIFORNIA

37 Chemehuevi Indian Tribe of the Chemehuevi Reservation, California GREAT BASIN

38 Cher-Ae Heights Indian Community of the Trinidad Rancheria, California CALIFORNIA

39 Cherokee Nation, Oklahoma PLAINS

40 Cheyenne and Arapaho Tribes, Oklahoma (formerly the Cheyenne-Arapaho Tribes of Oklahoma) PLAINS

41 Cheyenne River Sioux Tribe of the Cheyenne River Reservation, South Dakota PLAINS

42 Chickasaw Nation, Oklahoma PLAINS

43 Chicken Ranch Rancheria of Me-Wuk Indians of California CALIFORNIA

44 Chippewa-Cree Indians of the Rocky Boy's Reservation, Montana PLAINS

45 Chitimacha Tribe of Louisiana SOUTHEAST

46 Choctaw Nation of Oklahoma PLAINS

47 Citizen Potawatomi Nation, Oklahoma PLAINS

48 Cloverdale Rancheria of Pomo Indians of California CALIFORNIA

49 Cocopah Tribe of Arizona SOUTHWEST

50 Coeur D'Alene Tribe of the Coeur D'Alene Reservation, Idaho PLATEAU

51 Cold Springs Rancheria of Mono Indians of California CALIFORNIA

52 Colorado River Indian Tribes of the Colorado River Indian Reservation, Arizona and California SOUTHWEST

53 Comanche Nation, Oklahoma PLAINS

54 Confederated Salish & Kootenai Tribes of the Flathead Reservation, Montana PLATEAU

55 Confederated Tribes and Bands of the Yakama Nation, Washington PLATEAU

56 Confederated Tribes of Siletz Indians of Oregon (previously listed as the Confederated Tribes of the Siletz Reservation) NORTHWEST COAST

57 Confederated Tribes of the Chehalis Reservation, Washington NORTHWEST COAST

58 Confederated Tribes of the Colville Reservation, Washington PLATEAU

59 Confederated Tribes of the Coos, Lower Umpqua and Siuslaw Indians of Oregon NORTHWEST COAST

60 Confederated Tribes of the Goshute Reservation, Nevada and Utah GREAT BASIN

61 Confederated Tribes of the Grand Ronde Community of Oregon NORTHWEST COAST

62 Confederated Tribes of the Umatilla Reservation, Oregon PLATEAU

63 Confederated Tribes of the Warm Springs Reservation of Oregon PLATEAU

64 Coquille Tribe of Oregon NORTHWEST COAST

65 Cortina Indian Rancheria of Wintun Indians of California CALIFORNIA

66 Coushatta Tribe of Louisiana SOUTHEAST

67 Cow Creek Band of Umpqua Indians of Oregon NORTHWEST COAST

68 Cowlitz Indian Tribe, Washington NORTHWEST COAST

69 Coyote Valley Band of Pomo Indians of California CALIFORNIA

70 Crow Creek Sioux Tribe of the Crow Creek Reservation, South Dakota PLAINS

71 Crow Tribe of Montana PLAINS

72 Death Valley Timbi-Sha Shoshone Band of California GREAT BASIN

73 Delaware Nation, Oklahoma PLAINS

74 Delaware Tribe of Indians, Oklahoma PLAINS

75 Dry Creek Rancheria of Pomo Indians of California CALIFORNIA

76 Duckwater Shoshone Tribe of the Duckwater Reservation, Nevada GREAT BASIN

77 Eastern Band of Cherokee Indians of North Carolina SOUTHEAST

78 Eastern Shawnee Tribe of Oklahoma PLAINS

79 Elem Indian Colony of Pomo Indians of the Sulphur Bank Rancheria, California CALIFORNIA

80 Elk Valley Rancheria, California CALIFORNIA

81 Ely Shoshone Tribe of Nevada GREAT BASIN

82 Enterprise Rancheria of Maidu Indians of California CALIFORNIA

83 Ewiiaapaayp Band of Kumeyaay Indians, California CALIFORNIA

84 Federated Indians of Graton Rancheria, California CALIFORNIA

85 Flandreau Santee Sioux Tribe of South Dakota PLAINS

86 Forest County Potawatomi Community, Wisconsin NORTHEAST

87 Fort Belknap Indian Community of the Fort Belknap Reservation of Montana PLAINS

88 Fort Bidwell Indian Community of the Fort Bidwell Reservation of California CALIFORNIA

89 Fort Independence Indian Community of Paiute Indians of the Fort Independence Reservation, California GREAT BASIN

90 Fort McDermitt Paiute and Shoshone Tribes of the Fort McDermitt Indian Reservation, Nevada and Oregon GREAT BASIN

91 Fort McDowell Yavapai Nation, Arizona SOUTHWEST

92 Fort Mojave Indian Tribe of Arizona, California & Nevada SOUTHWEST

93 Fort Sill Apache Tribe of Oklahoma PLAINS

94 Gila River Indian Community of the Gila River Indian Reservation, Arizona SOUTHWEST

95 Grand Traverse Band of Ottawa and Chippewa Indians, Michigan NORTHEAST

96 Greenville Rancheria of Maidu Indians of California CALIFORNIA

97 Grindstone Indian Rancheria of Wintun-Wailaki Indians of California CALIFORNIA

98 Guidiville Rancheria of California CALIFORNIA

99 Habematolel Pomo of Upper Lake, California CALIFORNIA

100 Hannahville Indian Community, Michigan NORTHEAST

101 Havasupai Tribe of the Havasupai Reservation, Arizona SOUTHWEST

102 Ho-Chunk Nation of Wisconsin NORTHEAST

103 Hoh Indian Tribe of the Hoh Indian Reservation, Washington NORTHWEST COAST

104 Hoopa Valley Tribe, California CALIFORNIA

105 Hopi Tribe of Arizona SOUTHWEST

106 Hopland Band of Pomo Indians of the Hopland Rancheria, California CALIFORNIA

107 Houlton Band of Maliseet Indians of Maine NORTHEAST

108 Hualapai Indian Tribe of the Hualapai Indian Reservation, Arizona SOUTHWEST

109 Iipay Nation of Santa Ysabel, California (formerly the Santa Ysabel Band of Diegueño Mission Indians of the Santa Ysabel Reservation) CALIFORNIA

110 Inaja Band of Diegueño Mission Indians of the Inaja and Cosmit Reservation, California CALIFORNIA

111 Ione Band of Miwok Indians of California CALIFORNIA

112 Iowa Tribe of Kansas and Nebraska PLAINS

113 Iowa Tribe of Oklahoma PLAINS

114 Jackson Rancheria of Me-Wuk Indians of California CALIFORNIA

115 Jamestown S'Klallam Tribe of Washington NORTHWEST COAST

116 Jamul Indian Village of California CALIFORNIA

117 Jena Band of Choctaw Indians, Louisiana SOUTHEAST

118 Jicarilla Apache Nation, New Mexico SOUTHWEST

119 Kaibab Band of Paiute Indians of the Kaibab Indian Reservation, Arizona GREAT BASIN

120 Kalispel Indian Community of the Kalispel Reservation, Washington PLATEAU

121 Karuk Tribe, California (formerly the Karuk Tribe of California) CALIFORNIA

122 Kashia Band of Pomo Indians of the Stewarts Point Rancheria, California CALIFORNIA

123 Kaw Nation, Oklahoma PLAINS

124 Kewa Pueblo, New Mexico (formerly the Pueblo of Santo Domingo) SOUTHWEST

125 Keweenaw Bay Indian Community, Michigan NORTHEAST

126 Kialegee Tribal Town, Oklahoma PLAINS

127 Kickapoo Traditional Tribe of Texas SOUTHWEST

128 Kickapoo Tribe of Indians of the Kickapoo Reservation in Kansas PLAINS

129 Kickapoo Tribe of Oklahoma PLAINS

130 Kiowa Indian Tribe of Oklahoma PLAINS

131 Klamath Tribes, Oregon PLATEAU

132 Kootenai Tribe of Idaho PLATEAU

133 La Jolla Band of Luiseño Indians, California (formerly the La Jolla Band of Luiseño Mission Indians of the La Jolla Reservation) CALIFORNIA

134 La Posta Band of Diegueño Mission Indians of the La Posta Indian Reservation, California CALIFORNIA

135 Lac Courte Oreilles Band of Lake Superior Chippewa Indians of Wisconsin NORTHEAST

136 Lac du Flambeau Band of Lake Superior Chippewa Indians of the Lac du Flambeau Reservation of Wisconsin NORTHEAST

137 Lac Vieux Desert Band of Lake Superior Chippewa Indians, Michigan NORTHEAST

138 Las Vegas Tribe of Paiute Indians of the Las Vegas Indian Colony, Nevada GREAT BASIN

139 Little River Band of Ottawa Indians, Michigan NORTHEAST

140 Little Traverse Bay Bands of Odawa Indians, Michigan NORTHEAST

141 Los Coyotes Band of Cahuilla and Cupeno Indians, California (formerly the Los Coyotes Band of Cahuilla & Cupeno Indians of the Los Coyotes Reservation) CALIFORNIA

142 Lovelock Paiute Tribe of the Lovelock Indian Colony, Nevada GREAT BASIN

143 Lower Brule Sioux Tribe of the Lower Brule Reservation, South Dakota PLAINS

144 Lower Elwha Tribal Community of the Lower Elwha Reservation, Washington NORTHWEST COAST

145 Lower Lake Rancheria, California CALIFORNIA

146 Lower Sioux Indian Community in the State of Minnesota PLAINS

147 Lummi Tribe of the Lummi Reservation, Washington NORTHWEST COAST

148 Lytton Rancheria of California CALIFORNIA

149 Makah Indian Tribe of the Makah Indian Reservation, Washington NORTHWEST COAST

150 Manchester Band of Pomo Indians of the Manchester-Point Arena Rancheria, California CALIFORNIA

151 Manzanita Band of Diegueño Mission Indians of the Manzanita Reservation, California CALIFORNIA

152 Mashantucket Pequot Tribe of Connecticut NORTHEAST

153 Mashpee Wampanoag Tribe, Massachusetts NORTHEAST

154 Match-e-be-nash-she-wish Band of Potawatomi Indians of Michigan NORTHEAST

155 Mechoopda Indian Tribe of Chico Rancheria, California CALIFORNIA

156 Menominee Indian Tribe of Wisconsin NORTHEAST

157 Mesa Grande Band of Diegueño Mission Indians of the Mesa Grande Reservation, California CALIFORNIA

158 Mescalero Apache Tribe of the Mescalero Reservation, New Mexico SOUTHWEST

159 Miami Tribe of Oklahoma PLAINS

160 Miccosukee Tribe of Indians of Florida SOUTHEAST

161 Middletown Rancheria of Pomo Indians of California CALIFORNIA

162 Minnesota Chippewa Tribe, Minnesota: Bois Forte Band (Nett Lake) NORTHEAST

163 Minnesota Chippewa Tribe, Minnesota: Fond du Lac Band NORTHEAST

164 Minnesota Chippewa Tribe, Minnesota: Grand Portage Band NORTHEAST

165 Minnesota Chippewa Tribe, Minnesota: Leech Lake Band NORTHEAST

166 Minnesota Chippewa Tribe, Minnesota: Mille Lacs Band NORTHEAST

167 Minnesota Chippewa Tribe, Minnesota: White Earth Band NORTHEAST

168 Mississippi Band of Choctaw Indians, Mississippi SOUTHEAST

169 Moapa Band of Paiute Indians of the Moapa River Indian Reservation, Nevada GREAT BASIN

170 Modoc Tribe of Oklahoma PLAINS

171 Mohegan Indian Tribe of Connecticut NORTHEAST

172 Mooretown Rancheria of Maidu Indians of California CALIFORNIA

173 Morongo Band of Mission Indians, California (formerly the Morongo Band of Cahuilla Mission Indians of the Morongo Reservation) CALIFORNIA

174 Muckleshoot Indian Tribe of the Muckleshoot Reservation, Washington NORTHWEST COAST

175 Muscogee (Creek) Nation, Oklahoma PLAINS

176 Narragansett Indian Tribe of Rhode Island NORTHEAST

177 Navajo Nation, Arizona, New Mexico & Utah SOUTHWEST

178 Nez Perce Tribe, Idaho (previously listed as Nez Perce Tribe of Idaho) PLATEAU

179 Nisqually Indian Tribe of the Nisqually Reservation, Washington NORTHWEST COAST

180 Nooksack Indian Tribe of Washington NORTHWEST COAST

181 Northern Cheyenne Tribe of the Northern Cheyenne Indian Reservation, Montana PLAINS

182 Northfork Rancheria of Mono Indians of California CALIFORNIA

183 Northwestern Band of Shoshone Nation of Utah (Washakie) GREAT BASIN

184 Nottawaseppi Huron Band of the Potawatomi, Michigan (formerly the Huron Potawatomi, Inc.) NORTHEAST

185 Oglala Sioux Tribe of the Pine Ridge Reservation, South Dakota PLAINS

186 Ohkay Owingeh, New Mexico (formerly the Pueblo of San Juan) SOUTHWEST

187 Omaha Tribe of Nebraska PLAINS

188 Oneida Nation of New York NORTHEAST

189 Oneida Tribe of Indians of Wisconsin NORTHEAST

190 Onondaga Nation of New York NORTHEAST

191 Osage Nation, Oklahoma (formerly the Osage Tribe) PLAINS

192 Otoe-Missouria Tribe of Indians, Oklahoma PLAINS

193 Ottawa Tribe of Oklahoma PLAINS

194 Paiute Indian Tribe of Utah: Cedar Band of Paiutes GREAT BASIN

195 Paiute Indian Tribe of Utah: Indian Peaks Band of Paiutes GREAT BASIN

196 Paiute Indian Tribe of Utah: Kanosh Band of Paiutes GREAT BASIN

197 Paiute Indian Tribe of Utah: Koosharem Band of Paiutes GREAT BASIN

198 Paiute Indian Tribe of Utah: Shivwits Band of Paiutes GREAT BASIN

199 Paiute-Shoshone Indians of the Bishop Community of the Bishop Colony, California GREAT BASIN

200 Paiute-Shoshone Indians of the Lone Pine Community of the Lone Pine Reservation, California GREAT BASIN

201 Paiute-Shoshone Tribe of the Fallon Reservation and Colony, Nevada GREAT BASIN

202 Pala Band of Luiseño Mission Indians of the Pala Reservation, California CALIFORNIA

203 Pascua Yaqui Tribe of Arizona SOUTHWEST

204 Paskenta Band of Nomlaki Indians of California CALIFORNIA

205 Passamaquoddy Tribe of Maine NORTHEAST

206 Pauma Band of Luiseño Mission Indians of the Pauma & Yuima Reservation, California CALIFORNIA

207 Pawnee Nation of Oklahoma PLAINS

208 Pechanga Band of Luiseño Mission Indians of the Pechanga Reservation, California CALIFORNIA

209 Penobscot Tribe of Maine NORTHEAST

210 Peoria Tribe of Indians of Oklahoma PLAINS

211 Picayune Rancheria of Chukchansi Indians of California CALIFORNIA

212 Pinoleville Pomo Nation, California (formerly the Pinoleville Rancheria of Pomo Indians of California) CALIFORNIA

213 Pit River Tribe, California: Big Bend Rancheria CALIFORNIA

214 Pit River Tribe, California: Likely Rancheria CALIFORNIA

215 Pit River Tribe, California: Lookout Rancheria CALIFORNIA

216 Pit River Tribe, California: Montgomery Creek Rancheria CALIFORNIA

217 Pit River Tribe, California: Roaring Creek Rancheria CALIFORNIA

218 Pit River Tribe, California: XL Ranch Rancheria CALIFORNIA

219 Poarch Band of Creek Indians of Alabama SOUTHEAST

220 Pokagon Band of Potawatomi Indians, Michigan and Indiana NORTHEAST

221 Ponca Tribe of Indians of Oklahoma PLAINS

222 Ponca Tribe of Nebraska PLAINS

223 Port Gamble Indian Community of the Port Gamble Reservation, Washington NORTHWEST COAST

224 Potter Valley Tribe, California CALIFORNIA

225 Prairie Band of Potawatomi Nation, Kansas PLAINS

226 Prairie Island Indian Community in the State of Minnesota PLAINS

227 Pueblo of Acoma, New Mexico SOUTHWEST

228 Pueblo of Cochiti, New Mexico SOUTHWEST

229 Pueblo of Isleta, New Mexico SOUTHWEST

230 Pueblo of Jemez, New Mexico SOUTHWEST

231 Pueblo of Laguna, New Mexico SOUTHWEST

232 Pueblo of Nambe, New Mexico SOUTHWEST

233 Pueblo of Picurís, New Mexico SOUTHWEST

234 Pueblo of Pojoaque, New Mexico SOUTHWEST

235 Pueblo of San Felipe, New Mexico SOUTHWEST

236 Pueblo of San Ildefonso, New Mexico SOUTHWEST

237 Pueblo of Sandia, New Mexico SOUTHWEST

238 Pueblo of Santa Ana, New Mexico SOUTHWEST

239 Pueblo of Santa Clara, New Mexico SOUTHWEST

240 Pueblo of Taos, New Mexico SOUTHWEST

241 Pueblo of Tesuque, New Mexico SOUTHWEST

242 Pueblo of Zia, New Mexico SOUTHWEST

243 Puyallup Tribe of the Puyallup Reservation, Washington NORTHWEST COAST

244 Pyramid Lake Paiute Tribe of the Pyramid Lake Reservation, Nevada GREAT BASIN

245 Quapaw Tribe of Indians, Oklahoma PLAINS

246 Quartz Valley Indian Community of the Quartz Valley Reservation of California CALIFORNIA

247 Quechan Tribe of the Fort Yuma Indian Reservation, California & Arizona SOUTHWEST

248 Quileute Tribe of the Quileute Reservation, Washington NORTHWEST COAST

249 Quinault Tribe of the Quinault Reservation, Washington NORTHWEST COAST

250 Ramona Band or Village of Cahuilla Mission Indians of California CALIFORNIA

251 Red Cliff Band of Lake Superior Chippewa Indians of Wisconsin NORTHEAST

252 Red Lake Band of Chippewa Indians, Minnesota NORTHEAST

253 Redding Rancheria, California CALIFORNIA

254 Redwood Valley Rancheria of Pomo Indians of California CALIFORNIA

255 Reno-Sparks Indian Colony, Nevada GREAT BASIN

256 Resighini Rancheria, California CALIFORNIA

257 Rincon Band of Luiseño Mission Indians of the Rincon Reservation, California CALIFORNIA

258 Robinson Rancheria of Pomo Indians of California CALIFORNIA

259 Rosebud Sioux Tribe of the Rosebud Indian Reservation, South Dakota PLAINS

260 Round Valley Indian Tribes of the Round Valley Reservation, California CALIFORNIA

261 Sac & Fox Nation, Oklahoma PLAINS

262 Sac & Fox Nation of Missouri in Kansas and Nebraska PLAINS

263 Sac & Fox Tribe of the Mississippi in Iowa PLAINS

264 Saginaw Chippewa Indian Tribe of Michigan NORTHEAST

265 Saint Regis Mohawk Tribe, New York (formerly the St. Regis Band of Mohawk Indians of New York) NORTHEAST

266 Salt River Pima-Maricopa Indian Community of the Salt River Reservation, Arizona SOUTHWEST

267 Samish Indian Tribe, Washington NORTHWEST COAST

268 San Carlos Apache Tribe of the San Carlos Reservation, Arizona SOUTHWEST

269 San Juan Southern Paiute Tribe of Arizona SOUTHWEST

270 San Manuel Band of Mission Indians, California (previously listed as the San Manual Band of Serrano Mission Indians of the San Manual Reservation) CALIFORNIA

271 San Pasqual Band of Diegueño Mission Indians of California CALIFORNIA

272 Santa Rosa Band of Cahuilla Indians, California (formerly the Santa Rosa Band of Cahuilla Mission Indians of the Santa Rosa Reservation) CALIFORNIA

273 Santa Rosa Indian Community of the Santa Rosa Rancheria, California CALIFORNIA

274 Santa Ynez Band of Chumash Mission Indians of the Santa Ynez Reservation, California CALIFORNIA

275 Santee Sioux Nation, Nebraska PLAINS

276 Sauk-Suiattle Indian Tribe of Washington NORTHWEST COAST

277 Sault Ste. Marie Tribe of Chippewa Indians of Michigan NORTHEAST

278 Scotts Valley Band of Pomo Indians of California CALIFORNIA

279 Seminole Nation of Oklahoma PLAINS

280 Seminole Tribe of Florida: Big Cypress Reservation SOUTHEAST

281 Seminole Tribe of Florida: Brighton Reservation SOUTHEAST

282 Seminole Tribe of Florida: Dania Reservation SOUTHEAST

283 Seminole Tribe of Florida: Hollywood Reservation SOUTHEAST

284 Seminole Tribe of Florida: Tampa Reservation SOUTHEAST

285 Seneca-Cayuga Tribe of Oklahoma PLAINS

286 Seneca Nation of New York NORTHEAST

287 Shakopee Mdewakanton Sioux Community of Minnesota NORTHEAST

288 Shawnee Tribe, Oklahoma PLAINS

289 Sherwood Valley Rancheria of Pomo Indians of California CALIFORNIA

290 Shingle Springs Band of Miwok Indians, Shingle Springs Rancheria (Verona Tract), California CALIFORNIA

291 Shoalwater Bay Tribe of the Shoalwater Bay Indian Reservation, Washington NORTHWEST COAST

292 Shoshone-Bannock Tribes of the Fort Hall Reservation of Idaho GREAT BASIN

293 Shoshone-Paiute Tribes of the Duck Valley Reservation, Nevada GREAT BASIN

294 Shoshone Tribe of the Wind River Reservation, Wyoming GREAT BASIN

295 Sisseton-Wahpeton Oyate of the Lake Traverse Reservation, South Dakota PLAINS

296 Skokomish Indian Tribe of the Skokomish Reservation, Washington NORTHWEST COAST

297 Skull Valley Band of Goshute Indians of Utah GREAT BASIN

298 Smith River Rancheria, California CALIFORNIA

299 Snoqualmie Tribe, Washington NORTHWEST COAST

300 Soboba Band of Luiseño Indians, California CALIFORNIA

301 Sokaogon Chippewa Community, Wisconsin NORTHEAST

302 Southern Ute Indian Tribe of the Southern Ute Reservation, Colorado GREAT BASIN

303 Spirit Lake Tribe, North Dakota PLAINS

304 Spokane Tribe of the Spokane Reservation, Washington PLATEAU

305 Squaxin Island Tribe of the Squaxin Island Reservation, Washington NORTHWEST COAST

306 St. Croix Chippewa Indians of Wisconsin NORTHEAST

307 Standing Rock Sioux Tribe of North & South Dakota PLAINS

308 Stillaguamish Tribe of Washington NORTHWEST COAST

309 Stockbridge Munsee Community, Wisconsin NORTHEAST

310 Summit Lake Paiute Tribe of Nevada GREAT BASIN

311 Suquamish Indian Tribe of the Port Madison Reservation, Washington NORTHWEST COAST

312 Susanville Indian Rancheria, California CALIFORNIA

313 Swinomish Indians of the Swinomish Reservation, Washington NORTHWEST COAST

314 Sycuan Band of the Kumeyaay Nation CALIFORNIA

315 Table Mountain Rancheria of California CALIFORNIA

316 Te-Moak Tribe of Western Shoshone Indians of Nevada: Battle Mountain Band GREAT BASIN

317 Te-Moak Tribe of Western Shoshone Indians of Nevada: Elko Band GREAT BASIN

318 Te-Moak Tribe of Western Shoshone Indians of Nevada: South Fork Band GREAT BASIN

319 Te-Moak Tribe of Western Shoshone Indians of Nevada: Wells Band GREAT BASIN

320 Thlopthlocco Tribal Town, Oklahoma PLAINS

321 Three Affiliated Tribes of the Fort Berthold Reservation, North Dakota PLAINS

322 Tohono O'odham Nation of Arizona SOUTHWEST

323 Tonawanda Band of Seneca Indians of New York NORTHEAST

324 Tonkawa Tribe of Indians of Oklahoma PLAINS

325 Tonto Apache Tribe of Arizona SOUTHWEST

326 Torres Martinez Desert Cahuilla Indians, California (formerly the Torres-Martinez Band of Cahuilla Mission Indians of California) CALIFORNIA

327 Tulalip Tribes of the Tulalip Reservation, Washington NORTHWEST COAST

328 Tule River Indian Tribe of the Tule River Reservation, California CALIFORNIA

329 Tunica-Biloxi Indian Tribe of Louisiana SOUTHEAST

330 Tuolumne Band of Me-Wuk Indians of the Tuolumne Rancheria of California CALIFORNIA

331 Turtle Mountain Band of Chippewa Indians of North Dakota PLAINS

332 Tuscarora Nation of New York NORTHEAST

333 Twenty-Nine Palms Band of Mission Indians of California CALIFORNIA

334 United Auburn Indian Community of the Auburn Rancheria of California CALIFORNIA

335 United Keetoowah Band of Cherokee Indians in Oklahoma PLAINS

336 Upper Sioux Community, Minnesota PLAINS

337 Upper Skagit Indian Tribe of Washington NORTHWEST COAST

338 Ute Indian Tribe of the Uintah & Ouray Reservation, Utah GREAT BASIN

339 Ute Mountain Tribe of the Ute Mountain Reservation, Colorado, New Mexico & Utah SOUTHWEST

340 Utu Utu Gwaitu Paiute Tribe of the Benton Paiute Reservation, California GREAT BASIN

341 Walker River Paiute Tribe of the Walker River Reservation, Nevada GREAT BASIN

342 Wampanoag Tribe of Gay Head (Aquinnah) of Massachusetts NORTHEAST

343 Washoe Tribe of Nevada & California: Carson Colony GREAT BASIN

344 Washoe Tribe of Nevada & California: Dresslerville Colony GREAT BASIN

345 Washoe Tribe of Nevada & California: Woodfords Community GREAT BASIN

346 Washoe Tribe of Nevada & California: Stewart Community GREAT BASIN

347 Washoe Tribe of Nevada & California: Washoe Ranches GREAT BASIN

348 White Mountain Apache Tribe of the Fort Apache Reservation, Arizona SOUTHWEST

349 Wichita and Affiliated Tribes (Wichita, Keechi, Waco & Tawakonie), Oklahoma PLAINS

350 Wilton Rancheria, California CALIFORNIA

351 Winnebago Tribe of Nebraska PLAINS

352 Winnemucca Indian Colony of Nevada GREAT BASIN

353 Wiyot Tribe, California (formerly the Table Bluff Reservation-Wiyot Tribe) CALIFORNIA

354 Wyandotte Nation, Oklahoma PLAINS

355 Yankton Sioux Tribe of South Dakota PLAINS

356 Yavapai-Apache Nation of the Camp Verde Indian Reservation, Arizona SOUTHWEST

357 Yavapai-Prescott Tribe of the Yavapai Reservation, Arizona SOUTHWEST

358 Yerington Paiute Tribe of the Yerington Colony & Campbell Ranch, Nevada GREAT BASIN

359 Yocha Dehe Wintun Nation, California (formerly the Rumsey Indian Rancheria of Wintun Indians of California) CALIFORNIA

360 Yomba Shoshone Tribe of the Yomba Reservation, Nevada GREAT BASIN

361 Ysleta Del Sur Pueblo of Texas SOUTHWEST

362 Yurok Tribe of the Yurok Reservation, California CALIFORNIA

363 Zuni Tribe of the Zuni Reservation, New Mexico SOUTHWEST

INDIAN TRIBAL ENTITIES WITHIN THE STATE OF ALASKA RECOGNIZED AND ELIGIBLE TO RECEIVE SERVICES FROM THE UNITED STATES BUREAU OF INDIAN AFFAIRS

1 Native Village of Afognak ARCTIC & SUBARCTIC

2 Agdaagux Tribe of King Cove ARCTIC & SUBARCTIC

3 Native Village of Akhiok ARCTIC & SUBARCTIC

4 Akiachak Native Community ARCTIC & SUBARCTIC

5 Akiak Native Community ARCTIC & SUBARCTIC

6 Native Village of Akutan ARCTIC & SUBARCTIC

7   Village of Alakanuk ARCTIC & SUBARCTIC

8   Alatna Village ARCTIC & SUBARCTIC

9   Native Village of Aleknagik ARCTIC & SUBARCTIC

10   Algaaciq Native Village (St. Mary's) ARCTIC & SUBARCTIC

11   Allakaket Village ARCTIC & SUBARCTIC

12   Native Village of Ambler ARCTIC & SUBARCTIC

13   Village of Anaktuvuk Pass ARCTIC & SUBARCTIC

14   Yupiit of Andreafski ARCTIC & SUBARCTIC

15   Angoon Community Association NORTHWEST COAST

16   Village of Aniak ARCTIC & SUBARCTIC

17   Anvik Village ARCTIC & SUBARCTIC

18   Arctic Village (See Native Village of Venetie Tribal Government) ARCTIC & SUBARCTIC

19   Asa'carsarmiut Tribe ARCTIC & SUBARCTIC

20   Native Village of Atka ARCTIC & SUBARCTIC

21   Village of Atmautluak ARCTIC & SUBARCTIC

22   Atqasuk Village (Atkasook) ARCTIC & SUBARCTIC

23   Native Village of Barrow Inupiat Traditional Government ARCTIC & SUBARCTIC

24   Beaver Village ARCTIC & SUBARCTIC

25   Native Village of Belkofski ARCTIC & SUBARCTIC

26   Village of Bill Moore's Slough ARCTIC & SUBARCTIC

27   Birch Creek Tribe ARCTIC & SUBARCTIC

28   Native Village of Brevig Mission ARCTIC & SUBARCTIC

29   Native Village of Buckland ARCTIC & SUBARCTIC

30   Native Village of Cantwell ARCTIC & SUBARCTIC

31   Chalkyitsik Village ARCTIC & SUBARCTIC

32   Cheesh-Na Tribe (formerly the Native Village of Chistochina) ARCTIC & SUBARCTIC

33   Village of Chefornak ARCTIC & SUBARCTIC

34   Native Village of Chenega (aka Chanega) ARCTIC & SUBARCTIC

35   Chevak Native Village ARCTIC & SUBARCTIC

36   Chickaloon Native Village ARCTIC & SUBARCTIC

37   Chignik Bay Tribal Council (formerly the Native Village of Chignik) ARCTIC & SUBARCTIC

38   Native Village of Chignik Lagoon ARCTIC & SUBARCTIC

39   Chignik Lake Village ARCTIC & SUBARCTIC

40   Chilkat Indian Village (Klukwan) NORTHWEST COAST

41   Chilkoot Indian Association (Haines) NORTHWEST COAST

42   Chinik Eskimo Community (Golovin) ARCTIC & SUBARCTIC

43   Native Village of Chitina ARCTIC & SUBARCTIC

44   Native Village of Chuathbaluk (Russian Mission, Kuskokwim) ARCTIC & SUBARCTIC

45   Chuloonawick Native Village ARCTIC & SUBARCTIC

46   Circle Native Community ARCTIC & SUBARCTIC

47   Village of Clarks Point ARCTIC & SUBARCTIC

48   Native Village of Council ARCTIC & SUBARCTIC

49   Craig Community Association NORTHWEST COAST

50   Village of Crooked Creek ARCTIC & SUBARCTIC

51   Curyung Tribal Council ARCTIC & SUBARCTIC

52   Native Village of Deering ARCTIC & SUBARCTIC

53   Native Village of Diomede (aka Inalik) ARCTIC & SUBARCTIC

54   Village of Dot Lake ARCTIC & SUBARCTIC

55   Douglas Indian Association NORTHWEST COAST

56   Native Village of Eagle ARCTIC & SUBARCTIC

57   Native Village of Eek ARCTIC & SUBARCTIC

58   Egegik Village ARCTIC & SUBARCTIC

59   Eklutna Native Village ARCTIC & SUBARCTIC

60   Native Village of Ekuk ARCTIC & SUBARCTIC

61   Ekwok Village ARCTIC & SUBARCTIC

62   Native Village of Elim ARCTIC & SUBARCTIC

63   Emmonak Village ARCTIC & SUBARCTIC

64   Evansville Village (aka Bettles Field) ARCTIC & SUBARCTIC

65   Native Village of Eyak (Cordova) ARCTIC & SUBARCTIC

66   Native Village of False Pass ARCTIC & SUBARCTIC

67   Native Village of Fort Yukon ARCTIC & SUBARCTIC

68   Native Village of Gakona ARCTIC & SUBARCTIC

69   Galena Village (aka Louden Village) ARCTIC & SUBARCTIC

70   Native Village of Gambell ARCTIC & SUBARCTIC

71   Native Village of Georgetown ARCTIC & SUBARCTIC

72   Native Village of Goodnews Bay ARCTIC & SUBARCTIC

73   Organized Village of Grayling (aka Holikachuk) ARCTIC & SUBARCTIC

74   Gulkana Village ARCTIC & SUBARCTIC

75   Native Village of Hamilton ARCTIC & SUBARCTIC

76   Healy Lake Village ARCTIC & SUBARCTIC

77   Holy Cross Village ARCTIC & SUBARCTIC

78   Hoonah Indian Association NORTHWEST COAST

79   Native Village of Hooper Bay ARCTIC & SUBARCTIC

80   Hughes Village ARCTIC & SUBARCTIC

81   Huslia Village ARCTIC & SUBARCTIC

82   Hydaburg Cooperative Association NORTHWEST COAST

83   Igiugig Village ARCTIC & SUBARCTIC

84   Village of Iliamna ARCTIC & SUBARCTIC

85   Inupiat Community of the Arctic Slope ARCTIC & SUBARCTIC

86   Iqurmuit Traditional Council ARCTIC & SUBARCTIC

87   Ivanoff Bay Village ARCTIC & SUBARCTIC

88   Kaguyak Village ARCTIC & SUBARCTIC

89   Organized Village of Kake NORTHWEST COAST

90   Kaktovik Village (aka Barter Island) ARCTIC & SUBARCTIC

91   Village of Kalskag ARCTIC & SUBARCTIC

92   Village of Kaltag ARCTIC & SUBARCTIC

93   Native Village of Kanatak ARCTIC & SUBARCTIC

94   Native Village of Karluk ARCTIC & SUBARCTIC

95   Organized Village of Kasaan NORTHWEST COAST

96   Kasigluk Traditional Elders Council ARCTIC & SUBARCTIC

97   Kenaitze Indian Tribe ARCTIC & SUBARCTIC

98   Ketchikan Indian Corporation NORTHWEST COAST

99   Native Village of Kiana ARCTIC & SUBARCTIC

100 King Island Native Community ARCTIC & SUBARCTIC

101 King Salmon Tribe ARCTIC & SUBARCTIC

102 Native Village of Kipnuk ARCTIC & SUBARCTIC

103 Native Village of Kivalina ARCTIC & SUBARCTIC

104 Klawock Cooperative Association NORTHWEST COAST

105 Native Village of Kluti Kaah (aka Copper Center) ARCTIC & SUBARCTIC

106 Knik Tribe ARCTIC & SUBARCTIC

107 Native Village of Kobuk ARCTIC & SUBARCTIC

108 Kokhanok Village ARCTIC & SUBARCTIC

109 Native Village of Kongiganak ARCTIC & SUBARCTIC

110 Village of Kotlik ARCTIC & SUBARCTIC

111 Native Village of Kotzebue ARCTIC & SUBARCTIC

112 Native Village of Koyuk ARCTIC & SUBARCTIC

113 Koyukuk Native Village ARCTIC & SUBARCTIC

114 Organized Village of Kwethluk ARCTIC & SUBARCTIC

115 Native Village of Kwigillingok ARCTIC & SUBARCTIC

116 Native Village of Kwinhagak (aka Quinhagak) ARCTIC & SUBARCTIC

117 Native Village of Larsen Bay ARCTIC & SUBARCTIC

118 Levelock Village ARCTIC & SUBARCTIC

119 Lime Village ARCTIC & SUBARCTIC

120 Village of Lower Kalskag ARCTIC & SUBARCTIC

121 Manley Hot Springs Village ARCTIC & SUBARCTIC

122 Manokotak Village ARCTIC & SUBARCTIC

123 Native Village of Marshall (aka Fortuna Ledge) ARCTIC & SUBARCTIC

124 Native Village of Mary's Igloo ARCTIC & SUBARCTIC

125 McGrath Native Village ARCTIC & SUBARCTIC

126 Native Village of Mekoryuk ARCTIC & SUBARCTIC

127 Mentasta Traditional Council ARCTIC & SUBARCTIC

128 Metlakatla Indian Community, Annette Island Reserve NORTHWEST COAST

129 Native Village of Minto ARCTIC & SUBARCTIC

130 Naknek Native Village ARCTIC & SUBARCTIC

131 Native Village of Nanwalek (aka English Bay) ARCTIC & SUBARCTIC

132 Native Village of Napaimute ARCTIC & SUBARCTIC

133 Native Village of Napakiak ARCTIC & SUBARCTIC

134 Native Village of Napaskiak ARCTIC & SUBARCTIC

135 Native Village of Nelson Lagoon ARCTIC & SUBARCTIC

136 Nenana Native Association ARCTIC & SUBARCTIC

137 New Koliganek Village Council ARCTIC & SUBARCTIC

138 New Stuyahok Village ARCTIC & SUBARCTIC

139 Newhalen Village ARCTIC & SUBARCTIC

140 Newtok Village ARCTIC & SUBARCTIC

141 Native Village of Nightmute ARCTIC & SUBARCTIC

142 Nikolai Village ARCTIC & SUBARCTIC

143 Native Village of Nikolski ARCTIC & SUBARCTIC

144 Ninilchik Village ARCTIC & SUBARCTIC

145 Native Village of Noatak ARCTIC & SUBARCTIC

146 Nome Eskimo Community ARCTIC & SUBARCTIC

147 Nondalton Village ARCTIC & SUBARCTIC

148 Noorvik Native Community ARCTIC & SUBARCTIC

149 Northway Village ARCTIC & SUBARCTIC

150 Native Village of Nuiqsut (aka Nooiksut) ARCTIC & SUBARCTIC

151 Nulato Village ARCTIC & SUBARCTIC

152 Nunakauyarmiut Tribe ARCTIC & SUBARCTIC

153 Native Village of Nunam Iqua (formerly the Native Village of Sheldon's Point) ARCTIC & SUBARCTIC

154 Native Village of Nunapitchuk ARCTIC & SUBARCTIC

155 Village of Ohogamiut ARCTIC & SUBARCTIC

156 Village of Old Harbor ARCTIC & SUBARCTIC

157 Orutsararmuit Native Village (aka Bethel) ARCTIC & SUBARCTIC

158 Oscarville Traditional Village ARCTIC & SUBARCTIC

159 Native Village of Ouzinkie ARCTIC & SUBARCTIC

160 Native Village of Paimiut ARCTIC & SUBARCTIC

161 Pauloff Harbor Village ARCTIC & SUBARCTIC

162 Pedro Bay Village ARCTIC & SUBARCTIC

163 Native Village of Perryville ARCTIC & SUBARCTIC

164 Petersburg Indian Association NORTHWEST COAST

165 Native Village of Pilot Point ARCTIC & SUBARCTIC

166 Pilot Station Traditional Village ARCTIC & SUBARCTIC

167 Native Village of Pitka's Point ARCTIC & SUBARCTIC

168 Platinum Traditional Village ARCTIC & SUBARCTIC

169 Native Village of Point Hope ARCTIC & SUBARCTIC

170 Native Village of Point Lay ARCTIC & SUBARCTIC

171 Native Village of Port Graham ARCTIC & SUBARCTIC

172 Native Village of Port Heiden ARCTIC & SUBARCTIC

173 Native Village of Port Lions ARCTIC & SUBARCTIC

174 Portage Creek Village (aka Ohgsenakale) ARCTIC & SUBARCTIC

175 Pribilof Islands Aleut Communities of St. Paul & St. George Islands ARCTIC & SUBARCTIC

176 Qagan Tayagungin Tribe of Sand Point Village ARCTIC & SUBARCTIC

177 Qawalangin Tribe of Unalaska ARCTIC & SUBARCTIC

178 Rampart Village ARCTIC & SUBARCTIC

179 Village of Red Devil ARCTIC & SUBARCTIC

180 Native Village of Ruby ARCTIC & SUBARCTIC

181 Native Village of Saint Michael ARCTIC & SUBARCTIC

182 Village of Salamatoff ARCTIC & SUBARCTIC

183 Native Village of Savoonga ARCTIC & SUBARCTIC

184 Organized Village of Saxman NORTHWEST COAST

185 Native Village of Scammon Bay ARCTIC & SUBARCTIC

186 Native Village of Selawik ARCTIC & SUBARCTIC

187 Seldovia Village Tribe ARCTIC & SUBARCTIC

188 Shageluk Native Village ARCTIC & SUBARCTIC

189 Native Village of Shaktoolik ARCTIC & SUBARCTIC

190 Native Village of Shishmaref ARCTIC & SUBARCTIC

191 Native Village of Shungnak ARCTIC & SUBARCTIC

192 Sitka Tribe of Alaska NORTHWEST COAST

193 Skagway Village NORTHWEST COAST

194 Village of Sleetmute ARCTIC & SUBARCTIC

195 Village of Solomon ARCTIC & SUBARCTIC

196 South Naknek Village ARCTIC & SUBARCTIC

197 Stebbins Community Association ARCTIC & SUBARCTIC

198 Native Village of Stevens ARCTIC & SUBARCTIC

199 Village of Stony River ARCTIC & SUBARCTIC

200 Sun'aq Tribe of Kodiak (formerly the Shoonaq' Tribe of Kodiak) ARCTIC & SUBARCTIC

201 Takotna Village ARCTIC & SUBARCTIC

202 Native Village of Tanacross ARCTIC & SUBARCTIC

203 Native Village of Tanana ARCTIC & SUBARCTIC

204 Tangirnaq Native Village (formerly Lesnoi Village (aka Woody Island)) ARCTIC & SUBARCTIC

205 Native Village of Tatitlek ARCTIC & SUBARCTIC

206 Native Village of Tazlina ARCTIC & SUBARCTIC

207 Telida Village ARCTIC & SUBARCTIC

208 Native Village of Teller ARCTIC & SUBARCTIC

209 Native Village of Tetlin ARCTIC & SUBARCTIC

210 Central Council of the Tlingit & Haida Indian Tribes NORTHWEST COAST

211 Traditional Village of Togiak ARCTIC & SUBARCTIC

212 Tuluksak Native Community ARCTIC & SUBARCTIC

213 Native Village of Tuntutuliak ARCTIC & SUBARCTIC

214 Native Village of Tununak ARCTIC & SUBARCTIC

215 Twin Hills Village ARCTIC & SUBARCTIC

216 Native Village of Tyonek ARCTIC & SUBARCTIC

217 Ugashik Village ARCTIC & SUBARCTIC

218 Umkumiut Native Village (previously listed as Umkumiute Native Village) ARCTIC & SUBARCTIC

219 Native Village of Unalakleet ARCTIC & SUBARCTIC

220 Native Village of Unga ARCTIC & SUBARCTIC

221 Native Village of Venetie Tribal Government (Arctic Village and Village of Venetie) ARCTIC & SUBARCTIC

222 Village of Wainwright ARCTIC & SUBARCTIC

223 Native Village of Wales ARCTIC & SUBARCTIC

224 Native Village of White Mountain ARCTIC & SUBARCTIC

225 Wrangell Cooperative Association NORTHWEST COAST

226 Yakutat Tlingit Tribe NORTHWEST COAST

INDIAN TRIBAL ENTITIES BY REGION

CHAPTER 1: NORTHEAST

Aroostook Band of Micmac Indians of Maine; Bad River Band of the Lake Superior Tribe of Chippewa Indians of the Bad River Reservation, Wisconsin; Bay Mills Indian Community, Michigan; Cayuga Nation of New York; Forest County Potawatomi Community, Wisconsin; Grand Traverse Band of Ottawa and Chippewa Indians, Michigan; Hannahville Indian Community, Michigan; Ho-Chunk Nation of Wisconsin; Houlton Band of Maliseet Indians of Maine; Keweenaw Bay Indian Community, Michigan; Lac Courte Oreilles Band of Lake Superior Chippewa Indians of Wisconsin; Lac du Flambeau Band of Lake Superior Chippewa Indians of the Lac du Flambeau Reservation of Wisconsin; Lac Vieux Desert Band of Lake Superior Chippewa Indians, Michigan; Little River Band of Ottawa Indians, Michigan; Little Traverse Bay Bands of Odawa Indians, Michigan; Mashantucket Pequot Tribe of Connecticut; Mashpee Wampanoag Tribe, Massachusetts; Match-e-be-nash-she-wish Band of Potawatomi Indians of Michigan; Menominee Indian Tribe of Wisconsin; Minnesota Chippewa Tribe: Bois Forte Band (Nett Lake); Minnesota Chippewa Tribe: Fond du Lac Band; Minnesota Chippewa Tribe: Grand Portage Band; Minnesota Chippewa Tribe: Leech Lake Band; Minnesota Chippewa Tribe: Mille Lacs Band; Minnesota Chippewa Tribe: White Earth Band; Mohegan Indian Tribe of Connecticut; Narragansett Indian Tribe of Rhode Island; Nottawaseppi Huron Band of the Potawatomi, Michigan (formerly the Huron Potawatomi, Inc.); Oneida Nation of New York; Oneida Tribe of Indians of Wisconsin; Onondaga Nation of New York; Passamaquoddy Tribe of Maine; Penobscot Tribe of Maine; Pokagon Band of Potawatomi Indians, Michigan and Indiana; Prairie Island Indian Community in the State of Minnesota; Red Cliff Band of Lake Superior Chippewa Indians of Wisconsin; Red Lake Band of Chippewa Indians, Minnesota; Saginaw Chippewa Indian Tribe of Michigan; Saint Regis Mohawk Tribe, New York (formerly the St. Regis Band of Mohawk Indians of New York); Sault Ste. Marie Tribe of Chippewa Indians of Michigan; Seneca Nation of New York; Sokaogon Chippewa Community, Wisconsin; Shakopee Mdewakanton Sioux Community of Minnesota; St. Croix Chippewa Indians of Wisconsin; Stockbridge Munsee Community, Wisconsin; Tonawanda Band of Seneca Indians of New York; Tuscarora Nation of New York; Wampanoag Tribe of Gay Head (Aquinnah) of Massachusetts

CHAPTER 2: SOUTHEAST

Alabama-Coushatta Tribes of Texas; Catawba Indian Nation (aka Catawba Tribe of South Carolina); Chitimacha Tribe of Louisiana; Coushatta Tribe of Louisiana; Eastern Band of Cherokee Indians of North Carolina; Jena Band of Choctaw Indians, Louisiana; Miccosukee Tribe of Indians of Florida; Mississippi Band of Choctaw Indians, Mississippi; Poarch Band of Creek Indians of Alabama; Seminole Tribe of Florida: Big Cypress; Seminole Tribe of Florida: Brighton; Seminole Tribe of Florida: Dania; Seminole Tribe of Florida: Hollywood; Seminole Tribe of Florida: Tampa Reservation; Tunica-Biloxi Indian Tribe of Louisiana

CHAPTER 3: ARCTIC & SUBARCTIC

Native Village of Afognak; Agdaagux Tribe of King Cove; Native Village of Akhiok; Akiachak Native Community; Akiak Native Community; Native Village of Akutan; Village of Alakanuk; Alatna Village; Native Village of Aleknagik; Algaaciq Native Village (St. Mary's); Allakaket Village; Native Village of Ambler; Village of Anaktuvuk Pass; Yupiit of Andreafski; Village of Aniak; Anvik Village; Arctic Village (See Native Village of Venetie Tribal Government); Asa'carsarmiut Tribe; Native Village of Atka; Village of Atmautluak; Atqasuk Village (Atkasook); Native Village of Barrow Inupiat Traditional Government; Beaver Village; Native Village of Belkofski; Village of Bill Moore's Slough; Birch Creek Tribe; Native Village of Brevig Mission; Native Village of Buckland; Native Village of Cantwell; Chalkyitsik Village; Cheesh-Na Tribe (formerly the Native Village of Chistochina); Village of Chefornak; Native Village of Chenega (aka Chanega); Chevak Native Village; Chickaloon Native Village; Chignik Bay Tribal Council (formerly the Native Village of Chignik); Native Village of Chignik Lagoon; Chignik Lake Village; Chinik Eskimo Community (Golovin); Native Village of Chitina; Native Village of Chuathbaluk (Russian Mission, Kuskokwim); Chuloonawick Native Village; Circle Native Community; Village of Clarks Point; Native Village of Council; Village of Crooked Creek; Curyung Tribal Council; Native Village of Deering; Native Village of Diomede (aka Inalik); Village of Dot Lake; Native Village of Eagle; Native Village of Eek; Egegik Village; Eklutna Native Village; Native Village of Ekuk; Ekwok Village; Native Village of Elim; Emmonak Village; Evansville Village (aka Bettles Field); Native Village of Eyak (Cordova); Native Village of False Pass; Native Village of Fort Yukon; Native Village of Gakona; Galena Village (aka Louden Village); Native Village of Gambell; Native Village of Georgetown; Native Village of Goodnews Bay; Organized Village of Grayling (aka Holikachuk); Gulkana Village; Native Village of Hamilton; Healy Lake Village; Holy Cross Village; Native Village of Hooper Bay; Hughes Village; Huslia Village; Igiugig Village; Village of Iliamna; Inupiat Community of the Arctic Slope; Iqurmuit Traditional Council; Ivanoff Bay Village; Kaguyak Village; Kaktovik Village (aka Barter Island); Village of Kalskag; Village of Kaltag; Native Village of Kanatak; Native Village of Karluk; Kasigluk Traditional Elders Council; Kenaitze Indian Tribe; Native Village of Kiana; King Island Native Community; King Salmon Tribe; Native Village of Kipnuk; Native Village of Kivalina; Native Village of Kluti Kaah (aka Copper Center); Knik Tribe; Native Village of Kobuk; Kokhanok Village; Native Village of Kongiganak; Village of Kotlik; Native Village of Kotzebue; Native Village of Koyuk; Koyukuk Native Village; Organized Village of Kwethluk; Native Village of Kwigillingok; Native Village of Kwinhagak (aka Quinhagak); Native Village of Larsen Bay; Levelock Village; Lime Village; Village of Lower Kalskag; Manley Hot Springs Village; Manokotak Village; Native Village of Marshall (aka Fortuna Ledge); McGrath Native Village; Native Village of Mekoryuk; Mentasta Traditional Council; Native Village of Minto; Naknek Native Village; Native Village of Nanwalek (aka English Bay); Native Village of Napaimute; Native Village of Napakiak; Native Village of Napaskiak; Native Village of Nelson Lagoon; Nenana Native Association; New Koliganek Village Council; New Stuyahok Village; Newhalen Village; Newtok Village; Native Village of Nightmute; Nikolai Village; Native Village of Nikolski; Ninilchik Village; Native Village of Noatak; Nome Eskimo Community; Nondalton Village; Noorvik Native Community; Northway Village; Native Village of Nuiqsut (aka Nooiksut); Nulato Village; Nunakauyarmiut Tribe; Native Village of Nunam Iqua (formerly the Native Village of Sheldon's Point); Native Village of Nunapitchuk; Village of Ohogamiut; Village of Old Harbor; Orutsararmuit Native Village (aka Bethel); Oscarville Traditional Village; Native Village of Ouzinkie; Native Village of Paimiut; Pauloff Harbor Village; Pedro Bay Village; Native Village of Perryville; Native Village of Pilot Point; Pilot Station Traditional Village; Native Village of Pitka's Point; Platinum Traditional Village; Native Village of Point Hope; Native Village of Point Lay; Native Village of Port Graham; Native Village of Port Heiden; Native Village of Port Lions; Portage Creek Village (aka Ohgsenakale); Pribilof Islands Aleut Communities of St. Paul & St. George Islands; Qagan Tayagungin Tribe of Sand Point Village; Qawalangin Tribe of Unalaska; Rampart Village; Village of Red Devil; Native Village of Ruby; Native Village of Saint Michael; Village of Salamatoff; Native Village of Savoonga; Native Village of Scammon Bay; Native Village of Selawik; Seldovia Village Tribe; Shageluk Native Village; Native Village of Shaktoolik; Native Village of Shishmaref; Native Village of Shungnak; Village of Sleetmute; Village of Solomon; South Naknek Village; Stebbins Community Association; Native Village of Stevens; Village of Stony River; Sun'aq Tribe of Kodiak (formerly the Shoonaq' Tribe of Kodiak); Takotna Village; Native Village of Tanacross; Native Village of Tanana; Tangirnaq Native Village (formerly Lesnoi Village (aka Woody Island)); Native Village of Tatitlek; Native Village of Tazlina; Telida Village; Native Village of Teller; Native Village of Tetlin; Traditional Village of Togiak; Tuluksak Native Community; Native Village of Tuntutuliak; Native Village of Tununak; Twin Hills Village; Native Village of Tyonek; Ugashik Village; Umkumiut Native Village (previously listed as Umkumiute Native Village); Native Village of Unalakleet; Native Village of

Unga; Village of Venetie (See Native Village of Venetie Tribal Government); Native Village of Venetie Tribal Government (Arctic Village and Village of Venetie); Village of Wainwright; Native Village of Wales; Native Village of White Mountain

CHAPTER 4: THE PLAINS

Absentee-Shawnee Tribe of Indians of Oklahoma; Alabama-Quassarte Tribal Town, Oklahoma; Apache Tribe of Oklahoma; Arapahoe Tribe of the Wind River Reservation, Wyoming; Assiniboine and Sioux Tribes of the Fort Peck Indian Reservation, Montana; Blackfeet Tribe of the Blackfeet Indian Reservation of Montana; Caddo Nation of Oklahoma; Cherokee Nation, Oklahoma; Cheyenne and Arapaho Tribes, Oklahoma; Cheyenne River Sioux Tribe of the Cheyenne River Reservation, South Dakota; Chickasaw Nation, Oklahoma; Chippewa-Cree Indians of the Rocky Boy's Reservation, Montana; Choctaw Nation of Oklahoma; Citizen Potawatomi Nation, Oklahoma; Comanche Nation, Oklahoma; Crow Creek Sioux Tribe of the Crow Creek Reservation, South Dakota; Crow Tribe of Montana; Delaware Nation, Oklahoma; Delaware Tribe of Indians, Oklahoma; Eastern Shawnee Tribe of Oklahoma; Flandreau Santee Sioux Tribe of South Dakota; Fort Belknap Indian Community of the Fort Belknap Reservation of Montana; Fort Sill Apache Tribe of Oklahoma; Iowa Tribe of Kansas and Nebraska; Iowa Tribe of Oklahoma; Kaw Nation, Oklahoma; Kialegee Tribal Town, Oklahoma; Kickapoo Tribe of Indians of the Kickapoo Reservation in Kansas; Kickapoo Tribe of Oklahoma; Kiowa Indian Tribe of Oklahoma; Lower Brule Sioux Tribe of the Lower Brule Reservation, South Dakota; Lower Sioux Indian Community in the State of Minnesota; Miami Tribe of Oklahoma; Modoc Tribe of Oklahoma; Muscogee (Creek) Nation, Oklahoma; Northern Cheyenne Tribe of the Northern Cheyenne Indian Reservation, Montana; Oglala Sioux Tribe of the Pine Ridge Reservation, South Dakota; Omaha Tribe of Nebraska; Osage Nation, Oklahoma (formerly the Osage Tribe); Otoe-Missouria Tribe of Indians, Oklahoma; Ottawa Tribe of Oklahoma; Pawnee Nation of Oklahoma; Peoria Tribe of Indians of Oklahoma; Ponca Tribe of Indians of Oklahoma; Ponca Tribe of Nebraska; Prairie Band of Potawatomi Nation, Kansas; Quapaw Tribe of Indians, Oklahoma; Rosebud Sioux Tribe of the Rosebud Indian Reservation, South Dakota; Sac & Fox Nation, Oklahoma; Sac & Fox Nation of Missouri in Kansas and Nebraska; Sac & Fox Tribe of the Mississippi in Iowa; Santee Sioux Nation, Nebraska; Seminole Nation of Oklahoma; Seneca-Cayuga Tribe of Oklahoma; Shawnee Tribe, Oklahoma; Sisseton-Wahpeton Oyate of the Lake Traverse Reservation, South Dakota; Spirit Lake Tribe, North Dakota; Standing Rock Sioux Tribe of North & South Dakota; Thlopthlocco Tribal Town, Oklahoma; Three Affiliated Tribes of the Fort Berthold Reservation, North Dakota; Tonkawa Tribe of Indians of Oklahoma; Turtle Mountain Band of Chippewa Indians of North Dakota; United Keetoowah Band of Cherokee Indians in Oklahoma; Upper Sioux Community, Minnesota; Wichita and Affiliated Tribes (Wichita, Keechi, Waco & Tawakonie), Oklahoma; Winnebago Tribe of Nebraska; Wyandotte Nation, Oklahoma; Yankton Sioux Tribe of South Dakota

CHAPTER 5: THE SOUTHWEST

Ak Chin Indian Community of the Maricopa (Ak Chin) Indian Reservation, Arizona; Cocopah Tribe of Arizona; Colorado River Indian Tribes of the Colorado River Indian Reservation, Arizona and California; Fort McDowell Yavapai Nation, Arizona; Fort Mojave Indian Tribe of Arizona, California & Nevada; Gila River Indian Community of the Gila River Indian Reservation, Arizona; Havasupai Tribe of the Havasupai Reservation, Arizona; Hopi Tribe of Arizona; Hualapai Indian Tribe of the Hualapai Indian Reservation, Arizona; Jicarilla Apache Nation, New Mexico; Kewa Pueblo, New Mexico (formerly the Pueblo of Santo Domingo); Kickapoo Traditional Tribe of Texas; Mescalero Apache Tribe of the Mescalero Reservation, New Mexico; Navajo Nation, Arizona, New Mexico & Utah; Ohkay Owingeh, New Mexico (formerly the Pueblo of San Juan); Pascua Yaqui Tribe of Arizona; Pueblo of Acoma, New Mexico; Pueblo of Cochiti, New Mexico; Pueblo of Isleta, New Mexico; Pueblo of Jemez, New Mexico; Pueblo of Laguna, New Mexico; Pueblo of Nambe, New Mexico; Pueblo of Picuris, New Mexico; Pueblo of Pojoaque, New Mexico; Pueblo of San Felipe, New Mexico; Pueblo of San Ildefonso, New Mexico; Pueblo of Sandia, New Mexico; Pueblo of Santa Ana, New Mexico; Pueblo of Santa Clara, New Mexico; Pueblo of Taos, New Mexico; Pueblo of Tesuque, New Mexico; Pueblo of Zia, New Mexico; Quechan Tribe of the Fort Yuma Indian Reservation, California & Arizona; Salt River Pima-Maricopa Indian Community of the Salt River Reservation, Arizona; San Carlos Apache Tribe of the San Carlos Reservation, Arizona; San Juan Southern Paiute Tribe of Arizona; Tohono O'odham Nation of Arizona; Tonto Apache Tribe of Arizona; Ute Mountain Tribe of the Ute Mountain Reservation, Colorado, New Mexico & Utah; White Mountain Apache Tribe of the Fort Apache Reservation, Arizona; Yavapai-Apache Nation of the Camp Verde Indian Reservation, Arizona; Yavapai-Prescott Tribe of the Yavapai Reservation, Arizona; Ysleta Del Sur Pueblo of Texas; Zuni Tribe of the Zuni Reservation, New Mexico

CHAPTER 6: THE GREAT BASIN & PLATEAU

Big Pine Band of Owens Valley Paiute Shoshone Indians of the Big Pine, California; Bridgeport Paiute Indian Colony of California; Burns Paiute Tribe of the Burns Paiute Indian Colony of Oregon; Chemehuevi Indian Tribe of the Chemehuevi Reservation, California; Coeur D'Alene Tribe of the Coeur D'Alene Reservation, Idaho; Confederated Salish & Kootenai Tribes of the Flathead Reservation, Montana; Confederated Tribes and Bands of the Yakama Nation, Washington; Confederated Tribes of the Colville Reservation, Washington; Confederated Tribes of the Goshute Reservation, Nevada and Utah; Confederated Tribes of the Umatilla Reservation, Oregon; Confederated Tribes of the Warm Springs Reservation of Oregon; Death Valley Timbi-Sha Shoshone Band of California; Duckwater Shoshone Tribe of the Duckwater Reservation, Nevada; Ely Shoshone Tribe of Nevada; Fort Independence Indian Community of Paiute Indians of the Fort Independence Reservation, California; Fort McDermitt Paiute and Shoshone Tribes of the Fort McDermitt Indian Reservation, Nevada and Oregon; Kaibab Band of Paiute Indians of the Kaibab Indian Reservation, Arizona; Kalispel Indian Community of the Kalispel Reservation, Washington; Klamath Tribes, Oregon; Kootenai Tribe of Idaho; Las Vegas Tribe of Paiute Indians of the Las Vegas Indian Colony, Nevada; Lovelock Paiute Tribe of the Lovelock Indian Colony, Nevada; Moapa Band of Paiute Indians of the Moapa River Indian Reservation, Nevada; Nez Perce Tribe, Idaho (previously listed as Nez Perce Tribe of Idaho); Northwestern Band of Shoshone Nation of Utah (Washakie); Paiute Indian Tribe of Utah: Cedar Band of Paiutes; Paiute Indian Tribe of Utah: Indian Peaks Band of Paiutes; Paiute Indian Tribe of Utah: Kanosh Band of Paiutes; Paiute Indian Tribe of Utah: Koosharem Band of Paiutes; Paiute Indian Tribe of Utah: Shivwits Band of Paiutes; Paiute-Shoshone Indians of the Bishop Community of the Bishop Colony; Paiute-Shoshone Indians of the Lone Pine Community of the Lone Pine Reservation; Paiute-Shoshone Tribe of the Fallon Reservation and Colony, Nevada; Pyramid Lake Paiute Tribe of the Pyramid Lake Reservation, Nevada; Reno-Sparks Indian Colony, Nevada; Shoshone-Bannock Tribes of the Fort Hall Reservation of Idaho; Shoshone-Paiute Tribes of the Duck Valley Reservation, Nevada; Shoshone Tribe of the Wind River Reservation, Wyoming; Skull Valley Band of Goshute Indians of Utah; Southern Ute Indian Tribe of the Southern Ute Reservation, Colorado; Spokane Tribe of the Spokane Reservation, Washington; Summit Lake Paiute Tribe of Nevada; Te-Moak Tribe of Western Shoshone Indians of Nevada: Battle Mountain Band; Te-Moak Tribe of Western Shoshone Indians of Nevada: Elko Band; Te-Moak Tribe of Western Shoshone Indians of Nevada: South Fork Band; Te-Moak Tribe of Western Shoshone Indians of Nevada: Wells Band; Ute Indian Tribe of the Uintah & Ouray Reservation, Utah; Utu Utu Gwaitu Paiute Tribe of the Benton Paiute Reservation, California; Walker River Paiute Tribe of the Walker River Reservation, Nevada; Washoe Tribe of Nevada & California: Carson Colony; Washoe Tribe of Nevada & California: Dresslerville Colony; Washoe Tribe of Nevada & California: Woofords Community; Washoe Tribe of Nevada & California: Stewart Community; Washoe Tribe of Nevada & California: Washoe Ranches; Winnemucca Indian Colony of Nevada; Yerington

Paiute Tribe of the Yerington Colony & Campbell Ranch, Nevada; Yomba Shoshone Tribe of the Yomba Reservation, Nevada

CHAPTER 7: THE NORTHWEST COAST

Angoon Community Association; Chilkat Indian Village (Klukwan); Chilkoot Indian Association (Haines); Confederated Tribes of the Chehalis Reservation, Washington; Confederated Tribes of the Coos, Lower Umpqua and Siuslaw Indians of Oregon; Confederated Tribes of the Grand Ronde Community of Oregon; Confederated Tribes of Siletz Indians of Oregon (previously listed as the Confederated Tribes of the Siletz Reservation); Coquille Tribe of Oregon; Cow Creek Band of Umpqua Indians of Oregon; Cowlitz Indian Tribe, Washington; Craig Community Association; Douglas Indian Association; Hoh Indian Tribe of the Hoh Indian Reservation, Washington; Hoonah Indian Association; Hydaburg Cooperative Association; Jamestown S'Klallam Tribe of Washington; Ketchikan Indian Corporation; Klawock Cooperative Association; Lower Elwha Tribal Community of the Lower Elwha Reservation, Washington; Lummi Tribe of the Lummi Reservation, Washington; Makah Indian Tribe of the Makah Indian Reservation, Washington; Metlakatla Indian Community, Annette Island Reserve; Muckleshoot Indian Tribe of the Muckleshoot Reservation, Washington; Nisqually Indian Tribe of the Nisqually Reservation, Washington; Nooksack Indian Tribe of Washington; Organized Village of Kake; Organized Village of Kasaan; Organized Village of Saxman; Petersburg Indian Association; Port Gamble Indian Community of the Port Gamble Reservation, Washington; Puyallup Tribe of the Puyallup Reservation, Washington; Quileute Tribe of the Quileute Reservation, Washington; Quinault Tribe of the Quinault Reservation, Washington; Samish Indian Tribe, Washington; Sauk-Suiattle Indian Tribe of Washington; Shoalwater Bay Tribe of the Shoalwater Bay Indian Reservation, Washington; Sitka Tribe of Alaska; Skagway Village; Skokomish Indian Tribe of the Skokomish Reservation, Washington; Snoqualmie Tribe, Washington; Squaxin Island Tribe of the Squaxin Island Reservation, Washington; Stillaguamish Tribe of Washington; Suquamish Indian Tribe of the Port Madison Reservation, Washington; Swinomish Indians of the Swinomish Reservation, Washington; Central Council of the Tlingit & Haida Indian Tribes; Tulalip Tribes of the Tulalip Reservation, Washington; Upper Skagit Indian Tribe of Washington; Wrangell Cooperative Association; Yakutat Tlingit Tribe

CHAPTER 8: CALIFORNIA

Agua Caliente Band of Cahuilla Indians of the Agua Caliente Indian Reservation; Alturas Indian Rancheria; Augustine Band of Cahuilla Indians; Bear River Band of the Rohnerville Rancheria; Berry Creek Rancheria of Maidu Indians of California; Big Lagoon Rancheria Reservation; Big Sandy Rancheria of Mono Indians of California; Big Valley Band of Pomo Indians of the Big Valley Rancheria; Blue Lake Rancheria; Buena Vista Rancheria of Me-Wuk Indians of California; Cabazon Band of Mission Indians; Cachil DeHe Band of Wintun Indians of the Colusa Indian Community of the Colusa Rancheria; Cahto Indian Tribe of the Laytonville Rancheria, California; Cahuilla Band of Mission Indians of the Cahuilla Reservation; California Valley Miwok Tribe, California; Campo Band of Diegueño Mission Indians of the Campo Indian Reservation; Capitan Grande Band of Diegueño Mission Indians of California: Barona Group of Capitan Grande Band of Mission Indians of the Barona Reservation; Capitan Grande Band of Diegueño Mission Indians: Viejas (Baron Long) Group of Capitan Grande Band of Mission Indians of the Viejas Reservation; Cedarville Rancheria; Cher-Ae Heights Indian Community of the Trinidad Rancheria; Chicken Ranch Rancheria of Me-Wuk Indians of California; Cloverdale Rancheria of Pomo Indians of California; Cold Springs Rancheria of Mono Indians of California; Cortina Indian Rancheria of Wintun Indians of California; Coyote Valley Band of Pomo Indians of California; Dry Creek Rancheria of Pomo Indians of California; Elem Indian Colony of Pomo Indians of the Sulphur Bank Rancheria; Elk Valley Rancheria; Enterprise Rancheria of Maidu Indians of California; Ewiiaapaayp Band of Kumeyaay Indians; Federated Indians of Graton Rancheria; Fort Bidwell Indian Community of the Fort Bidwell Reservation of California; Greenville Rancheria of Maidu Indians of California; Grindstone Indian Rancheria of Wintun-Wailaki Indians of California; Guidiville Rancheria of California; Habematolel Pomo of Upper Lake; Hoopa Valley Tribe; Hopland Band of Pomo Indians of the Hopland Rancheria; Iipay Nation of Santa Ysabel (formerly the Santa Ysabel Band of Diegueño Mission Indians of the Santa Ysabel Reservation); Inaja Band of Diegueño Mission Indians of the Inaja and Cosmit Reservation; Ione Band of Miwok Indians of California; Jackson Rancheria of Me-Wuk Indians of California Jamul Indian Village of California; Karuk Tribe, California (formerly the Karuk Tribe of California); Kashia Band of Pomo Indians of the Stewarts Point Rancheria; La Jolla Band of Luiseño Indians, California (formerly the La Jolla Band of Luiseño Mission Indians of the La Jolla Reservation); La Posta Band of Diegueño Mission Indians of the La Posta Indian Reservation, California; Los Coyotes Band of Cahuilla and Cupeño Indians, California (formerly the Los Coyotes Band of Cahuilla & Cupeño Indians of the Los Coyotes Reservation); Lower Lake Rancheria; Lytton Rancheria of California; Manchester Band of Pomo Indians of the Manchester-Point Arena Rancheria; Manzanita Band of Diegueño Mission Indians of the Manzanita Reservation; Mechoopda Indian Tribe of Chico Rancheria; Mesa Grande Band of Diegueño Mission Indians of the Mesa Grande Reservation; Middletown Rancheria of Pomo Indians of California; Mooretown Rancheria of Maidu Indians of California; Morongo Band of Mission Indians, California (formerly the Morongo Band of Cahuilla Mission Indians of the Morongo Reservation); Northfork Rancheria of Mono Indians of California; Pala Band of Luiseño Mission Indians of the Pala Reservation; Paskenta Band of Nomlaki Indians of California; Pauma Band of Luiseño Mission Indians of the Pauma & Yuima Reservation; Pechanga Band of Luiseño Mission Indians of the Pechanga Reservation; Picayune Rancheria of Chukchansi Indians of California; Pinoleville Pomo Nation, California (formerly the Pinoleville Rancheria of Pomo Indians of California); Pit River Tribe: Big Bend Rancheria; Pit River Tribe: Likely Rancheria; Pit River Tribe: Lookout Rancheria; Pit River Tribe: Montgomery Creek Rancheria; Pit River Tribe: Roaring Creek Rancheria; Pit River Tribe: XL Ranch Rancheria; Potter Valley Tribe; Quartz Valley Indian Community of the Quartz Valley Reservation of California; Ramona Band or Village of Cahuilla Mission Indians of California; Redding Rancheria, California; Redwood Valley Rancheria of Pomo Indians of California; Resighini Rancheria; Rincon Band of Luiseño Mission Indians of the Rincon Reservation; Robinson Rancheria of Pomo Indians of California; Round Valley Indian Tribes of the Round Valley Reservation; San Manuel Band of Mission Indians, California (previously listed as the San Manual Band of Serrano Mission Indians of the San Manual Reservation); San Pasqual Band of Diegueño Mission Indians of California; Santa Rosa Band of Cahuilla Indians, California (formerly the Santa Rosa Band of Cahuilla Mission Indians of the Santa Rosa Reservation); Santa Rosa Indian Community of the Santa Rosa Rancheria; Santa Ynez Band of Chumash Mission Indians of the Santa Ynez Reservation; Scotts Valley Band of Pomo Indians of California; Sherwood Valley Rancheria of Pomo Indians of California; Shingle Springs Band of Miwok Indians, Shingle Springs Rancheria (Verona Tract); Smith River Rancheria; Soboba Band of Luiseño Indians; Susanville Indian Rancheria; Sycuan Band of the Kumeyaay Nation; Table Mountain Rancheria of California; Torres Martinez Desert Cahuilla Indians, California (formerly the Torres-Martinez Band of Cahuilla Mission Indians of California); Tule River Indian Tribe of the Tule River Reservation; Tuolumne Band of Me-Wuk Indians of the Tuolumne Rancheria of California; Twenty-Nine Palms Band of Mission Indians of California; United Auburn Indian Community of the Auburn Rancheria of California; Wilton Rancheria, Wiyot Tribe, California (formerly the Table Bluff Reservation—Wiyot Tribe); Yocha Dehe Wintun Nation, California (formerly the Rumsey Indian Rancheria of Wintun Indians of California); Yurok Tribe of the Yurok Reservation

FURTHER RESOURCES

Books and Articles

Adamson, Thelma. *Folk-tales of the Coast Salish.* University of Nebraska Press, 2009.

Anderson, David G., and Kenneth E. Sassaman, Eds. *The Paleoindian and Early Archaic Southeast.* University of Alabama Press, 1996.

"Arctic and Circumpolar Regions." In *Encyclopedia of Archaeology,* Ed. Deborah M. Pearsall. Elsevier/Academic Press, 2008.

Baraga, Frederic. *Chippewa Indians in 1847.* Studia Slovenica, 1976.

———. *The Diary of Bishop Frederic Baraga: First Bishop of Marquette, Michigan,* Ed. Regis M. Walling and N. Daniel Rupp. Wayne State University Press, 1990.

Blackhawk, Ned. *Violence over the Land.* Harvard University Press, 2006.

Briggs, Kara. "Pat Courtney Gold." *American Indian* (Fall/Winter 2002), 23–24.

Burch, Ernest S., Jr. *The Inupiaq Eskimo Nations of Northwest Alaska.* University of Alaska Press, 1998.

Cave, Alfred A. *The Pequot War.* University of Massachusetts Press, 1996.

Christie, John C., Jr., "The Catawba Indian Land Claim: A Giant among Indian Land Claims." *American Indian Culture and Research Journal* (No. 1, 2000), 173–82.

Conley, Robert. *The Cherokee Nation: A History.* University of New Mexico Press, 2005.

Copway, George. *Life, Letters and Speeches.* University of Nebraska Press, 1997. Originally published in 1847 as *The Life, History and Travels of Kah-ge-ga-gah-bowh,* expanded and republished as *The Life, Letters and Speeches of Kah-ge-ga-gah-bowh or G. Copway, Chief Ojibway Nation;* S. W. Benedict, 1850.

———. *The Traditional History and Characteristic Sketches of the Ojibway Nation.* Charles Gilpin, 1850. Reprinted as *Indian Life and Indian History, by an Indian Author: Embracing the Traditions of the North American Indians Regarding Themselves, Particularly of That Most Important of All the Tribes, the Ojibways;* Albert Cosby and Co., 1858.

Crowell, Aron, Rosita Worl, Paul C. Ongtooguk, and Dawn D. Biddison, Eds. *Living Our Cultures, Sharing Our Heritage: The First Peoples of Alaska.* Smithsonian Books, 2010.

Dauenhauer, Nora, and Richard Dauenhauer, Eds. *Haa Ḵusteeyí, Our Culture: Tlingit Life Stories.* University of Washington Press; Sealaska Heritage Foundation, 1994.

Dauenhauer, Nora, Richard Dauenhauer, and Lydia Black. *Anóoshi Lingít Aaní Ká / Russians in Tlingit America: The Battles of Sitka, 1802 and 1804.* University of Washington Press; Sealaska Heritage Institute, 2008.

Densmore, Frances. *Chippewa Customs.* Minnesota Historical Society, 1979.

Dowd, Gregory E. *War under Heaven: Pontiac, the Indian Nations, and the British Empire.* Johns Hopkins University Press, 2002.

Drake, James D. *King Philip's War: Civil War in New England, 1675–1676.* University of Massachusetts Press, 1999.

Edmunds, R. David. Tecumseh: *The Quest for Indian Leadership.* Pearson Longman, 2007.

"Eskimos about Bering Strait." Annual Report 18 of the Bureau of American Ethnology. Smithsonian Institution, 1899.

Fitzhugh, William W. "Yamal to Greenland: Global Connections in Circumpolar Archaeology." In *Archaeology: The Widening Debate,* ed. Barry Cunliffe, Wendy Davies, and Colin Renfrew. Oxford University Press, 2002.

Fitzhugh, William W., and Aron Crowell, Eds. *Crossroads of Continents: Cultures of Siberia and Alaska.* Smithsonian Institution Press, 1988.

Fitzhugh, William W., and Susan A. Kaplan. *Inua: Spirit World of the Bering Sea Eskimo.* Smithsonian Institution Press, 1982.

Grafe, Steven L. *Peoples of the Plateau: The Indian Photographs of Lee Moorhouse, 1898–1915.* University of Oklahoma Press, 2005.

Haida Dictionary, comp. Erma Lawrence. Society for the Preservation of Haida Language and Literature, 1977.

Handbook of North American Indians. Vols. 5–15 and 17, William C. Sturtevant, gen. ed. Smithsonian Institution, 1978–2008.

Hinton, Leanne. "Breath of Life/Silent No More: The Native California Language Restoration Workshop." *News of Native California* (Fall 1996), 13–16.

———. *Flutes of Fire: Essays on California Indian Languages.* Heyday Books, 1994.

Hinton, Leanne, and Susan L. Roth. *Ishi's Tale of Lizard.* Farrar, Straus and Giroux, 1992.

Hinton, Leanne, and Lucille Watahomigie, Eds. *Spirit Mountain: An Anthology of Yuman Story and Song.* Sun Tracks, vol. 10. Sun Tracks and University of Arizona Press, 1984.

Hunn, Eugene, and James Selam. *Nch'i-wana, "the Big River": Mid-Columbia Indians and Their Land.* University of Washington Press, 1990.

Jonaitis, Aldona. *Art of the Northwest Coast.* University of Washington Press; Douglas and McIntyre, 2006.

Josephy, Alvin M., Jr. *500 Nations: An Illustrated History of North American Indians.* Gramercy, 1994.

Kidwell, Clara Sue. *Choctaws and Missionaries in Mississippi, 1818–1918.* University of Oklahoma Press, 1995.

Kohl, Johann Georg. *Kitchi-Gami: Life among the Lake Superior Ojibway.* Minnesota Historical Society Press, 1985.

Lambert, Valerie. *Choctaw Nation: A Story of American Indian Resurgence.* University of Nebraska Press, 2007.

Lawson, John. *A New Voyage to Carolina.* University of North Carolina, 2001 [1709]. Available online at http://docsouth.unc.edu/nc/lawson/lawson.html.

Luthin, Herbert W., Ed. *Surviving through the Days: Translations of Native California Stories and Songs; A California Indian Reader.* University of California Press, 2002.

McGhee, Robert. *Ancient People of the Arctic.* University of British Columbia Press, 2001.

McWhorter, L. V. *Yellow Wolf: His Own Story.* Caxton Printers, 1986.

Montaigne, Fen. "A River Dammed." *National Geographic* (April 2001), 2–33.

Morrison, David A. *Inuit: Glimpses of an Arctic Past.* Canadian Museum of Civilization, 1995.

Nichols, John D., and Earl Nyholm (Otchingwanigan). *A Concise Dictionary of Minnesota Ojibwe.* University of Minnesota Press, 1995.

Rawls, James. *Indians of California: The Changing Image.* University of Oklahoma Press, 1984.

Relander, Click. *Drummers and Dreamers.* Northwest Interpretive Association, 1986.

Remini, Robert V. *Andrew Jackson and His Indian Wars.* Viking, 2001.

Richter, Daniel K. *The Ordeal of the Longhouse: The Peoples of the Iroquois League in the Era of European Colonization.* University of North Carolina Press, 1992.

Ruby, Robert H., and John Arthur Brown. *John Slocum and the Indian Shaker Church.* University of Oklahoma Press, 1996.

Sarris, Greg. *Keeping Slug Woman Alive: A Holistic Approach to American Indian Texts.* University of California Press, 1993.

Secrest, William B. *When the Great Spirit Died: Destruction of the California Indians, 1850–1860.* Word Dancer Press, 2003.

Serris, Greg. *Mabel McKay: Weaving the Dream.* University of California Press, 1994.

Smith, Paul, and Robert Warrior. *Like a Hurricane: The American Indian Movement from Alcatraz to Wounded Knee.* W. W. Norton, 1996.

Splawn, A. J. *Ka-Mi-Akin: The Last Hero of the Yakimas.* Caxton Printers, 1980.

Suttles, Wayne. *Coast Salish Essays.* Talonbooks; University of Washington Press, 1987.

Swanton, John R. "Early History of the Creek Indians and Their Neighbors." Smithsonian Institution, Bureau of American Ethnology, Bulletin No. 73, 1922.

Tanner, Helen Hornbeck, Ed. *Atlas of Great Lakes Indian History.* University of Oklahoma Press, 1987.

Treuer, Anton. *The Assassination of Hole in the Day.* Minnesota Historical Society Press, 2010.

———. *Living Our Language: Ojibwe Tales and Oral Histories.* Minnesota Historical Society Press, 2001.

———. *Ojibwe in Minnesota.* Minnesota Historical Society Press, 2010.

Walker, Deward E., Jr., and Virginia Beavert. *The Way It Was (Anaku Iwacha Yakima Indian Legends).* Consortium of Johnson O'Malley Committees, Region IV, State of Washington.

Warren, William W. *History of the Ojibway People.* Minnesota Historical Society Press, 1984.

White, Richard. *The Middle Ground: Indian, Empires, and Republics in the Great Lakes Region, 1650–1815.* Cambridge University Press, 1992.

Wickman, Patricia R. *The Tree That Bends: Discourse, Power, and the Survival of the Maskókí People.* University of Alabama Press, 1999.

Wood, Peter H., Gregory A. Waselkov, and M. Thomas Hatley. *Powhatan's Mantle: Indians in the Colonial Southeast.* University of Nebraska Press, 1989.

Wright, J. Leitch, Jr. *The Only Land They Knew: The Tragic Story of the American Indians in the Old South.* Free Press, 1981.

Wright, Robin. *Northern Haida Master Carvers.* University of Washington Press; Douglas and McIntyre, 2001.

———. *A Time of Gathering: Native Heritage in Washington State.* University of Washington Press, 1991.

Yahgulanaas, Michael. *Red: A Haida Manga.* Douglas and McIntyre, 2009.

Yamane, Linda. *When the World Ended, How Hummingbird Got Fire, How People Were Made: Rumsien Ohlone Stories.* Oyate Press, 1995.

Yoder, Janet, Vi Hilbert, and Jeanette Weston. *Writings about Vi Hilbert.* 2nd ed. Lushootseed Research, 1993.

DVD

Gold, Pat Courtney. *Northwest Basket Weavers: Honoring Our Heritage.* A Mimbres Fever Production, 2006.

Websites

California Indian Basketweavers Association
CIBA preserves, promotes, and perpetuates California Indian basketweaving traditions.
www.ciba.org/

California Indian Library Collections
The California Indian Library Collections Project has duplicated archived sound recordings, photographs, and textual materials (such as books, journal articles, unpublished manuscripts, and field notes) and installed them in northern and central California libraries.
http://www.mip.berkeley.edu/cilc/brochure/brochure.html

California Indian Storytellers Association
CISA is committed to providing a storytelling forum for the indigenous people of the Americas.
www.cistory.org/

Native Languages of the Americas
A nonprofit organization dedicated to the survival of Native American languages
www.native-languages.org/

Society for the Study of Indigenous Languages of the Americas
SSILA was founded in December 1981 as the international scholarly organization representing the languages of the native peoples of North, Central, and South America
http://www.ssila.org/

Chapter One: Northeast

ANTON TREUER is Ojibwe and a professor of Ojibwe at Bemidji State University, Minnesota. Dr. Treuer is the author of *Ojibwe in Minnesota, The Assassination of Hole in the Day, Awesiinyensag: Dibaajimowinan Ji-gikinoo'amaageng, Living Our Language: Ojibwe Tales and Oral Histories, Aaniin Ekidong: Ojibwe Vocabulary Project,* and *Omaa Akiing.* He is also the editor of the *Oshkaabewis Native Journal,* the only academic journal of the Ojibwe language. A graduate of Princeton University and the University of Minnesota, Dr. Treuer has sat on many organizational boards and has received awards and fellowships from the National Endowment for the Humanities, the National Science Foundation, the MacArthur Foundation, the Bush Foundation, and the John Simon Guggenheim Foundation.

Chapter Two: Southeast

KARENNE WOOD is an enrolled member of the Monacan Indian Nation. She is the director of the award-winning Virginia Indian Heritage Program at the Virginia Foundation for the Humanities and is a Ph.D. candidate and Ford Fellow in anthropology at the University of Virginia, working to revitalize indigenous languages and cultural practices. She has worked at the National Museum of the American Indian as a researcher and held a four-year gubernatorial appointment as chair of the Virginia Council on Indians. Wood is the author of *Markings on Earth,* which won the North American Native Authors Award for Poetry.

Chapter Three: Arctic/Subarctic

WILLIAM W. FITZHUGH is an anthropologist specializing in peoples and cultures of northern Canada, Alaska, Russia, Scandinavia, and Mongolia. Dr. Fitzhugh's research features the evolution of northern maritime adaptations, circumpolar culture contacts, cross-cultural studies, and culture change. His research expeditions have taken him throughout the North. Fitzhugh has published widely and has organized numerous museum exhibitions on Arctic subjects. His current research involves early Alaskan Eskimo culture and art, studies of Bronze Age Mongolia, and the effects of early Basque and European contacts on Native cultures in Labrador and the Gulf of St. Lawrence.

Chapter Four: Plains

GEORGE P. HORSE CAPTURE, SR. is an A'aninin Gros Ventre born in 1937 at Fort Belknap Indian Reservation, Montana. He graduated from Butte High School in 1956 and joined the U.S. Navy. Horse Capture participated in the 1969 Alcatraz movement. He earned a bachelor's degree in anthropology from the University of California, Berkeley, in 1974 and a master's in history at Montana State University in Bozeman and taught at the College of Great Falls, Montana, until 1979. Consulting as a writer and lecturer on cultural topics, Horse Capture became a curator at the Buffalo Bill Historical Center in Cody, Wyoming, and a senior manager at the National Museum of the American Indian in New York City and Washington, D.C. He retired in 2005 and moved to Great Falls, where he and his wife KayKarol can be found powwowing somewhere with their grandchildren.

Chapter Five: Southwest

THERESA LYNN FRAIZER is a Laguna/Hopi/Chippewa. She currently serves as a systems specialist for the Gallup McKinley County Schools in New Mexico, where she was previously an award-winning classroom teacher. Fraizer, who has a master's degree in educational leadership, is also the executive director of the Gallup Inter-Tribal Indian Ceremonial Association, which celebrated its 89th year in August 2010. Since 1985, she has owned Corn Silk Studio, where she is also an artist. Fraizer has been recognized as a world-class painter and potter in traditional and contemporary ceramic and clay art.

Chapter Six: Great Basin & Plateau

MILES R. MILLER is a Yakama who was born and raised in the Yakima Valley of Washington. As a beadwork artist, he creates tradition-inspired designs in a contemporary fashion. His beadwork has been exhibited at the Columbia Center for the Arts and at the Institute of American Indian Arts Museum. He was a longtime board member for the Indigenous Arts Action Alliance and has been published in *Red Ink* magazine. Miller has interned at such institutions as the Peabody Museum of Archaeology and Ethnology, the School for Advanced Research, and the National Museum of the American Indian. He completed his B.A. degree at Evergreen State College, Olympia, Washington, in 2005 and received his M.A. in museology at the University of Washington in 2008.

Chapter Seven: Northwest Coast

MIRANDA BELARDE-LEWIS is a member of the Takdeintaan clan of the Tlingit Nation and is also an enrolled member of the Zuni Pueblo. She holds a bachelor's degree in cultural anthropology from the University of Arizona. Belarde-Lewis has served as an art handler at the Institute of American Indian Arts Museum and a fellowship coordinator at the National Association of Tribal Historic Preservation Officers. She is an author, artist, mother, and Ph.D. student of information science at the University of Washington.

Chapter Eight: California

JILL NORWOOD is Tolowa, Karuk, and Yurok, enrolled with the Smith River Rancheria. She obtained her B.A. in psychology from the University of Maryland and has worked at the Smithsonian Institution since 1992. In her first position there, she worked with young children at the Smithsonian Early Enrichment Center to develop age-appropriate curricula based on the Smithsonian's collections. In 1999, Norwood moved to the Smithsonian's National Museum of the American Indian, where she develops professional development opportunities for tribal museum staff and coordinates the internship program.

INDIAN NATIONS
OF NORTH AMERICA

Anton Truer, Karenne Wood, William W. Fitzhugh,
George P. Horse Capture, Sr., Theresa Lynn Fraizer,
Miles R. Miller, Miranda Belarde-Lewis, Jill Norwood

Published by the National Geographic Society

John M. Fahey, Jr., *President and Chief Executive Officer*

Gilbert M. Grosvenor, *Chairman of the Board*

Tim T. Kelly, *President, Global Media Group*

John Q. Griffin, *Executive Vice President; President, Publishing*

Nina D. Hoffman, *Executive Vice President;
    President, Book Publishing Group*

Prepared by the Book Division

Barbara Brownell Grogan, *Vice President and Editor in Chief*

Marianne R. Koszorus, *Director of Design*

Susan Hitchcock, *Senior Editor*

Carl Mehler, *Director of Maps*

R. Gary Colbert, *Production Director*

Jennifer A. Thornton, *Managing Editor*

Meredith C. Wilcox, *Administrative Director, Illustrations*

Staff for This Book

Susan Straight, *Editor*

Maryann Haggerty, Anne Cherry, Stephen Hyslop, *Text Editors*

Kevin Eans, Robert Waymouth, *Illustrations Editors*

Carol Farrar Norton, *Art Director*

Linda Makarov, *Designer*

Matt Chwastyk, Steven D. Gardner, Gregory Ugiansky,
    and XNR Productions, *Map Research and Production*

Judith Klein, *Production Editor*

Lewis Bassford, *Production Manager*

Miriam Stein, *Ilustrations Research*

Marshall Kiker, *Illustrations Specialist*

Al Morrow, *Design Assistant*

Samantha Foster, Caitlin Mertzlufft, Andy Tybout, *Interns*

Manufacturing and Quality Management

Christopher A. Liedel, *Chief Financial Officer*

Phillip L. Schlosser, *Vice President*

Chris Brown, *Technical Director*

Nicole Elliott, *Manager*

Rachel Faulise, *Manager*

Robert L. Barr, *Manager*

The National Geographic Society is one of the world's largest non-profit scientific and educational organizations. Founded in 1888 to "increase and diffuse geographic knowledge," the Society works to inspire people to care about the planet. It reaches more than 325 million people worldwide each month through its official journal, *National Geographic,* and other magazines; National Geographic Channel; television documentaries; music; radio; films; books; DVDs; maps; exhibitions; school publishing programs; interactive media; and merchandise. National Geographic has funded more than 9,000 scientific research, conservation and exploration projects and supports an education program combating geographic illiteracy. For more information, visit nationalgeographic.com.

For more information, please call 1-800-NGS LINE (647-5463) or write to the following address:

National Geographic Society
1145 17th Street N.W.
Washington, D.C. 20036-4688 U.S.A.

Visit us online at www.nationalgeographic.com

For information about special discounts for bulk purchases, please contact National Geographic Books Special Sales: ngspecsales@ngs.org

For rights or permissions inquiries, please contact National Geographic Books Subsidiary Rights: ngbookrights@ngs.org

ISBN: 978-1-4262-0664-1
978-1-4262-0665-8 (Deluxe)

Library of Congress Cataloging-in-Publication Data

Indian nations of North America / by Anton Treuer ... [et al.];
foreword by Herman J. Viola.
    p. cm.
Includes bibliographical references and index.
ISBN 978-1-4262-0664-1 -- ISBN 978-1-4262-0665-8 (deluxe)
1. Indians of North America. I. Treuer, Anton.
E77.I4139 2010
970.004'97--dc22

                    2010026728

Printed in U.S.A.

10/RRDW/2